I0333298

VISIONS AND REVISIONS IN SANSKRIT NARRATIVE

Studies in the Sanskrit Epics and Purāṇas

VISIONS AND REVISIONS IN SANSKRIT NARRATIVE

Studies in the Sanskrit Epics and Purāṇas

EDITED BY RAJ BALKARAN
AND MCCOMAS TAYLOR

Australian National University
ANU PRESS

ASIAN STUDIES SERIES MONOGRAPH 19

Australian
National
University

ANU PRESS

Published by ANU Press
The Australian National University
Canberra ACT 2600, Australia
Email: anupress@anu.edu.au

Available to download for free at press.anu.edu.au

ISBN (print): 9781760465896
ISBN (online): 9781760465902

WorldCat (print): 1394053659
WorldCat (online): 1394054036

DOI: 10.22459/VRSN.2023

This title is published under a Creative Commons Attribution-NonCommercial-NoDerivatives 4.0 International (CC BY-NC-ND 4.0) licence.

The full licence terms are available at
creativecommons.org/licenses/by-nc-nd/4.0/legalcode

Cover design and layout by ANU Press.

This book is published under the aegis of the Asian Studies editorial board of ANU Press.

This edition © 2023 ANU Press

Contents

List of illustrations vii

Foreword ix
Wendy Doniger

Preface xi

Contributors xiii

Introduction: Visions and revisions of Sanskrit narrative 1

1. Narrative argument and interlocutory frames in the *Mahābhārata* 11
   Greg Bailey
2. Āstīka, black magic and apotropaic ritual: Peacemaking brahmins and the snake sacrifice in the *Mahābhārata*'s Ādiparvan 37
   Adam Bowles
3. Transitions and transmissions in the *Mahābhārata*: Revisiting the Ugraśravas/Śaunaka frame dialogue 65
   Brian Black
4. Battling inner conflicts: Dhṛtarāṣṭra and Saṃjaya in the Udyogaparvan of the *Mahābhārata* 93
   Angelika Malinar
5. The Ambopākhyāna reconsidered: Reading Ambā's story as part of the Rāma Jāmadagnya myth cycle 127
   Brian Collins
6. Claiming the narrative: Subjectivity and intertextuality in the Ambopākhyāna 153
   Zuzana Špicová
7. Bhīma: The shadow king 175
   Sudha Berry
8. Some moral tasting notes on the Udyogaparvan of the *Mahābhārata* 197
   James M. Hegarty

9. The *Bhagavadgītā*'s determinism and world literature 227
Simon Brodbeck

10. Mineral, vegetal, animal or divine? The flying palace Puṣpaka's manifold metamorphoses 251
Danielle Feller

11. From Ayodhyā to the Daṇḍaka: Rāma's journey in exile according to the Jain *Rāmāyaṇas* 275
Eva De Clercq

12. Gembedded narratives: Jewelled peacetime tales of Rāma's exile and Rāvaṇa's domicile as alternative afterlife anticipations in the *Vālmīki Rāmāyaṇa* 291
Shubha Pathak

13. Train stations, enterprising priests and the deadly blows of *kuśa* grass: Reading the purāṇas with a magic-realist lens 315
Laurie L. Patton

14. Textures of purāṇic transmission: A contemporary vernacular exposition of a Sanskrit purāṇa 337
Sucharita Adluri

15. The Śivaśarmopākhyāna of the *Padma Purāṇa* as a bizarre compendium of epic and purāṇic tales of *Pitṛbhakti* 369
Nicolas Dejenne

16. Same, same but different: The Tamil *Kāñcippurāṇam* and its Sanskrit source 387
Jonas Buchholz

17. The 'purāṇification' of the death of Kṛṣṇa 417
Christopher R. Austin

18. Lambs, lightning, nakedness and fire: Polythetic networks and literary elaborations of the Purūravas–Urvaśī narrative 441
McComas Taylor

List of illustrations

Figures

Figure 5.1 The descent of Rāma Jāmadagnya 133

Figure 5.2 Rāma Jāmadagnya at the intersection of *cirañjīvins* (horizontal in italics) and avatāras (vertical in bold) 134

Figure 5.3 The expected union of the three sons of Śaṃtanu and the three Kāśi princesses with their expected offspring 138

Figure 5.4 The epic's account of the descents of Dhṛtarāṣṭra, Pāṇḍu and Vidura 138

Figure 8.1 Moral tasting notes for the Udyogaparvan 218

Figure 8.2 Moral tasting notes for the Udyogaparvan, by embassy 218

Plates

Plate 10.1 *Puṣpaka as a flying palace. Rāma leaves Laṅkā on Puṣpaka*. Opaque watercolour and gold on paper, c. 1650. Himachal Pradesh, Pahari School. The San Diego Museum of Art 255

Plate 10.2 *Puṣpaka as a swan. Rāma, Sītā and Lakṣmaṇa fly back to Ayodhyā on Puṣpaka*. From: *Tulsi Ramayan*, Tej Kumar Book Depot, date unknown 259

Plate 10.3 *Garuḍa-Puṣpaka*. Garuḍa (holding a snake in his claws and with lotus-like back feathers) carries a canopy sheltering Hanumān, Rāma, Sītā and Lakṣmaṇa 263

Plate 10.4 The *vimāna* of the Virūpākṣa Temple, Hampi (Karnataka), c. fifteenth–sixteenth century 267

Plate 10.5 Keshava Temple, Somnathpur (Karnataka), c. 1268 268
Plate 10.6 The Puṣpaka temple 271

Tables

Table 8.1 Five moral 'foundations' for humans 200
Table 8.2 Moral tasting notes of the council of Upaplavya 205
Table 8.3 Moral tasting notes of the second embassy 212
Table 8.4 Moral tasting notes of the third embassy 215
Table 8.5 Moral tasting notes of the fourth embassy 217
Table 14.1 Dhruva Narrative (Pathak 1999) 341

Foreword

Wendy Doniger

I am so happy to see this volume, which generously bows with cupped hands to my own effort in this field some 30 years ago, *Purāṇa Perennis*. So much has happened in the intervening period, both in the study of the two great Sanskrit epics and, to an only slightly lesser extent, in the study of the purāṇas, that a thorough re-evaluation is long overdue. And, more importantly, so much has happened in our own lives and therefore in the questions that we now ask of texts. We no longer just ask about dynastic history (a subject about which the Sanskrit purāṇas are poorly equipped to answer and that therefore gave the purāṇas an undeserved reputation for historical inaccuracy) or about the ties between the purāṇas and earlier texts (an approach that foolishly limited discussions to theological, philosophical and mythological matters). Now scholars look at these old texts through new lenses, asking about the relationship between economic and social classes, about racism, classism and sexism and about the role that Sanskrit texts did or did not play in the development of vernacular literatures. These, and other equally pressing questions, are brilliantly confronted by the essays in the present volume.

The editors have gathered the leaders in this broad field (four of them, I am proud to say, my own students), scholars of literature, history, religion, linguistics, anthropology, sociology and cultural studies more broadly conceived. These scholars have brought to bear an exciting range of linguistic sources and theoretical toolboxes. After providing broad-ranging explorations of Sanskrit narrative as a whole and the two great Sanskrit epics in particular, they have gone on to include detailed and intense discussions of a number of key episodes in those epics and in several purāṇas. The result is a book that goes both broad and deep, raising new questions even as it challenges and reformulates some of the old questions that have dominated the discussion for too long. Key episodes of the *Mahābhārata* and the *Rāmāyaṇa* are given stunning new interpretations, and the purāṇas are newly examined in the light of magic realism, contemporary vernacular expositions, bizarre compendia with epic and Tamil texts and polythetic networks.

The result is a collection of essays that, despite their wonderful range of approaches, are clearly talking about the same subject—a rich and fascinating ocean of stories (to coin a phrase). The essays are written with grace and wit, making the heavy scholarship light for the reader. I cup my hands to honour the editors and authors, and to thank them.

Preface

Sanskrit narrative is the lifeblood of Indian culture, encapsulating and perpetuating insights and values core to Indian thought and practice. Eclipsed by colonial preoccupation with philosophical treatises, these texts are finally beginning to receive the scholarly attention they deserve. The tide is turning in terms of 'old-school slicing and dicing' of these texts for philological and historicist aims. This volume showcases 18 of the foremost scholars across the globe, who accord these texts the integrity and dignity they deserve in an unprecedented collaboration. The last time this was attempted, on a much smaller scale, was a generation ago, with *Purāṇa Perennis* (1993). The scholars featured here broach a variety of Sanskrit narrative texts, employing novel methods and theory to meaningfully engage them. Given that the field has been shaped and driven by the efforts of the preeminent scholars showcased in this project, it is high time for this *Visions and Revisions in Sanskrit Narrative* volume.

Contributors

Sucharita Adluri is an associate professor of Asian religions in the Department of Philosophy and Comparative Religion at Cleveland State University. Trained in the history of religions at the University of Pennsylvania, her work encompasses the social and religious history of the Sanskrit intellectual and devotional traditions of South India. A focus of her current research is the promulgation of the *Viṣṇu Purāṇa*, textually and performatively.

Christopher Austin completed his PhD at McMaster University in Hamilton, Ontario, and is an associate professor of religious studies in the Department of Classics at Dalhousie University in Halifax, Nova Scotia, where he teaches widely across all major religious traditions of South and East Asia. His principal areas of research are in the Sanskrit epic *Mahābhārata* and particularly its supplement, *the Harivaṃśa*, the biographical traditions of Kṛṣṇa's life, his son Pradyumna and early Vaiṣṇavism.

Greg Bailey, formerly reader in Sanskrit, is an honorary research fellow in the School of Linguistics and Culture at La Trobe University, Melbourne. He has published translations and studies of the *Gaṇeśa Purāṇa*, Bhartṛhari's *Śatakatrayam*, books on early Buddhism and Australian politics and many articles on Sanskrit literature. He has also published two novels, one of which was on early Buddhism.

Raj Balkaran is a self-employed scholar of Sanskrit narrative texts, focusing on the *Devī Māhātmya*, the *Mārkaṇḍeya Purāṇa* and the epics. He is the author of *The Goddess and the King in Indian Myth* (Routledge 2019), *The Goddess and the Sun in Indian Myth* (Routledge 2020), *The Stories behind the Poses* (Leaping Hare Press 2022), and a number of chapters and journal articles. He teaches online courses at the Oxford Centre for Hindu Studies and hosts the *New Books in Indian Religions* podcast. See rajbalkaran.com for more information.

Sudha Berry is a corporate lawyer and independent scholar with an abiding passion for the Indian epics, particularly the *Mahābhārata*. She was trained at the University of Toronto and the School of Oriental and African Studies, University of London. Her research employs literary analysis to uncover thematic relationships related to the depiction of nature. Her MA thesis, 'Sacred wilderness of resources', examined the role of the wilderness in the *Āraṇyakaparvan*. This was further explored in her paper 'Mountains in the Āraṇyakaparvan of the Mahābhārata'. She is currently working on expanding her study of the character of Bhīma, first presented in this volume.

Brian Black received his MA and PhD at SOAS University of London and is a lecturer in the Department of Politics, Philosophy and Religion at Lancaster University. His research interests include Indian religion and philosophy, comparative philosophy, the use of dialogue in Indian religious and philosophical texts, and Hindu and Buddhist ethics. He is author of the books *The Character of the Self in Ancient India: Priests, Kings, and Women in the Early Upaniṣads* (SUNY, 2008) and *In Dialogue with the Mahābhārata* (Routledge, 2020).

Adam Bowles is an associate professor in Asian religions at the University of Queensland. He has published three volumes about the *Mahābhārata*, two of which are translations of the *Karṇaparvan* published with the Clay Sanskrit Library (2006, 2008). The other, *Dharma, Disorder and the Political in Ancient India: The Āpaddharmaparvan of the Mahābhārata* (Brill, 2007), is a study of one of the didactic corpora belonging to the *Śāntiparvan*. He has also edited, with Simon Brodbeck and Alf Hiltebeitel, *The Churning of the Epics and Purāṇas* (Dev Publishers, 2018). His most recent publication is 'The Gṛhastha in the Mahābhārata', which appeared in the volume edited by Patrick Olivelle, *Gṛhastha: The Householder in Ancient Indian Religious Culture* (Oxford University Press, 2019). While continuing to research aspects of the *Mahābhārata* and early South Asian cultural history, he is also working on a large project titled the 'Queensland Atlas of Religion'.

Simon Brodbeck studied at Clare College, Cambridge, and SOAS University of London. He has worked at the universities of Edinburgh and London and, since 2008, at Cardiff University, where he is a reader in religious studies. His books include *Gender and Narrative in the Mahābhārata* (co-edited with Brian Black, Routledge, 2007), *The Mahābhārata Patriline: Gender, Culture, and the Royal Hereditary* (Routledge, 2009) and *Krishna's Lineage: The Harivamsha of Vyāsa's Mahābhārata, Translated from the Sanskrit* (Oxford University Press, 2019).

Jonas Buchholz is a postdoctoral researcher at the research unit 'Hindu Temple Legends in South India' at the Heidelberg Academy of Sciences and Humanities. His research focuses on the Sanskrit and Tamil mythological texts (*sthalamāhātmyas/talapurāṇams*) that deal with the Śaiva temples of the South Indian temple town of Kanchipuram. Other research interests include the relationship between Tamil and Sanskrit literatures as well as manuscript studies.

Brian Collins is the Drs Ram and Sushila Gawande Chair in Indian Religion and Philosophy at Ohio University, where he is also the chair of the Department of Classics and Religious Studies. He is the author of two books on Hindu myth, *The Head Beneath the Altar: Hindu Mythology and the Critique of Sacrifice* (Michigan State University Press, 2014) and *The Other Rāma: Matricide and Varṇicide in the Mythology of Paraśurāma* (SUNY, 2020), and a book of intellectual biography, *The Magic of the Combinatory Mind: The Forgotten Life of 20th Century Austrian Polymath Robert Eisler* (Palgrave, 2021). He is the co-editor of a book on Indian horror films called *Bollywood Horrors: Religion, Violence, and Cinematic Fears in India* (Bloomsbury, 2020). He is working on a new book project entitled 'The View from the Killing Post: Toward a Global Victimology of Human Sacrifice'.

Eva De Clercq is as associate professor of Indian languages and cultures at Ghent University in Belgium, where she teaches mainly Sanskrit, but also Prakrit and Apabhramsha, religious traditions of India and South Asian literature. She conducts research on premodern Indian literature, especially in Apabhramsha. The second volume of 'Life of Padma', a translation of the Jain Rāmāyaṇa poem *Paumacariu of Svayambhudeva*, will soon be published as part of the Murty Classical Library of India series by Harvard University Press.

Nicolas Dejenne is a lecturer in Indian studies at the University Sorbonne Nouvelle-Paris 3, France, and an associate researcher with the French Institute of Pondicherry. After his PhD dissertation (in French), 'From epic Rāma Jāmadagnya to contemporary Paraśurāma: Representations of a hero in India', his prime field of study has remained Sanskrit epics and purāṇas with a special interest in reinterpretations and uses of their characters and episodes in specific cultural contexts (especially Western Maharashtra since the early modern period and contemporary rewritings of the Paraśurāma story). The history of Indian studies in Europe represents another main area of research and teaching. He has co-edited special issues of *Archiv Orientální* (vol. 86[2], 2018) and *DESI: Diasporas: Études des Singularités Indiennes* (vol. 4, 2019), and is the co-editor, with Anne Castaing and Claudine Le Blanc, of the forthcoming *Dictionnaire Encyclopédique des Littératures de l'Inde*, a collective project involving more than 100 contributors.

Danielle Feller was born in Switzerland. After studying at the universities of Lausanne (Switzerland) and Poona (India), she obtained her doctoral degree in 2001 from the Department of South Asian Studies at the University of Lausanne. Her PhD thesis was published by Motilal Banarsidass in 2004 as *The Sanskrit Epics' Representation of Vedic Myths*. She has taught Sanskrit at the University of Geneva and, since 2003, Indian religions and Sanskrit at the University of Lausanne. Her main areas of interest and her publications concern the Sanskrit epics and kāvya literature.

James Marcel Hegarty is a professor of Sanskrit and Indian religions at Cardiff University, Wales. He is fascinated by the history of religions in South Asia. He has written on Hindu, Buddhist, Jain, Sikh and Christian traditions in the region. In particular, he is interested in how religious texts, and especially religious stories, are used by South Asians to communicate and negotiate their understanding of themselves and the world around them. This includes not just what we ordinarily associate with religion, such as ideas of god or gods, or the nature of the good life, but also other forms of knowledge, such as the way in which the past is understood, political life and language itself. He is the author of *Religion, Narrative and Public Imagination in South Asia* (Routledge, 2012), as well as numerous scholarly articles on Sanskrit and vernacular religious texts and their role in South Asian history and culture.

Angelika Malinar studied Indology and philosophy at the University of Tübingen, Germany, where she gained her PhD. She held positions at the University of Tübingen, Free University Berlin and SOAS University of London. Since 2009, she has been a professor of Indology at the University of Zurich. Key areas of her research are epic and purāṇic literature, the interplay between literary forms and intellectual discourse in classical and modern Indian literature and philosophy, and the formation and institutionalisation of Hindu religious traditions in the past and present. Her numerous publications include *The Bhagavadgītā: Doctrines and Contexts* (Cambridge University Press, 2009), *Time in India: Concepts and Practices* (as editor, Manohar, 2007) and the multivolume *Brill's Encyclopedia of Hinduism* (co-editor).

Shubha Pathak is an associate professor of philosophy and religion at the American University, Washington, DC. She is a historian of religions interpreting epic myths originating in Greece, India and Rome to illuminate their paradigmatic pantheons and their authors' creative understandings of their places in the universe. Her monograph *Divine Yet Human Epics: Reflections of Poetic Rulers from Ancient Greece and India* (Harvard University Press, 2014) shows how divinity-favoured and divinity-favouring bardic kings in the primary Greek and Sanskrit epics articulate and address their respective audiences' existential needs. Her edited volume *Figuring Religions: Comparing Ideas, Images, and Activities* (SUNY Press, 2013) demonstrates the methodological advances made by applying metaphor and metonymy theories in comparative religious studies. A past chair of the American Academy of Religion's Hinduism Unit, she is a steering committee member of AAR's *Mahābhārata* and Classical Hinduism Seminar.

Laurie L. Patton is author or editor of 10 books and 60 articles on early Indian religions and theory in the study of religion, including most recently *Who Owns Religion? Scholars and Their Publics in the Late Twentieth Century* (Chicago University Press, 2019). She is also the author of three books of poetry and translator of the *Bhagavadgītā*. Patton served as president of the American Academy of Religion in 2019 and was elected to the American Academy of Arts and Sciences in 2018 in two categories: philosophy and religion, and educational leadership. She is a professor of religion and the seventeenth (and first female) president of Middlebury College, in Vermont. Previously, she was the Robert F. Durden Professor of Religion and the dean of arts and sciences at Duke University, the Charles Howard Candler Professor of Religions at Emory University, and an assistant professor of religion at Bard College. She earned her PhD from the University of Chicago in 1991.

Zuzana Špicová studied Czech language and literature, comparative literature and Indology (Sanskrit and Bangla) at Charles University, Prague. She is finishing her PhD thesis, '"For Bhīṣma's destruction": Ambā, Śikhaṇḍinī and Śikhaṇḍin in the Mahābhārata'. In her research, which is mostly connected to the *Mahābhārata* and Bengali literature, she applies narratological and comparative approaches to both ancient and modern texts. She has presented various papers at conferences such as the World Sanskrit Conference in Vancouver and Sanskrit Traditions in the Modern World in Oxford, and translated some works of Saratchandra Chattopadhyay—most notably, *Debdas*—into Czech.

McComas Taylor is a reader in Sanskrit at The Australian National University, Canberra. His research lies at the intersection of contemporary critical theory and Sanskrit narrative texts, especially the genres of kathā and purāṇa. He is interested in the sources of textual authority and the role text plays in the production of 'truth'. His writing explores the ways in which texts become influential in society, shape discourse and are in turn shaped by discourse. In *Seven Days of Nectar* (Oxford University Press, 2017), he applied performance theory to explore contemporary oral renditions of the *Bhāgavata Purāṇa*. His most recent book is a blank-verse rendering of *The Viṣṇu Purāṇa: Ancient Annals of the God with Lotus Eyes* (ANU Press, 2021)—the first new English translation in nearly 200 years. Taylor is an active member of the International Association of Sanskrit Studies and was instrumental in bringing the Eighteenth World Sanskrit Conference to Australia in 2023.

Introduction: Visions and revisions of Sanskrit narrative

Told and retold in manifold vernacular and regional manners, ancient Sanskrit stories are the lifeblood of Indian culture: they articulate, encapsulate and perpetuate insights and values core to Indic thought and practice. Eclipsed by colonial preoccupation with philosophical treatises for far too long, these stories are finally able to bask in the scholarly attention they deserve, as evidenced by this present volume. The tide has at long last turned in terms of 'old-school slicing and dicing' of Sanskrit narrative texts for philological and historicist aims *alone*. While such approaches are unquestionably important, they need not dominate the study of Sanskrit stories as stories.

This volume showcases 18—a number as auspicious as it was unplanned, at least on behalf of the editors—of the foremost scholars across the globe coming together in significant collaboration to accord Sanskrit stories the integrity, dignity and authority they deserve. The last time this was attempted, on a much smaller scale, was a generation ago (30 years to be exact) with the 1993 publication of the landmark collection of papers entitled *Purāṇa Perennis: Reciprocity and Transformation of Hindu and Jaina Texts* edited by Wendy Doniger (1993). The successive publications from the Dubrovnik International Conference on Sanskrit Epics and Purāṇas have also provided an important conduit for scholarly writings in this area. Stimulated by the success of both the epic and the purāṇa sections at recent World Sanskrit Conferences in Bangkok (2015) and Vancouver (2018),[1] there has been a further upwelling and consolidation of interest in these genres and a need for a coordinated outlet for recent scholarly production. In response to this steady growth of interest in studies of Sanskrit narrative, we invited established and emerging scholars to contribute to this volume, which we hope will become, in a sense, the successor to *Purāṇa Perennis*. This present

1 See Balkaran and Taylor (2019).

volume pays homage to that one and aims to honour the ways in which the field has flourished in the intervening decades. The scholars featured here broach a variety of Sanskrit narrative texts, employing novel methods and theories to meaningfully engage them. Given that the field has been shaped and driven by the efforts of the preeminent scholars showcased in this project, it is high time for this *Visions and Revisions of Sanskrit Narrative* volume.

It was in fact while working with McComas Taylor on co-editing the 2018 proceedings of the World Sanskrit Conference that the vision for this volume dawned on Raj Balkaran. Not only was McComas a sharp and amiable collaborator, but also his affiliation with The Australian National University provided the necessary institutional grounding for the brainchild of that dreamy self-employed scholar. Dreaminess notwithstanding, Raj assured McComas he would shoulder the administration required for the volume if McComas would handle the courting of ANU Press—and so a deal was struck. We editors were delighted at ANU Press's interest in this proposal especially as its open-access publishing would allow us to offer the fruits of this collaboration to anyone interested, free of charge. So, Raj embarked on a rather surreal experience of approaching esteemed scholar after esteemed scholar, all of whom accepted his cheeky invitation. And suffice to say the surrealism culminated when Wendy Doniger herself agreed to consecrate the volume with her Foreword, bringing the journey full circle as it were.

As for the title of the volume, it came to Raj as both a vision and a revision as he reviewed and revised a title he had used in the context of work on the Indian goddess entitled 'Visions and revisions of the Hindu goddess: Sound, structure, and artful ambivalence in the Devī Māhātmya' (Balkaran 2019). Visions are ways of looking at text, and revisions are ways of looking again, in the twinned senses of revising and re-envisioning. The papers in this collection enact both visions and revisions of the two most significant bodies of Sanskrit narratives, the genres of epic and purāṇa. The *Mahābhārata* and *Rāmāyaṇa* dating from the beginning of the Common Era and the 18 great purāṇas from the first millennium are the primary sources of Hindu mythology, theology, orthodoxy and orthopraxis. These texts are pillars of Indic thought and have shaped cultures and societies from Afghanistan in the west to Bali in the east, and from Sri Lanka in the south to the Himalaya in the north. The impact of Sanskrit narrative on the life of Indian religions cannot be overstated: these texts—and the tales they contain—have encoded and disseminated values from various strata of Hinduism for millennia. They perpetuate the cultural ethos of Indic traditions.

Freda Matchett begins her *Blackwell Companion to Hinduism* introduction to the Purāṇas with something Doniger notes at the end of her introduction to *Purāṇas Perennis*—that is, an invitation to readers to 'sally forth into the living jungle of texts known as the Purāṇas' (Doniger 1993: xii). Matchett aptly comments on the hint of danger innate to Doniger's metaphor, calling narrative travellers to proceed with caution into an exciting—and potentially perilous—domain. Purāṇic narratives are vast, heterogeneous materials whose contents largely transcend the way they describe themselves. Moreover, notes Matchett, their modern printed and bound incarnations obscure for 'readers' the extent to which these works are 'more accurately described as performances, intended to be seen, heard, and enjoyed. Unless some appreciation of this is present, today's reader of the Purāṇas fails to understand them' (Matchett 2003: 129). Despite scholars' best efforts to date a particular purāṇic text, one must acknowledge that these works result from generations of poets and bards accumulating materials on a dynamic, lived process. Irrespective of whether ancient India was marked with the exact bardic culture featured within these story-worlds, it was marked by the idealisation of such bardic culture, as evidenced in the Sanskrit epics and purāṇas. And this comes as no surprise within a cultural context so steeped in performance as a means of celebrating and perpetuating its values. Nevertheless, these works bear the marks of conscious redaction—indeed, sophisticated narrative design that readily invites interpretation.

Some chapters in this volume apply tried and true methodologies to novel questions, while others are experimental (Hegarty), exploratory (Pathak) and indeed provocative (Brodbeck). Yet, all are ultimately philological in the sense that they are based on close readings of the respective source texts. Like a latā creeper entwining a mango tree, these different approaches curl through the branches of this collection of papers—nine on the *Mahābhārata*, four on the *Rāmāyaṇa* and six on the purāṇas—and, we hope, bind them together as a meaningful and informative whole. In addition to showcasing the rich content of Sanskrit narrative, we hereby equally aim to showcase diverse and innovative methods of reading such narratives, particularly as synchronic wholes.

Greg Bailey's Chapter 1, 'Narrative argument and interlocutory frames in the *Mahābhārata*', looks closely at the sessions with the sage Mārkaṇḍeya, the Mārkaṇḍeyasamasyāparvan, in the epic's third book, the *Book of the Forest*. The Pāṇḍavas have a great deal of time on their hands to leverage perhaps the most important function of the forest in Sanskrit narrative, as a locus of learning. Bailey's interest is in how the interlocutory framing devices deployed here serve to guide the interpretation of this section, purposefully interweaving narrative and homiletic (śāstric) material to do so. He also shows the role of these frame narratives in smoothly shifting gears to advance various subjects that would otherwise present as unrelated to one another. Bailey's contribution, too, entails examining the epic's portrayal of the behaviour of brahmins.

Adam Bowles continues the examination of brahmins in the epic's opening book with his contribution in Chapter 2. Bowles takes a deep dive into the character of Āstīka to decipher what he represents within the labyrinthine 'preamble' to Vaiśaṃpāyana's narration of the *Mahābhārata*. Bowles proposes that Āstīka is 'the culminating exemplar of the thematic thread of the peacemaking brahmin, a model of brahminhood opposed to other, necessarily less propitious, brahmin exemplars—a thematic thread to which the epic's authors deliberately allude'. Āstīka is compared with other (imperfect) peacemaking brahmins in the epic such as Ṛcīka, Ruru the lizard-brahmin and Śamīka.

Brian Black's Chapter 3 emphasises a theme common to several chapters in this volume: narrative structure. Black specifically looks at the transition in the transmitters of the text from bards to brahmins. He offers a close reading of the opening frame of the epic 'to bring attention to the rich potential in considering the literary dimensions of the *Mahābhārata*, without supposing that all tropes, metaphors and motifs correspond to a historical reality'. His chapter focuses on the story-world within the text of the epic rather than the historical world behind it. As Black writes, 'regardless of the history of the *Mahābhārata*'s transmission, the epic's own account is that it originated among brahmins, not bards'. He shows that the epic is very much in transition, trying to sort out how to present itself in a post-Vedic world. His chapter also focuses on yet another theme common to several contributions: the role of brahmins in this post-Vedic world.

The subsequent four contributions all focus on the crucial Udyogaparvan, or 'Book of Effort', detailing the various embassies and efforts undertaken to avert the war. Angelika Malinar's Chapter 4 probes the narrative frame of the battle books—that is, the dialogical exchange between the Kuru king Dhṛtarāṣṭra and his charioteer-bard Saṃjaya. Malinar notes that the intradiegetic interactions between Dhṛtarāṣṭra and Saṃjaya, which have yet to be studied in detail, play a significant role in the epic's narrative structure.

Her chapter, too, adopts a literary approach to analyse the structure and content of Dhṛtarāṣṭra and Saṃjaya's crucial exchange. Her analysis draws parallels between this exchange and dramatic literature.

The following two chapters focus on the story of Ambā (the Ambopākhyāna, *Mahābhārata*, 5.170–193), the princess whom Bhīṣma abducts as a bride for his brother. Bhīṣma returns her, learning that she was already betrothed, but Amba's fiancée rejects her on her return. She then approaches Bhīṣma to marry her, but he refuses based on his famous vow of lifelong celibacy. Vowing revenge, Ambā returns as the warrior Śikhaṇḍin to defeat Bhīṣma in the great war. Before destroying herself so that she will be reborn as Śikhaṇḍin, Ambā approaches Rāma Jāmadagnya (Bhīṣma's former guru) for aid, but he, too, refuses her. Brian Collins's Chapter 5 argues that Ambā's story serves as the Rāma Jāmadagnya 'exit myth' from the epic, while also reinforcing important elements of his wider mythology, especially his relationship with his mother, Reṇukā, and his status in South Indian village cults as a servant of Devī.

In Chapter 6, Zuzana Špicová pays special attention to the narrator of Ambā's story, Bhīṣma—'a highly developed character invested in the narrated events, as well as a skilled narrator'. Špicová highlights the subjectivity of an array of associations attached to Bhīṣma, which invariably colour his rendition of Ambā's story. Špicová rightly emphasises: 'When evaluating a story in the *Mahābhārata*, at least three things must be considered: the narrator, the listener and the circumstances.' The same could be said of all Sanskrit narrative. Špicová also examines the intertextuality between Ambā's story and that of other *pativratā* women—Sītā, Sāvitrī, Damayantī and Śakuntalā—to illuminate the way in which 'Bhīṣma [is] authoritatively claiming Ambā's narrative'.

Sudha Berry in Chapter 7 closely examines a highly understudied character in the epic: the formidable Pāṇḍava Bhīma. She argues that while Yudhiṣṭhira and Arjuna represent idealised versions of the dharmic king, Bhīma embodies 'the dark underbelly of *rājadharma*, which is the grunt-work required for the establishment and maintenance of rule'. Far from the 'unthinking, buffoonish glutton he is generally assumed to be', Bhīma is essential to the Pāṇḍavas achieving their goal, representing the pragmatic *realpolitik* required of *kṣatriya* rulers. His loyalty is unwavering, as is his drive to regain their kingdom. In the words of Berry, 'Bhīma neither prevaricates nor shirks from the necessary grit and gore required to win and maintain the kingdom'.

James Hegarty's experimental Chapter 8 examines the moral content of the courtly debates that take place in this book and which are so pivotal to the overarching plot of the epic. Hegarty draws on the work of the evolutionary psychologist and theorist of religion and politics Jonathan Haidt, who argues for a universalistic approach to morality as something innately human. Hegarty uses Haidt's work to consider the very 'moral foundations of the back and forth of negotiations in the Udyogaparvan', shedding light on the 'universal significance of the *Mahābhārata* as a nuanced response to the complex dynamics of family, politics, warfare and much else'.

Simon Brodbeck's Chapter 9 controversially argues that while the *Bhagavadgītā* is a salient and successful example of 'world literature', it is anomalous—first, in that it takes a prowar position, and second, in so far as it adopts a stance of 'philosophical and theological determinism, which is opposed to the idea of human free will that has been widespread in cultures ancient and modern'.

In the first of three chapters on the *Rāmāyaṇa*, Danielle Feller examines the *Rāmāyaṇa*'s story of the divine flying palace (*vimāna*) called Puṣpaka ('Little Flower') in Chapter 10. Feller examines the various metamorphoses the Puṣpaka undergoes in the *Rāmāyaṇa* and beyond, from a self-moving mineral artefact to one associated with animals, drawn by geese, to a deified flying palace worshipped by Rāma himself. Feller draws on the architectural treatise *Samaraṅganasūtradhāra*, in which Puṣpaka refers to a flower-shaped temple adorned with floral and plant motifs.

In Chapter 11, Eva De Clercq compares the Vālmīki *Rāmāyaṇa*'s portrayal of Rāma's journey to forest exile with that of Jain *Rāmāyaṇa* retellings. She notes: 'Whereas in the Vālmīki *Rāmāyaṇa*, Rāma, Sītā and Lakṣmaṇa spend 10 years visiting *āśrama*s in the forest and protecting sages, before settling in Pañcavaṭī, in the Jain accounts, the visits to *āśrama*s are largely replaced with visits to cities, helping rulers in need and marrying princesses.' De Clercq argues that the Jain retellings adopt these changes to align their story of Rāma with Jain universal history, representing Rāma and Sītā as the ideal lay couple and emphasising the forest as the domain of ascetics alone.

Shubha Pathak's Chapter 12 examines the epic's use of precious stones as related to Rāma's and Rāvaṇa's respective fates. Pathak argues that an examination of precious stones in the epic 'reveals its immediate inter-sectarian polemics emblematic of the non-Weberian *nivṛtti* (otherworldliness)/*pravṛtti* (thisworldliness) dynamics seen previously to animate the contemporaneous *Vyāsa Mahābhārata*'.

In the first of six chapters on the purāṇas, Chapter 13, Laurie L. Patton offers an innovative method for reading texts of this genre. She examines sections of the *Agni* and *Vāyu* purāṇas with an eye to reading them as something other than unwieldy fantastical/theological works. Patton advocates a method of reading these texts to reveal the motivation behind the compendium-like compositions as being like those of some contemporary postcolonial writers. Her chapter specifically draws on the theory of magic realism as a genre that interlaces realistic descriptions of the everyday with fantastical, supernatural elements.

In Chapter 14, focused on contemporary Telugu exposition (*pravacana*) of the *Viṣṇu Purāṇa*, Sucharita Adluri offers an exciting insight into the life of the narrative. Her study focuses on the role of the expounders, 'trained in reciting and interpreting the purāṇas and who incorporated material both oral and written in their delivery in temples or other performance spaces'. She specifically examines the way the story of Dhruva (the Dhruvacaritra) is expounded by the contemporary Telugu expositor Samaveda Shanmukha Sharma, shedding light on the crucial interplay between a written purāṇa and its vernacular rendition in oral performance.

Nicolas Dejenne explores the Purāṇic 'meta-myth' pertaining to filial piety (*pitṛbhakti*) in Chapter 15. He examines the second section of the *Padma Purāṇa*, which advances this theme in both its didactic and its narrative passages. He looks at the story of the brahmin Śivaśarman and the ways in which he tests the obedience of his five sons. He also examines the story's 'four plus one' structure—a common setup in Indian myth. Keeping in line with the connection between structure and content, Dejenne invites scholars to study the *Padma Purāṇa* 'at the level of *khaṇḍa*s, or even smaller and more homogeneous portions of *khaṇḍa*s, [which] could prove to be the most fruitful way to shed light on their dominant themes and their organisation'.

Jonas Buchholz examines the relationship between two related genres in Chapter 16, the Sanskrit *sthalamāhātmya Kāñcīmāhātmya* and the Tamil *talapurāṇam Kāñcippurāṇam*. He draws on the ways in which the two texts relate to one another and charts the extent to which the latter, an eighteenth-century text by Civañāṉa Muṉivar, closely models itself on the earlier Sanskrit text at the narrative level. Buchholz argues that Tamil *talapurāṇam* authors such as Muṉivar draw from Sanskrit sources in this manner to partake of the religious authority associated with the Sanskrit language, while the more ambitious poetic agenda that they pursued allowed them to assert the status of the Tamil language.

In Chapter 17 on the 'purāṇification' of the death of Kṛṣṇa, Christopher Austin examines portrayals of this event to illuminate the process of thematic development across the *Mahābhārata*, *Harivaṃśa* and *Viṣṇu Purāṇa*. Austin aims to historicise the popular mythic reading of the *Mahābhārata*, which privileges purāṇic themes. Purāṇification 'involves a shift away from the *Mahābhārata*'s *kālavāda* and *aṃśāvatarana* constructs, which nonetheless deserve to be examined and understood on their own terms'. He brings into focus the distinct vision found in the three source texts, notwithstanding the intertextuality between them.

The final chapter, Chapter 18 by McComas Taylor, examines iterations of the enigmatic Vedic dialogue between the king Purūravas and his divine lover, Urvaśī. This was reworked in various subsequent Sanskrit texts, including the *Kathāsaritsāgara*, *Harivaṃśa* and multiple purāṇas. Taylor demonstrates the way these iterations morph to suit the aims of the respective contexts of their authors, who 'add their own innovations to progress their discursive projects: to glorify the deity, to amuse their audience or to validate a sacred place'.

The chapters here explore narrative through what we refer to as a 'literary lens'. How this term was understood and interpreted was left up to the individual authors. The chapters in this collection, while varied, all engage with narrative as literature in a broad sense. As pedestrian as it may sound, these stories are studied herein *as stories*. The inclination to do so bespeaks not a shortage of impact on their behalf as powerful stories, but rather the relative paucity of attention paid to them as such throughout the history of Western scholarship. The contributions herein draw on a range of contemporary theoretical approaches, with particular interest in intertextuality, narrative structure, narrative authority, characterisation, social context, dialogue and performance. In the succinct and sage words of one of the anonymous reviewers of this volume (both of whom we thank): 'So far as there is a common theme [across the contributions to this volume], it is the need to understand each text on its own terms'. As such, it is our hope that the chapters will facilitate audiences appreciating the beauty, power and agency of these ancient Sanskrit stories.

Raj Balkaran,
Toronto, January 2023

McComas Taylor,
Canberra, January 2023

References

Balkaran, Raj. 2019. Visions and revisions of the Hindu goddess: Sound, structure, and artful ambivalence in the Devī Māhātmya. *Religions* 10(5): 322. doi.org/10.3390/rel10050322.

Balkaran, R. and Taylor, M. (eds). (2019). *Purāṇic Studies: Proceedings of the Purāṇa Section of the 17th World Sanskrit Conference*. Vancouver, BC: University of British Columbia.

Doniger, R. (ed.). (1993). *Purāṇa Perennis: Reciprocity and Transformation of Hindu and Jaina Texts*. Albany: SUNY Press.

Matchett, Freda. (2003). The Purānas. In Gavin Flood (ed.), *The Blackwell Companion to Hinduism*, pp. 129–43. Hoboken, NJ: Blackwell. doi.org/10.1002/9780470998694.ch7.

1

Narrative argument and interlocutory frames in the *Mahābhārata*

Greg Bailey

Abstract

The Mahābhārata 3.196–206 involves instruction on *dharma* given by the sage Mārkaṇḍeya to Yudhiṣṭhira. Its principal feature is the instruction given to the brahmin Kauśika by the wife of a householder and a low-caste seller of meat. This chapter demonstrates how the principal arguments about the question of a brahmin's *dharma* are enhanced by the contrast between the primary frame interlocutors, who introduce the basic narrative and push it along, and the episodic interlocutors, who talk about the difficulties of interpreting *dharma* and with their own behaviour strenuously support *svadharma* as this might be interpreted by the brahmins. There is a difference between the two levels in that the episodic interlocutors are describing and reflecting on their own lived experiences, in contrast with Yudhiṣṭhira, who is constantly being reminded of the difficulty of adhering strictly to his *svadharma* when he finds consistent interpretations of *dharma* so difficult to grasp. The contrast in the interlocutory frames beautifully illustrates the dilemma he faces and the behavioural problems the brahmins—representing a kind of faux institution—must have encountered in the changing social conditions of early historical India.

Introduction

If the overarching battle plot, the leadup to it and its denouement are considered, could we say that the interlocutory system is the main mode of organising the content of the *Mahābhārata*? This question arises out of the recognition that so many episodes in the *Mahābhārata*, especially the non-battle books, superficially appear to not relate directly to the main plot. Of course, this assumes that the epic is defined by the main plot, when in fact it is much more complicated in both its explicit and its implicit themes. A prime function of the interlocutory system is to introduce these lesser narratives—of various genres—in such a way that they will not seem fundamentally out of place in the immediate context where they appear. In this sense, the interlocutory system facilitates the flow—and various other flows—of the narrative whether in an oral recitation or read as a text.

One other area that is worthy of attention in this study is the question of vocatives, in the sense that the names they denote define the relationships between the interlocutors. Equally, they also provide a further confirmation of the fundamental themes of what the interlocutors narrate—that is, the fundamental themes of the *Mahābhārata* itself.

There are four interlocutory levels in the *māhātmya* narrated from 3.196 to 3.206, and the interaction between the levels guides the interpretation of the narrated content. It is especially the contrast between what I call the primary frame interlocutor (PFI) and the episodic interlocutor (EI), which is extremely valuable in defining Yudhiṣṭhira's struggles throughout the *Mahābhārata*. What is also fundamental is to contrast the functioning of both sets of interlocutors—that is, the episodic interlocutors, who play only a small role in the *Mahābhārata*, tell us, directly and indirectly, much about those who play a major role. We should not, however, underestimate the extent to which the *māhātmya*s stand as independent narratives. They demonstrate perfect coherence and a temporal horizon that includes all three tenses as opposed to the virtually one-dimensional time frame marking the narrative activity of the primary frame interlocutor.

The basic narrative summarised

Mārkaṇḍeya is addressing the Pāṇḍavas in the Kāmyaka forest about a range of topics.[1] In the set of chapters (3.196–206) under study, he is exclusively addressing Yudhiṣṭhira, who pushes along the narrative by asking about the law:

> Then King Yudhiṣṭhira, best of the Bharatas, asked Mārkaṇḍeya of great glory a question about the law [*dharmapraśnam*][2] which was exceedingly difficult to explain. Illustrious man, I want to hear this superb story of the greatness of women and the subtle law as it is told by you as it really is, brahmin. (3.196.1–2)

Mārkandeya then begins narrating a *kathā* about an orthodox brahmin named Kauśika who is performing *tapas* under a tree when a bird drops its dung on him. He glances at it angrily and it drops down dead. Filled with remorse, he goes begging and meets a housewife from whom he requests food. As she is getting a dish, her husband arrives and she feeds him first. She remembers the brahmin and he expresses anger towards her. In responding, she proceeds to give him a lengthy disquisition about a woman's obligation towards her husband and describes in several verses the ideal brahmin.

Kauśika is mollified by this. She then instructs him to go to Mithilā, where he will meet a seller of meat, called *dharmavyādha*,[3] who will instruct him further in *dharma*. He goes to Mithilā and receives from him a rather lengthy exposition on *dharma*, *svadharma/svakarma* and ontology. Then the *dharmavyādha* takes Kauśika to his own parents' house and introduces him to his parents, who declare the *dharmavyādha* to be an obedient son. Finally, he reveals to Kauśika he was once a brahmin who was reborn as a *śūdra* because of a sage's curse. Kauśika declares he truly acts like a brahmin and then returns to his own parents' house. Yudhiṣṭhira declares his satisfaction at hearing the *māhātmya* and then asks to hear more.

1 See also Bailey (2016).

2 This compound occurs in only one other place in the *Mahābhārata*, at 2.61.54.

3 'A hunter due to his [*sva*] *dharma*' and not through choice. This seems to be a title rather than a name. Apart from Kauśika, only the primary frame interlocutors are given names.

Primary frame interlocutors

The primary frame interlocutors are those who begin the narrative of the *māhātmya* and see it through to the end. Using Mangels's (1994) language, we might refer to them as 'narrating characters', though the narrated characters—the episodic interlocutors—in the episodes they narrate are themselves also narrating characters, even if in a much more limited space. Superficially, the PFI appears to play a minimal role across the whole of the *māhātmya*, yet each level must be examined in relation to the other.

In these chapters, Vaiśaṃpāyana, Mārkaṇḍeya and Yudhiṣṭhira are the PFIs, though the first appears only once to introduce the dialogue between the other two. In that sense, their interlocutory activity could be said to lie on the second/third level of the *Mahābhārata* interlocutory frame, but Vaiśaṃpāyana's introduction of Mārkaṇḍeya in this chapter, even where he has been speaking at length since the beginning of the *Mārkaṇḍeyasamasyāparvan*, has the effect of tying this episode into the larger *Mahābhārata* narrative. Arguably, though, this has already been done by the continuing references to Yudhiṣṭhira as the second main PFI. Mārkaṇḍeya's narrating activity spreads across the entire 11 chapters, compared with Yudhiṣṭhira's presence in only the first (196) and the last (206).

A few times in Chapter 196 Yudhiṣṭhira expresses his concerns using the first person: 'I do not see [*paśyāmi*] anything more difficult than the terrible law of women' (8ab); 'They always do their own proper duty and that is difficult in my view [*me matam*]' (11cd); and 'Illustrious man, best of those who know about questions, I want to hear this question, best of the Bhṛgu family, I want to hear from you' (13). In that sense, his closeness to Mārkaṇḍeya is made clear and his emphasis on perceiving/seeing indicates where the ensuing narrative must go.

In every place where Mārkaṇḍeya speaks, it is simply to introduce the respective EIs when they speak or when they acknowledge that their request has been answered. On the surface, it seems the PFIs are playing minor roles to push the narrative along. Yet, the two narratives within the *māhātmya* that contain a simple plot are being told in response to Yudhiṣṭhira's questions. Therefore, both question and answer tell us as much about Yudhiṣṭhira himself and, of course, the interpretation of *dharma* as the prominent theme in the epic.[4] But there is more. In the plot, besides the conversation between Mārkaṇḍeya and Yudhiṣṭhira—if that is a plot—,there are apparent reversals where non-brahmins are instructing a brahmin in his own *svadharma*. Maybe this mirrors the reversal of a brahmin/sage (Mārkaṇḍeya) teaching *dharma* to a *kṣatriya* warrior (Yudhiṣṭhira), which is the orthoprax way that things should be done. Why should it be done like this except to strengthen the brahmin's claim to expertise in *dharma*, which is accepted even by those of lesser status than the brahmin?

It is surely also noteworthy that Mārkaṇḍeya, as the 'omniscient narrator', could have easily given Yudhiṣṭhira the normative answers to the questions he put, yet he chooses to answer them through the framework of the EIs.

Episodic interlocutors

EI 1 is Kauśika, EI 2 is the *kutumbinī* and EI 3 is the *dharmavyādha*, with EI 4 and EI 5 intervening later as the *dharmavyādha*'s parents and the *ṛṣi* who curses the brahmin who in a later birth became the *dharmavyādha*. The two plots in which these interlocutors play the fundamental roles are introduced by Mārkaṇḍeya and therefore are separated from each other by the interlocutory activity of the PFI. This is so even where the two episodes operate within the same frame of narrated time, distinguished only by their different locations and the interaction of Kauśika, who provides the temporal and personal continuities with the other EIs and the two plots.

What emerges unambiguously in the speeches of the second and third EIs is the extent to which their expositions are dependent on existing opinions on dharmic matters—opinions seemingly beyond reproach. They are using their own immediate behaviour—feeding one's husband first and remaining in an inauspicious job—and traditionally handed down teachings to justify their own positions. Both appear on the surface to offend Kauśika's sensibilities, yet they are entirely consistent with the householder's view[5] of how society

4 Mangels writes on the contrast between the heroic ethos and *dharma* as a kind of abstract author: 'As already explained in the presentation of Schmid's structure of communication the abstract author as a noticeable instance in the text is not graspable, however in the arrangement of the text on the whole it can be understood' (Mangels 1994: 44–45).

5 On the centrality of the householder in the interpretation of this passage, see Thayanithy (2018).

should be run. The point is that both narrative action and expository teachings are being utilised to make a fundamental point about the ambiguity of *dharma*, otherwise called *sūkṣmatā*.

Let us note initially that the EIs are depicted doing much more expositing than acting, even though the only actions undertaken by the PFIs are speech acts. In the cases of EI 2 and EI 3 it is their status that is seemingly highlighted as the fundamental condition requiring them to provide dharmic expositions. That is, their status is intended to be contrasted with what they say: a lower-class man and a woman giving advice to a brahmin who is supposed to be orthoprax and an expert in the sources of *dharma*. And, apart from speech acts, it is EI 1 who acts most when he kills the *balākā* and makes the trip to Mithilā. This, then, is the basic plot of these 12 chapters, which is made racier by some actions that would seem repugnant to typical brahmin thinking, if such a thing exists.

Episodic interlocutors and their interactions

The episode of Kauśika is set in an entirely undefined past, presumably before the events leading up to the *Mahābhārata* war, though there is no temporal marker giving it any specificity (see 2d, *uccārayan sthitaḥ*, referring to Kauśika). The narrated action involving the EIs has the past, present and future shaping it, as well as at least three different geographical locations: the village, Mithilā and the forest where the brahmin (*dharmavyādha*) is cursed to become a *śūdra*. In contrast, Mārkaṇḍeya's interaction with Yudhiṣṭhira occurs in the present—for as long as it takes to narrate the *māhātmya*—without any indications of temporal difference being given, except at the end, where the conclusion of the narration is indicated in the past tense (cf. 3.206.31).[6]

Perhaps ironically, the brahmin Kauśika has been introduced in stereotypical terms as the ideal of what a brahmin should be. He is the best of the twice-born, learns the Vedas, is rich in austerities and is habituated to the law. And when he is introduced, he is studying the Vedas with their limbs and the Upaniṣads.[7] So, he is as perfect as could be in terms of *varṇa* affiliation.

6 *etat te sarvam ākhyātaṃ nikhilena yudhiṣṭhira* | *pṛṣṭavān asi yaṃ tāta dharmaṃ dharmabhṛtāṃ vara* ||

7 *kaś cid dvijātipravaro vedādhyāyī tapodhanaḥ* | *tapasvī dharmaśīlaś ca kauśiko nāma bhārata* || *sāṅgopaniṣadān vedān adhīte dvijasattamaḥ* | (197.1–2ab).

What more could one ask for? Hence, he is called *dvijasattama*. But surely the point is that this is a stereotype, a list of adjectives used throughout Sanskrit literature to describe the ideal brahmin. Here it is more striking because his subsequent behaviour seems to belie it—though it is unclear why, since the two misdemeanours he makes are hardly of great moment if one compares them with other catastrophic events in the *Mahābhārata*, especially the actions of brahmin warriors who populate the pages of this text.

Kauśika is meditating under a tree when a *balākā* drops its dung on him, leading him to curse it. He then comes begging to a pure village (*grāme śucīni*, 197.7),[8] where he meets the woman (called *kutumbinī*, 197.8).[9] All this is told in the past tense, except for the two imperatives *dehi* and *tiṣṭha* in verse eight, the first spoken by the brahmin, the second by the married woman, but both embedded in the narrated past in Mārkaṇḍeya's narration. These are surely highly significant because they require a response from at least one subject, if not both. But the narration here reverts to Mārkaṇḍeya until verse 18, when the first of the EIs begins with a single sentence, berating the wife.

The brahmin initially takes a haughty position towards the woman. But even before this he shows a degree of individual reflection when, after having killed the bird, he is described thus by the PFI: 'By his compassion the brahmin was severely troubled and grieved over her, "Overpowered by hate and emotion I have done what should not be done", the learned man said repeatedly before going to a village to beg for food' (197.5e–6). Note the initial loss of control and how quickly he changes when he thinks about what he has done. Also note the move to the first person, even where Mārkaṇḍeya is describing the narrative in the third person, which has occurred before only in the case of Yudhiṣṭhira.

As soon as Kauśika reaches a house, a very brief vocal exchange occurs. 'Give!' he was demanding, and then the woman said, 'Wait!' (197.8ab).[10] This shift to the imperative gives some actuality to the narrative, which until now has been spoken in the past tense, with the contrast between these two imperatives being a portentous introduction to the second EI (the wife). Now the narrative reverts to the PFI 1, who speaks in the third person.

8 The idea of purity is also reflected in the housewife going to clean a dish when the brahmin initially asks for food: *śaucaṃ tu yāvat kurute bhājanasya kuṭumbinī* (197.8cd), and *sādhvācārā śucir dakṣā kuṭumbasya hitaiṣiṇī* (197.14ab).

9 Also in Chapter 198, *strī* (8), *sādhvī* (10, 17, 19), *asitekṣaṇā* (11), *saṃyatendriyā* (15), *śubhekṣaṇā* (16), *yaśasvinī* (17) and, in the vocative, *varāṅaṅgane* (18) and *śobhane* (43).

10 *dehīti yācamāno vai tiṣṭhety uktaḥ striyā tataḥ* |

He tells that while Kauśika awaits his food the woman's husband suddenly arrives and she caters to him first, acting exactly as a wife loyal to her husband should. The description given from verse 10c–16 reiterates what Yudhiṣṭhira had already said in Chapter 196, with great emphasis placed on obedience (*patiśuśrūṣaṇe ratā*, 197.13d; *kurvatī patiśuśrūṣāṃ*, 16c) to her husband, her larger household, gods and guests (*śuśrūṣaṇaparā nityaṃ*, 15c). Equally, she is constantly in control of her senses (*satataṃ saṃyatendriyā*, 15d), unlike the brahmin. As such, what we are given here is a description of the ideal wife where the criterion is *pativratā*, all unambiguously reminding us of Yudhiṣṭhira's initial request. Given that Mārkaṇḍeya is offering an evaluative statement, it could have hardly been placed in the first person in the voice of the woman, though this does happen with the *dharmavyādha* later in the narrative.

Finally, she remembers the brahmin, is embarrassed and gives him some food. In opening the dialogue, Kauśika is abrasive: 'What is this? Lovely woman, you tell me "Wait!" and whilst making me stop you do not dismiss me' (197.18).[11] The language is strong, especially the open-ended question at the beginning, and we must wonder whether he assumes she is of a lower class[12] than him, completely ignoring her husband or whether it is just because she is a woman. What we are given is a very angry brahmin—not anticipated in the themes raised in Chapter 196 by either of the two PFIs—whose anger has been expressed in violence towards an innocent bird[13] and now towards a woman who was showing obedience towards her husband in the manner explicitly suggested by Yudhiṣṭhira in his initial comments about a woman's lot (196.7–11b). Does this mean the implied audience outside the text is being asked whether her obligation to feed the brahmin as a guest is greater than that to her husband, and that a brahmin's request outweighs her dharmic requirement to treat her husband first?

Before she can answer, the PFI intervenes, describing the physical and mental condition of the brahmin and, in so doing, opening the possibility of a new dialogue between the two EIs, also suggesting what the tone of this might be. He also brings Yudhiṣṭhira (197.12d) into the frame, pointing to a new development in the narrative and emphasising this change. Mārkaṇḍeya said: 'The good woman having seen the brahmin hot with anger,[14] virtually

11 *kim idaṃ bhavati tvaṃ māṃ tiṣṭhety uktvā varāṅgane | uparodhaṃ kṛtavatī na visarjitavaty asi ||*
12 The fact this is a pure village suggests brahmin status.
13 Another female, as noted by Thayanithy (2018: 196).
14 Cf. 197.4a, *tataḥ kruddhaḥ*, and 197.4c, *bhṛśaṃ krodhābhibhūtena*.

blazing with fiery energy, spoke in a conciliatory manner [*sāntapūrvam*], Indra of men' (3.197.19). The *sāntapūrvam* indicates an awareness that she may have been wrong or that she is dealing with someone of a higher class. In her defence, she says: 'Please be patient with me, brahmin, as my husband is my great deity. He too was hungry and tired when he arrived, he who I obeyed.'[15] Here, again, she reiterates words about obedience as full justification for her behaviour.

But Kauśika upbraids her further, saying in a strident tone:

> A brahmin is not more important! You made your husband more important. Living under the law of the household you are treating [*ava-man*] the brahmins with contempt. Even Indra bows to them, let alone men on earth. Arrogant woman, you do not know? You have not heard this from your elders. Because brahmins are like fire, they can burn up even the Earth. (197.21–22)

This is close to being a threat and at the least is a statement of self-importance based on class difference, though whether gender difference is coming into play here is more difficult to say. And, without subtlety, he asserts the fiery nature of brahmins—already demonstrated in relation to the female bird and in the appearance of his body as perceived by the woman.

His statement, of course, demands a response, but one might have thought it would be left to the husband. Yet, the woman now shows her wisdom in a lengthy speech directly contradicting the impression the brahmin has of her. She immediately declares that she did not treat with contempt the brahmins who are the equals of gods, asking for his forgiveness and then revealing her understanding of the power of the brahmins by providing examples of prominent brahmin ascetics taken from myth (197.26). Then she reiterates one of the basic themes of the *māhātmya* up to this point:

> Faultless brahmin, forgive me this transgression. The rule of the woman who is obedient to her husband [*patiśuśrūṣayā dharmaḥ*], that is pleasing to me, brahmin. Even amongst all the gods, my husband is my supreme god. Without qualification I must obey his law [*dharmam*], excellent brahmin. Behold this particular fruit of obedience to the husband [*śuśrūṣāyāḥ phalaṃ paśya patyur*], brahmin, though which I knew the female crane was angrily burnt by you. (197.28–30)

15 *kṣantum arhasi me vipra bhartā me daivataṃ mahat | sa cāpi kṣudhitaḥ śrāntaḥ prāptaḥ śuśrūṣito mayā* || (197.20).

Again, she is using herself as an example to illustrate Yudhiṣṭhira's concerns, not just mouthing platitudes, so bringing it to life, at least in a narrative sense. She then declares that 'anger is the enemy in the body' and for the next six verses states the qualities of the brahmins, where each verse ends with the phrase: 'Him the gods know to be a brahmin' (31–36).[16] This is clearly formulaic as it occurs elsewhere in the *Mahābhārata* and in some Buddhist texts. What she is doing here is establishing an authoritative basis on which stands her knowledge of 'what is a correct brahmin', backing this up with an esteemed authority, the gods. Her repetition of the appropriate phrase strengthens this authority. In verses 38–40ab, she goes beyond this by giving a kind of executive summary, and a fuller statement of her sources:

> Those people who know the law say that a brahmin's wealth is his learning, self-control, honesty and constant restraint of the senses, and they say the supreme law is truth and honesty, best of the brahmins [38]. The constant law is difficult to know, but it is established on the truth and the elders proclaim [*vṛddhānuśāsanam*] that the law is authorised by revelation [39]. Best of brahmins, the law is certainly subtle and is considered in many ways. And although you know the law, and you are devoted to your own learning and pure, it is my opinion, however, that you, illustrious man, truly do not know the laws [*na tu tattvena bhagavan dharmān vetsīti me matiḥ*] [40].

This takes us back to Mārkaṇḍeya's opening description of the brahmin (197.1), while omitting the reference to his capacity as a *tapasvin*, empowering him to destroy the crane with a single glance. Her final statement about him is, of course, highly significant, based as it is on her judgement of what a brahmin should be as confirmed in all the authentic sources she has just cited. So, she says unequivocally that here is a brahmin who does not understand *dharma*, the interpretation and living out of which are supposed to be the brahmin's speciality. And it is a very strong statement considering one might expect her own status to be lower than that of the brahmin—perhaps highlighted by using 12 vocatives between 197.20 and 197.42, where she calls him *dvijottama* (four times), *dvijasattama* (once), other words for brahmin three times, *anagha* (twice) and *anindita* (once). All these undergird his formal status as she sees him and the final two offer him praise as an ideal brahmin. Does this use of vocatives, in conjunction with the refrain *taṃ*

16 See Bailey (2011).

devā brāhmaṇaṃ viduḥ, undercut his status as a brahmin, without for all that denying his brahmin status—that is, he is a brahmin who does not know *dharma*? But what could this mean?

If this is not enough, she then gives him a suggestion as to where he can learn *dharma*, introducing the *dharmavyādha*, the third EI:

> There is a man, obedient to his mother and father [*mātāpitṛbhyāṃ śuśrūṣuḥ*], who speaks the truth and has conquered his senses. He is a hunter dwelling in Mithilā. He will proclaim the laws to you. Go there at your desire and good wishes to you, best of brahmins. Even if I have spoken all too much, please forgive me, blameless man, because women should not be harmed by anyone, those men who know the law. (197.41–42)

Straight away she is reiterating the importance of obedience—a trait modelling her defence of her own behaviour, but significantly signalling it is not a brahmin who will be telling him about *dharma*, but someone of a much lower class. And her final comment, too, seems to be indicating on her part a deference to his *varṇa* status and the possibility of violence. That is, her status is lower than his, yet she can still proclaim to him what he should know by virtue of being a brahmin.

This persuades Kauśika for, in parting, he says: 'I am pleased with you. Good wishes to you, and my anger has gone, splendid woman. The upbraiding you declared is absolutely the best for me. May you be blessed. I will go and improve myself, splendid woman' (197.43). His change in attitude is total, presumably because of the lecture. Yet, apart from an excess of anger, it is still unclear why Kauśika does not know *dharma* in the appropriate way.

What would be the difference if Mārkaṇḍeya had just stated these prescriptions immediately to Yudhiṣṭhira at the end of Chapter 196? In providing their exposition within a particular plot framework, a 'living' example is given of the clash between social status and dharmic behaviour. Even though 'fictional', it brings out in a more vibrant manner what would be only a set of prescriptions if given in the typical manner of *dharmaśāstra*. Though what has been said at length by the woman and the brahmin's response have been narrated by Mārkaṇḍeya, his use of direct speech by the two participants gives what is said a sense of immediacy, much more so than if he had just summarised it himself. In presenting it within a particular plot structure, he further emphasises the problem of the subtlety of *dharma* and reiterates the *duṣkara* nature of a woman's role, whether she should show allegiance to her husband or to someone defined solely by class identity.

At this point, Mārkaṇḍeya intervenes appropriately since there is to be the introduction of a new plot setting and of a third EI. In so doing, he sets off Kauśika's confrontation with the wife as a separate narrative unit, while maintaining its continuity with the next narrative unit and the theme of the complete *māhātmya*. He offers four verses about the transformation in Kauśika's thinking before he goes to Mithilā:

> Having reflected about the astonishing thing [*tad āścaryam*] the woman had proclaimed, the brahmin, scolding himself, appeared as if he had done something wrong. Thinking that the path of the law was subtle [*dharmasya sūkṣmāṃ gatim*], he then said, 'With trust in what must be, I am going to Mithilā. It is said the perfected hunter who knows the law dwells in it. Right now I am going to him to ask about the law. He is rich in austerities.' Having considered this and fully confident in his mind about the woman's speech, and on account of the female crane and the law-filled, auspicious words, filled with curiosity he set out for Mithilā. (198.1–4)

Here, the *āścaryam* seemingly refers to the housewife's knowledge of the *balākā* and her auspicious words about *dharma*. So, he proposes to ask the *vyādha* about *dharma*, even though it is unclear what he might be able to tell him given what the women has already told him. Mārkaṇḍeya is raising the stakes somewhat by further emphasising the theme of the subtlety of *dharma*, while mostly highlighting the brahmin's own response to what the woman said, perhaps implying his own lack of knowledge of what he should have known. In any case, these are interpretative words on his part, once more partially foreshadowing what will come in the next section—words reiterating for the reader/hearer what this *māhātmya* is about. Without them, the future narrative could be less dramatic than it seems.

Following this, the PFI in only four verses describes Kauśika's journey to Mithilā. The brevity of this again points to the importance of the dialogue that follows. His meeting with the *vyādha* (EI 3) is described by the PFI in the third person, in a manner suggestive of tentativeness on both sides. For initially, the brahmin watches the ascetic (*tapasvinam*, 198.10) selling buffalo meat and venison on the street, but he stays at one side until the *vyādha* senses his presence.[17] It is at this point that the long interaction begins that proceeds from chapters 198 to 205, dominated by the expositions of the *dharmavyādha*. But already in 198.12–13, he shows his special nature, properly greeting the brahmin, while declaring: 'Since you were told by that faithful wife, "You must go to Mithilā", I know entirely the purpose for why you have come here' (198.13).[18] How could he have known this? Unless he is more than just a seller of meat, setting up the expectation for a future answer to the mystery.

Now the narrative reverts to PFI 1, who points out that the brahmin was extremely happy when he heard these words and considered this to be the second astonishing thing (*dvitīyam idam āścaryam*, 198.14). Hence, this is a further qualification as to why the *vyādha* must be taken seriously, and another reference to the astonishment the brahmin felt after his meeting with the woman. It also builds a sense of awe, highlighting the stakes at play.

The *vyādha* takes him to his own home and treats him as he would an honoured guest. After this, Kauśika makes a statement that does not seem to have been anticipated in what either Mārkaṇḍeya or Yudhiṣṭhira said at the beginning of 196, as if a new theme is being introduced: 'It seems to me [*pratibhāti me*] that this activity is not suitable for you. Young fellow, I am extremely pained with your horrific activity' (198, 18). Significant here is the phrase *pratibhāti me*—already used several times (196.5 and 196.7 by Yudhiṣṭhira) as a means of expressing doubt. This is the cue for the *vyādha* to begin the first of his long expositions, which proceeds for the next 75 verses. Are we to assume there is some doubt about everything that is said in respect of the correct *dharma*, although this seems to be totally resolved at the end of this text? The *vyādha* begins by justifying the vocation he has, not yet in the manner of an autobiography, but in terms of his present duties and the cause of his degraded position:

> This job is suitable for my family and came from my father and grandfather. Do not be angry towards me, brahmin, whilst I observe my own law. My own job that I maintain was previously ordained by Dhātṛ, and, best of brahmins, I zealously obey my elderly parents. I speak the truth, I do not grumble, and I give according to my capacity and I live by what is left over from the gods, guests and

17 The title *dharmavyādha* occurs at 198.9 for the first time.

18 *ekapatnyā yad ukto 'si gaccha tvaṃ mithilām iti | jānāmy etad ahaṃ sarvaṃ yadarthaṃ tvam ihāgataḥ* ||

> dependants. I despise nothing and I do not condemn somebody more powerful. Previous actions that have been done follow the doer, best of brahmins. (198.19–22)

What more need be said? Maybe it is initially unexpected that a *vyādha* should have such an understanding, but this is nothing compared with what he teaches in the next six chapters. These show an extremely comprehensive knowledge of brahminical *dharma*, emphasising how the king should ensure the differences between the classes and the consequences of not following *dharma*. Between verses 19 and 27, derivatives of *kṛ* occur 12 times, with the opposition between *vikarma* and *svakarma* strongly asserted in verses 25–26. While rather general, this strongly sustains the decision of the *vyādha* to maintain his vocation even if it is seen as unacceptable from a brahmin's perspective. In short, he is arguing for the validity of class distinctions and the accompanying division of labour.

At 198.55, he introduces the category of the learned (*śiṣṭa*) with the statement that 'the conduct of the learned is difficult to achieve [*sudurlabhaḥ*]', reinforcing the difficulty of practising certain forms of behaviour, as already brought up by the PFI 2 (196.12; and *duṣkara*, 5, 7, 8 and 11). This provides a pretext for the intervention of PFI 1 as it superficially signals a change of direction, with Mārkaṇḍeya saying: 'Then, best of men, the very insightful brahmin asked the hunter by the law, "How can I know the conduct of the learned [*śiṣṭācāraṃ*]?"' (198.56). Arguably, the *vyādha* could have been portrayed continuing his exposition, but the PFI's intervention surely puts stress on the *śiṣṭācāra* and on the fact that a brahmin who was earlier said to be *mahāprājña* should need to know this at all. In the beginning, this seems to relate to conduct required of the brahmin and his appropriate qualifications before going on to treat dharmic behaviour as the foundation of society.

From 198.57, the *vyādha* continues, with the word *śiṣṭa* occurring 24 times between verses 57 and 94, and 14 times as part of a compound with *ācāra*—all confirming the sense of authority acquired by the transmission of learning over time. This is displayed explicitly in verse 78: 'The highest law is spoken in the Vedas and the lower in the treatises on the law, and the conduct of the learned. This is the threefold characteristic of the learned.' In the final verse of Chapter 198, he concludes his exposition of the teaching of the learned and demonstrates his own modesty: 'Brahmin, bull of the brahmins, having put before you the qualities of conduct of the learned, everything has been told to you as I have heard and understood it' (198.94). The point being that, as in all these expositions of *dharma* in the *Mahābhārata*, the teachings come from someone else and the speaker simply transmits them. This is reflected elsewhere in this chapter where the expression *śiṣṭāḥ śiṣṭasaṃmatāḥ* (198.81 and 83) is used twice.[19]

The EI 3 has seemingly given his own proper ending to his disquisition, but at the beginning of 199, the PFI intervenes again even where this might seem unnecessary. He simply states that the *dharmavyādha* began speaking, possibly strengthening the conclusion to the exposition given in the final verse of the previous chapter. These brief interventions are always designed to provide a smooth flow between the narration of subjects. The *dharmavyādha* simply returns to his own situation and reiterates that he does perform a horrific job (*ahaṃ hy ācare karma ghoram*, 199.1) but this is all due to past bad karma, foreshadowing the telling of what his previous deed was. Much of the rest of the chapter is taken up justifying his violent occupation and arguing quite strongly that violence is an integral part of life.

Two points are important here. The first is the stress he places on the dharmic justification for the job (derivatives of *kṛ* occurring nine times in three verses, 14–17). He says:

> Considering 'this is my own law', I will not give it up, best of brahmins. And knowing 'It is due to past acts', I will live by this job. Brahmin, of one who abandons his own job, this is considered not the law here. But whoever is devoted to his own job, that is definitely considered to be the law. (199, 14–15)[20]

The use of *iti* three times possibly gives a further sense of formality and authority to the explanation. Here, we might have expected the intervention of the PFI, but this does not happen and the *vyādha* continues, though shifting to a different subject. He makes an argument that violence is integral to life, as in so many places where things are killed (*han*). This is done in a rhetorical sense because he makes statements such as: 'They consider ploughing to be good, but it is thought there is considerable violence in that. Men who plough with ploughs kill many things dwelling on the ground, and many other living things. Is that obvious to you [*kiṃ pratibhāti te*]?' (199.19).[21] Verses 21–27 continue in a similar vein, each (except for 21) ending in the

19 Meaning that they are being communicated twice: by Mārkaṇḍeya and the *dharmavyādha*.

20 *svadharma iti kṛtvā tu na tyajāmi dvijottama | purākṛtam iti jñātvā jīvāmy etena karmaṇā || svakarma tyajato brahmann adharma iha dṛśyate | svakarmanirato yas tu sa dharma iti niścayaḥ ||*

21 *kṛṣiṃ sādhv iti manyante tatra hiṃsā parā smṛtā | karṣanto lāṅgalaiḥ puṃso ghnanti bhūmiśayān bahūn | jīvān anyāṃś ca bahuśas tatra kiṃ pratibhāti te ||*

phrase *kiṃ pratibhāti te*, where the *vyādha* is putting the responsibility back on to the brahmin, hence inviting him to make a dialogue, as it were, or just a judgement. Equally, it takes us back to the similar phrases found in 198.18, 196.5 and 196.7. These verses seem to be saying that the very ideas of killing and of living creatures living off other living creatures do not need to be justified by reference to *śruti* or the affirmation of the *śiṣṭa*—that it is obvious in itself.

Then follow a few verses stating that some ascetics devoted themselves to nonviolence (*ahiṃsāyāṃ tu niratā yatayo*, 199.29) but violence is still a reality in the world. The *vyādha* even extends violence to rudeness between kinsmen and friends. Finally:

> In the world much can be seen that is topsy-turvy, best of brahmins, and what is not the law is connected with the law. Is that obvious to you? One can talk in many ways about actions which are lawful and unlawful, however, he who is devoted to his own job wins great renown. (199, 33–34)[22]

After a set of arguments and rhetorical questions, this certainly seems an appropriate place to end as the *vyādha* has fully justified his own reason to continue what is seen by a brahmin as a *krūram karma*. Yet, in arguing this, he is supporting the position taken by the brahmin *varṇa* on the nature of society.

Yet, he is still not finished, and at the beginning of 200 the PFI 1 intervenes again, not to change the subject, but to enable the arguments to be refined and reminding us to whom he is speaking: 'Yudhiṣṭhira, the hunter by the law, best of those who uphold the law, once more cleverly said this to the bull of brahmins' (200.1). Is it to be expected that the *vyādha* is called 'best of those who uphold the law' here, given the expertise he has revealed on *dharma* in the previous chapter? It has not been used of Kauśika up to this point. But the *vyādha* wants to give further development to the meaning of *dharma*, so immediately raises yet again the difficulties of its understanding: 'It is said that the standard of the law of the venerable is revelation. For the way of the law is subtle [*sūkṣmā gatir hi dharmasya*], greatly ramified and endless' (200.4). Already the *sūkṣmā gatir* has been suggested in 198.2a and it will come up elsewhere in these chapters, perhaps as a means of

22 *bahu loke viparyastaṃ dṛśyate dvijasattama | dharmayuktam adharmaṃ ca tatra kiṃ pratibhāti te || vaktuṃ bahuvidhaṃ śakyaṃ dharmādharmeṣu karmasu | svakarmanirato yo hi sa yaśaḥ prāpnuyān mahat ||*

explaining why a brahmin ascetic who has not done anything evil needs such a sophisticated instruction in *dharma*. Then, for the next 20 verses, he gives an instruction on karma, how it dominates everything, taking up a theme common elsewhere in Book 3 and the *Mahābhārata* generally. At this point, he becomes metaphysical and begins talking about the difference between the *jīva* and the *śarīra*, as they are affected by karma.

Now the EI 1 breaks in again, asking about the eternality of the *jīva* (200.25). In so doing, he creates the conditions for an extension of what is being discussed, as the EI 3 had closed the previous discussion in a statement about the absoluteness of karma. As such, the *vyādha* leaves the discussion of karma to focus on ontology. This involves a discourse on karmic consequences, rebirth, *duḥkha*, *saṃsāra* and eventually *mokṣa*, with a continued adherence to *dharma*. These verses (30–52) are dominated by references to *dharma* and *duḥkha* (verses 33–37, five times).

Near the end of this chapter, the *vyādha* mentions 'repressing the senses [*indriyāṇāṃ nirodhena*]'. This provides a cue for the EI 1 to change the direction of the narrative and ask a question about the senses and how they can be restrained (200.53–54)—possibly an oblique reference to his failure to react in a restrained manner towards the bird that dropped its dung on him. Given this is the end of the chapter, it provides the opportunity for the PFI to ease the transition between the different subjects, even if this has already been done at the end of the previous chapter.

Chapter 201 continues further with ontology, having the *vyādha* now talk about the foundational nature of the mind and how its functioning can produce adherence to either *dharma* or *adharma*. The chapter is broken in half by Kauśika, who continues his intense praise of the *vyādha* in saying: 'You speak joyfully[23] about law, which has no speaker. In my opinion you are certainly a very great sage with divine powers' (201.12). At which the *vyādha* continues to stress that he is speaking the wisdom of the brahmins: 'I will say whatever is pleasing to them, best of brahmins. Having bowed to the brahmins hear my brahmin knowledge' (201.14). He then goes on to talk about the *sāṃkhyan* elements, finishing with the twenty-fourth. This concludes that chapter—again, at an appropriate point because the totality of the elements has been enumerated, but it foreshadows what the next chapter will be.

23 Taking *sūnṛtaṃ* as an adverb.

Chapter 202 begins with the PFI 1 breaking in: 'As such spoken to by the hunter by the law, Bhārata, the brahmin asked for a further tale [*kathām*] for increasing the joy in his mind' (202.1). Is it significant that *kathā* is used, as it normally designates a running narrative that has a plot, whereas what we are given here is primarily a descriptive ontology, a list with accompanying clarifications?

Kauśika then asks to hear about the five *mahābhūta*s and the *vyādha* immediately outlines their characteristics. Then, from verse 17, he begins talking about the *indriya*s and the need to control them.[24] At the beginning of Chapter 203, the PFI 1 and the EI 1 and EI 3 emerge again to signal a slight change in the direction of the disquisition that is being given:

> Mārkaṇḍeya said, 'When this had been explained subtly by the hunter by *dharma*, descendant of Bharata, the attentive brahmin once more asked about a subtle matter. The brahmin said, "Of *sattva*, *rajas* and *tamas* as they truly are, you should tell me the characteristics truly, carefully now whilst I am listening."[25] The hunter said, "Look here, I will tell you what you are asking me. Listen to their separate qualities as I talk."' (203.1–3)

What seems significant here is the repetition of *sūkṣma* (twice) in 203.1, reminding us of the theme of the subtlety of *dharma* found in earlier verses of this section.[26] It is possibly telling us—and the hearer, who is more important than us as onlookers—how difficult it is to understand this kind of material. And then, as if to confirm this perception of its difficulty, Kauśika asks to hear about the qualities of the three *guṇa*s in a verse where *yathātatham*, *tattvena* and *yathāvad* all occur, each having almost identical meanings (unless they are being used adverbially) and specifying the exactitude by which he wants the explanation to be given. Of these, *tattvena* occurs several times in earlier and later chapters, with *yathātatham* occurring only at 198.56.

24 Verses 21–23 are reminiscent of *Kaṭha Upaniṣad* (3.3–6), where the need to control the mind receives most focus at the end of the chapter.

25 *sattvasya rajasaś caiva tamasaś ca yathātatham | guṇāṃs tattvena me brūhi yathāvad iha pṛcchataḥ* || (203.2).

26 As noted by Ramanujan (1991: 435): 'It is not *dharma* or right conduct that the *Mahābhārata* seems to teach, but the *sūkṣma* or subtle nature of *dharma*—its infinite subtlety, its incalculable calculus of consequences, its endless delicacy. Because *dharma-sūkṣmatā* is one of the central themes that recur in an endless number of ways, the many legal discussions are a necessary part of the action.' See also Thayanithy (2018); Hudson (2013).

The *guṇa*s are explained in a dynamic sense where one moves from *tamas*, to *rajas* and then to *sattva*, which leads to *vairāgya* (203.9), and when there is no exertion and the opposites are appeased, one of a lower class can become of a higher class. The *vyādha* then brings this to an end and asks what the brahmin wishes to hear now. The brahmin's response is highly specific and he advances the discussion by asking 'what happens to the body fire when it reaches the element earth, and how does the wind by its particular location actuate [*vartayate*] a person?' (203.14).[27]

Once more, the PFI breaks in, but why? Mārkaṇḍeya said, 'Yudhiṣṭhira, this question directed [*samuddiṣṭaṃ*] by the brahmin, the *vyādha* spoke to the great brahmin' (203.14). The narrative could have continued simply with the *vyādha* speaking, but perhaps because it is such a specific question it was thought that an atypical form of indicating a new question was appropriate. There are no vocatives used in either of these verses, only the dative *brāhmaṇāya mahātmane*, which gives focus to Kauśika. From 203.15 to 203.28, the different forms of *prāṇa* are explained. More general teachings follow, which return to ethical behaviour and nonviolence, and the chapter finishes with these words:

> That man who completely gives up both unhappiness and happiness [*duḥkhaṃ sukhaṃ cāpy*], he attains Brahma and by detachment goes beyond the end. As I heard all this in summary [*yathāśrutam idaṃ sarvaṃ samāsena*], best of brahmins, all this to you I have narrated. What more do you want to hear? (203.50–51)

He points out yet again that none of what the *vyādha* says is original to him. Once more, he gives an appropriate conclusion to the content he had been expositing and an invitation to a new subject, the point being this: what more could he say about this subject of ontology and ascetic behaviour?

At this point, the PFI 1 intervenes again and the verses following indicate that this section of homiletic teaching has been completed. Mārkaṇḍeya said:

> Yudhiṣṭhira, when the entire teaching about release [*mokṣadharme*] had been narrated, the brahmin, really joyful in his heart spoke to the hunter by *dharma*: 'You have related everything with appropriate argumentation [*nyāyayuktam*]. There appears to be nothing in the world about the laws that is unknown to you.' (204.1–2)

27 Translated by van Buitenen (1975: 631).

This could have been an appropriate ending for this set of chapters as all the relevant teachings seem to have been completed. Yet, at least two implied questions have still to be answered: the conditions under which Kauśika encountered first the woman and then the *vyādha* still must be explained, as does the *vyādha*'s expertise in *dharma* when he is not a brahmin. Hence, the reason for the entry of the PFI 1 again:

> The hunter said, 'Best of brahmins, the law of mine is quite clear. Look at it, by which I have gained this success, bull of brahmins. Get up, illustrious man. Quickly enter my house and please visit my father and mother, knower of the law.' (204.3–4)

It could be significant that the *vyādha* calls Kauśika *dharmajña* here (though he has already called him *dharmabhṛtāṃ vara* at 200.16), indicating perhaps that Kauśika is now to be treated as one who knows *dharma* given the instruction he has had. At this point, the interlocutory system becomes more complex with the introduction of a new set of speakers and the need for the PFI to narrate what is narrative action rather than expository teaching. Mārkaṇdeya provides a brief description of the house and tells how, on entering, the *vyādha* fell at his parents' feet, bowing. The parents can be called EI 4 and immediately begin a dialogue, telling their son, called *dharmajña*, to rise, saying that 'the law will protect you' (204.8). They say he has treated them as a deity and that, 'by your personal devotion you are endowed with the restraint of the brahmins' (204.9cd), indicating that they see him as functioning like a brahmin. What they emphasise is the honouring of his parents.

Now Kauśika intervenes and asks after the parents' health in a formalised manner and they respond in an equal manner. In verse 16, the PFI 1 intervenes again. Mārkaṇḍeya said: '"Absolutely," the brahmin replied to these two happily. Now the hunter by the law made this statement which was full of meaning' (204.16). The brahmin's words are in response to the two parents wishing him well, but it seems unnecessary for Mārkaṇḍeya to intervene here unless it is to mark the transition from the parents to the brahmin to the *vyādha* speaking again. Now the *vyādha* intervenes and declares that he treats his parents like gods (204.17, 20) and further: 'My life, wife, sons and friends exist for them. With my wife and sons I always show obedience to them [*śuśrūṣāṃ nityam eva karomy aham*]' (204.22). In the end, he repeats: 'This is the eternal law for the one who lives in the householder stage' (204.27ef). This would surely seem to be an appropriate ending for this chapter, but the narrative reverts to the PFI 1 at the beginning of Chapter 205:

> Now that he had introduced both his parents to the brahmin, the *vyādha*, whose self is the law, spoke once more to the brahmin: 'My sight has become developed. Behold the power of austerities. For that purpose you were told by her—who is entirely obedient to her husband [*patiśuśrūṣaparayā*] and is disciplined and habituated to the truth—'Go to Mithilā. In Mithilā there lives a hunter. He will proclaim the laws to you.' (205.1–3)

This sets a context for both the past events and the future, establishing continuity between the two, and provides the temporal armature for the narrative plot in which the three EIs are involved. Now occurs a dialogue between the brahmin and the *vyādha* that confirms the brahmin has understood the *pativratā*'s prediction and this then leads on to the hunter's story of why he is a *vyādha*. He now tells Kauśika what he has done:

> Best of brahmins, you have offended your mother and father, because without their permission you left their house, blameless man. What you did was inappropriate according to the duties prescribed in the Vedas. These two ascetics [*tapasvinau*] have become blinded with grief for you. Go and appease them. Do not let the great law pass you by. You are an ascetic [*tapasvī*], your soul is the law and you are always devoted to the law, but all this is useless for you. Go quickly and really please them. Have faith in me, brahmin. Don't do anything else. Now go, brahmin sage. I am saying what is the best for you. (205.7–10)

This fits perfectly with the theme of obedience to one's parents or spouse that has run through this set of chapters. But why was the metaphysical material included? Was it to demonstrate how complete the *vyādha* was in his knowledge of the law?

The two final chapters (205–6) deal with Yudhiṣṭhira's request to hear the *māhātmya* to its completion and an explanation of the foresight of the faithful wife, in a manner that the *vyādha* has already given of himself. The *vyādha* now praises Kauśika, saying he is like a deity and he is vowed to the law. He instructs him explicitly to go to care for his parents as 'I can see no other higher law than that at all' (205.13cd).[28] In response, Kauśika begins to speak again, heaping praise on the *vyādha*, declaring that he has rescued him as he was falling to Hell (205.15). But now he asks the *vyādha* about his status as a *śūdra*: 'The law is always difficult to understand for one who lives in the *śūdra* class. I do not think you are a *śūdra*, for fate was the instrument

28 On which, see Thayanithy (2018: 195–96, 198).

of this. In consequence of the ripening of karma you attained this status as a *śūdra*' (205.19). Which brings into play the *karmavipāka* aspect of this entire narrative. To which the *vyādha* explains that he was a brahmin in a previous body, 'studying the Vedas, highly skilled, and expert in the limbs of the Vedas. Brahmin, I gained this situation because of mistakes I made' (205.22)[29]—thus advancing the narrative by requiring an explanation of this mistake.

At the beginning of 206.1–2, EI 5 is introduced by the *vyādha* in the third person. He is the seer who cursed the *vyādha* when he was a brahmin, hence a third tale referring to events that occurred in an earlier time, again reaffirming the explicit temporal frame of this statement. From 206.3 to 206.5, there is a brief dialogue between the hunter and the *ṛṣi*, in which the curse is stated with its accompanying mitigation. He learnt archery with the king, went out hunting and, by mistake, shot a *muṇi*, who cursed him to be born as a *śūdra*. The *muṇi* mitigates the curse by saying he will become a sage of the law and serve his parents, that he will remember his past life and become a brahmin again when the curse is ended (206.4–5).

Kauśika continues to praise him, saying that though he is a *śūdra* he is really a brahmin: 'Even now I have no doubt that you are a brahmin' (206.10e–12). And, from 15 to 26, the *vyādha* offers another disquisition about wisdom and not giving into despair, to which the brahmin responds:

> You are a man who has acquired wisdom, you are wise and your intellect is broad. Because you are satiated with knowledge and you know the law I do not grieve for you. I bid you farewell, good luck to you, and may the law protect you. There should be no carelessness in regard to the law, best of those who uphold the law. (206.27–28)

Kauśika does not grieve because he knows the *vyādha* will continue to perform his own duty. Adherence to *svadharma*—irrespective of how grisly it might be—is what he must do if he is to advance towards regaining his brahmin status.

At this point, the PFI re-enters the narrative to declare the hunter's agreement and the brahmin's return to his parents and his total obedience to them (*sarvāṃ śuśrūṣāṃ kṛtavāṃs*, 206.30). The final few verses are simply a brief dialogue between the two PFIs indicating that the narration is complete.

29 *ahaṃ hi brāhmaṇaḥ pūrvam āsaṃ dvijavarātmaja | vedādhyāyī sukuśalo vedāṅgānāṃ ca pāragaḥ | ātmadoṣakṛtair brahmann avasthāṃ prāptavān imam ||*

Episodic interlocutors and the sources of their authority

What is most striking about the dharmic expositions of EI 2 and EI 3 is their capacity to teach about *dharma* while simultaneously alluding to its subtlety and difficulty of interpretation. It is easier to exercise obedience to your parents than it is to untangle the inconsistencies of *dharma*, which extend even to ontology. Equally striking, if not more so, is the constant appeal to authorities beyond themselves made by the EIs. References are often made to *śrūyate śruti* (199.12; 199.5, 9; 200.23), *iti niścayaḥ* (199.15),[30] *vṛddhānām iti bhāṣitam* (200.2), *tat satyam iti dhāraṇā* (200.4), *ācāraś ca satāṃ dharmaḥ* (198.70), *śrutipramāṇo dharmaḥ syād iti vṛddhānuśāsanam* (197.39cd), *dharmaḥ sa ca satye pratiṣṭhitaḥ* (198.69), *atrāpi vidhir ucyate* (199.13), *iti smṛtam* (202.11) and *yathāśrutam idaṃ sarvaṃ* (203.51). In addition, there are many references to the *śiṣta* in Chapter 198 to which I have already alluded. As such they are just communicating what they have heard from other traditional sources and applying them to their own situation.

All the appeals to authority are found in statements made by the EIs, never by the PFIs. In part, this is because the woman and the *dharmavyādha* are justifying their own roles, whereas Kauśika does not justify his own actions; he simply listens. Why do EI 2 and EI 3 need to justify their own actions? Is it because they feel that, from the brahmin's perspective, they are not up to scratch? This seems to be one possible conclusion that can be drawn from the teachings and the positions in which they find themselves in relation to Kauśika.

The kind of certainty associated with these sources, especially used as a collective, is somewhat contrasted—contradicted would be too strong a word—with the occurrence of the verb *pratibhāti* at various points in the text, used by Yudhiṣṭhira and then by the *dharmavyādha*. Whether or not used with an interrogative particle, it can convey the sense of doubt, or at least of questioning. In the use of this by Yudhiṣṭhira, Kauśika and the *dharmavyādha* (10 times in 199.19, 20, 22–27 and 33), the final use is perhaps the most significant:

30 And *iti* occurring 23 times to indicate a source of authority.

> In the world much can be seen that is topsy-turvy, best of brahmins, and what is not the law is connected with the law. Is that obvious to you [*tatra kim pratibhāti te*]? One can talk in many ways about actions which are lawful and unlawful, however, he who is devoted to his own job wins great renown. (199.33–34)

This both justifies the *dharmavyādha* in his own occupation and highlights the real difficulties of interpreting *dharma* in the manner Yudhiṣṭhira already brought up in Chapter 196. Arguably, it brings together one of the PFIs with two of the EIs, though I would rather see it as Yudhiṣṭhira mirroring Kauśika, as both feel remorse for violence they have committed or will commit.

Conclusion

While the interpretative emphasis in these 11 chapters will necessarily centre on the two separate, though closely related *kathā*s of the brahmin Kauśika and the education he receives, it also interrogates the conduct and attitude of Yudhiṣṭhira, if only because he is the initial questioner. But for those who know the text, it is essential the underlying themes of this *ākhyāna* are read in relation to Yudhiṣṭhira, who is so well known as the *dharmarāja*. The subtlety of *dharma* in the face of problems of its correct interpretation is epitomised in the behaviour of Kauśika, and through him of Yudhiṣṭhira, whose doubts about correct *dharma* and his own dharmic role are legion throughout the *Mahābhārata*.

Yet, if the teachings on *dharma* are exposited with a high degree of clarity in this *māhātmya*—even in the face of its continually professed subtlety—it is still necessary to ask why these teachings had to be given, and why they must be given continually. I note, too, that they are delivered in terms of a narrative plot, in which two of the principal characters are a compromised brahmin and an ex-brahmin. Not only is there entertainment value in adopting this approach, it also must reflect the fluidity of rigid adherence to dharmic prescriptions in changing urban and even rural environments. Of course, the entire subject of dharmic fluidity under straitened circumstances dominates the main narrative of the *Mahābhārata* in which many of the prominent characters experience great difficulty conforming with their karmically defined identities. Though the teachings on *dharma* may have been designed to develop the framework of a 'perfect world', there is a constant recognition through the two epics and purāṇas that the world can never be like this. Furthermore, it is a question of (*sva*) karma and (*sva*) *dharma* being brought together here as they are in so many parts of the *Mahābhārata*.

In the final analysis, the two *kathā*s told in the *māhātmya* are human-interest stories. The method is the same as that used in contemporary electronic and print journalism when a particular law or government policy is illustrated within the context of a life event of a particular individual. That is, instead of simply stating what the formal, more abstract aspect of a prescribed mode of conduct might be, they show how it works effectively/ineffectively in recognisable life situations.

What would be the difference if Mārkaṇḍeya, in answering Yudhiṣṭhira's questions, had just stated the prescriptions immediately at the end of Chapter 196? In providing their exposition within a particular plot framework, a 'living' example is given of what can go wrong when ascription of social status is given against what is dharmic behaviour. Even though 'fictional', it brings out in a more vibrant manner what would be only a set of prescriptions if given in the typical manner of *dharmaśāstra*. Though what has been said at length by the housewife, to which the brahmin has responded, has been narrated by Mārkaṇḍeya, his use of direct speech in allowing the EIs to speak gives to what is said a sense of immediacy, much more so than if he had just summarised it himself. Emotional judgements come into play, then justifications are given for lifestyles initially frowned on by Kauśika. Use of the sophisticated interlocutory system is the key for allowing this to happen.

In the final analysis, this *māhātmya* contains 433 verses and, of these, arguably 48 relate to interlocutory activity, with all these ultimately recited by the PFIs (Mārkaṇḍeya and Yudhiṣṭhira) but including Mārkaṇḍeya's narration of the EIs' interlocutory activity. This amounts to about 12 per cent of the total. Though seemingly small in comparison with the verses describing narrated action, the interlocutory system remains highly significant, because it is so successful in advancing the narrative smoothly and incorporating subjects that on the surface seem quite different to each other.

References

Primary text

Sukthankar, Vishnu Sitaram (ed.). (1933–66). *The Mahābhārata*. [19 vols.] Poona, India: Bhandarkar Oriental Research Institute.

Secondary texts

Bailey, Greg. (2011). 'Him I call a brahmin': Further instances of intertextuality between the *Mahābhārata* and some Pāli texts. In B. Tikkanen and A.M. Butters (eds), *Pūrvāparaprajñābhinandanam: East and West, Past and Present—Indological and Other Essays in Honour of Klaus Kartunnen*. Studia Orientalia No. 110, pp. 3–19. Helsinki: Finnish Oriental Society.

Bailey, Greg. (2016). Introductory notes on the literary structure of the *Mārkaṇḍeyasamāsyāparvan*. In V. Adluri and J. Bagchee (eds), *Argument and Design: The Unity of the Mahābhārata*, pp. 127–60. Leiden, Netherlands: Brill. doi.org/10.1163/9789004311404_006.

Collins, Brian. (2020). *The Other Rāma: Matricide and Genocide in the Mythology of Paraśurāma*. Albany, NY: SUNY Press.

Hudson, Emily. (2013). *Disorienting Dharma: Ethics and the Aesthetics of Suffering in the Mahābhārata*. New York, NY: Oxford University Press. doi.org/10.1093/acprof:oso/9780199860760.001.0001.

Mangels, A. (1994). *Zur Erzähltechnik im Mahābhārata* [*On the Narrative Technique in the Mahābhārata*]. Hamburg: Verlag Dr. Kovac.

Ramanujan, A.K. (1991). Repetition in the *Mahābhārata*. In A. Sharma (ed.), *Essays on the Mahabhārata*, pp. 419–43. Leiden, Netherlands: E.J. Brill.

Sathaye, A. (2015). *Crossing the Lines of Caste: Viśvāmitra and the Construction of Brahmin Power in Hindu Mythology*. New York, NY: Oxford University Press. doi.org/10.1093/acprof:oso/9780199341108.001.0001.

Thayanithy, Maithili. (2018). Can the subaltern speak? Revisiting the expositions of dharma in the *Mahābhārata*. In S. Brodbeck, A. Bowles and A. Hiltebeitel (eds), *The Churning of the Epics and Purāṇas*, pp. 189–208. New Delhi: Dev Publishers and Distributors.

van Buitenen, J.A.B. (1975). *The Mahābhārata. Volume 2, Book 2: The Book of the Assembly Hall. Book 3: The Book of the Forest*. Chicago, IL: University of Chicago Press. doi.org/10.7208/chicago/9780226223681.001.0001.

2

Āstīka, black magic and apotropaic ritual: Peacemaking brahmins and the snake sacrifice in the *Mahābhārata*'s Ādiparvan

Adam Bowles

Abstract

The opening chapters of the Ādiparvan of the *Mahābhārata* present an intricate weaving together of stories and thematic motifs. This chapter will analyse the opposing, yet complementary, motifs of violent brahmins and peacemaking brahmins in various stories of the Ādiparvan, which culminate in Āstīka's halting of Janamejaya's snake sacrifice. It will further analyse the semiotics of aspects of the ritual setting that play with motifs deriving from the ritual tradition of the Atharvaveda. In the process, it will propose an explanation for the peculiar morphology of 'Āstīka' and Āstīka's 'meaning'.

Introduction

This chapter develops some ideas related to the character of Āstīka that seek to explain his meaning within the labyrinthine complexity of the Ādiparvan's preamble to Vaiśaṃpāyana's narration of the *Mahābhārata* (*Mbh*). It will focus on two aspects. First, it will propose that Āstīka is the culminating exemplar of the thematic thread of the peacemaking brahmin, a model of brahminhood opposed to other, necessarily less propitious, brahmin exemplars—a thematic thread to which the epic's authors deliberately allude. Second, it will suggest that in depicting both Janamejaya's snake sacrifice and Āstīka's peacemaking intervention in it, the *Mahābhārata*'s authors deployed apotropaic ritual ideas found especially in the Atharvaveda. Āstīka, in performing his peacemaking role and as a *vaidika* master of language, sublimates violence into verbal acts. These verbal acts suspend violence, but do not resolve the underlying enmity due to which violence is always imminent.

The complexity of the opening *upaparvans* in the *Mahābhārata*'s Ādiparvan is well acknowledged. Indeed, the metaphor of the labyrinth was used as far back as Winternitz (1926: 79). Its intersecting and overlapping themes, motifs and narrative devices include apocalyptic violence, revenge cycles, co-named protagonists, the ambivalent status of snakes (*nāga*, *sarpa*) and imperilled rituals. Causal explanations of violent events are layered in complex ways. The revenge cycles are suffused with a narrative aesthetic of reciprocal justice. Its contradictions and repetitions have led to higher critical analyses—for example, by Mehta (1973; cf. Adluri 2011) on the 'double introduction' and Shee (1986: 1–30) on the two versions of Parikṣit's assassination. Even so, such repetitions and retellings are important parts of the preamble's narrative texture, offering different viewpoints and explanatory details of the events culminating in the sacrifice of snakes at King Janamejaya's *sarpasatra*.

As Minkowski (2007: 398–400) and Hiltebeitel (2002: 114–15) have argued, the cycles of vengeful violence leading up to Vaiśaṃpāyana's narration to Janamejaya of the story of his ancestors during the snake sacrifice, in Hiltebeitel's words, 'underlie and enfold the rivalry between the Pāṇḍavas and Kauravas'—a point similarly made by Mahesh Mehta (1971: 51–52) in regard to the story of the rival sisters Kadrū and Vinatā (*Mbh*, 1.14–35) told in the Āstīkaparvan. Hiltebeitel was following a line of thought, instigated by Minkowski, revising Sukthankar's thesis that the brahmin line descending from Bhṛgu, whose members (which include our outer frame interlocutor Śaunaka) were therefore called Bhārgava, were a significant 'causeway' in the recessional history of the *Mahābhārata*. The Bhārgavas had, according to this theory, 'Bhṛguised' the *Mahābhārata* (Sukthankar 1936; Goldman 1977). Minkowski (2007) largely overturned this thesis, not because of the lack of prominence of Bhārgavas, but rather because they are generally negatively cast as perpetuators of violent and destructive deeds, making the narrativising of Bhārgava stories a better fit for the *Mahābhārata* than Sukthankar had supposed.

The pattern of violence enmeshed in rivalries prompted by slights is evident in the brahmin Rāma Jāmadagnya's repeated genocidal slayings of *kṣatriya*s to avenge his father's slaying at the hand of the Haihaya princes (*Mbh*, 1.2.2–8), thereby sustaining a generational feud; in Janamejaya's being cursed to experience an 'unseen danger' in return for his brothers' abuse and beating of a dog (1.3.1–9); in the brahmin Uttaṅka's smoking out of the snakes in their underworld to avenge Takṣaka's theft of earrings (1.3.158) and Uttaṅka's transferral of his vengeance on to Janamejaya by telling him that Takṣaka had killed his father (1.3.185–95); in the brahmin Ruru's stomping on snakes in revenge for his wife being bitten by a snake (1.9); in the rivalry between the sisters Kadrū and Vinatā, which itself results in the creation of birds and snakes and their interspecies rivalry that entertains cosmogonic and eschatological themes (1.14–30); in the brahmin Śṛṅgin's curse of Parikṣit to die at Takṣaka's bite to avenge Parikṣit's slight against his father, Śamīka (1.36.8–1.40; 1.45–46); and in Janamejaya's *sarpasatra*, which is an act of revenge for the assassination of Parikṣit, his father (1.47–1.53.26). The perpetrators of these violent and vengeful acts are frequently brahmins, though they culminate in the genocidal sacrifice of the *kṣatriya* Janamejaya (who 'makes people tremble'), and the victims are often snakes. But usually, it is also brahmins who attempt to bring these violent and genocidal episodes to a close—sometimes succeeding, especially so in the case of the brahmin-*nāga* Āstīka.

These revenge narratives display a logic of justice, in which the reckoning for an infraction mirrors aspects of the events characterising the original infraction. This pattern is a common motif in the *Mahābhārata*'s narrative aesthetics of justice, most tellingly in the felling of the four Dhārtarāṣṭra generals, Bhīṣma, Droṇa, Karṇa and Śalya, whose deaths are at once part of a cycle of human revenge and a playing out of the cosmological consequences of their breach of social and cultural norms (Hiltebeitel 1990: 244–86; Bowles 2008: xviii–xl). In each case, the mode of their demise reflects as consequence an aspect of the violation of such norms that each represents. The narrative aesthetics of justice in the *Mahābhārata* have a jurisprudential parallel in the idea of *lex talionis* (the 'law of retaliation'), in which the redress for a 'criminal' act is equal to the crime: an 'eye for an eye', as the so-called ancient Babylonian Code of Hammurabi would have it (Bottéro 1992: 156–84) and various biblical texts restate (Jackson 1998). The Indic version of this legal provision—apparently common to many ancient societies—operates within the telos of the law of *karman*, in which an act produces a consequent effect (Rocher 1983: 69; Yelle 2010: 187–88). As far as the narrative aesthetics of the *Mahābhārata* are concerned, the device produces neat refractions of cosmic justice—not necessarily reducible to such a simple equation as 'an eye for an eye', but nevertheless recognisable through an aesthetic resemblance between act and consequence—that confirm the implicit and integral link between social norms and cosmic stability. This cosmologically enframed ethics is a crucial part of the epic's plot and a key constituent of its normative claims.

Most of the material leading up to Janamejaya's snake sacrifice concerns two things: the snake sacrifice and events related to it, and Śaunaka's family, the Bhārgavas. I will not here give a summary of the intricate details of all the stories in these opening sections of the Ādiparvan, for which there are other sources (for example, Earl 2011; van Buitenen 1973). I will focus primarily on the stories of Rāma Jāmadagnya, the two Rurus, Śamīka and his son Śṛṅgin, and Āstīka and Janamejaya's sacrifice.

Rāma Jāmadagnya and his grandfather Ṛcīka

Ugraśravas introduces the story of Rāma Jāmadagnya very early in the *Mahābhārata*, if only obliquely. When explaining to the sages led by Śaunaka, who become his interlocutors and who are engaged in a 12-year *satra* in the Naimiṣa Forest, how he came to be before them, Ugraśravas reports:

> *samantapañcakaṃ nāma puṇyaṃ dvijaniṣevitam |*
> *gatavān asmi taṃ deśaṃ yuddhaṃ yatrābhavat purā |*
> *pāṇḍavānāṃ kurūṇāṃ ca sarveṣāṃ ca mahīkṣitām ||*
>
> [I went to that sacred land frequented by brahmins called Samantapañcaka, where the Pāṇḍavas, Kurus, and all the rulers of the Earth had a battle long ago.] (*Mbh*, 1.1.11)

Ugraśravas hereby introduces a region that is either the same as or within Kurukṣetra ('the field of the Kurus')—a name with Vedic pedigree for the region where the Kuru war will take place. Samantapañcaka—a name that appears to be inaugurated in the *Mahābhārata*—is conferred on this region due to the violent deeds of the brahmin Rāma Jāmadagnya, who is a

Bhārgava and ancestor of Śaunaka, Ugraśravas's primary interlocutor. With this ever-so-brief allusion, Ugraśravas links together the *kṣatriya* apocalypse perpetrated by Rāma Jāmadagnya, the *kṣatriya* apocalypse perpetrated by the Kuru heroes about which the bard has just heard and will soon tell, both taking place on the sacred fields of Kurukṣetra, and the apocalyptic snake sacrifice of Janamejaya from which he has just come (*Mbh*, 1.1.8; Fitzgerald 2002: 106).

Ugraśravas's brief reference to Samantapañcaka has not passed the notice of the seers to whom he speaks and, in a style that is typical of the *Mahābhārata*, they ask to hear about it in full (*sarvam*) at the beginning of Chapter 2. Ugraśravas responds:

> *śuśrūṣā yadi vo viprā bruvataś ca kathāḥ śubhāḥ |*
> *samantapañcakākhyaṃ ca śrotum arhatha sattamāḥ ||*
> *tretādvāparayoḥ saṃdhau rāmaḥ śastrabhṛtāṃ varaḥ |*
> *asakṛt pārthivaṃ kṣatraṃ jaghānāmarṣacoditaḥ ||*
> *sa sarvaṃ kṣatram utsādya svavīryeṇānaladyutiḥ |*
> *samantapañcake pañca cakāra rudhirahradān ||*
> *sa teṣu rudhirāmbhassu hradeṣu krodhamūrcchitaḥ |*
> *pitṝn saṃtarpayām āsa rudhireṇeti naḥ śrutam ||*
> *atha rcīkādayo 'bhyetya pitaro brāhmaṇarṣabham |*
> *taṃ kṣamasveti siṣidhus tataḥ sa virarāma ha ||*
> *teṣāṃ samīpe yo deśo hradānāṃ rudhirāmbhasām |*
> *samantapañcakam iti puṇyaṃ tatparikīrtitam ||*
> *yena liṅgena yo deśo yuktaḥ samupalakṣyate |*
> *tenaiva nāmnā taṃ deśaṃ vācyam āhur manīṣiṇaḥ ||*
> *antare caiva saṃprāpte kalidvāparayor abhūt |*
> *samantapañcake yuddhaṃ kurupāṇḍavasenayoḥ ||*
> *tasmin paramadharmiṣṭhe deśe bhūdoṣavarjite |*
> *aṣṭādaśa samājagmur akṣauhiṇyo yuyutsayā ||*
> *evaṃ nāmābhinirvṛttaṃ tasya deśasya vai dvijāḥ |*
> *puṇyaś ca ramaṇīyaś ca sa deśo vaḥ prakīrtitaḥ ||*
> *tad etat kathitaṃ sarvaṃ mayā vo munisattamāḥ |*
> *yathā deśaḥ sa vikhyātas triṣu lokeṣu viśrutaḥ ||*
>
> [Finest brahmins, if you want to listen as I narrate these auspicious, most excellent stories, you can hear about the place known as Samantapañcaka. At the juncture of the Tretā and Dvāpara epochs,

> the finest wielder of weapons, Rāma, driven by his indignation, repeatedly annihilated the warrior class. Rising against the entire warrior class, his radiance that of fire, he created five blood lakes at Samantapañcaka through his own valour. We've heard that, his anger swelling, he satiated his ancestors with blood amid those lakes the water of which was blood. Then his ancestors, led by Ṛcīka, approached that bull among brahmins and restrained him, saying, 'Quell your anger!' Then he stopped indeed. That holy land near to those lakes with their waters of blood is called 'Samantapañcaka'.[1] The wise say that with whatever feature a land is observed to be endowed, by that name alone that land shall be known.
>
> When the interval of the Kali and Dvāpara epochs had arrived, there was a battle on Samantapañaka between the Kuru and Pāṇḍava armies. On that land of supreme merit devoid of the defects of the earth, eighteen *akṣauhiṇī* armies gathered with eagerness for battle. And so resulted the name of that land, brahmins. That land was proclaimed to us as holy and beautiful. All this I have described to you, finest of sages—how this land famed in the three worlds was named.] (*Mbh*, 1.2.2–12)

This is the first time we are properly introduced to this 'best of brahmins', who, in his post-*Mahābhārata* career, becomes famous as Paraśurāma ('Rāma with an axe'), one of the *avatāra*s of the god Viṣṇu.[2] This is an epitome of the Rāma Jāmadagnya story rather than it being told in its entirety, as was requested. These and other elements of it are sprinkled throughout the *Mahābhārata*, often appearing at critical junctures (Fitzgerald 2002: 104) and often told more than once.

Goldman (1977: 136) has suggested that the Rāma myth is a 'deliberate creation of the epic bards intended to incorporate, in one complex, almost every highly charged feature of the Bhṛguid cycle'. The two most complete accounts are at 3.115–17, in which Rāma's companion Akṛtavraṇa narrates it to Yudhiṣṭhira when the latter has arrived at Rāma's mountain residence, Mahendra; and at 12.48–49, in which Kṛṣṇa narrates it to Yudhiṣṭhira as they travel to Kurukṣetra in preparation for Yudhiṣṭhira receiving his postwar education from the Kuru *paterfamilias* Bhīṣma. In these other accounts, which vary in some respects, we learn that the proximate cause of Rāma's

1 '[The place] consisting of five adjacent [lakes].' The lakes are sometimes referred to as *rāmahrada* ('Rāma's lakes').

2 Śiva gives Rāma Jāmadagnya an axe in 13.14.137–38 and 13.18.11; however, the name Paraśurāma does not appear in the *Mahābhārata*.

destructive rage was a desire to avenge the slaying of his father, Jamadagni, by the reckless *kṣatriya* sons of the Haihaya king Arjuna Kārtavīrya. Indeed, Rāma Jāmadagnya famously does so 21 times before he is stopped.

In the above version of Rāma Jāmadagnya's apocalypse, Rāma is stopped by his ancestors (*pitṛ*s), led by his grandfather Ṛcīka, after Rāma has satiated them with the blood from the blood-lakes of Samantapañcaka (*Mbh*, 1.2.6). Ṛcīka's prominence in this respect is interesting for several reasons. Hiltebeitel (2002: 116) has noted that Rāma Jāmadagnya's extermination of *kṣatriya*s reflects a larger 'multigenerational feud' between Bhārgavas and *kṣatriya*s, which begins with the Bhārgava Aurva's birth to avenge the slaughter of the Bhṛgus by the kin of their former patron, King Kṛtavīrya (1.169–71). Aurva's son, Ṛcīka, became master of the martial sciences (*dhanurveda*) for the destruction of *kṣatriya*s, though he defers his destructive urges to the next generation, Jamadagni, who also defers it to his son, Rāma Jāmadagnya, the brahmin with 'the characteristics of a *kṣatriya*' (*brāhmaṇaṃ kṣatradharmāṇaṃ*), by whom, we know, the feud is fully realised (13.56.4–11).[3] Though Ṛcīka apparently has a stake in Rāma's apocalypse against *kṣatriya*s, he is also frequently at the centre of moves to stop him. Both *Mbh* 3.117.9–10 and *Mbh* 14.29.20 restate the thrust of the above discussed version in 1.2; once Rāma has completed his twenty-first slaughter, his ancestors, led by Ṛcīka, ask him to stop.[4] It is significant that this occurs after Rāma has satiated them with the *tarpaṇa* offering made to ancestors, where the offering—the blood of the slain *kṣatriya*s—has satisfied their longstanding grudge, leading them to call off the feud.

There is a further instance of Ṛcīka and Rāma's other (unnamed) ancestors intervening to stop Rāma fighting. Towards the end of the Udyogaparvan (*Mbh*, 5), Bhīṣma describes the battle he has with Rāma Jāmadagnya, who trained him in the martial arts. Rāma has been asked to fight as Ambā's champion after Bhīṣma's failed attempt to have her married to his brother left her with a sullied reputation. As the fearsome battle takes place, attempts are made to stop them fighting, employing arguments highlighting their opposing yet complementary identities. At one point, after Nārada and

3 The passage appears in an account of how the *kṣatriya* Viśvāmitra became a brahmin. Immediately after Rāma is described as *brāhmaṇaṃ kṣatradharmāṇaṃ*, Viśvāmitra is described as *kṣatriyaṃ viprakarmāṇaṃ* ('the *kṣatriya* behaving as a brahmin'). There is a point being made here regarding the mixing up of *varṇa*s.

4 Aurva's ancestors similarly call on him to halt his destructive urge (*Mbh*, 1.170.20–21). In *Mbh* 12.49.57–59, it is Rāma Jāmadagnya's priest Kaśyapa who stops him, on which see Fitzgerald (2002: 102–3).

eight other Vedic scholars standing in the sky have convinced Bhīṣma to resist deploying the sleep-inducing *prasvāpa* weapon, Rāma encounters his ancestors, who circle him and appeal to him to stop fighting:

> *mā smaivaṃ sāhasaṃ vatsa punaḥ kārṣīḥ kathaṃ cana |*
> *bhīṣmeṇa saṃyugaṃ gantuṃ kṣatriyeṇa viśeṣataḥ ||*
> *kṣatriyasya tu dharmo 'yaṃ yad yuddhaṃ bhṛgunandana |*
> *svādhyāyo vratacaryā ca brāhmaṇānāṃ paraṃ dhanam ||*
> *idaṃ nimitte kasmiṃś cid asmābhir upamantritam |*
> *śastradhāraṇam atyugraṃ tac ca kāryaṃ kṛtaṃ tvayā ||*
> *vatsa paryāptam etāvad bhīṣmeṇa saha saṃyuge |*
> *vimardas te mahābāho vyapayāhi raṇād itaḥ ||*
>
> [Son, don't again do something so rash as this, going into battle with Bhīṣma, especially since he's a *kṣatriya*! Joy of the Bhṛgus, this is a *kṣatriya*'s *dharma*—battle. Vedic recitation and pursuing vows are the best treasure of brahmins. For a certain cause, we had advised you to bear arms—a terrible thing! And you have done that deed. Enough with this clash you're having in battle with Bhīṣma, mighty-armed son. Retire from the battlefield now!] (*Mbh*, 5.186.10–13)

As is often the case in the *Mahābhārata*, reminders of proper *kṣatriya* and brahmin behavioural norms are important. The epic poets have composed this passage in light of the earlier deeds of Rāma, in which he slaughtered the *kṣatriyas* in pursuing—as confirmed here (since he bore arms on their advice)—a longstanding grudge of his ancestors. Their appeal to him to desist from battle means more than this battle; he must desist from all battles and assume more appropriate brahmin occupations. At first, they are unsuccessful and Rāma refuses to withdraw. Then, 'led by Ṛcīka' (*Mbh*, 5.186.23), the sages turn their attention to Bhīṣma. He, too, refuses to retreat. The sages, together with Bhīṣma's mother, take to the battlefield to obstruct the combat, and finally Rāma's ancestors convince him to lay down his weapons (5.186.30).

As others have recognised, the telling of the story of Rāma Jāmadagnya so early in the *Mahābhārata* foregrounds prominent themes that will subsequently recur: apocalyptic violence, cycles of revenge and brahmin avengers. Yet, it also introduces another theme—that of the brahmin as agent of peace. While Ṛcīka is hardly a perfect appeaser of violence—his intervention coming only once he has been satisfied with the blood of those against whom he held a grudge—he serves to establish the archetype of the brahmin peacemaker.

Ruru and Ruru

The story of Ruru (*Mbh*, 1.8–12), another Bhārgava ancestor of Śaunaka, fills the second half of the Pulomaparvan. Ruru falls in love with a beautiful *apsaras* called Pramadvarā and requests to marry her. Not long before the wedding, she steps on a sleeping snake, which bites her and she dies. Ruru retreats to the forest and grieves. Wanting to revive her, Ruru is told by an envoy (*dūta*) of the gods that there is only one way: he must give her half his life. Ruru agrees and Yama makes it so. Ruru swears an oath to kill all snakes to avenge Pramadvarā's death. While making good on his promise, he hits a lizard by mistake. The lizard appeals to Ruru to not kill him, for he is not a snake, but a lizard, who was once the brahmin seer Ruru.

Ruru the once-brahmin lizard now tells Ruru the ancestor of Śaunaka his story. Ruru once frightened a brahmin engaged in an *agnihotra* with a fake (*tārṇa*, 'made of grass') snake, in consequence of which the brahmin cursed Ruru to be a harmless (*avīrya*) snake, which is to say, a lizard. Ruru begs that he lift the curse and the brahmin promises it will be once Ruru the lizard sees his namesake, Pramati's son Ruru, to whom he is just now relating his story. This condition met, Ruru resumes his proper form (*svarūpa*) and offers the other Ruru a brief ethical discourse. Nonviolence (*ahiṃsā*) is the highest law (*dharma*); a brahmin should never kill a living thing; *ahiṃsā*, speaking the truth and forgiveness (*kṣamā*) are the highest law of a brahmin, even more so than preserving the Veda. The *dharma* of the *kṣatriya*, on the other hand, involves meting out punishment (*daṇḍadhāraṇa*), fierceness (*ugratva*) and protecting people (*prajānāṃ paripālanam*), for which he offers as an example Janamejaya's 'long ago' (*purā*) massacre (*hiṃsana*) of the snakes (*Mbh*, 1.11.16). The snakes' rescue, he continues, was due to an eminent brahmin known as Āstīka, though he says neither why nor how this was done. The Bhārgava Ruru wants to hear further about the massacre and Āstīka, and he ends up hearing the whole story from his father, Pramati, though we do not.

There are some odd temporal things going on here, since Ruru, the former lizard speaking to the Bhārgava Ruru (Śaunaka's grandfather, great-grandfather or even great-great-grandfather),[5] seems to know about

5 The relationship of Śunaka to Śaunaka, whose name is a patronymic derived from Śunaka, is uncertain. The constituted text of the Critical Edition describes Ruru as Śaunaka's *pūrvapitāmaha* ('great-grandfather'), which would make Śunaka Śaunaka's grandfather. However, a significant number of northern manuscripts, and almost all the southern manuscripts, have *pūrvapitāmaha* modifying Śunaka. Passage *223, inserted in Grantha manuscripts after another account of the lineage at 1.8.1–2, says that Śaunaka was Śunaka's son, as does 13.31.62. Cf. Hiltebeitel (2002: 113n.68); Brodbeck (2009: 248–49).

Janamejaya's 'long ago' snake sacrifice, as does Ruru's father, Pramati, even though Ugraśravas—who is telling all this to Śaunaka and the other seers—has supposedly just travelled from the very same sacrifice, the saga of the Bhāratas having been told in its intervals. Even so, in the story of Ruru, we can see some common themes and motifs, co-named protagonists, reciprocal justice (*lex talionis*), imperilled rituals, revenge, apocalyptic violence and the ambivalent status of snakes. The brahmin Ruru pursuing a snake apocalypse is halted by the former brahmin now lizard (now brahmin again) Ruru, who proceeds to impart an idealised ethical discourse to his co-named protagonist and links it to the story of the exemplary apocalypse-ending brahmin Āstīka.

Śamīka and Śṛṅgin

The story of Śamīka and his son Śṛṅgin is also the story of the death of Parikṣit. It is told twice, at 1.36.8–1.40 and 1.45–46. These two narratives are divided by a second telling of the story of Āstīka and his parents, both of whom were called Jaratkāru. We will look at this shortly. The multiple versions of these stories probably reflect 'seams' in the *Mahābhārata*'s compositional process and history. The interlocutory dynamics give weight to Monika Shee's (1986) suggestion that the first iteration of the Parikṣit story is 'secondary', though the temporal implications of 'secondary' can remain only vague at best.[6] Such issues need not detain us here.

While largely similar in outline, the two Parikṣit stories have different emphases and details. The former (*Mbh*, 1.36.7–1.40) is more expansive on the interactions between the brahmin sage Śamīka and his son Śṛṅgin, while the second shifts the focus to the encounter between Takṣaka and the brahmin Kāśyapa, who potentially could act as Parikṣit's saviour. Further, the second version introduces the Vaiśaṃpāyana/Janamejaya interlocutory frame, through which much of the epic from here will be experienced.

While tracking a wounded deer on a hunting trip, Parikṣit comes across a sage (*muni*) in the forest. He asks the sage whether he has seen the deer, but the sage does not answer due to his vow of silence. Parikṣit gets angry, picks

6 Both the story of Parikṣit beginning at 1.36.8 and the resumption of the story of Jaratkāru at 1.41 occur without *praśnas* from Śaunaka, though this is the *Mahābhārata*'s typical interlocutory structure. The first Parikṣit story (*Mbh*, 1.36.8–1.40) begins abruptly. If it were to be lifted out, both the Jaratkāru story and the Parikṣit story would begin in similar ways, with questions from the 'audience' (in the case of Parikṣit 2, from both Śaunaka and Janamejaya) and a *nirukta* of each protagonist's name (1.36.3–4 for Jaratkāru and 1.45.13 for Parikṣit).

up a dead snake and, in a near recapitulation of Ruru's insult to the sage that led to him becoming a lizard, drapes it on the sage's shoulders. The sage does not move, but in due course the sage's son, Śṛṅgin, finds out and becomes furious—in part, according to the first version, because his friend Kṛśa teases him about it. Śṛṅgin curses Parikṣit to be killed by the snake Takṣaka within seven days. Śṛṅgin and his father, Śamīka, are marked as opposites, though the latter is named only in the first version. Śamīka's name means 'pacifier', as reflected in his exceedingly calm response to Parikṣit throwing the dead snake around his shoulders, but also because of his attempts to appease his son's curse. Śṛṅgin, on the other hand, means 'horned', and symbolically encodes his aggressive response to Śamīka being insulted.[7] Śamīka warns Parikṣit of his impending assassination. A brahmin called Kāśyapa gets wind of the curse and—knowing the remedy to snakebites, which Brahmā had earlier conferred on him (*Mbh*, 1.18.11)—sets out to Parikṣit's city to heal him and make some money in the process. Takṣaka encounters Kāśyapa while both are on the way to Hastināpura and Takṣaka buys him off to stop him offering his healing services to Parikṣit. Takṣaka hears of the apotropaic devices Parikṣit has put in place after being forewarned by Śamīka and sends some snakes disguised as ascetics with gifts of fruit, leaves and water. Takṣaka uses his power of illusion to hide in a piece of fruit disguised as a worm. Parikṣit, thinking the threat over, places the worm on his throat and, as it emerges from the fruit, it expands and circles Parikṣit's neck. But he is no constrictor: Takṣaka burns him with the fire of his poison (1.40.1–5).

Only in the first version does Śamīka rebuke Śṛṅgin for his overly impetuous response to Parikṣit's insult. This rebuke falls into two parts, 1.37.20–27 and 1.38.3–12, divided by Śṛṅgin's *mea culpa*. In the first part, Śamīka counsels Śṛṅgin on ascetic propriety: 'This is not the *dharma* of ascetics' (*naiṣa dharmas tapasvinām*), he begins. People such as they should forgive (*kṣantavya*) such churlish acts as Parikṣit's, 'for *dharma* violated violates' (*dharmo hi hato hanti*). Ascetics and kings share a mutual obligation; while kings provide safety for ascetics to pursue *dharma* as they please (*yathāsukham*), in return, kings receive a portion of their merit (*dharma*) (*Mbh*, 37.23–24). Parikṣit was a good king, who had protected them just like his great-grandfather (presumably Pāṇḍu); his mischief was due to him being hungry, tired, wretched and ignorant of the sage's vow. In the second part, Śamīka reminds Śṛngin of the immense power he has accrued due to his austerity (*tapas*), which, when coupled with uncontrolled anger (*kopa*), becomes dangerous

7 Śṛṅgin was 'born from a cow' (*Mbh*, 1.46.2).

(as his words cursing Parikṣit to die demonstrate). He therefore counsels him to give up his anger and adopt the proper life of the ascetic wanderer (*yati*), nurturing tranquillity (*śama*) and forgiveness (*kṣamā*).

Takṣaka and Kāśyapa meet on the way to Hastināpura. In the first version, Takṣaka doubts the brahmin's ability to cure those he bites. He sets Kāśyapa a test to bring back to life a tree that he burns, which he passes. Takṣaka realises that he must pay off Kāśyapa to succeed in assassinating Parikṣit (*Mbh*, 1.39.13–17), though 1.39.19 provides Kāśyapa with an out: his 'divine knowledge' (*divyajñāna*) allowed him to see that Parikṣit's life was on the wane (*kṣīṇāyus*). The second version does not mention the test when it narrates Takṣaka and Kāśyapa's meeting. Rather, the emphasis is on the latter's desire for wealth (1.46.16–21; Kāśyapa is *dhanalipsu*, 'eager for wealth', in 1.46.19); Kāśyapa is a trope for the greedy brahmin as gun for hire whose ethics can be priced. The test is introduced into the latter version only when Janamejaya asks again about the encounter between Takṣaka and Kāśyapa (1.46.26–27) to clarify what was said between them; the king wants to be sure whom to blame. It turns out there was a witness. A man gathering kindling had hidden in the tree and overheard the conversation. Though he had been burnt along with the tree by Takṣaka, he was also revived by Kāśyapa—a detail missing from the earlier version. Janamejaya now has his witness and evidence and lays the blame squarely on Takṣaka. Now we can see the main point of the second telling of this story: it provides an effective transition into the setting of Janamejaya's revenge-seeking *sarpasatra*, preparations for which begin in the next chapter. The tone is jurisprudential; not only did Takṣaka realise the curse of Śṛṅgin, but also he lured away Parikṣit's potential saviour (his 'great transgression', *mahān atikramaḥ*). The pattern of reciprocal justice (*lex talionis*)—well established in the preceding stories and an integral feature of epic deaths—now escalates into an instance of what Robert Goldman (2021) has called 'collective punishment', with Janamejaya plotting the inferno of a grand sacrifice of snakes to avenge his father's death at the hands of the snake who wields fire-like poison.

Āstīka and Kāśyapa

We earlier noted that the story of the two Rurus in the Pulomaparvan closes with Ruru the Bhārgava seeking an explanation for the exemplary apocalypse-ending brahmin Āstīka. Śaunaka begins the next *parvan* (*Mbh*, 1.13) asking about Janamejaya's sacrifice and Āstīka's role in it. The tale of Āstīka is then told twice in his eponymous *parvan*—first, in relatively brief form in 1.13, and then in much more detail together with substantial backstories in the subsequent chapters involving the sisters Kadrū and Vinatā and their children (respectively, the snakes and the two birds Garuḍa and Aruṇa), the churning of the ocean of milk to produce the *amṛta* and its theft and return. The beginning point of the second narration of the story of Āstīka and his co-named parents is to some degree arbitrary, since the backstories explain why the snakes were to be sacrificed and why Āstīka was to be born to halt their sacrifice. A reasonable starting point is 1.33, when Vāsuki anxiously confers with his fellow snakes to explore ways to avert the curse seemingly steering them to their demise, which leads to the story of Āstīka and his parents in 1.34. This account is interleaved with the first telling of Parikṣit's assassination starting at 1.36.7, and then resumes from 1.41 to 1.44. Once again, while the purpose of this chapter is not a higher critical analysis, the seams of composition are somewhat evident.

The short version of the story in 1.13 begins with Āstīka's father, Jaratkāru, a great celibate ascetic. While wandering, the ascetic encounters his ancestors (who do not recognise him) hanging upside-down in a cave. When asked why, they explain that the last of their descendants is an ascetic, who therefore does not fulfil the necessary rituals and obligations that sustain them in Heaven. Jaratkāru confesses his identity and they beg him to marry and have a son. Jaratkāru agrees to do so, if his wife bears the same name as him and is offered to him as alms. After he struggles to find a wife, eventually, the snake (*nāga*) Vāsuki offers his sister, Jaratkāru. The offering is explained as a means to appease the curse of the mother of snakes (Kadrū) that all snakes shall be burnt in the fire of Janamejaya's sacrifice (*Mbh*, 1.13.35). The two Jaratkārus have a son, Āstīka, who then frees the snakes from their curse at Janamejaya's sacrifice (1.13.40). The close of the chapter explains the theology that in this case forms the basis of a critique of celibate asceticism, since Jaratkāru ends up going to Heaven having fulfilled the 'three debts' of an orthodox ritualist (1.13.41–42)—to the gods through sacrifices, to the seers (*ṛṣi*s) through Vedic study (*brahmacarya*) and to his ancestors through ensuring the perpetuation of the family (*saṃtati*). In the last case, this ensures the continued performance of the ancestral rites (*pitṛmedha*s) that sustain ancestors in the heavens, the absence of which led to Jaratkāru's ancestors' initial plight. Jaratkāru's son, Āstīka, in becoming a good Brahmanical ritualist (trained, it should be noted, by a Bhārgava, the son of Cyavana, who is presumably Pramati: *Mbh*, 1.44.18; Brodbeck 2009: 234), saves both his paternal and his maternal lines. We recognise again the beguiling motif of the co-named protagonists, as well as the theme of apocalyptic violence—in this case, the key frame story of the sacrifice of snakes, which makes Āstīka an exemplar of our peacemaking brahmin archetype.

The expanded version explains how the *nāga* Vāsuki came to give his sister Jaratkāru to the brahmin Jaratkāru (*Mbh*, 1.33–35). Vāsuki takes counsel with his brothers to figure out a way to avert their mother's curse, but does not like their propositions, some of which involve killing some of or all the participants in the sacrifice—a reminder of the potential virulence of snakes. Their arguing reveals a division between those snakes who abide by the law and those who do not (1.33.19). Then Elāpatra speaks up, recalling overhearing Brahmā say there are too many snakes (see also 1.18.9–10). Nevertheless, only the virulent snakes set on evil (*pāpacāra*) will die; the pious ones (*dharmacārin*) will not (1.34.9–10). A brahmin named Āstīka, begotten by Jaratkāru with a namesake virgin, will halt the sacrifice and save them. Vāsuki is encouraged by Elāpatra to offer his sister, who is such a one, as alms when Jaratkāru comes begging; Vāsuki agrees (1.35). The snakes have found their saviour; and, unlike Kāśyapa, he cannot be bought.

After the intercession of the first narration of Parikṣit's assassination, the Āstīka story resumes from 1.41. It is broadly similar to the first version (*Mbh*, 1.13), but with some significant additional details. When Vāsuki offers his sister, the *nāginī* Jaratkāru, the once celibate ascetic Jaratkāru further insists that he will not support her and will leave her if she displeases him (1.42–43). The first condition Vāsuki readily agrees to; he is concerned only with the rescue of the snakes. The second condition threatens briefly to derail Vāsuki's plan. One day, Jaratkāru the brahmin falls asleep. His dutiful wife wakes him, in fear that he will neglect his religious duty (*dharmalopa*) by failing to perform his *agnihotra* at dusk (1.43.16–20). Jaratkāru the brahmin is insulted and leaves never to return (1.43.39). Vāsuki panics, but his sister reassures him that before departing, her husband had confirmed she was pregnant (1.44.10) and so Āstīka was born and raised in Vāsuki's court and taught the Vedas by Cyavana's Bhārgava son—presumably, Pramati (1.44).

After the second narration of Parikṣit's assassination (*Mbh*, 1.45–46), in 1.47, Janamejaya asks his *ṛtvij* priests whether they know of a rite to lead Takṣaka and his kin into the fire. They do, and preparations for the rite begin. The *sūtradhāra*, the architect measuring out the sacrificial enclosure, foretells that a brahmin will stop the sacrifice from being concluded. Janamejaya orders that no-one be allowed to enter whom he does not know. The *ṛtvij* priests conducting the sacrifice don black attire (1.47.18) and offer the snakes into the fire, killing millions. Takṣaka takes refuge with Indra and Vāsuki begins to despair (1.48). Jaratkāru summons her son and explains to him the purpose for which he was born. As expected, he was stopped from entering the sacrifice by gatekeepers; but Āstīka, the son of a reluctant sacrificer, sings the praises of Janamejaya's sacrifice and of Janamejaya, and they let him in (1.49). Janamejaya is impressed and wants to give him a boon; his priests tell him to wait until Takṣaka arrives. Learning that Takṣaka is taking refuge with Indra, Janamejaya makes some offerings in the fire until Indra appears with Takṣaka in the hem of his robe. Janamejaya orders that his priests hurl Takṣaka into the fire. But as the snake writhes helplessly towards the fire, the *ṛtvij* priests suggest that Janamejaya now offer the boon to Āstīka (1.51.12–14), which he does. Āstīka chooses that the sacrificial session be stopped—a request Janamejaya is reluctant to concede, offering riches instead (1.51.19). But Āstīka, unlike Kāśyapa, cannot be bought and he insists on stopping the rite to save his mother's line (*mātṛkula*; 1.51.20). The *sadasya* priests, seated and observing the rite, declare the boon must be honoured (1.51.23). Janamejaya wonders why Takṣaka remains suspended above the fire, as does Śaunaka, who is hearing this from Ugraśravas the bard. The last explains (1.53.5) it was due to Āstīka yelling three times, 'Stop! Stop!' (*tiṣṭha tiṣhta*). The effects of the boon are seemingly in force, subverting the mantras of the *ṛtvij* priests; boons—important devices in epic narratives—are typically binding utterances. Janamejaya concedes and calls off the sacrifice. Āstīka, half-brahmin and half-snake, has brought the annihilation of snakes to an end. And, perhaps, enhanced the reputation of brahmins as peacemakers in the process.

Peacemaking brahmins and the name 'Āstīka'

The startling role of violent brahmins as perpetuators or abetters of extraordinarily violent acts is juxtaposed with their opposites: peacemaking brahmins who attempt to bring cycles of violence to a close and sometimes succeed. Rāma Jāmadagnya is stopped by his ancestors led by Ṛcīka. Ruru the lizard-brahmin counsels his namesake Ruru against his snake apocalypse avenging his betrothed's death by snakebite, in the process regaining his brahminhood. Śamīka unsuccessfully intervenes in the assassination of Parikṣit that is prompted by a curse from his son, Śṛṅgin. Āstīka, the brahmin-*nāga*, halts King Janamejaya's ritual snake apocalypse, showing in the process that he cannot be bought off as was Parikṣit's potential saviour, the snake-lore expert Kāśyapa. If not perfect peacemakers, these brahmins can nevertheless be identified by their common purpose.

Some of the apocalyptically violent acts invite readings that see such episodes as reflecting tropes for the rivalries between the two apex social classes of brahmins and *kṣatriyas*. We see this especially in Rāma Jāmadagnya's pursuit of revenge against *kṣatriyas* for his father's death at the hands of the Haihaya princes (the continuation of an older feud) and Śṛṅgin's cursing of Parikṣit to die by snakebite for disrespecting his father. In the Ruru and Āstīka (Parikṣit) stories, the rivalry manifests between snakes and brahmins in the first case and snakes and *kṣatriyas* in the second. Yet, the narratives of Śamīka and Śṛṅgin, on the one hand, and Āstīka (and Takṣaka and Vāsuki), on the other, intersect and pivot on their entanglement in the destiny of Parikṣit, thereby underscoring the mutuality of the destinies of brahmins, *kṣatriyas* and snakes. In working to subvert the violence instigated by their anger-filled brahmin counterparts, the peacemaker brahmins typically foreground the complementarity of brahmins and *kṣatriyas* (especially kings). Ṛcīka, Ruru and Śamīka counsel their violent antipodes on proper brahmin behaviour, while simultaneously asserting the *kṣatriya*'s normative monopoly on violence (Ruru even uses the example of King Janamejaya); Āstīka—brahmin and *nāga*—does not engage in such discourse, but rather demonstrates his virtues through his peacemaking deeds and his mastery of language.

The thread of peacemaker brahmins culminates in Āstīka's intervention in Janamejaya's *sarpasatra*. Ruru explicitly draws attention to the interlocking themes through his use of Janamejaya and Āstīka as models of forms of idealised behaviour (*Mbh*, 1.11.16–17). The interlocking semiotics are also evoked by the rhyming homophony between the names Ṛcīka, Śamīka and Āstīka. Indeed, this might in part explain the peculiar phonology of the last name.

Ugraśravas explains Āstīka's name with a *nirukta*—an 'etymological' pun:

> *astīty uktvā gato yasmāt pitā garbhastham eva tam* |
> *vanaṃ tasmād idaṃ tasya nāmāstīketi viśrutam* ||
>
> [Since his father had said as he departed for the forest, 'There is (*asti*)', even while he was in the womb, his name was renowned as Āstīka.] (*Mbh*, 1.44.20)

In its narrative context, this evokes Āstīka's father's uttering of the verb *asti* ('there is') to confirm to his wife the existence of the foetus in her womb when he abandoned her in a fit of pique. This reflects how Jaratkāru the snake woman reports this news to Vāsuki:

> *pṛṣṭo mayāpatyahetoḥ sa mahātmā mahātapāḥ |*
> *astīty udaram uddiśya mamedaṃ gatavāṃś ca saḥ ||*
>
> [I questioned that great man of great austerity about the child. He said to me, pointing to my womb, 'There is', and then departed.] (*Mbh*, 144.10)

The brahmin Jaratkāru was somewhat more expansive:

> *asty eṣa garbhaḥ subhage tava vaiśvānaropamaḥ |*
> *ṛṣiḥ paramadharmātmā vedavedāṅgapāragaḥ ||*
>
> [There is a child in you, fortunate lady, who will be a seer equal to Agni, the essence of the highest law, a paragon of the Veda and its supplements.] (*Mbh*, 1.43.38)

Jaratkāru predicts Āstīka's dharmic piety and *vaidika* excellence. Yet, his response to Jaratkāru the snake woman's question is reduced in subsequent tellings to merely the copula functioning as an existential verb. While the context is to some degree rather ordinary, the emphasis placed on the expression invites strong readings. Hiltebeitel (2002: 63n.14), for example, taking it to mean 'He of whom one says it is' (cf. Adluri 2001: 163),[8] reads Āstīka as an implicit affront to the 'spiralling violence' of the snake sacrifice, which accords with the epic's treatment of heresy (*nāstikyam*) and heretics (*nāstika*), though he recognises that the ritual does not quite evoke 'the *real* Nāstika opposition of Buddhists, Jains, Ājīvakas, and Materialists' (Hiltebeitel 2002: 163). For Doniger O'Flaherty (1986: 18–19), this is precisely what it means, asserting that Āstīka is a cipher for orthodoxy in noting its 'obvious contrast' with the word *nāstika*, 'the usual Hindu word for a heretic'. She further suggests that the story of Āstīka is an 'affirmation of good religion (in which one does not sacrifice snakes) against bad religion (in which one does sacrifice snakes)'. But not all of this is convincing, not least because the proper antonym for *nāstika* is *āstika*, not *āstīka*, with its longer medial vowel—the reading adopted in the constituted text of the Critical Edition.[9] Nor is it a contrast explicitly drawn by the text itself. The term *nāstika* (the antonym of which is *āstika*) typically refers to a denier of the validity of the Veda—a *vedanindaka*, as *Mānavadharmaśāstra* 2.11 has it—who therefore

8 Cf. Hiltebeitel (2002: 174): '[T]he "Ontologically" all-important Āstīka.'

9 The spelling of this name varies in the manuscripts. In his note to 1.13.37, Sukthankar indicates that 'here and below', most southern recension manuscripts show *astīka*. In a similar note at 1.34.13, he reports that 'here and below the [manuscripts] vary at random between *āstīka*, *astīka* and *āstika*'.

refuses to participate in the ritual practices the Veda espouses.[10] The pivotal point, therefore, that makes one a *nāstika* or an *āstika* is not whether one sacrifices snakes, but rather whether one sacrifices at all and acknowledges as authoritative those texts that encode the sacrifice. The participants and sponsors and the rite itself hardly conform to this definitional requirement. The good/bad religion binary is similarly problematic, since it reduces a complex labyrinth of revenge, violence and moral reckoning to a simple question of who is good and who is bad; if anything, the *Mahābhārata* works hard to make *us* think hard about such simple reductions.

The rhyming homophony of the triad Āstīka, Ṛcīka and Śamīka underscores their interrelationship as peacemaking brahmins. The derivations of Ṛcīka and Śamīka are readily explained by the addition of the suffix *-īka* to the roots *ṛc* ('to praise') and *śam* ('to be calm, tranquil'), respectively, thereby producing agentive nominals expressing the sense of the root;[11] Ṛcīka is the 'extoller' or 'praiser',[12] while Śamīka is the calm, tranquil 'pacifier'. The grammatical derivation of the name 'Āstīka' is more problematic. Containing the element *asti* ('there is'), the conjugated third-person singular form of the existentially functioning copula, and showing *vṛddhi* vowel strength on the initial vowel,[13] *āstīka* parts from the morphology of primary derivatives with the *-īka* suffix. On the other hand, it potentially reflects secondary (*taddhita*) derivations with either *-īka* or *-ika*, though the *Aṣṭādhyāyī* only indicates the former for a very limited set of nominals.[14] With such derivational possibilities in mind, it seems rather likely that *āstīka* is a fit-for-purpose neologism—the

10 Similar usages in the *Mahābhārata* that oppose the *nāstika* to the Veda can be found at 3.188.22, 5.35.40, 7.76.4. 12.12.4, 12.15.33, 12.162.8, 12.255.4 and 13.107.60. The term *nāstika* appears 87 times in the *Mbh* (including passages excluded from the constituted text), some of which are explored by Hopkins (1901: 86–90). Further analysis of these could reveal other gradations of meaning, as discussed, for example, by Nicholson (2012) in relation to medieval doxographies.

11 Pāṇini (Vasu 1891–98) does not appear to discuss *-īka* as a *kṛt pratyaya* (yet does as a *taddhita pratyaya* in restricted domains, see below), though Whitney (1973: 450) includes it as a subset of *-ka* and compares it with primary derivatives with *-aka*/*-āka* (see also *Aṣṭādhyāyī*, 3.1.133 and 3.2.155, wherein the root vowels in most cases undergo strengthening) and *-uka* (see also *Aṣṭādhyāyī*, 3.2.154).

12 Unlike the case with Śamīka, it is not clear what significance lies in this name in the context of the narratives that concern Ṛcīka, though he is thrice called *japatāṃ vara* ('finest of chanters'; *Mbh*, 12.49.23, 25; 13.4.18) and once *kaviputra* (12.49.7). The verb is rarely used, being largely restricted to the *Ṛg Veda* (6.38.2, 6.49.3, 7.70.6, 8.38.1).

13 Though see Note 9.

14 See *Aṣṭādhyāyī* (Vasu 1891–98), 4.4.59 and 5.3.110. Secondary derivations with *-ika* typically require *vṛddhi* gradation on the initial vowel. The broad meaning of the *-ika* affix ('knowing', 'possessing' or 'relating to' the base form; cf., for example, *dhārmika*) is rather appealing in this regard. The secondary derivation of a nominal from *asti* showing *vṛddhi* vowel strength already has a precedent with *āstika* (which some relate, as we have seen, to Āstīka), formed with the affix *-ka*, as described (together with *nāstika* and *daiṣṭika*) at *Aṣṭādhyāyī*, 4.4.60.

poets phonologically modelling the word from the base *asti* to both echo the names of Āstīka's fellow brahmin peacemakers and elevate the existential semantic domain of the underlying verb. The morphological links of *āstīka* to *ṛcīka* and *śamīka*, and Āstīka's role in stopping the *sarpasatra* itself, point to him manifesting his father's proclamation '*asti*' as an agent of existence over annihilation.

The power of words

If Āstīka embodies existence as such, the epic's poets marshalled a provocative ritual assembly for him to exercise this embodiment. Vedic antecedents to the epic *sarpasatra* have been noted in the *Pañcaviṃśa Brāhmana* (25.15) and various *śrautasūtra*s (Caland 1931: 640–42; Minkowski 1989: 413–16, 2007: 386–91; Kinjawadekar 1993). Caland suggests these exemplars provide the 'prototype' of Janamejaya's *sarpasatra* in the *Mahābhārata*, but Minkowski notes the ways in which it has been reworked. While Janamejaya is the royal patron *yajamāna* of the epic's *sarpasatra*, a *satra* typically only involves brahmins, who are at once and equally the ritual's *yajamāna*s and officiants (Minkowski 1989: 413). Further, and crucially, the Vedic antecedents describe a ritual performed by and for serpents, who therefore receive its benefits (Minkowski 2007: 388). The *Mahābhārata sarpasatra* is, rather, a sacrifice *of* snakes, undertaken as an exercise in vengeance against a virulent enemy; all its officiants, participants and beneficiaries are human.

The *Mahābhārata* is fond of reworking Vedic ritual ideas and motifs. It is aware of the uniqueness of its *sarpasatra*. Janamejaya's priests tell him that it was fashioned for him by the gods (*devanirmita*) and is described in a purāṇa (*Mbh*, 1.47.6). Both Minkowski (2007: 391) and Hiltebeitel (2002: 115) have suggested a connection to the 'black magic' associated with the term *abhicāra* (cf. Winternitz 1926: 75), which is rooted in rites and mantras of the Atharvaveda, the compositionally early but canonically late *saṃhitā* of the Veda. The word *abhicāra* is not found in this passage, as Hiltebeitel recognises; nevertheless, aspects of the rite are suggestive, eliciting a foreboding mood, not least that its purpose is a massacre. The presiding *hotṛ* priest is called Caṇḍabhārgava, the 'cruel Bhārgava', evoking the violent tendencies of other Bhārgavas already encountered. He seems particularly invested in Takṣaka's death, since on the advice of the *sadasya*s he stops Janamejaya offering Āstīka the boon that will ultimately enable him to halt the rite until Takṣaka has arrived (*Mbh*, 1.51.2–4; Hiltebeitel 2002: 115); as the story of Ruru shows,

Bhārgavas have had trouble with snakes before and perhaps see themselves benefiting from the *sarpasatra*. Portentously, all the presiding *ṛtvij* priests don black robes. The semiotics of robe colour are not entirely clear,[15] but we witness the same motif again in a parallel episode preceding the *sarpasatra* in time but following it in narrative order, when Agni appears in black robes before Arjuna and Kṛṣṇa to seek their assistance in burning the Khāṇḍava forest, destroying Takṣaka's native forests and most of his family (*Mbh*, 1.214.31).[16] In the later sixfold classificatory scheme of *abhicāra* found in tantric contexts, the *māraṇa* rites involving killing and murder—to which Janamejaya's *satra* would belong, if it is indeed *abhicāra*—are associated with the colour black (Türstig 1985: 102, 106–7).

Even so, not all *abhicāra* rites are so macabre. The sixfold tantric typology of *abhicāra* described by Türstig (1985: 107–8) includes a category of *śānti* ('pacification') rites for removing diseases, for pacifying curses and for warding off malevolent beings, of which snakes are one. According to Türstig (1985: 108), their main purpose is to 'counteract other types of *abhicāra*' (see also Bloomfield 1899: 66). The Atharvaveda (AV) and its ritual manuals contain numerous mantras and rites for warding off snakes or for neutralising snake venom (AV, 3.26, 3.27, 5.13, 6.56, 7.56, 7.88, 10.4, 12.1.46), as do other Vedic texts;[17] in its account of the Vedic *sarpasatra*, the *Baudhāyana Śrautasūtra* says that whoever undertakes it will not be harmed by snakes (Minkowski 1989: 414). The *Arthaśāstra* (4.3.1–2, 35–39, 42–44) charges officials (probably principally the *purohita*; 1.9.9) with protecting the realm from snakes using mantra, medicines and Atharvan *abhicāra* devices.

Such apotropaic devices are reflected in Āstīka's role in the *sarpasatra* and its aftermath, to which Minkowski (1989: 416) has again pointed the way. Apotropaic ritual devices have already been alluded to in the narrations of Parikṣit's assassination. Kāśyapa was granted the *sarpavidyā* ('snake lore') by Brahmā and planned to use it to save Parikṣit in return for payment, only for Takṣaka to buy him off before he could get there. Parikṣit himself, forewarned by Śamīka of Takṣaka's plans, deploys apotropaic devices in an

15 Information on robe colour in *abhicāra* rites is scant. I have found only one instance of black robes in a rite from an *Atharvavedapariśiṣṭa* described by Türstig (1985: 92).

16 Agni needs their assistance because Takṣaka's ally Indra keeps raining. Arjuna counters the rain with his arrows. The temporal logic makes this the beginning of the Pāṇḍava/*nāga* feud culminating in the *sarpasatra* (Minkowski 2007: 390–91).

17 See, for example, *Āśvalāyana Gṛhyasūtra*, 2.3; *Pāraskara Gṛhyasūtra*, 2.14; *Śāṅkhāyana Gṛhyasūtra*, 4.18; and *Hiraṇyakeśin Gṛhyasūtra*, 2.16.8—all of which cite the first half of AV 10.4.3 as an apotropaic mantra.

unsuccessful effort to ward off the snake. In the case of Āstīka, he returns to his mother (Jaratkāru) and uncle (Vāsuki) once the *sarpasatra* has been stopped and tells them what happened; the snakes offer him a boon, with which he chooses to turn his 'tale of *dharma*' (*dharmākhyānam*), the story of the stopping of the *sarpasatra*, into an apotropaism: those who recite it will have no danger (*bhaya*) from snakes (*Mbh*, 1.53.20). The effect of this promise is subsequently reproduced in two stanzas that are to function like apotropaic mantras (1.53.22–23):

> *jaratkāror jaratkārvāṃ samutpanno mahāyaśāḥ |*
> *āstīkaḥ satyasaṃdho māṃ pannagebhyo 'bhirakṣatu ||*
> *asitaṃ cārtimantaṃ ca sunīthaṃ cāpi yaḥ smaret |*
> *divā vā yadi vā rātrau nāsya sarpabhayaṃ bhavet ||*

> [Born of Jaratkāru to Jaratkāru, his renown immense and his promises true, may Āstīka protect me from snakes.

> Whoever recalls Asita, Ārtimat, and Sunītha, whether in the day or night, shall have no fear of serpents.]

The significance and referentiality of *asita* ('white'), *ārtimat* ('suffering') and *sunītha* ('good leader') are not clear; perhaps they are references to mantras, as the seventeenth-century commentator Nīlakaṇṭha suggests and as some authorities follow (Monier-Williams 1899; Sörensen 1904; Mehendale 1993–2007). One Kashmiri manuscript (K_3) has a marginal note in a second hand suggesting they refer to the three great *nāga*s Śeṣa, Vāsuki and Takṣaka. Böhtlingk and Roth (1855–75) take them to be names for snakes (at least for Asita and Ārtimat), as do van Buitenen (1973: 123) and Ganguli (1884: 160).[18] In a note to these verses in the critical apparatus of the Critical Edition, Sukthankar expressed the view that these two verses are 'a somewhat irrelevant interruption in the narrative of the *sūta*, and are probably an *old* interpolation' (1933–66: Vol. 1, 229–30). He nevertheless rightly included them in the constituted text since the manuscript evidence is conclusive.

The verses have a reception history that closely links Āstīka to apotropaic function. A passage in the supplement to the *Ṛg Veda* known as the *Ṛgveda Khila* (*RvKh*) interlocks Āstīka, this passage and the apotropaic traditions

18 Ganguli's translation has appeared in numerous subsequent editions, including at the *Internet Sacred Text Archive* (available from: www.sacred-texts.com/index.htm). In some of these, the name Asita has been mysteriously substituted with Astika (*sic.*) (for example, at: www.sacred-texts.com/hin/m01/m01059.htm). Some southern recension manuscripts (T $G_{1.3.6}$) show *astīka* (*sic.*) for *asita*.

of the Atharvaveda. *RvKh* 2.1, an apotropaic hymn directed at snakes, presents a composite of materials (Scheftelowitz 1906: 69–71).[19] The first verse incorporates AV 5.30.8a (the verse targets *yakṣa* ['illness'] in a hymn for long life) in its first line, the first quarter of *Ṛg Veda* 2.1.1 directed at Agni in its last line,[20] separated by AV 10.4.9cd,[21] *ghanena hanmi vṛśikam ahiṃ daṇḍenāgatam* ('I kill the scorpion that's come with a club and the snake with a staff'). Verses three and four reflect *Suparṇādhyāya* 2.1–2 (Charpentier 1920: 213–14). The connection to Āstīka comes in two ways. First, *Mbh* 1.53.22ab appears in variant form at *RvKh* 2.1.9. Second, *RvKh* 2.1.5–6 incorporates two verses, explicitly referencing Āstīka, which also appear in an expansion of *Mbh* 1.53.22–23 in a significant number of northern recension *Mahābhārata* manuscripts (lines 2–5 of *463):[22]

> *sarpāpasarpa bhadraṃ te gaccha sarpa mahāviṣa* |[23]
> *janamejayasya yajñānte āstīkavacanaṃ smara* ||
> *āstīkavacanaṃ smṛtvā yaḥ sarpo na nivartate* |
> *śatadhā bhidyate mūrdhni śiṃśavṛkṣaphalaṃ yathā* ||
>
> [Snake away, snake! Good luck to you! Snake, your poison is strong. Leave! Recall Āstīka's words at the end of Janamejaya's sacrifice. The snake that recalls Āstīka's words, but does not retreat, is rent at the head into a hundred pieces, like the fruit of a *śiṃśa* tree.][24]

Demonstrating the circulation of these stanzas, they also appear in the editions of the *Garuḍa Upaniṣad* by Weber (1885: 162) and Wojtilla (1975: 388)—another text using mantras to ward off snakes and remedy snake poison (Slouber 2017: 23, 26–27).

---

19 The connection of *RvKh* 2.1 to Āstīka is noted by Minkowski (1989: 416), though he does not note the links to the *Ṛg Veda* and the AV.

20 This line, absent in the Müller edition (1966: 521), becomes somewhat difficult to understand in its new context, since it is divorced from its finite verb. Presumably, Agni is evoked due to the assistance fire provides in warding off snakes.

21 AV 10.4 is a reasonably common source for apotropaic mantras targeted at snakes. See Note 17. *Kauśika Sūtra* 32.20 (Bahulkar 1994: 225) quotes verse 1 of 10.4 and addresses it to Takṣaka.

22 I give the text as it appears in the *Mahābhārata* Critical Edition. The readings of *RvKh* and the *Garuḍa Upaniṣad* (see below) vary sometimes from the *Mbh* (though some *Mbh* manuscripts are closer to the *RvKh* and *Garuḍa Upaniṣad*). The sense, nevertheless, is broadly the same. Slouber (2017: 26) gets Minkowski (1989: 416ns69, 70) slightly wrong here: passage *463 was rightly excluded from the constituted text of the Critical Edition according to the principles followed by Sukthankar—a decision Minkowski does not dispute.

23 Variants of this line appear twice in the *RvKh*: in the first line of 2.1 and in slightly different form in the second line of 2.1.9.

24 With thanks to Robert Goldman for pointing out an error I had earlier made in understanding the last line. As Prof. Goldman suggested, this is likely a reference to the 'shattered head' motif analysed by Witzel (1987).

Āstīka: Peacemaker, wordsmith

If Āstīka is the embodiment and agent of existence and the culminating exemplar of the peacemaking brahmin in the preamble to Vaiśaṃpāyana's telling of the *Mahābhārata* to Janamejaya, it is interesting to recognise the devices he uses to draw the violence to a close and the legacy he leaves to, so to speak, maintain the peace. In both cases, Āstīka shows himself to be an expert in the uses of language and the power of words. It is perhaps telling in this regard that on two occasions (1.141.1 and 1.53.26) he is referred to as a *kavi* ('sage', 'poet')—a title used for a select few in the *Mahābhārata*, including, for example, Vyāsa, Vidura, Agni and Śukra (Kāvya) Uśanas.

The motivation for stopping the *sarpasatra* comes from those most severely affected by it, the *nāgas*. Āstīka is a product of an alliance underpinned by mutual interest, the desire of the brahmin Jaratkāru's ancestors to be sustained in the heavens by a descendent who can perform the rituals (see *Mbh*, 1.53.24) and the desire by Vāsuki and his kin to save the *nāgas* from annihilation. The mutual interest produces a brahmin archetype invested in the survival of snakes. Āstīka, his father tells us (1.43.38), will be a paragon of the Veda, and so it comes to pass with his training under a Bhārgava—in this case, an agent in the stalling of a violent cycle. Having already promised his maternal uncle Vāsuki that he will lift the curse on the snakes by pleasing Janamejaya with 'words filled with benedictions' (*vāgbhir maṅgalayuktābhiḥ*; 1.49.20), Āstīka gains entry to the sacrificial arena by singing the praises of Janamejaya's sacrifice (1.50.1–10) and Janamejaya himself (1.50.11–16). The formulaic *stotra* has the desired effect and Janamejaya offers him the boon (*vara*), with which Āstīka requests the rite be stopped. Despite the efforts of the presiding *ṛtvij* priests to accelerate the close of the sacrifice and entice Takṣaka to the fire (using mantras), and despite Janamejaya's efforts to offer alternative boons, primarily in the form of riches, Āstīka sticks to his choice. Janamejaya concedes to Āstīka's request only after Takṣaka is suspended in the air, but the boon has already been offered, accepted and actualised: Takṣaka is suspended due to Āstīka's thrice pronounced 'Stop! Stop!' The boon Āstīka extracts from Janamejaya due to his praise works like an apotropaic mantra protecting snakes from humans. Āstīka, seemingly realising the binding effect of boons in a way that Janamejaya does not, again demonstrates his capacity for using powerful words to powerful effect.

In the aftermath of the stopping of the rite, there is joy and excitement, and Janamejaya is generous to a fault. But there is no expression of forgiveness, no commitment to a resolution of an underlying enmity and danger. Rather, the latent potential for further violence is tacitly recognised; Āstīka chooses as his boon from his own snake kin that when 'brahmins and other men' recite his *dharmākhyānam* (his 'story of what's right'), they will have no danger (*bhaya*) from snakes—an apotropaism subsequently reproduced in simpler form by Ugraśravas with the mantras of *Mbh* 1.53.22–23, the first of which refers directly to Āstīka, as do those in the expanded version that appears in the *ṚvKh* and *Garuḍa Upaniṣad*. Apotropaic mantras, while often expressions of violence (as, for example, in the Ādiparvan's expanded collection) sublimate violent deeds with verbal deeds. Āstīka, an embodiment of 'existence', supplants the remedy for virulent snakes of slaughtering them en masse with apotropaic stories and mantras that preserve the lives of humans and snakes alike, while recalling the capacity of each for violence.

The ending of cycles of revenge reflecting reciprocal forms of justice is engendered—not through a final and ultimate victory—but through a stalemate brought about by Āstīka's utterances, which effect a suspension of conflict. Āstīka, agent of existence and agent of peace, demonstrates the primacy of language in arresting violence. His flattering praise of Janamejaya and his sacrifice extract from the king the boon, the binding quality of which Āstīka recognises (as do the *sadasya*s; *Mbh*, 1.51.23). In calling out 'Stop! Stop!' and thereby halting Takṣaka's decent into the flames, Āstīka actualises the boon before Janamejaya gives his largely redundant verbal consent. Āstīka's subsequent determination that his *dharmākhyānam* be an apotropaism against the virulence of snakes, and the still further production of apotropaic mantras evoking Āstīka's special relationship with snakes to protect humans from them, are a recognition that peace is a 'warding off' of violence. Snakes—whether real or metaphoric—are endemic after all.

References

Primary text

Sukthankar, Vishnu Sitaram (ed.). (1933–66). *The Mahābhārata*. [19 vols.] Poona, India: Bhandarkar Oriental Research Institute.

Secondary texts

Adluri, Vishwa. (2011). Frame narratives and forked beginnings: Or, how to read the Ādiparvan. *Journal of Vaishnava Studies* 19: 143–210.

Bahulkar, S.S. (1994). *Medical Ritual in the Atharvaveda Tradition*. Pune, India: Tilak Maharashtra Vidypeeth.

Bloomfield, M. (1899). *The Atharva-Veda and the Gopatha-Brāhmaṇa*. Strasbourg, France: Verlag von Karl J. Trübner.

Böhtlingk, O. and Roth, R. (1855–75). *Sanskrit Wörterbuch, herausgegeben von der kaiserlichen Akademie der Wissenschaften, bearbeitet von Otto Böhtlingk und Rudolph Roth* [*Sanskrit Dictionary Published by the Imperial Academy of Sciences, Edited by Otto Böhtlingk and Rudolph Roth*]. Saint Petersburg, Russia: Eggers.

Bottéro, Jean. (1992). *Mesopotamia: Writing, Reasoning and the Gods*. Chicago, IL: University of Chicago Press.

Bowles, Adam. (2008). *Mahābhārata Book 8. Karṇa: Volume 2*. New York, NY: New York University Press.

Brodbeck, S. (2009). *The Mahābhārata Patriline: Gender, Culture and the Royal Hereditary*. Farnham, UK: Ashgate.

Caland, W. (1931). *Pañcaviṃśa-Brāhmaṇa. The Brāhmaṇa of Twenty Five Chapters*. Calcutta, India: Asiatic Society of Bengal.

Charpentier, Jarl. (1920). *Die Suparṇasage: Untersuchungen zur altindischen Literatur- und Sagengeschichte* [*The Legend of Suparṇa: Studies in the History of Ancient Indian Literature and Legends*]. Uppsala, Sweden: A.-B. Akademiska Bokhandeln.

Doniger O'Flaherty, Wendy. (1986). Horses and snakes in the Adi Parvan of the Mahabharata. In Margaret Case and Gerald Barrier (eds), *Aspects of India: Essays in Honor of Edward Cameron Dimock*, pp. 16–44. New Delhi: Manohar.

Earl, James W. (2011). *Beginning the Mahābhārata: A Reader's Guide to the Frame Stories*. Woodland Hills, CA: South Asian Studies Association.

Fitzgerald, James. (2002). The Rāma Jāmadagnya 'thread' of the Mahābhārata: A new survey of Rāma Jāmadagnya in the Pune text. In Mary Brockington (ed.), *Stages and Transitions: Temporal and Historical Frameworks in Epic and Purāṇic Literature*, pp. 89–132. Zagreb: Croatian Academy of Sciences and Arts.

Ganguli, K.M. (1884). *The Mahabharata of Krishna-Dwaipayana Vyasa: Adi Parva*. Calcutta, India: Bharata Press.

Goldman, Robert. (1977). *Gods, Priests, and Warriors: The Bhṛgus of the Mahābhārata*. New York, NY: Columbia University Press.

Goldman, Robert. (2021). *Ā Garbhāt*: Murderous rage and collective punishment as thematic elements in Vyāsa's *Mahābhārata*. In Nell Shapiro Hawley and Sohini Sarah Pillai (eds), *Many Mahābhāratas*, pp. 37–52. Albany, NY: SUNY.

Hiltebeitel, Alf. (1990 [1976]). *The Ritual of Battle: Krishna in the Mahābhārata*. Albany: SUNY Press.

Hiltebeitel, Alf. (2002). *Rethinking the Mahābhārata: A Reader's Guide to the Education of the Dharma King*. New Delhi: Oxford University Press.

Hopkins, E. Washburn. (1901). *The Great Epic of India: Its Character and Origin*. New York, NY: Charles Scribner's Sons.

Jackson, Bernard S. (1998). An aye for an I: The semiotics of 'lex talionis' in the Bible. In Roberta Kevelson, William Pencak and J. Ralph Lindgren (eds), *New Approaches to Semiotics and the Human Sciences: Essays in Honour of Roberta Kevelson*, pp. 127–49. New York, NY: Peter Lang.

Kinjawadekar, Mandakini Ashok. (1993). Sarpasattra: Development of the legend. *Bulletin of the Deccan College Post Graduate and Research Institute* 53: 215–17.

Mehendale, M.A. (1993–2007). *Mahābhārata, Cultural Index*. Pune, India: Bhandarkar Oriental Research Institute.

Mehta, Mahesh. (1971). The evolution of the Suparṇa saga in the *Mahābhārata*. *Journal of the Oriental Institute, Baroda* 21: 41–65.

Mehta, Mahesh. (1973). The problem of the double introduction to the Mahābhārata. *Journal of the American Oriental Society* 93: 547–49. doi.org/10.2307/600175.

Minkowski, C.Z. (1989). Janamejaya's sattra and ritual structure. *Journal of the American Oriental Society* 109(3): 401–20. doi.org/10.2307/604141.

Minkowski, C.Z. (2007 [1991]). Snakes, sattras and the Mahābhārata. In A. Sharma (ed.), *Essays on the Mahābhārata*, pp. 384–400. Delhi: Motilal Banarsidass.

Monier-Williams, M. (1899). *A Sanskrit–English Dictionary: Etymologically and Philologically Arranged with Special Reference to Cognate Indo-European Languages*. Oxford, UK: The Clarendon Press.

Müller, F. Max. (1966 [1892]). *Rig-Veda-Samhitā: The Sacred Hymns of the Brāhmans together with the Commentary of Sāyaṇāchārya. Volume IV*. Varanasi, India: Chowkhamba Sanskrit Series Office.

Nicholson, Andrew J. (2012). Doxography and boundary-formation in late medieval India. In Piotr Balcerowicz (ed.), *World View and Theory in Indian Philosophy*, pp. 103–18. Delhi: Manohar.

Rocher, Ludo. (1983). Karma and rebirth in the Dharmaśāstras. In W. Doniger O'Flaherty (ed.), *Karma and Rebirth in Classical Indian Traditions*, pp. 61–89. Delhi: Motilal Banarsidass.

Scheftelowitz, J. (1906). *Die Apokryphen des Ṛgveda (Khilāni)* [*The Apocrypha of the Ṛgveda (Khilāni)*]. Indische Forschungen 1 [Indian Research 1]. Breslau, Germany: Verlag von M. & H. Marcus.

Shee, Monika. (1986). *Tapas und Tapasvin in den erzählenden Partien des Mahābhārata* [*Tapas and Tapasvin in the Narrative Sections of the Mahābhārata*]. Reinbek, Germany: Dr Inge Wezler, Verlag für orientalistische Fachpublikationen.

Slouber, Michael. (2017). *Early Tantric Medicine: Snakebite, Mantras, and Healing in the Gāruḍa Tantras*. New York, NY: Oxford University Press.

Sörensen, S. (1904). *An Index to the Names in the Mahabharata with Short Explanations and a Concordance to the Bombay and Calcutta Editions and P.C. Roy's Translation*. London: Williams & Norgate.

Sukthankar, V.S. (1936). Epic studies VI: The Bhṛgus and the Bhārata—A text-historical study. *Annals of the Bhandarkar Oriental Research Institute* 18: 1–76.

Türstig, H.-G. (1985). The Indian sorcery called Abhicāra. *Wiener Zeitschrift für die Kunde Süd- und Ostasiens und Archiv für Indische Philosophie* [*Vienna Journal of South and East Asian Studies and Archive of Indian Philosophy*] 29: 69–117.

van Buitenen, J.A.B. (1973). *The Mahābhārata. Volume 1, Book 1: The Book of the Beginning*. Chicago, IL: University of Chicago Press. doi.org/10.7208/chicago/9780226217543.001.0001.

Vasu, S.C. (1891–98). *The Aṣṭādhyāyī of Pāṇini*. [7 vols.] Allahabad, India: Indian Press.

Weber, A. (1885). Die Garuḍopaniṣad [The Garuḍopaniṣad]. *Indische Studien* [*Indian Studies*] 17: 161–67.

Whitney, W.D. (1973 [1924]). *Sanskrit Grammar*. Delhi: Motilal Banarsidass.

Winternitz, Moriz. (1926). The serpent sacrifice mentioned in the Mahābhārata. *Journal of the Bombay Branch, Royal Asiatic Society* 2: 74–91.

Witzel, Michael (1987). The case of the shattered head. *Studien zur Indologie und Iranistik* 13/14: 363–415.

Wojtilla, G. (1975). The 'longer' recension of the Garuḍopaniṣad. *Acta Orientalia Academiae Scientiarum Hungaricae* [*Oriental Journal of the Hungarian Academy of Sciences*] 29(3): 385–92.

Yelle, Robert A. (2010). Hindu law as performance: Ritual and poetic elements in Dharmaśāstra. In T. Lubin, D.R. Davis and J.K. Krishnan (eds), *Hinduism and Law: An Introduction*, pp. 183–92. Cambridge, UK: Cambridge University Press. doi.org/10.1017/CBO9780511781674.016.

3

Transitions and transmissions in the *Mahābhārata*: Revisiting the Ugraśravas/ Śaunaka frame dialogue

Brian Black[1]

Abstract

The focus of this chapter will be on the literary significance of the *Mahābhārata*'s framing of the dialogue between Ugraśravas and Śaunaka. By taking a literary, rather than historical, approach to the dialogue between Ugraśravas and Śaunaka, I hope to explore some of the ways in which this opening scene characterises the *Mahābhārata* as a whole, including what

1 I wrote this paper in 2010 for an edited volume that was never published. The working title of that volume was 'Revisiting Transitions in Indian History'. It was due to be edited by Ranabir Chakravarti and Kumkum Roy. In the meantime, this paper has circulated among friends and colleagues and has been cited in two publications of which I am aware: Adluri (2011: 192) and Brodbeck (2009: 245n.40). Although I might have approached this paper differently now, because it has already been circulated among and cited by other scholars, I leave it almost unchanged from the version I submitted for publication more than 10 years ago. I am grateful to Raj Balkaran and McComas Taylor for inviting me to submit this paper to this volume. I would like to thank the following people for their helpful feedback during the Revisiting Transitions seminar in Delhi in March 2007: Naina Dayal, Shonaleeka Kaul, Meenakshi Mukherjee, Kumkum Roy, Shalini Shah, Romila Thapar and Mudit Trivedi. Additionally, I would like to thank Simon Brodbeck, Yulia Egorova, Jim Fitzgerald and Alf Hiltebeitel for reading earlier drafts of this paper and offering useful suggestions. I am also grateful to the British Arts and Humanities Research Council for funding the project 'Epic Constructions: Gender, Myth, and Society in the Mahābhārata', under which the research for this paper was carried out.

type of text it aspires to be, what types of audiences it intends to address and what types of authority it attempts to invoke. As we will see, the complexities of the outer-frame dialogue often elicit more questions than they solve, but by investigating these issues, I hope to bring attention to the rich potential in considering the literary dimensions of the *Mahābhārata*, without supposing that all tropes, metaphors and motifs correspond to a historical reality.

Introduction

Historians have tended to regard the *Mahābhārata* as representing important transitions within Indian history. Romila Thapar (2000: 131), for example, has suggested that the epic reflects 'something of a transitional condition between two rather different structures, the societies of the lineage-based system and that of the monarchical state'. Despite such assertions, the *Mahābhārata* remains a troublesome text for historians both because of its composite nature—containing textual material likely to represent several different historical periods—and because of its mythic scope in relating the deeds of gods and demigods alongside those of mortals. As such, it is very difficult to determine the relationship, if any, between the episodes recorded in the text and events that occurred in Indian history.

Despite such limitations in linking the narrative to historical changes, the *Mahābhārata* is correctly regarded as a transitional text, if for no other reason than the fact that transition is a major theme within the literary world of the text. Throughout both the main narrative and its abundance of embedded stories, the *Mahābhārata* portrays several radical temporal, cultural and religious changes, such as the transformation from one *yuga* to another, shifting attitudes about *dharma* and a change from ritualism to devotionalism. Furthermore, the text itself represents a shift from the revealed authority of the Vedas (*śruti*) to a new type of religious literature based on the memory of a lost tradition (*smṛti*).[2]

The focus of this chapter will be on another transition that has long been associated with the *Mahābhārata*: the change in the transmitters of the text from bards to brahmins. As we will see, this portrayal of the epic's origins has been closely tied to the assumption that the outer frame of the story,

2 As Sheldon Pollock (1997) has demonstrated, both *śruti* and *smṛti* claim Vedic status. But whereas *śruti* designates the Vedic texts that have remained intact, traditional accounts present *smṛti* as that which has been remembered from lost Vedic sources.

featuring the dialogue between Ugraśravas and Śaunaka, can be read as representing the compositional history of the text. Part of the problem with this hypothesis is, as I will suggest, that it naively assumes that this scene depicts a historical process, while it neglects to examine the ways in which the frame story can add to our appreciation of the literary construction of the text. By taking a literary, rather than historical, approach to the dialogue between Ugraśravas and Śaunaka, I hope to explore some of the ways this opening scene characterises the *Mahābhārata* as a whole, including what type of text it aspires to be, what types of audiences it intends to address and what types of authority it attempts to invoke. As we will see, the complexities of the outer-frame dialogue often elicit more questions than they solve, but by investigating these issues, I hope to bring attention to the rich potential in considering the literary dimensions of the *Mahābhārata*, without supposing that all tropes, metaphors and motifs correspond with a historical reality.

Ugraśravas as bard: Why does a *sūta* narrate the *Mahābhārata*?

For most audiences of the epic in India today, the *Mahābhārata*'s outer-frame story features the episode in which Vyāsa, the author of the text, dictates his tale to Gaṇeśa, who puts the brahmin's words into writing. The impetus for transcribing the epic came from the god Brahmā, who visited Vyāsa when he was concerned about how he should communicate his work to his students. Despite the ubiquity of this episode among modern tellings of the *Mahābhārata*, this is not the story that frames most of the manuscripts that were considered when constructing the Critical Edition.[3] Instead, the critically reconstituted text begins with an episode in which the *sūta* Ugraśravas approaches a group of brahmin *ṛṣi*s and recites the tale that he claims to have heard told by Vaiśampāyaṇa at King Janamejaya's snake sacrifice.

It has always seemed curious to me that a text that declares itself to be as authoritative and exhaustive as does the *Mahābhārata*—at times even claiming for itself Vedic status—would feature a *sūta*[4] as the main narrator

3 See Fitzgerald (1991: 152).

4 One of the problems in understanding Ugraśravas's role as the *Mahābhārata*'s main narrator revolves around the ambiguity of the term *sūta*, which sometimes seems to mean 'bard', on other occasions seems to be a name for a charioteer and on yet other occasions can mean both or neither. Shubha Pathak (2006: 133) attributes this ambiguity to the merging of two different textual traditions.

of its outer frame. This central role attributed to Ugraśravas has tended to be explained in terms of the theory that the *Mahābhārata* originated among professional storytellers and was later appropriated by brahmins. V.S. Sukthankar explicitly connected the theory about the text's transmission to the dialogue between Ugraśravas and Śaunaka, seeing the frame story as 'an unconscious admission' that the *Mahābhārata* originated among bards and was appropriated by a specific group of brahmins, the Bhṛgu clan:

> The Bhārgava influence is implied in the person of the Kulapati Śaunaka. The *sūta*, who used to recite the poem in the Heroic Age, is kept on, with due regard to traditional usage, to give the new recension a setting appropriate to it and indicating the source at the same time. (Sukthankar 1936: 73)[5]

It is not my intention to argue that the *Mahābhārata* was not originally composed by bards; indeed, there are other grounds besides the frame story that suggest bardic origins.[6] Rather, my aim here is to point out that even if the *Mahābhārata* originated among professional storytellers, it is extremely unlikely that Ugraśravas as a literary character is meant to represent such a bardic background. According to the *Mahābhārata*'s own representation of its compositional history, it did not originate among *sūta*s, but was authored by the brahmin Vyāsa, who taught it as the fifth Veda to his five brahmin students, who, in turn, went in separate directions to recite the *Mahābhārata* in public.[7] As we will see, the text provides conflicting accounts of how the *sūta*s—Ugraśravas and his father, Lomaharṣaṇa—learned the *Mahābhārata*, but all such explanations agree that they learned it from brahmins: either from Vyāsa himself or from his student Vaiśaṃpāyana.[8] Furthermore, the outer-frame narrative reminds us on several occasions that Śaunaka and the

5 More recently, Vassilkov (1995: 251) sums up this view: the *Mahābhārata* is a 'heroic epic of the classical type. On the other hand, it is well known that at a certain stage of its development in the oral tradition the *Mbh* was revised by brahmins who tried to make it into a religious and didactic work, a Dharmaśāstra'. See also Brockington (1998: 20, 155).

6 For theories about the oral history of the text, see de Jong (1975); and Vassilkov (2002). See also Sharma (2000) for possible links between *sūta*s and the *śloka* compositional style. Hiltebeitel (2001b: 4) has challenged such theories of bardic origins, calling the orality of the *Mahābhārata* a literary trope.

7 Vyāsa's five brahmin students are Vaiśaṃpāyana, Sumantu, Jaimini, Paila and his son Śuka (*Mbh*, 1.57.74–75); a different list includes Śuka, Nārada and Asita Devala (1.1.63–64); and, as we have seen, Vyāsa is also said to have taught Lomaharṣaṇa (1.13.7).

8 As we will see, Ugraśravas gives two different explanations for how he knows the *Mahābhārata*: at the very beginning of the text, he claims to have heard Vaiśaṃpāyana's narration at the *sarpasatra* (*Mbh*, 1.1.10), while at the beginning of the Paulomaparvan, he attributes his knowledge to learning from his father (1.5.4–5). Ugraśravas also gives two different explanations for how his father knows the text: on one occasion he says his father learned from Vaiśaṃpāyana (1.5.4–5), while later he says his father was Vyāsa's student (1.13.6–8).

brahmins of the Naimiṣa Forest have already heard everything that Ugraśravas has to tell them.[9] Thus, regardless of the history of the *Mahābhārata*'s transmission, the epic's own account is that it originated among brahmins, not bards.[10]

Rather than look for a historical explanation for Ugraśravas's role as a narrator, we might be better advised to examine what literary purpose he serves. One way to explore his literary role as narrator is to see how he compares with other narrators within the text. With the inclusion of at least 67 *upākhyānas* (Hiltebeitel 2005: 467), not to mention numerous embedded teachings, dialogues and other stories, there is a long list of *Mahābhārata* characters who assume the role of narrator at one time or another. However, there are four speakers whose narration frames large portions of the narrative: 1) Ugraśravas, the main speaker in the text's outer frame; 2) Vaiśaṃpāyana, the main speaker in the text's inner frame; 3) Saṃjaya, who narrates Books 6–10; and 4) Bhīṣma, the main speaker in Books 12–13.

Among these narrators, Ugraśravas seemingly has the most in common with Saṃjaya, who is also a *sūta*. However, the parallels between Ugraśravas and Saṃjaya as storytellers are limited for two reasons. One is because Saṃjaya repeats events that he witnesses at first hand, while Ugraśravas recounts a text he has learned (more on this distinction below). The other difference is that Saṃjaya has a special power to enhance his narration: the divine eye (*divya cakṣus*) he receives from Vyāsa (*Mbh*, 6.2.9–13, 6.16.5–10).

In fact, the text's two other narrators, Vaiśaṃpāyana and Bhīṣma, receive some form of narratorial assistance as well. Vaiśaṃpāyana is not only a brahmin, but also one of Vyāsa's five students. If that is not enough to authorise him as the *Mahābhārata*'s narrator to King Janamejaya, he recounts the text under the specific instruction of Vyāsa (*Mbh*, 1.54.21–22), who remains present for the text's recital.

Bhīṣma, despite not being a brahmin, is described by his mother, Gaṅgā, as having learned the Vedas from Vasiṣṭha, as knowing all the *śāstras* known by Uśanas and Bṛhaspati and as knowing all the weapons known by Rāma Jāmadagnya (*Mbh*, 1.94.31–36). As Alf Hiltebeitel (2001a: 276–77) points

9 After the Pauṣyaparvan, for example, the sages make a point of describing what Śaunaka already knows (*Mbh*, 1.4.4–5). As Hiltebeitel (2001b: 103) comments: 'Ugraśravas can hardly feel much esteemed at hearing that Śaunaka already knows "completely" all such stories as Ugraśravas might tell him.'

10 As Hiltebeitel (2001b: 13n.51) observes, this is the case for both the *Mahābhārata* and the *Rāmāyaṇa*: '[I]n each Sanskrit epic the transmission goes in the reverse, from Brahmans to bards.'

out, these celestial teachers described in the Ādiparvan account for many of the sources that he cites in the Śānti and Anuśāsanaparvans. Yet, the time spent in Heaven with his mother is not enough to authorise Bhīṣma as Yudhiṣṭhira's postwar instructor on *dharma* and the duties of a king. Like Saṃjaya, Bhīṣma begins his narration only after receiving the divine eye—although Bhīṣma receives it from Kṛṣṇa rather than from Vyāsa (*Mbh*, 12.52.15–22). Bhīṣma makes clear that receiving divine vision is what gives him the traditional knowledge to be Yudhiṣṭhira's teacher: 'I behold all the laws [*dharma*] pronounced by the Vedas and by the final portions of the Vedas [*vedānta*], because of the boon you have granted me' (12.54.19).[11] Even despite such a divine endorsement, Bhīṣma's authority to narrate seems to be a concern throughout both the Śānti and Anuśāsanaparvans, as he continually makes clear who his sources are, often citing Bṛhaspati and Manu in particular. If that is not enough, Vyāsa is present for most of his narration.

In these examples, we see that the other major narrators within the *Mahābhārata* have some special authority to narrate that is additional to their class status or their *paraṃparā*. Vaiśaṃpāyana and Saṃjaya derive their authority directly from Vyāsa, while Bhīṣma receives authority from both Vyāsa and Kṛṣṇa. When all the narrators receive direct endorsement in one way or another from Vyāsa, the fact that Ugraśravas does not contributes to the questions about his narratorial authority.

Ugraśravas as narrator: The problem of the double explanation

Equally problematic is how Ugraśravas learns the *Mahābhārata* in the first place. In the very first scene of the *Mahābhārata*, Ugraśravas approaches a group of brahmins who are conducting a 12-year ritual in the Naimiṣa Forest. After a brief exchange, the brahmins ask Ugraśravas to recount the *Mahābhārata*: 'Tell us the story of old [*purāṇam*] that was imparted by the great *ṛṣi* Dvaipāyana' (*Mbh*, 1.1.15). Ugraśravas begins with several preliminaries—providing invocations, a cosmology, a brief history of the composition and transmission of the text, three plot summaries and various *phalaśrutis*—before narrating the epic's first story, the Pauṣyaparvan (1.3).

11 Translations based on those of van Buitenen and Fitzgerald.

Yet, after the Pauṣyaparvan, we again hear of Ugraśravas's arrival in the Naimiṣa Forest. This time, however, before recounting any stories to the brahmins, he must wait for their leader, Śaunaka, to finish performing a ritual. When Śaunaka arrives, he asks Ugraśravas to begin his narration of the *Mahābhārata* with an account of the Bhṛgu clan—Śaunaka's own family. Ugraśravas obliges by reciting the Paulomanparvan, and subsequently relates the Āstīkaparvan, after which the main story of the *Mahābhārata* begins.

Mahesh Mehta (1973: 547) has described the 'double introduction' to the *Mahābhārata* as 'two blocks [that] are put together without any attempt at organic combination—a strange patchwork!' Yet, he has proposed that despite their 'incongruous juxtaposition', there are threads that link them together, suggesting they 'belong to the same redactoral agency' (Mehta 1973: 549).

In addition to the textual problems with the double introduction, both accounts provide different explanations for how Ugraśravas has learned the *Mahābhārata*. In the first introduction (*Mbh*, 1.1.1–26), Ugraśravas informs his brahmin hosts that he recently returned from King Janamejaya's snake sacrifice, where he heard Vaiśaṃpāyana recount the great stories that make up the *Mahābhārata* (1.1.10). Then the *sūta* reports that he has also visited numerous sacred fords (*tīrtha*s) and sanctuaries (*āyatana*s), including the location of the war between the Kauravas and Pāṇḍavas. Ugraśravas's travels along the pilgrimage circuit demonstrate his bardic credentials, as, according to the *Mahābhārata* itself, such locations were venues for performing oral legends; meanwhile, his presence at the snake sacrifice, where he hears Vyāsa's student Vaiśaṃpāyana recite the *Mahābhārata*, places him in a line of oral transmission that is just one person removed from the epic's composer.

The second introduction begins with the same sentence as the first, but subsequently Ugraśravas's arrival is portrayed quite differently. Rather than wait for the brahmins to be seated and for them to offer him a seat, Ugraśravas folds his hands at his forehead and is the first to speak, asking the brahmins: '[W]hat do you wish to hear, what should I tell you?' (*Mbh*, 1.4.2). They reply that they will ask him to tell stories later, but first they must wait for Śaunaka, who is in the fire hall attending to the ritual. While they are waiting, the brahmins make a point of describing what their leader already knows. When Śaunaka finally arrives, he takes his 'most respected seat' (*āsanaṃ paramārcitam*) and then speaks to Ugraśravas: 'Your father, my boy, formerly learned all the stories of old. Have you learned them all too, son of Lomaharṣaṇa?' (1.5.1).

Crucially, throughout his conversation with Śaunaka, Ugraśravas never mentions that he has been to King Janamejaya's *sarpasatra*,[12] nor does he say he has toured any pilgrimage sites. Rather, the first glimpse of how Ugraśravas has learned the *Mahābhārata* comes from Śaunaka's question. Of course, at this point, Śaunaka is not asking to hear the *Mahābhārata* per se, but rather to hear an account of his own ancestors, the Bhṛgus—an account that becomes part of the *Mahābhārata* through Ugraśravas's narration. Nevertheless, when responding to Śaunaka, Ugraśravas confirms that he has received his learning from his father, who had learned from Vaiśaṃpāyana: 'All that was formerly learned perfectly and was formerly narrated perfectly by the great-spirited Vaiśaṃpāyana and the brahmins, that was learned by my father and has been perfectly learned by me' (*Mbh*, 1.5.4–5).

At the beginning of the Āstīkaparvan, Ugraśravas again presents himself as his father's student:

> This *itihāsa*, known as a *purāṇa*, was recited by Kṛṣṇa Dvaipāyana to the dwellers of the Naimiṣa Forest. My father, the bard Lomaharṣaṇa, Vyāsa's student [*śiṣyo vyāsasya*], was once asked by the brahmins to tell it. Therefore, I have listened to it. I will now relate it just as I have heard it. (*Mbh*, 1.13.6–8)

Here, apparently in addition to teaching the *Mahābhārata* to his five students, Vyāsa is said to have recited the Āstīkaparvan to brahmins in the Naimiṣa Forest; crucially, Ugraśravas adds that his own father, rather than learning this story from Vaiśaṃpāyana and his successors, had learned it directly from Vyāsa, as his student. Additionally, Ugraśravas claims that his father had once recited the Āstīkaparvan to brahmins.

Śaunaka, seemingly unperturbed by the different presentations of Lomaharṣaṇa's *paraṃparā*, observes that Ugraśravas narrates like his father: 'You speak like your father; we are very pleased. Your father was always ready to please us. Tell us now this story as your father told it' (*Mbh*, 1.14.2–3). Here, Śaunaka verifies Ugraśravas's claim that his father had narrated this tale to brahmins and suggests that he had heard such tales from Lomaharṣaṇa himself. Ugraśravas then confirms that he has learned to narrate like his father: 'I will tell the Āstīka story as I heard it from my father' (1.14.4).

---

12 I use the form *satra* instead of *sattra* throughout, as this is how the word appears in the *Mahābhārata*. As Simon Brodbeck (2009: 125) suggests, the *Mahābhārata*'s different representation of this term could indicate that it represents its *satra* rituals differently from how *sattra*s are described in Vedic texts.

As we can see from these exchanges, in addition to the 'problem of the double introduction', the *Mahābhārata*'s outer-frame story also presents the problem of two modes of transmission.[13] In the Paulomaparvan, Ugraśravas does not mention attending King Janamejaya's *sarpasatra*, while in the opening scene, when Śaunaka is not yet present, Ugraśravas does not mention learning from his father. The most well-known explanation for the double introduction is the one offered by Sukthankar (1944: 11): that each version was at one point the opening frame for a different version of the *Mahābhārata*, and that both have been included in the final redaction because both were 'too good to lose'.

Yet, when we approach the double introduction as a narratorial question, rather than merely a textual one, another intriguing possibility emerges: rather than two versions of the same scene, these two accounts could represent two different narrations. This is indicated when Ugraśravas, addressing the Naimiṣa brahmins in the first introduction, refers to his narration to Śaunaka in the second introduction: 'I will narrate to you the entire Bhārata tale from the Pauloman tale onwards, as it was told at Śaunaka's *satra*' (*Mbh*, 1.2.30). As the second introduction begins at the Paulomanparvan, this remark suggests that Ugraśravas is telling the Naimiṣa brahmins that he will narrate to them what he had already told Śaunaka on a previous occasion.

Subsequently, after listing the *Mahābhārata*'s 100 books, Ugraśravas tells his audience: 'These one hundred *parvan*s were previously recited by the great-spirited Vyāsa. They were again narrated by Ugraśravas, son of Lomaharṣaṇa, in the Naimiṣa Forest, but in eighteen books' (*Mbh*, 1.2.70–71). Again, this scene indicates a narration by Ugraśravas that has already happened. Of course, such passages could be explained away in terms of sloppy editing, and the fact that Ugraśravas refers to himself in the third person suggests there is some confusion here. However, these two references to the second introduction within the first introduction should also give us pause to consider whether our final redactors had in mind one Naimiṣa frame or two.

It is certainly possible that Ugraśravas has recited the *Mahābhārata* in the Naimiṣa Forest before, and to some of the same brahmins. Ugraśravas tells the Naimiṣa brahmins, for example, that poets have recited the epic before, are reciting it now and will recite it again in the future (*Mbh*, 1.1.24).

13 The end of the *Mahābhārata* seems to recognise the first introduction, with Ugraśravas concluding that he has narrated everything that was told by Vaiśaṃpāyana, rather than everything that had been told by his father (*Mbh*, 18.5).

Furthermore, we know that the Naimiṣa Forest had already been the setting for at least two other narrations: one by Vyāsa and one by Lomaharṣaṇa. Indeed, as Hiltebeitel (2001b: 100–1) points out, when the Naimiṣa brahmins ask Ugraśravas to narrate the *Mahābhārata* in the first introduction, they seem to have a certain familiarity with what the *sūta* is about to recount: '[W]hat the *ṛṣis* want to hear is something that has clearly passed through the hands of such Brahmans as themselves.' Of course, Hiltebeitel is making a different point: that the outer frame generally presents the *Mahābhārata* as the type of text that would be known by brahmins such as those in the Naimiṣa Forest. Yet, if the episode featuring Śaunaka represents a previous occasion, this would also help explain some of the differences between the two introductions concerning the interactions between Ugraśravas and the Naimiṣa brahmins. The first introduction, for example, describes in more detail the courteous exchanges between the *sūta* and his brahmin hosts, with Ugraśravas waiting for the brahmins to speak before speaking and only taking a seat after his hosts have been seated. By contrast, in the second introduction, Ugraśravas begins speaking immediately on his arrival. Thus, if the first introduction came chronologically after the second, this would help clarify why the Naimiṣa brahmins are more respectful towards him than they were earlier: now they know he can spin a fine tale because they have already experienced his storytelling abilities.

Although the outer frame is open to this reading, I do not want to emphasise this point too strongly; it is not clear that such an interpretation would offer a better explanation for the 'problem of double introduction' than those offered by Sukthankar and Mehta. Additionally, such a scenario presents a major chronological inconsistency: if, in the second introduction, Ugraśravas had not yet been to Janamejaya's snake sacrifice, how is he able to narrate this episode to Śaunaka?

While such a blatant temporal problem might seem to discount the possibility of two different Naimiṣa frames, there are hints of a similarly complex chronology even if we take the two introductions as one continuous scene, with Śaunaka making a late entrance. At the beginning of the first introduction, when the Naimiṣa brahmins ask Ugraśravas to tell them the *Mahābhārata*, they seem to know already some of the details, not only about the epic in a general sense, but also as it has been narrated at the snake sacrifice: 'Tell us the story of old [*purāṇam*] ... [W]e wish to hear it just as Vaiśaṃpāyana, at Dvaipāyana's request, repeated it at King Janamejaya's *satra*' (*Mbh*, 1.1.15–18). Of course, Ugraśravas has not come directly from the snake sacrifice, as he has already told the seers that on the way to the Naimiṣa Forest he has visited many *tīrtha*s and *āyatana*s, as well as making a stop at the holy site of Samantapañcaka; so, it is possible that word of Janamejaya's sacrifice had already reached his brahmin interlocutors before Ugraśravas arrived. But even if we can produce a chronological explanation, it seems clear that the two accounts of how Ugraśravas has learned the *Mahābhārata* do not fit comfortably together.

Unlike Mehta and Sukthankar, I am not interested in speculating about the process and relative sequence by which different sections were incorporated into the text. Rather, my aim here is to draw attention to the fact that—whichever way we try to explain the double introduction: as one continuous scene, as two different frames or as two versions of the same scene—the outer frame contains two explanations for Ugraśravas's education: an overdetermined justification that could suggest that the authority of Ugraśravas as a narrator was a concern for the redactors, and perhaps one for which they struggled to find a satisfactory explanation. But, as we will see, this double explanation also places Ugraśravas equally within two very different types of lineages of transmission.

The second introduction presents a lineage that resembles a Vedic *paraṃparā*, with Ugraśravas learning the tradition from his father, who learned it from Vyāsa and/or his student. Although Ugraśravas and his father are not brahmins themselves, the father to son transmission, combined with a lineage that goes directly back to Vyāsa, gives the appearance of an orthodox mode of transmission. The first introduction, however, is seemingly much more problematic. Although Ugraśravas's claim to have heard the *Mahābhārata* at Janamejaya's *sarpasatra* places him closer to Vyāsa in terms of the history of the text's transmission, this explanation seems to open more complications, as Ugraśravas is the student neither of Vyāsa nor of Vaiśaṃpāyana. In fact, in this account, his only means of knowing the *Mahābhārata* seems to be overhearing the text as it was narrated to someone else.

Eyewitnesses and eavesdroppers

Ugraśravas, of course, is not the only narrator who legitimises his claim to knowledge by means of his presence at a particular place and time. Another example of eavesdropping as the means for narratorial authority appears in Ugraśravas's account of the Āstīkaparvan, as he describes the events leading up to the snake sacrifice. Ugraśravas mentions that King Janamejaya once asked his ministers to report a conversation between Takṣaka, the king of the snakes, and the brahmin Kaśyapa. However, when Janamejaya asks to hear this exchange, he is concerned about how his ministers could possibly recount a conversation they did not themselves witness—a dialogue that was seemingly not witnessed by anyone at all: 'I first wish to hear the dialogue between the king of snakes and Kaśyapa in the forest, which was without inhabitants. Who witnessed and heard what came to be heard by you?' (*Mbh*, 1.46.26–27). The ministers respond that a man who was collecting branches just happened to have climbed a tree when he overheard the conversation. Later this man recounted the dialogue in the city where the ministers were present. The ministers tell Janamejaya that what they related to him about this encounter was exactly as they had heard it from the eyewitness himself (1.46.31). Crucially, after hearing this explanation, King Janamejaya makes his fateful decision to conduct the snake sacrifice.

Similarly, when Śakuntalā recounts her family origins to Duḥṣanta, she presents her own biography in the words of her father as spoken in a conversation with a *ṛṣi*—a dialogue she claims to have overheard (*Mbh*, 1.65–66). As I have discussed elsewhere (Black 2007b), eavesdropping is often offered as a plausible explanation for how female characters know what they know, particularly when their words could be called into question. Both Draupadī (3.33.56–58) and Sulabhā (12.308.181–84), for example, describe occasions when they overheard brahmins teaching their fathers when they need to explain how they have been educated in traditional knowledge. Perhaps Ugraśravas, as a *sūta* who might not have been accepted formally as Vaiśaṃpāyana's student, is relying on eavesdropping for similar reasons.[14]

Significantly, Vyāsa, who is credited with composing the *Mahābhārata* from his own mind, also resorts to eavesdropping to explain how he knows what he knows—suggesting, of course, that even he was not outside the question of how he derived his authority as composer or narrator. In the Strīparvan (*Mbh*, 11.8.20–44), for example, the divine plan that Vyāsa reveals to Dhṛtarāṣṭra is one he overheard when it was discussed in Indra's assembly hall.

On other occasions, his authorial status derives from being an eyewitness. When Jamanejaya first asks Vyāsa to recite the *Mahābhārata*, he says to him: 'The actions of the Kurus and Pāṇḍavas, you have seen them with your

14 However, Ugraśravas tells Śaunaka that his father, Lomaharṣaṇa, was the student of Vyāsa (*Mbh*, 1.13.6–8) and Vaiśaṃpāyana (1.5.4–5).

own eyes [*pratyakṣadarṣivān*], Sir. I want you to tell me, twiceborn' (*Mbh*, 1.54.18). Vaiśaṃpāyana will subsequently tell Janamejaya (1.55.2, 1.56.12), as Ugraśravas tells the Naimiṣa brahmins (1.1.23), that the *Mahābhārata* is Vyāsa's 'thought entire' (*mataṃ kṛtsnam*), but here, when Vyāsa is first asked to speak about the Pāṇḍavas and Kauravas, Janamejaya addresses Vyāsa more as a chronicler than as a textual composer.

Similarly, when Bhīṣma narrates an account of Vyāsa and Śuka in the Śāntiparvan, he spells out how he has come to know about the scene where Śuka achieves *mokṣa*. As Bhīṣma explains to Yudhiṣṭhira, Vyāsa was not present to witness Śuka's final liberation, but this event was observed by several *ṛṣi*s, who reported back to Vyāsa, from whom Bhīṣma learned about it. As Hiltebeitel (2001a: 261) comments: 'Bhīṣma thereby indicates who [beside Śuka] witnessed the wonder of Śuka's liberation, which Vyāsa has just missed, and thus how Bhīṣma could have gotten this missing moment of the tale.' Such scenes indicate the complexity of Vyāsa's double role as both the text's divinely inspired composer and a participant within the narrative. Vyāsa is portrayed as both a Vedic *ṛṣi* who sees the text with his mind's eye and a 'historical' witness who provides a testimony of the events he observes at first hand.

In returning to the question of why Ugraśravas is the main narrator, we have perhaps elicited more questions than provided answers. But if questions remain as to why a *sūta* would be the text's main narrator, it is instructive to observe that the *Mahābhārata* seems to have struggled with this question as well. As is evident with episodes throughout the text, such as Draupadī's polyandrous marriage, the death of Bhīṣma and the death of Kṛṣṇa,[15] the *Mahābhārata* tends to provide multiple explanations for situations that are considered controversial or problematic. Seen in this light, the double explanation is worth noting because it indicates a possible tension within the text itself.

We might also consider reading the Ugraśravas narration within the context of the text's claim to reach an audience that is much larger and more inclusive than that of the Vedas. Although the Critical Edition does not contain the

15 For a discussion of these three episodes, see Black (2021): Draupadī's marriage (pp. 57–81), Bhīṣma's death (pp. 49–52) and Kṛṣṇa's death (pp. 169–71).

well-known description of the epic as a text 'for women and śūdras',[16] the *Mahābhārata* does seem to regard itself as delivering a universal message. In addition to the numerous *phalaśruti*s throughout the text that address audiences beyond those who are male and of the twice-born classes, Vyāsa himself, in the Śāntiparvan, instructs his disciples to teach his story to members of all four *varṇas* (12.314.45). Given the author's own instruction to his students, what better way to reach a diverse and inclusive audience than to have Brahmanical knowledge communicated by someone of lower birth. Indeed, without making any claims about the 'real' history of the text, this scenario seems to be the one that the *Mahābhārata* tells about its own transmission: originating among brahmins, but learned by *sūta*s such as Ugraśravas, who, implicitly, share such tales and legends with a wide audience, particularly when they frequent popular pilgrimage sites, such as the ones Ugraśravas visited before arriving in the Naimiṣa Forest. If this is indeed the *Mahābhārata*'s own account of its transmission, perhaps the double explanation of Ugraśravas's narratorial credentials is part of depicting him as a transitional character: as both inside and outside the Brahmanical textual tradition. He can trace his educational lineage back to the composer himself, but at the same time he is at the margins of that tradition, eavesdropping on the epic at King Janamejaya's sacrifice.

Śaunaka the Bhārgava

While Sukthankar's theory of the *Mahābhārata*'s compositional history takes Ugraśravas to represent the text's bardic origins, a more recent hypothesis suggests that Śaunaka and the Naimiṣa brahmins are symbolic of a Brahmanical authorial committee. In his provocative book *Rethinking the Mahābhārata: A Reader's Guide to the Education of the Dharma King*, Alf Hiltebeitel (2001b) has challenged several widespread assumptions about the compositional history of the epic. In response to the commonly accepted theory that the *Mahābhārata* was composed in distinct stages over up to 1,000 years (500 BCE – 500 CE), Hiltebeitel (2001b: 20) suggests the text was put together in a much shorter period—at most, a 'couple of generations'; instead of positing bardic origins, Hiltebeitel proposes that the

16 This description of the *Mahābhārata* appears in the *Bhāgavata Purāṇa* (1.4.25), which says that Vyāsa composed his story out of compassion for women, *śūdras* and uneducated twice-borns. Nonetheless, there are several individual *phalaśrutis* throughout the text that offer rewards for *śūdras* and women (see, for example, 12.327.104–5; see also Black 2007b: 55–56, for *phalaśrutis* that specifically address a female audience).

Mahābhārata was originally composed by brahmins. Moreover, according to Hiltebeitel (2001b: 19–20), the brahmins who composed the epic were part of a 'committee' or 'team' who had the patronage of a minor king or merchant. As Hiltebeitel speculates, Śaunaka and the brahmins of the Naimiṣa Forest represent part of this authorial committee.

I have considerable appreciation for Hiltebeitel's theory of the text's history and transmission, particularly as he bases most of his speculations on a close reading of the stories the epic tells about itself—'how the text itself portrays those who compose, transmit, and receive it as audiences' (2001b: 29). Nevertheless, while Śaunaka and the Naimiṣa brahmins are depicted as major players in the transmission of the text, at no point does the *Mabhābhārata* suggest they were involved in any compositional activities, such as authorship or editing. Thus, it seems unlikely that the brahmins in the frame story reflect an authorial or editorial team. Rather than assume that Śaunaka and the Naimiṣa brahmins are depictions of the epic's authors, I would like to examine the role that Śaunaka plays within the literary world of the text. Or, following Hiltebeitel's (2001b: 110) own advice, I would like to explore Śaunaka as a literary character.[17]

Although he is usually not considered a central character, Śaunaka has the prominent role of being the *Mahābhārata*'s primary listener. Of the four main framing dialogues that structure the text, three feature a king as the primary audience—namely, Janamejaya, Dhṛtarāṣṭra and Yudhiṣṭhira—and in all three cases, the stories and teachings that the king hears are connected to his ability to rule and his claim to regal power.[18] In the examples of these three royal auditors it is clear that listeners depicted in the *Mahābhārata* are well chosen receivers who often have something to learn from what they hear.

In his role as the text's primary listener, much has been made of Śaunaka being a member of the Bhārgava family of brahmins,[19] particularly in the context of Sukthankar's theory of Bhṛguisation.[20] As we have seen, Sukthankar's

17 See also Patton (2011).

18 Janamejaya hears the *Mahābhārata* at his *sarpasatra*, where he interrupts his massacre of the snakes, hence stopping, or at least pausing, a cycle of violence that has continued for several generations; Dhṛtarāṣṭra not only hears in detail the tragedies of the war, but also is repeatedly instructed by Saṃjaya that his own actions and inactions contributed to the war and, consequently, to the deaths of his sons; Yudhiṣṭhira learns discourses on *nīti* and *dharma* as he prepares to assume the position of king.

19 Members of the Bhārgava family are descendants of the *ṛṣi* Bhṛgu, who is one of the 10 *ṛṣi* composers of hymns in the *Ṛg Veda*. Although the term *Bhṛgu* appears in the *Ṛg Veda*, this word is first associated with a particular sage or as the ancestor of the Bhārgava clan in the Brāhmaṇas (Goldman 1977: 150n.14).

20 See also Goldman (1977); Minkowski (1991); Brockington (1998); and Hiltebeitel (2001b: 105–18).

theory assumes that the *Mahābhārata* was not only composed by bards and appropriated by brahmins, but also appropriated by a specific group of brahmins: the Bhārgavas. Śaunaka plays a pivotal role in this theory, as he, being a descendent of Bhṛgu, represents the Bhārgava appropriation of the text. Recently, scholars such as Minkowski (1991) and Hiltebeitel (2001b) have rejected the suggestion that the Bhṛgus were compilers and/or editors of the text. As Minkowski ponders: 'Why should we assume that in India a distinct group could take hostage the product of an entire culture, an epic, moreover, that itself suggests a history of conforming to the interests of its listeners?' (1991: 400). But, even if it is unlikely that Śaunaka represents an appropriation of the text, his family identity is nonetheless an integral part of his character in the frame story.

Indeed, the two stories that Ugraśravas narrates to Śaunaka in the outer frame feature a Bhārgava brahmin in a prominent role.[21] Ugraśravas's first story to Śaunaka is prompted by the brahmin's request to hear about the history of his own family. After recounting a family genealogy[22] and an episode about Bhṛgu cursing Agni, the story resumes several generations later, with Ruru, whose fiancée Pramadvarā is killed by snakebite. Through an act of truth (*satyakrīya*), Ruru revives his bride-to-be, but only after giving up half his own life. Yet, even after bringing his bride back from the dead, Ruru swears to take revenge by killing all snakes. He then goes around lashing snakes with a stick, but one day strikes a lizard instead. This lizard, as it turns out, is a sage who has been cursed because he had frightened another sage with a snake. The lizard tells him he is acting like a *kṣatriya*: that brahmins should observe *ahiṃsā* and leave the killing to the *kṣatriya*s. He then tells Ruru about Āstīka, who saved the snakes from extermination through his inspiring song of praise to Janamejaya. Rather than narrating this story himself, however, the lizard instructs Ruru to learn it from a brahmin. Subsequently, Ruru returns to his father, Pramata, who tells him the story.

Yet, we never hear Pramata tell the tale, as the beginning of the Āstīkaparvan returns to the dialogue between Ugraśravas and Śaunaka. Ugraśravas's account of the Āstīkaparvan begins with the rivalry between the two wives of Kaśyapa: Kadrū, the mother of the snakes, and Vinatā, the mother of two birds, one of which is Garuḍa. This story weaves together several other

21 The Pauṣyaparvan also features a prominent Bhārgava and addresses the *sarpasatra*, but Śaunaka is not present to hear this tale.

22 The genealogy of Śaunaka's branch of the family is presented as follows: Bhṛgu (+ Pulomā) > Cyavana Bhārgava > Pramati (+ Ghṛtācī) > Ruru (+ Pramadvarā) > Śunaka.

tales, including the churning of the milk ocean, the stealing of *soma* and the battle between the *devas* and *asuras*, before relating the death of Parikṣit and how Āstīka—who was taught by Cyavana, son of Bhṛgu—interrupted Janamejaya's sacrifice to save the snakes from extermination.

As we can see, the stories of Ruru and Āstīka connect Śaunaka personally with the snake sacrifice, which both stories set up to be the primary lenses through which Śaunaka will view the *Mahābhārata*'s main narrative (Minkowski 1991). Additionally, a number of themes that appear generally in Bhārgava stories link closely with the account of Janamejaya's snake sacrifice, particularly the recurring motif of genocidal vendettas, with the Bhārgavas often depicted as the ones who attempt to exterminate entire populations.[23] Rāma Jāmadagnya, who kills off the entire *kṣatriya* population 21 times, is well known, but the theme of near-extermination also appears in other Bhārgava stories, such as the story of Aurva (*Mbh*, 1.169–71), in which, in this case, the Bhārgavas are the victims of genocide, with the *kṣatriyas* not even sparing the unborn Bhārgava children.

Another Bhārgava story with relevance to Śaunaka—although it is not included in the outer frame—is the tale of King Vītahavya, the founder of Śaunaka's branch of the Bhārgava family. As narrated by Bhīṣma to Yudhiṣṭhira in the Anuśāsanaparvan (*Mbh*, 13.31), King Vītahavya was born a Śāryāta king and is depicted as a 'particularly murderous warrior' (Goldman 1977: 112). In another episode of near-genocide, Vītahavya and his sons kill all the sons and soldiers of King Divodāsa. However, King Divodāsa manages to escape and, subsequently, holds a sacrifice with the aid of his priest Bharadvāja for the sake of having a son. Subsequently, Pratardana is born and, when he reaches maturity, he attempts to avenge his father's family by marching against King Vītahavya and killing all his sons in a single battle. Fearing for his own life, Vītahavya flees to Bhṛgu's ashram. When King Pratardana shows up—keen to complete extermination of the Vītahavya clan—he asks the brahmin to surrender the king, with Bhṛgu replying that there are no *kṣatriyas* in his ashram. Because of Bhṛgu's inherent truthfulness, this declaration transforms Vītahavya into a brahmin, and Vītahavya ends up being the founder of Śaunaka's branch of the family.

23 As Goldman (1977: 5) points out, the Bhārgavas are often portrayed in a rather negative light: 'The central concern of the Bhṛgus appear from the mythology to have included death, violence, sorcery, confusion and violation of class roles [*varṇāśramadharma*], intermarriage with other varṇas [*varṇasaṃkara*] and open hostility to the gods themselves. In addition, several of the Bhārgava sages are shown in the epic to have engaged with impunity in such activities as theft, drinking liquor, and killing a woman, acts that are condemned unequivocally in the law texts as especially improper for brahmins.'

The story of Vītahavya brings up several recurring themes that have relevance to Śaunaka and the tales he hears in the outer frame. For example, it portrays the founder of Śaunaka's side of the family as originally being a king. As such, Śaunaka is reminded that Ruru, who was accused of acting too much like a *kṣatriya*, was not his only ancestor whose status as a brahmin was somewhat ambiguous. This story also reveals that Vītahavya, once he was pronounced a brahmin, did not receive his Vedic education by means of the traditional method, but rather learned the Vedas from the virtue of Bhṛgu's words.

As we can see, one of most significant aspects of Śaunaka's character as depicted in the frame story is as a figure who links themes found in Bhārgava stories with the portrayal of Janamejaya's snake sacrifice, as well as with other tales of violence and mass destruction found throughout the *Mahābhārata*. If we begin to reconsider with Minkowski (1991: 400) 'the process that brought the Bhṛgu material into the *Mahābhārata*', a possible clue could be that Śaunaka is not the narrator of the epic, but its foremost listener. In other words, if Minkowski (1991: 400) is correct in assuming that the *Mahābhārata* has 'a history of conforming to the interests of its listeners', rather than supposing that the *Mahābhārata* was appropriated *by* Bhṛgus, we could consider the possibility that, conversely, it was framed or modified *for* them—or, more likely, a community of listeners who were familiar with Bhārgava lore. Without any external evidence, such a suggestion remains highly speculative; and, as I have already suggested, it is not at all clear that the frame story should be read as depicting the historical transmission of the text. However, when considering the *Mahābhārata*'s own portrayal of its transmission, we should keep in mind that Śaunaka is depicted as neither author nor appropriator of the text, but rather, as its main listener.

Śaunaka as listener

Although Śaunaka's role as a Bhārgava is clearly important, there is much more to him than being a member of this famous family. Along with his participation in the outer-frame dialogue,[24] characters with the name Śaunaka appear on four other occasions in the *Mahābhārata*'s main story, three of

24 After the opening section of the text (*Mbh*, 1.1–54), the outer-frame dialogue is referred to directly only on a few other occasions: 2.46.4; 15.42–43 (when Kṛṣṇa brings Parikṣit back to life); and at the very end of the epic (18.5). Additionally, as Hiltebeitel has argued, the narrative returns to the outer-frame dialogue at several points in the Nārāyaṇīya, in passages that either have not been included in the Critical Edition or have been misattributed to other speakers (for further discussion, see Hiltebeitel 2006).

them in the Āraṇyakaparvan. The name Śaunaka is a patronym that can refer to any descendent of Śunaka, so we cannot assume that all appearances of this name necessarily refer to the same person.[25] However, as we will see, there are similar characteristics among these Śaunakas and, in one case in particular, when the text seems to be referring to a different Śaunaka, the narrative playfully connects this personage to the one who is listening to Ugraśravas in the outer frame.

In the Āraṇyakaparvan, which depicts the Pāṇḍavas during their 12-year exile, the heroes encounter numerous *ṛṣis*, brahmins and storytellers, including Vyāsa, Mārkaṇḍeya, Nārada, Dhaumya, Baka Dālbhya, Bṛhadaśva and Lomaśa. Significantly, Śaunaka appears as the first of these eminent sages to offer the Pāṇḍavas a teaching (*Mbh*, 3.2.14–79). On this occasion, he is described as a knower of *sāṃkhya* and yoga; and his reference to King Janaka suggests he is familiar with upanishadic lore.[26]

Śaunaka also appears as one of several *ṛṣis* who are in attendance during Baka Dālbhya's instruction to Yudhiṣṭhira (*Mbh*, 3.27.23).[27] Notable names among those present on this occasion are Vyāsa, Nārada and Bṛhadaśva. Although it is not clear what Śaunaka does after Baka Dālbhya's lesson, it is possible he stays around to hear the Nala story, which is suggested by the fact that the story's narrator, Bṛhadaśva, has also seemingly been present among the Pāṇḍavas since listening to Baka Dālbhya. Additionally, Śaunaka appears in a list of *ṛṣis* who accompany the Pāṇḍavas on part of their tour of *tīrtha*s (3.83.102–4).[28] Among the more familiar names here are Vyāsa and Vālmīki, as well as Vedic *ṛṣis* such as Kāśyapa, Viśvāmitra, Gautama, Asita Devala, Bharadvāja, Vasiṣṭha and the upaniṣadic teacher Uddālaka.[29]

25 As Patton (2011: 131) remarks, even if we take these and other instances of the name to be referring to different personages, there are nonetheless several similarities among them: a 'set of literary characteristics that constellate around this name'.

26 For further discussion of the connections between characters with the name Śaunaka in the Upaniṣads and the *Mahābhārata*, see Black (2017). For Śaunaka as contributing to the *Mahābhārata*'s presentation of itself as an Upaniṣad, see Black (2021: 2).

27 The full list is: Dvaipāyana, Nārada, Jāmadagnya, Pṛthuśravas, Indradyumna, Bhāluki, Kṛtacetas, Sahasrapād, Karṇaśravas, Muñja, Lavaṇāśva, Kaśyapa, Hārīta, Sthūnakarṇa, Agniveśya, Śaunaka, Ṛtavāk, Bṛhadaśva, Ṛtavasu, Urdhvaretas, Vṛṣāmitra, Suhotra and Hotravāhana.

28 Here, the list is: Vālmīki, Kāśyapa, Ātreya, Kauṇḍinya, Viśvāmitra, Gautama, Asita Devala, Mārkaṇḍeya, Gālava, Bharadvāja, Vasiṣṭha, Uddālaka, Śaunaka and his son Vyāsa, Durvāsas and Jābāli. It is also notable that, according to this list, Śaunaka has a son.

29 During this journey, they hear the following *upākhyānas*: *Agastya* (*Mbh*, 3.94–108), *Ṛṣyaśṛṅga* (3.110–13), *Kārtavīrya* (3.115–17), *Sukanyā* (3.122–25), *Māndhātar* (3.126), *Jantu* (3.127–28), *Śyena-Kapotīya* (3.130–31), *Aṣṭāvakra* (3.132–34) and *Yavakrīta* (3.135–39). Interestingly, among the places they go with the Pāṇḍavas is the Naimiṣa Forest (3.93.1).

In these two lists, Śaunaka is mentioned along with textual composers such as Vyāsa and Vālmīki; storytellers within the *Mahābhārata*, such as Mārkaṇḍeya and Bṛhadaśva; and Vedic *ṛṣis* such as Vasiṣṭha and Bharadvāja. Although only his name is mentioned, in these instances, we are offered a glimpse of Śaunaka's character through his association with composers, storytellers and immortal sages: he is confirmed as an authoritative teacher, whose presence contributes to establishing the reliability of other speakers and the orthodoxy of their teachings. Moreover, on these two occasions, he is present as a listener—that is, cast in the same role as the Śaunaka in the outer-frame dialogue. In this way, Śaunaka is presented as a key listener within the text, as well as the primary listener to the text as a whole.[30]

In a fourth occurrence of a character with the same name in the main story, Śaunaka Indrota[31] appears in the Śāntiparvan (*Mbh*, 12.146–8). Although the inclusion of his given name could distinguish Indrota from the other Śaunakas, this episode makes teasing allusions to the text's outer-frame dialogue. In this episode, Śaunaka Indrota features in a dialogue with King Janamejaya, who, we might remember, is the primary listener to Vaiśaṃpāyana's recital of the *Mahābhārata* in the epic's inner-frame dialogue. Thus, the narrative presents its audience with the baffling scenario of Yudhiṣṭhira listening to a story about Janamejaya,[32] who is his brother Arjuna's yet-to-be-born grandson. Considering the temporal complexities of such a situation, it would certainly not strain any further narrative plausibility if this Śaunaka were the same as the one in the text's outer frame. But even if they are not the same person, it is hard to imagine that the epic poets did not at least intend for Śaunaka Indrota to call to mind Śaunaka the Kulapati,[33]

30 It is noteworthy that the portrayal of Śaunaka as a primary listener, or interlocutor, is consistent with the appearances of personages sharing the name Śaunaka in other textual contexts, particularly the Upaniṣads (see Black 2017). For example, in the *Chāndogya Upaniṣad* (4.3.5–7), Śaunaka Kapeya is the audience to whom a *brahmacārin* poses a riddle; while in the *Muṇḍaka Upaniṣad* (1.3), a 'great householder' (*mahāśāla*) named Śaunaka learns from Aṅgiras—a scenario that is repeated at the beginning of the *Brahma Upaniṣad* (see Olivelle 1992). The beginning of the *Nāradaparivrājaka Upaniṣad* (c. 1150 CE) appears to be modelled on the outer frame of the *Mahābhārata*, with Narāda arriving in the Naimiṣa Forest to find Śaunaka and a group of *ṛṣis* performing a 12-year *satra* (see Olivelle 1992).

31 This name also appears in the *Śatapatha Brāhmaṇa* (8.5.3.5).

32 This story refers to Janamejaya as a descendant of Parikṣit (*Mbh*, 12.146.3), making it clear that this is the same king who performs the *sarpasatra* in the inner-frame story. See Fitzgerald's note (2004: 768).

33 *Kulapati*, which appears on two occasions to designate Śaunaka (*Mbh*, 1.1.2; 1.4.1), probably means something like 'leader' (see Hiltebeitel 2001b: 99, 103). Another designation used to describe Śaunaka is *gṛhapati* (1.4.11).

who appears at the beginning of the text.[34] Assuming that this is the case, this dialogue playfully puts the listeners of the outer and inner dialogues in conversation with each other.

Furthermore, the dialogue between Śaunaka and Janamejaya addresses themes explored in the text's frame stories. In this episode from the Śāntiparvan, Janamejaya retreats to the forest in shame after accidentally killing a brahmin. While in the forest, he seeks the advice of the wise sage Śaunaka, who instructs the king to perform a ritual and to make a promise never to harm brahmins again. Śaunaka then praises the king for his efforts to make up for his past deeds and reinstates him as king. That a character named Śaunaka can assist King Janamejaya in expiating his sins connects this story to two of the tales that Śaunaka the Kulapati hears at the beginning of the *Mahābhārata*: one in which Āstīka, a relative of Śaunaka, interrupts King Janamejaya's snake sacrifice; the second in which Ruru, Śaunaka's 'grandfather',[35] does not go through with his vow to kill all snakes. Taken together, all three stories seem to connect the name Śaunaka with the capacity for making up for past sins and putting an end to horrible cycles of violence.

As we can see from the stories of the outer frame, as well as other tales directly related to him, Śaunaka's identity as a member of the Bhārgava clan is a vital link in connecting several themes that appear in stories of Bhārgavas, with the account of Janamejaya's snake sacrifice and several episodes in the *Mahābhārata*'s main story. Additionally, in his role as a brahmin listener, Śaunaka serves to legitimise Ugraśravas's narration. A possible implication is that Ugraśravas's story cannot be the fifth Veda that it aspires to be without being sanctioned by Śaunaka and his colleagues.[36] Fitzgerald makes

34 Adam Bowles (2007: 318) has recently made similar observations: the Śaunaka of the outer frame 'is nowhere called Indrota, suggesting that the two should not, strictly speaking, be identified as the one person. But we should be wary of concluding that the choice of interlocutors is an unknowing coincidence, and we could perhaps regard the authors or redactors as engaging in a bit of playfulness by vaguely suggesting, or leaving it open for the audience to conclude, that the principle audiences of the two tellings of the *Mbh* described in the *Mbh* itself are here engaging in a conversation of their own.'

35 Śaunaka's family tree is ambiguous. The Anuśāsanaparvan depicts him as Śunaka's son, but the Ādiparvan suggests that Ruru is his great-grandfather, thus making Śunaka, referred to as *pūrvapitāmaha* ('forefather'), his grandfather, rather than father. As Hiltebeitel (2001b: 113n.68) comments, the Ādiparvan genealogy is 'short', giving Śaunaka no father to close the descent line. See also Goldman (1977: 165n.66).

36 Indeed, throughout the *Mahābhārata*, Vedic authority is often established more through the text's listeners than through its speakers—a point suggested by Vaiśaṃpāyana at the beginning of his narration to Janamejaya, when he says, twice, that the *Mahābhārata* should be recited to brahmins (*Mbh*, 1.56.28–29). Additionally, when Ugraśravas tells the Naimiṣa brahmins that reciting even a quarter of the *Mahābhārata* to brahmins performing a *śraddha* will bring food and drink to his ancestors, perhaps he is effectively providing the authorising criteria for his own recitation (1.1.203).

a similar point in describing how the presence of brahmins contributes to the *Mahābhārata*'s self-proclaimed Vedic status: the 'enthusiasm for the text by Śaunaka's company is not only a rhetorically important endorsement of the text, legitimising and recommending it as reliable teaching, it implies a necessary feature of the text's being a Veda' (Fitzgerald 1991: 164).

Conclusion

As several scholars have explored (for example, Witzel 1987; Minkowski 1989), framing techniques are an important characteristic of several ancient Indian religious texts.[37] While different texts employ this organisational structure differently, one of the most recurring uses is to lend authority to a particular doctrine within a text or to the whole text. The Upaniṣads and Buddhist Nikāyas are relatively straightforward in this respect, as they link specific teachings to authoritative individuals such as Yājñavalkya or the Buddha. Through the figure of Vyāsa, as well as the inclusion of teachings from famous teachers such as Bṛhaspati, Kṛṣṇa, Nārada and others, the *Mahābhārata* seems to use its dialogical structure in similar ways. Yet, as we have seen, the dubious authority of several of its narrators, combined with the multivocality of its narration, make the epic's use of frame dialogues much more complex and ambiguous.

Perhaps the best way to understand Ugraśravas's narration is as operating in tandem with the other major recitals within the text. While the Ugraśravas narration takes place at an all-brahmin ritual,[38] Vaiśaṃpāyana's telling is during a royal ritual, with a much wider audience. Meanwhile, Saṃjaya's reportage of the war is delivered in Dhṛtarāṣṭra's court, with Gāndhārī and the wives of many of the combatants listening as well;[39] Bhīṣma's postwar instruction to Yudhiṣṭhira is set outside, near the battlefield, with Kṛṣṇa, Satyaki, Bhīma, Arjuna, the twins, Kṛpa, Yuyutsu, Saṃjaya and Draupadī in attendance; and the Pāṇḍavas hear a number of tales during their wanderings in the forest, particularly at pilgrimage sites—exactly the sorts of places from where Ugraśravas has just come when he arrives in the Naimiṣa Forest.

37 See also Matchett (2002); Adluri (2011); Appleton (2015); Esposito (2015); and Hiltebeitel (2015).

38 Although Hiltebeitel (2001b: 166) suggests that the wives of the brahmin ritualists could also have been in attendance. See also Black (2007b: 60–62).

39 For a discussion about the role of Gāndhārī as a listener to Saṃjaya's report of the war, see Black (2007b: 62–65).

In other words, the numerous narrators of the *Mahābhārata* connect the telling of the epic to different possible contexts of reception, as well as to the various types of listeners who are present in each location.

Among other things, the many voices, settings and audiences of the *Mahābhārata* can be seen as part of its transitional character from *śruti* to a new type of post-Vedic religious text. It is well known that the *Mahābhārata* links itself to the Vedic tradition through its claim to be a fifth Veda, but, as Sukthankar (1998: 23) (reflecting on Dahlmann) reminds us: '[T]hroughout Indian antiquity, above all things, the *Mahābhārata* was recognised as a "dhamma-saṁhita, as a smṛti".' What has been largely overlooked, however, is the wide range of textual descriptions the *Mahābhārata* uses to refer to itself. As Hiltebeitel observes, the two most frequent designations are *ākhyāna* (on 14 occasions) and *itihāsa* (on eight occasions). Other terms the text uses for self-description are *purāṇa*, *kathā*, *śāstra*, *upaniṣad* and *carita*.[40] Hiltebeitel (2005: 465) suggests that, by means of 'its multiple self-designations', the *Mahābhārata* 'sustains itself as a multigenre work'.

This array of self-descriptions could run parallel with the multiple voices, but it also could be seen as betraying a certain ambiguity, even uncertainty, among the composers and editors as to what type of text the *Mahābhārata* aspires be. In this way, the *Mahābhārata* is very much a text in transition—still in the process of deciding how to define itself in a post-Vedic world. Ugraśravas and Śaunaka emerge as integral participants in representing this transition.

References

Primary text

Sukthankar, Vishnu Sitaram (ed.). (1933–66). *The Mahābhārata*. [19 vols.] Poona, India: Bhandarkar Oriental Research Institute.

Secondary texts

Adluri, Vishwa P. (2011). Frame narratives and forked beginnings: Or, how to read the Ādiparvan. *Journal of Vaishnava Studies* 19(2): 143–210.

40 See Hiltebeitel (2005: 465) for the full list of terms and their references.

Appleton, Naomi. (2015). The Buddha as storyteller: The dialogical setting of *Jātaka* stories. In Brian Black and Laurie Patton (eds), *Dialogue in Early South Asian Religions: Hindu, Buddhist, and Jain Traditions*, pp. 99–112. Farnham, UK: Ashgate.

Belvalkar, Shripad Krishna. (1947). Saṃjaya's 'divine eye'. *Annals of the Bhandarkar Oriental Research Institute* 27: 310–31.

Black, Brian. (2007a). *The Character of the Self in Ancient India: Priests, Kings, and Women in the Early Upaniṣads*. Albany: SUNY Press.

Black, Brian. (2007b). Eavesdropping on the epic: Female listeners in the *Mahābhārata*. In Simon Brodbeck and Brian Black (eds), *Gender and Narrative in the Mahābhārata*. London: Routledge.

Black, Brian. (2017). The Upaniṣads and the Mahābhārata. In Signe Cohen (ed.), *The Upaniṣads: A Complete Guide*, pp. 186–99. New York, NY: Routledge.

Black, Brian. (2021). *In Dialogue with the Mahābhārata*. London: Routledge. doi.org/10.4324/9780367438142.

Bodewitz, H.W. (1973). *Jaiminīya Brāhmaṇa: I, 1–65. Translation and Commentary, with a Study: Agnihotra and Praṇāgnihotra*. Leiden, Netherlands: E.J. Brill.

Bowles, Adam. (2007). *Dharma, Disorder and the Political in Ancient India: The Āpaddharmaparvan of the Mahābhārata*. Leiden, Netherlands: Brill.

Brockington, John. (1998). *The Sanskrit Epics*. Leiden, Netherlands: E.J. Brill. doi.org/10.1163/9789004492677.

Brodbeck, Simon. (2009). *The Mahābhārata Patriline: Gender, Culture, and Royal Hereditary*. Aldershot, UK: Ashgate Press.

de Jong, J.W. (1975). Recent Russian publications on the Indian epic. *Adyar Library Bulletin* 39: 1–42.

Esposito, Anna Aurelia. (2015). Didactic dialogues: Communication of doctrine and strategies of narrative in Jain literature. In Brian Black and Laurie Patton (eds), *Dialogue in Early South Asian Religions: Hindu, Buddhist, and Jain Traditions*, pp. 79–98. Farnham, UK: Ashgate.

Fitzgerald, James L. (1991). India's fifth Veda: The Mahābhārata's presentation of itself. In Arvind Sharma (ed.), *Essays on the Mahābhārata*. Leiden, Netherlands: E.J. Brill.

Fitzgerald, James L. (2002). The Rāma Jāmadagnya 'thread' of the Mahābhārata: A new survey of Rāma Jāmadagnya in the Pune text. In Mary Brockington (ed.), *Stages and Transitions: Temporal and Historical Frameworks in Epic and Purāṇic Literature*. Zagreb: Croatian Academy of Sciences and Arts.

Fitzgerald, James L. (trans.). (2004). *The Mahābhārata Books. 11: The Book of Women; Book 12: The Book of Peace, Part One*. Chicago, IL: Chicago University Press. doi.org/10.7208/chicago/9780226252513.001.0001.

Ganguli, K.M. (trans.). (1993 [1883–96]). *The Mahābhārata of Krishna-Dwaipayana Vyasa Translated into English Prose from the Original Sanskrit Text*. [12 vols.] New Delhi: Munshiram Manoharlal.

Goldman, Robert. (1977). *Gods, Priests, and Warriors: The Bhṛgus of the Mahābhārata*. New York, NY: Columbia University Press.

Hiltebeitel, Alf. (2001a). Bhīṣma's sources. In Klaus Karttunen and Petteri Koskikallio (eds), *Vidyārṇavavandanam: Essays in Honor of Asko Parpola*. Studia Orientalia 94. Helsinki: Finnish Oriental Society.

Hiltebeitel, Alf. (2001b). *Rethinking the Mahābhārata: A Reader's Guide to the Education of the Dharma King*. Chicago, IL: Chicago University Press.

Hiltebeitel, Alf. (2005). Not without subtales: Telling laws and truths in the Sanskrit epics. *Journal of Indian Philosophy* 33(4): 455–511. doi.org/10.1007/s10781-005-7050-9.

Hiltebeitel, Alf. (2006). The Nārāyaṇīya and the early reading communities of the Mahābhārata. In Patrick Olivelle (ed.), *Between the Empires: Society in India 300 BCE to 400 CE*. New York, NY: Oxford University Press. doi.org/10.1093/acprof:oso/9780195305326.003.0010.

Hiltebeitel, Alf. (2015). Dialogue and apostrophe: A move by Vālmīki? In Brian Black and Laurie Patton (eds), *Dialogue in Early South Asian Religions: Hindu, Buddhist, and Jain Traditions*, pp. 37–77. Farnham, UK: Ashgate.

Killingley, Dermot. (1997). The paths of the dead and the five fires. In Peter Connolly and Sue Hamilton (eds), *Indian Insights: Buddhism, Brahmanism and Bhakti—Papers from the Annual Spalding Symposium on Indian Religions*. London: Luzac Oriental.

Matchett, Freda. (2002). Some reflections on the frame-narrative of the Bhāgavatapurāṇa. In Mary Brockington (ed.), *Stages and Transitions: Temporal and Historical Frameworks in Epic and Purāṇic Literature*. Zagreb: Croatian Academy of Sciences and Arts.

Mehta, M. (1973). The problem of the double introduction to the Mahābhārata. *Journal of the American Oriental Society* 93(4): 547–50. doi.org/10.2307/600175.

Minkowski, Christopher. (1989). Janamejaya's sattra and ritual structure. *Journal of the American Oriental Society* 109: 401–20. doi.org/10.2307/604141.

Minkowski, Christopher. (1991). Snakes, sattras and the Mahābhārata. In Arvind Sharma (ed.), *Essays on the Mahābhārata*. Leiden, Netherlands: E.J.Brill.

Minkowski, Christopher. (2001). The interrupted sacrifice and the Sanskrit epics. *Journal of Indian Philosophy* 29(1–2): 169–86. doi.org/10.1023/A:10175515 11325.

Olivelle, Patrick (trans.). (1992). *Saṃnyāsa Upaniṣads: Hindu Scriptures on Asceticism and Renunciation*. New York, NY: Oxford University Press.

Olivelle, Patrick (trans.). (1998). *The Early Upaniṣads: Annotated Text and Translation*. New York, NY: Oxford University Press.

Pathak, Shubha. (2006). Why do displaced kings become poets in the Sanskrit epics? Modeling *dharma* in the affirmative *Rāmāyaṇa* and the interrogative *Mahābhārata*. *International Journal of Hindu Studies* 10: 127–49. doi.org/ 10.1007/s11407-006-9018-0.

Patton, Laurie. (2011). Traces of Śaunaka: A literary assessment. *Journal of the American Academy of Religion* 79(1): 113–35. doi.org/10.1093/jaarel/lfq062.

Pollock, Sheldon. (1997). The 'revelation' of 'tradition': Śruti, smṛti, and the Sanskrit discourse of power. In Siefried Lienhard and Irma Piovano (eds), *Lex et Litterae: Essays on Ancient Indian Law and Literature in Honour of Professor Oscar Botto*. Turin, Italy: CESMEO.

Sharma, Arvind. (2000). Of śūdras, sūtas and ślokas: Why is the Mahābhārata preeminently in the anuṣṭubh metre? *Indo-Iranian Journal* 43(3): 225–78. doi.org/10.1163/000000000124994047.

Sukthankar, Vishnu S. (1936). Epic studies 6: The Bhṛgus and the Bhārata—A text-historical study. *Annals of the Bhandarkar Oriental Research Institute* 18(1): 1–76.

Sukthankar, Vishnu S. (1944). *Critical Studies in the Mahābhārata*. Poona, India: Bhandarkar Oriental Research Institute.

Sukthankar, Vishnu S. (1998 [1957]). *On the Meaning of the Mahābhārata*. Delhi: Motilal Banarsidass.

Thapar, Romila. (2000). Society and historical consciousness: The itihāsa-purāṇa tradition. In *Cultural Pasts: Essays in Early Indian History*. New Delhi: Oxford University Press.

van Buitenen, J.A.B. (trans.). (1973). *The Mahābhārata. Volume 1, Book 1: The Book of the Beginning*. Chicago, IL: University of Chicago Press. doi.org/10.7208/chicago/9780226217543.001.0001.

van Buitenen, J.A.B. (trans.). (1975). *The Mahābhārata. Volume 2, Book 2: The Book of the Assembly Hall; Book 3: The Book of the Forest*. Chicago, IL: University of Chicago Press. doi.org/10.7208/chicago/9780226223681.001.0001.

Vassilkov, Yaroslav. (1995). The Mahābhārata's typological definition reconsidered. *Indo-Iranian Journal* 38(3): 249–56.

Vassilkov, Yaroslav. (2002). Indian practice of pilgrimage and the growth of the Mahābhārata in the light of new epigraphical sources. In Mary Brockington (ed.), *Stages and Transitions: Temporal and Historical Frameworks in Epic and Purāṇic Literature*. Zagreb: Croatian Academy of Sciences and Arts.

Witzel, Michael. (1987). On the origin of the literary device of the 'frame story' in old Indian literature. In Harry Falk (ed.), *Hinduismus und Buddhismus: Festschrift für Ulrich Schneider* [*Hinduism and Buddhism: Festschrift for Ulrich Schneider*], pp. 340–414. Freiburg, Germany: Hedwig Falk.

4

Battling inner conflicts: Dhṛtarāṣṭra and Saṃjaya in the Udyogaparvan of the *Mahābhārata*

Angelika Malinar

Abstract

Kuru king Dhṛtarāṣṭra and his companion Saṃjaya belong to the few epic characters with intra and extradiegetic functions. They feature in the narration of the *Mahābhārata* as interlocutors establishing the narrative frame of the battle books and in the epic narrative as 'narrated' characters. In academic studies, the two characters do not receive much attention. The intradiegetic interactions between Dhṛtarāṣṭra and Saṃjaya, in particular, have not been studied in great detail, although they play a significant role in the epic narrative. This significance will be explored by dealing with the narrative function of these interactions in the Udyogaparvan (UdP), in which the two characters feature prominently. Their prominent role suits the main task of the UdP: the narration of the negotiations about war and peace. Drawing on a literary studies approach, the analysis focuses on the literary structure and the topics of their conversations and explores connections with dramatic literature.

Introduction

Kuru king Dhṛtarāṣṭra and his companion Saṃjaya belong to the few epic characters with intra and extradiegetic functions.[1] In academic studies, the two characters have not received much attention, except when dealing with the epic's narrative frames[2] and its depiction of guilt and grief.[3] The intradiegetic interactions between Dhṛtarāṣṭra and Saṃjaya have not been studied in great detail, although they play a significant role in the narrative. One reason for this neglect is that the two are often treated as 'minor' characters when compared with the fighting heroes—the 'major' characters who have attracted considerable scholarly attention. Major characters are considered to drive the action and be equipped with individual traits and personal histories. However, the criteria for measuring 'minor' and 'major' parts vary, as is the case with Saṃjaya. Apart from Saṃjaya being the son of Galvagaṇi, a *sūta* (charioteer, bard), we do not know much about his provenance, appearance or exact position at Dhṛtrāṣṭra's court. He is variously called 'bard', 'charioteer',[4] 'advisor' and 'factotum' (Mangels 1994: 97). Such vagueness is often typical of a minor figure, as is pointed out by Mangels (1994: 143), who talks of the '*kleine Sūta Saṃjaya*', but at the same time emphasises Saṃjaya being perhaps one of the most prolific intradiegetic narrators.

Unlike Saṃjaya, sufficient information about Dhṛtarāṣṭra's provenance and character traits is given to make him a major character. Furthermore, as one of the few protagonists, the blind king lives through almost the entire narrated time; he accompanies the epic plot from its prehistory to almost the end of the epic. He took responsibility for the Pāṇḍavas and widowed Kuntī and had the young boys educated together with his own sons. He supported Duryodhana's intrigue to lure the Pāṇḍavas away from Hāstinapura. But then he arranged for the partition of the kingdom (Book 1). He half-heartedly tried to prevent the dice game and declared the conversion of the Pandavas' enslavement into exile (Book 2). At the end of the exile, he tried to prevent the war (Book 5) and then functioned as a counterpart of Saṃjaya in the intradiegetic narrative frame of the battle books (6–9). After the

1 Apart from the epic author Kṛṣṇa Dvaipāyana Vyāsa and the frame-dialogue partners Janamejaya and Vaiśampāyana, who by default feature as narrated figures within the narrative frame constituted by Ugraśravas and Śaunaka; sage Nārada also belongs to this group (see Malinar 2015).

2 See Mangels (1994); Minkowski (1989: 406 ff.); Hiltebeitel (2001: 57–61); Malinar (2005); and Hämeen-Anttila (2019).

3 See Hill (1993); and Hudson (2007, 2013).

4 Sharma (2000: 263n.45) deals with the meaning and caste status of *sūta* as charioteer and bard and suggests that, in Saṃjaya, the sense of charioteer also blends with the meaning of bard.

war, he appeared on the battlefield (Book 11), then moved to Yudhiṣṭhira's residence and performed together with Yudhiṣṭhira the memorial offerings for the dead heroes (Book 12). Finally, he decided to retreat to the forest with Gāndhārī and Kunti (Book 14), where all three died (Book 15). When seen from a literary perspective, Dhṛtarāṣṭra is a complex character as he is given intradiegetic and extradiegetic functions: he is the narrated character, interlocutor of an intradiegetic frame and narrator of an abridged version of the epic. In some parts of the epic (the UdP, for instance), his thoughts and emotions are narrated extensively. In these instances, his advisors, Saṃjaya and Vidura, play an important role as well. The interactions with the advisors complicate the figure of the blind king and point to his essential role in the unfolding of the epic narrative.

This role has, however, been rather neglected in *Mahābhārata* research.[5] Dhṛtarāṣṭra has mostly been dismissed as a ridiculous 'secondary character', a 'failed' and 'morally inferior' figure who cannot control his feelings, pushes aside normative and moral concerns and does not care for religious-philosophical knowledge. He is mostly viewed as a weak king, an old man prone to laments and self-pity. In one of the few studies that deals with Dhṛtarāṣṭra, Hill (1993) has pointed out that the blind king's role is not so 'minor' when considering the question of who is responsible for the course of events. But he concludes that the king's characterisation as 'chronically indecisive' is less complex than Yudhiṣṭhira's since the former refuses responsibility by pointing to the workings of fate. In addition, Saṃjaya's advice shows inconsistencies (Hill 1993: 11). Hudson (2007, 2013) views Dhṛtarāṣṭra as a negative example of the epic's central message that one must overcome grief by facing the consequences of one's deeds (*karman*) instead of putting the blame on 'fate'. In focusing mostly on what the king's advisors say, Hudson (2013: 142) claims that the epic depicts the aged king as 'morally wanting' and encourages 'our increasing estrangement' from him. In Hill's view, the epic presents *karman* and fate as closely linked. For Hudson, they signify different viewpoints. She argues that Dhṛtarāṣṭra refuses to embrace the *karman* doctrine that would help him accept that he is both agent and victim of suffering. Hill and Hudson raise important points about the certainly ambiguous, even dubious role of Dhṛtarāṣṭra in the configuration of the epic's much-debated moral messages. However, the focus on the moral

5 In studies dealing with the mythological and Vedic background of the epic, Dhṛtarāṣṭra is connected to the gods Bhaga (Dumézil 1959) and Varuṇa (Johnsen 1966); von Simson (1984: 211) accepts the latter identification and furthermore connects the blind king to Venus, the Evening Star (p. 198).

of the tale results in discussing only selected passages without dealing with their literary context, and the exchanges between the king and his advisors are not studied in greater detail. To explore the role of Dhṛtarāṣṭra and his interactions with Saṃjaya (and Vidura) in unfolding the epic plot and its narrative semantics, a more comprehensive approach to the texts is necessary, which also addresses the interplay between literary structures and religious-philosophical ideas. Otherwise, there is the risk of passing judgements on the protagonists while neglecting the literary character of the epic and the complexity of the issues it raises.[6]

Methodological considerations

The following discussion focuses on the depiction of Dhṛtarāṣṭra and the interactions with Saṃjaya in the UdP in which the two characters feature prominently. By drawing on a literary studies approach, the analysis deals with the literary structure and the topics of their conversations. It will ask which narrative domains the two characters occupy and what is their role in the epic's narrative semantics. Their prominent role is intrinsically connected to the main task of the UdP: the narration of negotiations about war and peace, which mark a turning point in the plot and the transition to battle books. In the UdP, the major characters of both parties are assembled again. It is the first time they assemble after the dice game and the last time before the battle, in which many of them will die and thus leave the narrative as acting characters. The UdP offers a detailed account of how they are tied to each other in ways that lead to war. The conflict between the two parties is not a neat opposition since it is depicted both as a clash of interests and values and as a drama of conflicting emotions that entwines the characters across the two parties. The protagonists fight with and for each other, but some also wrestle with themselves, with emotional conflicts and with the ambiguity of norms and values. All this amounts to a complex constellation that the epic poets present with great care and effort. Consequently, a considerable part of the action in the UdP consists of debating these conflicts in character speech. These speeches present arguments, admonishments and advice, but also express emotions.

6 Employing a psychological perspective, Hudson (2007) detects in Dhṛtarāṣṭra 'prideful arrogance' paired with an inability to act (p. 38), 'weaknesses as a father' (p. 45) and other flaws that prevent 'his moral awakening' (p. 47). In a more nuanced discussion of Dhṛtarāṣṭra as being both an agent and a victim of suffering for the overall message of the epic (to overcome suffering), Hudson (2013) explores selected passages in which the old king is listening to his advisors (Vidura and Saṃjaya).

The display of emotions is a characteristic feature of the interactions between Dhṛtarāṣṭra and Saṃjaya. Their conversations increase the dramatic tension by unfolding the king's inner conflict, which is mirrored and at the same time intensified by Saṃjaya's often reproachful comments. Other characters in the UdP—Yudhiṣṭhira, for instance—also struggle with the question of what is the right or wrong course of action, draw on normative and moral premises and calculate loss and profit. However, Dhṛtarāṣṭra is the only one wrestling with an inner emotional and intellectual conflict that is deepened by his being aware of it and by the constraints he suffers due to his blindness. Saṃjaya responds to the king's struggle not so much with arguments and instructive tales as with emotionally tinged rebuke. The elaborated narration of this conflict suggests that the epic composers had intentions other than merely showing up the aged king as a 'failed', 'morally wanting' character who cannot overcome his emotions by heeding law and better knowledge. The narration of the emotional dimensions of familial discord points to the intention to explore what seems to puzzle Dhṛtarāṣṭra most: the love (*sneha*) for his son. His fate lies not in grief and fear, but in being attached to a son who seems undeserving of his love. Seen from this perspective, the figure of Dhṛtarāṣṭra entwines epic discourses of fate and guilt with those of parental and familial love. Thereby the affective dimensions driving the epic narrative come to the fore and Dhṛtarāṣṭra plays a vital role in this respect. The aged king occupies a narrative domain that points to the limitations of law, reason and knowledge when used to counter unconditional (parental) love. This love is highly ambiguous. On the one hand, it is something deeply human and constitutes an elementary bond of sociality and, on the other, considered dangerous when undermining other bonds.

While most characters display emotions at some point in the narrative, not all are characterised by their emotionality or an emotional conflict, as is the case with Dhṛtarāṣṭra. When emotions feature prominently in the epic, they imbue it with drama. In these instances, the narration includes the articulation and display of emotions (fainting, shedding tears and so on) and thus shows features that connect it to theatrical plays.[7] Furthermore, the

7 See Malinar (2007b) on Arjuna displaying theatrical *bhāva*s at the beginning of the *Bhagavadgītā*; and Tubb (1991) and Hudson (2013) for Ānandavardhana's reading of the epic from the perspective of the *rasa* theory.

UdP draws on drama also in using the display of emotions and the staging of speeches as literary devices. In such instances, the narration turns into an ornately crafted drama.[8]

In dealing with the intradiegetic functions of the conversations embedded in the Janamejaya–Vaiśampāyana frame and the presentation of Dhṛtarāṣṭra and Saṃjaya as 'narrated figures',[9] narratological approaches and terminology are employed.[10] This literary studies approach entails distinguishing between the different levels of narration and how they influence the depiction of the agency of the protagonists (such as focalisation) and exploring how the characters relate to the fictional world of the epic. Since the following analysis focuses on the interactions between characters, their ways of relating to the events are of particular importance. This means paying attention to the different modalities that structure the story's fictional world and the relationships of the protagonists to that world. In literary theory, these modes are referred to as 'narrative modalities' or 'propositional attitudes' and play an essential role in narrative semantics—the organisation of meaning creation in the story's fictional world.[11] One narrative modality can organise a plot as a whole, but different modalities can be combined, resulting in a complex story (Doležel 1976, 1980). In drawing on philosophical terminology, these modalities are called ontological (what is accepted as real, possible and so on), deontic (norms, notions of obligation, permission, prohibition), axiological (morality, notions of good and bad, indifference), epistemic (belief, knowledge, ignorance) and so on (Ryan 1985). The modalities also shape the characters' thoughts and actions in the world of the story. Their respective 'modal systems' or 'propositional attitudes' constitute the 'world-representing acts of individuals'. They reveal 'relative worlds of the narrative universe (epistemic or knowledge worlds, hypothetical worlds, intention worlds, wish worlds, moral values, obligation worlds, and alternate worlds)' (Ronen 1990: 839). These 'relative worlds' comprise different components that influence a character's relationship to the fictional world and can

8 This dramatic quality connects the narration of the UdP with that of the dice game, in addition to the frequent references to the dice game in the UdP. These features of the epic narration will be explored in a separate study.

9 Conversations within the 'outer' narrative frame (Ugraśravas–Śaunaka) and the exchanges between Saṃjaya and Dhṛtarāṣṭra as interlocutors constituting the narrative frame of the battle books will be included in a separate study. As the analysis primarily deals with the literary structure, text-historical aspects connected with the two protagonists (as pointed out by Mangels 1994) will not be addressed here.

10 See Genette (1998); and Bal (2009). Some elements of this approach have been used for studying the epic, by Minkowski (1989); Mangels (1994); Malinar (2005, 2015, 2017, 2022).

11 See Todorov (1971); Pavel (1980); Doležel (1976, 1988); Ronen (1990).

produce inner tensions as well as conflicts with other characters. A typical constellation is a clash between 'wish-world' and 'obligation-world' when the desired object is undesirable because of normative rules prohibiting its acquisition (in the *Mahābhārata*, for instance, Yudhiṣṭhira's claim for his property necessitates waging war against his relatives). This structure can be further complicated if conflicting axiological and moral propositions are at stake that would remove normative premises (for instance, when breaching the norm produces something 'good'; in the *Mahābhārata*, Yudhiṣṭhira's war against his relatives and breaking the *kṣatriya* code of conduct aim to restore righteousness). In such a constellation, any action taken could produce undesirable results and confront decision-makers with dilemmas.

The characters' modal systems are connected to the organisation of the plot in various ways. Characters may share, for instance, the same ontological assumptions (in the *Mahābhārata*, they accept the existence of gods, demons and so on), but follow divergent normative ones (in the *Mahābhārata*, they champion different interpretations of what is *dharma* or the norms of action). Therefore, the plot may be semantically homogeneous at one level but partitioned and heterogeneous at another.[12] Furthermore, the 'relative worlds' expressed by the protagonists may receive different degrees of authorisation (by a narrator, for instance). When there is no solid or persistent authorisation of one of these worlds in the narration, the possible meaning of an event in the plot and even the plot can become an issue. Such a literary strategy invites different views and interpretations. An example of this is the UdP's juxtaposition of 'decided' and 'hesitant' characters. In letting the protagonists voice their propositional attitudes, the UdP points to the reasons, motifs and emotions that resulted in the decision for the war. Because the decision-making is made an element of the plot, it remains an issue even after the war, provoking doubts, complaints and accusations. From a literary point of view, the absence of a final say about how to interpret the course of events is not accidental but results from the epic poets' deliberate effort to unfold the heterogeneity of the 'relative worlds' of the characters. Seen from

12 See Pavel (1980) on different constellations; and Doležel (1976), who distinguishes between stories organised through a single modal system (for instance, mystery stories through the epistemic mode) and more complex ones.

contextual and intertextual perspectives, the inclusion of conflicting, even contradictory, views in the storyline points to the coexistence of different narrations and interpretations of the epic.[13]

The narration of the Udyogaparvan

In the UdP, Dhṛtarāṣṭra and Saṃjaya are depicted as being actively involved in the events before they assume the function as interlocutors in the framing of the battle books. They resume their roles as narrated characters after Duryodhana's death when Saṃjaya loses the 'divine eyesight' that made him the overall narrator during the battle (10.9.58). The two characters stay in the narrative until Book 15, in which Dhṛtarāṣṭra plays an important role again, while Saṃjaya recedes into the background. As mentioned, the depiction of the two characters must not be analysed apart from the literary context: the deliberations on war and peace. The UdP unfolds a complex constellation of entwined decision-making,[14] which marks the transition to the battle, which is the next major plot event. The narration of the UdP is characterised by many verbal interactions that in some instances imbue the book with features of drama. The dramatic quality of some of the scenes match a book in which the 'action' driving the narrative comprises mainly debates and conversations. This feature is also supported by the alternation between the two major scenes of action: Dhṛtarāṣṭra's court and Yudhiṣṭhira's headquarters. The alternation between the two is organised through switches to the extradiegetic frame (the dialogue between Vaiśampāyana and Janamejaya), whereas most of the information about what is happening *en scène* is circulated by the

13 In an earlier study, I analysed the deliberations as a literary representation of a conflict of values and an intellectual and normative crisis attested to in contemporary non-literary sources, and about the socio-historical contexts in the which the epic was probably composed (Malinar 2007b). In the following, the focus is on their literary function (see also Malinar 2022). From a text-historical perspective, Hill (1993: 20) explains the contradictions and the inconclusiveness of the epic's treatment of guilt and responsibility for the catastrophe as follows: 'Those who are looking for a logically well-founded solution to the problem of individual responsibility will not find it in the *Mahābhārata*'s treatment of the incidents. Given the manner in which the *Mahābhārata* grew over centuries, its solution to the problem is, not surprisingly, more of A+B+C than A or B or C.'

14 For a more detailed discussion of this constellation, see Malinar (2022). This entwinement can also be traced at the level of arguments and a conflict of values; see Malinar (1996, 2007b). Viewing the UdP as an account of a wrong decision made by only one party or character—namely, Dhṛtarāṣṭra (Hudson 2013: 117n.33)—reduces its complexity. See Hill (1993) on the inconclusive representation of 'guilt' in the epic.

protagonists themselves.[15] Furthermore, in several instances, extradiegetic narration is used to set the stage for character speech. Before discussing some of the interactions in greater detail, a general outline is given of their placement in the UdP and of the entwined structure of the deliberations and the divergent propositional attitudes of the characters.

The sequence of negotiations starts at *Mbh* 5.20–21 when Yudhiṣṭhira's envoy, the (nameless) house-priest of Drupada, is sent to Duryodhana's court to claim a share of the kingdom. The priest formulates the claim's legal basis, mentions the mistreatment and humiliation suffered by the Pāṇḍavas and stresses their military strength (*Mbh*, 5.20). This speech receives mixed reactions, revealing the disaccord among the Kauravas (5.21). While Bhīṣma supports the claim, Karṇa rejects it as unfounded. Dhṛtarāṣṭra sides with Bhīṣma. This dissent already demonstrates the positions staked out in the following deliberations. While Duryodhana, his friend Karṇa and his maternal uncle Śakuni reject all claims and are ready to wage war, the elders—in particular, Dhṛtarāṣṭra and Bhīṣma—keep the decision-making process going as they want to prevent the destruction of the family. This constellation resembles the one on Yudhiṣṭhira's side, with the critical difference that he appears reluctant to enforce his claim. His hesitancy is occasionally supported by one of his brothers but is regularly criticised by his brother-in-law Kṛṣṇa, and his wife Draupadī.[16] In this constellation, Dhṛtarāṣṭra emerges as a figure fulfilling a narrative function like that of Kṛṣṇa in that they both counteract certain attitudes of the two primary opponents. While Dhṛtarāṣṭra urges his son to find a peaceful solution (counteracting proneness to war), Kṛṣṇa insists that Yudhiṣṭhira should not relinquish his claims (counteracting reluctance to war). Dhṛtarāṣṭra's failure is mirrored in Kṛṣṇa's success. Consequently, both, but mostly Dhṛtarāṣṭra, are made responsible by other characters for the disastrous war. On the other hand, when focusing on the propositional attitudes accorded to the protagonists, it becomes clear that Dhṛtarāṣṭra's wrestling with the situation resonates with the depiction of Yudhiṣṭhira. Both express contradictions between the modal

15 According to van Buitenen (1978: 134), '69 out of 196 chapters' are 'strictly speaking irrelevant to the action' as they contain 'other stories'—namely, Vidura's speeches during Dhṛtarāṣṭra's vigil, the Sanasujatīya (which is not exactly a 'story', but rather a didactic text extending Vidura's sleep-inducing talk) and the 'bizarre' story of Ambā. Van Buitenen seems to overlook the fact that, except for Sanatsujata, we are dealing here with exceptionally long character speeches (in comparison with the rest of the UdP), which take in one case the form of an insomnia antidote (Vidura) and contain essential *ad hominem* passages (see below).

16 Draupadī had also earlier urged her husband to fight Duryodhana—for instance, in her discussion with Yudhiṣṭhira at *Mbh* 3.32–35. See Malinar (2007a).

systems that motivate their actions in the world of the story. This tension contrasts with Duryodhana's determined stance, which resembles Kṛṣṇa's. Both appear as uncompromising and unbending heroes (although in quite different ways) as they display a quite homogeneous set of propositional attitudes. The exchanges between characters—to a considerable extent conveyed through envoys—reveal the divergent ways in which they relate to the events that drive the plot. In so doing, the bonds between them also come to the fore—bonds that turn into grounds for their separation. When seen from this perspective, Dhṛtarāṣṭra and Yudhiṣṭhira are close to each other in their struggling with the affective dimension of the familial bonds (and not only dharmic ones), which is not an issue for Duryodhana and Kṛṣṇa. In this way, the UdP prepares the transition not only to the battle books but also to the postwar situation, in which Dhṛtarāṣṭra and Yudhiṣṭhira reunite in performing the death rituals and living together in Indraprastha until the old king retires to the forest. The conflict between the two parties is settled with the generational transition completed. The interactions between Dhṛtarāṣṭra and Saṃjaya serve to highlight these aspects of the epic narrative.

Dhṛtarāṣṭra and Saṃjaya in the UdP

Before discussing the interactions between Dhṛtarāṣṭra and Saṃjaya in more detail, I will give an overview of their placement in the UdP. The first interaction between Dhṛtarāṣṭra and Saṃjaya takes place after Drupada's house-priest has delivered the message that the Pāṇḍavas demand their share of the kingdom (5.20). Afterwards, Bhīṣma and Karṇa have an argument (5.21), which Dhṛtarāṣṭra interrupts by taking sides with the former and rebuking the latter. He dismisses the house-priest and announces that he will send Saṃjaya to Yudhiṣṭhira's headquarters at Upaplavya (5.22). Chapters 5.23–31 cover Saṃjaya's diplomatic mission. With Saṃjaya's return (5.32), the scene of action changes back to Hāstinapura, where it remains until 5.69. In the next chapter (5.70), we are taken back to the side of the Pāṇḍavas, and their reactions to Saṃjaya's mission are related (5.70–81). This is followed by an account of Kṛṣṇa's journey to the Kuru court (5.82) and the reactions to his arrival (83–91). Saṃjaya plays no role in the events during Kṛṣṇa's sojourn (5.92–135), but he reappears when he reports to Dhṛtarāṣṭra a conversation he overheard between Kṛṣṇa and Karṇa (5.138–41). The narration returns to the Pāṇḍavas' place, where Kṛṣṇa reports what has happened and the decision is made to march the troops to Kurukṣetra (5.145–51). Vaiśampāyana relates that Duryodhana is informed about this move and orders his army to march out (152). At 5.156.2, Dhṛtarāṣṭra, who stays behind in Hāstinapura, asks Saṃjaya to tell him what is going on. Before Saṃjaya does what the old king asks, he voices another round of reproaches. This exchange establishes the intradiegetic narrative frame (Dhṛtarāṣṭra–Saṃjaya) up to 5.194.22, where the UdP ends by switching back to Vaiśampāyana as the extradiegetic narrator (5.195–96). Let us have a closer look at some of these interactions.

Dhṛtarāṣṭra's instruction (*Mbh*, 5.22)

In his first speech in the UdP (5.22), Dhṛtarāṣṭra tells Saṃjaya to go to Upaplavya. He instructs him to pay homage to Yudhiṣṭhira and congratulate him on mastering the undeserved exile. Saṃjaya should also declare that the Pāṇḍavas will quickly 'find their peace in us' (*teṣāṃ śāntir vidyate' smāsu*; 5.22.2) when they, who were wronged, remain favourable (or subservient). This statement can be read as demanding quiescence in suggesting that the Pāṇḍavas should desist from war so that an arrangement can be found. Dhṛtarāṣṭra then talks about the Pāṇḍavas and his son Duryodhana and concludes his speech urging Saṃjaya to do whatever it takes to prevent war. He stresses that he wants peace with the Pāṇḍavas (*dhṛtarāṣṭraḥ pāṇḍavaiḥ śāntim īpsuḥ*; 5.22.36). Dhṛtarāṣṭra's praise of the Pāṇḍavas is combined with reproachful remarks about Duryodhana. The comparison of the opponents results in fears and worries about the war that motivate the king's suing for peace. He states that he has never seen any falseness in the Pāṇḍavas, who behave perfectly and remain generous to their friends. On the Kuru side, they have no enemy but one, his son. Dhṛtarāṣṭra regards him as evil, false, dull-witted (*manda*), lacking all the qualities he finds in the Pāṇḍavas. But he also views his son as a young man indulging in his blossoming masculinity, which makes him think that he did splendidly so far. Only a child (*bāla*) would think that the Pāṇḍavas should give up their share of the kingdom. Being neither a child nor a young man, Dhṛtarāṣṭra concludes that this share should be handed over (22.9). On this note, his thoughts come back to the Pāṇḍavas and their allies, who are not only powerful but also devoted to Yudhiṣṭhira's cause (*bhakta*, *bhaktimat*; 22.18, 20) and will undoubtedly destroy his line of the family. The king closes his speech (in which the word 'fate' is not mentioned) with praise of Kṛṣṇa's valour. He stresses the latter's Viṣṇu-like invincibility that makes his heart tremble (which is again contrasted with Duryodhana's false judgement). However, the king's fear of Kṛṣṇa is surpassed by that of Yudhiṣṭhira's wrath (*manyu*). Now, says Dhṛtarāṣṭra, it is Saṃjaya's task to prevent the destruction of the Kurus and do everything to pacify the Pāṇḍavas.

Apart from revealing the motive for dispatching Saṃjaya, this speech is an excellent example of the contrasting appraisal of the two parties, which is a characteristic feature of the old king's discourses (see also 5.51–52). Duryodhana, in particular, is regularly called *manda* ('dull-witted'), *durbuddhi* and *durātman*. As an assessment voiced by the 'villain's' own father,[17] it stresses the epic composer's partiality for the Pāṇḍavas and the legitimacy of their claim. However, it also highlights the conflict that turns Dhṛtarāṣṭra's inability to follow his insights into a character trait that is complicated because he is aware of it. This complication unfolds further in the conversations that take place after Saṃjaya's return from his mission (narrated at 5.23–31).[18]

Samjaya's 'unofficial' message (*Mbh*, 5.32)

It seems remarkable that Saṃjaya's 'official' report about his mission is preceded by a speech in which he blames Dhṛtarāṣṭra for the wrong that has been done to the Pāṇḍavas. This speech takes place on his return from Upaplavya (5.32). It sets the stage for the further depiction of Dhṛtarāṣṭra's inner conflict, which is one of the drivers of the deliberations in the UdP. From a literary point of view, it also serves to redirect the focus of the narration back to the side of the Kurus and thus entwines the two scenes of action. This entwinement is brought about by a *mise-en-scène* of Saṃjaya's entrance and his emotionally tinged speech.[19] Extradiegetic narrator Vaiśampāyana's task is to set the stage. He relates that having carried out Dhṛtarāṣṭra's order, Saṃjaya reached Hāstinapura late in the evening, quickly entered the palace and spoke to the doorkeeper (32.2). The narration now switches to character speech. Saṃjaya orders the doorkeeper to announce his return to the king and that he wants to speak to him. Next, we listen to the doorkeeper's announcement, followed by Dhṛtarāṣṭra's slightly impatient reply to summon his envoy immediately. When the scene of action changes again, Vaiśampāyana offers a glimpse into the king's chamber. The king sits on the lion-throne surrounded by 'wise and noble Aryas', when Saṃjaya greets him politely (32.6). Next, Saṃjaya reports that he went to the Pāṇḍavas and conveys Yudhiṣṭhira's greetings. Dhṛtarāṣṭra asks about Yudhiṣṭhira, and

17 Unsurprisingly, this echoes similar views on the side of the Pāṇḍavas.

18 Saṃjaya's conversations with Yudhiṣṭhira and Kṛṣṇa cannot be dealt with within the scope of this chapter. For an analysis of the arguments, see Malinar (1996, 2007b); and for their role in the narration of decision-making, see Malinar (2022).

19 Furthermore, it anticipates a pattern of introducing reports and thus of narrating events, which is a characteristic feature of Saṃjaya in his role as an intradiegetic narrator of the battle books.

this sets off Saṃjaya's reproachful reply. At first, he states that Yudhiṣṭhira is well, even better than before. He is cheerful, learned, intelligent and virtuous, and values harmlessness (*ānṛśaṃsya*) more than *dharma*[20] and *dharma* more than 'piling up wealth'. On this note, Saṃjaya states that seeing the constraint (*niyama*) under which Yudhiṣṭhira is living in the household of the Matsya king is like seeing a man who struggles as he is yoked or directed by another (*paraprayukta*), like a wooden puppet on a string. Using a metaphor that in the epic mainly illustrates the working of fate (*daiva*, *diṣṭi*) or a divine disposer (*vidhātṛ*), Saṃjaya hints at Dhṛtarāṣṭra (and implicitly Duryodhana) as the 'other' who is holding Yudhiṣṭhira down, playing the part of fate in the Pāṇḍavas' life. For him, it is a fate made by man; it is caused by *karman*: 'I think that fate is *karman* following a man.'[21] This line of thought is pursued further when he next points to Dhṛtarāṣṭra and his *karmadoṣa* ('damaging, sinful acts'). The damage done by his master is a recurrent topic in Saṃjaya's reproachful speeches.[22] This is typically combined with a reference to the dice game as the moment when Dhṛtarāṣṭra gave in to the will of his son.

Seeing what exile and incognito life at the court of Virāṭa have done to Yudhiṣṭhira seems to have touched a chord with Saṃjaya, who probably knows very well what it means to be 'yoked to another'. In any case, his sympathies do not result in lament, in trying to rouse Dhṛtarāṣṭra's compassion, but in indignation about the unfair treatment, which, in his view, is unworthy of his master and threatens to ruin both reputation and fortune. He points out that Yudhiṣṭhira has shed evil (*pāpa*) like a snake its old skin and cast it off to Dhṛtarāṣṭra. The blame (*upakrośa*) is now on the latter, whose *karman* has become a part of him, like a limb, and will accompany him to the yonder-world (32.15). Influenced by his son (*putravaśānuga*), he is hoping to enjoy wealth without the Pāṇḍavas. But this is what low-born men do, not someone like him; it is unlike him. Not being foolish and with all the resources (counsellors, and so on) at his disposal, Saṃjaya wonders how Dhṛtarāṣṭra could commit such a cruel deed (*anānṛśaṃsyaṃ karma*; 32.19). Should Yudhiṣṭhira counter 'the evil with evil', the new evil has already been cast off on Dhṛtarāṣṭra, who must take the blame (*nindā*; 32.21). Saṃjaya

20 On *ānṛśaṃsya*, see Hiltebeitel (2001: 206–14).

21 *Manye paraṃ karma daivaṃ manuṣyāt* (*Mbh*, 5.32.12). Van Buitenen translates: 'I think *karman* is fate that exceeds the man.' While 'exceeds' suits the idea of transmigration in pointing to consequences of *karman* that exceed a man's present life, the context of the passage suggests that the emphasis here is on the point that the consequences of a deed stick to the doer; they catch up with him unescapably like fate. This is what is also pointed out in the next verse when Saṃjaya talks about Dhṛtarāṣṭra's sinful acts.

22 See also Mangels (1994: 104); Hill (1993).

makes clear that he views fighting against one's relatives to enforce one's claims, as Yudhiṣṭhira seems ready to do, as sinful.[23] Yet, the king's wrongful actions allow Yudhiṣṭhira to pass on the blame.

Next, Saṃjaya cites King Bali, who examined the qualities (virtues) of what is achieved by acts and concluded that time (*kāla*) is the cause of everything. The sense organs are the seats of all knowledge and one should cater to them. However, others say that all depends on *karman*. Saṃjaya adopts this position, again championing the *karman* doctrine, when he exclaims: 'I blame you for the hostility between the Bhāratas!' (32.27). He accuses his master of being the only person in the world who has fallen under the control of his sons (*vaśaṃ gantā*; 32.28) and reminds him that he praised his greedy son at the dice game. He asks the blind king to see (*paśya*; 32.28) that without peace, destruction is inevitable and says that the king cannot protect the Earth because he is powerless (*durbalyatvāt*; 32.29). With this scathing remark, Saṃjaya ends his address, says he is tired from the ride home, announces that he will convey Yudhiṣṭhira's message the next day and exits, leaving a silent Dhṛtarāṣṭra alone. The speech sets the tone for his other rebukes in the UdP and it sets the stage for what happens next: Dhṛtarāṣṭra awaits a sleepless night. The following conversation with Vidura shows that the king has heard and understood his envoy well. Conversely, the king's conversation with Vidura is significant also for the characterisation of Saṃjaya, and therefore shall be included in the analysis.[24]

Vidura's double-edged discourse (*Mbh*, 5.32–40)

The scene remains the same and character speech continues; Vaiśampāyana's only task is to inform us that the king spoke to his doorkeeper. Dhṛtarāṣṭra orders the doorkeeper to summon Vidura, his brother and confidant. Again, the doorkeeper has his word (cf. 5.32.4). As before with Saṃjaya, Vaiśampāyana briefly describes the setting of the following conversation by relating that Vidura, 'with folded hands', approached the king, who was lost in thought. Dhṛtarāṣṭra relates that Saṃjaya has returned and blamed him (*garhayitvā*; 33.9) for the Pāṇḍavas' misery. Tomorrow Yudhiṣṭhira's message will be announced in the assembly. Tormented by fears and worries about this message, the old king's limbs are burning and he cannot find

23 In a similar vein during his mission in Upaplavya, Saṃjaya tried to persuade Yudhiṣṭhira to abstain from war (see *Mbh*, 5.25). See Malinar (2007b) on these arguments and their connection to the *Bhagavadgītā*, and Malinar (2022) on Yudhiṣṭhira's reaction to this message.

24 This triangular constellation is another echo of the dice game. See Hudson (2013) on the actions of the two advisors at the dice game.

sleep. Therefore, Vidura should give soothing speeches to fight off his inner turmoil (33.12). These statements stress the impact of Saṃjaya's reproach and the tension created in the king by postponing the official message to the next day. The king's waking is narrated in 12 chapters (5.33–45, more than 650 verses including the Sanatsujatīya) and is thus made an element of the epic narrative.[25] According to van Buitenen (1978: 134), these chapters do not function as a retardation that would create suspense for an extradiegetic audience. However, this does not mean they are 'irrelevant to the action' as van Buitenen states because the epic composers continue very carefully by elaborating Dhṛtarāṣṭra's inner conflict as an essential element of the action that is driving the UdP as a whole. The king's waking is an occasion to address this conflict at still other levels of discourse—namely, gnomic-śāstric knowledge about *dharma* and *artha* (Vidura) and religious-philosophical instruction (Sanatsujāta).[26]

Vidura's instructions are marked by a remarkable contrast between a rather noncommittal, and indeed tiring, listing of gnomic-śāstric knowledge and more personal addresses warning the king of further wrongdoing. At first, these addresses are placed at the end of each speech and then interspersed in the gnomic parts.[27] These latter parts with their listing of proverbial wisdom could well have the desired 'sleep-inducing' effect.[28] But the passages in which Vidura admonishes the king to give the Pāṇḍavas their due and warns him of the destruction of the family achieve the exact opposite: they are veritable wake-up calls that prevent the king from falling asleep. Vidura's personal addresses complement Saṃjaya's rebukes in both style and content. Dhṛtarāṣṭra's sparse but significant reactions to Vidura's counterpoints provide further insights into the king's inner conflict.

Vidura makes the following points: Dhṛtarāṣṭra has raised and educated the sons of his brother; he now should continue to act like the father they see and seek in him. He should give them their share of the kingdom and live

25 It should be noted that the waking (*prajagāra*) is also included in the summary of contents at *Mbh* 1.2.50.

26 In van Buitenen's (1978: 180–81) view, the first provides admonishment and warning, the second hope and consolation. He also connects the speeches to the UdP's general tendency to demonstrate the undesirability of war and doubts 'that this effort of stalling is a narrative device to increase suspense on the part of the listener or reader'. Instead, the UdP treats the war as a 'moral embarrassment'. This view seems to be a rather one-sided interpretation of the complex entwinement of the war and peace debates. On the role of grief in the epic in general, see Hudson (2013).

27 *Mbh*, 5.33.103–4; 34.78–83; 35.66–67; 36.68–72; 37.18–19, 38–42, 59–60; 38.43–44; 39.2–6, 15–30, 68–70.

28 Van Buitenen (1978: 180) speaks of 'Vidura's relentlessly incessant rainy-season pitter-patter of peanuts of wisdom that should have lulled to sleep the most insomniac of warriors'.

happily together with all the sons. In this way, he will no longer be suspected (*tarkaṇīya*; 33.104). This cryptic remark seems to point to the precarious position of Dhṛtarāṣṭra as the custodian of his brother's sons, who are, when seen from the perspective of kinship rules, no less his sons than those born to him.[29] Therefore, his social reputation as father and king depends on treating all his sons fairly. Dhṛtarāṣṭra's affection for Duryodhana amounts to a partiality that casts doubt on his righteousness and moral fibre. This interpretation is corroborated when Vidura next warns the king that his own sons' *buddhi* ('faculty of judgement') is obsessed with their hostility towards the Pāṇḍavas, and they therefore misjudge the situation. Such misjudgement indicates that the gods have settled on someone's destruction. Therefore, Yudhiṣṭhira must rule the kingdom as he has all the qualities needed (34.78–83). In the next personal address at the end of 5.35, Vidura tells the king he must not adhere to the idea that he will prosper by placing the power (*aiśvarya*) in Duryodhana. He should behave like a father to the Pāṇḍavas, who treat him as one (35.66–67). In the middle of Vidura's next recital of gnomic sayings (5.36), the old king suddenly reacts to what is said about the topic of the desirability of detachment. This sudden reaction demonstrates that parallel to the gnomic discourse, not only Vidura but also Dhṛtarāṣṭra are pondering their anxieties. While Vidura brings his worries home in perorations, Dhṛtarāṣṭra suddenly exclaims that his mind is constantly upset as he has wronged Yudhiṣṭhira, who will destroy his 'dull-witted' (*manda*) sons (36.47). He urges Vidura to tell him something that does not upset him; however, Vidura seems unwilling to comply. He ends his speech by reminding the king that he did not listen to him before (at the dice game) and urges him to do better now and stop Duryodhana. Then he will live happily together with the Pāṇḍavas in a single kingdom (36.68–72). All this is repeated in the following speech with three personal addresses emphasising the advantages of having family and kingdom united under Yudhiṣṭhira's rule (37.18–19, 38–42, 59–60). Vidura compares such a union with the profitable alliance between tigers (Pāṇḍavas) and the forest (Kurus). At the end of the next speech, Vidura compares Duryodhana's imminent downfall with that of King Bali, who was also intoxicated by power (38.43–44). Dhṛtarāṣṭra replies that all is a matter of fate and man is like a puppet on a string, subject to what has been ordained (39.1).

29 In his interpretation of the *Mbh* as mirroring the structure of a potlatch ritual, Held (1935: 302–3) has discussed this kinship structure emphasising the issue of seniority in the conflict of the two 'phratries', and notes Dhṛtarāṣṭra's ambiguous paternal agency when coping with the conflicting claims of his own and his adopted 'sons'.

Vidura seems to have understood that his brother alludes here to what is fate for him: to his son to whom he is attached and emotionally dependent like a puppet on a string. Assuming such understanding explains why Vidura immediately turns to the topic of love. Says Vidura: 'The one becomes beloved for his gifts, the other for his pleasant words, the third for his power of spells and herbs, but he who is loved is loved.'[30] With the last line, Vidura touches the heart of the matter: the riddle of groundless, even undeserved, love and the drama of loving an apparently undeserving person—here, a ruthless son and an intransigent, self-indulgent warrior. The drama is heightened by the presence of an obviously better candidate for such love: a virtuous and righteous son, Yudhiṣṭhira. Vidura alludes to this when he points out that a loved one should be characterised by good deeds, suggesting an intrinsic connection between love and virtue. However, Dhṛtarāṣṭra's reply confirms the line 'who is loved is loved'. Despite all objections and against his better knowledge, he loves Duryodhana better. He replies that what Vidura is saying is well meant and correct, but 'I cannot bear to give up my son. Where there is law, there is victory' (39.7). At the end of 5.40, he also discloses how this fateful and fatal love works:

> Every time my resolve has settled thus in favour of the Pāṇḍavas, it again turns around to Duryodhana, when I am near to him. Fate cannot be overcome by any mortal being. What is done is only fate, I think. Human acts are just useless. (*Mbh*, 5.40.29–30)[31]

These statements end the conversation with Vidura, which is followed by the Sanatsujatīya. Furthermore, they make clear that at the centre of Dhṛtarāṣṭra's thought is not fate in general,[32] but Duryodhana and the love he feels for him constitute his fate.

---

30 *priyo bhavati dānena priyavādena cāparaḥ | mantraṃ mūlabalenānyo yaḥ priyaḥ priya eva saḥ* (*Mbh*, 5.39.3; translation by van Buitenen 1978), with the note (p. 545) on the verse, in which van Buitenen rejects the reading of the Critical Edition and reads *mantramūlabalenānyo.*

31 *sā tu buddhiḥ kṛtāpy evaṃ pāṇḍavān prati me sadā / duryodhanaṃ samāsādya punar viparivartate // na diṣṭam abhyatikrāntuṃ śakyaṃ martyena kena cit / diṣṭam eva kṛtaṃ manye pauruṣaṃ tu nirarthakam* // (*Mbh*, 5.40.29–30). A similar statement is given at 5.156.6, in the last exchange with Saṃjaya in the UdP (see below).

32 Hill (1993) focuses on fate as a power on to which some characters shift the blame for what is happening. In his view, Dhṛtrāṣṭra ultimately absolves himself of responsibility, while Yudhiṣṭhira seems to admit that he failed during the dice game. Neither the king's awareness of the wrong he has done nor the significance of the type of love Dhṛtarāṣṭra is struggling with is considered. But the epic's composers have explored the ambiguities of human action in the case not only of Yudhisthira, as Hill rightfully argues (1993: 20), but also of Dhṛtarāṣṭra.

In other instances, the king uses the word *sneha* for this kind of love,[33] which he seems to represent like no other character in the epic. It is a trait that determines his role in the epic no less strongly than the dysfunctional condition caused by his blindness.

In his study of contemporary notions of love, Hara (2007: 87) notes that *sneha* is an emotional type of love associated with the element water and distinguished from *kāma*—fiery love that is driven by an egotistic desire for an object. *Sneha* is described as a deeply felt affection and attachment, an emotion defying explanation. The word is often used when dealing with familial and friendship bonds and often entails empathy, understanding and unwavering partiality for the beloved. It is viewed as an emotion that establishes social bonds that are not driven by self-interest or other purposes. Its groundless, unreasonable character makes it a powerful force that is difficult to control and can even result in self-destructive actions (Hara 2007: 90–92). For this reason, it is also viewed as a form of folly that must be controlled and overcome. Otherwise, it will undermine a law-abiding and prosperous life (*dharma* and *artha*) and drive a person to act against his or her self-interest. On the other hand, the disregard for self-interest distinguishes this kind of love from egotistic *kāma* and is also presented as motivating altruism and self-sacrifice. This ambiguity is addressed in the epic in stories depicting the willingness to sacrifice oneself for love[34] as well as in religious-philosophical and dharmic discourses warning of the dangers of *sneha*.[35] The conflicts it causes are elaborated in the figure of Dhṛtarāṣṭra, who wrestles with this love because he is aware of its detrimental effects.

Dhṛtarāṣṭra's blindness does not make him blind to this conflict, which he experiences as his fate. He thus sees the consequences of this fatal love, and even sees his *buddhi*, his faculty of judgement's resolve, slipping away from him and turning back to this son again and again. Other characters also struggle with the king's reversals, especially Saṃjaya, Vidura and Yudhiṣṭhira. The last mentioned bitterly complains about this love and the partiality it entails, which prevents his paternal uncle and social father from deciding in his favour, and from loving him. The knowledge of the old king's conflict is carefully circulated in the narrative so that it becomes a well-known fact for

33 See, for instance, *Mbh* 3.10.3 to Vyāsa and at 15.5.4 to Yudhiṣṭhira.

34 See, for instance, the story of the Śārṅkakas (*Mbh*, 1.220–25), the conversation between a brahmin and his wife in the Baka story (1.145–46), the story of Śibi at *Mbh* 3.131 and the conversation between a vulture and a jackal (12.149).

35 See, for instance, the instruction of Yudhiṣṭhira by Sāṃkhya and Yoga expert Śaunaka at *Mbh* 3.2.

most characters. Since the conflict is an essential element of the narrative, its elaboration takes up a considerable part of the UdP. It produces paradoxes and contradictions that puzzle not only the characters confronted with it but also extradiegetic audiences.[36] The nightly conversation with Vidura is thus by no means 'irrelevant to the action' (van Buitenen 1978: 134), since it is in accordance with the concern of the UdP to not only relate the events that lead to the marching out of the armies, but also depict the inner conflicts and the emotional entanglements that make war inevitable. Furthermore, Vidura's double-edged discourse complements Saṃjaya's rebukes by including a different level of discourse, in which 'sleep-inducing' recounting of gnomic knowledge is used as the foil for sounding 'wake-up calls'. Furthermore, these wake-up calls reveal Vidura's view on how the conflict should be resolved: by making Yudhiṣṭhira king of a single kingdom. Only when Dhṛtarāṣṭra makes clear that he will not give up Duryodhana does Vidura shift his position and propose to give 'some little villages' (*grāmaka*) to the Pāṇḍavas so they can earn their livelihood (39.19).[37] Vidura's discourse and the solution he proposes are also critical for delineating Saṃjaya's role in the UdP. In contrast to Vidura, Saṃjaya does not advocate that Yudhiṣṭhira should become the only ruler. However, with his emotionally tinged, reproachful speeches, he attacks Dhṛtarāṣṭra at a more personal level than Vidura. Furthermore, Vidura's partiality for the cause of the Pāṇḍavas is further emphasised when Kṛṣṇa chooses to stay with Vidura during his mission at Hastināpura. This points to his being involved in the conflict also as a member of the family. In contrast to him, Saṃjaya is a member of Dhṛtarāṣṭra's household, with various tasks, and he shows no inhibition in reproaching and scolding his master, in displaying an emotional involvement. In a rather dramatic way, these traits come to the fore in the interactions between Dhṛtarāṣṭra and Saṃjaya when they meet again the next morning.

36 In one of the rare interventions by the extradiegetic audience represented by King Janamejaya, he asks his bard Vaiśampāyana, who had just narrated the heated debate during Kṛṣṇa's mission in Dhṛtarāṣṭra's assembly hall, why no-one stopped Duryodhana (*Mbh*, 5.104).

37 This can be interpreted as hinting at the 'five-villages' demand, which Yudhiṣṭhira had asked Saṃjaya to convey to Duryodhana (*Mbh*, 5.31.19–20). Vidura also suggests that Dhṛtarāṣṭra compensates Duryodhana's offences and thereby strengthens his reputation (30.30). He urges the king to treat all his sons (which includes the Pāṇḍavas) equally to ensure his prosperity (30.68–70).

Saṃjaya's fainting and the verbal exchange with Dhṛtarāṣṭra (*Mbh*, 5.49–53)

The account of Dhṛtarāṣṭra's sleepless night is followed by that of the events of the next morning, which include another moment of drama: Saṃjaya's fainting in the assembly hall. At *Mbh* 5.46, narrator Vaiśampāyana describes the setting and the pompous entry of the Kaurava heroes to the assembly hall, comparing them with the gods arriving at the residence of Indra. Again, the doorkeeper has a word announcing that 'our envoy' has returned 'on the chariot ... with the horses from Sindh' (46.13). In marking the change of speakers, Vaiśampāyana adds that Saṃjaya, wearing earrings, jumped off the chariot and quickly entered the hall (46.14). This scene is one of the rare instances in which we learn more about Saṃjaya than his name and provenance (see above on 'minor' characters). At 5.49, Dhṛtarāṣṭra asks him about Yudhiṣṭhira's reaction to the armies arrayed against him and whether his advisors recommend war or peace to him, 'who is furious because of the deception [committed] by the dull-witted [that is, Duryodhana]' (49.3).[38] Saṃjaya replies that his brothers, his allies and the people revere and trust Yudhiṣṭhira. But when Dhṛtarāṣṭra asks about the troop strength, there is no reply. Vaiśampāyana is switched in to relate what happened (49.10): 'Saṃjaya apparently was ruminating on something for a moment when he heaved a loud, long sigh. Then by accident, for no obvious reason the *sūta* became dismayed [lit., dismay seized him].'[39] At this point, the narration switches back to character speech and thereby turns the spotlight directly on what is happening. The primarily dramatic function of this switching (allowing audiences to follow the narrative as if it were happening presently) can also be seen when we hear 'a man in the assembly' informing Dhṛtarāṣṭra that Saṃjaya has fainted and fallen to the ground. Unconscious Saṃjaya does not say a word, reports the man. The king explains that Saṃjaya beheld the Pāṇḍavas and this has undoubtedly upset his mind (*manas*; 49.12). This comment, like Vaiśampāyana's interpretation that Saṃjaya was overwhelmed by dismay (*kaśmala*), leaves the exact cause of the turmoil unexplained.[40]

---

38 This remark confirms Dhṛtarāṣṭra's opinion about his son's character expressed in his instruction to Saṃjaya (*Mbh*, 5.22) and elsewhere in the epic.

39 *niḥśvasya subhṛśaṃ dīrghaṃ muhuḥ saṃcintayann iva | tatrānimittato daivāt sūtaṃ kaśmalam āviśat* | (*Mbh*, 5. 49.10). The expression 'dismay seized him/entered him' points to an intense and sudden emotional turmoil and is used in other instances in the epic, as has been pointed out by Hara (2006). See, for instance, the description of Arjuna's breakdown at the beginning of the *Bhagavadgītā* (cf. Malinar 2007b).

40 Without discussing the passage in any detail, Mangels (1994: 143) claims that Saṃjaya went into a sort of trance and connects this to the 'divine eye' given to him before the battle. Hiltebeitel (2001: 57) follows this interpretation.

Next, a recovered Saṃjaya clarifies that neither fear nor despair made him faint; rather, it was seeing 'the warrior sons of Kuntī emaciated by the constraints of living in the house of the Matsya king' (49.14; translation by van Buitenen 1978). This statement connects the fainting to what happened the night before. In his nightly speech, Saṃjaya had also stressed his dismay because of the constraints put on the Pāṇḍavas (32.12). The scene also recalls the sleepless night an upset (*udvejita*) Dhṛtarāṣṭra awaited afterwards. Once again, the epic poets take great care to direct attention to the emotional undercurrents that imbue the relationships between the characters and lend them a dramatic, lively form. At the same time, they entwine the events of the morning with those of the night before (the message before the official report is alluded to, the king's nightly turmoil echoed in the fainting of Saṃjaya). In Sanskrit drama, fainting belongs with the shedding of tears, sweating and so on to the so-called *sāttvika-bhāva*s: intense psychophysical reactions to events.[41] When protagonists show these reactions (or actors in a drama do that on purpose), this points to an intense inner involvement with the events that would otherwise remain invisible. According to the *Nāṭyaśāstra*, the mind (*manas*) is the seat of this engagement, producing images, thoughts, emotions, memories and so on, and in this way contributes to the development of the *rasa* and the meaning of a play. In the epic, these reactions are likewise employed to highlight that a character is emotionally and mentally overwhelmed.[42] Fainting shows that something quite dramatic has happened as the mental processes completely overtake the body. For this reason, it can also be interpreted as pointing to physical and mental weakness and thus can be used in drama for different purposes. Fainting is only occasionally used in the epic—perhaps most strikingly at the beginning of Book 9. When Saṃjaya returns from the battlefield and reports Duryodhana's death, Dhṛtarāṣṭra, Vidura and Gāndhārī and all the wives of the Kurus faint and fall unconscious to the ground—a sight that makes Saṃjaya cry (9.1.37–48). Since Dhṛtarāṣṭra is generally characterised as engaged in mental, inner processes due to his blindness, it is no surprise that he faints twice on this occasion.[43] The two fainting scenes underline the solid affective relationship between the king and his confidant.

41 See *Nāṭyaśāstra* 6.23; see also Malinar (2010).

42 See Dhṛtarāṣṭra's comment about the fainting (*Mbh*, 5.49.13) or Arjuna's display of *sāttvika-bhāvas* at the beginning of the *Bhagavadgītā*. See Malinar (2007b: 59–60).

43 See *Mbh* 3.7.2, when Dhṛtarāṣṭra faints after Vidura joined the Pāṇḍavas after the dice game.

Saṃjaya's following report of the troop strength describes the Pāṇḍavas and their allies in glowing terms and stresses their readiness for war. Dhṛtarāṣṭra reacts to his assessment. As in the earlier instruction of Saṃjaya (5.22; see above), Dhṛtarāṣṭra formulates his thoughts and emotions (often addressing Saṃjaya directly) regarding the Pāṇḍavas, starting with Bhīma (5.50), moving on to Arjuna (5.51) and ending with Yudhiṣṭhira (5.52). He again speaks unfavourably about his son. However, he now draws a more nuanced picture in that he also blames Bhīma for the bleak situation. He openly expresses his fear of Bhīma, which has him heaving 'long, hot sighs' in his sleepless nights.[44] Past and future actions are entwined when Dhṛtarāṣṭra, with his inner eye, sees 'cruel and impatient' Bhīma wielding his club and killing his 'dull-witted' sons (50.2–9). In the past, Bhīma has proved most hostile, always opposing his paternal uncle. Dhṛtarāṣṭra recounts how Bhīma tormented his cousin-brothers in their childhood, which made his heart tremble. For him, Bhīma is the cause of the breach (*bheda*) in the family (*sa eva hetur bhedasya*; 50.12). He states that he could not control him then, how should he now when Bhīma seeks revenge for the mistreatment he suffered from his 'evil sons' (*duṣputrair*; 50.17) and therefore cannot be pacified? Using lively imagery and metaphors, Dhṛtarāṣṭra foretells what Bhīma will do to his sons and elders. He despairs of his inability to avert it, to change what is his fate: 'Fate always prevails, especially over man's efforts: for even though I see the others' triumph, I do not bridle my sons' (5.50.47; translation by van Buitenen 1978). As if alluding to Sāṃkhya teachings, he offers his opinion about the use of knowledge (*jñāna*) in such situations: 'I do not think that knowledge is [useful] for warding off pain, Saṃjaya. For when it is too strong it is hurting knowledge as well' (50.53).[45] Even sages, free of attachments, are sympathetic when watching how people are faring. For Dhṛtarāṣṭra, knowledge does not work as an antidote to intense suffering and he sees himself in the good company of 'sages, who have freed themselves [*nirmukta*]' but are still moved when people are happy or suffer. Here, Dhṛtarāṣṭra casts himself as being touched by what happens, although his sympathies are scaled and partial in that they are commanded by his love for Duryodhana. There is no help for him in this respect and teachings about overcoming both happiness and suffering by knowledge alone do not give him solace. In growing despair, the aged king exclaims: 'Of what in the end am I capable in this great danger,

44 This is another reference to the turmoil the king underwent the previous night.

45 *na tu manye vighātāya jñānaṃ duḥkhasya saṃjaya | bhavaty atibale hy etaj jñānam apy upaghātakam* (*Mbh*, 5.50.53). *Sāṃkhyakārikā* teaches that knowledge (*jñāna*) of Saṃkhya is the instrument for warding off (*abhighātaka*) the 'threefold suffering'.

for I see in my thoughts the perdition of the Kurus ... What am I to do, how am I to do it, where am I going, Saṃjaya!' (50.56, 59ab; translation by van Buitenen 1978). In this highly emotional peroration, Dhṛtarāṣṭra assumes a role like that he accorded previously to Vidura, when the latter warned—to no avail—that the dice game would lead to the downfall of the Kurus. Now Dhṛtarāṣṭra himself is warning that he is already grieving for those who must fight the Pāṇḍavas. However, he warns not only what awaits them from the Pāṇḍavas, but also of himself. Pointing to the limitations of his knowledge and the range of actions, he presents himself as doomed by 'fate': the groundless love for his son.

In a much less excited tone, Dhṛtarāṣṭra next turns to the other Pāṇḍavas, reviewing Arjuna's prowess (5.51) and Yudhiṣṭhira's virtues (5.52) in a way that resembles his earlier speech (5.22; see above). He concludes that war cannot be won and urges the Kauravas to seek peace:

> Not to war were best, I think—listen to me, Kurus ... This is my last attempt at peace, to appease my mind. If you do not want war, let us strive for peace. Yudhiṣṭhira will not ignore you, if you sue for peace, for he loathes lawlessness, pointing at me as the cause of it. (UdP, 5.52.14–16; translation by van Buitenen 1978)

It seems Dhṛtarāṣṭra has indeed listened to Saṃjaya's first address of the previous night that the blame will be put on him should he not seek peace.

Dhṛtarāṣṭra has hardly finished his speech when Saṃjaya rebukes him again (5.53). After agreeing that war will result in disaster, Saṃjaya says that he does not understand how this wise king could subject himself to his son (53.2). He accuses him of having betrayed the Pāṇḍavas from the beginning. He did not act towards them as a father and therefore wields no authority: 'An ill-wisher [*drogdhā*] is not regarded as a teacher [*guru*]' (53.4). Saṃjaya continues the personal attack by raising further doubts about Dhṛtarāṣṭra's moral integrity, even his maturity. He recalls how the king behaved during the dice game—that he was 'gloating' (van Buitenen 1978: 317) like a little boy (*kumāravat*; 53.5, 10) when he heard that his party had won and the Pāṇḍavas had gone into exile. He did not object to the offences after the dice game, nor did he consider his downfall when learning that his sons had 'won the entire kingdom' (53.6).[46] Next, Saṃjaya reminds Dhṛtarāṣṭra of the fact that he initially possessed only the paternal, inherited kingdom of the Kurus together with uninhabited areas (*sajaṅgala*), while the Pāṇḍavas conquered their kingdom on their own and presented it to him; they even rescued his sons. Now, Dhṛtarāṣṭra thinks he had done all this. Having lost his reputation, the other kings now despise him and have sided with the Pāṇḍavas. Saṃjaya admonishes him to restrain 'the evil man, your son, with all means' and reminds him that already at the dice game he and Vidura had warned him, and thus he should not grieve (53.18). All his lamentations about the strength and virtues of the Pāṇḍavas are pointless because he behaves as though he were a powerless man. After this sharp attack, Duryodhana speaks up next, objecting to his father's concerns and stressing the superiority of the Kaurava heroes. He insists that one must not accept that Yudhiṣṭhira makes himself the king of only one kingdom (5.54.10). Dhṛtarāṣṭra intervenes and pleads with Duryodhana not to wage war ('turn away from war, for there are no circumstances in which war is condoned ... return to Pāṇḍu's sons what is rightfully theirs'; 5.57.2, 4; translation by van Buitenen 1978). Finally, he even declares that he will give up his son (5.57.19). To Duryodhana's reassuring speeches (50.60–62),[47] seconded by Karṇa, his father gives no further reply. When all falls silent and everyone has left the assembly hall, Dhṛtarāṣṭra turns again to Saṃjaya and asks him to tell him more about the strengths and weaknesses of both parties (5.65–69).[48]

Transition to the frame dialogue (*Mbh*, 5.156)

Saṃjaya's third, and relatively brief, rebuke reacts to Dhṛtarāṣṭra's request to report what is happening after the armies marched to Kurukṣetra. This request prepares the dialogue frame for the narration of the battle, which is later authorised by Vyāsa (6.2.9–13).[49] In this short speech, the king states that he thinks fate is supreme and human efforts are pointless. Again, it is

46 Van Buitenen (1978: 317) translates 'while knowing full well that they themselves had won the entire kingdom', understanding the '*iti*' sentence as referring not to the dice game, but to the Pāṇḍavas' expansion described in the following stanzas. My rendering suggests that Saṃjaya continues castigating Dhṛtarāṣṭra's immature delight when knowing that 'they' (that is, his side) had won the entire kingdom. It prevented him from foreseeing that this would result in the very ruinous confrontation he is now fearing. Then, in the following verse, Saṃjaya reminds him that this 'entire' kingdom only exists because of the Pāṇḍavas' efforts.

47 See Malinar (2012) for an analysis of these speeches.

48 As mentioned before, Saṃjaya's report cannot be dealt with in the scope of this chapter.

49 See Mangels (1994: 94–96) for a discussion of the manuscript evidence regarding this frame in the UdP.

his fate that is on his mind, his inability to control his son and to act for his own good and prevent destruction. As in the nightly conversation with Vidura, Dhṛtarāṣṭra describes the working of this fate as a power that affects the proper functioning of his *buddhi*, his faculty of judgement. Although he sees the harmful effects of his son's actions, his insight 'is turning around' (*parivartate*) to his son as soon as he is close to him (5.156.6).[50] He concludes that things are as they are and what must happen will happen. Citing common knowledge, he reinterprets fate in terms of *kṣatriyadharma*, stating that giving up one's life is honoured as the law of warriors. Whether this indicates that the king has come to terms with fate and imminent disaster or that he has given up is hard to tell.

Once again, Saṃjaya is unwilling to accept his master's view. He admonishes him not to blame Duryodhana alone, nor fate or time as it was under his watch that the Pāṇḍavas were cheated at the dice game. Once again, we see Saṃjaya insisting on the workings of *karman* as the mechanism that explains what happened to the Bhāratas. He has no sense of the emotional dimensions that undermine reasonable action and the complexity of the conflicts driving the events. In his view, power and resources are all at his master's disposal and, since he cannot understand why the old king fails to use them, he berates him again. The pattern of interaction between the two protagonists is also characteristic of their verbal exchanges as interlocutors of the intradiegetic dialogue frame of the battle books. While the two change their literary function in becoming involved in the narration of the epic, their well-established, quite personal relationship is maintained. Despite Saṃjaya's official promotion to what could be called 'bard', when he receives the 'divine eye' from Vyāsa (*Mbh*, 6.2), he does not turn into a distant observer, relating what happens without showing reactions. Instead, he remains defined and shaped by his unique relationship with the king, being a confidant and trusted household member. This brings the discussion back to the question of the identity of Saṃjaya as a literary character so strongly associated with King Dhṛtarāṣṭra, and thus to some general considerations that follow from the analysis of their interactions in the UdP.

50 Van Buitenen (1978) translates 'my mind is perverted', which downplays, in my view, the emotional dimension of the king's inability.

Dhṛtarāṣṭra and Saṃjaya as literary characters

Dhṛtarāṣṭra's speeches in the UdP are intrinsically connected to the multifaceted role he plays in the negotiations. He is wrestling with conflicting thoughts and emotions to an extent that can only be compared with Yudhiṣṭhira. In both cases, this wrestling sometimes results in inconsistent statements, which other characters view primarily as signs of weakness. In the case of Dhṛtarāṣṭra, such inconsistencies result in admonishments and reproaches from his companions, which are often accompanied by reminders of the dice game. Saṃjaya and Vidura repeatedly recall the Pāṇḍavas' deception and their warnings to the king about the dire consequences. They urge the king not to make the same mistake again by not paying heed to what they say and what he knows only too well. Indeed, Dhṛtarāṣṭra is shown to intervene when he sues for peace and warns Duryodhana that this battle cannot be won and he should be satisfied with ruling half the kingdom. His failed interventions confirm what he sees with his 'eyesight of insight' (*prajñācakṣus*) and this includes the love for his son that makes him weak because it lets him ignore his interests. Being blind, Dhṛtarāṣṭra follows the events from inside, voicing what he sees and knows with the 'eyesight of insight'—an epithet used often when referring to him.[51] The blind king's conflicting thoughts and feelings reflect what he sees with his 'eyesight of insight', which switches back and forth between memories of the past and sightings of the future. Voicing all this in confounding ways marks his involvement in the events of the UdP. His relationship to the events is driven by conflicting axiological and normative premises and his unconditional love for his son. The display of his inner conflict is as inhibited by his blindness[52] as is his power as father and king. According to the contemporary interpretation of 'seeing' as a sensory faculty, blindness is a defect that keeps the fiery dimensions (*tejas*) of experiencing and relating to the world inside due to the defect in the eyes, the outer site

51 This 'signature' attribute is noted in academic studies but rarely explored in connection to the king's role in the narrative (see Malinar 2005). Mangels (1994) is more interested in the 'divine eye' accorded to Saṃjaya, which belongs to a somewhat different set of faculties. Without providing textual evidence, Hiltebeitel (2001: 66n.121) regards it as an 'ironic epithet', as does Hudson (2007: 49n.14).

52 According to Held (1935: 301), Dhṛtarāṣṭra's blindness is a poetic device that was used to justify the Pāṇḍavas' claim to the right of the throne.

of the sense of seeing (also called *dvāra*, 'door').[53] While the inner sense of seeing is functioning and enables him to know and see with the 'eyesight of insight', Dhṛtarāṣṭra cannot use the power of the 'eye-beam' when relating to the world and acting in it. Not only are the eyes crucial for perceiving and knowing the world, but also he lacks the operational capacity of the eyes, which allows one to show all kinds of emotions and to influence others.[54] As he cannot participate in these dimensions of life, the king is consumed by and preoccupied with thoughts and emotions he cannot communicate and express fully. It is not only old age, but also the inhibited capacity of expression and agency that make him weak, sleepless, brooding and lamenting. Tears appear in his eyes, but not the redness of fury or the intensity of sidelong glances. Blindness robs him of this possibility of wielding power and authority, as a king, head of the family and father. All these aspects are carved out in the epic's characterisation of Dhṛtarāṣṭra.[55]

His speeches in the UdP reveal the range of his inner vision and show him to be mainly preoccupied with the family and the affective entanglements of its members. They present a vision and version of a divisive past that inform his sightings of the future. However, when his insight should guide the king's actions in the present, the 'eyesight of insight' is destabilised by Duryodhana's presence. This situation is described in the speeches quite precisely as the turning around of *buddhi* ('faculty of judgement'). The 'eyesight of insight' enables him to look into the dreadful future of war but also keeps him aware of missed chances in the present when he watches his resolve fade again and again. So, it is an eyesight that works quite clearly and vividly when recalling past events and foreseeing the future but becomes unclear and hazy when coping with the present. From a literary point of view, this accords the figure of Dhṛtarāṣṭra analeptic and proleptic narrative functions that are important for unfolding the epic narrative. His speeches in the UdP are, to a considerable extent, sightings of the future. They are visions of the much-quoted 'end of time' and contain vivid descriptions

53 In the general parallelism drawn between the senses and the elements in philosophical discourse, the eyes are usually connected with fire (*tejas*), which illuminates the objects. The connection between the eyes and fire and light is, of course, much older and not only is connected to emotions and notions of power but also plays an essential role in knowledge discourses that highlight the intrinsic connection between seeing and knowing. See Hara (2006).

54 For a study of the semantics of 'being blind' (*andha*), see Hara (2006). For a discussion of instances of 'veiling' the eye to conceal emotions, see Malinar (2005).

55 The impact of Dhṛtarāṣṭra's blindness can also be seen in his limited mobility. He lives through the epic mostly confined to the house, sitting on the throne. It seems significant that we see him departing from this statue-like confinement only after all his fears and sightings have come true—when he moves to Indraprastha, takes part in the death rites and then departs to the forest, his final destination.

of the heroes, their virtues and achievements, how they will appear on the battlefield and so on. In this way, Dhṛtarāṣṭra emerges as a quite future-oriented character.[56] 'Future' in a literary work, of course, means heading for the unfolding of the plot and bringing the story to its end. Since Dhṛtarāṣṭra will survive the war, he is thus also looking at his own future. It is a future that reunites him with Yudhiṣṭhira in becoming a member of his household. Therefore, it is no surprise that Dhṛtarāṣṭra's speeches focus mainly on the Pāṇḍavas and their virtues. Genealogically speaking, they are the family's and Dhṛtarāṣṭra's future as he will move to them as they had moved to him after their father's death. In this way, the generational transition of power comes full circle with the original, but now expanded, unity of the kingdom re-established, although at a very high cost. Thus, grief and sorrow remain with the old king as does his unconditional love for Duryodhana.

Dhṛtarāṣṭra's conflict and awareness of it imbue the narrative with an emotional drama that enriches the epic's messages about the proper and improper ways to pursue *dharma* and *artha* from a position of (unrequited) paternal love. The old king is not worried or fearful for his own life but terrified by foreseeing the destruction of the Kurus and the death of Duryodhana. He fears for Duryodhana, whom he loves and favours despite all his flaws. Dhṛtarāṣṭra is not blind with love, but quite aware of his son's flaws. He knows that he should give him up and enforce peace; he must not be lectured about his unreasonableness. This could explain why Saṃjaya is not trying to reason with him but just blames him for the injustice that results from what he (and others) view as unmerited love and who resent him for this.[57]

Saṃjaya's three speeches of rebuke are given in moments of the narrative that epitomise the conflict between Dhṛtarāṣṭra's expressed wish to prevent the war and his 'fate'—the inability to stop his son. The speeches offer a reading of events that allows the old king[58] to be blamed without completely effacing Yudhiṣṭhira's insistence that obtaining his share is sinful because it entails killing family members.

56 This position is also corroborated by his appearance in the extradiegetic frame in Book 1, where he recounts the sequence of events, which delineate the epic plot (*Mbh*, 1.1.88–161). The connections between the extra- and intradiegetic appearances will be explored in a separate study.

57 This is particularly true for Yudhiṣṭhira, who resents Duryodhana being favoured by father-substitute Dhṛtarāṣṭra. In a similar vein, he resents Draupadī's alleged preference for Arjuna (*Mbh*, 17.2.6) and appears as a character who is more admired than loved.

58 Mangels (1994: 104) calls this a 'motif' in Saṃjaya's speeches without dealing with them in greater detail, which is also true of Hudson (2013). Hill (1993) takes a closer look and detects 'contradictions' in some passages without analysing individual speeches in context.

The directness and personal character of Saṃjaya's rebukes suggest he is in the UdP cast not as a 'bard' relating past events, but as an advisor and confidant of the king who is also entrusted with various tasks, such as acting as an envoy. Furthermore, the UdP presents some of the interactions between him and his master by drawing on elements of drama. The bluntness of Saṃjaya's rebukes and the tasks he is carrying out for Dhṛtarāṣṭra resonate with a character typical of Sanskrit drama: the *vidūṣaka*. Although Saṃjaya is certainly not the buffoon—the comical figure teasing the leading hero (*nāyaka*) of classical theatre—his role in the epic echoes other, probably earlier appearances of a figure who acted towards a leading character as companion, servant and critic. In his study of the background of the figure, Kuiper (1979: 208) points to the generally accepted etymology of *vidūṣaka* as 'corrupter' ('*Schlechtmacher, Schimpfer*') and deals with the connections to Vedic ritual verbal contests that feature the figure of the opponent, and to the appearance of the reviler in the Mahāvrata ritual. He points out that the *Nāṭyaśāstra* also presents the *vidūṣaka* as meeting the leading character, the king, on an equal footing and is presented in this way in older dramas of Bhasa and Kālidāsa (Kuiper 1979: 205, 211). Kuiper (1979: 209) concludes: '[I]n the relationship that must originally have existed between the hero and his "friend" there was, in fact, an element of contest ... He was a "tegenspeler", a fellow-player and "counter-actor".'

Paying attention to the possible connections and allusions to features of theatrical plays in the depiction of the interactions between Dhṛtarāṣṭra and Saṃjaya could offer a more comprehensive perspective on their role in the epic and invites further study. As a pair, they introduce an element of emotionality and trust that allows the display and articulation of the inner conflicts of the old king, which are echoed and intensified by Saṃjaya's rebukes. However, it must also be noted that the epic narration employs elements of drama only selectively. Saṃjaya's rebukes resonate with the emotional dimensions of what the king is struggling with, while at the same time trying to delimit them in focusing mainly on failures and wrongdoing. Only rarely does Saṃjaya point the finger at the king's painful love for his son as the uncontrollable, bottomless force with which Dhṛtarāṣṭra struggles, and which is beyond Saṃjaya's comprehension. The pair and their interactions play a prominent role in the UdP, in which verbal exchanges and reports of them drive and constitute the action. The process of decision-making manifests the fateful entwinement of the characters and conflicting propositional attitudes. The UdP explores this entwinement in the elaborate narration of the thoughts, arguments and emotions expressed and exchanged by the characters in assembly halls or in private. It thus presents a critical transition in the epic narrative and a counterpoint to the following battle books that focus on the violence of war. In their various interactions, the old king and his companion both shape and mirror this transition. At the end of the UdP, their literary roles start to change in this transition as they take their new positions as interlocutors in the narrative frame of the battle books.

References

Primary text

Sukthankar, Vishnu Sitaram (ed.). (1933–66). *The Mahābhārata*. [19 vols.] Poona, India: Bhandarkar Oriental Research Institute.

Secondary texts

Bal, Mieke. (2009). *Narratology: Introduction to the Theory of the Narrative*. Toronto: University of Toronto Press.

Bremond, Claude. (1980). The logic of narrative possibilities. *New Literary History* 11(3): 387–411. doi.org/10.2307/468934.

Doležel, Lubomír. (1976). Narrative modalities. *Journal of Literary Semantics* 5: 5–14. doi.org/10.1515/jlse.1976.5.1.5.

Doležel, Lubomír. (1980). Truth and authenticity in narrative. *Poetics Today* 1(3): 7–25. doi.org/10.2307/1772407.

Doležel, Lubomír. (1988). Mimesis and possible worlds. *Poetics Today* 9(3): 475–96. doi.org/10.2307/1772728.

Dumézil, Georges. (1959). La transposition des dieux souverains mineurs en héros dans le Mahābhārata [The transposition of minor sovereign gods into heroes in the Mahābhārata]. *Indo-Iranian Journal* 3: 1–16. doi.org/10.1163/000000059792938062.

Genette, Gerard. (1998). *Die Erzählung* [*The Story*]. Paderborn, Germany: Fink.

Hämeen-Anttila, V. (2019). To make the short story long: The development of the frame-story structure in Sanskrit narrative; the Vedic and epic models. Doctoral dissertation, University of Helsinki.

Hara, Minoru. (1979). Śraddhāviveśa. *Indological Taurinensia* 7: 261–73.

Hara, Minoru. (2006). A note on the Sanskrit word 'andha'. *Indo-Iranian Journal* 49(3–4): 273–303. doi.org/10.1007/s10783-007-9004-7.

Hara, Minoru. (2007). Words for love in Sanskrit. *Rivista degli studi orientali* [*Journal of Oriental Studies*] [NS] 80(1–4): 81–106.

Held, G.J. (1935). *The Mahābhārata (An Ethnological Study)*. London: Kegan Paul.

Hill, Peter. (1993). Individual responsibility in the Mahābhārata. *South Asia: Journal of South Asian Studies* 16(2): 3–20. doi.org/10.1080/00856409308723180.

Hiltebeitel, Alf. (2001). *Rethinking the Mahābhārata: A Reader's Guide to the Education of the Dharma King*. Chicago, IL: Chicago University Press.

Hudson, E.T. (2007). Listen but do not grieve: Grief, paternity, and time in the laments of Dhṛtarāṣṭra. In S. Brodbeck and B. Black (eds), *Gender and Narrative in the Mahābhārata*, pp. 35–52. London: Routledge.

Hudson, E.T. (2013). *Disorienting Dharma: Ethics and the Aesthetics of Suffering in the Mahābhārata*. New York, NY: Oxford University Press. doi.org/10.1093/acprof:oso/9780199860760.001.0001.

Johnsen, G. (1966). Varuṇa and Dhṛtarāṣṭra. *Indo-Iranian Journal* 9(4): 245–65. doi.org/10.1163/000000066790086549.

Kuiper, F.B.J. (1979). *Varuṇa and Vidūṣaka: On the Origin of the Sanskrit Drama*. Amsterdam: North Holland Publishing.

Malinar, Angelika. (1996). *Rājavidyā: Das königliche Wissen um Herrschaft und Verzicht* [*Rājavidyā: The Royal Knowledge of Domination and Renunciation*]. Studien zur Bhagavadgītā [Studies in the Bhagavadgītā]. Wiesbaden, Germany: Harrassowitz.

Malinar, Angelika. (2005). 'Blindheit' und 'Sehen' in der Erzählung des Mahābhārata ['Blindness' and 'seeing' in the narrative of the Mahābhārata]. In A. Luther (ed.), *Odyssee-Rezeptionen* [*Odyssey Receptions*], pp. 73–94. Frankfurt, Germany: Verlag Antike.

Malinar, Angelika. (2007a). Arguments of a queen: Draupadī's views on kingship. In S. Brodbeck and B. Black (eds), *Gender and Narrative in the Mahābhārata*, pp. 79–96. London: Routledge. doi.org/10.1017/CBO9780511488290.

Malinar, Angelika. (2007b). *The Bhagavadgītā: Doctrines and Contexts*. Cambridge, UK: Cambridge University Press.

Malinar, Angelika. (2010). Schauspieler in ihren Rollen: Zur Deutung der sāttvika-bhāvas im Nāṭyaśāstra [Actors in their roles: On the interpretation of the sāttvika-bhāvas in the Nāṭyaśāstra]. In K. Steiner & H. Brückner (eds), *Indisches Theater: Text, Theorie, Praxis* [*Indian Theatre: Text, Theory, Practice*], pp. 7–26. Wiesbaden, Germany: Harrassowitz.

Malinar, Angelika. (2012). Duryodhana's truths: Kingship and divinity in Mahābhārata 5.60. In J.L. Brockington (ed.), *Battle, Bards and Brāhmins: Papers of the 13th World Sanskrit Conference. Volume II*, pp. 51–79. New Delhi: Motilal Banarsidass.

Malinar, Angelika. (2015). Nārada and the Pāṇḍavas: Regulating domestic life in the Mahābhārata. In A.A. Esposito, H. Oberlin, B.A. Viveka Rai and K.J. Steiner (eds), *'In Her Right Hand She Held a Silver Knife with Small Bells ...': Studies in Indian Culture and Literature*, pp. 157–76. Wiesbaden, Germany: Harrassowitz. doi.org/10.2307/j.ctvc5pg6c.19.

Malinar, Angelika. (2017). Narrating Sāṃkhya philosophy: Bhīṣma, Janaka and Pañcaśikha at Mahābhārata 12.211–12. *Journal of Indian Philosophy* 45(4): 609–49. doi.org/10.1007/s10781-017-9315-5.

Malinar, Angelika. (2022). Entwined decision-making in the Mahābhārata. In J. Koch, Helmar Kurz, Mrinal Pande and Annika Strauss (eds), *Practices of Transformation—Transformation of Practices: Essays in Honour of Helene Basu*, pp. 99–123. Münster, Germany: Olms.

Mangels, A. (1994). *Zur Erzähltechnik im Mahābhārata* [*On the Narrative Technique in the Mahābhārata*]. Hamburg, Germany: Kovač.

Minkowski, C.Z. (1989). Janamejaya's sattra and ritual structure. *Journal of the American Oriental Society* 109(3): 401–20. doi.org/10.2307/604141.

Pavel, Thomas G. (1980). Narrative domains. *Poetics Today* 1(4): 105–14. doi.org/10.2307/1771889.

Ronen, Ruth. (1990). Paradigm shift in plot models: An outline of the history of narratology. *Poetics Today* 11(4): 817–42.

Ryan, Marie-Laure. (1985). The modal structure of narrative universes. *Poetics Today* 6(4): 717–55. doi.org/10.2307/1771963.

Sharma, A. (2000). Of śūdras, sūtas, and ślokas: Why is the Mahābhārata preeminently in the anuṣṭubh metre?' *Indo-Iranian Journal* 43(3): 225–78. doi.org/10.1163/000000000124994047.

Todorov, Tzvetan. (1971). *Poétique de la prose* [*Poetics of Prose*]. Paris: Éditions du Seuil.

Tubb, Gary. (1991). Śāntarasa in the Mahābhārata. In A. Sharma (ed.), *Essays on the Mahābhārata*, pp. 171–203. Leiden, Netherlands: Brill.

van Buitenen, J.A.B. (trans. & ed.). (1978). *The Mahābhārata. Volume 3, Book 4: The Book of Virāṭa. Book 5: The Book of the Effort.* Chicago, IL: Chicago University Press. doi.org/10.7208/chicago/9780226223711.001.0001.

von Simson, Georg. (1984). The mythic background of the Mahābhārata. *Indological Taurinensia* 12: 191–223.

5

The Ambopākhyāna reconsidered: Reading Ambā's story as part of the Rāma Jāmadagnya myth cycle

Brian Collins

Abstract

In the Ambā episode of the *Mahābhārata*, Bhīṣma abducts the princess Ambā as a bride for his brother, then releases her when she asks to be returned to the man to whom she was already betrothed. When her betrothed refuses her, Ambā returns to Bhīṣma and asks him to marry her. Bhīṣma, sworn to celibacy, also refuses. Twice rejected and rightly blaming Bhīṣma for her predicament, Ambā seeks revenge—first, by asking for aid from Bhīṣma's former guru, Rāma Jāmadagnya, and then, when Rāma is unable to defeat him and goes into permanent exile, by committing suicide to be eventually reborn as the warrior Śikhaṇḍin to defeat Bhīṣma herself. In this chapter, I will reframe this narrative by reading it as part of the myth cycle of the mostly peripheral figure of Rāma Jāmadagnya, arguing that it serves as his 'exit myth' from the epic while also reinforcing important elements of his wider mythology, especially his relationship with his mother, Reṇukā, and his status in South Indian village cults as a servant of Devī.

Introduction

In the third volume of his never-to-be-completed translation of the *Mahābhārata* for the University of Chicago Press, J.A.B. van Buitenen suggests the Ambā episode of the Udyogaparvan (5.170–97) is evidence of the epic's mytho-genetic properties. He argues that the long and complicated story, which is unique to the epic, sprang from an epic author's lack of an explanation for Śikhaṇḍin's invulnerability to Bhīṣma. Demonstrating that all the individual elements in the story are found elsewhere in the *Mahābhārata*, he conjectures that storytellers cobbled together a lot of unrelated elements to provide an explanation:

> The point I am trying to make ... is that within a half a millennium of the composition of the text, a minor element ... could create a new legend, an instant tradition, which is acceptable not only because it is entirely epigonic in character, drawing on materials already there, but also because it is so utterly appropriate: the great Bhīṣma, fearfully famed for his abjuration of women, in the end finds his undoing at the hand of one of them, whom he had cheated out of her rightful marriage. It has no precursors, and to my knowledge no successor. This last battle of Rāma is not part of his later biography as an *avatāra* of Viṣṇu. (van Buitenen 1978: 178)

Van Buitenen's analysis of the myth is plausible, if dismissive (he finds it 'ridiculous' and has quite a bit of fun imagining how the mythmakers came up with such an outlandish story). But it is not exhaustive, as shown in subsequent studies by Vishwa Adluri, Wendy Doniger, Alf Hiltebeitel, Veena R. Howard and Stephanie W. Jamison. These studies have focused on issues of *dharma*, gender, Vedic ritual, the larger *Mahābhārata* narrative and the elements of Śaivism and Śaktism in the story.

There are valuable insights to be gained from all these approaches, but in this chapter, I will do something different and attempt to reframe the Ambā episode as part of the myth cycle of Rāma Jāmadagnya, the warrior sage to whom Ambā appeals for help and who duels with his former pupil Bhīṣma on her behalf. Rāma Jāmadagnya, like Ambā-Śikhaṇḍin, is a creature of the epic, with no narratives preceding his appearance in the *Mahābhārata*.[1] But,

1 Making an argument about him that resembles van Buitenen's analysis of Ambā, Robert Goldman describes all the epic myths of Bhārgava Brahmins (of which Rāma Jāmadagnya is the most famous) as 'metamyths'. He concludes that the Rāma Jāmadagnya cycle, which he calls 'a pastiche of Bhārgava motifs and themes', is 'a deliberate creation of the epic bards intended to incorporate, in one complex, almost every highly charged feature of the [Bhārgava] cycle' (Goldman 1977: 135–36).

unlike Ambā-Śikhaṇḍin, Rāma Jāmadagnya is subsequently elevated to the status of an *avatāra* and starts to appear in many purāṇas and temple legends beginning in the ninth century CE. With varying degrees of emphasis, narratives of his two most notable mythic exploits—decapitating his mother, Reṇukā, and annihilating 'thrice-seven' generations of *kṣatriya*s—are repeated throughout this literature, in which he is frequently known as Paraśurāma ('Rāma with the Axe')—a name that does not appear in the *Mahābhārata*.

But his defeat in a duel with Bhīṣma in the Ambopākhyāna is one of the two episodes that rarely travels beyond the boundaries of the epic (the other is his training and subsequent cursing of Karṇa). In light of this fact, I decided to leave both these episodes out of my overall analysis of the myth cycle as I worked on turning my dissertation on Rāma Jāmadagnya into a book (Collins 2020a). Having reconsidered that decision, I will argue two things in this chapter: first, that we should read the Ambā story as an 'exit myth' of Rāma Jāmadagnya, about which I will say more below; and second, that Ambā's relationship with Rāma Jāmadagnya sets up a connection to Devī that develops further in his later mythology. But first, we need a brief telling of Ambā's story.

The Ambā story

At the end of the Udyogaparvan, as the great battle between the Pāṇḍavas and the Kauravas draws near, the warrior guru Bhīṣma tells the eldest Kaurava, Duryodhana, that he will not take up arms against Śikhaṇḍin, a prince fighting on the side of the Pāṇḍavas. Alarmed, Duryodhana asks him why. Bhīṣma responds by retelling a story that has already been recounted in *Mbh* 1.96 by Vaiśaṃpāyana. It begins with Bhīṣma having renounced the throne and taken a vow of celibacy so that his father, Śaṃtanu, can marry the much younger Satyavatī with the promise that her sons will inherit his kingdom. After siring two sons named Citrāngada and Vicitravīrya with Satyavatī, Śaṃtanu dies and Citrāngada takes the throne. But when Citrāngada is killed in a duel with a *gandharva* (also named Citrāngada), his brother, Vicitravīrya, is still too young to rule, so Bhīṣma becomes the regent.

When Vicitravīrya comes of age, Bhīṣma decides to attend the *svayaṃvara* of the three princesses Ambā, Ambikā and Ambālikā and kidnap them as brides for his brother. Ambikā and Ambālikā happily agree to the marriage, but their older sister, Ambā, tells Bhīṣma that she has already chosen a husband

and asks to be allowed to return to him. Bhīṣma agrees and lets her go back to her intended husband, King Śālva, who happens to be the same man whom Bhīṣma humiliated by killing his charioteer and defeating him in battle in front of a huge crowd at the sisters' *svayaṃvara*. This is where the narrative in 1.96 ends, so now Bhīṣma tells Duryodhana the rest of the story.

Unsurprisingly, Ambā's intended husband refuses to take her back after she has been in the house of the man who shamed him so publicly and spectacularly, so he orders her to return to Bhīṣma. Ambā correctly sees the futility of this course of action and, after blaming Śālva, her father and herself for her misfortune, she settles on Bhīṣma as the root cause of her situation and goes to a hermitage to practise asceticism in hopes of finding a way to avenge herself on him. Her maternal uncle Hotravāhana then suggests that she visit Rāma Jāmadagnya.

She first meets his disciple Akṛtavraṇa, who sees that she is troubled and asks her why. She tells him her story and, making reference to the paradigmatic Vedic cattle raid, expresses her wish to see Rāma Jāmadagnya 'kill Bhīṣma as Indra killed Vṛtra' (*Mbh*, 5.176.42). Soon, Rāma Jāmadagnya arrives on the scene and, on hearing her story, he regretfully informs her that he cannot fight Bhīṣma, recalling a promise he made after the annihilation of the *kṣatriya*s that he can only take up arms again at the request of brahmin women. At this point, Akṛtavraṇa reminds Rāma Jāmadagnya of another pledge he made after he wiped out the *kṣatriya*s:

> After you defeated all the kṣatriyas you promised the brahmins: 'Whenever a brahmin, a kṣatriya, a vaiśya, or a śudra becomes a brahmin-hater, I will kill him in battle. As a shelter for frightened ones coming for refuge, afraid for their lives, I can never abandon them as long as I live. If an arrogant man defeats the entire kṣatriya class in battle, I will kill him.' (*Mbh*, 5.177.14–15)

The pledge to kill the 'arrogant man' who does what he himself has done and wipes out the *kṣatriya*s is certainly a strange promise and it does not occur in either of the epic's versions of Rāma Jāmadagnya's 21-fold annihilation of the *kṣatriya*s. The meaning of the phrase could be that even the man strong enough to wipe out all the *kṣatriya*s would not be strong enough to defeat him. Whatever the case, Rāma Jāmadagnya remembers making the promise even if we do not and agrees to try to persuade Bhīṣma to do the honourable thing and, failing that, to kill him.

The next day, Rāma Jāmadagnya goes to see Bhīṣma and, speaking as his guru, orders him to take Ambā back. When that fails, the two agree to meet on the field of battle. After he duels with Bhīṣma for several days, Rāma Jāmadagnya's ancestors appear and convince him to abandon the fight and return, defeated, to his hermitage on Mount Mahendra. After the duel ends with no relief for Ambā, she takes matters into her own hands and starts to practise austerities in hopes of being granted a boon by the gods. Finally, Śiva appears and grants Ambā the boon of being born a man in her next life, at which point she immolates herself in the sacrificial fire.

But in her next life, she is born as a princess named Śikhaṇḍinī, although her parents dress and raise her as a boy. After Śikhaṇḍinī's wedding, the princess whom she marries learns the truth and word is sent back to her father, Hiraṇyavarman. Furious, Hiraṇyavarman threatens to dethrone Śikhaṇḍinī's father if this rumour is proved true. To save her father's kingdom, Śikhaṇḍinī finds a *yakṣa* and convinces him to temporarily trade genital organs with her, so that when the brahmin sent by Hiraṇyavarman comes to inspect his 'son-in-law', he finds a man, 'Śikhaṇḍin'.

Meanwhile, Kubera, king of the *yakṣa*s, finds out what the *yakṣa* has done and curses him to remain a woman (and Śikhaṇḍin to remain a man) until Śikhaṇḍin's death. Therefore, Bhīṣma explains to Duryodhana, even though the Pāṇḍava warrior Śikhaṇḍin has the body of a man, Bhīṣma still considers him a woman whom *dharma* forbids him to attack. Ultimately, this will doom Bhīṣma when the Pāṇḍavas, using Śikhaṇḍin as a human shield, line up behind him and fill Bhīṣma with arrows until he can fight no more.

The Rāma Jāmadagnya–Bhīṣma connection

Elsewhere, I have written about the thematic connection of Rāma Jāmadagnya, Droṇa and Aśvatthāman (Collins 2021b). Based on Alexis Sanderson's (2009) epigraphical findings that Indian kings who had converted to Vaiṣṇavism and Śaivism between the fifth and the eighth centuries commonly proclaimed their commitment to upholding the *varṇa* system and Johannes Bronkhorst's (2016) argument that Sanskrit mythology provided a model for a new post-Vedic *kṣatriya*–brahmin relationship, I argued that brahmins who felt threatened by the spread of Buddhism and the decline of Vedic ritual and who wanted to protect their privilege and distinctive identity could have done so by embracing narratives of such powerful and dangerous brahmin warriors.

These myths of enraged brahmins, usually connected to Śiva, who unleash terrible destruction before being severely punished for it, would have served as warnings to kings not to forget the potentially destructive power of brahmins' command over the sacrifice. And, through the element of exile or punishment, they would have also reassured the brahmins themselves that they still regarded violence as inherently impure. The connection between Rāma Jāmadagnya and Aśvatthāman specifically is especially clear on this last point since both figures are later recognised as *cirañjīvins* whose immortality is sometimes imagined to be a punishment for their violent actions.

There are reasons to argue for a similarly clear connection between Rāma Jāmadagnya and Bhīṣma (apart from the fact that both figures were portrayed by the Burkinabé actor and *griot* Sotigui Kouyaté in the Peter Brook production). First, both have a 'mother' who is not a mother and in both stories this figure is named Satyavatī. In Rāma Jāmadagnya's story, Satyavatī is a princess married to the Bhārgava sage Ṛcika. After the marriage, she asks his clan patriarch, Bhṛgu, to help her give birth to an ideal brahmin son and to help her mother give birth to an ideal *kṣatriya* son. Bhṛgu agrees and infuses a rice pudding with *brahman* for Satyavatī to consume and infuses another with *kṣatra* for her mother.

But the women accidentally mix up the ritual and Bhṛgu predicts that Satyavatī will give birth to a brahmin who will act like a *kṣatriya* and her mother will give birth to a *kṣatriya* who will act like a brahmin. Horrified, Satyavatī convinces Bhṛgu to defer the prediction for one generation, effectively rejecting the child she is now carrying. As a result, she gives birth to the pure brahmin Jamadagni. Jamadagni in turn sires the *kṣatriya*-natured brahmin Rāma Jāmadagnya, who *should* have been Satyavatī's son.

In Bhīṣma's story, Satyavatī is the younger woman who agreed to marry his father if Bhīṣma would renounce the throne and promise never to marry or have children. Bhīṣma's mother is the goddess Gangā, but it is on Satyavatī's behalf that he kidnaps Ambā, Ambikā and Ambalikā as brides for his half-brother. Later, balking at Satyavatī's request that he break the vow he made for her and do it himself, he has Vyāsa impregnate his widowed sisters-in-law Ambikā and Ambālikā. Perhaps significantly, Bhīṣma justifies his plan of having a brahmin ascetic sire sons with *kṣatriya* widows by telling Satyavatī the story of Rāma Jāmadagnya having done the same thing after he killed 21 generations of *kṣatriya* men.

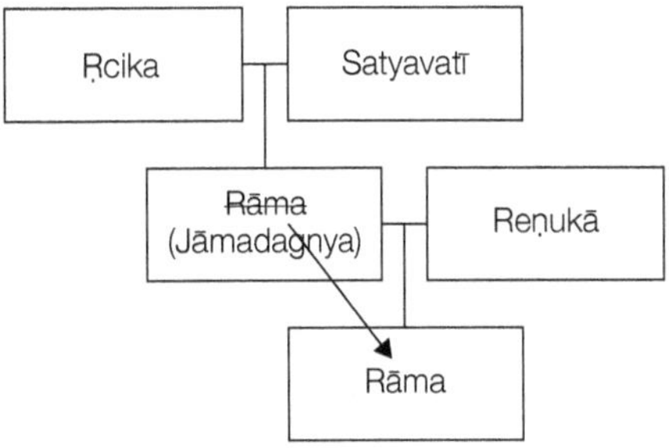

Figure 5.1 The descent of Rāma Jāmadagnya
Source: Author's depiction.

Another connection is the fact that both Rāma Jāmadagnya and Bhīṣma are notably unmarried and childless—although this is explained only in Bhīṣma's case—and each has some power over death. In later traditions, Rāma Jāmadagnya is a *cirañjīvin*. He is not described this way within the *Mahābhārata*, but he is at the very least a figure from a distant former age who appears to still be alive at the end of the epic. For his part, Bhīṣma has the boon of choosing the moment of his death, which he received from his father after making his terrible vow.

The duel with Bhīṣma as an 'exit myth'

As I have argued elsewhere, in the post-epic tradition, Rāma Jāmadagnya is unique in his dual identification as both *avatāra* and *cirañjīvin*. He was probably first recognised as an *avatāra* by the Pāñcarātrins not long after the composition of the *Sanatkumāra Saṃhitā* around 800 CE (see Collins 2020b: 169–77). His identification as a *cirañjīvin* is harder to trace, but I would argue that his inclusion in the group (probably around the same time, but independently) is a result of his thematic connection to Aśvatthāman, the epic's other brahmin warrior who perpetrates terrible and disproportionate acts of violence to avenge his father's death. But in the epic where he originates, Rāma Jāmadagnya is best understood as a proto-*cirañjīvin* whose presence links the sacrificial battle at Kurukṣetra to another mythical annihilation of *kṣatriya*s—namely, the one he himself perpetrated in a previous age when he killed 21 generations of them in a rapidly escalating feud that began with a cattle raid.

			Matsya				
			Kurma				
			Varāha				
			Vāmana				
			Narasiṃha				
Aśvatthāman	*Bali*	*Hanumān*	***Rāma Jāmadagnya***	*Kṛpa*	*Vibhīṣaṇa*	*Vyāsa*	*Mārkaṇḍeya*
			Rāma				
			Kṛṣṇa				
			Buddha				
			Kalki				

Figure 5.2 Rāma Jāmadagnya at the intersection of *cirañjīvins* (horizontal in italics) and avatāras (vertical in bold)

Source: Author's depiction.

Other than his annihilation of the *kṣatriyas*, which takes place well outside the time frame of the main events of the epic, Rāma Jāmadagnya is involved in only one battle in the *Mahābhārata*: the spectacular duel with his former pupil Bhīṣma that ends with the brahmin warrior withdrawing after days of pitched combat. The duel with Bhīṣma is what I would call one of the 'exit myths' of Rāma Jāmadagnya—an episode in which he enters the main narrative just long enough to be written out of it so that his absence requires no further explanation.

In the regional purāṇas, dramas and temple legends focused on Rāma Dāśarathi, where most of Rāma Jāmadagnya's exit myths are found, the necessity of his exit is clear: there cannot be two *avatāras* at the same time, much less two *avatāras* named 'Rāma'. The *Viṣṇudharmottara Purāṇa*, composed by Pāñcarātrins in Kashmir between 600 and 1000 CE, is one of the first major purāṇic accounts of the myth to appear after the redaction of the *Mahābhārata*. In it, Śiva tells Rāma Jāmadagnya twice that he will have to give up his *tejas* and lay down his arms (except to protect women and brahmins) when he meets Rāma Dāśarathi (see Collins 2020b: 174–75). The oft-told story of Rāma Dāśarathi establishing his superiority over Rāma Jāmadagnya and forcing him into permanent exile appears in a wide array of textual traditions, including both Vālmīki's and Kṛttivāsa's *Rāmāyaṇas*, the Oriya *Jagamohana Rāmāyaṇ*, the Marāṭhī *Śrī Rāmavijaya*, the *Madhava*

Kandali Rāmāyaṇa, the *Brāhmāṇḍa Purāṇa* and Bhavabhūti's eighth-century drama the *Mahāvīracarita* (see Nagar 2006: 40–100); Choudhary 2010: 142–48).

For evidence that we should read Bhīṣma's defeat of Rāma Jāmadagnya as a similar denigration of the latter, let us look at how Bhīṣma responds to his guru's command to take back Ambā. After initially greeting Rāma Jāmadagnya with joy and reverence, Bhīṣma insults him, saying that since he does not act like a guru, he will not obey him as a guru. Finally, Bhīṣma challenges Rāma Jāmadagnya with a spiteful and boastful rant that throws his violent past back in his face:

> Go and return to Kurukṣetra, War-lover! I will meet you in battle there, strong-armed ascetic. There where you purified your father long ago, Rāma, I will kill and then purify you. Go quickly, war-crazed Rāma! I will dispel your legendary pride, you who call yourself a brahmin. You always boast in crowds, 'I single-handedly wiped out all the kṣatriyas in the world.' Listen to this: Back then, Bhīṣma was not yet born. A kṣatriya that is my equal would have dispelled your pride and lust for battle. But now I, strong-armed Bhīṣma, the destroyer of enemies, *have* been born. And I will take away your pride, Rāma, do not doubt it. (*Mbh*, 5.178.33–38)

Lynn Thomas also sees the duel between Bhīṣma and Rāma Jāmadagnya as an analogue of Rāma Jāmadagnya's duel with Rāma Dāśarathī in the *Rāmāyaṇa*. In both stories, she notes, 'the battle is witnessed by representatives of most of the world's inhabitants (gods, *ṛṣi*s, etc.), and the cosmic significance of this not uncommon phenomenon is emphasised by phrases which suggest the fate of the world is in the balance' (Thomas 1996: 69).[2]

The results of Rāma Jāmadagnya's battles with Rāma and Bhīṣma are not defeat so much as an acknowledgement that his time has passed. Explaining why he was unable to defeat Bhīṣma as promised, Rāma Jāmadagnya regretfully explains to Ambā: 'This is the limit of my power. This is the limit of my strength' (*Mbh*, 5.187.3). In the later literature, beginning with the *Rāmāyaṇa* and the *Viṣṇudharmottara Purāṇa*, this same idea of limitation is transformed into a sense—reflective of his dual identity as an *avatāra* and a *cirañjīvin*—that his power and relevance on Earth are less long-lived than is he.

2 See also Choudhary (2010: 110).

While the *Mahābhārata* does not mention him transferring his mantle to the next *avatāra*, as he does with Rāma Dāśarathī, Rāma Jāmadagnya's excoriation and humiliating defeat at the hands of his former pupil serve to convey the same message. There are also obvious references throughout the text to see this battle as the end of his career. For his duel with Bhīṣma, Rāma Jāmadagnya returns to the site where he made five lakes of *kṣatriya* blood in a prior age. And, after two days of battle, his ancestors approach Rāma Jāmadagnya and tell him to lay down his bow (presumably forever) and practise austerities. They also address him twice as *vatsa* ('calf')—a term I will have more to say about later (*Mbh*, 5.186.10–15).

After Rāma Jāmadagnya's ineffectual efforts to intervene in what I will argue below is a transformation of a traditional cattle-raiding story—which is especially humiliating given that an earlier cattle theft had occasioned his total annihilation of the *kṣatriya*s—the story resumes and Ambā, now reborn as Śikhaṇḍin, does what Rāma Jāmadagnya (of all people) could not do, and exacts her bloody revenge. What the Amba-Upakhyāna gives us is a cattle-theft story that serves as an ignominious exit for the brahmin warrior just as the theft of his father's calf serves as his violent but grand entrance—first, as tragedy, then as farce.

Ambā's abduction and the theft of Jamadagni's calf

In the cases in which his exit myth centres on a battle of the two Rāmas, the winner is elevated and the loser is displaced. But the story of his duel with Bhīṣma does something other than just displace Rāma Jāmadagnya. It plays with one of the elements of his main myth: the cattle raid. The Ambā story in the Udyogaparvan, I argue, can best be understood as a transformation of the same Indo-European cattle-raid mytheme employed to such dramatic effect at the close of the previous book, the Virāṭaparvan, when the Pāṇḍavas end their period of exile and accompany the first raising of Arjuna's standard in 13 years with a show of force to repel an attempted raid by the Kauravas on the cattle of Matsya.

Ruth Katz Arabagian has observed that the 'predominant subject of Indo-European heroic literature is successful warfare for the winning of wealth and kingdom' and that it is 'most often realized in one of two guises: as a theme of cattle raiding, or a theme of bride stealing' (1984: 107). The Ambā story presents a superimposition of these two themes that is rooted in Vedic ritual while also serving as an inversion of the cattle raid that began Rāma Jāmadagnya's true entrance into the epic (the attempted theft of his family's wishing cow by King Kārtavīrya, which sets his annihilation of the *kṣatriya*s into motion), creating two bookends that contain his epic career.

Returning to Bhīṣma's abduction of Ambā and her sisters, an obvious question arises: why does Bhīṣma kidnap three brides for his younger brother? The easiest way to explain this is to take the story of the bride-napping in 1.96 as an earlier narrative than the longer and more elaborate Ambā story in the Udyogaparvan. If we ignore for a moment Citrāngada's strange and senseless death in 1.95 at the hands of a *gandharva* who coincidentally bears his name (and who promptly ascends to Heaven and disappears from the narrative after the deed is done), we have three brides for three brothers.

From there, we can imagine a version of this story in which Bhīṣma, Citrāngada and Vicitravīrya are the oldest, middle and youngest sons of Śaṃtanu, respectively—all three in need of wives to carry on their line. Quite literally, the names Ambā, Ambikā and Ambālikā are progressively diminutive forms of the word for 'mother' (helpfully equated by Hiltebeitel [2011a: 374] to the Spanish, 'Mama, Mamita, Mamacita'). Their names (which also have Vedic ritual significance, as Jamison and Hiltebeitel have pointed out) suggest that Ambā is meant to 'mother' children for the oldest brother (Bhīṣma), Ambikā for the middle brother (Citrāngada) and Ambālikā for the youngest brother (Vicitravīrya). But of course, Bhīṣma cannot marry, so Ambā is left out.

There are two details in the text that go along with the 'three brides for three brothers' model. First, the next generation of Kurus consists also of three brothers: Dhṛtarāṣṭra, Pāṇḍu and Vidura. But since Ambā is missing, the text introduces an unnamed slave girl who has sex with Vyāsa when he comes to impregnate Ambikā a second time—something he does not attempt with Ambālikā for reasons that are never explained. Second, it is noteworthy that the only suitor we hear about Bhīṣma defeating is Śālva, the intended husband of Ambā, implying that he specifically challenged and defeated him to win her.

To be clear, I am not arguing that some lost earlier recension of the *Mahābhārata* story had Bhīṣma kidnapping three brides for himself and his two brothers. I am suggesting, rather, that the epic narrative intentionally departs from the expectations set up by the numerical structure of its mythic episodes. This creation of tension by playing against structure is analogous to the way that a film might deliberately play against the expectations set up by its genre, as in Disney's *Frozen* (2013)—a fairytale in which the princess does not need the prince to save her, which plays against expectations set up in virtually every Disney princess movie since *Snow White and the Seven Dwarfs* (1937).

Hiltebeitel has made a convincing case that Vyāsa's impregnation of the two queens and the slave woman is a mythic representation of the Vedic Aśvamedha (2011b: 269–75). I, too, see a ritual context in this myth, but there is also a 'puzzle' (to use Hiltebeitel's term) that operates at the level of the narrative itself. If I were to say, 'I am now going to tell you a story about three princes, three princesses, and their three sons', you would expect to hear something more like the story represented in Figure 5.3 than the confusing patriline in Figure 5.4. In the Ambā episode, the text sets up an expected narrative of three brides for three brothers from which it then departs using a series of unexpected plot twists—some of them (like the death of Citrāngada) a bit unconvincing.

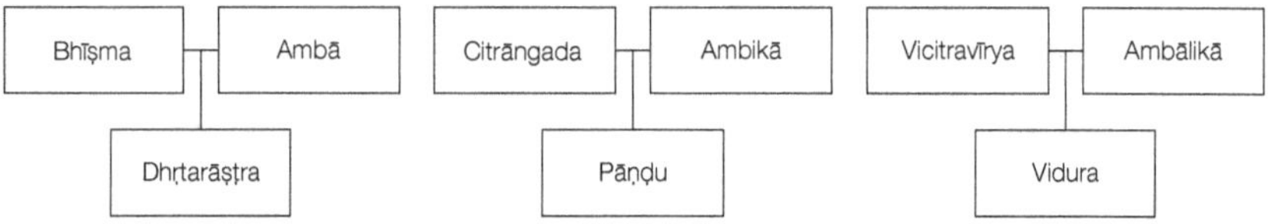

Figure 5.3 The expected union of the three sons of Śaṃtanu and the three Kāśi princesses with their expected offspring

Source: Author's depiction.

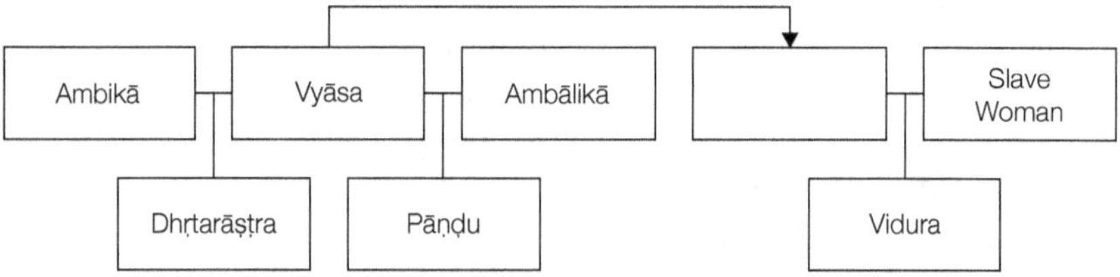

Figure 5.4 The epic's account of the descents of Dhṛtarāṣṭra, Pāṇḍu and Vidura

Source: Author's depiction.

All this is to say that the epic establishes a deep connection between Ambā and Bhīṣma at the level of structure—a structure that is made more intelligible to the reader the more the narrative plays against it. This structural connection is reinforced at the (much more complex) narrative level: after carefully analysing and recapitulating the story thus far for the audience, Ambā places the ultimate responsibility for her predicament on Bhīṣma in an inner monologue in 5.173.1–10. She then undertakes a sacred vow to become the only being in the world who can defeat him in battle, in 5.188.18, explicitly saying 'For the death of Bhīṣma!' before stepping into the fire.

Now, let us turn to the cattle-raid element in the story of Rāma Jāmadagnya, the most detailed versions of which are found in 3.115–17 and 12.49. One day a king of the Haihaya clan named Arjuna Kārtavīrya, who has received 1,000 arms as a boon from the gods, comes to Jamadagni's hermitage while on a hunting trip and either he steals (in the Araṇyakaparvan) or his wicked sons steal (in the Śāntiparvan) the calf of the milking cow from the hermitage. Rāma Jāmadagnya, who has been away on a journey, returns to find the calf missing and goes after Kārtavīrya to avenge the theft, cutting off Kārtavīrya's thousand arms with his arrows before finally killing him. But while he is still away and the hermitage is unprotected, the slain king's sons sneak in and kill Jamadagni in retaliation. When Rāma Jāmadagnya returns to find his father dead, he swears revenge on all *kṣatriya*s, vowing to wipe them out 21 times over. In fulfillment of his vow, he kills 21 generations of *kṣatriya*s and fills five lakes with their blood at the site that will later become Kurukṣetra, before he makes a sacrifice in which he gives away the earth that he has conquered and goes into exile to spend the rest of his days in meditation.

Significantly, in both epic versions of Rāma Jāmadagnya's extermination of the *kṣatriya*s, the event that starts the conflict is the theft of a calf (*vatsa*) from his father's hermitage. Also in both versions, the slaying of his father happens when Rāma Jāmadagnya is out retrieving that calf. While there are differences concerning who is responsible for the theft in the two versions of the story, both agree that the calf was the stolen animal and that Jamadagni's death happened while Rāma Jāmadagnya was out retrieving that calf. In the Ambā story, I argue, the stolen calf reappears in the form of Ambā, and she is once again calling for the help of Rāma Jāmadagnya.

Evidence of this identification appears throughout the text. First, Hotravāhana, the sage who sends Ambā to Rāma Jāmadagnya for help in defeating Bhīṣma, addresses her twice as *vatsa* ('calf') in 5.175, as does Akṛtravraṇa, once in 5.176. Second, when Śālva sends Ambā away in 5.172.22, he does so by telling her that he fears Bhīṣma and she is '*bhīṣmaparigrahaḥ*'. Van Buitenen translates this compound as 'Bhīṣma's chattel', taking it (correctly, I think) to mean that Śālva sees Ambā as Bhīṣma's spoils of war in the form of livestock, rather than simply as 'dependent on Bhīṣma', which the compound could also plausibly mean (1978: 498). Finally, as the result of a curse from Bhīṣma's mother during her austerities, Ambā is somehow spiritually bifurcated, with one part of her transformed into an ugly, twisted and crocodile-infested creek in Vatsabhūmi ('Calf-Land') before what is left of her is reborn as Śikhaṇḍin. The final splitting off of part of Ambā at Vatsabhūmi before she is reborn seems to suggest that there is nothing left of the stolen, wandering calf from the first part of the story in the warrior Śikhaṇḍin.

There is also an echo of Rāma Jāmadagnya's main myth in his failure to protect or avenge Ambā. When Kārtavīrya or his sons abduct the calf from Jamadagni's hermitage and Rāma Jāmadagnya takes her back, he is appropriating for himself the paradigmatic *kṣatriya* duty of protecting and raiding livestock. From then on, and especially in his massacre of the warrior class, he is himself more *kṣatriya* than brahmin. But when he fails to bring back the '*vatsa*'—that is, Ambā—he not only fails to uphold his *kṣatriya*-like vows to protect all who come to him for help. He also fails in a task that the text has prompted us to regard as a variant form of cattle-raiding: the paradigmatic activity of the Indo-European warrior class.

The destructive goddess, the rejected Dakṣiṇā and the demonic Kṛtyā

Noting that the only two hymns addressed to Durgā in the *Mahābhārata* are found on either side of Ambā's story in the Udyogaparvan, Veena Howard argues that the text goes to some lengths to identify Ambā (which is another name for Durgā) with the terrifying Mother Goddess:

> Even though the traditional conventions of battle prohibit women from participating in battle, I focus on the resemblance of Ambā's acts with those of Mother Durgā, who symbolises the feminist value of defying patriarchal structure. No one's consort, Durgā depends on no male figure. She singly embodies raw power and does not hesitate to decapitate demons ... Ambā's rage, intense austerities, her autonomy, and single-minded focus to kill Bhīṣma evoke Goddess Durgā, who defeats demons impossible even for gods. (Howard 2019: 240)

Asko Parpola has argued against the consensus based on archaeology and art history that Durgā's presence in India does not pre-date the arrival of the Kuṣāṇas from Afghanistan around the middle of the first millennium CE. He concludes instead that the Indus Valley civilisation worshiped a Durgā-like goddess connected to a lion or tiger who presided over fertility, death and war and underwent a sacred marriage at the New Year festival that involved the death and rebirth of the bridegroom in the form of a bull or a human male sacrificial victim. He also argues for the continuity of this practice in the Vrātya rituals associated with Indo-European-language speakers coming into South Asia from southern Central Asia between 2000 and 1700 BCE (Parpola 2015: 255).

The Vrātyas were a martial band of priests who supposedly conducted their violent sacrifices in the middle of the forest and the dead of winter and who kept the sacrificial gift for themselves. Before Jan Heesterman's important and influential re-evaluation of the Vrātyas in 1962, the prevailing scholarly opinion was that they were a non-Vedic group of antinomian ascetics and that their central ritual, the Vrātyastoma, was a conversion rite that allowed them to purify themselves and enter the brahmin fold (see Collins 2010: 63). But Heesterman argued convincingly that the rites of the Vrātyas were in fact a central part of the ancient Vedic sacrifice that was gradually marginalised as the Vrātyas themselves were demonised by brahmin priests. Their exclusion, according to Heesterman (1962: 19), was a result of 'a shift of ritual thinking in which the ritual universe and its brahmin guardians came to be viewed as pure as against the impure profane world'.

In other words, certain elements of the purāṇic Durgā myth could have been brought to South Asia by the Kuṣāṇas, but they were absorbed into a world view that already had traces of an older version of Durgā in the deep layers of its ritual system.[3] I propose two places in the Vedic literature where we might look for signs of this proto-Durgā, both of which are thematically connected to the figure of the rejected wife, which Ambā surely is.

3 The way that an imported Durgā might be reshaped through association with the traces of her predecessor is a process that must be thought out. One imperfect analogue can be found in language, in which common word stocks undergo transformation and differentiation through the process of linguistic change before being reunited with their distant cognates by the movement of speakers. I will take two examples from children's literature as that is where one is apt to find alliteration and punning. The first example is the 'Ghost Host' in the Haunted Mansion ride at the Disneyland theme park. The idea behind the name 'Ghost Host' is to play on the resemblance of the two words and the differences in meaning to create a new and evocative phrase. The second example is *The Hostile Hospital*, the title of a children's book by Daniel Handler, who writes under the pen-name Lemony Snicket. In both cases, the alliterative or punning phrases are intended as juxtapositions of meaning, bringing two semantic fields into a state of overlap. In reality, we could also say that all this language play is contained within the single semantic field (greatly expanded through generations of language change) of the *PIE word *ghosti-s*, which gives us the words *host*, *hostile*, *hospital* and (debatably) *ghost*.

The first is the Kṛtyā, a demoness described in *Ṛg Veda* 10.85, 'The Marriage of Sūryā', which is still commonly recited at weddings (see Collins 2014: 221–23; 2020a: 42). Verses 28–30 describe the Kṛtyā's origin in the blood that stains the bride's gown on the night of her defloration:

> 28. The purple and red appears, a Kṛtyā; the stain is imprinted [on the gown]. The wife's family prospers and her husband is bound in the bonds.
>
> 29. Throw away the gown, and distribute money to the priests. [The stained gown] becomes a Kṛtyā walking on two feet and, like the wife, it draws close to the husband.
>
> 30. The [husband's] body becomes ugly and pale if the husband covers his penis with his wife's robe out of his evil desire.[4]

The Kṛtyā, born of blood and sex, is the double of the wife created when she loses her virginity and, one might add, her autonomy. It is the power of the feminine, bringing misery to the husband's family and prosperity to the wife's household. The hymn tells us that the woman can be absorbed safely into her new family only if the bloody gown/Kṛtyā is disposed of and the officiating priests are paid off. If not dealt with properly, it will become a kind of succubus.

Verse 28 uses the word *bandha*, which is the same word used for the fetters that bind the victim to the sacrificial post, when describing the husband being placed in bonds. And verse 30 tells us that if the husband should reciprocate and succumb to evil desires by penetrating the gown sexually, the Kṛtyā will possess him and make him deformed and pale. A few verses later, the hymn returns to the bloody gown:

> 34. [The gown] burns, it bites, and it has claws, as dangerous as poison to eat. Only the priest who knows the Sūrya hymn can receive the bridal gown.
>
> 35. Butchering, carving, and dividing it into pieces, behold the forms of Sūryā, which only the priest can purify.[5]

4 Based on a translation in Jamison and Brereton (2014: 1524).

5 Based on a translation in ibid.

In verse 34, the Kṛtyā takes a demonic and dangerous form that only a priest who knows this verse can handle. The final verse has the priest cutting up the Kṛtyā, using the words *āśasana*, *viśasana* and *adhivikartana*—the last term usually applied especially to an animal carcass.

We have in this story a rough outline of the paradigmatic Devī myth of India in which the male gods temporarily cede their power to a domesticated goddess like Pārvatī so that she can kill a powerful demon. In the *Mārkaṇḍeya Purāṇa*, where, as Raj Balkaran (2018, 2020) has noted, there is a deep connection between Devī and Sūrya, the demon she slays and whose blood she drinks is Raktabīja ('Blood-Seed'). This Devī-Sūrya connection could explain why the Kṛtyā passage is about the transformation of Sūrya's feminine counterpart, Sūryā, 'the archetypal bride' of the *Ṛg Veda* (Jamison and Brereton 2014: 52). One other provocative piece of evidence is the use of '*kṛtya*' to denote a fierce goddess who receives blood sacrifices, but the usage is only attested in Sanskrit lexicons (Monier-Williams 2009: 303).

In this argument (which I have made before, but with less confidence), I am taking a cue from the recent work of David Gordon White, examining a range of Sanskrit, Celtic and Arthurian myths sometimes identified as forms of an Indo-European mytheme in which a hero must win and possess the goddess of sovereignty (Śrī in Sanskrit, Flaith in Old Irish) if he wants to rule the land. But White identifies the core of the story behind them all as something much older: an encounter between a hero and a demon at the grove or pond for which it serves as a *genius loci* (2020: 159–61). More generally, White argues that behind the rites, gods and goddesses of nearly all official religions (Vedic religion included) is something better understood as 'daemonology'—the term he gives to the various approaches ordinary people have taken to deal with the problems of everyday life and the spirit beings who cause them, cure them, or both (see Collins 2021a).

The second possible proto-Durgā appears in the Vedic Rājasūya sacrifice: a wife of a certain kind is explicitly connected to the ceremonial cattle raid that is part of the ritual. The figure of the Parivṛktī, or 'avoided wife', represented by Indra's consort Indrāṇi, is considered essential to the cattle raid's success and is 'homologized to the rejected Dakṣiṇā [or gifted cow]' (Jamison 1996: 107). To interpret this part of the rite, Jamison turns to the *Kāṭhika Saṃhitā*, in which the gods reject the demons' gift of a cow and send her back to the demons, where she becomes a hyena and annihilates them:

> In this set of stories ... a Dakṣiṇā [that is, a cow given as a priestly gift] is rejected by the intended recipients. Refusing a gift without cause is a terrible insult and leads to hostile relations ... and the rejected cow is transformed into a fierce, wild female beast—lioness, tigress, or female hyena depending on the text—who ravages the herd. (Jamison 1996: 106; see also Jamison 1991: 93–96)

The violent and uncontrollable nature of the rejected cow or wife and the danger she presents have a flipside in that she can also be used as a weapon against others, guaranteeing the cattle raid's success. Likewise, when she is rejected both by her intended husband and by the celibate Bhīṣma who had sent her to him, Ambā functions much like the dangerous figure of the Parivṛktī. The authors of the epic appear to be making a triple identification of the rejected wife who is also a cow and the rejected cow that becomes the demon-destroying hyena when they have Ambā transform herself into the warrior Śikhaṇḍin—a human weapon that decisively turns the tide of battle against the Kauravas. It is only because of Śikhaṇḍin, literally leading the Pāṇḍava company as a human shield, that Arjuna can successfully defeat the practically invincible Bhīṣma on the field of battle.

I contend that the rejected Dakṣiṇā also plays a role in the post-epic stories of Rāma Jāmadagnya in the form of the Kāmadhenu (or 'Wishing Cow'), who takes the place of Jamadagni's calf in the purāṇic literature. This transposition is likely a result of influence from the myth of Viśvāmitra, who in *Mbh* 13.56.12 is explicitly named as the *kṣatriya* with a brahmin nature born to Satyavatī's mother (that is, Rāma Jāmadagnya's uncle and mirror image). His rivalry with the pure brahmin Vasiṣṭha is at the centre of the Viśvāmitra mythos and at the centre of this rivalry is the Kāmadhenu.

It begins when the king Viśvāmitra visits Vasiṣṭha's hermitage on a hunting trip and is amazed to find that a forest-dwelling ascetic can feed his entire royal retinue with a magic cow—here, referred to with the proper name Nandinī. In this story, narrated by a *gandharva*, Viśvāmitra tries to buy the cow but the brahmin Vasiṣṭha refuses to give her up:

> Vasiṣṭha replied, 'This cow is used for the gods, for guests, and for the ancestors, and also to make ghee for the sacrifice; this Nandinī of mine cannot be given away, not even for your kingdom, good sir.' Viśvāmitra said, 'I am a kṣatriya, and you are but a mendicant, engaged in ascetic practice and contemplation. How could brahmins have any valor with their placid and subdued nature? If you don't give me the cow that I want for a hundred million [coins], then I will not be deviating from my personal moral code as I take away your cow by force.'

> 'You are a powerful king,' said Vasiṣṭha. 'A kṣatriya of great valor. Just do whatever you want, but do it quickly—don't deliberate on it.'
>
> The gandharva said: When he received this reply, Pārtha, Viśvāmitra forcefully seized the cow Nandinī, who had the appearance of a swan or the moon. Struck by whips and goads, being pushed around here and there, Vasiṣṭha's blessed Nandinī began to bellow. She came before him and stood there looking up expectantly. And even though she was being repeatedly beaten, she did not move away from his hermitage. 'I hear you crying, my dear,' said Vasiṣṭha, 'as you scream out again and again. But, my Nandī, you are being stolen away by force, and I am just a passive brahmin.' (*Mbh*, 1.165.17–24)[6]

Following this exchange, Viśvāmitra's men try to take the cow's calf, which proves to be the last straw for her. The cow grows enraged and produces enormous foreign armies from her dung, urine and spittle. Viśvāmitra surrenders to the overwhelming forces arrayed against him and is convinced by what he has seen to renounce his *kṣatriya* status to become a brahmin (*Mbh*, 1.165.35–45).

A divine magical cow named Surabhī or Kapilā with the power to grant wishes takes the place of the calf stolen from Jamadagni's hermitage in both the *Brahmavaivarta Purāṇa* and the *Padma Purāṇa*, where she is a boon granted by Indra to Jamadagni. The *Brahmavaivarta* describes armies emerging from the cow in the same way as in the Viśvāmitra story and the *Padma* has the cow fight back herself, attacking Kārtavīrya's men before disappearing back to Indraloka. The cow does much the same thing in the *Brahmāṇḍa Purāna*, but in the *Bhāgavata Purāṇa*—the only place where she is called Kāmadhenu—Kārtavīrya's men are able to steal her and hold her until Rāma Jāmadagnya gets her back (Choudhary 2010: 59–60).

The behaviour of cows resisting their abductors recalls elements of the myth of Durgā's dangerous transformation as well as the figures of the Dakṣiṇā and the Parivṛktī. As I have argued above, the epic connects Ambā to Bhīṣma at the structural as well as the narrative levels. It seems plausible, then, that the Ambā story is a transformation of the earlier Dakṣiṇā story told in the *Kāṭhika Saṃhitā*—one in which she is the cow-turned-lioness, the Pāṇḍavas are the *devas* and the Kauravas are the *asuras*.

6 Translated by Adheesh Sathaye, available from: global.oup.com/us/companion.websites/fdscontent/uscompanion/us/static/companion.websites/9780199341115/chapter_2.pdf.

But why does the epic have Rāṃa Jāmadagnya, whom Ambā chooses as her champion, intervene in a way that does not even affect the outcome before she transforms into Śikhaṇḍin and destroys Bhīṣma herself? My answer, which I will explain in the conclusion, is that the epic is introducing an element of his character that will be further developed in South Indian myth and ritual: Rāma Jāmadagnya's role as servant of the goddess.

Conclusion: Ambā, Reṇukā and the goddess

Arabagian argues that the earliest strata of Indo-European bride-napping and cattle-raiding stories reflect the struggle between the Indo-European settlers and indigenous peoples. Later epic stories of this type, on the other hand, come out of a subsequent period of internal struggle in which the Indo-Europeans have absorbed the indigenous culture and its goddess tradition, which they attempt to 'domesticate' (Arabagian 1984: 118). Arabagian sees the promiscuously sexual and violent female warrior Queen Medb from the *Táin Bó Cúailnge* as an Irish analogue to Ambā and identifies both as examples of a 'humanized reflection of the goddess of Sovereignty' arising out of the contact between Indo-Europeans and indigenous goddess-worshippers (1984: 116).

As Parpola has demonstrated, there are good reasons to believe that a proto-Durgā goddess came from West Asia into the Indus Valley long before the Vedic people, and that her main ritual was preserved by the Vrātyas before they were written out of the Vedic tradition themselves. We can see shadows and traces of this proto-Durgā in the Parivṛktī, the rejected Dakṣiṇā and the Kṛtyā—the last identification supported by White's contention that the earliest forms of gods and goddesses could be preserved as the 'daemons' associated with sickness, childbirth and fecundity.

As I wrote at the beginning of this chapter, my purpose here is to reread the Ambopakhyāna as part of the Rāma Jāmadagnya myth cycle. I have already argued that his duel with Bhīṣma is an 'exit myth' analogous to the many myths of Rāma Dāśarathī defeating and replacing him in post-epic literature. Now, for the final part of my rereading, I will argue that the connection to Devī introduced by the Ambā story represents a theme that is picked up on in later myths glorifying his mother, Reṇukā, as a form of Devī.

First, I want to point out an important connection between Ambā and Reṇukā: both die and are resurrected in some form as part of their myth cycle. Ambā, in a popular motif, commits suicide by walking into a sacrificial fire so she can be reborn as Bhīṣma's destroyer. Reṇukā is decapitated by Rāma Jāmadagnya himself at Jamadagni's command after she wets her clothes when she sees a *gandharva* prince bathing in a stream and is then resurrected by Jamadagni at Rāma Jāmadagnya's request. In the epic, Reṇukā's re-capitation goes smoothly, but this is not so in myths from Maharashtra and Tamil Nadu that focus on Reṇukā as a goddess in her own right and identify her post-matricide form with the headless goddesses Chinnamastā and Lajjāgauri or the 'transformed' goddess Māriyamman.

In South Indian myths and rituals recorded and examined by Biardeau and Hiltebeitel (1988: 77), Rāma Jāmadagnya is identified with the 'Buffalo King' Pōttu Rāja or Pōrma<u>nn</u>a<u>n</u>, who is also the Buffalo Demon slain by Devī and converted into one of her devotees (see Collins 2020b: 138). He is typically shown holding a demon's head, which is usually the last head of the hundred-headed demon slain by Devī that would kill her were he to allow it to hit the ground (Hiltebeitel 1988: 76–82). Biardeau's analysis of a 17-day Tamil festival dedicated to Māriyamman shows Pōttu Rāja having become the sacrificial post and Reṇukā having been assimilated to Durgā:

> The goddess who decapitates the buffalo-demon has by implication offered herself for decapitation. Her warrior's sacrifice is what saves the world. Reṇukā is first sacrificed by her son in an act that would be more monstrous than self-sacrifice. She is then replaced with substitute victims: the *kṣatriya*s, who proved to be dangerous to the wellbeing of the cosmic order, *dharma*. (Biardeau 1993: 83–84)

Ambā's story does not play a major part in the Paraśurāma myth cycle that develops after the composition of the epic. But her role as the fierce resurrected battlefield goddess who is alone capable of defeating the seemingly invincible enemy standing in the way of re-establishing *dharma* is clearly passed on to Reṇukā in the forms of Chinnamastā, Lajjāgauri and Māriyamman. I will conclude with one last interesting bit of folklore: the silk-weaving Khatri caste, who claim descent from Rāma Jāmadagnya's archenemy Kārtavīrya Arjuna, offer monthly goat sacrifices to his mother, whom they recognise as their caste goddess 'Reṇukāmba' (Choudhary 2010: 298–99).

References

Primary texts

Ananthanarayana, H.S. and Lehman, W.P. (eds). (2020). *Ṛg Veda*. [Online.] Göttingen Register of Electronic Texts in Indian Languages (GRETIL). Available from: www.sub.uni-goettingen.de/ebene_1/fiindolo/gretil.htm#Samh.

Bhāgavata Purāṇa with the Commentary of Śrīdhara. (1972). Benares, India: Pandita Pustakalaya.

Bhatt, G.H. and Shah, U.P. (eds). (1960–75). *The Vālmīki Rāmāyaṇa: Critical Edition*. [7 vols.] Baroda, India: Oriental Institute.

Brahmāṇḍa Purāṇa. (1857). Bombay, India: Venkateshvara Sagara Press.

Brahmavaivarta Purana. (1981). Allahabad, India: Hindi Sahitya.

The Viṣṇudharmottara Purāṇa. (1912). Bombay, India: Veṅkaṭeśvara Steam Press.

Secondary texts

Adluri, Vishva. (2016). The divine androgyne: Crossing gender and breaking hegemonies in the Ambā-Upākhyāna of the Mahābhārata. In Vishwa Adluri and Joydeep Bagchee (eds), *Argument and Design: The Unity of the Mahābhārata*, pp. 275–319. London: Brill. doi.org/10.1163/9789004311404_011.

Arabagian, Ruth Katz. (1984). Cattle raiding and bride stealing: The goddess in Indo-European heroic literature. *Religion* 14: 107–42. doi.org/10.1016/S0048-721X(84)80005-6.

Balkaran, Raj. (2018). The splendor of the sun: Brightening the bridge between Mārkaṇḍeya Purāṇā and Devī Mahātmyā in light of Navarātri ritual timing. In Caleb Simmons, Moumita Sen and Hillary Rodrigues (eds), *Nine Nights of the Goddess: The Navaratri Festival in South Asia*, pp. 23–38. Albany: SUNY Press.

Balkaran, Raj. (2020). *The Goddess and the Sun in Indian Myth: Power, Preservation and Mirrored Māhātmyas in the Mārkaṇḍeya Purāṇa*. London: Routledge. doi.org/10.4324/9780429322020.

Biardeau, Madeleine. (1993). Paraśurāma. In Yves Bonnefoy, Wendy Doniger and Gerald Honigsblum (eds), *Asian Mythologies*, pp. 82–84. Chicago, IL: University of Chicago Press.

Biardeau, Madeleine. (2004). *Stories about Posts: Vedic Variations around the Hindu Goddess*. Chicago, IL: University of Chicago Press.

Bronkhorst, Johannes. (2016). *How the Brahmins Won: From Alexander to the Guptas*. Leiden, Netherlands: Brill. doi.org/10.1163/9789004315518.

Choudhary, Pradeep Kant. (2010). *Rāma with an Axe: Myth and Cult of Paraśurāma Avatāra*. Delhi: Aakar Books.

Collins, Brian. (2010). Headless mothers, magic cows, and lakes of blood: The Paraśurāma cycle in the Mahābhārata and beyond. PhD dissertation, University of Chicago.

Collins, Brian. (2014). *The Head Beneath the Altar: Hindu Mythology and the Critique of Sacrifice*. East Lansing, MI: Michigan State University Press.

Collins, Brian. (2020a). Monsters, *masala*, and materiality: Close encounters with Hindi horror movie ephemera. In Ellen Goldberg, Aditi Sen and Brian Collins (eds), *Bollywood Horrors: Religion, Violence, and Cinematic Fears in India*, pp. 21–43. London: Bloomsbury Academic. doi.org/10.5040/9781350143180.ch-001.

Collins, Brian. (2020b). *The Other Rāma: Matricide and Genocide in the Mythology of Paraśurāma*. Albany: SUNY Press.

Collins, Brian. (2021a). Of demons and disciplines: *Old Thiess, a Livonian Werewolf: A Classic Case in Comparative Perspective* by Carlo Ginzburg and Bruce Lincoln, and *Daemons Are Forever: Contacts and Exchanges in the Eurasian Pandemonium* by David Gordon White. *Religious Studies Review* 47(1).

Collins, Brian. (2021b). Paraśurāma, Droṇa, and Aśvatthāman: A comparative study of brahmin warriors in the Mahābhārata. In Marcello do Martino and Claudia Santi (eds), *NOMEN NVMEN: Espressioni del sacro tra storia delle religioni, linguistica e archeologia, Atti del convegno Università degli Studi della Campania 'Vanvitelli', Santa Maria Capua Vetere—15–16 Aprile 2019* [*NOMEN NVMEN: Expressions of the Sacred between the History of Religions, Linguistics and Archaeology: Proceedings of the Conference 'Vanvitelli', University of Campania, Santa Maria Capua Vetere, 15–16 April 2019*], pp. 177–92. Lugano, Italy: Agora & Co.

Deshpande, N.A. (1988). *The Padma Purāṇa*. Delhi: Motilal Banarsidass.

Doniger, Wendy. (1999). *Splitting the Difference: Gender and Myth in Ancient Greece and India*. Chicago, IL: University of Chicago Press.

Goldman, Robert P. (1977). *Gods, Priests and Warriors: The Bhṛgus of the Mahābhārata*. New York, NY: Columbia University Press.

Heesterman, Jan. (1962). Vrātya and sacrifice. *Indo-Iranian Journal* 6: 3–37. doi.org/10.1163/000000062791616002.

Hiltebeitel, Alf. (1988). *The Cult of Draupadī. Volume 1: Mythologies—From Gingee to Kurukṣetra*. Chicago, IL: University of Chicago Press.

Hiltebeitel, Alf. (2011a). *Dharma: Its Early History in Law, Religion, and Narrative*. New York, NY: Oxford University Press.

Hiltebeitel, Alf. (2011b). Epic aśvamedhas. In Vishwa Adluri and Joydeep Bagchee (eds), *Reading the Fifth Veda: Studies on the Mahābhārata. Essays by Alf Hiltebeitel. Volume 1*, pp. 259–78. Leiden, Netherlands: E.J. Brill.

Howard, Veena R. (2019). Narrative of Ambā in the Mahābhārata: Female body, gender, and the namesake of the divine feminine. In Veena R. Howard (ed.), *The Bloomsbury Research Handbook of Indian Philosophy and Gender*, pp. 217–47. London: Bloomsbury. doi.org/10.5040/9781474269612.ch-010.

Jamison, Stephanie W. (1991). *The Ravenous Hyenas and the Wounded Sun: Myth and Ritual in Ancient India*. Ithaca, NY: Cornell University Press.

Jamison, Stephanie W. (1996). *Sacrificed Wife/Sacrificer's Wife: Women, Ritual, and Hospitality in Ancient India*. New York, NY: Oxford University Press.

Jamison, Stephanie and Brereton, Joel P. (2014). *The Rigveda: The Earliest Religious Poetry of India*. Oxford, UK: Oxford University Press.

Kṛttibāsa, Shanti Lal Nagar and Nagar, Suriti. (1997). *Kṛttivāsa Rāmāyaṇa*. Delhi: Eastern Book Linkers.

Monier-Williams, Monier. (2009). *An English–Sanskrit Dictionary*. New Delhi: Asian Educational Services.

Nagar, Shantilal. (2006). *Paraśurāma (An Incarnation of Viṣṇu)*. Delhi: B.R. Publishing Corporation.

Parpola, Asko. (2015). *The Roots of Hinduism: The Early Aryans and the Indus Civilization*. New York, NY: Oxford University Press. doi.org/10.1093/acprof:oso/9780190226909.001.0001.

Sanderson, Alexis. (2009). The Śaiva age: The rise and dominance of Śaivism during the early medieval period. In Shingo Einoo (ed.), *Genesis and Development of Tantrism*, pp. 41–349. Tokyo: Institute of Oriental Culture.

Sathaye, Adheesh. (2015). *Crossing the Lines of Caste: Viśvāmitra and the Construction of Brahmin Power in Hindu Mythology*. Oxford, UK: Oxford University Press. doi.org/10.1093/acprof:oso/9780199341108.001.0001.

Sukthankar, V.S. (1976). *The Mahābhārata: Text as Constituted in Its Critical Edition*. Poona, India: Bhandarkar Oriental Research Institute.

Thomas, Lynn. (1996). Paraśurāma and time. In Julia Leslie (ed.), *Myth and Mythmaking: Continuous Evolution in Indian Tradition*, pp. 63–86. Richmond, UK: Curzon Press.

van Buitenen, J.A.B. (trans. & ed.). (1973). *The Mahābhārata. Volume 1, Book 1: The Book of the Beginning*. Chicago, IL: University of Chicago Press. doi.org/10.7208/chicago/9780226217543.001.0001.

van Buitenen, J.A.B. (trans. & ed.). (1975). *The Mahābhārata. Volume 2, Book 2: The Book of the Assembly Hall. Book 3: The Book of the Forest*. Chicago, IL: University of Chicago Press. doi.org/10.7208/chicago/9780226223681.001.0001.

van Buitenen, J.A.B. (trans. & ed.). (1978). *The Mahābhārata. Volume 3, Book 4: The Book of Virāṭa. Book 5: The Book of the Effort*. Chicago, IL: University of Chicago Press. doi.org/10.7208/chicago/9780226223711.001.0001.

White, David Gordon. (2020). *Dæmons Are Forever: Contacts and Exchanges in the Eurasian Pandemonium*. Chicago, IL: University of Chicago Press. doi.org/10.7208/chicago/9780226715063.001.0001.

6

Claiming the narrative: Subjectivity and intertextuality in the Ambopākhyāna

Zuzana Špicová

Abstract

The Ambopākhyāna (*Mbh*, 5.170–93) is one of the few autobiographical narratives of the *Mahābhārata*. As such, the basis for any interpretation should always be the fact that it is narrated by Bhīṣma, who is a highly developed character invested in the narrated events, as well as a skilled narrator. His narration of the story of Ambā and Śikhaṇḍin can therefore be seen as subjective and potentially unreliable and influenced (actively or passively) by the vast 'library' of the narratives he knows and often shares with his listeners (most prominently in the Śāntiparvan and the Anuśāsanaparvan). The subjectivity of his narration will be observed in differences between this version of certain events and the versions of other narrators or himself at a later point, and the intertextuality on the palimpsest-like relation with the stories of *pativratā* women—Sītā, Sāvitrī, Damayantī and Śakuntalā—to show Bhīṣma authoritatively claiming Ambā's narrative.

Subjectivity and intertextuality

Subjectivity in the *Mahābhārata* is not as widely discussed as it should be, given it is a vital concept that lies in the very structure of the text. Because of the polyphonic[1] nature of the text, it is crucial to pay attention to narrators of different portions: most, if not all, of the *Mahābhārata*'s narrators are personalised to various degrees and personalised narrators are by definition prone to subjectivity, be it by slightly preferring one topic or character over another or by interpreting certain events, characters and fictional facts in a profoundly subjective manner. Personalised narrators can also deliberately present some of the events and fictional facts falsely, thus becoming unreliable. Contrary to later literary conventions, events and fictional facts of this story-world are only very rarely presented in a completely unequivocal and objective manner. Most of the narration is presented from someone's point of view and/or moulded for a specific audience. Important events are re-narrated and reinterpreted several times, with different things emphasised each time.

There are various narrators in the *Mahābhārata*, both the 'outer-frame' narrators such as Ugraśravas Sauti and Vaiśaṃpāyana, who is the reliable voice of the implied author, and narrator-characters who must be taken as subjective and occasionally unreliable.[2] Every character has an individual narrative or 'personal script' based on the events presented in the *Mahābhārata*. He or she can never know everything that is going on nor are they able to see all the implications of an event, and they organise and interpret the events according to their own knowledge, personality and memory. The more a character is developed and the more experience and relationships with other characters he or she has, the more subjective they can be as narrators. When evaluating a story in the *Mahābhārata*, at least three things must be considered: the narrator, the listener and the circumstances. A single story can be narrated differently by different narrators, such as the stories of Rāma Jāmadagnya by Akṛtavraṇa (*Mbh*, 3.115–17) and Kṛṣṇa (12.49); by a single narrator to different listeners—for example, Kṛṣṇa's different accounts of Bhīṣma's death to Gaṅgā (13.154.29–32) and Vasudeva (14.59.8–12); or in different

1 For the importance of polyphony and dialogue in the *Mahābhārata*, see Hiltebeitel (2001); Fitzgerald (2003); and Black (2007: 57), who speaks about the *Mahābhārata*'s 'complexly interwoven dialogical structure' and the importance of various primary and secondary (eavesdropping) audiences; or Reich (1998), who interprets the *Mahābhārata* quite aptly as a 'battlefield of a text'.

2 For differences between narrators and audiences, I especially follow Genette (1980); Phelan (2017); Bal and Tavor (1981); Booth (1983).

circumstances. It can be theorised that Mārkaṇḍeya's version of Rāma's story (the Rāmopākhyāna, 3.257–76) has a happy ending and does not include the later problems known from the *Rāmāyaṇa* because the goal is to cheer up Yudhiṣṭhira and not make him even more depressed. A certain part of any narration can be omitted—creating gaps in narration—both because of it being uninteresting in general, to a certain recipient and/or under certain circumstances (which is mostly the case of *events I* and can often be filled with *schemata*—scripts and frames, as defined by Emmott and Alexander 2009: 411), and because of the narrator's conscious aim to hide it from the recipient (typically *events II*).[3] Every narration by a personalised character must be evaluated in the terms of the narrator's subjectivity (personal script, including the narrator's knowledge), authority (or power to influence) and reliability (presenting events in accordance with 'reality' or with the implied author). The combination of these terms—high subjectivity and authority paired with suspected or proved unreliability—can lead to a reading that will reveal the way the narrator attempts to claim the narrative. The next step is to compare the narrator's version of the events with the implied author's textual signs, and to evaluate how successful the narrator was in convincing various audiences of his or her claims.

In this chapter, I will show that Bhīṣma's narration of the Ambopākhyāna is highly subjective and intertextual and that stories of *pativratās* lie in the background of the Ambopākhyāna as a referential frame. Bhīṣma as the narrator uses the narratives and patterns to show Ambā in a bad light, comparing her with the great, determined and faithful women of the *upākhyānas*, and thus subtly presenting her flaws to the recipients—primarily to Duryodhana and other characters. In other words, not only can and should these heroines be compared, but also the text explicitly invites us to do so and to draw certain conclusions. I will also show that even though Bhīṣma successfully claimed Ambā's narrative inside the story-world, audiences of the whole text can nevertheless see her from a completely different point of view if they recognise the subjectivity and intertextuality of Bhīṣma's

3 The difference between *events I* and *events II*, as used in modern narratology, is that *events I* are considered every change of predicate, whereas *events II* are those with an undeniable importance to the story—'an interpretation- and context-dependent type of narration that implies changes of a special kind' (Hühn 2009: 80). Omitting an *event I* is therefore usually insignificant, but omitting an *event II* in a personalised narration is a very strong signal of possible unreliability. The typical signs of unreliability, as defined by Phelan and Martin (1999: 94–95), are misreporting, misreading and mis-regarding, underreporting, underreading and under-regarding. Omitting an *event II* would be a case of underreporting.

narration and see the narrative in a wider context in which Śikhaṇḍin, whom Bhīṣma recognises as Ambā reborn, causes his death; the events of the whole text eventually betray Bhīṣma's authoritative claims.

Upākhyānas and intertextuality

The relationship between the parts and the whole of the *Mahābhārata* is a complex one. Sources are incorporated into it through quoting or paraphrasing and there is 'interreferentiality between the whole and its parts' (Hiltebeitel 2016: 21). There are various *upākhyānas* whose main (or central) character is a woman,[4] the most important and best-known being the Śakuntalopākhyāna (*Mbh*, 1.62–69), the Sāvitryopākhyāna (3.277–83), the Nalopākhyāna (3.50–78) and, to a certain degree, the Rāmopākhyāna (3.257–76).[5] All these stories are narrated by men, primarily to other men, with an occasional woman as a secondary listener (such as Draupadī in the Vanaparvan), and often glorify the *pativratā* ideal of a woman who, despite adversity and suspicion of her own husband, remains perfectly faithful to him, as attested by gods. This seems to be the primary ideal woman of the *Mahābhārata*. Shalini Shah (2012: 80) even calls the epics 'the vehicle for the popularisation of this *dharma*'. Narrators of these *upākhyānas* can be seen as reliable, as there are no overt signs of unreliability. The Śakuntalopākhyāna (*Mbh*, 1.62–69) is narrated by the reliable voice of the implied author, Vaiśaṃpāyana, to Janamejaya, which ensures as much reliability as the audiences can get in the *Mahābhārata*. The *ṛṣi*s who narrate most of the *upākhyānas* in the Vanaparvan are not as well known as characters of the main story and therefore are usually not subjective enough to be suspected of unreliability or any great agenda. Mārkaṇḍeya, a Bhārgava *brahmarṣi* and the narrator of the Rāmopākhyāna (3.257–76) and the Sāvitryopākhyāna (3.277–83), is a constant presence in the forest, narrating various stories to Yudhiṣṭhira, and later is mentioned as one of Bhīṣma's most prominent sources, even of the information about Kṛṣṇa's glory (for example, in the

4 In Hiltebeitel's list (2016: 28, 31), there is only one *upākhyāna* mentioned as narrated by a woman (Kuntī to Pāṇḍu, *Mbh*, 1.112) and four *upākhyānas* primarily about women with four others in which a woman can be seen as the main heroine as well.

5 All these *upākhyānas* and their heroines have invited a plethora of interpretations from different perspectives over the years, including feminist, theological, philosophical and psychoanalytical approaches. From the most recent scholarship, see, for example, Chakravarti (2009) and Dhand (2004) about women in the *Mahābhārata*; Shah (2012) about *pativratās* in general; Brodbeck (2013) about Sāvitrī; and Adluri (2016) or Howard (2020) about Ambā.

Viśvopākhyāna, 6.61–64). On the other hand, Bṛhadaśva, the narrator of the Nalopākhyāna (3.50–78), is more of a one-story *ṛṣi*: he is mentioned only in passing before his narration and quite forgotten afterwards.

In another famous *upākhyāna* about a woman, the Ambopākhyāna (*Mbh*, 5.170–93), the situation, circumstances, style of the narration and even the heroine herself are different. Veena Howard (2020: 235) explicitly says that 'Ambā is not a *pativrata* woman' and contrasts her story with the stories of *pativratā*s (p. 219). On the other hand, some authors, such as Roberto Morales-Harley (2019: 7), have recognised Ambā's devotedness towards Śālva and see her as a *pativratā*. She can also be seen as one of the 'aggressive' women of the *Mahābhārata*; Andrea Custodi, mentioning Draupadī[6] and other heroines, argues that

> this current of feminine vengeance—which I might also argue drives the major events of the epic—is an important strand of femininity in the *Mahābhārata* not articulated in the *strīdharma* that constitutes the dominant conscious discourse on femininity in the epic. (Custodi 2007: 220)

Ambā is certainly a multilayered character if her *pātivratya* and personality in general can be such points of contention. How can these contrary images of Ambā be reconciled? I argue that there are different Ambās for different audiences. There is an Ambā for those who only know the Ambopākhyāna and there is another Ambā when we consider other fragments of her story, including those narrating the story of Śikhaṇḍin; there is an Ambā for those who accept Bhīṣma's framing of her life story and another for those who do not.

The story of Ambā and Śikhaṇḍin

The story of the kidnapping of Ambā and her life events is mentioned on a few occasions in the text. Since both Vaiśaṃpāyana's and Bhīṣma's narrations are understandably favourable towards Bhīṣma, he is presented as the hero, which is not self-evident. If someone else narrated the story,

6 Draupadī is both an 'aggressive' woman seeking vengeance for her humiliation by the Kauravas and one of the *pativratā* women. She is also closely connected to Ambā, who, in her next life as Śikhaṇḍin, becomes her sibling. For the aggressive behaviour in the *Mahābhārata* and in the Rāmāyaṇa, as well as for comparison of the heroines in question, see Sutherland (1989).

especially someone from Śālva's or Ambā's families, Bhīṣma could have been presented as a villain of the Rāvaṇa type: the kidnapper of a married woman who fights against her rightful husband.

The most prominent *events II* of the story concerning the characters of Ambā/Śikhaṇḍin and Bhīṣma include Ambā's engagement to Śālva (narrated as an *analepsis* in at least two contradictory versions), the abduction of the three princesses of Kāśi, Bhīṣma's victorious fight against the assembled kings and/or Śālva, his victory over Rāma Jāmadagnya, Ambā's austerities and death, her rebirth as Drupada's daughter Śikhaṇḍinī, her sex change, Bhīṣma's defeat/death and Śikhaṇḍin's death. The beginning of the story is partly narrated in the Ādiparvan (*Mbh*, 1.96.1–51, by Vaiśaṃpāyana). It is narrated in full (except for Bhīṣma's and Śikhaṇḍin's deaths, which come later in the narration) in the Ambopākhyāna (5.170–93, by Bhīṣma). The events are summarised or alluded to on various occasions in the Udyogaparvan (5.49.31–34, by Saṃjaya; 5.145.15–40, by Bhīṣma in Kṛṣṇa's narration; 5.166.1–9, by Bhīṣma again). It is also found in the Bhīṣmaparvan (several mentions, mostly by Dhṛtarāṣṭra and Saṃjaya) and in the Anuśāsanaparvan (13.44.37–54, by Bhīṣma). These are only the most important occurrences. Ambā's story (and especially the story of Śikhaṇḍin) thus continues in the reliable discourses of Saṃjaya and Vaiśaṃpāyana.

These events are mentioned and narrated from different perspectives by different character-narrators to different listeners and with different intentions, and often present a considerably varied set of fictional facts that are sometimes complementary and sometimes contradictory. However, it seems that Bhīṣma managed to almost monopolise and thus claim the narration of Ambā's misfortune, being the main source of information about the events for the next generations and the audience. It is worth noting that he is the only character who is given the chance to narrate his perspective of the events, and not only once, but several times throughout the text. Most poignantly, Ambā's and/or Śikhaṇḍin's own perspective, which would be narrated by herself/himself, is completely omitted. Ambā's perspective is always narrated by Bhīṣma (or briefly by Vaiśaṃpāyana) and Śikhaṇḍin only once alludes to the fight between Bhīṣma and Rāma Jāmadagnya. Even then it is not from his own experience or memory, but *mayā śrutaṃ* ('heard by me') (*Mbh*, 6.104.43). Similarly, none of the other characters who are still alive and present in the time around the Kurukṣetra War—namely, Bāhlīka, Vyāsa, Nārada or Rāma Jāmadagnya—comments on this episode (except for Gaṅgā in the Anuśāsanaparvan, and she does not bring any new information). Most other characters of the story-world quote only Bhīṣma's own words when the events concerning Ambā or Śikhaṇḍin are in question.

Bhīṣma as narrator

It is crucial to note that the most influential version of Ambā's story, the Ambopākhyāna (*Mbh*, 5.170–93), is narrated to Duryodhana by Bhīṣma, who is a subjective and occasionally unreliable narrator.[7] It must also be noted that Bhīṣma's presentation of the fictional facts and events that are connected predominantly to the character of Ambā undergoes a certain evolution from the Ādiparvan to the Udyogaparvan to the Anuśāsanaparvan. These changes can be read as Bhīṣma's attempts to gradually diminish his guilt in Ambā's ruined life.

It is also crucial to bear in mind that Bhīṣma is a skilled narrator who knows a variety of stories,[8] as shown predominantly in the Śāntiparvan and the Anuśāsanaparvan, in which Bhīṣma names some of the narrators and characters of the most influential stories about *pativratā*s among his sources—most prominently, Mārkaṇḍeya (for example, 12.310.24, 13.17.169). He even mentions Sāvitrī herself when talking about various types of marriages at 13.45.5, only a few verses after alluding to Ambā, so he is apparently aware of this story. The fact that there is no need to narrate the story in detail here means he presumes his audience, the Pāṇḍavas, is aware of it. The story of Śakuntalā is narrated by Vaiśaṃpāyana to Janamejaya as part of the history of the Kaurava family. It is safe to assume that Bhīṣma (and perhaps even his audience in the Udyogaparvan, Duryodhana and the Kauravas) knew at least some of the stories of *pativratā* women (quite probably the story of Śakuntalā and Sāvitrī) and the traditional sequence of events. I suggest that the author(s) of the Ambopākhyāna took this into consideration, so Bhīṣma tries to present Ambā as an anti-*pativratā* and seems to succeed.

7 For the account of Bhīṣma's possible unreliability, see Špicová (2019). Even though scholars usually at least mention that Bhīṣma is the narrator of the *Mahābhārata* (for example, Howard 2020: 220; Adluri 2016: 275), they do not seem to consider it a thoroughly narrative-changing feature. The narrative aptness of Bhīṣma as the narrator is also sometimes commented on (van Buitenen 1978: 178; Howard 2020: 222), but generally Vaiśaṃpāyana's narration in the Ādiparvan and Bhīṣma's autodiegetic narration in the Udyogaparvan are treated in the same way.

8 For more about Bhīṣma as a narrator and about his sources, see Hiltebeitel (2014).

The *pativratā* genre and its schemata

The stories of *pativratās* share several similar traits. They are usually stories about a woman (role: wife) who: 1) chose her own husband (role: husband); 2) was kidnapped (role: villain) and/or was left by her husband and returned/ was returned to him; 3) faced his suspicion; and finally 4) was happily reunited with him thanks to her unwavering *pātivratya*, which won her the intervention of gods (role: gods) and/or the power to convince her husband by the means of her own *tapas* channelled through a '*tena satyena*' sentence. In other words, first, the heroine is presented as a strong and independent woman who chooses her own husband and follows him anywhere. Then there is an external crisis (a physical separation) that is solved by the husband or herself, followed by an internal crisis (suspicion), which is solved by the gods. There can be additional roles of a helper, a father, a maternal relative, a treacherous relative and so on, but the basic structure operates with the four main roles of the wife, the husband, the villain and the god(s). The sequence of events, the way of narration and common motifs and roles show that this type of *pativratā* narrative can be seen as a genre or at least a subgenre of its own. Recognising a genre has a prominent communicative function between the author(s) and the reader(s) (Martin 2005: 10), as well as between the narrator and the recipient. It profoundly influences the way the audience perceives the story. The events that constitute the *pativratā* genre and create the fitting script for the audiences will be presented and then compared with the Ambopākhyāna's treatment of them to show that the Ambopākhyāna is narrated as a take on the *pativratā* genre.

Event 1: *Svayaṃvara*

The *svayaṃvara* is one of the most common means of marrying off a high-status *kṣatriya* daughter in the *Mahābhārata*'s story-world, be it a proper *svayaṃvara* with hosts of kings invited (such as the *svayaṃvara* of Draupadī, Ambā and Damayantī) or a *svayaṃ-vara* in the loose sense of a woman choosing her own husband (which is the case of Śakuntalā and Sāvitrī). In the formal *svayaṃvara*, there is often the idea of the princess in question being *vīryaśulkā*—that is, heroism must be shown to 'pay' for the bride, sometimes heroism of a specific type, chosen by the father of the bride (Draupadī, Sītā). As Brockington (2006: 35) rightly notes, 'the initiative in the matter is normally with the fathers'.

In the traditional *svayaṃvara* narrative of the *upākhyāna*s, the bride, who seems to be fully adult (cf. Brockington 2006: 38), chooses her husband herself. She usually informs the groom and/or her father that the husband has been chosen by her using the word *vṛta*. A common motif is that the bride has chosen her groom even before the formal *svayaṃvara* and considers that to be irrevocable: a woman can only choose a husband once. Interestingly, most of the greatest *pativratā*s have chosen their husbands on their own, even without their father's knowledge or approval—a fact that is often overlooked and presented as a specific trait of Ambā. Veena Howard (2020: 224) claims that Ambā 'defies the normative tradition by choosing a bridegroom (*vara*) for herself in secret'. I argue that this is, in fact, a typical feature of a *pativratā* woman and the starting point of Bhīṣma's intertextual play.

When Śakuntalā—possibly the most famous *pativratā* of the Bhāratas, being the mother of the eponymous Bharata—talks to her father, Kaṇva, after his return to the *āśrama*, she informs him that she has chosen Duḥṣanta as her husband (*Mbh*, 1.67.31). Śakuntalā has chosen Duḥṣanta without her father's knowledge in a *gāndharva* marriage but asks for his permission as soon as possible. It is also worth noting that she asked for a *śulka* before the marriage—namely, that her son would be the king. Damayantī first promises Nala that she will choose him at the *svayaṃvara* (3.53.11). Later, she uses the same *vṛtaḥ* at the *svayaṃvara* to denote that she has chosen Nala and cannot choose anyone else, even using '*tena satyena*' sentences here to force the gods to reveal themselves (3.54.17–19). Damayantī has chosen her husband even before the marriage and it is shown very clearly that she cannot accept anyone else, and the gods are forced to agree. Sāvitrī finds herself in a similar situation. She chooses her own husband without consulting anyone, even though her father explicitly sent her to find a husband herself (3.278.10). When warned that Satyavat will die very soon, she nevertheless refuses to choose anyone else (3.278.26).

Ambā's svayaṃvara

Having these three great *pativratā*s and their husband-choosing process in mind, Ambā's story can be perceived with great sympathies towards Ambā, at least in the beginning. This event (as well as the kidnapping) is available to us in two important versions: the Ādiparvan version of Vaiśaṃpāyana and the Udyogaparvan version of Bhīṣma. In the plot, Ambā choosing her own husband is presented as an *analepsis* in her own speech after she has been kidnapped and the marriage preparations have begun. The Ādiparvan version of this speech is more concise than the Udyogaparvan one, spanning only three lines (*Mbh*, 1.96.48–49). The Ādiparvan version is very clear: she chose mentally the lord of Saubha, was chosen by him, it was also her father's wish and she would have chosen him at the *svayaṃvara* as well.[9] There is hardly anything improper anyone could find in her speech. On the contrary, she seems to be a dutiful daughter and a *pativratā*—like Damayantī or Śakuntalā.

Bhīṣma's two changes in the events known from the Ādiparvan that are the strongest signs of his narratorial unreliability (that is, changing 'it was also my father's wish' to 'without my father's knowledge' and omitting his fight against Śālva) result in effectively diminishing his guilt and opening Ambā's morality to questioning. In Bhīṣma's version, the fact she would have chosen Śālva at the *svayaṃvara* is also dropped and instead it is said that she was *in love* with someone else (5.17.6–7). Choosing a husband on her own, and especially choosing without her father's knowledge, implies that the lovers have already met, and the conspicuously similar wording of Ambā's and Śakuntalā's requests to Bhīṣma and Kaṇva, respectively, also implies that there could have been a *gāndharva* marriage between Ambā and Śālva, making Ambā the wife of another and therefore a wholly undesirable person in the Kaurava household. Be it a dutiful daughter and wife as presented in the Ādiparvan or the (still *pativratā*) woman longing for another man in the Udyogaparvan, Ambā is shown in the tradition of the great *pativratā*s by both Vaiśaṃpāyana and Bhīṣma.

Event 2: Separation

There are two main variations of the separation event: the heroine is kidnapped by another man and the heroine is abandoned by her husband. Most of the heroines undergo both: Damayantī is left by Nala in a forest and then harassed by a hunter, while Sītā is kidnapped by Rāvaṇa and then left by Rāma. Śakuntalā and Sāvitrī are left by their husbands in the forest. Duḥṣanta leaves and Satyavat dies but the effects are similar: the heroine is left alone in an inimical world. Kidnapping an unmarried woman constitutes a *rākṣasa*

9 Roberto Morales-Harley (2019: 4) recognises that this is exactly Ambā's argumentation: '[T]hrough a svayaṃvara, she is already married to Śālva ... Once she became Śālva's wife, through the rite of svayaṃvara, she cannot be Vicitravīrya's wife through the rākṣasa vivāha.' Veena Howard (2020: 226) also notes that 'Ambā finds herself involved with *gandharva* and *rākṣasa* marriages: one by love [Śālva], the other by abduction [Bhīṣma].' And in a footnote: 'If Ambā and Śālva both have chosen one another in love, they have performed what is known as *gandharva* marriage (voluntary union of a maiden and her lover) as Śakuntalā does in Book I' (Howard 2020: 244).

type of marriage (which often brings heirs to the dynasty—for example, the kidnapping of Ambā's sisters or of Subhadrā; *Mbh*, 1.211–13), whereas kidnapping a married woman is a sin (in the 'main events' most prominently Draupadī, 3.248–56). Indeed, it is often considered outright rape. Doniger (2014: 353) says that Ambā is 'socially, if not physically, raped by Bhishma'. Similarly, Custodi (2007: 218) claims that 'Bhīṣma symbolically and socially rapes Ambā'. There is certainly the idea that kidnapping a married woman makes her somewhat tainted[10] and unsuitable to remain a wife.

The story of Nala and Damayantī is narrated earlier in the Vanaparvan than the story of Rāma and Sītā and is set in earlier times (it is earlier in terms of both the story and the plot). It can be therefore assumed that the story of Sītā is somehow aware of the story of Damayantī. Damayantī sets the ideal for a *pativratā* extremely high. She is left by her husband in the forest (3.59–60) and later harassed by a strange man (3.60.25–38), yet never ceases to be greatly devoted to Nala. When she finds out her husband has left her in the forest, she cries and laments for some time in one of the most famous episodes of the whole *Mahābhārata*, but she never blames Nala for it. Thanks to her *pātivratya*, she manages to kill a man who is trying to force himself on her, setting a dangerous precedent for other wives (3.60.37–38). After this failed kidnapping, Damayantī enters an *āśrama* and tells the ascetics about her father and her husband, Nala. The ascetics promise her that she will be reunited with Nala and she continues to look for him without a single doubt about her husband.

Probably the most famous story of a kidnapped wife is that of Sītā. The Rāmopākhyāna is narrated by the *ṛṣi* Mārkaṇḍeya to Yudhiṣṭhira, answering his question about Draupadī's abduction. After getting Draupadī back, Yudhiṣṭhira goes to the *munis* and specifically asks Mārkaṇḍeya, among others ('Is there someone more unfortunate than me?'; 3.257.10), a very important question: 'How is it possible that a man like Jayadratha kidnapped Draupadī, as she never committed a sin?' (3.257.5–7). This is a pregnant question. There seems to have been an underlying presumption (either of Yudhiṣṭhira or in general) that a woman who is kidnapped and/or raped deserved it because of her own sin or generally not being sufficiently devoted to her husband. This is probably made stronger by the story of Damayantī, who could not be kidnapped thanks to her *pātivratya*. The story of Rāma and

10 Simon Brodbeck (2013: 539–40) discusses the 'tainted' status of Draupadī and Sītā and compares it with that of Sāvitrī.

Sītā, presented here as an answer to this question, is a rebuttal of this view, and Sītā in the *Mahābhārata* paradoxically improves the status of women.[11] If a woman as perfect as Sītā was kidnapped, it cannot be a woman's fault. Sītā is shown to be struggling with Rāvaṇa and, similarly to Damayantī, only thinking about Rāma all the time (3.264.42). She also says she would prefer death to becoming Rāvaṇa's wife (3.264.49–51).

Ambā's abduction

Both these stories are present in the story of Ambā as an underlying current, even though the situation is slightly different as she is not known to be a wife when she is being kidnapped and, even after the kidnapping, her status is uncertain. Bhīṣma sees her as Śālva's wife and Śālva as Bhīṣma's property. In the Ādiparvan version of her story, we find a transgression against a normal *svayaṃvara* clearly stated. It is not the women or the father, but Bhīṣma who does the choosing (*Mbh*, 1.96.6). Bhīṣma continues with a lengthy explanation of why his deed is dharmic and even laudable, showing thus that it was not, in fact, self-evident, otherwise there would be no need for his speech. Later he also fights against the assembled kings in general and against Śālva in particular, and it is only after the preparations for the wedding are afoot that Ambā claims she wants to be sent to Śālva, thus revealing her status as 'another's wife'. She is not explicitly said to have struggled when Bhīṣma was kidnapping her (neither by Vaiśaṃpāyana nor by Bhīṣma) or to have made speeches about preferring death, not to mention any attempt to slay Bhīṣma through her *tapas*—yet. The Udyogaparvan version is very similar, only instead of having a speech about different types of marriage, Bhīṣma informs Duryodhana that he knew the girls were *vīryaśulkā*, thus legitimising the abduction in a different way (5.170.13–14).

Apart from this and the fact that Bhīṣma omitted the fight against Śālva, the narrative is much the same in its main events. The difference becomes obvious only later with events that are presented only from Bhīṣma's perspective and cannot be compared with the versions of a reliable discourse. Bhīṣma adds new information about the kidnapping, or at least a new confusion. During Ambā's dialogue with her intended husband (in which he expresses his suspicion, see below), Śālva claims, among other things, that she was

11 The *Rāmāyaṇa*, which presents a more famous version of this story and even more so the later tradition, somehow nullifies this betterment of women's lot through the last part, which includes Rāma's abandonment of Sītā, regardless of her virtue proven by gods, making Sītā's virtue in effect vain.

happy when she was being carried away by Bhīṣma (5.172.6). It comes as no surprise that Ambā protests here very strongly, saying that she was taken by force and against her will, but to no avail (5.172.8–9). It is not clear which is true because the narrator does not provide us with an unequivocal answer, but it is enough to plant a seed of suspicion about Ambā's *pātivratya* in the audience's mind. In any case, there are no markers of a *pativratā*, which were mentioned in the narratives of Damayantī and Sītā. Most prominently, there is no struggle against the kidnapper, and there is even a deliberate uncertainty about Ambā's emotions while she was being kidnapped in Bhīṣma's account, which goes directly against everything the *pativratā* women were doing. After leaving Śālva's city, Ambā also blames herself (among others) and regrets not jumping from the chariot (5.173.4). Again, these are Ambā's thoughts as presented by Bhīṣma, who is very invested in not portraying Ambā as a *pativratā* as that would show him as a Rāvaṇa-type villain. She also blames her father for organising the *svayaṃvara* and for making the girls *vīryaśulkā* (5.173.3, 5), as well as Bhīṣma, Śālva and the Creator himself (5.173.6), before she quickly decides that she should get revenge on Bhīṣma (5.173.8). Like Damayantī, she finds refuge with ascetics, but instead of listening to their advice—which is not unanimous anyway—she is bent on revenge and gets them (or, specifically, their visitor, Rāma Jāmadagnya) to fight for her.

Taking into the picture the shift between the stories of Damayantī and Sītā, Ambā should not have been blamed for her kidnapping by Bhīṣma. In any case, the audiences from Janamejaya upwards (including the flesh-and-blood audience) would be sympathetic to Ambā if Bhīṣma had not started the anti-*pativratā* narrative through a visible absence of certain markers. The only event that could be read as a *pativratā* marker here is Ambā's later determination to kill the 'villain', Bhīṣma. This event goes beyond the scope of the Ambopākhyāna and therefore also beyond the scope of Bhīṣma's narration.

Event 3: Suspicion

The third event is probably the richest in intertextuality of the *upākhyāna*s. Every *pativratā*—Śakuntalā, Sītā, Damayantī—faces suspicion from her husband that eventually gives her a chance to prove beyond doubt her *pātivratya*. Even Sāvitrī, who does not face the suspicion literally, must prove her *pātivratya* to the god(s) so she can be reunited with her husband.

In the story of Śakuntalā, Duḥṣanta promises to send for Śakuntalā but never does so. She is eventually sent to him by Kaṇva when their son is six years old. Śakuntalā does not ask Duḥṣanta to accept her, just to accept their son as the *yuvarāja* (1.68.15–17). She only claims her right as Duḥṣanta gave her this promise as her *śulka* before the *gāndharva* marriage. Duḥṣanta voices his suspicion (1.68.18–19) and Śakuntalā's immediate reply is certainly a passionate one. She mentions that all the gods are witnesses to a person's bad deeds, calls herself a *pativratā* (1.68.33a), threatens that if he does not do as she says, his head will burst into a hundred pieces (1.68.35), follows with a lengthy speech about the importance of a wife and a son, and reminds him of her parentage and their marriage. Duḥṣanta accuses her of lying, which is highly paradoxical here as the audience knows that it is in fact him who lies (the narrator informs us explicitly in 1.68.18), then continues with his suspicion and even calls her a harlot (*puṃścalī*; 1.68.75, 79). Śakuntalā reacts with another speech about truth, goodness and virtue, and leaves. Her speeches do not help to persuade the king; it is the bodiless voice that authoritatively claims that Duḥṣanta is indeed the father of Śakuntalā's son and that he should accept both. Duḥṣanta rejoices, claims that he did not have any suspicion but merely pretended to have them so the people would not consider him impure (1.69.35–36), and explains it to Śakuntalā as well (1.69.40–42).

In the Nalopākhyāna, Nala suspects Damayantī of trying to marry for the second time and complains about the frail nature of women (3.74.21–23), even though Damayantī has been perfectly virtuous. After Nala's suspicion, she replies with a long speech, explaining what happened and advocating her innocence (2.75.1–6). She invites gods who are the witnesses of human deeds to kill her if she ever committed a sin, even in her mind (3.75.7–10). The gods indeed come to vouch for Damayantī's innocence: Vāyu attests that Damayantī never committed a sin, she was protected by them and orders Nala to be reunited with his wife. Flowers fall from Heaven, other auspicious omens occur and Nala accepts Damayantī again (3.75.11–16).

A very similar motif can be found in the Rāmopākhyāna. When Rāma finally defeats Rāvaṇa and summons Sītā, he is seized by suspicion and tells her to go wherever she wishes (3.275.10), continuing with his explanation: 'How could someone like us, knowing the rules of dharma, keep a woman who went to the hands of another? I cannot enjoy you, Maithilī, virtuous or sinful, like an oblation licked by a dog' (3.275.12–13).[12] It is clearly stated that he does not care much about her conduct but the mere fact that she was in the *rākṣasa*'s house is enough to send her away. Sītā reacts more passively than Śakuntalā: instead of trying to argue with her husband, she simply falls down (3.275.14). Immediately, gods, *yakṣa*s, *ṛṣi*s and even Rāma's father, Daśaratha, appear to vouch for her chastity (3.275.17–19). Only then is Sītā confident enough to speak for herself: if she is guilty in any way, let the gods kill her (3.275.23–24). The gods immediately tell Rāma that Sītā is telling the truth, is innocent and that Rāma should accept her. Brahmā even adds that Sītā was protected by the curse of Nalakūbara and by Brahmā himself. After Daśaratha allows Rāma to return to the kingdom, Rāma agrees. Rāma's suspicion is also overcome only by the voice of gods, and it is worth noting that Sītā did not have to try to prove her case before the gods appeared.

Śālva's suspicion

With these very powerful narratives, which share the main structure of this event, the stage is set for Śālva's suspicion in the Ambopākhyāna. Ambā reaches a situation very similar to that of Śakuntalā, Damayantī and Sītā. Like Sītā, she is returned to her (intended) husband after being kidnapped by another and, like Śakuntalā and Damayantī, she actively returns to him on her own accord and argues her case. A reader or listener who is aware of these patterns and recognises these stories as belonging to the same (sub) genre should explicitly expect a similar outcome—that is, the appearance of gods and their vouching for her innocence. This could be the most important script of the *pativratā* genre and the expectations of the audience should be very high here.

Ambā comes to Śālva and simply says that she came because of him (*Mbh*, 5.172.3c), to which Śālva immediately replies with suspicion, claiming that he does not want her as a wife and asking how a king like him could accept a woman who belonged to another man (5.172.5–7). Śālva calls Ambā *anyapūrvā* (which is basically what she claimed to be so Bhīṣma would dismiss her) and accuses her of going with Bhīṣma happily. He expresses the same sentiment as Rāma, especially when saying that *asmadvidho rājā* could not accept such a woman and expresses fear of Bhīṣma. Ambā protests and

12 *kathaṃ hy asmadvidho jātu jānan dharmaviniścayam | parahastagatāṃ nārīṃ muhūrtam api dhārayet || suvṛttāṃ asuvṛttāṃ vāpy ahaṃ tvām adya Maithili | notsahe paribhogāya śvāvalīḍhaṃ havir yathā ||*.

systematically rebuts every claim of his: she was taken by force and crying (5.172.8–9), Śālva should accept her as she is blameless, spurning those who are faithful is not praised (5.172.10) and Śālva should not be afraid of Bhīṣma because he allowed Ambā to go to Śālva and did not want her for himself (5.172.11–13). What follows bears a striking similarity to Śakuntalā's words and resembles a '*tena satyena*' sentence: Ambā swears that she never belonged to another man (5.172.14–16). Her words are without success as Śālva does not believe her, even though Ambā tries to persuade him with many other words (5.172.17–18). The narrative has so far followed the suspicion event very closely and the audience could—and even should—expect a divine intervention when everything seems lost. However, Ambā never calls the gods for help, and they do not appear. When Ambā says she will leave and Śālva does not try to persuade her to stay, she informs him that she will find a refuge with the good. Śālva replies that he is afraid of Bhīṣma and sends her away (5.172.22) and Ambā leaves the city in tears (5.172.23). The greatly anticipated gods never appear, forcing the audience to update the script because of this 'plot twist'—to re-evaluate their view of the Ambopākhyāna as a *pativratā* genre and, in effect, to question Ambā's character.

The *pativratā* (sub)genre

The great *pativratā*s of the *Mahābhārata* often fall into extreme misfortune, are left by their husbands and yet manage to be reunited with them thanks to their *pātivratya*. In the story of Sāvitrī, there is no suspicion about the heroine's virtue, yet she proves her *pātivratya* from the very beginning. After she mentally chooses Satyavat to be her husband, she does not choose another even though she is told that he will die soon. She must prove her *pātivratya* to the god Yama, and only after that is her husband restored to life. Sāvitrī creates a model for *pativratā*s who are supposed to be able to do anything thanks to their *pātivratya*, even cheat death. Damayantī is a similar icon for the conduct of *pativratā*s. When Nala leaves her, she only blames herself and never Nala and is still trying to find him (*Mbh*, 3.60). It is therefore made clear that even after a woman is deserted by her husband, she can be reunited with him if she is devoted enough.

There are various events and motifs known from the stories of *pativratā* women that can be observed in the Ambopākhyāna in a realised or unrealised yet expected form. Bhīṣma as the narrator of this episode is trying to portray Ambā as an anti-*pativratā*. First, he shows her in situations strikingly similar to those of the famous *pativratā*s: she chooses her husband herself, is kidnapped and faces her (intended) husband's suspicion. Following this pattern, the audience, as a narrative necessity, anticipates the script to continue in the same way: the gods or celestial voices are expected to vouch for her innocence. This event is, however, strikingly absent; the script has to be re-evaluated, the roles shift and the audience's expectations must change significantly. This 'plot twist' can result in feeling sympathy towards Ambā, especially in the modern flesh-and-blood reader, but it can also warn the audience that she is not, in fact, a *pativratā*; she is a bad woman and a liar. It also suggests that her chosen husband perhaps was not Śālva but Bhīṣma or that she truly happily exchanged Śālva for Bhīṣma when the great warrior appeared (as Śālva suggests in his speech), and only asked to be returned to Śālva when she found out that she was intended to become the wife not of Bhīṣma, but of his cowardly younger half-brother Vicitravīrya. All these options are opened by Bhīṣma's intertextual play.

The fight between Rāma Jāmadagnya (who plays the role of the god here) and Bhīṣma can be seen as Ambā's second *svayaṃvara*—a mock-*svayaṃvara* (like the one of Damayantī), or even an anti-*svayaṃvara* as both heroes fight, in essence, to get rid of her. When Ambā is asked to choose between Śālva (to marry) and Bhīṣma (to kill), she chooses the latter. Rāma asks Bhīṣma to accept her into his household but Bhīṣma refuses with words similar to those of the husbands of the *pativratā*s (5.178.21). After the fight, even Rāma abandons her, claiming that he did whatever he could and advises her to go wherever she wants, ideally to find refuge with Bhīṣma (5.187.1–4). Śālva is now forgotten by both Bhīṣma as the narrator and Ambā herself; she is depicted as thinking only of Bhīṣma (which is, however, still narrated by Bhīṣma). Her devotion in ascetic practices is more than a match to the asceticism of the *pativratā*s, but completely twisted:[13] Ambā practises asceticism not to marry a man, to be reunited with him or to keep him alive, but to kill him.

The Ambopākhyāna in the plot

The timing and circumstances of Bhīṣma's narration are also not unimportant. He narrates the story just before the battle at Kurukṣetra to inform Duryodhana that there is someone Bhīṣma will not be able to

13 According to Bhīṣma as the narrator, to Gaṅgā, who curses her to become a crooked river, and also to the wider context of the story-world (see, for example, *Mbh*, 6.39.4–6, which is part of the *Bhagavadgītā*).

fight against: the Pāñcāla warrior Śikhaṇḍin, who used to be a woman. On Duryodhana's question about why he would not fight against him, Bhīṣma replies with the—in fact, unnecessary—story of Ambā. For Duryodhana's purposes, it would suffice to narrate the second part about the sex change, yet Bhīṣma decides to narrate the story of a woman who is totally devoted to his death. So, if we consider the wider context, the question remains: Ambā is portrayed as an anti-*pativratā* by Bhīṣma, but who is the *pati*? Is it Śālva, as the first part of the story suggests, or is it, in fact, Bhīṣma? And is it possible that Ambā's devotion to Bhīṣma brought about what he wanted: his death? Bhīṣma died exactly the way he wanted to and it would not have been possible without Ambā's devotion to his death. It can be argued that even if, in Bhīṣma's own narration, Ambā is wilfully presented as Śālva's anti-*pativratā* using the context of the abovementioned *pativratā* stories, when the wider context is considered, she can be seen as the perfect *pativratā* for the lifelong *brahmacārin* Bhīṣma: a *pativratā* who went to great pains, including self-immolation and a rebirth aimed at meeting him again, to ensure that his ultimate wish came true.

On the other hand, when Ambā's and Śikhaṇḍin's stories are read as one, Bhīṣma's unwillingness or even inability to fight Śikhaṇḍin can be interpreted in the same terms as the hunter's and Rāvaṇa's inability to touch Damayantī and Sītā, and Ambā's efforts to kill Bhīṣma as the *pativratās*' and/or their husbands' determination to kill the abductors. This would betray Bhīṣma's interpretation of Ambā's life and show him as the villain of the story. The Ambopākhyāna would then be the answer to the question 'How would the *pativratā* genre look from the villain's point of view?'. Furthermore, this reading can be endorsed by Bhīṣma's continuous insistence that his fall was caused not by Śikhaṇḍin in any way, but by Arjuna (for example, *Mbh*, 6.114.54–61). We can read it as Bhīṣma's last attempt to claim Ambā and Śikhaṇḍin's narrative: if gods did not appear for her when she wanted to return to Śālva and if her *tapas* did not bring about Bhīṣma's death, she was a sinful woman and he is a hero. But if it did—and the text seems to imply that this is the case, even though it is careful not to give a readymade answer—Bhīṣma can be seen as a villain and Ambā as a successful woman in the line of *pativratās* who slayed her abductor thanks to her own *tapas* and with the help of gods. Even with Bhīṣma claiming Ambā's narrative and with all the narrators being favourable to Bhīṣma (to the point of calling Śikhaṇḍin a *rākṣasa* reborn; 1.161.87, 15.39.14), events of the wider context seem to suggest that a reading seeing Ambā as a *pativratā* heroine and condemning Bhīṣma is also a legitimate part of the subjective and polyphonic text that is the *Mahābhārata*.

References

Primary text

Sukthankar, Vishnu Sitaram (ed.). (1933–66). *The Mahābhārata*. [19 vols.] Poona, India: Bhandarkar Oriental Research Institute.

Secondary texts

Adluri, Vishwa. (2016). The divine androgyne: Crossing gender and breaking hegemonies in the Ambā-Upākhyāna of the Mahābhārata. In Vishwa Adluri and Joydeep Bagchee (eds), *Argument and Design: The Unity of the Mahābhārata*, pp. 275–319. Leiden, Netherlands: Brill. doi.org/10.1163/9789004311404.

Bal, Mieke and Tavor, Eve. (1981). Notes on narrative embedding. *Poetics Today* 2(2): 41–59. doi.org/10.2307/1772189.

Black, Brian. (2007). Eavesdropping on the epic: Female listeners in the Mahābhārata. In Simon Brodbeck and Brian Black (eds), *Gender and Narrative in the Mahābhārata*. London: Routledge.

Booth, Wayne C. (1983 [1961]). *The Rhetoric of Fiction*. Chicago, IL: University of Chicago Press. doi.org/10.7208/chicago/9780226065595.001.0001.

Brockington, John L. (2006). Epic svayamvaras. In Raghunath Panda and Madhusudan Mishra (eds), *Voice of the Orient: A Tribute to Prof Upendranath Dhal*. Delhi: Eastern Book Linkers.

Brodbeck, Simon. (2013). The story of Sāvitrī in the Mahābhārata: A lineal interpretation. *Journal of the Royal Asiatic Society* 23(4): 527–49. doi.org/10.1017/S1356186313000424.

Chakravarti, Uma. (2009). *Of Meta-Narratives and 'Master' Paradigms: Sexuality and the Reification of Women in Early India*. New Delhi: Center for Women's Development Studies.

Custodi, Andrea. (2007). 'Show you are a man!' Transsexuality and gender bending in the characters of Arjuna/Bṛhannaḍā and Ambā/Śikhaṇḍin(ī). In Simon Brodbeck and Brian Black (eds), *Gender and Narrative in the Mahābhārata*. London: Routledge.

Dhand, Arti. (2004). *Woman as Fire, Woman as Sage: Sexual Ideology in the Mahābhārata*. Albany: SUNY Press.

Doniger, Wendy. (2014). *On Hinduism*. New York, NY: Oxford University Press. doi.org/10.1093/acprof:oso/9780199360079.001.0001.

Emmott, Catherine and Alexander, Marc. (2009). Schemata. In Peter Hühn (ed.), *Handbook of Narratology*. Berlin : Walter de Gruyter.

Fitzgerald, James L. (2003). The many voices of the Mahābhārata. *Journal of the American Oriental Society* 123(4): 803–18. doi.org/10.2307/3589969.

Genette, Gerard. (1980). *Narrative Discourse: An Essay in Method*. Ithaca, NY: Cornell University Press.

Hiltebeitel, Alf. (2001). *Rethinking the Mahābhārata: A Reader's Guide to the Education of the Dharma King*. Chicago, IL: University of Chicago Press.

Hiltebeitel, Alf. (2011). Weighting orality and writing in the Sanskrit epics. In Vishwa Adluri and Joydeep Bagchee (eds), *Reading the Fifth Veda: Studies on the Mahābhārata—Essays*. Boston: Brill.

Hiltebeitel, Alf. (2014). Bhīṣma's sources. *Studia Orientalia Electronica* 94: 261–78. Available from: journal.fi/store/article/view/43975.

Hiltebeitel, Alf. (2016). Not without subtales: Telling laws and truths in the Sanskrit epics. In Vishwa Adluri and Joydeep Bagchee (eds), *Argument and Design: The Unity of the Mahābhārata*. Leiden, Netherlands: Brill.

Howard, Veena R. (2020). Narrative of Ambā in the Mahābhārata: Female body, gender, and the namesake of the divine feminine. In Veena R. Howard (ed.), *The Bloomsbury Research Handbook of Indian Philosophy and Gender*, pp. 217–48. London: Bloomsbury Academic. doi.org/10.5040/9781474269612.ch-010.

Hühn, Peter. (2009). Event and eventfulness. In Peter Hühn (ed.), *Handbook of Narratology*. Berlin: Walter de Gruyter.

Martin, Richard P. (2005). Epic as genre. In John Miles Fowley (ed.), *A Companion to Ancient Epic*. London: Blackwell.

Morales-Harley, Roberto. (2019). Ambā's speech to Bhīṣma (Mbh 1.96.48–49). In Robert P. Goldman and James Hegarty (eds), *Proceedings of the 17th World Sanskrit Conference, Vancouver, Canada, July 9–13, 2018. Section 4: Epics*. Vancouver, BC: Department of Asian Studies, University of British Columbia. Available from: wsc.ubcsanskrit.ca/proceedings.

Phelan, James. (2017). Reliable, unreliable, and deficient narration: A rhetorical account. *Narrative Culture* 4(1): 89–103. doi.org/10.13110/narrcult.4.1.0089.

Phelan, James and Martin, Mary Patricia. (1999). The lessons of 'Weymouth': Homodiegesis, unreliability, ethics, and *The Remains of the Day*. In David Herman (ed.), *Narratologies: New Perspectives on Narrative Analysis*, pp. 88–109. Columbus: Ohio State University Press.

Reich, Tamar Chana. (1998). *A Battlefield of a Text: Inner Textual Interpretation in the Sanskrit Mahābhārata*. Chicago, IL: University of Chicago.

Shah, Shalini. (2012). On gender, wives and 'pativratās'. *Social Scientist* 40(5–6): 77–90.

Špicová, Zuzana. (2019). Bhīṣma, an (un)reliable narrator. In Robert P. Goldman and James Hegarty (eds), *Proceedings of the 17th World Sanskrit Conference, Vancouver, Canada, July 9–13, 2018. Section 4: Epics*. Vancouver, BC: Department of Asian Studies, University of British Columbia. Available from: wsc.ubcsanskrit.ca/proceedings.

Sutherland, Sally. (1989). Sītā and Draupadī: Aggressive behavior and female role-models in the Sanskrit epics. *Journal of the American Oriental Society* 109(1): 63–79. doi.org/10.2307/604337.

van Buitenen, J.A.B. (1978). Introduction. In J.A.B. van Buitenen (trans. & ed.), *The Mahābhārata. Volume 3, Book 4: The Book of Virāṭa. Book 5: The Book of the Effort*. Chicago, IL: Chicago University Press. doi.org/10.7208/chicago/9780226223711.001.0001.

7

Bhīma: The shadow king

Sudha Berry

Abstract

Bhīma is the second eldest of the five Pāṇḍavas in the *Mahābhārata*, known for his cartoonish characterisation as a huge man with large appetites, a formidable warrior lauded for his brute strength and a passionate partner to Draupadī. Together with his younger brother Arjuna, he is recognised as a pivotal warrior on the Pāṇḍava side. What is less appreciated is Bhīma's embodiment of a successful *kṣatriya* king counselling a pragmatic *rājadharma* (the rules or laws relating to kings) in pursuit of the throne. In contrast with Yudhiṣṭhira, who performs the ceremonial and leadership functions, and Arjuna, who embodies the ideal king, Bhīma performs the military and administrative functions of kingship in the shadow of the ideal kingly depictions of his more luminary brothers. This view of Bhīma as the shadow king is at odds with his conventional image, which does not credit him in this regard.

Introduction

The analysis of Bhīma's character in the *Mahābhārata* as one of the three senior Pāṇḍavas has been explored by significant past scholarship, establishing that Yudhiṣṭhira, Bhīma and Arjuna embody different but complementary qualities that are markers of kingship in the *Mahābhārata*. Yudhiṣṭhira is the heir to the throne of his father, Pāṇḍu, embodies *dharma* and always has his eye on *mokṣa* but lacks the will and strength required to rule independently and must rely on Kṛṣṇa and his brothers to fill the gap. It is evident that although Yudhiṣṭhira is the apparent king, Arjuna, who possesses skill, strength and discrimination, is often held up as the ideal king. Bhīma is recognised largely for his martial success arising from his innate strength, massive appetite and size, loyalty to the Pāṇḍava cause and to his family, his terrible deeds, which are rākṣasic in nature, and his devotion, bordering on slavishness, to Draupadī, the common wife of the Pāṇḍavas. Contrary to this commonly held characterisation of Bhīma, this chapter will argue that he represents the figure of a pragmatic, successful *kṣatriya* king whose pursuit of rule is fuelled by *kāma* directed at the communal achievements of his family rather than his own interests. Together with Kṛṣṇa, Draupadī and Arjuna, he is constant in counselling a pragmatic *rājadharma*, the pursuit of which is necessary if the kingdom is to be regained. This is not to deny the predominant understanding of his character but rather to appreciate that his character displays a facet of kingship that is in counterpoint to the apparent king (Yudhiṣṭhira) and the ideal king (Arjuna) of the *Mahābhārata*.

This chapter presents a view of Bhīma over the span of the *Mahābhārata*, employing a synchronous literary analysis that is necessary to obtain an overarching view of his character. There could be occasions when adopting a non-synchronous approach is fruitful (Austin 2011: 130)[1] or having a rigorous methodology for synchronous readings with a view to narrative frames such as that proposed by Balkaran (2021) is useful, but neither of these seems appropriate for the scope and focus of this chapter because the character of Bhīma is mostly contained within the main narrative frame. Accordingly, the picture of Bhīma as the shadow king presented in this chapter is that garnered by analysing his actions and relationships over the course of the *Mahābhārata*—a picture that has been hiding in plain sight for centuries.

1 Analysing two mirroring passages that more or less bookend the *Mahābhārata*, Austin has suggested that although he would normally adopt a synchronous approach, a non-synchronous approach can sometimes provide greater insight into the text.

Mythic symbolism of Bhīma and his brothers

The line of scholarship to which this chapter is indebted and incremental was initiated by the groundbreaking work of Wikander, Dumézil and Biardeau, as incorporated by Hiltebeitel. Hiltebeitel summarises the principal findings of Wikander and Dumézil as follows, with respect to the functions represented by the Pāṇḍavas and their common wife, Draupadī: '[t]he eldest Pāṇḍava, king Yudhiṣṭhira, has both sacerdotal and juridical traits; the next two brothers, Arjuna and Bhīma, have pronounced warrior characteristics; and the twins and Draupadī have associations, respectively, with pastoralism and the earth's fecundity' (Hiltebeitel 2011a: 597).[2]

Biardeau (1981: 91) takes this understanding further, associating the sannyāsic Yudhiṣṭhira with the sāttvic quality of *mokṣa* ('liberation') and making him the ideal king at a moment of world crisis who leads the warriors to salvation at the end: 'He rules as Dharma-Yama rules, by destroying and making room for a new world in order to save *dharma* and the three worlds.' She sees the energetic and violent Bhīma as the opposite of Yudhiṣṭhira, devoted to *kāma* ('desire'), as he is the one who is 'born as an answer to this embodied threat to the existence of earth ... at the lowest point of the world crisis' and as such

> upholds the interests of life in this world, and is the strong and bloody warrior who treats his victims on the battlefield [Duḥśāsana, Duryodhana, etc.] as well as outside [Jarāsandha, Kīcaka, many *rākçasas*] without any consideration for the warrior's code of honour. (Biardeau 1981: 91)

She argues that this is because 'desire for life requires violence [*hiṃsā*] because every living being is threatened in its very existence by a stronger one' (Biardeau 1981: 91).

Yudhiṣṭhira's passivity, propensity for renunciation, indecisiveness, weakness, inability to refuse dice (van Buitenen 1975: 232; *Mbh*, 3.6.9),[3] vacillation and lack of prowess in battle all highlight the fact that he does not have

2 As the twins do not feature prominently and are not relevant to the argument, they will not be explored in any detail.

3 It is remarkable that even after the kingdom has been lost in the rigged dice game and the Pāṇḍavas are in exile, Yudhiṣṭhira muses to Bhīma about the reason for Vidura's visit to them in the forest and whether it means another invitation to play dice. Shockingly, he acknowledges that if he were to be invited again, he would be unable to refuse yet again.

the wherewithal to prevail against the challenges of rule and exile without assistance, principally from Bhīma and Arjuna. Arjuna—the Nara to Kṛṣṇa's Nārāyaṇa, favoured by the gods and adept in the arts—is lauded as the warrior par excellence, capable of heroic deeds and yogic austerities, whose achievements in obtaining divine weapons and mastery on the battlefield are instrumental to the eventual transcendence of the Pāṇḍavas. Pointing out the various facets of Arjuna's special relationship with Kṛṣṇa, Biardeau (1981: 88) regards Arjuna as 'the figure of the ideal king, in spite of Yudhiṣṭhira's being the apparent king of the story'.

Whether Yudhiṣṭhira or Arjuna is the ideal king, it is obvious that Bhīma is never overtly depicted as the ideal king, although his role in crushing enemies—arguably a kingly function—is well recognised, as for example, in Draupadī's description of him in the following words to her abductor Jayadratha:

> *mahābhujaṁ śālam iva pravṛddham ... etasya karmāṇy atimānuṣāṇi |*
> *bhīmeti śabdo 'sya gataḥ pṛthivyām ||*
> *nāsyāparāddhāḥ śeṣam ihāpnuvanti |*
> *nāpy asya vairaṁ vismarate kadā cit ||*
> *vairasyāntaṁ saṁvidhāyopayāti |*
> *paścāc chāntiṁ na ca gacchaty atīva ||*
>
> [Strong-armed, like a full-grown śāla tree ... The feats he has done are more than human. And the cry of him on this earth is: He's Bhima! No quarter from him will the guilty receive, Nor will his enmity be forgotten; Having put an end to the feud he will come To serenity afterward but not too quickly.] (van Buitenen 1975: 718–19; *Mbh*, 3.254.9–11)

The first part of the picture of Bhīma painted by Draupadī is the typical one describing his appearance and praising his strength and his feats. The second part, however, is more interesting. She describes him as the dreadful hand of justice whose actions are praised by the Earth. We will see later in this chapter the correlation between Draupadī as Śrī and the Earth. By referring to the Earth's cry greeting Bhīma, Draupadī is highlighting her own reliance on him. From the person who perhaps knows him best, he is described as serene after he has acted to enforce *dharma*, implying that the extremity of his actions is paired with a degree of self-mastery and control that enables him to return to equilibrium after the actions have been successfully completed. This description shows Bhīma embodying the necessary functions of an effective king wielding the rod of punishment (*daṇḍa*): to be aware of *dharma*, acting selflessly and strongly in meting out justice to those who violate *dharma* and returning to a sense of serenity after the deed is done. Bhīma's characterisation is usually of the bombastic, passionate, unruly *kṣatriya*, which is so vividly painted that his role as the law-abiding, dharmic enforcer does not usually come to the fore. Yet, his self-restraint is also recognised by his mother, Kuntī, when after a long absence from her sons, she prefaces her query about Bhīma's welfare to Kṛṣṇa as follows:

> *parākrame śakrasamo vāyuvegasamo jave* |
> *maheśvarasamaḥ krodhe bhīmaḥ praharatāṁ varaḥ* ||
> *krodhaṁ balam amarṣaṁ ca yo nidhāya paraṁtapaḥ* |
> *jitātmā pāṇḍavo 'marṣī bhrātus tiṣṭhati śāsane* ||
> *tejorāśiṁ mahātmānaṁ balaugham amitaujasam* |
> *bhīmaṁ pradarśanenāpi bhīmasenaṁ Janārdana* |
> *taṁ mamācakṣva vārṣṇeya katham adya vṛkodaraḥ* ||
>
> [And Wolf-Belly ... in speed the equal of a wind gust, in anger the match of the great God ... the enemy burner who controlled his anger, strength and impatience ... master of himself in spite of his fury, who obeys his brother's behest, that mass of splendor, storm flood of power, boundlessly august, great-spirited Bhīmasena who strikes terror with his appearance.] (van Buitenen 1975: 368–69; *Mbh*, 5.88.25)

What's in a name?[4]

A common epithet for Bhīma is Wolf-Belly (Vṛkodara),[5] signifying his rapacious appetite (van Buitenen 1971: 360; *Mbh*, 1.12.185.5).[6] This is obviously a reference to his physical appetite, but the term also describes Bhīma's appetite for life (or, in Biardeau's words, *kāma*) and his bottomless capacity for action. Whether evading assassination as a child, carrying the

4 I am deeply grateful to Renate Söhnen-Thieme as a senior scholar of the *Mahābhārata* for her exactitude and generous guidance in providing comments that improved this chapter generally and this section in particular.

5 One of the meanings of this term listed in Monier-Williams (1899: 1008) is a class of demons attendant on Śiva. This is yet another marker of Bhīma's association with Rudra-Śiva.

6 When instructing Draupadī as a new bride in domestic matters, her mother-in-law, Kuntī, asks her to divide all the food collected in two: one half for Bhīma and the other half to be shared among the rest of the family.

entire family to safety from the House of Lac (3.13.75), vanquishing *rākṣasas* or obtaining victory against enemies in battle, particularly when they are outside the towns in the forest or in the mountains—Bhīma is responsible for saving the family from danger time and again.

Bhīma's parentage, like that of his brothers, is half-human, half-divine. His nominal human father, Pāṇḍu, yearning for sons but unable to father them because of a curse that would result in his death if he touched his wives, learns of the mantra that his first wife, Kuntī, received from the sage Durvāsas in her youth. This magical mantra empowered her to conceive a child from whichever god on whom she meditated and called. At Pāṇḍu's direction and behest, seeking first a son who would be 'law-minded', she obtains the eldest, Yudhiṣṭhira, from the god Dharma; then, seeking a son whose strength would grant dominion (*prāhuḥ kṣatraṁ balajyeṣṭhaṁ balajyeṣṭhaṁ sutaṁ vṛṇu*) (van Buitenen 1973: 255; *Mbh*, 1.7.114.5), she obtains Bhīma from the wind god Vāyu; and then, seeking a 'superior son who will be supreme in the world' (*putro lokaśreṣṭho*), she obtains Arjuna from the god Indra, king of the gods. She shares the mantra with Pāṇḍu's childless second wife, Mādrī, who obtains the twin sons, Nakula and Sahadeva, by calling on the Aśvins, the two divine charioteers considered to be the physicians of Heaven.

At Bhīma's birth, a disembodied voice proclaims: 'O Bhārata: He is born to be strong over all that is strong! [*sarveṣāṁ balināṁ śreṣṭho jāto 'yam iti bhārata*].' He displays his strength immediately, shattering a mountain by falling on it with his diamond-hard body, when his mother, Kuntī, startled by a tiger, inadvertently drops him from her lap (van Buitenen 1973: 255; *Mbh*, 1.114.11–13). While the birth of each of the Pāṇḍavas is heralded by a disembodied voice—indeed, Arjuna's birth receives star billing with an extended paean of praise—it is only Bhīma who immediately provides proof of his innate prowess. The baby Yudhiṣṭhira can hardly extol the law and the baby Arjuna will have to be schooled to develop his gifts, but baby Bhīma's essential nature is already on display. While he will also be tutored, his innate nature is radiant from his birth to his end.

The narrative refers to him at this point as Bhīma, however, he is named later with the rest of his brothers by mountain-dwelling seers who call him Bhīmasena (van Buitenen 1973: 259; *Mbh*, 1.115.20), which is translated by Monier-Williams (1899: 758) as 'having a formidable army'—a quintessentially *kṣatriya* name.

The name of Bhīṣma, the Kuru elder who is the caretaker of the kingdom while the nominal rulers are minors, is translated as 'terrible' or 'dreadful' (Monier-Williams 1899: 758)—the name given to him by a disembodied heavenly voice in response to his oath of celibacy. As suggested by the similarities of their names, there is also a resonance in the stories of Bhīma and Bhīṣma. Each has the capacity to be king, but each forgoes the realisation of his innate capacity in favour of others. Bhīṣma does so voluntarily, vowing to abandon his birthright in favour of the son of his father's second wife and eschewing matrimony to satisfy her that neither he nor his descendants will ever challenge her son as king. Bhīma is automatically excluded from rule by the law of male primogeniture, which dictates that he will always be subservient to Yudhiṣṭhira and must curtail his activities and ambitions accordingly. This consequence is accepted and never challenged by Bhīma, who subsumes any personal ambitions to the communal welfare of the family. The sacrifice of Bhīṣma and Bhīma relates to rule of the kingdom; each relinquishes his personal ambitions to rule for the sake of others who assume rule in his stead.

There is a further inference to be drawn from their similar names: a feature that is clearly detailed in the Bhīṣma story is that, like him, Bhīma, based on his abilities and nature, is the one who ought to have been king. This aspect is alluded to by Karve (1969: 56) when she imagines the dying Draupadī saying to Bhīma with her last breath: 'In our next birth be the eldest, Bhima; under your shelter we can all live in safety and joy.' I believe Karve's *naroti* ('dry coconut shell'), deliberately straying from the critical edition of the *Mahābhārata*, speaks not only to her reading of Draupadī's estimation of Bhīma as her husband and principal protector but also to the many endured vicissitudes that could have been avoided had Bhīma been king.

An association with the god Śiva is embedded in Bhīma's name as it is associated with Rudra-Śiva and the name Bhīṣma is also a name of Śiva. As Kevin McGrath (2017: 52–53) has remarked, Bhīma 'is repeatedly likened to the deity Rudra, being *raudrātmā*, and he is said to be: *atiṣṭhat tumule bhīmaḥ śmaśāna iva śūlabhṛt* (6.58.61) "Bhīma stood in the tumult like the Trident Bearer in a burning ground"'. Śiva is the god known for being out of the ordered norms of the Vedic fire rituals transacted by brahmins between humans and the gods making offerings in return for blessings. Being outside these norms means that Śiva is unpredictable, unregulated and unbiddable. These characteristics combined with his power and propensity to anger make him awesome, terrible, dreadful and so on—characteristics that could be described as those of *rākṣasa*s. Bhīma's power and tendency to violence and wrath are well-defined characteristics, as indeed is his affinity to *rākṣasa*s seen particularly in his deeds, which are so outside *dharma* as to be rākṣasic in nature.

Bhīma and *rākṣasas*

There are two sets of encounters between Bhīma and *rākṣasa*s given prominence in the text, mainly involving their killing by Bhīma.[7] The first set involves the killing of Hiḍimba, Baka and Baka's brother Kirmīra—all in extended encounters in single combat. The first set follows a pattern of Bhīma clearing the area of the threat posed by the *rākṣasa* in question to either the surrounding population or even to the Pāṇḍavas and Kuntī. These killings symbolise Bhīma's defeat of these *rākṣasa*s, fulfilling the *kṣatriya* ruler's role of eradicating threats to the populace and thereby bringing about peace. The first set of killings also cements his connection with *rākṣasa*s through his encounter with the rākṣasic Hiḍimbā, sister of Hiḍimba, whom she betrays in favour of Bhīma. With Kuntī's blessing, accompanied by strange strictures about how they can spend time together, Bhīma and Hiḍimbā enjoy a brief but pleasure-filled marriage, eventually resulting in the birth of their son, Ghaṭotkaca (*Mbh*, 1.143.35).

The second set of killings of unnamed *rākṣasa*s, Maṇimat and other, unnamed *yakṣa*s who bar his entry into territories reserved for the gods and higher beings is harder to fathom and occurs when Bhīma barges his way into these realms in search of the fragrant flowers demanded by Draupadī in the *Saugandhikaparvan* (3.146 ff.).

The first-named *rākṣasa* episode given prominence in the narrative is the killing of Hiḍimba. After Bhīma carries the Pāṇḍavas and Kuntī to safety from the House of Lac, they take shelter in a forest while Bhīma stands watch. He encounters the rākṣasic Hiḍimbā, sent by her carnivorous brother Hiḍimba to capture all of them so that he can make a meal of them to share with her. As the others are asleep, she sees Bhīma standing guard and is captivated by his appearance. She assumes a charming human body and approaches him, offering to fly with all of them away from the danger posed by Hiḍimba. Witnessing his sister's appearance and sensing her lust for Bhīma,

7 See Gitomer (2007) for a revealing comparison of Bhīma as depicted in the *Mahābhārata* and Bhaṭṭa's *Veṇisaṃhāra*, illustrating Bhīma's rākṣasic nature.

the enraged Hiḍimba arrives and a battle between him and Bhīma ensues, at the end of which Bhīma kills Hiḍimba. There are no weapons mentioned and the fight sounds like hand-to-hand combat. Hiḍimbā asks Kuntī to be allowed to marry Bhīma, and their union produces Ghaṭotkaca, who will be useful to the Pāṇḍavas, initially in carrying them to the remote Mount Kailāsa (van Buitenen 1975: 497; *Mbh*, 3.145.15) when their own strength fails (3.145 ff.). Later he is summoned to fight on the Pāṇḍava side, and he does so courageously, using his magical powers and tremendous strength in fighting the Kaurava army.

In the company of Hiḍimbā, Bhīma enjoys suprahuman experiences, flying and visiting magical realms not normally available to humans. Hiḍimbā flies him up into these environs where they disport themselves. Via Hiḍimbā, Bhīma is invited into the world of *rākṣasa*s and fathers a son with suprahuman characteristics—a son who will be sacrificed as cannon fodder when Karṇa uses a divine weapon to kill Ghaṭotkaca instead of saving it to kill Arjuna as he had planned (*Mbh*, 7.154.48–50). This episode marks Bhīma's entry into the world of *rākṣasa*s by invitation, because he is loved by a *rākṣasī*, and here, too, the force that propels him into this world is that of *kāma*—this time, not initiated by him but nevertheless enjoyed by him. In any event, ever conscious and true to his *rājadharma*, he remarks that after he has killed Hiḍimba, those who walk in the forest will be able to do so without oppression (1.141.10).

In the Baka story, the Pāṇḍavas and Kuntī are living in disguise as brahmins in the house of a brahmin. Their host is in sorrow because it is now his turn to send a person from his family as a sacrifice, together with food to the *rākṣasa* Baka. Offering to alleviate this problem, Kuntī offers Bhīma instead of the host's family as the sacrificial offering, as she is confident that Bhīma will overpower Baka (*Mbh*, 1.145 ff.). The brahmin host complains to Kuntī that the local king is incompetent and has not taken care of this menace because of which the people suffer (1.148.10). Bhīma takes the food demanded by Baka to him but ignores the enraged Baka and eats it all himself before engaging with him in battle. When Baka is felled, Bhīma leaves his body by the town gate and the townsfolk, believing that a brahmin has rid them of Baka, rejoice, instituting a brahmin festival. It is notable that Kuntī arranges Bhīma's confrontation with Baka for two reasons: first, as a mark of gratitude for their brahmin host and, second, to follow *kṣatriyadharma* and *rājadharma* as she asserts that the rewards for doing so are many (1.150.20). As in the previous killing of *rākṣasa*s, the agent for relieving the populace from the misery of Baka is Bhīma, as he fulfills the *rājadharma* and *kṣatriyadharma* of providing safety and security, which the local king has failed to do.

The pattern is repeated in the killing of Kirmīra, Baka's brother and a friend of Hiḍimba, who seeks revenge for their killings. Instead, he is killed by Bhīma, thereby rendering the forest safe and pest-free (*Mbh*, 3.12.50).

The wanton destruction, killing and rampage on Gandhamādana Mountain and in Kubera's domain by Bhīma do not follow the earlier pattern of killing *rākṣasa*s to eradicate threats to safety. It is also puzzling that Bhīma is chastised by Yudhiṣṭhira, but only mildly by Kubera (*Mbh*, 3.158.35–45), whose friend, the *yakṣa* Maṇimat, was killed by Bhīma while mounting a defence of Kubera's realm. Sent on a mission to collect flowers by Draupadī, Bhīma takes his time, frolics, kills, plunders flowers and so on. This is also the setting, in a mythical landscape away from society, where Bhīma's heroic initiation takes place (Laine 1989: 42–43) and where he is humbled by his elder half-brother Hanumān (3.146.14 ff.). Feller (2005) has analysed these passages in detail, so I will make only some incremental comments here. In these instances, Bhīma is completely unrestrained, outside society and unburdened by the concerns of *dharma* and the opinions of others. He is free to express his elemental nature without societal consequences and when he does so, he overpowers various suprahuman classes of beings in their own domain. Perhaps this is why Kubera does not protest too loudly: he and his followers are no match for the mighty Bhīmasena. As to why Bhīma chooses to indulge in these acts, one can only posit that it is the expression of his elemental nature as the destructive force of the wind. Biardeau (1981: 91) explains the significance of Bhima's descent from Vāyu, who represents *prāṇa*, which is 'the first and last manifestation of life and movement', and 'Prabhañjana, the breaker, one of the symbols of physical strength in its most violent form'.

When Bhīma is restrained and bested, it is by his elder brother Hanumān, who demonstrates a way of being where his formidable strength is yoked to *bhakti*. Both are the sons of the god Vāyu, but Hanumān's realm is accompanied by a gentle, perfumed breeze, whereas Bhīma moves like a windstorm. In these passages, high in the mountains, concerns about kingship and *rājadharma* fade and the unfettered Bhīma is free to express his elemental nature. When he does so, there is no-one, including Kubera and his *rākṣasa*s, except Hanumān, who embodies the same nature as Bhīma, who can stop him.

Bhīma and Duryodhana: One another's *bhāga*

Each of the five Pāṇḍavas is born a year apart from his senior sibling and the eldest, Yudhiṣṭhira, is born a year after Gāndhārī became pregnant (van Buitenen 1973: 255; *Mbh*, 1.7.114). Gāndhārī is married to Pāṇḍu's blind brother, Dhṛtarāṣṭra, who is acting as regent under the supervision of Bhīṣma, while Pāṇḍu, Kuntī and Mādrī live as ascetics in the forest. Gāndhārī's pregnancy is long and tortured and she gives birth to a mass of flesh that is divided into a hundred pots, each portion gestating at different times and each culminating in the birth of a son (1.107.19–27). The eldest of Gāndhārī's 100 sons is Duryodhana, who is born after his cousin Yudhiṣṭhira, but at the same time as Kuntī gives birth to her second son, Bhīma (van Buitenen 1973: 255; *Mbh*, 1.114.14).

Yudhiṣṭhira is the eldest Pāṇḍava and heir to the throne and should be paired with Duryodhana, who is the eldest Kaurava and seeks to usurp him. However, throughout the *Mahābhārata*, the keenest rivalry is not between Yudhiṣṭhira and Duryodhana but rather between Bhīma and Duryodhana. The symmetry between Bhīma and Duryodhana is evident from the outset and is established by their birth on the same day. That symmetry matures into rivalry during childhood games among the cousins when, without malintent, Bhīma's brute strength plagues his Kaurava cousins and continually humiliates them. These experiences inform Duryodhana's desire to bring Bhīma down by trickery, believing that once it is accomplished, he will overpower both Yudhiṣṭhira and Arjuna (van Buitenen 1973: 265; *Mbh*, 1.119.25):

> The Bhāga, or 'appointed opponent', of Yudhiṣṭhira, the heir apparent is Śalya ... Yudhiṣṭhira's maternal uncle ... There is no symmetry between these two chiefs in the poem apart from the fact of their equal and opposing kinship status. This is despite the fact that individual combat should, by *kṣatriya* custom, only occur between warriors of like rank. (McGrath 2017: 90–91)

The pairing of Yudhiṣṭhira with Śalya highlights the fact that Yudhiṣṭhira is merely the titular king who did not have the capacity to rule independently. While noting that 'Duryodhana's Bhāga is Bhīma', McGrath (2017: 90–91) states: 'There is a condition of asymmetry here whose reasoning is not explicit.' However, I argue that if we appreciate Bhīma's ability, strength and will to rule, the reasoning behind this pairing becomes obvious: both Bhīma and Duryodhana are 'the man who would be king' and each is the mirror of the other. Bhīma's actions, un-dharmic though they may be, are performed on the side of *dharma*, whereas Duryodhana's conformity to *kṣatriyadharma* in battle is performed for an un-dharmic reason, which is the usurpation of the throne against the recognised societal norm of male primogeniture.

At least in childhood, the main Pāṇḍava is Bhīma, and vanquishing him by any means becomes Duryodhana's obsession. At this point, neither Yudhiṣṭhira nor Arjuna is seen as a threat and it is Bhīma who is the thorn in the side of Duryodhana. The twins Nakula and Sahadeva are not even contenders because 'their only aim is to serve their brothers' purposes' (Biardeau 1981: 89). When poisoning Bhīma, tying him in chains and drowning him all fail, Duryodhana conceives of killing all the Pāṇḍavas and Kuntī in the House of Lac. When Kuntī is alerted to this danger by Vidura, of all her sons, Bhīma is the one to whom she turns for assistance and protection. He assures her and ensures their escape by carrying his mother and siblings away to safety. He guards them while they sleep in the forest and is their main protector from the dangers of the forest in the *Ādiparvan* (*Mbh*, 1.143).

While Bhīma takes the lead and shoulders the burden, there is neither assistance nor protest from either Yudhiṣṭhira or Arjuna until they encounter the *rākṣasa* Baka, who bars their entry to the forest. While Bhīma battles Baka with trees used as clubs, Arjuna taunts him and offers to kill Baka if Bhīma is unable to do it himself. This interchange marks Arjuna's emerging presence and skill in arms, which will lead to his eventual transcendence as the *kṣatriya* par excellence in the narrative. Gradually but inexorably, the sole reliance on Bhīma as the mighty protector of the Pāṇḍavas transitions to a tripartite force of Kṛṣṇa for policy and counsel and Bhīma and Arjuna for victory in battle. This reliance is reflected in Yudhiṣṭhira's words while vacillating about whether to send the trio against the Magadhan king Jarāsaṃdha, who is killed in single combat by Bhīma:

> *bhīmārjunāv ubhau netre mano manye janārdanam* |
> *manaścakṣurvihīnasya kīdṛśaṁ jīvitaṁ bhavet* ||
>
> [Bhīma and Arjuna are my eyes, Janardana I deem my mind: what kind of life shall be left for me when I have lost my eyes and my mind?] (van Buitenen 1975: 61; *Mbh*, 2.15.1)

It is this trio that eventually brings about the defeat of the Kauravas and, in particular, the death of Duryodhana by Bhīma. Kṛṣṇa tells Arjuna that Bhīma will be unable to vanquish Duryodhana except by deceit. In turn, Arjuna points to his thigh and Bhīma, understanding the gesture, attacks Duryodhana below the waist, against *kṣatriyadharma*, shattering his thighs, and thus fulfilling his vow of vengeance. When Balarāma, Kṛṣṇa's brother and teacher to both Duryodhana and Bhīma, is shocked by this act, Kṛṣṇa defends Bhīma, but Balarāma remains repulsed and Kṛṣṇa must restrain him from attacking Bhīma (Matilal 2002: 117; *Mbh*, 9.59.17–19). Adding a further action beyond the pale, Bhīma places his foot on the head of the dying Duryodhana, attracting censure from everyone around. He responds with characteristic boldness to Yudhiṣṭhira: '*tavādya pṛthivī ... tāṃ praśādhi mahārāja* [now the Earth is yours, rule it, Mahārāja!]' (*Mbh*, 9.59.39; McGrath 2017: 108). Yet, even while chiding him, Yudhiṣṭhira reminds Bhīma that this action is at odds with his reputation as 'righteous Bhīma' (*dhārmiko bhīmaseno*) (Meiland 2007: 329–31; *Mbh*, 9.58.17). Bhīma's deeds and attitude at this moment underline his recognition that the mere defeat of the Kauravas is insufficient. A complete annihilation of the world order represented by Duryodhana is necessary. The humiliation of Duryodhana, marked by the smashing of his beautiful thighs (*ūrū babhañja*; the perfected form of the verb √*bhañj*, 'to break'), harks back to the crumbling of the mountain at Bhīma's birth (*śilāṁ gātrair acūrṇayat*). The smashing of the mountain immediately after his birth is Bhīma's potential, which is self-restrained and only partially realised in his smashing of Duryodhana's thighs. This is because his innate ability is restrained by *dharma*; whether we see this as Bhīma's own self-mastery or as Yudhiṣṭhira's leadership of the Pāṇḍavas' cause, the result—that Bhīma never achieves his full potential—is the same. If he were to have been given free rein, as the son of the god Vāyu and like the god Śiva, he could have instigated *pralaya*[8]—a complete destruction of the world—however, this would have prevented Yudhiṣṭhira's rule. Accordingly, in devotion to the Pāṇḍavas' cause and the *rājadharma* that is necessary to allow it to be established, he pulls back, but not without his foot on Duryodhana's head signifying the crushing of the enemy of *dharma*.

8 See Biardeau (1981: 91) for the significance of Bhīma's descent from Vāyu, who represents *prāṇa* ('breath, breathing', pl. 'life'), both at 'the first and last manifestation of life and movement' and at its annihilation.

Protector, partner and servant of Draupadī/Śrī

Bhīma's other key pairing is with Draupadī, the common wife of the Pāṇḍavas. While in exile with Kuntī, the Pāṇḍavas attend the *svayaṃvara* of Draupadī disguised as brahmins. For extended periods after Draupadī is 'won' at her *svayaṃvara*, Arjuna is absent—with Kṛṣṇa, on military campaigns, conducting austerities to win divine weapons or with the gods in Indraloka. Although all the Pāṇḍavas have secondary wives, the narrative displays Arjuna's greater emotional involvement with Subhadrā—whom he abducts with her brother Kṛṣṇa's knowledge and consent—than he displays with Draupadī. In contrast, Bhīma is ever-present with Draupadī and their relationship is portrayed as compatible, warm and full-blooded. When Draupadī is lost in the dice match, it is only Bhīma among all her husbands who is enraged at her plight and protests to Yudhiṣṭhira against the injustice (*Mbh*, 2.61.1–6, 10). He castigates Yudhiṣṭhira, threatens to burn his arms and is barely restrained from proceeding by Arjuna (2.61.7–9).

Bhīma and Draupadī are often on the same side of the argument urging Yudhiṣṭhira to commence war and their extended exhortations to Yudhiṣṭhira on *rājadharma* are significant and passionate. Bhīma urges Yudhiṣṭhira to action against Magadha by highlighting the need for both strength and policy in an effective king:

> *anārambhaparo rājā valmīka iva sīdati* |
> *durbalaś cānupāyena balinaṁ yo 'dhitiṣṭhati* ||
> *atandritas tu prāyeṇa durbalo balinaṁ ripum* |
> *jayet samyaṅ nayo rājan nītyārthān ātmano* ||
>
> [A king without enterprise collapses like an anthill, and weak is the king who governs a strong one without policy. But a weak king who is enterprising can often defeat a strong enemy, if his policy is right, and win the goals that are of benefit to oneself!] (van Buitenen 1975: 60–61; *Mbh*, 2.14.7)

Draupadī continues her extended berating of Yudhiṣṭhira by urging action, asking why their treatment by the Kauravas and their pitiable condition in the forest do not enrage or motivate Yudhiṣṭhira to action (*Mbh*, 3.28.1 ff.). Of Bhīma, she says: 'The powerful man could have killed all the Kurus, but the Wolf-Belly suffered it, waiting for your grace [*kurūn api hi yaḥ sarvān hantum utsahate prabhuḥ | tvatprasādaṁ pratīkṣaṁs tu sahate 'yaṁ vṛkodaraḥ ||*]' (van Buitenen 1975: 285).

Bhīma goes so far as to question Yudhiṣṭhira's manliness. As he is the closest in age to Yudhiṣṭhira—his almost constant companion, counsellor, advocate, strongman and executor—one has the sense that, among all the brothers, it is only Bhīma who can stretch the bounds of decorum so far:

> *bhavān dharmo dharma iti satataṁ vratakarśitaḥ |*
> *kaccid rājan na nirvedād āpannaḥ klībajīvikām ||*
>
> [You are Law, and crying Law! you emaciate yourself always with your vows; but is it possible, king, that despair has prompted you to the life of a eunuch?] (van Buitenen 1975: 287; *Mbh*, 3.34.11)

After the bitter end of the war, when Yudhiṣṭhira wants to renunciate and Arjuna, on behalf of Draupadī and the twins, speaks harshly, counselling against it, it is Bhīma who intervenes—'it seems, to try to soften Arjuna's harshness' (Hiltebeitel 2011b: 349). In contrast to his spirited exhortations to Yudhiṣṭhira, he is also the regulator of his younger brothers, who follow his lead either in restraining themselves in deference to Yudhiṣṭhira or in urging action: 'Out of deference you, great king, and in a spirit obedient to the Law, the Gandiva bowman has not burst into violence yet [*na kiṁ cit sāhasaṁ kṛtam*]. I constantly keep [*mayā nityaṁ*] Sahadeva and Nakula in check [*nivāritau*]' (van Buitenen 1975: 809; *Mbh*, 3.299.22–23).

The symbolism of Draupadī as Śrī (the goddess of prosperity or beauty and the Earth's fecundity) has been well established, and Laine (1989: 46) remarks that '[s]everal stories in the Bhārata's twelfth book tell of Indra's realisation that sovereignty is given to those whom Śrī chooses; on the epic level, Draupadī's choice of a husband [*svayaṃvara*] is a symbolic gift of sovereignty'. Of all the brothers, Bhīma is the one on whom Draupadī calls time and again to revenge dishonour, to protect her or even to indulge her fancies, and Bhīma is ever ready to comply. He seems pliable to her demands and this relationship is most obviously demonstrated in the *Saugandhikaparvan* (*Mbh*, 3.146–53, 3.157–59), when she twice calls on him to fetch her fragrant flowers. These seemingly fanciful requests nevertheless initiate adventures for Bhīma, which result in heroic initiations that are consistent with his personality (Laine 1989: 40–41). In Feller's insightful study of these passages, she argues that the flowers represent immortality and that, despite having requested the fragrant lotuses twice, Yudhiṣṭhira rather than Draupadī is the recipient, because

Bhīma's rampage to obtain them in realms forbidden to humans symbolises stealing immortality from Heaven, and that Yudhisthira, as Dharma's son, could 'never condone such a revolutionary and dissident act' (2012: 94).[9]

If we regard Draupadī as the Earth/Śrī, I suggest that we can see her in this role looking for a powerful protector at a time of world crisis and she chooses only Bhīma from the five Pāṇḍavas to fulfill this function. I posit that, seen in this context, the golden lotuses and Aśvatthāman's divine armour (which is the subject of another of Draupadī's vengeful and unreasonable requests to Bhīma) can all be interpreted as symbols of kingship, in addition to the lotuses being symbols of immortality, as Feller suggests. In each case, Draupadī taunts Bhīma with the achievements of others, exhorts him to action and, after he returns to Draupadī with the desired prizes, she turns the prizes—that is, the lotuses and the armour—over to Yudhiṣṭhira, the rightful king and the embodiment of Dharma. I regard this repeated motif as the symbolic anointing (*abhiṣeka*) of Yudhiṣṭhira by Draupadī as Śrī, bestowing on him the symbols of kingship. Bhīma's un-dharmic actions are necessary for the establishment of dharmic rule, which is for the benefit of society and thereby also the Earth/Śrī, whose agency transmutes Bhīma's un-dharmic acts into the necessary components of *rājadharma* and the practice of *kṣatriyadharma* that is required for its execution.

Bhīma is commanded by Draupadī because her presence as Śrī connotes kingship, which is what he desires, and his terrible strength and deeds that stand outside society are required to appease her demands.[10] His devotion to her personal protection can also be seen as his devotion to the kingdom. As the agents of the un-dharmic actions required to establish *dharma*, Bhīma and Draupadī are essentially rajasic in nature, whereas the ideal dharmic king (that is, Yudhiṣṭhira) is sāttvic in nature. In contrast, Arjuna—ever the 'middle Pandava'—combines both sāttvic qualities (seen in his austerities and devotion to Krsna) and rajasic qualities (as the supreme warrior). In this way, I argue that we can understand *rājadharma* as being a composite of both sāttvic and rajasic elements represented by the two extremes of Yudhiṣṭhira and Bhīma, with Draupadī as the Earth/Śrī choosing the appropriate agent for the appropriate action.

9 I am indebted to Danielle Feller for her comments on my original thinking about this chapter and, in the true spirit of scholarly collaboration and generosity, for her assistance in sourcing and sharing materials I was unable to access.

10 'And it is important to remember that Draupadī and Bhīma's collaboration against Yudhiṣṭhira constitutes a very real and literal opposition to Dharma—they desire the justice of a revenge that cannot be contained within the notion of dharma' (Gitomer 2007: 302).

Conclusion

The *Mahābhārata* seduces us with stories of *dharma*, heroism, *yoga*, renunciation and *bhakti*. All these ideals intertwine in a majestic symphony of such beauty and detail that our gaze is forever drawn up towards them. As a result, we fail to appreciate the depiction of the real, which runs parallel with those ideals and provides the necessary counterpoint bass note to the melodic symphony. If Yudhiṣṭhira and Arjuna represent the embellished ideals of the dharmic king held up to the light in the melody of the narrative, Bhīma is forever striking the bass notes, embodying the pragmatic *kṣatriya* king in their shadow, illustrating the dark underbelly of *rājadharma*, which is the grunt-work required for the establishment and maintenance of rule. Bhīma neither prevaricates nor shirks from the necessary grit and gore required to win and maintain the kingdom. While he may rail against Yudhiṣṭhira, his unswerving loyalty is never in doubt. Yudhiṣṭhira and Arjuna work to regain sovereignty, however, it is Bhīma who has the true and abiding lust for the kingdom. This is recognised by Dhṛtarāṣṭra, whose lamenting words display his foreboding, primarily of Bhīma, as the looming threat to the life of his sons:

> *na pāpakaṁ dhyāsyati Dharmaputro dhanaṁjayaś cāpy anuvartate tam* |
> *araṇyavāsena vivardhate tu bhīmasya kopo 'gnir ivānilena*
> *sa tena kopena vidīryamāṇaḥ karaṁ kareṇābhinipīḍya vīraḥ* |
> *viniḥśvasaty uṣṇam atīva ghoraṁ dahann ivemān mama putrapautrān* ||
>
> [The son of Dharma won't think of misdeeds, And Dhanaṃjaya surely follows his course; But in his forest-exile there is growing In Bhima a wrath as fire in the wind. That hero driven by that great fury And beating his fist in the palm of his hand Does heave a most gruesome, searing sigh And he puts my sons and grandsons on fire.] (van Buitenen 1975: 673; *Mbh*, 3.225.18–19)

Bhīma's eye is firmly on the goals of this world appropriate to *rājadharma*—first, on the *kāma* to the throne as his family's birthright and, second, on *artha*, but only as a means to the practice of *rājadharma*. He leaves *dharma*, unrelated to *rājadharma*, and *mokṣa* to his brothers Yudhiṣṭhira and Arjuna. The ambit of his activities may be more restrained than that of Yudhiṣṭhira and Arjuna, but within that limited space that he has self-defined as the scope of his action, he has a depth of knowledge and fierceness of commitment that are unchallenged.

We are given a glimpse of what rule by Bhīma might have looked like in the story of Nala and Damayantī that follows closely Bhīma's discourse on *rājadharma* directed at Yudhiṣṭhira (*Mbh*, 3.49.5–24). The story is contained within the *Āraṇyakaparvan*, where Damayantī's father is also named Bhīma and is the king of Vidarbha.[11] Damayantī's description of her father is a picture of the sort of king the Pāṇḍava Bhīma might have been had he been allowed to rule:[12]

> *rājā vidarbhādhipatiḥ pitā mama mahārathaḥ* |
> *bhīmo nāma kṣitipatiś cāturvarṇyasya rakṣitā* ||
> *vsūyāśvamedhānāṁ kratūnāṁ dakṣiṇāvatām* |
> *āhartā pārthivaśreṣṭhaḥ pṛthucārvañciteksaṇaḥ* ||
> *brahmaṇyaḥ sādhuvṛttaś ca satyavāg anasūyakaḥ* |
> *śīlavān susamācāraḥ pṛthuśrīr Dharmavic chuciḥ* ||
> *samyag goptā vidarbhāṇāṁ nirjitāriganaḥ prabhuḥ* |

> [The sovereign king of Vidarbha is my warlike father, he the lord of the land Bhīma, protector of the society of the four classes. He has offered up great sacrifices of rich stipends, the Royal Consecration and Horse Sacrifice, that eminent prince, with eyes that are wide, handsome, and curved. He is brahminic, virtuous in his conduct, truthful in his speech, unprotesting, decorous, and strict, widely famed, Law-wise, and pure. A perfect herdsman is he of the Vidarbhas, a lord who has vanquished the band of his enemies, and sir, know that I, his daughter, seek help from thee!] (*Mbh*, 3.49.5–24)

Bhīma the king practices what Bhīma the hero is known to espouse: support for the traditional order, strength to protect his populace and conduct the sacrifices enjoined on his station. He is at the apex of his society, able to follow the eternal *dharma* that kings do not request: '*na hi yācanti rājāna eṣa Dharmaḥ sanātanaḥ* [kings do not request, this is the eternal *dharma*]' (*Mbh*, 3.152.9; McGrath 2017: 54).

---

11 A mapping of the two Bhīmas is beyond the scope of this chapter but as an indicator of the reflection of the hero in the king, the king Bhīma is twice referred to as *bhīmaparākramaḥ* (*Mbh*, 3.66.1, 3.78.3), which is a common term for the hero Bhīma both before (3.48.8, 3.50.5) and after (3.146.13, 72; 3.195.8; 3.276.6) this in the *Āraṇyakaparvan*.

12 See Hiltebeitel (2001: 215–39) for an analysis of the 'mirror effect' of this story to the larger epic narrative; however, to the best of my knowledge, Hiltebeitel does not highlight the resonance between the hero Bhīma and the king Bhīma.

Arjuna is the much-vaunted audience of the *Bhagavadgītā* and espouses the doctrine of *karma* and non-attachment; however, it is Bhīma who continually acts energetically and purposefully in the interests of others rather than his individual self. Like Bhīṣma, Bhīma's sublimation of his immense potential to rule in favour of Yudhiṣṭhira can be regarded as the ultimate sacrifice. Duryodhana represents what Bhīma could have chosen to become: a usurper and a 'man who would be king'. Instead, Bhīma accepts a secondary role in the service of the traditional order despite possessing the advantages of inherent gifts from his father, Vāyu, and the benefits of his *rākṣasa* affiliation. He demonstrates his *rājadharma* by protecting his family, vanquishing *rākṣasa*s, successfully conducting military campaigns and counselling the pursuit of action to regain the throne. His partnering with and devotion to Draupadī further augment the pursuit of a dharmic world order for the benefit of the Earth. There is an honesty in his brutality that reflects the necessary actions to establish suzerainty.

He is far from the unthinking, buffoonish glutton he is generally assumed to be. Rather, together with Kṛṣṇa, Arjuna and Draupadī, Bhīma is a key engine for the achievement of the Pāṇḍavas, whose success is indebted to his devotion to the traditional order and to the family and to which his actions and energies are directed. In the *Mahābhārata*, a text devoted to *dharma*, he is a secondary actor, albeit still the necessary shadow king. In a text extolling *realpolitik* such as Machiavelli's *Prince* or the *Arthaśāstra*, he would take centre-stage. It is therefore only fitting that the poets place him at the head of the chariots when Yudhiṣṭhira enters Hastināpura as king (*dharmarājapurogās tu bhīmasenamukhā rathāḥ*; *Mbh*, 9.12.45) and that he is the one whom Yudhiṣṭhira nominates as the crown prince:

> *paurajānapadān sarvān visṛjya kurunandanaḥ*
> *yauvarājyena kauravyo bhīmasenam ayojayat* (*Mbh*, 12.41.8)

References

Adarkar, Aditya. (2008). The Mahābhārata and its universe: New approaches to the all-encompassing epic. *History of Religions* 47(4): 304–19.

Austin, Christopher R. (2011). 'Draupadī's fall: Snowballs, cathedrals, and synchronous readings of the 'Mahābhārata'. *International Journal of Hindu Studies* 15(1): 111–37. doi.org/10.1007/s11407-011-9101-z.

Balkaran, Raj. (2021). Synchronic strategy: Rules of engagement for Sanskrit narrative literature. *Journal of Dharma Studies* 4(2): 199–221. doi.org/10.1007/s42240-021-00099-x.

Biardeau, Madeleine. (1969–72). *Conférences de Mlle Madeleine Biardeau: étude du mythe-cadre du Mahābhārata. Annuaire de l'EPhE, Section des Sciences Religieuses* [*Lectures by Miss Madeleine Biardeau: Study of the frame-myth of the Mahābhārata. EPhE Directory, Section of Religious Sciences*], 77(1969–70): 168–73; 78(1970–71): 151–61; 79(1971–72): 139–46. Paris: École pratique des hautes études.

Biardeau, Madeleine. (1981). Salvation of a king in the Mahābhārata. *CIS* [NS] 15(1–2): 75–97. doi.org/10.1177/006996678101500107.

Brockington, Mary. (2001). Husband or king? Yudhiṣṭhira's dilemma in the Mahābhārata. *Indo-Iranian Journal* 44(3): 253–63. doi.org/10.1023/A:1012637404940.

Ernest, Phillip. (2006). True lies: Bhīma's vows and the revision of memory in the Mahābhārata's code. *Annals of the Bhandarkar Oriental Research Institute* 87: 273–82.

Feller, Danielle. (2005). Hanumān's jumps and their mythical models. In Petteri Koskikallio (ed.), *Parallels and Comparisons, Proceedings of the Fourth Dubrovnik International Conference on the Sanskrit Epics and Purāṇas*, pp. 193–219. Zagreb: Croatian Academy of Sciences and Arts.

Feller, Danielle. (2012). Bhīma's quest for the golden lotuses (Mahābhārata 3.146–153 and 3.157–159). In John Brockington (ed.), *Battle, Bards and Brāhmins: Papers of the 13th World Sanskrit Conference. Volume 2*, pp. 79–99. Delhi: Motilal Banarsidass.

Gitomer, David L. (2007). Rākṣasa Bhīma: Wolfbelly among ogres and brahmans in the Sanskrit Mahābhārata and the Veṇisaṃhāra. In Arvind Sharma (ed.), *Essays on the Mahābhārata*, pp. 298–323. Delhi: Motilal Banarsidass.

Hiltebeitel, Alf. (1990). *Ritual of Battle: Krishna in the Mahābhārata*. Albany: SUNY Press.

Hiltebeitel, Alf. (2001). *Rethinking the Mahābhārata: A Reader's Guide to the Education of the Dharma King*. Chicago, IL: University of Chicago Press.

Hiltebeitel, Alf. (2011a). *Dharma: Its Early History in Law, Religion, and Narrative*. Oxford, UK: Oxford University Press. doi.org/10.1093/obo/9780195399318-0001.

Hiltebeitel, Alf. (2011b). Reading the Fifth Veda: Studies on the Mahābhārata. In Vishwa Adluri and Joydeep Bagchee (eds), *Essays by Alf Hiltebeitel. Volume I*. Leiden, Netherlands: Brill Academic Publishing.

Karve, Irawati. (1969). *Yugānta: The End of an Epoch*. Pune, India: Poona Deshmukh Prakashan.

Laine, James W. (1989). Initiation visions of the Pāṇḍavas. In James W. Laine, *Visions of God: Narratives of Theophany in the Mahābhārata*. Publications of the De Nobili Research Library. Volume 16, pp. 37–57. Leiden, Netherlands: Brill.

Matilal, Bimal. (2002). *Philosophy, Culture and Religion: The Collected Essays of Bimal Krishna Matilal—Ethics and Epics*. Edited by Jonardon Ganeri. Oxford, UK: Oxford University Press.

McGrath, Kevin. (2017). *Raja Yudhistira: Kingship in the Epic Mahabharata*. Ithaca, NY: Cornell University Press. doi.org/10.7591/9781501708220.

Meiland, Justin (trans.). (2007). *Mahabhárata Book Nine (Volume 2): Shalya*. New York, NY: NYU Press. doi.org/10.2307/j.ctt1bmzmqm.

Monier-Williams, M. (1899). *A Sanskrit–English Dictionary: Etymologically and Philologically Arranged with Special Reference to Cognate Indo-European Languages*. Oxford, UK: The Clarendon Press. Available from: www.sanskrit-lexicon.uni-koeln.de/scans/MWScan/2020/web/index.php.

Smith, John D. (revision by). (n.d.). *The Mahābhārata*. Edited by Muneo Tokunaga. [Critical Edition Online.] Pune, India: Bhandarkar Oriental Research Institute. Available from: bombay.indology.info/mahabharata/statement.html.

Smith, John D. (2009). Consistency and character in the Mahābhārata. *Bulletin of the School of Oriental and African Studies* 72(1): 101–12. doi.org/10.1017/S0041977X09000056.

Sörensen, S. (2006). *An Index to the Names in the Mahābhārata*. Delhi: Motilal Banarsidass.

Sukthankar, V.S. (1942). *On the Meaning of the Mahābhārata*. Delhi: Motilal Banarsidass.

van Buitenen, J.A.B. (trans. & ed.). (1973). *The Mahābhārata. Volume 1, Book 1: The Book of the Beginning*. Chicago, IL: University of Chicago Press. doi.org/10.7208/chicago/9780226217543.001.0001.

van Buitenen, J.A.B. (trans. & ed.). (1975). *Mahābhārata. Volume 2, Book 2: The Book of the Assembly Hall. Book 3: The Book of the Forest*. Chicago, IL: University of Chicago Press. doi.org/10.7208/chicago/9780226223681.001.0001.

van Buitenen, J.A.B. (trans. & ed.). (1978). *Mahābhārata. Volume 3, Book 4: The Book of Virāṭa. Book 5: The Book of the Effort*. Chicago, IL: University of Chicago Press. doi.org/10.7208/chicago/9780226223711.001.0001.

8

Some moral tasting notes on the Udyogaparvan of the *Mahābhārata*

James M. Hegarty

Abstract

This chapter explores the nature of moral deliberation in the Udyogaparvan of the *Mahābhārata*. It focuses on the moral content of the courtly debates contained in the Udyogaparvan, which are so central to the narrative progression of the *Mahābhārata*. The work of the noted psychologist Jonathan Haidt is used to explore the moral foci of the Udyogaparvan and the nature of moral debate in the text. The chapter shows that the debates of the Udyogaparvan centre on a series of recurrent moral concerns, which are enumerated and explored in Haidt's work. It is the argument of this chapter that the exploration of these recurrent moral concerns helps to explicate the moral saliency of the *Mahābhārata* in South Asia (across linguistic, cultural and religious boundaries) in new ways and further facilitates comparative analyses of religious texts.

Introduction

Nīlakaṇṭha, the great commentator on the *Mahābhārata*, repeated a widespread view held by the learned brahmins of his day that the *Mahābhārata*'s teachings on the *dharma* (or 'righteous acts') of kings were perpetually authoritative and not just for the *kṣatriya* or warrior caste.[1] Nīlakaṇṭha, moreover, felt that the relevance of the *Mahābhārata* was not limited to its teachings on how to rule; it was, in his view, a text of universal, and universalising, religious significance. This was because it was based on Vedic knowledge, even where the original Vedic source was now lost to humankind.[2] While some may consider that rootedness in the Veda makes this claim a distinctively Hindu one, it is, in fact, from the perspective of the individual committed to the truth of the Veda, as Nīlakaṇṭha was, universal.[3] This chapter explores a somewhat different line of argument, but, like Nīlakaṇṭha, it stresses both the moral relevance and the universal underpinnings of the *Mahābhārata*. It focuses on the fifth book, the Udyogaparvan, in which the two branches of the royal family at the heart of the tale seek to avert—with rather different degrees of commitment—all-out war between them.

The existing scholarship on the Udyogaparvan, as is perfectly appropriate, emphasises the place of this *parvan* in the *Mahābhārata* as a whole and in the history of the development of Hindu religious and political thought more generally. In his introduction to his translation of the Udyogaparvan, van Buitenen does an excellent job of identifying the parallels between the great Sanskrit manual of statecraft, the *Arthaśāstra*, and the Udyogaparvan. For van Buitenen, the *Arthaśāstra*'s ideal-typical account of the conduct of diplomacy informs the form and content of the various diplomatic engagements of the Udyogaparvan. He is less clear, however, on the relationship between the several parts of the Udyogaparvan taken as a whole. For example, the night-time homily given by the sage advisor Vidura to the confused King Dhṛtarāṣṭra is, for van Buitenen, something of a trite rehash of materials better expressed elsewhere, while Sanatsujāta's philosophical teachings, which constitute a freestanding *upaniṣad*, are not much more than a foreshadowing of the *Bhagavadgītā*. Van Buitenen thus treats the Udyogaparvan in a way that is sensitive but disjointed. He offers instead, in his introduction, a long meditation on the theory of myth and the relevance of historical method as they pertain to the *Mahābhārata* taken as a whole (or not, which is rather the point of his discussion). Elsewhere, van Buitenen

1 He was writing in the second half of the seventeenth century in Benares, India, in his *Bhāratabhāvadīpa* or *Light on the Inner Significance of the (Mahā)Bhārata*, as cited and discussed by Minkowski (2010).

2 In the *smṛtyadhikaraṇa* of the Mīmāṃsāsūtra (1.3.1–2). See Minkowski (2005: 240–41), where he cites some of Nīlakaṇṭha's remarks. See also Müller (1860: 94); Pollock (1997).

3 Something McComas Taylor explores adroitly and to great effect in his work on 'regimes of truth' in relation to the *Pañcatantra* and the *Bhāgavata Purāṇa*. See Taylor (2007, 2008, 2016).

offers masterful elucidations of the ways in which the *Mahābhārata* evokes other ideas and practices only to subvert them or, at the very least, comment on them (the patterning of the Dyūtaparvan after the Vedic royal consecration ritual, the *rājasūya*, being a case in point) and yet here the parallels are elucidated but not definitively explored. The *Mahābhārata* and *Arthaśāstra* are, for van Buitenen, in learned agreement, but not *in conversation*, at least not in the Udyogaparvan. Angelika Malinar adopts a more subtle and sensitive approach to the debates of the Udyogaparvan, but she focuses on characterising the nature of their contribution to a larger debate about kingship, the *Bhagavadgītā* and the transition from lineage to state systems (ground covered in a more historical mode by Romila Thapar and many others before and since). My approach to the Udyogaparvan in this chapter is somewhat different and more than a little experimental (for which I beg the reader's indulgence and patience). It focuses on the moral content of the courtly debates contained in the Udyogaparvan, which are central to the narrative progression of the *Mahābhārata*. My exploration will pursue a more universalist line of inquiry, in which I consider the *moral foundations* of the back and forth of negotiations in the Udyogaparvan. This more universalist approach develops the work of the evolutionary psychologist and theorist of religion and politics Jonathan Haidt. Haidt argues for an approach to morality as *innate* to our species. He sums up his approach as follows:

> I defined innateness as 'organised in advance of experience,' like the first draft of a book that gets revised as individuals grow up within diverse cultures. This definition allowed me to propose that the moral foundations are innate. Particular rules and virtues vary across cultures, so you'll get fooled if you look for universality in the finished books. You won't find a single paragraph that exists in identical form in every human culture. But if you look for links between evolutionary theory and anthropological observations, you can take some educated guesses about what was in the universal first draft of human nature. (Haidt 2012: 178)

Haidt characterises five moral 'foundations' for humans, as shown in the columns in Table 8.1.

Table 8.1 Five moral 'foundations' for humans

	Care/harm	Fairness/ cheating	Loyalty/ betrayal	Authority/ subversion	Sanctity/ degradation
Adaptive challenge	Protect and care for children	Reap benefits of two-way partnerships	Form cohesive coalitions	Forge beneficial relationships within hierarchies	Avoid contaminants
Original triggers	Suffering, distress or neediness expressed by one's child	Cheating, cooperation, deception	Threat or challenge to group	Signs of dominance and submission	Waste products, diseased people
Current triggers	Baby seals, cute cartoon characters	Marital fidelity, broken vending machines	Sports teams, nations	Bosses, respected professionals	Taboo ideas (communism, racism)
Characteristic emotions	Compassion	Anger, gratitude, guilt	Group pride, rage at traitors	Respect, fear	Disgust
Relevant virtues	Caring, kindness	Fairness, justice, trustworthiness	Loyalty, patriotism, self-sacrifice	Obedience, deference	Temperance, chastity, piety, cleanliness

Source: From Haidt (2012: 146).

He explains them as follows:

> The *Care/harm* foundation evolved in response to the adaptive challenge of caring for vulnerable children. It makes us sensitive to signs of suffering and need; it makes us despise cruelty and want to care for those who are suffering.
>
> The *Fairness/cheating* foundation evolved in response to the adaptive challenge of reaping the rewards of cooperation without getting exploited. It makes us sensitive to indications that another person is likely to be a good (or bad) partner for collaboration and reciprocal altruism. It makes us want to shun or punish cheaters.
>
> The *Loyalty/betrayal* foundation evolved in response to the adaptive challenge of forming and maintaining coalitions. It makes us sensitive to signs that another person is (or is not) a team player. It makes us trust and reward such people, and it makes us want to hurt, ostracise, or even kill those who betray us or our group.

> The *Authority/subversion* foundation evolved in response to the adaptive challenge of forging relationships that will benefit us within social hierarchies. It makes us sensitive to signs of rank or status, and to signs that other people are (or are not) behaving properly, given their position.
>
> The *Sanctity/degradation* foundation evolved initially in response to the adaptive challenge of the omnivore's dilemma, and then to the broader challenge of living in a world of pathogens and parasites. It includes the behavioral immune system, which can make us wary of a diverse array of symbolic objects and threats. It makes it possible for people to invest objects with irrational and extreme values—both positive and negative—which are important for binding groups together. (Haidt 2012: 178–79)

I will explore the significance of Haidt's theory, using his fivefold foundation of morality, to the debates of the Udyogaparvan.[4] On the basis of this, I will suggest that an approach that is theoretically informed by Haidt's evolutionary psychology can shed new light on the universal significance of the *Mahābhārata* as a nuanced response to the complex dynamics of family, politics, warfare and much else. I will, in this way, join Nīlakaṇṭha in making universal claims for the significance of the *Mahābhārata*, albeit on rather different foundations. I do this in a spirit of experiment and in the desire to model and stimulate new modes of engagement with ancient texts (most especially those that open new avenues for the comparison of materials from diverse contexts and stimulate new readings of both well-known and less well-explored materials). Inevitably, this chapter therefore sits somewhat adjacent to continuing debates about the *Mahābhārata* that are more literary or historical in their focus.

My title requires some explanation. In *The Righteous Mind: Why Good People Are Divided by Politics and Religion* (2012), Haidt compares his moral 'foundations' to 'taste receptors' and makes recurrent use of the metaphor of a 'moral palate'. This is, of course, a metaphor well-known to Sanskrit intellectual tradition in the context of dramaturgy and formal

4 To this list of five, Haidt adds a provisional sixth foundation: liberty/oppression. Haidt (2012: 215) characterises this as: 'We added the Liberty/oppression foundation, which makes people notice and resent any sign of attempted domination. It triggers an urge to band together to resist or overthrow bullies and tyrants. This foundation supports the egalitarianism and antiauthoritarianism of the left, as well as the don't-tread-on-me and give-me-liberty anti-government anger of libertarians and some conservatives.' I do not make use of this additional foundation in the present analysis. It is described as provisional and seems, much more than others, to reflect contemporary, and particularly American, political polarities.

aesthetics, where the dominant mode of a work was explored in terms of its *rasa* or flavour. What follows, then, is a set of very exploratory 'moral tasting notes' for one of the most debate-intensive books of the *Mahābhārata*, the Udyogaparvan.

The debates of the Udyogaparvan

In this chapter, I follow the core courtly debates of the Udyogaparvan across its four main 'embassies', by which I refer to occasions in which an individual or group is sent from one court to another for the purpose of negotiation and/or remonstration. I will not explore the substories told to justify positions in the text, though I will touch on one of the more important of them, which is that of Indra and the slaying of Vṛtra and the consequent reign of the human Nahuṣa as king of the gods. I will also leave to one side the major separate and distinct dialogues of the text—namely, those between King Dhṛtarāṣṭra and his advisor, Vidura, and between King Dhṛtarāṣṭra and the sage Sanatsujāta, both of which occur during the blind king's long dark night of the soul (I have explored these dialogues elsewhere; see Hegarty 2019). My primary focus is on the patterns of exchange in the Udyogaparvan and the characterisation of their moral foundations or 'flavours'. I will point, however, to the ways in which aspects of the Indra/Vṛtra/Nahuṣa story, the theophany of Kṛṣṇa and the myopic focus on royal power in Duryodhana's speeches and embassies are morally and metaphysically relevant to the debates of the embassies of the Udyogaparvan.

By way of context, for those not overly familiar with the Udyogaparvan, it is structured around the back and forth between the two sets of cousins who are in conflict in the *Mahābhārata*, the Pāṇḍavas and the Kauravas. The five Pāṇḍava brothers, led by the eldest, Yudhiṣṭhira, have just completed 13 years in exile, which stipulated that the final year should be spent incognito. This period was spent in disguise in the court of King Virāṭa of the Matsyas, in Upaplavya, where we initially find the Pāṇḍavas considering their position. The other, far more numerous, set of cousins, the Kauravas, is to be found in Indraprastha, where they, too, led by King Dhṛtarāṣṭra and his boorish son Duryodhana, are debating their next steps. In both courts, different assessments of the recent past are heard and, in both courts, there is disagreement about what constitutes the right and the politic thing to do. The issues raised are not resolved, as one court sends embassies to the other. Against this backdrop of two very polarised groups of cousins, Kṛṣṇa, as both god and chieftain, plays a critical role. The word *udyoga* literally means an 'effort' or a 'preparation' and the text is true to its moniker, in terms of both its diplomatically intensive content and its role in preparing the characters and readers of the text for the war that is to come.

The council of Upaplavya (*Mbh*, 5.1–6)

Dominant flavours: *Fairness* and *cheating*

Kṛṣṇa opens the proceedings. His initial statement regarding the situation of the Pāṇḍava brothers is anchored in the specifics of the wrongdoings of their cousins and opponents, the Kauravas. He wastes no time in enumerating the nature of the latter's misdeeds. He focuses on the following accusations: the Kauravas tricked Yudhiṣṭhira, the senior Pāṇḍava brother; they plundered the kingdom of the Pāṇḍavas; and finally, they sought to harm the Pāṇḍavas as children. The *mithyācāra*—the deceitful means, as the Sanskrit has it—of the Kauravas are thus made clear. Kṛṣṇa's emphasis on the moral rectitude of the Pāṇḍavas is equally clear. He suggests that Yudhiṣṭhira is always preoccupied with that which is right (*dharma*) and that which is useful (*artha*). The brothers, according to Kṛṣṇa, only wish to regain that which they won for themselves. Kṛṣṇa closes with a suggestion that an envoy be sent to the court of King Dhṛtarāṣṭra to establish the intentions of Duryodhana.

I will pause for an initial application of Haidt's typology of moral concerns. Kṛṣṇa's objections to the conduct of the Kauravas centre on the following:

- *Harm:* the Kauravas sought to harm the Pāṇḍavas as children.
- *Cheating:* the Kauravas cheated the Pāṇḍavas at dice.
- *Betrayal:* the Kauravas abused the parameters of the coalition of cousins.
- *Subversion:* the Kauravas took the kingdom and imposed the conditions of exile based on the improper use of power and rank (chiefly, though left unstated by Kṛṣṇa at this point, as a consequence of the weakness of Dhṛtarāṣṭra and his reliance on explanations of events in terms of the power of fate [*daiva*] and time [*kāla*]).

The rectitude of the Pāṇḍavas is, essentially, the inverse of this. They have, in Kṛṣṇa's view, never reacted to the abuse heaped on them. They are thus *caring*, *fair*, *loyal* and properly respectful of *authority* and its responsible and appropriate use.

Kṛṣṇa's point of view is most certainly not that of his senior brother, Balarāma. Balarāma makes clear that, in his view, Yudhiṣṭhira lost his head and the game of dice was entirely fair and above board. For Balarāma, Yudhiṣṭhira did not act as someone in his position should. Balarāma sees no issue in Śakuni's victory over Yudhiṣṭhira at dice, where the former acted as Duryodhana's nominated representative. Balarāma makes these points to urge the council to take up a conciliatory stance in their negotiations with Duryodhana and the Kauravas. Balarāma's counterposition can be read as follows in terms of Haidt's moral foundation theory: Yudhiṣṭhira is guilty of an act of *subversion*; as Pāṇḍava king, he lost his head to the dice, which is not appropriate behaviour given his position in the social hierarchy. Balarāma considers Śakuni to have acted *fairly* on this basis.

Kṛṣṇa's charioteer and Pāṇḍava ally Sātyaki counters this view very forcefully. He suggests that Yudhiṣṭhira was too trusting. He does not believe Yudhiṣṭhira should prostrate himself for the return of his patrimony, nor does he accept the claim that the Pāṇḍavas were discovered during their exile (an accusation that is circulating and which we will hear repeated below). His concerns centre therefore on fairness, cheating and the proper respect for authority. His final points emphasise the moral acceptability of the killing of one's enemies and the risks of begging from them.

The next speaker, Drupada, King of Pañcāla, reinforces this view by suggesting that Duryodhana acts consistently in bad faith and that King Dhṛtarāṣṭra is blinded by love for his son. Here, again, *fairness*, *cheating* and the proper exercise of *authority* are the key issues. This being said, the debate ends with Drupada dispatching his old house brahmin to argue their cause and sow dissent in the ranks of the Kaurava court (protected by his status as an envoy and by the spectre of brahminicide—in a culture in which the killing of a brahmin is the worst sin imaginable—something reinforced in the Udyogaparvan itself with its famous story of Indra's double brahminicide, which I explore below).

I count 25 distinct moral claims made across the various speeches of the council of Upaplavya (see Appendix 8.1 for my detailed enumeration and coding). For my moral tasting notes, I am not, at present, interested in who says what, but rather what, morally, is given the most 'airtime'—or perhaps, given my central metaphor and title, what is chewed over more thoroughly—by those present at a given debate or set of debates. We can represent the 'moral tasting notes' of the council of Upaplavya as Table 8.2.[5]

5 The embassy that immediately proceeds this council adds nothing to these totals, so I offer the tasting notes here rather than with my examination of the embassy below.

Table 8.2 Moral tasting notes of the council of Upaplavya

Moral 'flavour'	Level of usage
Care/harm	3
Fairness/cheating	20
Loyalty/betrayal	5
Authority/subversion	11
Sanctity/degradation	0

The passage we have been considering is thus strongly flavoured with concerns about *fairness* and *cheating* (it is indeed fiery with indignation); the *subversion* of *authority* follows next on our moral palate (sour as it is), with diminishing notes of *loyalty* and *betrayal* (ever salty) and issues of *care* and *harm* (earthy and umami, as these are, at least in my imagination). We find—unsurprisingly, given it is a partisan gathering—a simple exchange of mostly mutually reinforcing positions in this initial debate. Only Balarāma demurs. We also observe Haidt's typology holding up quite well as I put it through its initial paces. Nothing has challenged or exceeded his categories thus far. We will see the unfolding debates pivot several times, however, and interrupted by other forms of discourse or events that are significant and, I will argue, usefully explicated in relation to Haidt's 'foundations' of morality. It is worth noting that the present debate offered nothing in relation to the moral centre of *sanctity/degradation*, which is something that the next exchange in the text addresses fulsomely, though it is not one of the four embassies of the Udyogaparvan that are central to my analysis. It is to this exchange I will now turn.

Kṛṣṇa's options, Śalya and the story of Indra, Vṛtra and Nahuṣa (*Mbh*, 5.7–18)

Dominant flavours: *Sanctity* and *degradation*

Kṛṣṇa heads to his home in Dvārakā after the council of Upaplavya; the *kṣatriya* tradition in the *Mahābhārata* is that a request for support in arms will be met on a first-come, first-served basis. Consequently, Kṛṣṇa finds himself visited by Arjuna for the Pāṇḍavas and Duryodhana for the Kauravas. He is napping when they arrive; Duryodhana arrives first, but Arjuna is seen first. It is thus debatable who is truly 'first' at this critical juncture. This complexity leads the wily Kṛṣṇa to promise his aid to both parties either as a noncombatant advisor or through the loan of his armies. Arjuna is given first choice. He selects Kṛṣṇa's aid as noncombatant advisor. Duryodhana is pleased to accept Kṛṣṇa's armies. Kṛṣṇa's brother, Balarāma, declares that he will not aid either party. Arjuna asks Kṛṣṇa to be his charioteer. This passage of only 37 verses is a momentous one. It gives us the critical pairing of Arjuna and Kṛṣṇa on one chariot, which will provide the setting for the *Bhagavadgītā*. It also neatly dramatises the personal, increasingly devotional, loyalty of the Pāṇḍavas to Kṛṣṇa and the paramount goal of military power for Duryodhana, whose focus on a more mundane form of *kṣatriya* supremacy is, as we will see, unrelenting.

The passage includes another important and parallel event regarding the leadership of the Kaurava armies by King Śalya. Śalya, a Pāṇḍava supporter, is tricked into offering a boon to Duryodhana; Duryodhana uses this boon to compel Śalya to act as the leader of his forces. Śalya will also serve as the charioteer of Karṇa in his battle with Arjuna. On hearing this, Yudhiṣṭhira asks Śalya to undermine the confidence of Karṇa while acting as his charioteer; Yudhiṣṭhira acknowledges that this act is *akartavya* (a gerundive meaning 'it should not be done') but nevertheless makes the request. Here, we find a distorted reflection of the relationship between Kṛṣṇa and Arjuna. Śalya will agree, at Yudhiṣṭhira's behest, to act as charioteer and provocateur to Karṇa. Śalya will undermine his passenger; disunity will be the hallmark of their relationship, as harmony is that of Arjuna and Kṛṣṇa.[6] Indeed, Karṇa's chariot, in a powerful metaphor of the limitations of his moral and metaphysical horizons, will sink into the mire of the battlefield just before his death.[7] Yudhiṣṭhira's request, alongside other misdeeds by the Pāṇḍavas during the war that is to come, will form the basis of further intratextual and extratextual controversies (beyond the scope of this chapter, but in proportion to the accusations of moral impropriety levelled against the Kauravas before the *Mahābhārata*'s main war).

It is at this point that Śalya tells the story of the victory of Indra over Vṛtra and Nahuṣa. Śalya explains that he intends to tell this tale to demonstrate that even the lord of the gods himself had his trials and tribulations. The tale is wonderfully rich, widely distributed in multiple tellings across South Asian literature and has been subject to numerous scholarly analyses, which I will not enumerate. It moves through the complex ramifications of a feud between the brahmin Tvaṣṭar Prajāpati and Indra. Indra kills the son

6 Kṛṣṇa will provide, through an extended act of philosophical persuasion and another well-timed theophany, higher knowledge in the *Bhagavadgītā* of the Bhīṣmaparvan, the book that follows the Udyogaparvan.

7 Notwithstanding other more complex symbolisms to be associated with this event.

of Tvaṣṭar, Triśiras, and incurs the sin of brahminicide. Tvaṣṭar, enraged, creates Vṛtra to destroy Indra. With Viṣṇu's aid, Vṛtra is killed by means of exploiting the 'small print' of his invulnerability (he cannot be killed by solid or liquid, by night or by day and so, inevitably, is slain by Viṣṇu-impregnated thunder-foam, which is, of course, neither solid nor liquid, at dusk, which is neither day nor night; this is the obvious ploy in retrospect!). Indra, now responsible for a double brahminicide, is overcome at the murderous ploy in which he has participated and retreats from the world in miniaturised form, choosing to hide in a lotus stalk. The gods anoint Nahuṣa, a human, to be their king in his absence. Nahuṣa proves to be more than a little despotic and lascivious.[8] He relentlessly pursues Indra's wife, Śacī, who resists his questionable charms. Meanwhile, Viṣṇu explains how Indra can expiate the sin of double brahminicide by means of ritual action (the very *aśvamedha* that Yudhiṣṭhira will perform after the terrible battle at Kurukṣetra). He does so and is cleansed of his sin. Śacī finds Indra, through the intercession of the goddess Upaśrutir ('Whisper' or perhaps 'Oracular Voice'). Indra suggests that Śacī make herself available to Nahuṣa on the condition that he appears on a wagon drawn by brahmin seers. While remonstrating with the seers, Nahuṣa's foot touches the head of Agastya. Because of this violation, he is cursed to spend 10,000 years in the form of a snake and is toppled from his position as king of the gods. Indra is thus returned to his high estate, cleansed of sin and reunited with Śacī.

This wonderfully rich story plays only a minor role in this chapter and I will detain us with only a few key observations drawing on the moral typology of Haidt (I will not seek to tabulate its content, as it is far less amenable to this treatment than a more straightforward moral debate). The story of Indra, Vṛtra and Nahuṣa is redolent with *sanctity* and *degradation* through the issue of both brahminicide (by Indra of Triśiras) and the physical humiliation of the brahmin Agastya (by Nahuṣa). It is filled with taboo, transgression and the ritual expiation of impurity. It is replete with beings invested with sacral power, in complex social hierarchies, who are themselves shot through with considerations of relative purity. With its graphic violence and emphasis on sexual possession and physical, but also symbolic, humiliation (most prominently, the foot on the brahmin's head, but also through beheadings and much else besides), it is a tale of moral disgust—a tale of sin and expiation. For Haidt, *sanctity* and *degradation* are those rules of moral behaviour that were, in our deep past, related to the avoidance of pathogens and parasites.

8 It is hard not to point to recent American political events here.

They are the moral impulses least amenable to the back and forth of debate. Instead, they engender the strongest and most visceral responses and are the locus of moral disgust. We find this moral centre being recurrently triggered in this tale. The story is also shot through with the agency of Viṣṇu. He is in the foam that kills Vṛtra and his advice provides the means by which Indra is rehabilitated from the sin of (double) brahminicide (a sin with no ritual expiation in *dharmaśāstra*). This allows Indra to advise his wife, Śacī, as to the means of defeating the despotic Nahuṣa, who stands, of course, as the proxy of Duryodhana in the main narrative of the Udyogaparvan, as Indra is Yudhiṣṭhira's. It is no accident that a story that places such emphasis on *sanctity* also emphasises its divine lynchpin, Viṣṇu. This is not insignificant to the action of the main plot of the *Mahābhārata*.

We are now in the position to observe how, in the content of the narration of the tale of Indra, Vṛtra and Nahuṣa, *sanctity* and *degradation* predominate. This is in marked contrast to the context of narration, in which we have seen, and will see, a strong emphasis on *fairness* and *cheating* with considerable emphasis also on the proper conduct of *authority* and the detailed examination of the recent past. This morally orthogonal discourse finds a complement and capstone in the theophany of Kṛṣṇa towards the end of the Udyogaparvan, which anchors both *sanctity* and human action in the revelation of its reality and substrate. Above and beyond the cut and thrust of moral and philosophical debate, the self-disclosure of God is the only meaningful power play. There is another contrastive moral discourse, but it lacks this heavyweight metaphysical anchorage. It is the 'might is right' philosophy of Duryodhana, which forms the core of his final mocking embassy to the Pāṇḍavas, when he sends the gambler's son Ulūka to beard his cousins mercilessly (in the fourth and final embassy that we will explore). For the present, it is sufficient to note that we will observe three types of moral discourse in the Udyogaparvan. One is anchored in the close reading of events to discern their morality (we have seen this already and might call it a discourse of *social justice*). Another is anchored in the sacred and the recognition of the underlying nature of reality, which, crucially, finds Viṣṇu/Kṛṣṇa at its apex as the divine being who encompasses and directs that reality (inclusive of fate and time). The third rejects the idea of the rules of engagement *in toto*, be they anchored in moralities, legalities or divine realities, and plumps instead for power in the here and now as the only determining factor. For this type of king, the pertinent question is not 'should I?' It is only ever the question, 'Can I?' We will see this play out across all the embassies of the Udyogaparvan, to which I will now turn.

The first embassy: King Drupada's brahmin in the Kaurava court (*Mbh*, 5.20–21)

Dominant flavours: *Fairness* and *cheating*

On arriving at the Karuava court, Drupada's unnamed brahmin leads with a reiteration of the moral concerns as they were laid out in the council at Upaplavya. It is a speech that even the pro-Pāṇḍava councillor of King Dhṛtarāṣṭra, Bhīṣma, calls *atitīkṣṇa* ('sharp'). Karṇa, interrupting his elder, moves the debate from one of varied moral issues, as reflected in the exchanges at Upaplavya, to a single moral and legal issue—that of *samaya* (or 'covenant'). For Karṇa, the dice game was fair, if asymmetric, and the consequent 'covenanted' period of exile was not duly honoured. There is but one moral issue here for Karṇa and it relates to *fairness* and *cheating*: the Kauravas have been fair; the Pāṇḍavas have not. Issues of *sanctity* and *degradation*, of godhead and brahmin supremacy count not at all.

Bhīṣma offers no further moral discourse. He does not attempt a rebuttal of the points made by Karna; instead, he recalls the court's attention to the prowess of the Pāṇḍavas in battle. The decision is subsequently taken to send the *sūta* ('charioteer') Saṃjaya to the court of King Yudhiṣṭhira. It is worth noting that even in this short sequence, the evident discord between Bhīṣma and Karṇa is exacerbated by the brahmin's blunt talk. In this way, our brahmin ambassador is true to the instructions given to him by his king, Drupada: he sows seeds of dissent even as he relays his message.

There is little need to tabulate the moral tasting notes of this embassy. We find, after a blunt speech by Drupada's brahmin, only one morally focused retort from a single, albeit important, interlocutor: Karṇa. Only Karṇa offers a rejoinder that is *morally engaged*. Indeed, he speaks directly to the dominant concern with *fairness* and *cheating* in the Pāṇḍavas' narrative of events. This absence of debate is itself significant. It reflects, from those sympathetic to the Pāṇḍavas, the absence of a convincing moral counterargument and, from those antipathetic to them, their reliance on arguments that are not morally focused. Dhṛtarāṣṭra, the blind Kaurava king—as is usual in the *Mahābhārata*—turns to metaphysics and the power of fate to determine events, while his son Duryodhana relies on a doctrine of brute force.

The second embassy: Saṃjaya among the Pāṇḍavas (*Mbh*, 5.22–31)

Dominant flavours: *Sanctity* and *degradation*

Saṃjaya's embassy is longer and more complex than that of Drupada's brahmin. It also introduces some themes and threads that begin to push us beyond the moral preoccupations of the debates of the Udyogaparvan. It brings together the discourse of *sanctity*—reflected in the tale of Indra, Vṛtra and Nahuṣa—with an assertion of the metaphysical supremacy of Kṛṣṇa, which will be further developed in Kṛṣṇa's embassy to the Kaurava court. A signal demonstration of this can be found in Dhṛtarāṣṭra's initial instruction to his faithful servant as he sends him to Yudhiṣṭhira's assembly, when he states:

no ced gacchet saṃgaraṃ mandabuddhis | tābhyāṃ suto me viparītacetāḥ
no cet kurūn saṃjaya nirdahetām | indrāviṣṇū daityasenāṃ yathaiva
mato hi me śakrasamo dhanaṃjayaḥ | sanātano vṛṣṇivīraś ca viṣṇuḥ

[Though false, and weak-of-mind, pray that my son seeks not
battle with those two men; pray they burn not the Kurus,
As Indra and Viṣṇu consumed their enemies.
For to my troubled mind, Arjuna is Indra's match,
And that Vṛṣṇi hero is Viṣṇu everlasting.] (*Mbh*, 5.22.31)

The *dvandva* (or 'list'; compound, *indrāviṣṇū*, which combines Indra and Viṣṇu into a single word) emphasises the close relationship of these deities even as, in the verse's culmination, the relationship of these gods to Arjuna and Kṛṣṇa is asserted. The closeness of the relationship of Arjuna and Kṛṣṇa is underscored in the previous verse with another *dvandva* in the celebrated line *kṛṣṇāv ekarathe sametau*, which can be translated as 'the two Kṛṣṇas are united on a single chariot'—an image that was brilliantly explored by Hiltebeitel (1984) almost four decades ago. It is worth noting the difference in the way in which King Dhṛtarāṣṭra expresses the relationships between Arjuna and Indra and between Kṛṣṇa and Viṣṇu. Arjuna's relationship to Indra is expressed in terms of equivalence, while that of Kṛṣṇa and Viṣṇu is expressed in terms of identity. Additionally, the adjective *sanātana* ('eternal' or 'everlasting') does some theological heavy lifting here. It underscores the preeminent status of Viṣṇu by placing him beyond time—the very force that

Dhṛtarāṣṭra tends to fall back on when excusing his inability to check the excesses of his son Duryodhana. In this way, Dhṛtarāṣṭra is acknowledging the divine status of Kṛṣṇa, albeit without any great impact on his decision-making processes. He is true to the optative mood he uses in the above: he wishes one thing, but always seems to do another.

Saṃjaya's embassy properly begins on his arrival at the court-in-exile of King Yudhiṣṭhira. There is an immediate asymmetry in the extent of the inquiries about the health of the king and the court between Saṃjaya and Yudhiṣṭhira. Saṃjaya asks only of Yudhiṣṭhira's close kin; Yudhiṣṭhira asks after the whole Kaurava court and broader community. This prefigures a shift in focus in the unfolding moral debate to issues of *care* and *harm*, *loyalty* and *betrayal* and, finally, *sanctity* and *degradation*. Yudhiṣṭhira's series of caring inquiries gives way (from 23.20), however, to a none-too-subtle emphasis on the military prowess of his brothers (the sort of undermining sabre-rattling that is critical to ambassadorial activity both in the Udyogaparvan and in the normative instructions of the *Arthaśāstra*).

Saṃjaya relates the message of Dhṛtarāṣṭra, whose emphasis is on the moral issues surrounding the pursuit of war in the abstract. These emphasise the *harm* that will be done and the need for *care* of one's kin. He also suggests that to live on after the killing of kin is *na sadhu* ('not right'). This moves us from the *care/harm* moral centre to that of *loyalty/betrayal* and studiously avoids the difficult terrain of *fairness* and *cheating*. Saṃjaya, in articulating these positions, tends to offer *bons mots* rather than examples, as befits the shift from the moral analysis of the past to moral exhortation based on anticipated transgression in the future. Saṃjaya's embassy, like that of any good politician avoiding controversy, seeks to refocus the debate. Of the 25 moral points made in the council of Upaplavya, only three are abstract moral injunctions, whereas in the embassy of Saṃjaya, we find only 10 of the 26 moral claims are concrete (see Appendix 8.1).

Yudhiṣṭhira's response is to discourse initially on the evils of desire and on Dhṛtarāṣṭra's hypocrisy. He points to the failure of the king and his son Duryodhana to listen to the words of their advisor, Vidura, on at least four occasions. His response suggests that it is the desire of Duryodhana for personal power and wealth—and Dhṛtarāṣṭra's failure to heed sound advice—that is making war inevitable. The proper exercise of *authority* requires that the person in a position of power is in control of their desires and does not *cheat*. The willingness to engage in the latter is evidence of a failure to properly wield the former. Yudhiṣṭhira returns, in closing, to his emphasis on the might of his brothers. The emphasis on desire gives Saṃjaya an opportunity to reframe the debate philosophically, which he is not slow to do.

Saṃjaya's response, in *adhyāya* 27, is thus interesting and constitutes a marked shift in the content of the moral debate so far. Saṃjaya does more than relay a message;[9] his is a far subtler approach. In the light of Yudhiṣṭhira's comments, he departs from the specifics of King Dhṛtarāṣṭra's message and shifts to a discourse of *sanctity* and *degradation*. However, it is one quite different from the very concrete, brahmin-centred and socially hierarchical emphasis of the Indra/Vṛtra/Nahuṣa narrative. Saṃjaya emphasises the following: the sanctity of life; the need to not perpetrate evil deeds; the need to live without desire or material possessions; and the inevitability of karmic consequence. He uses metaphors of disease and illness to characterise the existential predicament and emphasises the Vedas and ritual purity to address this. It is a more than slightly ascetic discourse even if ritually orthodox.[10] It emphasises *sanctity* and *degradation* in the abstract. Only Karṇa (and Balarāma), it seems, has sought to engage with the Pāṇḍavas on their own moral territory. Saṃjaya's embassy is one that, while perhaps aimed at Yudhiṣṭhira's weakness for the contemplative life, takes us to a different place morally. This is made clear in its moral tasting notes of the debate taken as a whole (Table 8.3).

Table 8.3 Moral tasting notes of the second embassy

Moral 'flavour'	Level of usage
Care/harm	6
Fairness/cheating	4
Loyalty/betrayal	7
Authority/subversion	11
Sanctity/degradation	13

The moral flavour profile of this embassy is in marked contrast with the previous one. Here, *fairness* and *cheating* are little more than background notes, while *sanctity* and *degradation* come to the fore, albeit closely followed by *authority* and *subversion*. Behind these, but ahead of *fairness* and *cheating*,

9 Van Buitenen explores the reasons for this in formal Arthaśāstraic terms; see his introduction to his translation of the Udyogaparvan (1978: 134–38).

10 It appears that Saṃjaya is attempting to jump the strands of the 'dharmic double helix', from the this-worldly to the renunciative. This brilliant metaphor for *dharmic* concerns is that of Raj Balkaran (2020).

are notes of *care* and *harm*, as well as *loyalty* and *betrayal*. In Haidt's terms, the relationship of this sort of discourse to *sanctity* and *degradation* is clear; after a series of more concrete accusations from Yudhiṣṭhira, Saṃjaya invokes a variety of symbolic threats to what Haidt calls the 'behavioural immune system' and urges Yudhiṣṭhira to flee from the very real, very personal moral threat of his circumstances. This is not a debate of rights and wrongs *à la* Upaplavya, but it is a deeply engaged, agent-centred means of subsuming all moral debate into the overarching threat to one's sanctity as a Vedically guided, ritually active, transmigratory being. This is not to say other moral flavours are not present, but the emphasis is on moving away from the emphasis on fairness and cheating to a more abstract and 'ethical' mode.

If the first Pāṇḍava council and embassy see them develop a specific set of moral grievances based on experience, the embassy from Dhṛtarāṣṭra to their court does nothing to address these. Instead, the verbatim message of Dhṛtarāṣṭra and the further imploring and manoeuvring of Saṃjaya seek to move the debate from what has happened to the moral uncertainty of the future and of existence more generally, for the royal household, the world at large and, now, for Yudhiṣṭhira personally, as someone in immediate danger of moral pollution and its attendant metaphysical consequences. As the Indra/Vṛtra/Nahuṣa narrative showed, the deep past hinges on the sanctity of the social hierarchy with the brahmin at its apex; the present is a locus of moral uncertainty; the future must be brought into alignment with the deep and not the proximate past.

Saṃjaya's position, notwithstanding his status as Dhṛtarāṣṭra's ambassadorial mouthpiece, is rather different to that of his king's. He enjoins action to avoid the metaphysical, personal consequences of sin. This is the force of Saṃjaya's statement '*jarāmṛtyū naiva hi tvaṃ prajahyāḥ*' (*Mbh*, 5.27.26), which can be translated as 'for you shall never throw off old age and death' and which has a force not unlike Socrates's emphasis on the 'care of the soul' in Plato's *Apology* (as explored in Christiansen 2000). One must live in anticipation of an afterlife. This is a long way from the moral laziness of Dhṛtarāṣṭra's attitude that fate conquers all or Duryodhana's emphasis on royal power in the here and now. The future is now yoked to spiritual self-interest in a way that weakens the likelihood of the resolution of the moral debates about the recent past precisely because one should not be invested in the outcome of these trivial events. This is a brilliant manoeuvre on Saṃjaya's part, which plays into Kṛṣṇa's hand, as we shall see.

Yudhiṣṭhira seeks neatly to sidestep Saṃjaya's increasingly personalised and ascetic emphasis by shifting the debate to that of the adjusted legal obligations of exigent circumstances (in Sanskrit, *āpaddharma*; lit., 'the obligations of misfortune'; *Mbh*, 5.28.3). He stops short, however, of this form of justification (essentially the moving of the moral and legal goalposts) and instead defers the matter to the judgement of Kṛṣṇa in its entirety.

Kṛṣṇa's response seeks to meet Saṃjaya on his own ground. Rather than move the goalposts, he adjusts the rules of the game once more. The movement from morality to ethics by Saṃjaya is built on by Kṛṣṇa, but with a more forceful metaphysical turn, which encompasses participation in the social order and puts moral and social engagement firmly back on the table. His is a discourse not on the inevitable consequences and spiritual pollutions attendant on acting in the world, but a hymn of praise to acting in accordance with one's prescribed role (foreshadowing the *Bhagavadgītā*). Ironically, if debatably, this brings us closer to Dhṛtarāṣtra's *kṣatriya* fundamentalism. His elaborate description of the inevitability and necessity of karma extends over 20 verses and encompasses the gods and the various *varṇa*s of society. His conclusion is that Duryodhana is in the wrong because he is not duly conscious of the relational, reciprocal, profoundly patterned nature of morality and the society that emerges from it and its divine substrate. This is not a moral debate; it is an invocation of a moral framework as a metaphysical reality anchored in the self-disclosure of God. To consider yourself above the law, or to consider yourself the law, is to be, in the memorable Sanskrit term, a *manyuvaśānugāmin* ('a slave to wilful wrath'). Kṛṣṇa brings the sanctity of the social structure that has the brahmin at its apex into alignment with the sanctity of the transmigratory being. He places 'himself' at the apex of Saṃjaya's moral framework and, in so doing, harmonises the exigencies of fate (Dhṛtarāṣṭra's obsession) with 'care for the soul' (Yudhiṣṭhira's concern, and also that of Vidura, the son and incarnations of Dharma, respectively). Only Duryodhana's position is left beyond the pale, incapable of harmonisation with either devotion or asceticism even if, in practice, a fanatic adherence to warrior *dharma* would look a lot like orthopraxy (until it went off the rails, as it has at this point in the *Mahābhārata*, and as it did for Nahuṣa).

The third embassy and its preparatory discussions: Kṛṣṇa in word and deed (*Mbh*, 5.47–93 and 5.122–35)

Dominant flavours: *Authority* and *subversion*, *fairness* and *cheating*

The third embassy, in both its preparation and its undertaking by Kṛṣṇa, returns us to the more concrete enumeration of the wrongs experienced by the Pāṇḍavas at the hands of the Kauravas. Only 10 of the 59 moral points that are enumerated (see Appendix 8.1) are in the abstract in this long sequence of arguments, punctuated by several important subtales (beyond the scope of this chapter). I tabulate the moral concerns evinced in this portion of the Udyogaparvan in Table 8.4.

Table 8.4 Moral tasting notes of the third embassy

Moral 'flavour'	Level of usage
Care/harm	19
Fairness/cheating	31
Loyalty/betrayal	21
Authority/subversion	32
Sanctity/degradation	6

It is immediately clear that we are returning to a moral profile similar to that of the council of Upaplavya and its subsequent embassy, with the exception that here there are notes of *sanctity* and *degradation*. I recognised these by the way in which purity and pollution seem to haunt the edges of the debates about Draupadī's molestation in the *sabhā* of Hastinapurā at the time of the dice match because she was in her menses. This is a fact that is mentioned only once in the Udyogaparvan—precisely in the present cluster of texts, at *Mbh* 5.88.85. The reference is an oblique one: Draupadī is said to be *ekavastra* ('in one garment').

What runs through the, by now, almost rote enumeration of injustice, however, is the recurrent emphasis on the godhead of Kṛṣṇa. This is a return to and amplification of the morally and metaphysically orthogonal discourse that I have already identified and explored. Arjuna acknowledges Kṛṣṇa's identity as Viṣṇu in a long enumeration of Kṛṣṇa's great deeds (*Mbh*, 5.47 ff.). This is delivered in thunderous *triṣṭubh*s with, initially at least, a central conditional refrain, *tadā yuddhaṃ dhārtarāṣṭro 'nvatapsyat* ('then that descendant of Dhṛtarāṣṭra will come to regret this war'). Directly after this speech, which is reported verbatim to the Kaurava court by Saṃjaya, Bhīṣma explicitly discloses the godhood of both Kṛṣṇa and Arjuna, as Nara and Nārāyaṇa, who are born again and again when it is time to do battle (*tatra tatraiva jāyete yuddhakāle punaḥ punaḥ*). Saṃjaya likewise emphasises the unity, perfection and divine qualities of Arjuna and Kṛṣṇa shortly thereafter, calling them *indraviṣṇusamau* ('the equal of Indra and Viṣṇu') at *Mbh* 5.58.11. However, much of this seems to emphasise the power of the Pāṇḍavas rather than to make a complex moral point.

The points made do stimulate, however, a theological retort from the warlike Duryodhana. He states that the gods do not concern themselves in human affairs. He then engages in self-praise that is close to a statement of his own godhead, as, for example, when he states—portentously or pretentiously, depending on your perspective: *devāsurāṇāṃ bhāvānām aham ekaḥ pravartitā* ('I alone set in motion the existence of gods and demons!'; *Mbh*, 5.60.14). This sort of statement has been interpreted as a refraction in the *Mahābhārata* of the historical rise of absolutism in post-Mauryan South Asia (see Malinar 2007: 36). In this context, however, it is hard not to read this assertion by Duryodhana as ironical or even bathetic in the light of what happens shortly thereafter—namely, the revelation of Kṛṣṇa's divine form in the Kaurava court. Before this, however, we have a series of passages, from 5.66 onwards, in which moral debate gives way to the frank assertion of Kṛṣṇa's divinity, culminating in the celebrated Sanskrit dictum *yataḥ kṛṣṇas tato jayaḥ* ('Where there is Kṛṣṇa, there is victory'). There follow, from Saṃjaya, words of deep devotion, which include etymological meditations on the names of God in a classically *bhakti* mode. Shortly after, Kṛṣṇa begins his embassy in the Kaurava court. Here, we find a back and forth between the more philosophical and abstract treatment of the nature of fate, time and human action with the more fine-grained debate on the specific wrongs done to the Pāṇḍavas. The debates go nowhere. Finally, at the close of Kṛṣṇa's embassy (at *Mbh*, 5.129.4–16), he reveals his *vidyutrūpa* (his 'brilliant form'). It is one that encompasses all being, and the assembled kings tremble before it. We have seen several both concrete and abstract arguments in the moral back and forth of the Udyogaparvan, but nothing like this. Where the moral *aporia* of the text gave rise to debates and to meta-moralities of various types (be they unrepentantly martial, ascetic or existentially engaged, but liberational), Kṛṣṇa's theophany connected definitively his views to his status as being itself. However, of itself, it can do little to resolve the moral minutiae of the Udyogaparvan and the debate about them persists within and beyond the *Mahābhārata* (indeed, to these are added new accusations pertaining to the conduct of the war by both sides).[11] Moral arguments stick. Essays on theology and philosophy tend not to, it seems.

The fourth embassy: Ulūka beards the Pāṇḍavas (*Mbh*, 5.157–60)

Dominant flavours: *Authority* and *subversion*

Ulūka repeats verbatim the words of Duryodhana to the Pāṇḍavas in this final, rather brief embassy. Duryodhana returns to the events of the recent past, but substantially alters the moral tone. There is no meeting of the Pāṇḍavas on their own terms. There is no use of moral or legal counterarguments to rebut their complaints, as Karṇa sought to do with his emphasis on the covenant or *samaya*. Instead, Duryodhana interprets the entire sequence of events from the dice game and the molestation of Draupadī on as an example of might making right. Duryodhana could and did, and that is that. *Authority* is all. The victor determines the moral order. It is possible to interpret some of his message as morally focused (see Appendix 8.1). The two most abstract 'moral' principles Duryodhana offers are the need to subjugate enemies and the need to regain anything one has lost. The tasting notes of this passage are consequently not complex (Table 8.5).

Table 8.5 Moral tasting notes of the fourth embassy

Moral 'flavour'	Level of usage
Care/harm	0
Fairness/cheating	0
Loyalty/betrayal	0
Authority/subversion	5
Sanctity/degradation	0

Duryodhana was not privy to the story of Nahuṣa. He would have been unlikely to listen in any case. This final embassy, on the very eve of hostilities, is one that does not detain itself with the subtleties of what has gone before,

11 This is not the last, or most celebrated, occasion on which Kṛṣṇa will reveal his divine form. He does so in the *Bhagavadgītā*. However, even God incarnate cannot guarantee an attentive audience. Arjuna will ask for a reprise of the *Bhagavadgītā* 'because he forgot' in the fourteenth book of the *Mahābhārata*, the Aśvamedhikaparvan.

be this moral minutiae or metaphysics. It is insulting and intended to undermine the Pāṇḍavas. In this, it is superficially effective, but it has little to add to the foregoing analyses.

Some moral tasting notes for the Udyogaparvan in summary

Figure 8.1 summarises my initial findings in relation to the four embassies of the Udyogaparvan by moral 'foundation'.

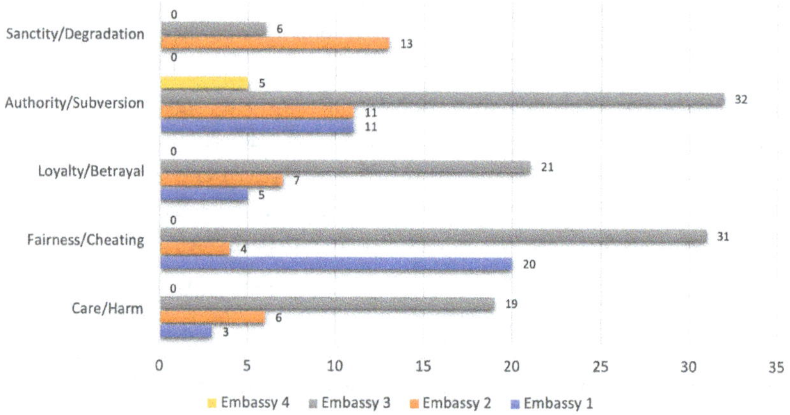

Figure 8.1 Moral tasting notes for the Udyogaparvan

Source: Author's summary.

Figure 8.2 summarises my initial findings by embassy.

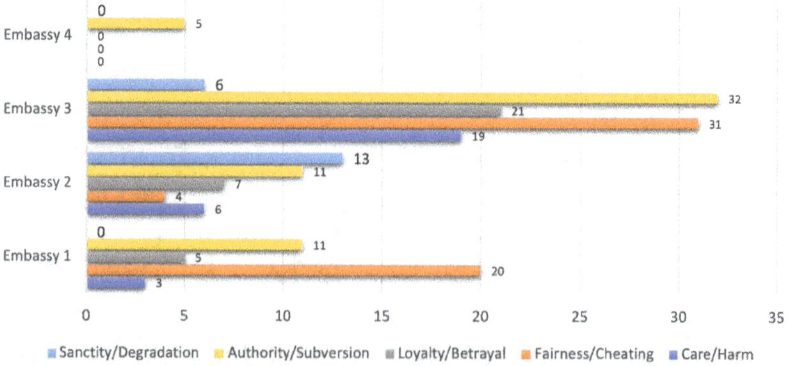

Figure 8.2 Moral tasting notes for the Udyogaparvan, by embassy

Source: Author's summary.

We can thus observe the flavour profile of the key debates of the Udyogaparvan and see clearly their similarities and differences, as discussed in detail above.

Conclusion

It is my hope that I have convinced you of at least the potential utility of Haidt's approach to morality as I have applied it to the *Mahābhārata*. I have no doubt this chapter is a first pass only. It is an attempt to provide, if not proof of concept, at least a suggestion of the need for further investigation. What, then, are the advantages of the approach adopted here? For the individual interpreting a text, it can lead to counterintuitive results. I coded as I went and found that I could not predict the outcome in terms of the moral profile of a given passage or set of passages. I am not insensible to the presence of confirmation bias in my coding, of course. This is not the first time I have read the Udyogapravan or the *Mahābhārata*. Without doubt, I have developed moral assumptions about the text and directly sought to apply Haidt's approach (thus, there is confirmation in two directions). For all that, I did not find the process to be a forced one. Indeed, I found it liberating to step away from the more established modes of classical Indological inquiry and use Haidt's typology, albeit as a heuristic only. I could then connect my results to more culturally specific ideas and arguments in the text, which I found to be illuminating, as I hope you did.

For comparison of the moral emphases and agendas of a variety of religious or political texts, there are also possibilities. I make one reference in passing to Plato's *Apology*, but it seems there is much to be said for an approach that sets out to compare moral 'tasting notes' drawn from materials from different times and places. The present approach also helps to explicate the moral saliency of the *Mahābhārata* in South Asia (across linguistic, cultural and religious boundaries). It has long been obvious that moral tales do not observe religious borders within and beyond South Asia. A cursory examination of the Buddhist *Jātaka*s and the Hindu *Pañcatantra* is sufficient to convince one of this. The moral discourse of the text, as reflected in my moral tasting notes, shows that the *Mahābhārata* is most satisfying to the moral palate. Additionally, if we accept for a moment Haidt's species-level claims, the *Mahābhārata* stimulates every one of our moral 'centres'. In this way, it is like a South Indian 'meal': nourishing to body and mind because it leaves nothing out. Yudhiṣṭhira's dice game, the Pāṇḍavas' exile and Draupadī's molestation, to name only a few examples, echo through the ages precisely because of their rich range of moral flavours and their deep connection to the central concerns of our day-to-day existence and all those who have gone before us. The *Mahābhārata*'s attempts to explain these moral *aporia* in more and less rarefied terms—theologically and philosophically rich as they are (in the mouth of a Saṃjaya or a Kṛṣṇa) or existentially myopic (in the 'live free or die' or 'man a god to man' mode of Duryodhana)—are equally compelling and never more brilliantly set forth and juxtaposed than in the Udyogaparvan. These, however, sit at one remove from the direct moral experience of the text—not moral flavours so much as essays. However, such an order of examination of the text, which begins with an anthropology of moral concerns and moves to culturally specific ideologies, is a novel one in this age of hyperspecialisation. Nīlakaṇṭha was not so wrong, it seems to me, when he contended that the significance and moral reach of the *Mahābhārata* were universal.

References

Balkaran, Raj. (2020). *The Goddess and the King in Indian Myth: Ring Composition, Royal Power and the Dharmic Double Helix*. London: Taylor & Francis.

Christiansen, Michel. (2000). 'Caring about the soul' in Plato's 'Apology'. *Hermathena* 169: 23–56.

De, Sushil Kumar. (1940). *The Udyogaparvan Being the Fifth Book of the Mahābhārata the Great Epic of India*. Poona, India: Bhandarkar Oriental Research Institute.

Haidt, Jonathan. (2012). *The Righteous Mind: Why Good People Are Divided by Politics and Religion*. London: Random House.

Hegarty, James. (2019). Models of royal piety in the Mahābhārata: The case of Vidura, Sanatsujāta and Vidurā. In Brian Black and Ram-Prasad Chakravarthi (eds), *In Dialogue with Classical Indian Traditions: Encounter, Transformation and Interpretation*, pp. 211–27. London: Taylor & Francis. doi.org/10.4324/9781351011136-13.

Hiltebeitel, Alf. (1984). The two Kṛṣṇas on one chariot: Upaniṣadic imagery and epic mythology. *History of Religions* 24(1): 1–26. doi.org/10.1086/462971.

Malinar, Angelika. (2007). *The Bhagavadgita: Doctrines and Contexts*. Cambridge, UK: Cambridge University Press. doi.org/10.1017/CBO9780511488290.

Minkowski, Christopher. (2005). On the success of Nīlakaṇṭha's Mahābhārata commentary. In F. Squarcini (ed.), *Boundaries, Dynamics and Construction of Traditions in South Asia*, pp. 225–52. Florence, Italy: Firenze University Press.

Minkowski, Christopher. (2010). Nilakantha's Mahābhārata. *Seminar: Special Issue: The Enduring Epic: A Symposium on Some Concerns Raised in the Mahābhārata* (608)(April). Available from: www.india-seminar.com/2010/608/608_c_minkowski.htm.

Müller, Max. (1860). *A History of Ancient Sanskrit Literature so far as it Illustrates the Primitive Religion of the Brahmans.* London: Williams & Norgate.

Pollock, Sheldon. (1997). Tradition as revelation: Śruti, smṛti, and the Sanskrit discourse of power. In S. Lienhard and I. Piobvana (eds), *Lex et Litterae: Essays on Ancient Indian Law and Literature in Honor of Oscar Botto*, pp. 395–417. Rome: Edizioni dell'Orso.

Taylor, McComas. (2007). *The Fall of the Indigo Jackal: The Discourse of Division and Pūrṇabhadra's Pañcatantra*. Albany: SUNY Press.

Taylor, McComas. (2008). What enables canonical literature to function as 'true'? The case of the Hindu purāṇas. *International Journal of Hindu Studies* 12(3): 309–28. doi.org/10.1007/s11407-008-9065-9.

Taylor, McComas. (2016). *Seven Days of Nectar: Contemporary Oral Performance of the Bhāgavata Purāṇa*. Oxford, UK: Oxford University Press. doi.org/10.1093/acprof:oso/9780190611910.001.0001.

van Buitenen, J.A.B. (trans. & ed.). (1978). *Mahābhārata. Volume 3, Book 4: The Book of Virāṭa. Book 5: The Book of the Effort*. Chicago, IL: University of Chicago Press. doi.org/10.7208/chicago/9780226223711.001.0001.

Appendix 8.1: Moral claims enumerated and coded according to Haidt's typology

The following are little more than the equivalent of 'fieldnotes', which I offer to the reader with a due sense of humility and contrition. This chapter employs Haidt's typology heuristically. I make no definitive claims that I have correctly identified the nature of a given moral observation, claim or injunction in the text. My hope is that I have not misrepresented the moral emphases of a given passage. This chapter is part of a larger project on 'public reason' in the *Mahābhārata*. It is thus exploratory and preparatory in the context of this larger project, for which I will find a more fine-grained and detailed means of presenting information such as that given below. Indeed, the publication of preliminary inquiries is an important means of refining one's approach.

Claims given in italics are abstract, while those not in italics are concrete. Abstract moral claims tend to take the form of exhortations, while concrete moral claims are anchored in specific events.

Key

CH: *Care/harm*

FC: *Fairness/cheating*

LB: *Loyalty/betrayal*

AS: *Authority/subversion*

SD: *Sanctity/degradation*

The council of Upaplavya (*Mbh*, 5.1–6) and the first embassy: King Drupada's brahmin in the Kaurava court (*Mbh*, 5.20–21)

Defeated with tricks—FC

Kingdom taken—FC/AS/LB

Stood their truth—FC

Abominable vow—FC/AS/LB

Domain plundered ... in a manner deceitful—FC/AS/LB

Submitted to great, unendurable hardship—FC/AS

Did not vanquish ... by virtue of their own splendour—FC/AS

The king and his brothers desire to see them well—CH/FC

The sons of ... only the wish to regain what [they] won for themselves—FC

They tried to kill ... when children—CH

Sought to seize domain—FC/AS

Who all abide by their personal *dharma*—FC/AS

He lost his head—AS/LB

And was soundly defeated—FC

He did not know the dice; he trusted them—FC

Should he prostrate himself for coming into his patrimony—AS

Who claim that the Kaunteyas were discovered—FC
No adharma *in killing enemies*—FC/AS
Begging from foemen brings on adharma—AS/FC
Dhṛtarāṣṭra loves his son—CH/LB
[A]pplies to a man who from the first wanted to act wisely—FC
Men who are loyal will accept the first bid—FC
We owe the Kurus and Pāṇḍavas the same loyalty—AS
Refuse out of arrogance and folly—FC
You know fully how the Kaurava acts—FC

The embassy of Saṃjaya (*Mbh*, 5.22–31)

Victory is defeat—CH/LB
Blessed are those that act for the sake of their kin—CH/LB
To live with your kinfolk dead is not right—CH/LB
Dhṛtarāṣṭra is addled by desire—FC/AS
Dhṛtarāṣṭra is partial, but expects others to be impartial—FC/AS
Dhṛtarāṣṭra wails, but took the advice of his son—AS
Dhṛtarāṣṭra embarked on *adharma* knowing it well—AS/LB/FC
Duryodhana failed to listen to trustworthy Vidura—AS/LB
Duryodhana is prey to his wrath and a lecher, evil, betrayer—AS/LB
Dhṛtarāṣṭra saw full well—LB
Do not destroy life—CH/SD
Do not reign by war—CH/SD
Perpetrate no sin—CH/SD
Live without desire—SD
Live without objects—SD
Dharma *must go before acts*—AS/SD
Obtaining the Earth without dharma *is pointless*—AS/SD
Gifts to brahmins are the highest estate—AS/SD
Yudhiṣṭhira lives in desire; he should practise yoga—AS/SD
Possessions and the search for them lead to adharma—AS/LB/SD
Do not pleasure your heartburning after death—SD
Deeds pursue one—FC/SD

Yudhiṣṭhira is known to be pure—SD

Deeds follow you—FC/SD

Desire leads to evil [with disease metaphors]—SD

Killing of relatives is a sin—CH/LB

Yudhiṣṭhira should take the road of the gods—SD

The embassy of Kṛṣṇa (including preparatory councils; *Mbh*, 5.47–93, 5.122–35)

The Kauravas have been greedy—FC/LB/AS

Draupadi was molested—FC/LB/AS/SD

Arjuna points to trickery—FC

The sons of Pāṇḍu were cheated—FC

He who betrays is not called a guru—FC

They took the rightful gains of the Pandavas—FC

The Kauravas gloated—LB/AS

Duryodhana must be abandoned and lamentation must be replaced with action—LB/AS

It was assumed Dhṛtarāṣṭra would stand by his covenant—FC/LB/AS

He would not give even five villages—FC

Greed kills good sense—FC/LB

Shamelessness kills dharma—AS

Modesty is best—AS

It is ill to rob people of their wealth—FC/LB/AS

Killing kinsmen is wrong—CH/LB

Kṣatriya dharma *is a violent one*—CH/AS

Survivors engage in feuds—FC/LB

When they left you in your loincloth, the Kauravas did not care—CH/AS

The Kauravas cheated you—FC

They hurt you with words—CH

They boasted—AS

They are drunk with power –AS

They are engaged in a feud—FC/AS

They are cruel-spoken—CH

They are quick to deceive—FC/AS
Duryodhana will die before sharing his wealth—AS/LB
He turns down his friends—LB
He has given up *dharma*—AS/SD
He loves the lie—FC
Duryodhana stole what was theirs—FC
Using a cheater—Śakuni—at dice—FC
Draupadi was molested—FC/LB/AS/SD
Duryodhana mistreated you when children—CH
He looted your kingdom—CH
Duryodhana sought to estrange me [Kṛṣṇa] from you—FC/LB
There was trickery—FC
When conciliation and generosity have failed, only the rod remains—AS
Those who should be killed must be killed or there is a sin by omission—FC/LB/AS
Draupadi cites her molestation—CH/FC/AS/SD
The fact of their unfair banishment—CH/FC
The fact of their poverty—CH/FC
Her separation from her children—CH/AS
That she was given away by her father—CH/LB
That she was cheated by her father-in-law—FC/LB/AS
That she has not seen her sons—CH
There was the theft of their kingdom—FC/LB/AS
There was their unfair defeat at dice—FC/LB/AS
There was their exile—FC/LB/AS
There was the molestation of Draupadī *in her menses*—CH/FC/AS/SD
There was manifest cruelty—CH
The Kauravas were misguided—AS
They overstepped their bounds—AS
Their minds were carried away by greed—LB
The Pāṇḍavas *agreed* to the dice game—FC
The dice were crooked—FC
Draupadī was molested—CH/LB/AS/SD

The language used in the *sabhā* was abusive—CH/AS
They sought to murder the Pāṇḍavas in the lacquer house plot—CH/LB/AS
The Kauravas have used poison, fetters and attempted murder—CH/LB/AS

The fourth embassy: Ulūka beards the Pāṇḍavas (*Mbh*, 5.157–60)

The test of the *kṣatriya* is upon you—AS
Avenge your grudge—AS
He who fights must subjugate his enemies—AS
He who fights must restore their kinship—AS
Yudhiṣṭhira should be a man—AS

9

The *Bhagavadgītā*'s determinism and world literature

Simon Brodbeck

Abstract

This chapter discusses two aspects of the *Bhagavadgītā* in light of the category of world literature.[1] In both cases, I will argue that if one understands world literature in a programmatic sense, the *Bhagavadgītā* is anomalous or heretical. Thus, despite being one of the most salient and successful examples of world literature, the *Bhagavadgītā* is an odd fit for the category. The first aspect discussed is the text's attitude to the Kurukṣetra War, which caused the deaths of more than one billion men. I will show that the *Bhagavadgītā* (*Bhg*) takes a pro-war position, particularly when understood through the surrounding text of the *Mahābhārata*. The second aspect discussed is the text's philosophical and theological determinism, which is opposed to the idea of human free will that has been widespread in cultures ancient and modern.

1 An earlier version of this chapter was presented at the Nehru Centre in London at a conference entitled 'The *Bhagavad Gītā*: Its Contemporary Relevance', 24–25 September 2015. I am grateful to the conference organisers and to the audience on that occasion, particularly Gabriella Burnel.

The *Bhagavadgītā* as a text of war

Consider the ethics of Arjuna Pāṇḍava's situation just before the Kurukṣetra War. What does Arjuna think his options are? To fight or not to fight. His preference for the latter seems to be based on his horror at the prospect of fighting, rather than on any clear alternative. He just does not think winning the war would be worth it. He says to Kṛṣṇa, his chariot-driver:

> Those for whose sake we want kingdom, enjoyments, and pleasures are drawn up here for battle, ready to give up their lives and wealth: teachers, fathers, sons, grandfathers, uncles, fathers-in-law, grandsons, brothers-in-law, and other relatives. Though they would kill me, slayer of Madhu, I wouldn't want to kill them even for the sovereignty of the triple-world; how much less, then, for the sake of the earth! What joy could there be for us, Janārdana, were we to kill Dhṛtarāṣṭra's sons? Were we to kill these murderers, evil would befall us; so we mustn't kill Dhṛtarāṣṭra's sons, our kinsmen. For how could we be happy having killed our family, Mādhava? ... It would be better for me if Dhṛtarāṣṭra's sons, armed with weapons, were to kill me in battle unresisting and unarmed ... Better in this world to live on alms without killing the mighty elders; for were I to kill the elders, eager though they are for worldly gain, in this very world I would taste pleasures smeared with blood. (*Bhg*, 1.33–37, 46; 2.5)[2]

When Arjuna says it would be better to live on charity, he does not say whose—perhaps the charity of the Kauravas or of some other relatives or friends, or perhaps the charity of strangers as an itinerant beggar.

The *Mahābhārata* is a great work of world literature, yet there is a problem when we view it from a humanitarian perspective. The war in the *Rāmāyaṇa* is fought against a great demon, to rescue a damsel in distress, so the *Rāmāyaṇa*'s bloodshed has a moral justification. It is like the Anglo-American myth of World War II: the goodies won and the demon was destroyed, but he would not have been destroyed without the action that was taken against him, so that action was justified, despite the collateral damage. If Hitler came again—God forbid—he should be cut down again. But in the Kurukṣetra War the destruction is on a different scale, and in human terms it is comparatively senseless. It is more like the millions dying on the Western Front during World War I—the 'Great War'. The message from *that* war was:

2 For the *Bhagavadgītā* text, see Belvalkar (1968). *Bhagavadgītā* translations are adapted from Cherniak (2008).

never again must so many die for so little. The Great War was called 'the war to end all wars'. Just weeks after it began, H.G. Wells published a book about it entitled *The War That Will End War* (1914). When the war ended on 11 November 1918, David Lloyd George told the UK House of Commons: 'At eleven o'clock this morning came to an end the cruellest and most terrible war that has ever scourged mankind. I hope we may say that thus, this fateful morning, came to an end all wars.'[3] The mistaken idea that the Great War would be the last war was perhaps the only way in which recent slaughter on such a scale could be comprehended or justified.

From the perspective of the analogy between the Great War and the Kurukṣetra War, we can read the *Mahābhārata* as the story of a human disgrace. More than a billion men died[4] because two sets of royal cousins could not resolve their differences any other way. Even after each set of cousins had been given half the ancestral kingdom, they restarted their feud. If we seek someone to blame, part of the blame falls on blind King Dhṛtarāṣṭra, who would not make his son Duryodhana behave; and part of it falls on Duryodhana himself, who would not even give his cousins five villages in which to live in peace. If one looks at it in this way (and it is *if*; see Brodbeck 2020), the Pāṇḍavas largely escape blame because they waged war as a last resort to rescue themselves from intolerable victimisation and, having embarked on it, they had to try their best to win. But winning does not make them happy. So, the war is a tragedy. We can hope that no-one will ever again be as intransigent as Duryodhana or as careless as Dhṛtarāṣṭra or as unlucky as the Pāṇḍavas. From this perspective—whereby war is an undesirable result—we can respect Arjuna's position: 'I will not fight.' Surely, it would have been morally correct to be a conscientious objector during the Great War.

The humanitarian perspective is a humanistic ethical perspective and it has implications for the understanding of world literature. If we want world literature to be literature that is good for the world, then knowing what we do about the damage that war does, we might want the world's great war stories to tell us *to* avoid war and *how* to avoid war. From this perspective, the *Mahābhārata* as a work of world literature would teach us how not to be like Duryodhana and Dhṛtarāṣṭra. And it can do that.

---

3 Available from: en.wikiquote.org/wiki/David_Lloyd_George.

4 Some 1,660,020,000 men were killed in the war, with a further 24,165 missing in action (*Mahābhārata*, 11.26.9–10). For the *Mahābhārata* text, see Dandekar (1971–76). The *Bhagavadgītā* is *Mahābhārata* 6.23–40 (vol. 2, pp. 1158–85).

There is no need to be programmatic about world literature. David Damrosch's definition is neutral: 'I take world literature to encompass all literary works that circulate beyond their culture of origin, either in translation or in their original language' (2003: 4). Nonetheless, a programmatic notion of world literature has some pedigree. In their *Manifesto of the Communist Party*, Karl Marx and Friedrich Engels made the connection between processes of globalisation and a new literary paradigm:

> In place of the old local and national seclusion and self-sufficiency, we have intercourse in every direction, universal inter-dependence of nations. And as in material, so also in intellectual production. The intellectual creations of individual nations become common property. National one-sidedness and narrow-mindedness become more and more impossible, and from the numerous national and local literatures, there arises a world literature. (Marx and Engels 1967: 46–47)

The history of the *Mahābhārata*'s interpretation includes a very important chapter, which took place largely after Marx and Engels wrote the above words, wherein the *Mahābhārata* was understood primarily as a national text, and the struggle of the Pāṇḍavas against the Kauravas was understood as a cipher for the nationalist struggle against the colonial British (Lothspeich 2009). But that interpretive perspective is dependent on its specific context. Other perspectives on the text are available and have often been evident—for example, the theosophical interpretation shared by Mahatma Gandhi, whereby the Kurukṣetra War is seen as one between opposed forces within the human psyche.[5]

Discussing the role played by Yugoslavia's various regional intelligentsias in creating the conditions for the Yugoslav wars of the 1990s, Aijaz Ahmad warns that

> the idea of a 'national literature' can quite easily cease to represent the legitimate cultural rights of a people and become a retrograde—even murderous—force as soon as it gets sundered from the more progressive moorings in ideas of cultural diversity and universalist civilization. (Ahmad 2000: 17)

5 On Gandhi's interpretation, see Sharpe (1985: 113–22); Robinson (2006: 60–64); and Davis (2015: 136–45). On its theosophical roots, see Sharpe (1985: 91–94, 117). Similar in this respect are the interpretations of V.S. Sukthankar (1957: 91–115), Bede Griffiths (Robinson 2006: 80–85), Swami Vivekānanda (pp. 86–87), Sarvepalli Radhakrishnan (p. 91), Swami Śivānanda (p. 97) and Annie Besant (p. 108).

The roots of mass killing may lie in ethnic or national exclusivism; so it is that '[w]riting that addresses some of the worst horrors and crimes of humankind, genocide and war, has a particular position in world literature', partly because of its potential to 'warn the future' (Thomsen 2008: 103, 106).

In this perspective, being a global ethical actor involves sitting in judgement on oneself and each other. So we respect Arjuna for taking his business so seriously, and that is a large part of the *Bhagavadgītā*'s contemporary relevance. But when Arjuna decides not to fight, that is just the start, for his decision is wrong. He does not understand the war or his own role in it. His journey in the *Bhagavadgītā* is the journey from thinking that he cannot and will not fight, to knowing that he must and will.

The *Mahābhārata* explains that Kṛṣṇa is the great god Viṣṇu Nārāyaṇa, who has been born on Earth, along with various other celestials, on a special mission of destruction, according to a divine plan. Details are given in *Mahābhārata* 1.58–61. From J.A.B. van Buitenen's summary of *Mahābhārata* 1.58:

> [I]t became the golden age. But the Asuras [demons], defeated by the Gods, reincarnate themselves in prideful and oppressive kings. Tyrranized, Earth seeks mercy from Brahmā, who orders that the Gods incarnate themselves. Indra and Nārāyaṇa compact to this purpose. The celestials descend, and wreak havoc on the demons. (van Buitenen 1973: 125)

Mahābhārata 1.61 gives details of which celestials descended as which humans. The celestial business is also mentioned after the war, in *Mahābhārata* 11.8. From James Fitzgerald's summary:

> [To Dhṛtarāṣṭra] Vyāsa recounts overhearing a past conversation among the Gods in which Viṣṇu told Earth that Duryodhana would soon be the occasion for the Gods' fulfilling their promise to relieve her of her burden. Vyāsa lectures Dhṛtarāṣṭra on his sons' wickedness and on the fact that they were born on earth in the interests of destruction. He tells him the Pāṇḍavas were blameless, while his sons were vile and harmed the earth. All this is the 'secret of the Gods'. (Fitzgerald 2004a: 29–30)

In the account given in *Harivaṃśa* 40–45,[6] the origin of the Earth's problem is slightly different (see Viethsen 2009; Brodbeck 2022: 103–17), but the solution is the same: massive destruction arranged by the gods, led by Viṣṇu.[7]

6 For the *Harivaṃśa* text, see Dandekar (1971–76, vol. 5).

7 On this 'secret of the gods', see also Fitzgerald (2004b: 56–59) and Hiltebeitel (2011: 571–80).

Emily Hudson (2013: 115, 138–39) seeks to stress that this explanation for the war is just one among many. Since this explanation is a secret that is not available to most of the protagonists, there are naturally others within the discourse, and to this extent Hudson is correct. But the divine explanation for the war is placed in a superordinate position for the listening King Janamejaya and for us, because it is presented in advance, before the story of the Pāṇḍavas and Kauravas begins, as a primary tool for that story's understanding. And the divine explanation must largely be sidelined if one wishes to focus on the *Mahābhārata* in terms of humanistic ethics.

The Kurukṣetra War was the main event, during which the massacre arranged by the gods occurred. But most of the characters acting in the war do not know or do not remember this 'secret of the gods'. Indra, for example, has incarnated a portion of himself as Arjuna, to kill in this battle; but Arjuna does not know this. Only Kṛṣṇa knows. Kṛṣṇa is the leader of the war party and he must ensure that the necessary destruction takes place. That is why he must make Arjuna fight. Kṛṣṇa is not able to say 'Remember yourself!' to Arjuna in the same straight way that he says it to Baladeva in *Harivaṃśa* 58 (Brodbeck 2019: 180–81), because Kṛṣṇa and Baladeva are Viṣṇu in a way that Arjuna is not, despite Arjuna and Kṛṣṇa's connection as the Nara–Nārāyaṇa pair (see Biardeau 1991), and despite their connection as two of the several Kṛṣṇas (alongside Vyāsa and Draupadī; see Hiltebeitel 1991). So Kṛṣṇa does not reveal the secret of the gods (the divine plan) to Arjuna in the *Bhagavadgītā* as such. But in the theophany of *Bhagavadgītā* 11, Kṛṣṇa shows Arjuna the results of the divine plan in advance. Arjuna, beholding the godhead, says:

> All those sons of Dhṛtarāṣṭra, and the armies of kings, and Bhīsma, and Droṇa, and [Karṇa] that son of a *sūta* and all our best warriors rush into your terrifying mouths with their horrible fangs; I can see some stuck between your teeth with their heads smashed. These heroes of the world of men pile into your blazing mouths like the many rivers running into the sea; as moths rush to their deaths in a burning flame, so these men accelerate into your mouths to meet their doom. (*Bhg*, 11.26–29)

Kṛṣṇa replies:

> I am Time, the destroyer of people, ripened, and here I am busy crushing people. Even without you, all the warriors drawn up in the opposing ranks will cease to exist. So get up and win your fame! Conquer your enemies and enjoy the full sovereignty. I have myself

> long since doomed them to perish; you just be the instrument, left-handed archer. Droṇa, and Bhīṣma, and Jayadratha, and Karṇa, and other heroic warriors too: kill them, for I have already slain them. Don't hesitate! Fight! You will conquer your rivals in the battle. (*Bhg*, 11.32–34)

The message to Arjuna is: you do not understand what is happening. You do not need to and you will not be able to. But it is under control; and it is out of your control. Because, as Kṛṣṇa goes on to say in *Bhg* 18:

> When you indulge your ego and think 'I won't fight', this resolution of yours is spurious, for nature [*prakṛti*] will force you to. Fettered by your proper activity, Kaunteya, which is determined by your very nature [*svabhāva*], you will do what in your confusion you don't want to do, even if it be against your will [*avaśo 'pi*]. (*Bhg*, 18.59–60)

The situation is special, because Kṛṣṇa is God and because Arjuna, Kṛṣṇa's cousin, brother-in-law and best friend, has God Viṣṇu as his best friend. How is that supposed to make the rest of us feel? As for Kṛṣṇa being God: becoming a person or some other kind of creature to affect the world is just something that God does sometimes. South Asian examples are given in the *Mahābhārata*, the *Rāmāyaṇa*, the Purāṇas, and in more recent texts (Granoff 1984). Examples could be multiplied, in South Asia and elsewhere.

Meeting God and then doing what he says is one thing. That is what I would do if it happened to me. But from our point of view, there is also the idea of a more general claim about human action, as if the myth of Kṛṣṇa and Arjuna were a dramatised illustration of an abiding prior certainty to human deeds. Does the *Mahābhārata*'s claim about divine business in human affairs only apply to Arjuna and his contemporaries in relation to the Kurukṣetra War for which this myth is told? Arguably, something more general is being said (Hill 2001: 345–52; Brodbeck 2004, 2010: 138–39).

The concept of free will

Here we move from considering the *Bhagavadgītā* as offending against a programmatic world-literature sensibility in terms of being pro-war to considering its offending against such a sensibility in terms of denying free will. Arjuna sees that there is no choice, because Kṛṣṇa already contains the future. It is a truth for all. Kṛṣṇa says:

> *īśvaraḥ sarvabhūtānāṃ hṛddeśe 'rjuna tiṣṭhati |*
> *bhrāmayan sarvabhūtāni yantrārūḍhāni māyayā ||*
>
> The lord sits in the heart *of every being*, Arjuna, and by magic power he makes *all the beings* put in the machine move about. (*Bhg*, 18.61; emphasis added)

This determinism complements Kṛṣṇa's Sāṃkhya-style discrimination of humans into two aspects: that of awareness, and that of activity, phenomena and substance. The aspect of awareness is called *ātman* ('the self'), *puruṣa* ('the person'), *kṣetrajña* ('the knower of the field') or *dehin* ('the one in the body'). It witnesses but cannot act. In terms of the human organism, the other aspect is the body, the senses and the mind, and this aspect is causally continuous with the rest of the world. So it is a mistake to appropriate agency to the self. Here there are three nice quotations:

> Deeds are everywhere performed by the modes of nature [*guṇa*s of *prakṛti*].[8] The one who has been deluded by their own ego [*ahaṃkāra*] thinks 'I am the doer', but the one who truly knows the two divisions—the division of modes and the division of actions—realises that the modes are acting upon each other and doesn't become attached, mighty-armed one. Those who are bewildered by nature's modes become attached to the actions of those modes. (*Bhg*, 3.27–29b)

> The disciplined one who knows the true reality of things should think 'I am doing nothing at all', remembering that when they see, hear, touch, smell, eat, walk, sleep, breathe, talk, excrete, grasp, and open and close their eyes, their senses and capacities are just acting upon their objects. (*Bhg*, 5.8–9)

> The one who sees that all actions are performed by nature [*prakṛti*] alone, and so sees themself as a non-agent, can truly see. (*Bhg*, 13.29)

According to these verses, the phenomenal world (which means not just the physical world) is causally complete, and thus the idea of one's responsibility for one's actions is problematic and potentially illegitimate as a product of the ego—the ego that Kṛṣṇa says we must suppress. This is perhaps the *Bhagavadgītā*'s most enduringly relevant message. It strikes at the root of human suffering.

8 The three *guṇas* ('modes', 'qualities', 'strands') of *prakṛti* are *sattva*, *rajas* and *tamas* ('clarity', 'passion' and 'darkness'), as described in detail in *Bhg* 14 and 17–18.

The suppression of the ego is a common theme in religious literature, and in Indian philosophy Kṛṣṇa is not alone in suggesting it. The pernicious nature of the idea of 'mine' is a recurring notion in the Mokṣadharmaparvan of *Mahābhārata* 12. In a nutshell: 'Absolutely everything that is conceived of with the idea of "mine" culminates in suffering' (*Mahābhārata*, 12.168.41, translation from Fitzgerald 2015: 132). But when the suppression of the ego involves the idea of determinism, it is also heresy, because generally we are held responsible for our actions. Conventional analysis attributes human actions to a self behind and above the personal pronoun 'I' and imagines that when this self initiates an action, it is also free not to. It imagines the self as agent 'I'.

The philosophical literature on the topics of free will and determinism is enormous and contains numerous definitions of both terms. Here, I effectively follow Peter van Inwagen's notion that 'the concept of free will should be understood in terms of the *power* or *ability* of agents to act otherwise than they in fact do' (1982: 49).[9] From this point of view, the idea of seeing the future in God's present body is powerful. Even if Arjuna saw it in dramatised or metaphorical form as warriors being crushed by God's teeth (rather than killed in battle at Kurukṣetra as they will in fact be), Kṛṣṇa implies that the world's current and past configurations imply all future configurations given the passage of time: 'I have myself long since doomed them to perish; you just be the instrument' (*Bhg*, 11.33cd).

In conventional terms, the principle of retributive justice seems to require the free will of an agentive self. This principle is presented in various religions in terms of our being rewarded or punished after death for what we did while alive—in heaven or hell or in the circumstances of future rebirth. And without thinking in post-mortem terms, legal theory involves philosophical justification of the nature and implications of moral responsibility within this life, and a host of discourses and operations, legal and otherwise, punish people, ostensibly for the common good. Thus, Kṛṣṇa's idea may seem to threaten the very system that protects us—the system, in which we collude, of ethical praise and blame. Clement of Alexandria wrote in his *Stromata*

9 Viewed in these terms, Schopenhauer (1985) and Double (1991), for example, argue, as Kṛṣṇa effectively does, that there is no free will. Schopenhauer (1985: 70–83) cites in agreement Luther, Vanini, Hume, Hobbes, Spinoza, Priestley, Voltaire and Kant. Scientific progress has implications for this issue: see, for example, Swinburne (2011); Wegner (2002), on 'the illusion of conscious will'; and Bohm (1983) and Norris (2000) on quantum mechanics and the principle of causation. 'The law of causality is established a priori as the general rule to which all objects of the external world are subject without exception' (Schopenhauer 1985: 28).

that 'neither praises nor censures, neither rewards nor punishments, are right, when the soul has not the power of inclination and disinclination, but evil is involuntary' (Roberts and Donaldson 1956: 319).

So, Kṛṣṇa's denial of free will has not been well received. For example, Ellen Jane Briggs (2008: 66–95) finds a counter-perspective in *Bhg* 13.22, where the *puruṣa* is described as the *anumantṛ* ('consenter' or 'approver'), and she proposes a 'libertarian interpretation' of the apparently deterministic verses, whereby they are not deterministic; but she stretches the text. More faithful—and more radical—is the view of Will Johnson:

> Krishna subsumes within himself both fate and agency ... In other words, the dichotomy between fate ... and human effort ... is collapsed ... In practical terms, this entails turning over the results of one's actions to the real actor, God, and relying entirely on his liberating power. (Johnson 1997: 99)

The brief discussion of the *Bhagavadgītā* in Edwin Bryant's paper on 'Agency in Sāṃkhya and Yoga' (2014: 33–37) emphasises the text's denial of the *puruṣa*'s agency, while admitting that various commentators had problems with this. The latter situation will no doubt continue to obtain. The denial of agency can seem to endorse irresponsible behaviour and the idea of being beyond good and evil. It has received a bad press, from the time of Kṛṣṇa through to the story of Charles Manson (Zaehner 1975) and beyond.

The divinity of the world

Kṛṣṇa is only peripherally talking about a philosophical system. He responds to Arjuna's emotional expression and begins from the individual's messy point of view. Thus, in the *Bhagavadgītā*, it is a question of 'facing the human condition not as anyone's problem but as my problem, that is, a first-person problem' (Kwak and Han 2013: 69). It is not so much about whether Arjuna *is held* responsible for his actions (and we for ours) as whether Arjuna *holds himself* (or we ourselves) responsible; whether we judge ourselves. Because if we do, we do so from a position of ignorance. In Albert Camus's *L'Étranger* (1942), after killing the Arab on the beach, Meursault does not judge himself.

At the start of the *Bhagavadgītā*, Arjuna does not know what to do. But what he will do is already within the configuration of the world. So he is told what to do, just as a tossed coin is told, by forces and circumstance, whether to land heads-up or tails-up. But the *Bhagavadgītā*'s determinism differs from the determinisms in philosophy books or in Camus, because in the *Bhagavadgītā* the world is divine. Kṛṣṇa explains that the various constituents of the psycho-physical world are part of him:

> My phenomenal nature [*prakṛti*] is divided into eight: earth, water, fire, air, ether, mind, understanding [*buddhi*], and ego. This is my lower nature, mighty-armed one; so know too my other, higher nature, namely the soul, by which this universe is sustained. Understand that all beings originate from my nature; I am the source of the whole universe, and its dissolution too. (*Bhg*, 7.4–6)

Further details are given concerning Kṛṣṇa's 'lower nature':

> The great elements, the ego, the understanding, and the unmanifest itself; the ten senses and the mind, and the five sense-realms; desire, aversion, pleasure, pain, the organism, consciousness [*cetanā*], and stability: together these are said to constitute the field with its modifications. (*Bhg*, 13.5–6)

This is the field that the 'knower of the field'—the *kṣetrajña*, *ātman*, *puruṣa* or *dehin*—knows. The 'great elements' mentioned at *Bhg* 13.5 are listed at 7.4: earth, water, fire, air and ether. The 'ten senses' are listed at *Sāṃkhya Kārikā* 26 as two groups of five, the sense-capacities and the action-capacities: seeing, hearing, smelling, tasting and touching; and voice-part, hand, foot, anus and genitals.[10] The 'five sense-realms' (the *tanmātras* of the *Sāṃkhya Kārikā*) are the sensations gathered by the five sense-capacities.

So Kṛṣṇa contains nature with all its modes and modalities, including every organism's senses and capacities and their objects—all the aspects onto which we are to displace our misplaced agency, according to Kṛṣṇa's advice, in a gesture of pure, truthful homage to him. This is the pantheism that the early Christian commentators found so distasteful (Plumptre 1878: 17–24, 110–22). But what they found distasteful—the lack of a safe distance between us and God—is what is most relevant: a message of basic acceptance, the opposite of alienation (Chakravarty 1955). Ted Honderich argues that determinism should evoke a response of affirmation and 'a celebratory philosophy of life' (1990: 171). Before him, Arthur Schopenhauer wrote that determinism and the denial of free will 'are the most abundant source of comfort and tranquility' (1985: 62).

10 For the *Sāṃkhya Kārikā* text, see Burley (2007: 163–79).

To step back and proceed chronologically. In his essay *On the Free Choice of the Will*, Saint Augustine asked: 'If sins come from the souls that God created, and those souls come from God, how is it that sins are not almost immediately traced back to God?' (King 2010: 5). In 1825, Wilhelm von Humboldt noted that the *Bhagavadgītā* 'implies a necessary fatalism', since 'the Godhead ... is, properly speaking, to be considered as the only moral agent' (1849: 126). In 1839, Schopenhauer wrote:

> [T]here is no shortage of ignoramuses who proclaim the freedom of the will as actually given ... But perhaps I am unfair to them, as it may be the case that they are not as ignorant as they seem but only hungry, and therefore, for a very dry piece of bread, teach everything that might please a lofty ministry. (Schopenhauer 1985: 45)

Catherine Robinson (2006: 73) finds R.D. Griffith in 1849 'objecting to what he thought of as a determinism that tended to fatalism and a reliance on the divine that detracted from moral responsibility'. As Eric Sharpe (1985: 37) puts it, in Griffith's view, 'simple obligation is powerless to provide the motive for right action'. Griffith writes:

> It will suffice to observe, that the doctrine [of the *Bhagavadgītā*] interferes with human responsibility and freedom; and whatever clashes with them, subverts itself. The transference of our actions and condition to Deity, subtracts from our moral feelings all healthful stimulus; it sheds upon us an unmanly indifference; it disorganizes the probationary and tentative economy with which we are allied; it blasts the charities of man's heart; it strips the spirit of ardour—it paralyzes its elasticity;—it breaks its wing. (Griffith 1849: xliii)

Verbiage. In 1863, Robert Caldwell, the bishop of Tirunelveli in Tamil Nadu, commented on the *Bhagavadgītā* with words that were laced with righteous disgust, but otherwise astute:

> According to the Gítá, God is the Soul of the world; its material cause, as well as its efficient cause. The world is his body, framed by himself out of himself. A consequence of this doctrine, a consequence which is distinctly taught again and again, is that God is all things, as containing all things. Every thing that exists is a portion of God, and every action that is performed is an action of God. The doctrine knows no limitations, and is incapable of being exaggerated. The basest animals that creep on the face of the earth have not merely been created by God for some good purpose, but are divine, inasmuch as they are portions of God's material form; and the most wicked actions which men, vainly fancying themselves free agents, are ever

> tempted to perform, are not only permitted by God, but are actually perpetrated by him, inasmuch as they are performed by his power and will, working out their ends through the human constitution, which is a part of himself. (Caldwell 1894: 25–26; also quoted in Murdoch 1894: 33)

A statue of Caldwell was erected on the promenade at Marina Beach, Madras, in 1968. W.S. Urquhart (1914: 490) similarly opined that 'we cannot acquiesce in a facile identification of God with the world, or a perhaps less facile merging of the world in God, if we are to have any secure foundation for morality, progress and religion'. At some level, Simone Weil felt this too (Bingemer 2006: 83–86). The moral agent within the human must be significantly non-divine so that it can be responsible.

How specifically Christian this objection is I am not sure. It sought to rescue morality against a legendary Oriental fatalism that was associated with belief in karma and rebirth. But is theology to be a by-product of social planning? Compare the perspective presented by Allen Ginsburg in his 1955 'Footnote to Howl':

> Holy! Holy! Holy! Holy! Holy! Holy! Holy! Holy! Holy! Holy!
> Holy! Holy! Holy! Holy! Holy!
>
> The world is holy! The soul is holy! The skin is holy! The nose is holy! The tongue and cock and hand and asshole holy![11]
>
> Everything is holy! everybody's holy! everywhere is holy! everyday is in eternity! everyman's an angel!
>
> The bum's as holy as the seraphim! the madman is holy as you my soul are holy! (Ginsburg 1994: 27)

Concluding discussion

The *Mahābhārata*'s (retrospective) pro-war stance for the good of the Earth is contrary to the idea that war is bad. The Kurukṣetra War was good and holy. But the theological frame offends the secular gaze and can offend the ongoing world-literature gaze. After all, in addition to being the champion of the war, Viṣṇu is also the champion of the Brahmanical class system, the

11 In this line, Ginsburg mentions two of the five sense-capacities ('skin', 'nose') and four of the five action-capacities ('tongue', 'cock', 'hand', 'asshole'); see *Sāṃkhya Kārikā* 26.

royalist system and the patrilineal gender system (on the theological level, the male God contains and surpasses female nature). In social terms, he embodies the *Ancien Régime*, the inheritance of privilege by birth, and all the myths spun to explain it. The only possible defence is offered: everyone gets what they deserve. Because of karma, the ribbon is tied in a bow.

The Kurukṣetra War as a population purge for the benefit of the Earth has an apocalyptic climate-crisis resonance. But if many more people must die, in masses, before their time, I hope they are not killed by each other.

If the divine pro-war position is offensive, so also is the determinism by which it is forced on Arjuna and the rest of us. We react against the reduction of our ego. We mount all manner of righteous defences on its behalf. Its reduction seems unethical and is certainly counterintuitive. Kṛṣṇa's advice is that the enemies are desire and anger (*Bhg* 3.37–43), but in so saying, he urges Arjuna—and, by implication, the rest of us—to try to counter those enemies, rather than just watching them do their work; and the very form of his repeated imperatives to Arjuna to 'Stand up!' and 'Fight!' can seem to imply a freely acting self (Sharma 1979: 534; Brodbeck 2010: 139).

Regarding the reduction of the ego, Sanskrit has first-person singular, dual and plural. The plural has been easily slipped into above—the 'we' or 'us' that Arjuna's position so beautifully evokes, fashioned as I please—and the dual is just me and you, dear reader, mixed in with other dual forms (self and, for example, parent, sibling, friend, lover, child, time, God). The reduction of the ego might be presented in terms of acting not for oneself but for another (as per the Good Samaritan in the Bible, Luke 10:25–37) or for a community of others (as per John 15:13: 'Greater love hath no man than this, that a man lay down his life for his friends').[12] One responds positively to the sentiment of the enlarged concern, but in a way, any 'we two' or any 'we' that I could imagine in advance would be my own ego writ large. So it is interesting to note the various kinds of 'we' that others attempt to co-opt one into (national, modern, social, and so on) and to imagine opting out of them. But opting out of one 'we' inevitably emphasises other kinds of 'we', and thus, eventually, a 'me'. By contrast, in the *Bhagavadgītā*, the reduction of the ego is presented in terms of acting for the world or God (Gelblum 1992).

12 For the Gospel texts, see www.nestle-aland.com/en/read-na28-online/. Translations are from www.kingjamesbibleonline.org.

Determinism is abominated. But in the *Bhagavadgītā* with Kṛṣṇa and Arjuna, and elsewhere in the *Mahābhārata*, determinism is presented as inclusion, where its opposite would be separation. There would only be separation if people were singled out to be judged one by one. And judgement is, in the first place, a trick of the ego. 'Judge not, that ye be not judged' (Matthew 7:1).

Why is the *Bhagavadgītā* a work of world literature? One might wish to take a neutral approach to world literature, following Damrosch (2003: 4: 'all literary works that circulate beyond their culture of origin, either in translation or in their original language'). From this perspective, the history of the *Bhagavadgītā*'s popularity since its first translation into English (Wilkins 1785) puts it immediately in that category. But that cannot be all there is to it. Since its first translation, the *Bhagavadgītā* has also been seen as world literature in a programmatic sense, and this has involved an interpretive overlay that, facilitated by the removal of the *Bhagavadgītā* from the larger *Mahābhārata*, has tended to de-emphasise the war's divine context and the implications of that context for Arjuna's freedom, and to emphasise aspects that travel better, as it were, such as Kṛṣṇa's message of selfless devotion to duty and the poetic power of his theophany. In this chapter, I have tried to remove the overlay, to reflect on what it obscures and why, and to show that when the war's divine context and its deterministic ramifications are appreciated, they are anomalous in a work of world literature in the programmatic sense.

When Johann von Goethe in 1827 opined that 'it is the time for world literature, and all must aid in bringing it about' (Bell 2016: 908; Schrimpf 1998: 362), this was a plan, and it was so in part, no doubt, because of his encounter with Sanskrit literature (specifically *Abhijñānaśākuntalam*, *Bhagavadgītā* and *Gītagovinda*). There is also no doubt that the *Bhagavadgītā*'s format as a meeting between human and God facilitates a universalist projection. But can we continue to imagine world literature in a programmatic sense after Goethe, Marx and Engels, the Great War, the Soviet Union, World War II, the Holocaust and the Cultural Revolution? If so, it must be progressive, anti-war and anti-slaughter. It must be compassionate for the greater good. And, after the blood spilled in the name of religion and the advances made in the name of science, world literature must also somehow be humanistic, perhaps secular, even anti-theological, so that sacred texts, many of which are primary works to be included in the category, are only included insofar as they have the same kind of inverted commas around them as has every other work. This is what it is now for the notion of world literature to be modern or up to date: it must be viewed postcolonially. To understand the violence of colonialism will be to understand the role of religion in facilitating it. And the notion of world literature must be supernational almost by definition, against the perversions of nationalism in the nineteenth, twentieth and twenty-first centuries. What is left? Some global ethical frame that seeks to encourage one to respect the other—where both oneself and the other are freely choosing agents. So, this imaginary notion of world literature must be anti-deterministic. What is left? People made of straw.

I would not want to be programmatic about world literature; but at the same time, I want it to be helpful, and I suspect that the *Bhagavadgītā* stands to be more helpful without the overlay. The tension is an interesting one. Quotations follow from Damrosch and Homi Bhabha, presented here to provoke further reflections:

> As we triangulate between our own present situation and the enormous variety of other cultures around and before us ... a degree of distance from the home tradition can help us to appreciate the ways in which a literary work reaches out and away from its point of origin. If we then observe ourselves seeing the work's abstraction from its origins, we gain a new vantage point on our own moment. The result may be almost the opposite of the 'fusion of horizons' that Friedrich Schleiermacher envisioned when we encounter a distant text;[13] we may actually experience our customary horizon being set askew, under the influence of works whose foreignness remains fully in view. (Damrosch 2003: 300)

> What of the more complex cultural situation where 'previously unrecognized spiritual and intellectual needs' emerge from the imposition of 'foreign' ideas, cultural representations, and structures of power[14] ... [T]here may be a sense in which world literature could be an emergent, prefigurative category that is concerned with a form of cultural dissensus and alterity, where non-consensual terms of affiliation may be established on the grounds of historical trauma. The study of world literature might be the study of the way in which cultures recognise themselves through their projections of 'otherness' ...

13 The horizons are the horizon of the text and the horizon of the interpreter. On the 'fusion of horizons', see Gadamer (2004: 304–6).

14 The quotations are from Goethe (as quoted by Bhabha 1994: 11). See Bell (2016: 911) and Schrimpf (1998: 364).

> If we are seeking a 'worlding' of literature, then perhaps it lies in a critical act that attempts to grasp the sleight of hand with which literature conjures with historical specificity ... As literary creatures and political animals we ought to concern ourselves with the understanding of human action and the social world as a moment when something is beyond control, but it is not beyond accommodation. (Bhabha 1994: 12)

Arjuna is in that moment, realising that fighting is beyond his control, but not beyond his accommodation. We are in that moment, too. But who is the 'we'?

Coda

To close—and to emphasise, in closing, the determinism of the *Bhagavadgītā*—I quote from the last chapter of Kṛṣṇa's story in the *Mahābhārata*, at the end of the *Harivaṃśa*'s Viṣṇuparvan. Kṛṣṇa and comrades have rescued Kṛṣṇa's grandson Aniruddha, and on the way home Kṛṣṇa tries to get Bāṇa's cows (Austin 2021). The cows take refuge in Varuṇa's ocean, Varuṇa fights Kṛṣṇa, Kṛṣṇa gets the better of Varuṇa and Varuṇa protests at length:

> Remember the unmanifest primordial matrix [*prakṛti*],[15] of which the manifest world is a sign. Shun the quality of darkness [*tamas*], momentous man. Why are you deluded by the quality of passion [*rajas*]? You always used to concentrate upon the quality of clarity [*sattva*], wise lord of yogis. Renounce the vices that stem from the five elements, and renounce the ego!
>
> I'm definitely older than this manifestation of Viṣṇu, and by dint of being your elder I deserve your respect. So why do you want to burn me here? Surely a fire can't fight against another fire. Put your anger aside, supreme warrior.
>
> No one will match you, for you're the source of the world. First, of course, you created the matrix, who dutifully transforms herself, through the ripening of karmic seeds, in accordance with good works that were performed previously. In the beginning, using only the matrix, you created this world that's made of fire and soma. So why

15 Here and below, the word *prakṛti* is translated as 'matrix'. In Cherniak's *Bhagavadgītā* translations above, it was translated as 'nature'. On *prakṛti*, see Ashton (2020).

> would you, of all people, esteem the likes of me? Brilliant god, you and you alone are forever the unconquerable, eternal, indestructible, changeless, self-born nurturer of beings. So protect me. You should protect me, impeccable god! Homage to you! You're the world's prime mover—it was promulgated by you alone.
>
> Great god, are you playing, like a child playing with its toys?
>
> I'm certainly not hostile towards the matrix, and nor am I harming her. The matrix exists within her transformations [*vikāra*s], supreme person, and when her transformations have ceased, you, as is your wont, carry on. You're the transformation of all the transformations in the house of transformation, faultless god, and you always transform the fools who don't know their duty. For indeed the matrix is always beset with faults through the quality of darkness, or stained through the quality of passion, and hence delusion occurs. But you know the precedent and the consequent, you know everything, you possess supernormal powers, and you're practically the patriarch himself, so why do you make us all go astray? (*Harivaṃśa*, 113.28c–40)[16]

The deterministic perspective is particularly evident as a capstone in the final paragraph. Varuṇa can be speaking of Arjuna when he says to Kṛṣṇa that 'you always transform the fools who don't know their duty'; and he is asking for us all, but most immediately himself, when he asks Kṛṣṇa, 'Why do you make us all go astray?' The *Bhagavadgītā*'s theological determinism seems to be too much for the modern ego to handle, and for Varuṇa.

One must be a fool who is transformed by God. One must fight, but not against God. In a way, Varuṇa has invited Kṛṣṇa to transform him; but after Varuṇa's speech, Kṛṣṇa laughs, avoids the questions and demands the cows. Varuṇa refuses to give them because he has promised to support Bāṇa, and Kṛṣṇa backs down and goes home. He only wanted them for his wife:

> Satyabhāmā told me to bring back some of Bāṇa's cows. She said it's because they drink the milk of those cows that the great demons don't grow old. She said I should please bring some back for her as long as it didn't hinder our mission, but that I mustn't set my heart on them if it would compromise our main task. (*Harivaṃśa*, 113.9–10)

In fact, Satyabhāmā had no need of these cows, because she had already received the boon of never getting old from Aditi (*Harivaṃśa* 92.60).

16 *Harivaṃśa* translations are adapted from Brodbeck (2019).

References

Ahmad, Aijaz. (2000). The Communist Manifesto and 'world literature'. *Social Scientist* 29(7–8): 3–30. doi.org/10.2307/3518232.

Ashton, Geoffrey. (2020). The puzzle of playful matters in non-dual Śaivism and Sāṃkhya: Reviving prakṛti in the Sāṃkhya Kārikā through Goethean organics. *Religions* 11(5): 1–38. doi.org/10.3390/rel11050221.

Austin, Christopher. (2021). Subrahmaṇya Kṛṣṇa: Stolen and unstolen cows in the Mahābhārata and Harivaṃśa. Paper presented at the international online seminar series 'Transdisciplinary Approaches to the Rāmāyaṇa and Mahābhārata', 24 June.

Bell, Matthew (ed.). (2016). *The Essential Goethe*. Princeton, NJ: Princeton University Press.

Belvalkar, Shripad Krishna (ed.). (1968). *The Bhagavadgītā, Being Reprint of Relevant Parts of Bhīṣmaparvan from B.O.R. Institute's Edition of the Mahābhārata*. Poona, India: Bhandarkar Oriental Research Institute.

Bhabha, Homi K. (1994). *The Location of Culture*. London: Routledge.

Biardeau, Madeleine. (1991). Nara et Nārāyaṇa. *Wiener Zeitschrift für die Kunde Südasiens* [*Vienna Journal of South Asian Studies*] 35: 75–108.

Bingemer, Maria Clara. (2006). War, suffering and detachment: Reading the *Bhagavad Gītā* with Simone Weil. In Catherine Cornille (ed.), *Song Divine: Christian Commentaries on the Bhagavad Gītā*, pp. 69–89. Leuven, Belgium: Peeters.

Bohm, David. (1983 [1980]). *Wholeness and the Implicate Order*. London: ARK Paperbacks.

Briggs, Ellen Jane. (2008). Freedom and desire in the Bhagavad Gītā. PhD thesis, University of Texas at Austin.

Brodbeck, Simon. (2004). Calling Kṛṣṇa's bluff: Non-attached action in the Bhagavadgītā. *Journal of Indian Philosophy* 32(1): 81–103. doi.org/10.1023/B:INDI.0000014005.76726.ea.

Brodbeck, Simon. (2010). Review of *Desire and Motivation in Indian Philosophy*, by Christopher G. Framarin. *Religious Studies* 46(1): 135–40. doi.org/10.1017/S0034412509990461.

Brodbeck, Simon (trans.). (2019). *Krishna's Lineage: The Harivamsha of Vyāsa's Mahābhārata*. New York, NY: Oxford University Press.

Brodbeck, Simon. (2020). The end of the Pāṇḍavas' year in disguise. *Journal of Hindu Studies* 13(3): 320–46. doi.org/10.1093/jhs/hiaa019.

Brodbeck, Simon. (2022). *Divine Descent and the Four World-Ages in the Mahābhārata—or, Why Does the Kṛṣṇa Avatāra Inaugurate the Worst Yuga?* Cardiff: Cardiff University Press. doi.org/10.18573/book9.

Bryant, Edwin F. (2014). Agency in Sāṃkhya and Yoga: The unchangeability of the eternal. In Matthew R. Dasti and Edwin F. Bryant (eds), *Free Will, Agency, and Selfhood in Indian Philosophy*, pp. 16–40. New York, NY: Oxford University Press. doi.org/10.1093/acprof:oso/9780199922734.003.0002.

Burley, Mikel. (2007). *Classical Sāṃkhya and Yoga: An Indian Metaphysics of Experience*. London: Routledge. doi.org/10.4324/9780203966747.

Caldwell, Robert. (1894 [1863]). *Bishop Caldwell on Krishna and the Bhagavad Gita. A Reprint of Remarks on the Late Hon. Sadagopah Charloo's Introduction to a Reprint of a Pamphlet, Entitled 'Theosophy of the Hindus', with a Preface by the Rev. J.L. Wyatt*. Madras, India: Christian Literature Society.

Camus, Albert. (1942). *L'Étranger* [*The Outsider*]. Paris: Gallimard.

Chakravarty, G.N. (1955). The idea of fate and freedom in the Mahābhārata. *Poona Orientalist* 20: 7–16.

Cherniak, Alex (trans.). (2008). *Mahābhārata Book Six: Bhīṣma. Volume One, Including the 'Bhagavad Gītā' in Context*. Clay Sanskrit Library. New York, NY: New York University Press & John and Jennifer Clay Foundation.

Damrosch, David. (2003). *What is World Literature?* Princeton, NJ: Princeton University Press.

Dandekar, R.N. (ed.). (1971–76). *The Mahābhārata Text as Constituted in its Critical Edition*. [5 vols.] Poona, India: Bhandarkar Oriental Research Institute.

Davis, Richard H. (2015). *The Bhagavad Gita: A Biography*. Princeton, NJ: Princeton University Press. doi.org/10.1515/9781400851973.

Double, Richard. (1991). *The Non-Reality of Free Will*. New York, NY: Oxford University Press.

Fitzgerald, James L. (trans.). (2004a). *The Mahābhārata, Volume 7: 11. The Book of the Women; 12. The Book of Peace, Part One*. Chicago, IL: University of Chicago Press.

Fitzgerald, James L. (2004b). Mahābhārata. In Sushil Mittal and Gene R. Thursby (eds), *The Hindu World*, pp. 52–74. New York, NY: Routledge.

Fitzgerald, James L. (2015). 'Saving Buddhis' in epic Mokṣadharma. *International Journal of Hindu Studies* 19(1–2): 97–137. doi.org/10.1007/s11407-015-9173-2.

Gadamer, Hans-Georg. (2004 [1975]). *Truth and Method*. Translated by Joel Weinsheimer and Donald G. Marshall. London: Continuum.

Gelblum, Tuvia. (1992). On 'the meaning of life' and the Bhagavad Gītā. *Asian Philosophy* 2(2): 121–30. doi.org/10.1080/09552369208575359.

Ginsburg, Allen. (1994). *Howl and Other Poems*. San Francisco, CA: City Lights Books.

Granoff, Phyllis. (1984). Holy warriors: A preliminary study of some biographies of saints and kings in the classical Indian tradition. *Journal of Indian Philosophy* 12(3): 291–303. doi.org/10.1007/BF00186686.

Griffith, R.D. (1849). An essay on the Bhagavat-Geeta. In J. Garrett (ed.), *The Bhagavat-Geeta, or Dialogues of Krishna and Arjoon; in Eighteen Lectures. Sanscrit, Canarese, and English: In Parallel Columns*, pp. xxxvii–lvii. Bangalore, India: Wesleyan Mission Press.

Hill, Peter. (2001). *Fate, Predestination, and Human Action in the Mahābhārata: A Study in the History of Ideas*. Delhi: Munshiram Manoharlal.

Hiltebeitel, Alf. (1991). Two Kṛṣṇas, three Kṛṣṇas, four Kṛṣṇas, more Kṛṣṇas: Dark interactions in the Mahābhārata. In Arvind Sharma (ed.), *Essays on the Mahābhārata*, pp. 101–9. Leiden, Netherlands: Brill.

Hiltebeitel, Alf. (2011). *Dharma: Its Early History in Law, Religion, and Narrative*. New York, NY: Oxford University Press. doi.org/10.1093/acprof:oso/9780195394238.001.0001.

Honderich, Ted. (1990). *The Consequences of Determinism: A Theory of Determinism, Volume 2*. Oxford, UK: Oxford University Press. doi.org/10.1093/acprof:oso/9780198242833.001.0001.

Hudson, Emily T. (2013). *Disorienting Dharma: Ethics and the Aesthetics of Suffering in the Mahābhārata*. New York, NY: Oxford University Press. doi.org/10.1093/acprof:oso/9780199860760.001.0001.

Humboldt, Wilhelm von. (1849 [1825–26]). Essay on the episode of the Mahabharat, known by the name of Bhagavat-Geeta (a lecture delivered in the Berlin Academy of Science, on the 30th June, 1825; and 15th June, 1826). Translated by G.H. Weigle. In J. Garrett (ed.), *The Bhagavat-Geeta, or Dialogues of Krishna and Arjoon; in Eighteen Lectures. Sanscrit, Canarese, and English: In Parallel Columns*, pp. 125–47. Bangalore, India: Wesleyan Mission Press.

Johnson, W.J. (1997). Transcending the world? Freedom (mokṣa) and the Bhagavadgītā. In Julius Lipner (ed.), *The Fruits of Our Desiring: An Enquiry into the Ethics of the Bhagavadgītā for Our Times*, pp. 92–104. Calgary, AB: Bayeux Arts.

King, Peter (ed. and trans.). (2010). *Augustine: On the Free Choice of the Will, On Grace and Free Choice, and Other Writings*. New York, NY: Cambridge University Press. doi.org/10.1017/CBO9780511844720.

Kwak, Duck-Joo and Hye-Chong Han. (2013). The issue of determinism and freedom as an existential question: A case in the Bhagavad Gītā. *Philosophy East and West* 63(1): 55–72. doi.org/10.1353/pew.2013.0003.

Lothspeich, Pamela. (2009). *Epic Nation: Reimagining the Mahabharata in the Age of the Empire*. Delhi: Oxford University Press.

Marx, Karl and Friedrich Engels. (1967 [1848]). *Manifesto of the Communist Party*. Moscow: Progress Publishers.

Murdoch, John. (1894). *Krishna as Described in the Vishnu Purana, Bhagavata Purana, and the Mahabharata, Especially the Bhagavad Gita; with a Letter to Mrs Annie Besant*. Madras, India: Christian Literature Society.

Norris, Christopher. (2000). *Quantum Theory and the Flight from Realism: Philosophical Responses to Quantum Mechanics*. London: Routledge.

Plumptre, Constance E. (1878). *General Sketch of the History of Pantheism, in Two Volumes. Volume I: From the Earliest Times to the Age of Spinoza*. London: Samuel Deacon & Co.

Roberts, Alexander and James Donaldson (eds). (1956). *The Ante-Nicene Fathers: Translations of the Writings of the Fathers down to A.D. 325. Volume II: Fathers of the Second Century*. Revised by A. Cleveland Coxe. Grand Rapids, MI: Wm. B. Eerdmans Publishing Company.

Robinson, Catherine A. (2006). *Interpretations of the Bhagavad-Gītā and Images of the Hindu Tradition: The Song of the Lord*. London: Routledge.

Schopenhauer, Arthur. (1985 [1841]). *On the Freedom of the Will*. Translated by Konstantin Kolenda. Oxford, UK: Basil Blackwell.

Schrimpf, Hans Joachim (ed.). (1998). Schriften zur literatur [Writings on literature]. In *Johann Wolfgang von Goethe: Werke. Hamburger Ausgabe* [*Works: Hamburg Edition*]. *Volume 12*, pp. 224–364. Munich: Deutscher Taschenbuch Verlag.

Sharma, Arvind. (1979). Fate and free will in the Bhagavadgītā. *Religious Studies* 15(4): 531–37. doi.org/10.1017/S0034412500011719.

Sharpe, Eric J. (1985). *The Universal Gītā: Western Images of the Bhagavadgītā. A Bicentenary Survey*. London: Gerald Duckworth & Co.

Sukthankar, Vishnu Sitaram. (1957). *On the Meaning of the Mahābhārata*. Bombay, India: Asiatic Society.

Swinburne, Richard (ed.). (2011). *Free Will and Modern Science*. Oxford, UK: Oxford University Press & The British Academy. doi.org/10.5871/bacad/9780197264898.001.0001.

Thomsen, Mads Rosendahl. (2008). *Mapping World Literature: International Canonization and Transnational Literatures*. London: Continuum.

Urquhart, W.S. (1914). Theism and pantheism in the Bhagavadgita. *The Calcutta Review* 278: 467–90.

van Buitenen, J.A.B. (trans.). (1973). *The Mahābhārata, Volume 1: 1. The Book of the Beginning*. Chicago, IL: University of Chicago Press. doi.org/10.7208/chicago/9780226217543.001.0001.

van Inwagen, Peter. (1982). The incompatibility of free will and determinism. In Gary Watson (ed.), *Free Will*, pp. 46–58. Oxford, UK: Oxford University Press.

Viethsen, Andreas. (2009). The reasons for Viṣṇu's descent in the prologue to the Kṛṣṇacarita of the Harivaṃśa. In Petteri Koskikallio (ed.), *Parallels and Comparisons: Proceedings of the Fourth Dubrovnik International Conference on the Sanskrit Epics and Purāṇas*, pp. 221–34. Zagreb: Croatian Academy of Sciences and Arts.

Wegner, Daniel M. (2002). *The Illusion of Conscious Will*. Cambridge, MA: Massachusetts Institute of Technology Press. doi.org/10.7551/mitpress/3650.001.0001.

Wells, H.G. (1914). *The War That Will End War*. London: Frank & Cecil Palmer.

Wilkins, Charles (trans.). (1785). *The Bhăgavăt-Gēētā, or Dialogues of Krēēshnă and Ărjŏŏn; in Eighteen Lectures; with Notes*. London: C. Nourse.

Zaehner, Robert Charles. (1975). *Our Savage God: The Perverse Use of Eastern Thought*. New York, NY: Sheed & Ward Inc.

10

Mineral, vegetal, animal or divine? The flying palace Puṣpaka's manifold metamorphoses

Danielle Feller

Abstract

The story of the divine flying palace (*vimāna*) called Puṣpaka ('Little Flower') is well known from the Vālmīki *Rāmāyaṇa*. Puṣpaka is created by the god Brahmā for Kubera. Subsequently, Rāvaṇa wrests the aerial car from Kubera and uses it to defeat the gods and other supernatural beings. When Rāvaṇa is killed by Rāma, Puṣpaka becomes Rāma's property. Later, Rāma wishes to return Puṣpaka to Kubera, but the god of riches sends it back. Here, I propose to investigate the series of metamorphoses of the flying palace in the Vālmīki *Rāmāyaṇa* and beyond. Depicted as a self-moving architectural construction made of precious metal and stone, Puṣpaka is also associated with animals, since it is sometimes drawn by *haṃsa*s ('geese') and is *īhāmṛgasamāyukta* ('embossed with an animal motif'). In pictorial representations, Puṣpaka is often shown as a hybrid between a bird and a palace or temple-like structure. In Book 7 of the *Rāmāyaṇa*, the flying palace is personified and can suddenly speak and bow. It even appears to acquire divine status, as it is worshipped by Rāma himself. The Uttarakāṇḍa promotes a vision of Puṣpaka as Rāma's *vāhana* (a mount belonging to a god), which both carries and symbolises the divinity. In architectural treatises, *vimāna* is a technical term for a pyramidal spire rising above the sanctum in temples of the southern or *drāviḍa* type. In the *Samarāṅgaṇasūtradhāra*, the name Puṣpaka is given to a flower-shaped temple adorned with floral and vegetal motifs, thus finally giving full sense to its name, 'Little Flower'.

Introduction

The Vālmīki *Rāmāyaṇa* provides us with the first and most detailed version of the story of the divine flying palace (*vimāna*) called Puṣpaka ('Little Flower'). Puṣpaka was created by the god Brahmā for the newly appointed god of riches, Kubera. Subsequently, the *rākṣasa* Rāvaṇa, Kubera's half-brother, wrests the aerial car from Kubera and uses it to defeat the gods and other supernatural beings. When Rāvaṇa is killed by Rāma in the battle of Laṅkā, Puṣpaka is given to Rāma. Thanks to the divine palace, Rāma can fly back quickly to Ayodhyā, his time of exile being over. Afterwards, Rāma wishes to return Puṣpaka to its first owner, Kubera, but the god of riches sends it back with a message that Rāma should keep it as a reward for his prowess.

The term *vimāna*, which means 'measurement' in Vedic literature, derives from the root *vi-mā-* ('to measure, mete out, pass over, traverse'). In the two Sanskrit epics,[1] the Vālmīki *Rāmāyaṇa* (*Rām*) and the *Mahābhārata* (*Mbh*), the term *vimāna* is used with four different meanings:[2]

1. In the first meaning of the term, *vimāna* designates a palace or a building of some size and height that must be built according to measurement.
2. It designates a palace-like flying structure the use of which is the prerogative of divine or semidivine beings, essentially as a means to circulate in Heaven or between Heaven and Earth. The gods come down to Earth on *vimāna*s to witness noteworthy events, and newly deceased and deified meritorious people go to Heaven on *vimāna*s.
3. It is synonymous with Puṣpaka, which is one representative of the second category.

1 References will be given throughout to the critical editions of these two texts: for the Vālmīki *Rāmāyaṇa*, Bhatt and Shah (1960–75); and for the *Mahābhārata*, Sukthankar (1933–66).

2 For a more detailed exposition of the different meanings of *vimāna* in the Sanskrit epics, see Feller (2022).

4. By semantic shift, the name of the conveyance used to reach Heaven came to designate Heaven itself, or at least one type of individual mini-heaven, complete with a palace, gardens, etcetera. This usage appears especially in some passages of the *Mahābhārata*'s Anusāśanaparvan.[3]

The divine *vimāna* Puṣpaka, which figures chiefly in the Vālmīki *Rāmāyaṇa*, can be considered the *vimāna* par excellence. It is a palatial construction made of all kinds of precious materials and able to fly about at will. It is also, as far as I am aware, the only *vimāna* that has a name and, we might even say, a personality of its own. I have examined elsewhere (Feller 2020) Puṣpaka's nature and its three consecutive owners: the god of riches, Kubera; the lustful *rākṣasa* Rāvaṇa; and the righteous prince Rāma—who stand, respectively, for *artha*, *kāma* and *dharma*. The divine palace's functions in the *Rāmāyaṇa* are threefold: narrative, allowing the tale to wind up quickly at the end of the war, since Rāma can fly back to Ayodhyā instead of walking; psychological, with Puṣpaka functioning as a status symbol that excites both admiration and envy; and theological, as the possession of the flying palace confers divine or quasi-divine status on its owner.

In this chapter, I investigate more closely the series of metamorphoses of the divine palace, both in the Vālmīki *Rāmāyaṇa* and in other texts. Initially depicted as a self-moving architectural construction of precious metal and stone, Puṣpaka is also associated with animals, since it is sometimes said to be drawn by *haṃsa*s (or 'geese'). But the greatest change takes place in Book 7 of the *Rāmāyaṇa*, the Uttarakāṇḍa, in which the flying palace is personified to a greater extent than before. It can suddenly speak and is more independent after becoming Rāma's property. It even appears to acquire divine status, as Rāma himself worships it. The authors of the Uttarakāṇḍa were likely trying to promote a new representation of Puṣpaka as Rāma's *vāhana*, in the sense of a mount belonging to a god, which carries and to some extent symbolises and represents the divinity.

In post-epic literature, *vimāna* becomes one of the many general terms that designate a temple. In the southern or *drāviḍa*-type temples, *vimāna* refers more specifically to the pyramidal spire that rises over the sanctum. In an architectural treatise, the *Samarāṅgaṇasūtradhāra*, the name Puṣpaka is given to a flower-shaped temple adorned with floral and vegetal motifs,

3 Also in the Vimānavatthu or 'The Stories about Vimānas', a Pāli Buddhist canonical text belonging to the Khuddakanikāya of the *Suttapiṭaka*.

finally giving full sense to its name, 'Little Flower'. We will examine Puṣpaka's various metamorphoses as the flying palace keeps shifting through mineral, animal, personified, divine and vegetal forms.

Mineral Puṣpaka

In the Vālmīki *Rāmāyaṇa*, Puṣpaka is depicted in a way that corresponds to the descriptions of divine *vimānas* we come across elsewhere in the epics: palace-like, huge and dazzling, made of all things precious and adorned with architectural elements (Plate 10.1). Its mineral nature is what strikes us first and foremost. This is how Puṣpaka is described in one of its first elaborate depictions in this text, as it appears to the monkey Hanumān's eyes while he is searching Rāvaṇa's palace for Sītā:

> *īhāmṛgasamāyuktaiḥ kāryasvarahiraṇmayaiḥ* |
> *sukṛtair ācitaṃ stambhaiḥ pradīptam iva ca śriyā* ||
> *merumandarasaṃkāśair ullikhadbhir ivāmbaram* |
> *kūṭāgāraiḥ śubhākāraiḥ sarvataḥ samalaṃkṛtam* ||
> *jvalanārkapratīkāśaṃ sukṛtaṃ viśvakarmaṇā* |
> *hemasopānasaṃyuktaṃ cārupravaravedikam* ||
> *jālavātāyanair yuktaṃ kāñcanaiḥ sthāṭikair api* |
> *indranīlamahānīla-maṇipravaravedikam* |
> *vimānaṃ puṣpakaṃ divyam āruroha mahākapiḥ* ||

> [It was supported by finely wrought pillars that were fashioned of gold and silver and embossed with an animal motif. It seemed ablaze with splendor. It was adorned everywhere with exquisite penthouses, which, resembling Mount Meru and Mount Mandara, seemed almost to scrape the sky. The great monkey then climbed the heavenly flying palace Puṣpaka, which had been finely wrought by Viśvakarman and which, with its golden staircases and its lovely raised platforms, resembled the blazing sun. Its ornamental skylights and windows were of gold and crystal; and its raised platforms were set with lovely emeralds and sapphires.] (*Rām*, 5.7.12–15; translations by Goldman and Sutherland Goldman 2017)

Plate 10.1 ***Puṣpaka as a flying palace. Rāma leaves Laṅkā on Puṣpaka.*** **Opaque watercolour and gold on paper, c. 1650. Himachal Pradesh, Pahari School. The San Diego Museum of Art**

Source: Wikimedia Commons.

This description—which teems with architectural terms such as pillars, staircases, platforms, skylights and windows—testifies to rather advanced architectural techniques. Puṣpaka is not only said to be made of mineral elements—such as gold, silver, crystal, emeralds and sapphires—it is also compared with the mountains Meru and Mandara. Moreover, as the context shows, Puṣpaka is here a part of Rāvaṇa's palace (also called *vimāna*), as it were. Hanumān finds the divine flying palace parked in a hall, as though it were encapsulated and indeed captive, as a spoil of war, in the larger stone enclosure of the *rākṣasa* king's mansion. The palace itself forms part of Rāvaṇa's citadel, which is built on the lofty Mount Trikūṭa, which is subsequently elaborately described when Rāma's army reaches Laṅkā in Book 6:

śikharaṃ tu trikūṭasya prāṃśu caikaṃ divispṛśam |
samantāt puṣpasaṃchannaṃ mahārajatasaṃnibham ||
śatayojanavistīrṇaṃ vimalaṃ cārudarśanam |
ślakṣṇaṃ śrīman mahac caiva duṣprāpaṃ śakunair api ||
manasāpi durārohaṃ kiṃ punaḥ karmaṇā janaiḥ |
niviṣṭā tatra śikhare laṅkā rāvaṇapālitā ||
sā purī gopurair uccaiḥ pāṇḍurāmbudasaṃnibhaiḥ |
kāñcanena ca sālena rājatena ca śobhitā ||
prāsādaiś ca vimānaiś ca laṅkā paramabhūṣitā |
ghanair ivātapāpāye madhyamaṃ vaiṣṇavaṃ padam ||
yasyāṃ stambhasahasreṇa prāsādaḥ samalaṃkṛtaḥ |
kailāsaśikharākāro dṛśyate kham ivollikhan ||

[There, reaching into the sky, stood one of the lofty summits of Mount Trikūṭa. Covered on all sides with flowers, it seemed to be made of gold. It was bright and lovely to behold, and its breadth was a hundred leagues. It was beautiful, grand, and majestic and impossible for even the birds to reach. It was impossible for men to scale, even in their imagination, let alone in reality. And there, on that peak, stood Laṅkā, under the protection of Rāvaṇa. The citadel was adorned with ramparts of gold and silver and with lofty gateway towers resembling white clouds. Indeed, Laṅkā was as magnificently adorned by its palaces [*prāsāda*] and mansions [*vimāna*] as are the heavens, Viṣṇu's middle step, with clouds at summer's end. In the city could be seen a palace [*prāsāda*] adorned with a thousand columns, which, seeming to scrape the sky, resembled the peak of Mount Kailāsa.] (*Rām*, 6.30.18–23; translation by Goldman and Sutherland Goldman 2017)

From these two juxtaposed descriptions, we can see how similarly the mountain, the citadel of Laṅkā, Rāvaṇa's palace and Puṣpaka are described: all are equally lofty, golden and seem to scrape the sky. More importantly for present purposes, all seem to be coterminous extensions of one another, as though they were different manifestations of an identical mineral essence. Unfolding in quasi-telescopic fashion, the mountain gives birth to the citadel, which in turn yields Rāvaṇa's palace, which contains Puṣpaka—imprisoned for the time being, but destined to soon fly free.

Animal Puṣpaka

Unlike most other heavenly *vimāna*s depicted in the Sanskrit epics (Feller 2022), Puṣpaka seems to be able to move through the air without being drawn by animals, nor is it said to have wheels or wings. As far as we can make out from the passages that describe it, the divine flying palace zooms about in quasi-magical fashion. It is said to be yoked to *haṃsa*s ('geese') only once in the Vālmīki *Rāmāyaṇa*,[4] in a passage that describes Rāma's return to Ayodhyā on board the majestic flying palace:

> *yayau tena vimānena*
> *haṃsayuktena bhāsvatā* |
> *prahṛṣṭaś ca pratītaś ca*
> *babhau rāmaḥ kuberavat* ||
>
> [Then Rāma departed in that radiant flying palace yoked to *haṃsa*s. Delighted in mind and body, he resembled Kubera himself.] (*Rām*, 6.110.23; translation by Goldman and Sutherland Goldman 2017)

The *haṃsa* or bar-headed goose (*Anser indicus*) is the god Brahmā's sacred bird. It flies particularly high in the sky in its yearly migrations over the Himalaya. Due to this characteristic, it is considered a symbol of the pure, liberated soul. Even though Puṣpaka is by no means the only *vimāna* said to be drawn by these birds,[5] the choice of *haṃsa*s to pull the flying palace serves as a reminder of its divine origins, for it was made for the newly appointed god of riches, Kubera, by Brahmā himself.[6]

4 And once in *Mbh* 9.46.27, where Puṣpaka is likewise said to be 'yoked to geese' (*haṃsa-yukta*).

5 See, for example, *Mbh* (3.246.31; 13.14.141; 13.109.52, 54) or *Rām* (3.68.6; 7.68.10).

6 Or by the divine architect Viśvakarman, on Brahmā's order. See Feller (2020: 329).

In the passage quoted above (*Rām*, 5.7.12), we furthermore read that Puṣpaka is 'supported by finely wrought pillars ... embossed with an animal [or wolf] motif' (*īhāmṛgasamāyuktaiḥ ... sukṛtair ācitaṃ stambhaiḥ*). Here, it appears as though the animals had become mere decorative items on the flying palace—a trend we can also witness in some *vimāna* descriptions of the *Mahābhārata*'s Anuśāsanaparvan (Feller 2022). Apart from these few references, Puṣpaka's link with the animal kingdom is scanty. But its association with *haṃsa*s has nevertheless left a lasting impression, for until today, many visual representations of Puṣpaka show the divine flying palace as drawn by geese, as a goose or swan or, more often, as a hybrid half-goose, half-palace (Plate 10.2). The half-palace, half-bird shape could have become a favourite because of its easily recognisable characteristics, which immediately signal Puṣpaka's identity.[7] Another reason this *haṃsa* shape met with success in the plastic arts, despite its meagre literary support, can be explained by the fact that in Book 7 of the Vālmīki *Rāmāyaṇa*, the Uttarakāṇḍa, Puṣpaka's personification is more pronounced than in the previous books. Its semi-architectural, semi-ornithomorphic appearance could be an ingenious way of accounting for both its original palace-like aspect and its personified behaviour. The latter certainly looks less odd in the case of a bird than in the case of a flying mansion, at least in the fable-like literary context of the *Rāmāyaṇa*, which is otherwise peopled by intelligent speaking monkeys, vultures and bears.

7 In this respect, we can draw a comparison with the *nāga*s ('snake-genii'). In the epics—especially in the *Mahābhārata*, where they play a great role—the *nāga*s, who are endowed with the power to change their form at will, appear either as snakes or as humans. But in the plastic arts, to make them immediately recognisable as *nāga*s, they are mostly shown as hybrid creatures, half-human and half-snake, with a human torso and a snake tail, or as humans with the characteristic uneven number of cobra-hoods sprouting from their neck and surrounding their human head.

Plate 10.2 *Puṣpaka as a swan. Rāma, Sītā and Lakṣmaṇa fly back to Ayodhyā on Puṣpaka.* From: *Tulsi Ramayan*, Tej Kumar Book Depot, date unknown

Source: Wikimedia Commons.

Personified and deified Puṣpaka

In the Uttarakāṇḍa, Puṣpaka appears personified to a greater extent than before and differentiates itself sharply from all the other *vimāna*s described in Sanskrit literature, as well as from the way it is described in the previous books of the *Rāmāyaṇa*. Whereas Puṣpaka is 'just' an inanimate heavenly flying palace under Kubera's and Rāvaṇa's ownership, it develops a personality of its own once it becomes Rāma's property. At the end of Book 6, after returning to Ayodhyā, Rāma sends Puṣpaka back to its first owner, Kubera (*Rām*, 6.115.48–50). Some time later, Rāma and his brothers are surprised to hear 'sweet words spoken from the sky' (*madhurāṃ vāṇīm antarikṣāt prabhāṣitām*; *Rām*, 7.41.2). Looking up, they see Puṣpaka hovering above them in the air. The beautiful flying palace explains to them that Kubera has ordered it to come back to Rāma and to continue to serve him as a reward for slaying Rāvaṇa. In *Rām* 7.66, an occasion arises for which Rāma requires Puṣpaka's help. This will be the last time the divine palace makes an appearance in the Vālmīki *Rāmāyaṇa*. Rāma needs Puṣpaka to tour the directions to locate and eliminate the source of evil, the *śūdra* Śambūka's unlawful austerities, which have caused the untimely death of a brahmin's son. Rāma merely has to think of Puṣpaka to make the golden flying palace appear:

manasā puṣpakaṃ dadhyāv āgaccheti mahāyaśāḥ ||
iṅgitaṃ sa tu vijñāya puṣpako hemabhūṣitaḥ |
ājagāma muhūrtena samīpaṃ rāghavasya vai ||
so 'bravīt praṇato bhūtvā ayam asmi narādhipa |
vaśyas tava mahābāho kiṃkaraḥ samupasthitaḥ ||

[He called to mind the Puṣpaka with the thought, 'Come!' When the Puṣpaka, adorned with gold, perceived Rāghava's intentions, it came at once into his very presence. Bowing humbly, he said, 'It is I, great-armed lord of men, your obedient servant, who has come.'] (*Rām*, 7.66.5c–7; translation by Goldman and Sutherland Goldman 2017)[8]

These characteristics and behaviour clearly evoke a sentient being rather than an inanimate palace. The fact that Puṣpaka bows (*praṇato bhūtvā*) and calls himself Rāma's servant (*kiṃkara*) even evokes an anthropomorphic appearance. How a flying palace can speak and bow is left unexplained by the text, but later commentators, as well as Kālidāsa in his Raghuvaṃśa 13.68, explain this by means of a presiding deity (*devatā*, *abhimānidevatā* or *adhidevatā*) residing in Puṣpaka and appearing and speaking when required.

Though not clearly expressed in the *Rāmāyaṇa*, this deification of Puṣpaka is nevertheless corroborated by the Uttarakāṇḍa in 7.40, where Rāma worships the heavenly palace as one would a divinity, before dismissing it:

kākutsthaḥ puṣpakaṃ samapūjayat |
lājākṣataiś ca puṣpaiś ca gandhaiś ca susugandhibhiḥ ||
gamyatāṃ ca yathākāmam āgacches tvaṃ yadā smare |
evam astv iti rāmeṇa visṛṣṭaḥ puṣpakaḥ punaḥ |
abhipretāṃ diśaṃ prāyāt puṣpakaḥ puṣpabhūṣitaḥ ||

8 *Padma Purāṇa* (Sṛṣṭikhaṇḍa, 1.35.61–63), which relates the Śambūka episode, contains practically the same wording: 'He, of great fame, mentally thought of the Puṣpaka aeroplane and ordered it, "Come [here]". Knowing the internal thought [of Rāma] that aeroplane, decorated with gold and moving according to [the occupant's] desire came near Rāma in a short time. He [the presiding deity of the aeroplane] joined the palms of his hands as a mark of humility and said: "O king, [here] I am. This servant, O you of mighty arms, stands before you' (Deshpande 1989: 464). My sincere thanks to Mary Brockington for pointing out this reference to me.

> [Kākutstha worshipped the Puṣpaka with parched grain, unhusked rice, flowers, and extremely fragrant perfumes, saying: 'Now you must depart as you wish. But you must return whenever I call you to mind.' Then, having said, 'May it be so!' the Puṣpaka was dismissed once again by Rāma. Adorned with flowers, the Puṣpaka departed in the direction of its choice.] (*Rām*, 7.40.10–11; translation by Goldman and Sutherland Goldman 2017)

Concerning this personification and deification of the *vimāna* Puṣpaka, which are quite unique because they do not seem to happen in the case of any other *vimāna*, I submit the hypothesis that the Uttarakāṇḍa is here trying to promote a new vision of Puṣpaka as Rāma's *vāhana*—a trend that runs parallel to its theological agenda of representing Rāma as the supreme god Viṣṇu.[9] A divine flying palace obviously *is* a *vāhana*, in the literal sense of a 'vehicle',[10] but I mean here *vāhana* in the sense of an (animal) mount belonging to a god that both carries and to some extent symbolises and represents the divinity. This concept was yet unknown to Vedic literature, in which the gods ride on *rathas* ('chariots') drawn mostly by horses.[11] The term *vāhana* is quite rare even in the epics. When it does occur, it is mostly used in battle descriptions, in the sense of an ordinary mount, horse, elephant or chariot. Yet, the concept of a *vāhana* as a god's typical mount makes a timid debut in the epics, even though the animals serving as *vāhanas* may not necessarily be called by that name.

9 See Brockington (1998: 393): 'Superficial hints of Rāma's exceptional status now became the basic theme of the *Uttarakāṇḍa*, in which the final stage was reached in the progress of Rāma from a heroic figure to an ideal model of the perfect ruler and finally to the *avatāra* of the supreme deity.'

10 It is probably in this meaning that Puṣpaka is called Kubera's *vāhana* in *Mbh* 9.46.27, which describes how Kubera became a god and received the divine *vimāna* after performing severe penance.

11 On the historical precedence of riding chariots drawn by horses over riding horses, see Gonda (1965: 95–114).

For instance, the *Rāmāyaṇa* knows the elephant Airāvata as Indra's mount (*Rām*, 7.35).[12] The *Mahābhārata* witnesses the birth of Garuḍa, explaining how the divine bird becomes both Viṣṇu's vehicle and the emblem on his banner (*dhvaja*) (*Mbh*, 1.29.16). The great epic also contains many accounts of the god Skanda's birth.[13] One explains how the young god receives his rooster (*kukkuṭa*) from Agni (*Mbh*, 3.218.32).[14] In other passages, we see how the god Śiva receives his bull[15] from Brahmā to use as his mount and to keep on his banner (*Mbh*, 13.76.27–28; 13.128.9–12). We see that the gods' favoured animals serve them as both mounts and emblems. Banners were of course initially meant to float above the chariots in battle. We see again, superimposed, the continuance of the Vedic custom of riding a chariot and the new trend of riding an animal mount.

Of course, unlike most other *vāhana*s, Puṣpaka is not an animal, even though it has some links to the animal kingdom, as we have seen. However, it shares several characteristics with the animal *vāhana*s belonging to other gods. It appears at once when its master requires its presence and carries him wherever needed. It is a sentient being who can speak and act of its own volition and has a life of its own when not serving the deity.[16] It is a hybrid creature and can be personified, or at least semi-personified, as for instance, Viṣṇu's eagle, Garuḍa, or Śiva's bull, Nandin.[17] It is even deified to some extent, since Rāma himself worships it. In this, Puṣpaka is again comparable to Viṣṇu's *vāhana*s, the divine bird Garuḍa and the great snake Śeṣa or Nandin, who at times receive their own separate cult within the perimeter of a temple dedicated to the main deity. We can further note that in some

12 Elsewhere, the epics also show Indra as the owner of a *vimāna* (for example, in *Mbh* 1.51.9) or of a *ratha*, which on occasion he generously lends to certain heroes (for example, to Arjuna in *Mbh* 3.43 and to Rāma in *Rām* 6.90–100).

13 For these, see Feller (2004: 115–20); and Mann (2012: Chs 2–4).

14 In Gupta times, this rooster usually becomes a peacock, perhaps as an emblem of imperial rule (see Mann 2012: 204). The god Skanda is often represented sitting on his peacock, but sometimes this bird figures on his banner as well. See, for instance, Bṛhat Saṃhitā 58.41, where Skanda is called *barhiketu* ('having a peacock on his banner') (cf. Sastri 1946). We can note that both the rooster and the peacock are very colourful birds belonging to the order Galliformes. They are indigenous to India and enjoy an omnivorous diet, scratching the ground in search of seeds and insects.

15 Nandin is also mentioned by name as Śiva's attendant in *Rām* 7.16, but there he appears in the unusual guise of a monkey (*Rām*, 7.16.12, 14), and not as a bull. Since Rāvaṇa makes fun of his monkey-shape, this provides Nandin with a pretext for cursing him that monkeys will bring about his destruction (*Rām*, 7.16.14–15).

16 Even though Rāma allows Puṣpaka to roam about as it likes (*Rām*, 7.40.11), the text never tells us what Puṣpaka is doing in its free time. Unlike some other *vāhana*s—Garuḍa, for instance—Puṣpaka does not seem to have any adventures on its own, independently of Rāma.

17 Shukla (1993: 283) remarks that both Nandin and Garuḍa are often represented (both in literature and in the plastic arts) as theri-anthropomorphic, or even as fully human, especially in Nandin's case.

modern devotional representations of Puṣpaka, the divine palace is depicted in the form of Garuḍa (and not as a *haṃsa*) carrying a temple-like pavilion on his back, which shelters Rāma, Sītā and their entourage (Plate 10.3). Although this proves nothing about the time in which the Uttarakāṇḍa was composed, it reveals a merging of identities between Puṣpaka and Garuḍa as Viṣṇu's/Rāma's *vāhana*s.

Plate 10.3 *Garuḍa-Puṣpaka*. Garuḍa (holding a snake in his claws and with lotus-like back feathers) carries a canopy sheltering Hanumān, Rāma, Sītā and Lakṣmaṇa

Source: Copy of an unidentified illustration seen on the internet. Drawing by Aryan Conus.

For the supreme god, or at least one of his manifestations, having a divine flying chariot as his *vāhana* seems singularly appropriate. If we make a comparison with another of Viṣṇu's *avatāras*, Kṛṣṇa, we see that one of his most popular representations is on a chariot, when he acts as Arjuna's charioteer in the Kurukṣetra War, guiding him simultaneously towards victory in battle and towards spiritual fulfillment by his recitation of the *Bhagavadgītā*. In the *Rāmāyaṇa*'s Uttarakāṇḍa, when Kubera sends Puṣpaka back to Rāma, he tells him the following highly meaningful words, here reported by Puṣpaka to Rāma:

> *sa tvaṃ rāmeṇa laṅkāyāṃ nirjitaḥ paramātmanā* |
> *vaha saumya tam eva tvam aham ājñāpayāmi te* ||
> *eṣa me paramaḥ kāmo yat tvaṃ rāghavanandanam* |
> *vaher lokasya saṃyānaṃ gacchasva vigatajvaraḥ* ||
>
> [You were won in Laṅkā by Rāma, who is the Supreme Spirit. And thus I command you, 'Gentle one, you must carry him.' It is my greatest desire that you should carry the delight of the Raghus (on his journeys through the world/the vehicle of the world). So go, free from any anxiety.'] (*Rām*, 7.40.7–8; translation by Goldman and Sutherland Goldman 2017, modified)

The key term here is *saṃyāna*, a neuter substantive that can mean 'going together', 'a journey', 'a vehicle, wagon, car'.[18] Various commentators interpret the phrase *lokasya saṃyānaṃ* in different ways. Some, taking *saṃyāna* in the sense of 'journey', interpret it as an accusative of direction meaning 'on his journey through the world' (*lokasya saṃyānam iti lokasaṃcaraṇam ity arthaḥ*), which is how Goldman and Sutherland Goldman translate it. Other commentators take it as an apposition to *rāghavanandanam* and gloss it—somewhat stretching the meaning of *saṃyāna*—as 'the refuge of the world' (*lokasya saṃyānaṃ lokasya śaraṇam*) (see Goldman and Sutherland Goldman 2017: 838–39). I propose to understand *saṃyāna* in the sense of 'vehicle': 'the vehicle of the world'. Since the term *saṃyāna* is a neuter, *saṃyānaṃ* can be taken either as a nominative, and as such refer to Puṣpaka,[19] or as an accusative, as an apposition to *rāghavanandanam*. The ambiguity could have been deliberate, but if we choose the second possibility, *lokasya saṃyānaṃ* designates Rāma as the

18 According to Monier-Williams's *Sanskrit–English Dictionary* (2009).

19 Goldman and Sutherland Goldman (2017: 839) note that 'Ck, Cm, and Ct understand the term to mean that the Puṣpaka has become an excellent vehicle for the attainment of any desired world, such as the earth, etc. [*lokasya bhūrādyaśeṣābhimatalokaprāpaṇasya saṃyānaṃ samīcīnayānabhūtas tvaṃ*].'

'vehicle of the world'. Indeed, as the supreme god, Rāma/Viṣṇu carries and contains the whole world and its population. He is furthermore the 'vehicle' by means of which his devotees can reach ultimate release.[20] Puṣpaka, who is ordered by Kubera to carry Rāma, thus holds an extremely prestigious function: no less than carrying the Supreme Being, who himself carries the whole world. Puṣpaka thus becomes the vehicle's vehicle. We see that there is a fusion between Rāma's and Puṣpaka's identities,[21] as is indeed commonly the case for a deity and his or her *vāhana*.[22]

Except for this incipient and rather sketchy *vāhana*-hood of Puṣpaka in the *Rāmāyaṇa*'s Uttarakāṇḍa, however, the divine flying palace did not, as far as I could ascertain, have a noteworthy destiny as Rāma's *vāhana* in other texts. Of course, we must consider the fact that many other versions of the Rāma-*kathā* deal with Puṣpaka summarily and only mention the heavenly palace while describing Rāma's flight back to Ayodhyā after the war. And many—such as the Rāmopākhyāna found in *Mahābhārata* 3.257–276, Bhaṭṭi's *Bhaṭṭikāvya*, Tulsidas's *Rāmacaritamānasa* and so on—dispense with the events of the Uttarakāṇḍa altogether. In their view, Puṣpaka is returned to the god of riches after Rāma's return to Ayodhyā and remains ever after in Kubera's possession as his inanimate *vimāna*.[23]

Vimāna as a temple

In later literature, the term *vimāna* acquires the meaning of 'temple'. As Kramrisch (1977: Vol. 1, p. 132) remarks: '[V]imāna ... has remained one of the most generally accepted names which designate a temple.' This meaning does not yet appear in the epics, for indeed temples, at least in the form in which they are known today, probably first appeared in north India only towards the end of the fourth century CE (see Dagens 2009: 11). In view

20 In a Buddhist context, the current known as Mahāyāna, 'The Great Vehicle', is likewise called a *yāna* ('vehicle') because it brings people to liberation.

21 This identical essence is also subtly underscored in the same passage, where Puṣpaka twice calls Rāma *saumya* (*Rām*, 7.40.2), and Kubera likewise calls Puṣpaka *saumya* (*Rām*, 7.40.6). *Saumya* can simply be translated as 'gentle', but the term of course derives from *soma*, the plant used in the sacrifice, the nectar of immortality or the Moon. Rāma and Puṣpaka, it seems, partake of the same somic nature.

22 Gonda's (1965: 83) remark that 'these animals which are more or less intimately or regularly connected with gods are, in the Vedic as well as the Hindu period, theriomorphic manifestations of an aspect of the god's essence or nature' could be extended to a divine flying palace.

23 See *Mbh* 3.158.35 and 3.175.68; Harivaṃśa 34.17. However, Puṣpaka is not Kubera's *vāhana*, as this god has a man for his *vāhana* and is often called *naravāhana*.

of our introductory remarks on the term *vimāna*,[24] this semantic shift from '(flying) palace' to 'temple' appears to be a logical development, from both a formal and a symbolic point of view. From a morphological point of view, palaces and temples share the same basic requirement for exact measurement as complex architectural constructions. Kramrisch (1977: Vol. 1, p. 133) cites the following definition: 'Vimāna is the name of the temple built according to tradition [*śāstra*] by the application of various proportionate measurements or various standards of proportionate measurement.'[25]

In some architectural treatises, the term *vimāna* becomes a technical term for a 'pyramidal form of superstructure that rises over the *garbha-gṛha* [sanctum]' in temples of the southern or *drāviḍa* type.[26] Lorenzetti says it 'comprises a succession of sloping storeys [*tala*, *bhūmi*], generally separated by a corniced moulding, *kapotapālī*' (2015: 79). Again, it is likely that the name *vimāna* was given to this type of spire because it had to be measured with utmost precision. Various types of spire-*vimāna*s are shown in Plates 10.4 and 10.5.

From a symbolic point of view, too, we can immediately perceive the connection between a temple and a heavenly *vimāna*: flying *vimāna*s are the abodes of celestial beings in paradise. Similarly, temples are the abodes of celestial beings on Earth. As Kramrisch (1977: Vol. 1, p. 133) remarks: 'The temple as Vimāna, proportionately measured throughout, is the house and body of god.' Similarly, Dagens (2009: 25) says: '*Un temple dans le monde indien, c'est ... la "maison d'un/du dieu"* [A temple in the Indian world is ... the "house of (a) god"].' It is thus a piece of Heaven that has come down to Earth.

24 See also Feller (2022).

25 Cf. *Īśānaśivagurudevapaddhati* 3.28.2, repeated in *Śilparatna* 16.2.

26 For a detailed exposition on *drāviḍa* temples, see Hardy (2007: Pt 5).

Plate 10.4 The *vimāna* of the Virūpākṣa Temple, Hampi (Karnataka), c. fifteenth–sixteenth century

Photo: Raymond Conus.

Plate 10.5 Keshava Temple, Somnathpur (Karnataka), c. 1268

Hardy (2007: 99) describes it: 'Three stellate vimanas share the mandapa, which is closed at the rear, open (with pierced screens) at the front. The temple is raised on a platform [*jagati*] within an enclosure [*prakara*].'

Photo: Raymond Conus.

Divine *vimānas* are also used as transportation between Heaven and Earth. The gods occasionally come down to Earth on their *vimānas* and newly deceased people ascend to Heaven on a *vimāna* acquired by their good deeds. Likewise, a temple is, *par excellence*, a place where the human and divine planes are believed to intersect, and where men can meet gods. The devotees are lifted along 'the spire's upward thrust' (Lorenzetti 2015: 22) by means of the sacrifices, gifts and prayers offered at the temple. As Kramrisch (1977: Vol. 1, p. 142) remarks: 'The temple is built as a work of supererogation, with the utmost effort in material means and the striving of the spirit so that the Prāsāda attains and leads to the Highest Point.'

While Kramrisch concentrates on the upward movement implied in both the building and the viewing of a temple, where the eye is naturally led up the elevation of the spire, Hardy remarks that the inverse downward movement is implied as well in a temple building and that the gods are thought to come down from Heaven and reside in the sanctum, which is right beneath the spire:

> At this point it can be noted that within the logic of Kramrisch's own metaphysical view, aspiration towards union with the divine must be inwards and upwards to the unity beyond form, while manifestation must be downwards and outwards from the one to the many: God is up there and comes down to earth. (Hardy 2011: 485)[27]

This downward movement is further explained on an architectural plane:

> The shrine is invested with a sense of movement that appears to originate at the tip of the finial, or a point just above it, progressing downwards from this point and outwards from the vertical axis, radiating all around, predominantly in the four cardinal directions. (Hardy 2007: 38)

Thus, a temple, even though it is static, remains the locus of upward, downward and radiating movements in a manner that is consistent with, and reminiscent of, its nature as a mobile, heavenly *vimāna*.

Even more potent than the prayers and oblations offered up by the devotees at the temple, the *building* of a temple was, over time, increasingly seen as a guarantee of future heavenly bliss:

> Let him who wishes to enter the worlds that are reached by sacrificial offerings and the performance of religious obligations [*iṣṭāpūrta*] build a temple to the gods, by doing which he attains both the results of sacrifice and the performance of religious obligations. (*Bṛhat Saṃhitā*, 55.2).[28]

In other words, by building a *vimāna* ('temple') according to *vimāna* ('measurement'), the devotee then climbs on a *vimāna* ('heavenly palace') and obtains a *vimāna* ('heavenly abode'). To sum up the evolution of the concept of *vimāna*, we might say that, starting out as an earthly human palace, transferred to Heaven as a godly palace, the *vimāna* has come full circle, taking root in the ground, but this time as the permanent residence of the gods on Earth.

27 Quoted nearly *verbatim* from Hardy (2007: 38).

28 Quoted in Kramrisch (1977: Vol. 1, p. 139). We see here that the Bṛhat Saṃhitā proceeds by equivalences, trying to establish practices that bring about the same merit as sacrificial performances.

Vegetal Puṣpaka

After this excursus on *vimāna* as a temple, let us return to Puṣpaka in conclusion. In a treatise on *vāstu*, the *Samarāṅgaṇasūtradhāra*[29] (*Ssd*), the name Puṣpaka is given to a flower-shaped temple adorned with floral and vegetal motifs (Plate 10.6). Hardy (2016: 132) doubts whether anyone ever built a temple of this kind, even though, as he notes, temples inspired by the shape of lotuses are quite common. Not only is the basic layout inspired by the design of a flower,[30] but also its walls abound in decorations representing vegetal motifs:

> The instructions for the Pushpaka luxuriate in flowery poetry. For example, the wall of the temple should be adorned with 'a garland of celestial maidens' [*vidyādharī mālā*] 'with flowers in their hands' [*mālā vidyādharī kāryā puṣpahastair alaṅkṛtā*] (*Ssd*, 57: 152). Many technical terms for temple architecture already have flower-like etymology: śṛṅga ('sprout'), kanda ('bulb'), mañjari ('blossom'), and so on. Here the floral characteristics of a temple blossom in profusion. (Hardy 2016: 132)

Thus, more than a millennium after the composition of the Vālmīki *Rāmāyaṇa*, Puṣpaka, which despite its appellation never had a particularly prominent connection with flowers,[31] finally realises the full potential of its name, 'Little Flower', even though this flower is sculpted in stone. We see that Puṣpaka has come full circle in its metamorphoses through every conceivable mode of being, starting from a mineral shape, then passing through animal, personified, divine and vegetal forms, the protean flying palace has returned to its original mineral manifestation. It is of special interest to note that in their semantic evolution, the terms *vimāna* and Puṣpaka have ultimately come to designate a temple or type of temple. Could this be because, in modern non-mythical times, the temple remains the only 'vehicle' in which humans still hope to be uplifted to Heaven?

29 The *Samarāṅgaṇasūtradhāra* is a 'compendious Vastu Shastra attributed to the legendary king Bhoja (ruled c. 1010–1055), Paramara ruler of Malwa in central India' (Hardy 2016: 126).

30 'The arrangement of the ground plan for the Puṣpaka should be in the shape of five flowers [*puṣpakasya talanyāsaḥ pañcapuṣpākṛtir bhavet*] (Ssd 57: 149)' (Hardy 2016: 132).

31 In the *Rāmāyaṇa*, it is once said to be adorned with golden lotuses (*hemapadmavibhūṣitam*; *Rām*, 6.109.23) and once to be decorated with flowers (*puṣpabhūṣitaḥ*; *Rām*, 7.4.11), after Rāma has worshipped it.

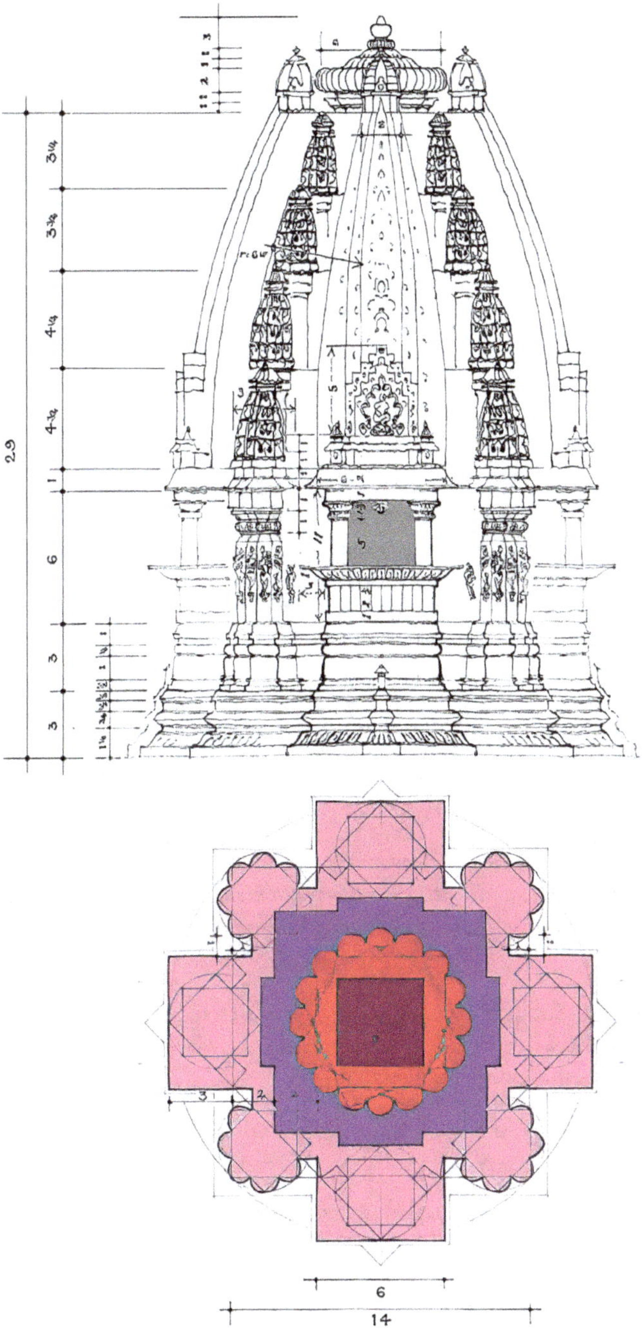

Plate 10.6 The Puṣpaka temple

Source: Reproduced by permission of the author from Hardy (2016: 131). My heartfelt thanks to Professor Hardy for allowing me to use his drawing.

References

Primary texts

Bhatt, G.H. and Shah, U.P. (eds). (1960–75). *The Vālmīki-Rāmāyaṇa.* [7 vols.] Baroda, India: Oriental Institute.

Sukthankar, Vishnu Sitaram (ed.). (1933–66). *The Mahābhārata.* [19 vols.] Poona, India: Bhandarkar Oriental Research Institute.

Secondary texts

Brockington, John L. (1998). *The Sanskrit Epics.* Leiden, Netherlands: Brill. doi.org/10.1163/9789004492677.

Dagens, Bruno. (2009). *Le temple indien miroir du monde* [*The Indian Temple: Mirror of the World*]. Paris: Les Belles Lettres.

Deshpande, N.A. (1989 [1939]). *The Padma-Purāṇa. Part II.* Delhi: Motilal Banarsidass.

Feller, Danielle. (2004). *The Sanskrit Epics' Representation of Vedic Myths.* Delhi: Motilal Banarsidass.

Feller, Danielle. (2020). Puṣpaka in the Vālmīki-Rāmāyaṇa. *Asiatische Studien/Etudes Asiatiques* 74(2): 325–48. doi.org/10.1515/asia-2019-0043.

Feller, Danielle. (2022). From palace to Heaven: Vimāna in the Sanskrit epics. In P.M. Rossi (ed.), *Liminal Spaces and Identity Transformations in South Asian Literatures and Arts: Essays in Honour of Professor Alexander Dubyanskiy*, pp. 43–67. Milan, Italy: Ledizioni.

Goldman, Robert and Sutherland Goldman, Sally J. (trans & eds). (2017). *The Rāmāyaṇa of Vālmīki: An Epic of Ancient India. Volume 7: Uttarakāṇḍa.* Princeton, NJ: Princeton University Press.

Gonda, Jan. (1965). *Change and Continuity in Indian Religion.* The Hague: Mouton & Co.

Hardy, Adam. (2007). *The Temple Architecture of India.* Chichester, UK: Wiley.

Hardy, Adam. (2011). The expression of movement in architecture. *The Journal of Architecture* 16(4): 471–97. doi.org/10.1080/13602365.2011.598698.

Hardy, Adam. (2016). Hindu temples and the emanating cosmos. *Religion and the Arts* 20: 112–34. doi.org/10.1163/15685292-02001006.

Kramrisch, Stella. (1977 [1946]). *The Hindu Temple*. [2 vols.] Delhi: Motilal Banarsidass.

Lorenzetti, Tiziana. (2015). *Understanding the Hindu Temple: History, Symbols and Forms*. Berlin: EB-Verlag.

Mann, Richard D. (2012). *The Rise of Mahāsena: The Transformation of Skanda-Kārttikeya in North India from the Kuṣāṇa to Gupta Empires*. Leiden, Netherlands: Brill. doi.org/10.1163/9789004218864.

Monier-Williams, Monier. (2009). *An English–Sanskrit Dictionary*. New Delhi: Asian Educational Services.

Sastri, P.S. (1946). *Varahamihira's Brihat-Samhita: With English Translation & Notes*. Bangalore, India: Soobbiah & Sons.

Shukla, D.N. (1993). *Vāstu-Śāstra. Volume II: Hindu Canons of Iconography and Painting*. Delhi: Munshiram Manoharlal.

11

From Ayodhyā to the Daṇḍaka: Rāma's journey in exile according to the Jain *Rāmāyaṇas*

Eva De Clercq

Abstract

In this chapter, I compare the journey of Rāma from Ayodhyā to the forest in the Vālmīki *Rāmāyaṇa* with the parallel episodes of the main Jain tradition of Rāma tellings. Whereas in the Vālmīki *Rāmāyaṇa*, Rāma, Sītā and Lakṣmaṇa spend 10 years visiting *āśrama*s in the forest and protecting sages before settling in Pañcavaṭī, in the Jain accounts, the visits to *āśrama*s are largely replaced with visits to cities, helping rulers in need and marrying princesses. I argue how these changes reflect the strategy of the Jain authors to bring the Jain Rāma narrative into line with the Jain universal history, how they allow a representation of Rāma and Sītā as the ideal lay couple and how they underscore the forest as the place for ascetics alone.

Introduction: *Rāmāyaṇa* and the forest

In his introduction to the Araṇyakāṇḍa, translator Sheldon Pollock (1991: 3–6) discusses some of the responses readers of the *Rāmāyaṇa* have had to the transition from the second book, Ayodhyākāṇḍa, to the third,

Araṇyakāṇḍa—that is, the spatial shift from the city to the forest. Classical Indology scholars of the late nineteenth and early twentieth centuries, beginning with Hermann Jacobi, experienced this transition as a rupture or a discontinuity in the narrative. They believed that the first part (that is, Ayodhyākāṇḍa) represents a work dealing with *dharma* and that the narrative in the Araṇyakāṇḍa is to be considered more as a 'romance', including various supernatural characters who were largely absent from the Ayodhyakāṇḍa. According to them, a possible reason for this discontinuity is the fact that the narrative of the *Rāmāyaṇa* combines two originally distinct narratives into one. Other scholars, including Pollock, do not see anything problematic in this shift to the forest and emphasise the presence of similar episodes of forest exile in other examples of Indian narrative literature, including the *Mahābhārata*, the Nalopākhyāna and the *Vessantara Jātaka*, to name a few, suggesting that a forest exile is a popular motif of the Indian epic genre.

In this chapter, I explore the dramatically distinctive way in which the shift from Ayodhyā to the forest and beyond is dealt with in a different, 'oppositional' set of *Rāmāyaṇa*s—more precisely, those by Jain authors—and how these changes can be explained within the overall Jain reframing of the narrative.

Rāmāyaṇa and Jainism

In the past 25 centuries or so, the story of the *Rāmāyaṇa* has been told and retold thousands of times by authors who freely adapted the story to their own requirements. Jain authors also composed adaptations in many literary languages, from Sanskrit, Prakrit and Apabhramsha to vernaculars such as Kannada, Gujarati and classical Hindi.[1] Characteristic of these Jain retellings is the fact that they are sometimes highly critical of the 'standard' popular versions attributed to Vālmīki or Vyāsa—here, probably representing authoritative Brahmanical epic and purāṇic authorship in general, rather than the author of the *Mahābhārata* and its Rāma narrative in the Rāmopākhyāna, specifically. Some commence with a list of episodes from the 'standard' version that they claim to be false and for which they offer another, often far more logical, explanation (see De Clercq and Vekemans forthcoming).

1 For an overview of different traditions within the Jain, see Kulkarni (1990). Recent studies by Gregory Clines (2018) and Adrian Plau (2018) deal with later Jain reworkings in Sanskrit and classical Hindi.

The story that the Jain authors offer is in many ways more coherent and therefore often makes sense at times when Vālmīki's story does not. This is, of course, initially due to the different way in which these Jain versions came about—namely, as works composed by a single identifiable author at one point in time, whereas the text of the *Rāmāyaṇa* of Vālmīki as we now have it, though more coherent than the *Mahābhārata*, is still a work of layers added on to a kernel over several centuries, as is accepted by most scholars. The basic Jain story is very similar to that of Vālmīki, narrating the life of Rāma, the Prince of Ayodhyā, whose wife, Sītā, is abducted by King Rāvaṇa of Laṅkā during their exile in the forest, and who, together with his brother Lakṣmaṇa, and with the help of the *vānara*s, vanquishes Rāvaṇa and is reunited with his beloved. Despite the existence of different Jain *Rāmāyaṇa* accounts and traditions (Kulkarni 1990), there appears to be a common Jain *Rāmāyaṇa* prototype that distinguishes itself in two features.

First, the Jains adapted the story to Jain ideology and to the concept of what has been termed the Jain universal history—a framework that the Jains themselves term (*mahā*)*purāṇa*. According to this framework, in every period, *śalākā-puruṣa*s or *mahāpuruṣa*s ('great men') are born in succession—the standard list numbering 63 such heroes, each with a specific mythic-historical role. They include the 24 *Tīrthaṃkara*s or *Jina*s, the 'prophets' of Jainism, 12 *cakravartin*s or 'universal emperors' and nine sets of a Baladeva, Vāsudeva and Prativāsudeva. The main characters of the *Rāmāyaṇa*, Rāma, Lakṣmaṇa and Rāvaṇa, are the eighth Baladeva, Vāsudeva and Prativāsudeva, respectively, of the current period, at the time of the fourteenth Tīrthaṃkara, Muni Suvrata. These categories of Baladevas, Vāsudevas and Prativāsudevas are sets of heroes and antiheroes who live simultaneously, their lives intertwined. As the names of these categories make clear, the biographies of Balarāma and Kṛṣṇa (Vāsudeva) must have been the inspiration for the Baladeva, Vāsudeva and Prativāsudeva categories; the Baladeva is always the older half-brother to the Vāsudeva and the Vāsudeva ends up killing their mortal enemy, the Prativāsudeva. So, here, Lakṣmaṇa kills Rāvaṇa, not Rāma.

The second commonality concerns the characterisation of the *rākṣasa*s and the *vānara*s. In the Jain narratives, they are not demons and monkeys, but humans belonging to two distinct branches of the Vidyādhara dynasty. How this Vidyādhara dynasty came into being is narrated in the biography of the first Tīrthaṅkara, Ṛṣabha, often included in the Jain *Rāmāyaṇa*s. Ṛṣabha, the founder of the Ikṣvāku dynasty of Ayodhyā and thus direct forefather to Rāma at the time of his renunciation, divided the realm among his relatives.

Two relatives, Nami and Vinami, were absent on this occasion and, later, when Ṛṣabha was already immersed in meditation, approached him to claim their land. Their presence near Ṛṣabha and the possible disturbance they posed to his meditation alerted Dharaṇendra, the lord of the *nāga*s—in Jainism, a class of serpent deities. He appeared there and offered the two men *vidyā*s and a territory comprising the two ranges of the Vaitāḍya mountains. Hence, their dynasty came to be known as that of the Vidyādharas ('*vidyā*-bearers'). Generations later, the *rākṣasa*s and *vānara*s rose as two closely allied branches within this dynasty.

These Jain *vidyā*s are portrayed as a kind of supernatural female entity, sometimes translated as 'genies', granting the person who possesses them certain powers—for example, the power to change one's appearance or size. These *vidyā*s are inherited through one's family, but they can also be gained through performing austerities. There are occasions when *vidyā*s are simply donated by one person to another. The Jain Rāma and Lakṣmaṇa, too, are described as possessing some *vidyā*s, though they are not part of the Vidyādhara dynasty. As Vidyādharas, the *vānara*s were named *vānara* ('monkeys') because their ancestral island was Vānaradvīpa ('Monkey Island') and because they had a monkey as their emblem. On the explanation for the name *rākṣasa*, Jain authors disagree: some say they are named after an early ancestor called Rakṣas, others say the name is linked to a *vidyā* called Rākṣasī and an island called Rākṣasadvīpa, which were donated to Toyadavāhana, the first king of the *rākṣasa* dynasty. In the second, less widespread Jain Rāma tradition (of Guṇabhadra's *Uttarapurāṇa*), however, the *vānara*s and *rākṣasa*s do not manifest themselves as such until they are opposite each other on the battlefield in Laṅkā; then, the Vidyādharas in Rāma's camp take on the form of monkeys, while those in Rāvaṇa's camp take on the form of demonic *rākṣasa*s. This transformation of the *vānara*s and *rākṣasa*s into humans is generally recognised as a tendency by the Jain authors to rationalise the story of Vālmīki.

For this chapter, I focus on the most authoritative tradition of Jain Rāma stories and its three closely related earliest texts—namely, the *Paümacariyaṃ*, in Māhārāṣṭrī by Vimalasūri (third–fifth centuries CE; hereinafter *PCV*), the *Padmapurāṇa* or *Padmacarita* in Sanskrit by Raviṣeṇa (678 CE; hereinafter *PCR*) and the Apabhramsha version, *Paümacariu* (ninth–tenth centuries CE; hereinafter *PCS*), by Svayambhūdeva. Of these three authors, Svayambhūdeva is the only one to mimic Vālmīki's division of the work into five *kāṇḍa*s: 1) Vidyādharakāṇḍa, 2) Ayodhyākāṇḍa, 3) Sundarakāṇḍa,

4) Yuddhakāṇḍa and 5) Uttarakāṇḍa.[2] With an Araṇyakāṇḍa not being part of the set, the events parallel to Vālmīki's Araṇyakāṇḍa are here transferred to the Ayodhyākāṇḍa. I begin with a summary of Vālmīki's account, comparing it with these texts.

From Ayodhyā to Citrakūṭa

Following the intrigues of Kaikeyī and receiving the news of Rāma's banishment, Rāma, Sītā and Lakṣmaṇa have set out on their journey towards a life as ascetics in the forest in the first part of the Ayodhyākāṇḍa, in *Sarga* 35 of the Vālmīki *Rāmāyaṇa*, as devastated family members and sympathisers trail after them. In *Sarga* 41, they leave the city in a chariot, still followed by a small group of aged brahmins, who eventually return to Ayodhyā after Rāma, Lakṣmaṇa and Sītā leave their campsite in the chariot early in the morning before the brahmins are awake. They traverse the land of Kosala, which is strewn with forests and villages, where the news of Rāma's exile has already reached, and cross several streams, as Rāma reminisces about royal hunting parties in the area (42–43), until they reach the fortified town (*durga*; 46.59) of Śṛṅgaverapura on the bank of the River Gaṅgā, where Guha, King of the Niṣādas, rules. Guha offers them his hospitality and even rule over his kingdom, but Rāma refuses given his resolve to stay true to his father's word and live in the forest as an ascetic (44–45).

On the third day of their exile, before crossing the Gaṅgā in a boat, Rāma orders the charioteer Sumantra to go back to Ayodhyā so that he can take the news to Kaikeyī that Rāma has indeed gone into exile in the forest. Rāma and Lakṣmaṇa put on the garb of ascetics, including matting their hair. With the aid of some Niṣāda boatmen, they cross the Gaṅgā, while Sītā pays obeisance to the sacred river (46). From this point, the three appear to be travelling through deep forest (48.2), as they head towards the confluence of the Gaṅgā with the River Yamunā (*prayāga*; 48.5), which is described as an isolated place (*avakāśo vivikto*; 48.20) where the sage Bharadvāja lives with his dependants. The three introduce themselves and Bharadvāja, who has heard of their plight, invites them to spend their exile in his hermitage. However, because the hermitage is near populated areas (*paura-jānapado*; 48.22),

2 For convenience's sake, I give the Sanskrit form of names and terms rather than the Prakrit or Apabhramsha forms.

Rāma fears people will come to visit them. Bharadvāja then suggests that they create an *āśrama* of their own on the sacred Mount Citrakūṭa, 10 *krośas* (37 kilometres) away.

After a night in Bharadvāja's *āśrama*, the three leave for Citrakūṭa (47–48). Following Bharadvāja's instruction, they cross the River Yamunā on a self-made raft, pass the great banyan tree Śyāma and spend the night on the riverbank, steadily abandoning their sadness over the events in Ayodhyā (49). The next day, six days after leaving Ayodhyā, they continue their journey and soon reach Mount Citrakūṭa, where Lakṣmaṇa builds them a hut and they settle (50).

The narration now reverts to Ayodhyā, where the charioteer arrives without Rāma, the city is still immersed in grief and Daśaratha soon dies of sadness, recollecting to Rāma's mother, Kausalyā, the curse that a sage put on him for accidentally killing his son a long time ago (51–58). As the palace and city are immersed even deeper in sorrow (59–61), on the advice of Vasiṣṭha, messengers are sent to bring back Bharata (62–65), who is infuriated with his mother, Kaikeyī, when he hears what has happened (66–72), and together with an enormous retinue, which appears to comprise almost the entire city, he goes in pursuit of Rāma. After meeting Guha (79–82) and Bharadvāja (83–86), who are both initially suspicious of Bharata's motives but later give him and his retinue a warm welcome, Bharata reaches Citrakūṭa, 2.5 *yojana*s (about 35 kilometres) away (87). Rāma, meanwhile, has settled into a life of tranquillity in Citrakūṭa near the Mandākinī River (88–89). This Citrakūṭa mountain has been identified with different places, one of which developed into the pilgrimage site of Chitrakoot in Bundelkhand (Law 1954: 73–74, 313–14). Bharata and his retinue arrive, bringing the news of Daśaratha's death (90–94). After Rāma's performance of the funeral libation to Daśaratha (95), Bharata and some others repeatedly urge Rāma to return to Ayodhyā and take up the role of king, but Rāma is resolved to stay in the forest for 14 years, staying true to Daśaratha's word (96–103). Bharata takes back slippers as representative of Rāma and rules the kingdom from Nandigrāma, awaiting Rāma's return (104–7).

The parallel Jain accounts are here considerably more condensed (about two chapters: *PCR*, 31.201–33.39; *PCV*, 31.112–33.11; *PCS*, 23–24) than the Sanskrit epic. On the evening of the day that they receive the news that Bharata will become the new king, and Rāma subsequently decides to live in exile somewhere in the south to facilitate his younger brother's early kingship, Rāma, Lakṣmaṇa and Sītā visit the Jina temple where they say goodbye to their mothers and depart for their forest exile about midnight, observing the nightly (erotic) activities of Ayodhyā's inhabitants. A small group of soldiers, not brahmins, follows them, but when they realise that Rāma is not going back, they return to Ayodhyā one by one. Rāma, Lakṣmaṇa and Sītā first reach the area of Pāriyātra near the River Gambhīrā. Neither of these geographical names corresponds to a place in Vālmīki's account, nor are they common in other Jain narrative texts, though Pāriyātra is known from Hindu purāṇic sources as a mountain to the west of Mount Meru and has otherwise been identified with a western part of the Vindhya Range (Law 1954: 20, 326) corresponding to the River Gambhir, which flows through that region and joins the River Shipra in Ujjain, or with the more northernly River Gambhir, a tributary of the Yamunā. The description of the area is limited and generic, leaving no clues for further identification. Before crossing the River Gambhīrā (without a boat), Rāma sends the remainder of the soldiers back to Ayodhyā, some of whom, out of sadness and disgust with the world, decide to become renouncers. The Jain accounts revert to Ayodhyā at this point, before Rāma has set up a fixed forest abode. In Ayodhyā, Daśaratha prepares to renounce the material world. Seeing the grief of her co-wives at the loss of their husband to renunciation and their sons to voluntary exile, Kaikeyī remorsefully requests Bharata to go after Rāma and bring him back. She joins Bharata and they catch up with Rāma, Sītā and Lakṣmaṇa near an unnamed lake after six days. Despite Bharata's request and Kaikeyī's regret, Rāma makes it clear that he cannot return to Ayodhyā out of respect for Daśaratha's truthfulness. Rāma ties the royal turban to Bharata's head. Bharata and Kaikeyī return to Ayodhyā, where Bharata reluctantly lives as a householder and king, resolved to hand over the kingdom to Rāma on his return and thereafter commence life as an ascetic. Rāma, Sītā and Lakṣmaṇa meanwhile travel through an area where there are *āśrama*s with various types of (Brahmanical) hermits and other communities, until they reach Citrakūṭa, which is described as a place of pleasant, dense forest inhabited by wild animals. From the names of towns that follow, the Citrakūṭa imagined by the Jain texts is different from the one in the Vālmīki *Rāmāyaṇa* and is identified with now-famous Chittorgarh in modern-day Rajasthan (Law 1954: 313–14). Thus, the journey from Ayodhyā is some 900 kilometres, making the four and a half months explicitly mentioned in all three texts a reasonable time for that distance. This identification of the Jain authors of Citrakūṭa with Chittorgarh parallels the historical shift westward of the Jain community, its interest and culture (see, for example, Dundas 2002: 113). This, in consequence, accounts for the later placement of Citrakūṭa on Rāma's travel route, compared with the Vālmīki *Rāmāyaṇa*, as well as the explicit mention of the 4.5-month period.

From Citrakūṭa to Daṇḍaka

In the final chapters of the Ayodhyākāṇḍa in the Vālmīki *Rāmāyaṇa*, sages flee the Citrakūṭa area, suffering attacks from *rākṣasas* (108), as do Rāma, Sītā and Lakṣmaṇa, who visit the ascetic couple Atri and Anasūyā. Sītā receives gifts from the female ascetic and tells her the story of her birth and wedding to Rāma (109–11). The Araṇyakāṇḍa begins with Rāma, Sītā and Lakṣmaṇa entering the Daṇḍaka Forest, which is described as a vast jungle with many *āśrama*s and ascetics. Rāma, Sītā and Lakṣmaṇa are invited in by these sages and Rāma pledges to protect them from the *rākṣasas* (1). As they proceed, they encounter a huge demonic being, Virādha, who wants to make Sītā his wife. Struck down by Rāma and Lakṣmaṇa, Virādha, as he lies dying, reveals himself to be a cursed *gandharva*, Tumburu, who can now return to Heaven (2–3). On the direction of Virādha, they go to the *āśrama* of the sage Śarabhaṅga, who directs them to the sage Sutīkṣṇa (4). On their way, they meet different kinds of ascetics, all of whom request the protection of Rāma (5). After their visit to Sutīkṣṇa's *āśrama*, they visit all the other sages in the Daṇḍaka Forest (6–7). Though Sītā expresses her worry about Rāma's pledge to protect the sages against the *rākṣasa*s, Rāma remains firm in his promise (8–9). Thus, they spend 10 years of their exile staying in the different *āśrama*s in the Daṇḍaka Forest (10). Returning to Sutīkṣṇa, Rāma asks him directions to the *āśrama* of the great sage Agastya, who conquered two demon brothers. Reaching Agastya, Rāma receives divine weapons from him, as well as directions to Pañcavaṭī, which is a suitable place 2 *yojanas* away where Rāma can settle in his own *āśrama* and stay in relative comfort for the rest of his exile (11–12). On their way to Pañcavaṭī, they encounter the vulture Jaṭāyus, who identifies himself as a friend of Daśaratha and offers to protect Sītā (13). Reaching Pañcavaṭī, Lakṣmaṇa builds them a hut and the trio settles there (14), until one day Rāvaṇa's sister Śūrpaṇakhā encounters them, setting in motion the events leading to Sītā's abduction and the eventual downfall of Rāvaṇa's rule.

In the Jain texts, Rāma, Sītā and Lakṣmaṇa ultimately also enter the Daṇḍaka Forest, but only after a long series of adventures that breaks with the narrative of the Vālmīki *Rāmāyaṇa*. This passage, amounting to about one-tenth of the entire text (in *PCS*, more than nine chapters, 24–34; in *PCV* and *PCR*, more than seven chapters, 33–40), is an innovation by the Jain authors, describing visits to various cities, most of which are not known from other Jain narrative literature.

After passing Citrakūṭa, Rāma, Sītā and Lakṣmaṇa reach the area of Avantī and settle under a tree to rest. On Rāma's instruction, Lakṣmaṇa goes in search of a village or city where they can get some food. Lakṣmaṇa sees an abandoned city and hears from a passer-by that it is Daśapura (*PCR*: Daśāṅgapura), which is identified by Law (1954: 280–81) as the modern city of Mandsaur in Malwa. The city is under siege from Siṃhodara, king of nearby Ujjayinī (Ujjain), because Daśapura's ruler, Vajrakarṇa, has taken a vow to not bow to anyone but the Jina. After the trio receives a meal from cordial Vajrakarṇa, Lakṣmaṇa goes to Siṃhodara pretending to be a messenger from Bharata, threatening war on Siṃhodara if he does not stop the siege of Daśapura. After a battle with Lakṣmaṇa, Siṃhodara is defeated and brought before Rāma. Vajrakarṇa and Siṃhodara become friends and each rules half the land, and they, as well as some other kings, offer their daughters in marriage to Lakṣmaṇa.

Rāma, Sītā and Lakṣmaṇa then proceed towards the city of Kūbara, where they meet its ruler princess, Kalyāṇamālā, who has reigned over the city disguised as a man since her father, Vālikhilya, was taken prisoner by a Mleccha king, Rudrabhūti (*PCR*: Raudrabhūti), in the Vindhya Range. Crossing the River Narmadā, they encounter and subdue the army of Mlecchas and request Rudrabhūti to release Vālikhilya. Vālikhilya returns to his city and Rudrabhūti becomes his subject.

Rāma, Sītā and Lakṣmaṇa head further south, crossing the River Tāpī and, in the village of Aruṇagrāma, entering the house of a brahmin, Kapila, who forces them to leave. They take shelter from the monsoon rains under a banyan tree. The *yakṣa* of the tree alerts his king, Pūtana, to the presence of the three strangers. Using his clairvoyance (*avadhi*), Pūtana builds them a beautiful city, Rāmapuri, as they sleep.[3] The next day, Kapila hears of the riches in this new city, which can be entered only by those who have received instruction in the Jain teachings. Wanting to also profit from this new wealth, Kapila immediately goes to a Jain temple, where he becomes a devout Jain layman and his greed vanishes. Together with his wife, he now enters the city of Rāmapuri, only to discover that the people for whom the *yakṣa* king built the city were those whom he had so brutally cast out of his home. He apologises for his former ignorance and receives many gifts from Rāma.

3 Note that K.R. Chandra (1970: 512) identifies this Rāmapuri, because of its association with *yakṣa*s, with Rāmagiri or contemporary Ramtek, the place where the *yakṣa* from Kālidāsa's *Meghadūta* sent his message. I prefer to follow Mirashi (1968) in identifying the city of Rāmagiri that is mentioned later and was equally built for Rāma, as contemporary Ramtek, due to its location just north of the Daṇḍaka Forest.

Eventually, he renounces the material world and becomes an ascetic. When the monsoon season is at an end, Rāma, Sītā and Lakṣmaṇa bid farewell to Pūtana, who makes the city disappear again.

They travel further and reach the city of Vijayapura (*PCR*: Vaijayantapura; *PCS*: Jīvanta)—another unidentified city—where the king's daughter, Vanamālā, had fallen deeply in love with Lakṣmaṇa after hearing of his many qualities. When her father, Pṛthivīdhara (*PCS*: Mahīdhara), hears that Lakṣmaṇa has left Ayodhyā to live in the forest, he decides to give his daughter to another man. Vanamālā thereupon plans to commit suicide. That night, Lakṣmaṇa observes her as she prepares to hang herself from a banyan tree and makes himself known. The next morning, she, together with Rāma, Sītā and Lakṣmaṇa, enters the city in celebration.

About the same time, Pṛthivīdhara receives a letter from Ativīrya (*PCS*: Anantavīrya), the King of Nandāvarta,[4] asking him to become an ally in a war against Bharata of Ayodhyā, who had refused to submit to Ativīrya. Rāma thinks of a plan and joins with Lakṣmaṇa and Pṛthivīdhara's sons and sons-in-law to enter Nandāvarta disguised as female dancers. Brought before the king, the dancers perform a play about the lives of the Tīrthaṃkaras, and Rāma sings the praises of Bharata, much to the irritation of Ativīrya. A battle ensues and Ativīrya is captured and made to accept Bharata's suzerainty. Ativīrya decides to renounce the world, leaving the throne to his son, who marries one of his sisters to Lakṣmaṇa and another to Bharata. Bharata goes to visit and praise Ativīrya.

In due course, Rāma, Lakṣmaṇa and Sītā leave Vijayapura and head towards the city of Kṣemāñjali, ruled by Śatrudamana (*PCS*: Aridamana). As Rāma and Sītā rest in a park nearby, Lakṣmaṇa enters the city, where he hears that Princess Jitapadmā is destined to marry the man who can stop the five *śakti*s of her father. Lakṣmaṇa enters the palace to take on the challenge and wins the hand of Jitapadmā. Rāma and Sītā are also brought into the city and, after celebrations, the trio continues their journey.

4 Chandra (1970: 513) believes that because of its relative proximity to Ramtek (as Rāmagiri or Rāmapuri), this Nandāvarta (or Nandyāvarta) could refer to the Vākāṭaka capital, Nandivardhana. It is interesting that, like Ativīrya, who forged an alliance through marriage with Bharata in 'imperial' Ayodhyā, the Vākāṭakas and the imperial Guptas, under whose rule the identification of Sāketa/Ayodhyā with the city of Rāma developed, also forged marriage alliances.

Moving further, they reach a city, Vaṃśasthala (*PCR*: Vaṃśasthadyuti), near a mountain, Vaṃśagiri (*PCR*: Vaṃśadhara), whose inhabitants are fleeing calamities caused by a vengeful god to disturb the austerities of two ascetics on the mountain. Rāma, Sītā and Lakṣmaṇa go towards the seers, chasing away the calamity by twanging their bows, and stand guard. The ascetics, Kulabhūṣaṇa and Deśavibhūṣaṇa, achieve *kevala* ('omniscience') and Indra and his retinue come to honour them. Rāma asks to hear the cause of this calamity and Kulabhūṣaṇa explains how their lives and that of the vengeful god had been entwined in previous existences. Rāma, Lakṣmaṇa and Sītā stay on this mountain and a city is built for them, Rāmagiri, with many temples to the Jinas.[5]

After this sequence of adventures, Rāma, Lakṣmaṇa and Sītā enter the Daṇḍaka Forest and rest near the River Karṇaravā. One day, two ascetics, Gupti and Sugupti, arrive there and Sītā serves them a meal, whereupon all kinds of divine phenomena occur, including a rain of gemstones. A vulture, Jaṭāyin, sees the gems and, on remembering his previous life as King Daṇḍaka, falls at the feet of the ascetics. The seer Sugupti tells Jaṭāyin's previous birth story, as well as how he became a Jain ascetic himself. Sītā vows to protect the bird. The ascetics leave and Rāma, Sītā and Lakṣmaṇa proceed on their journey through the forest in a chariot they received from the gods for giving food to the ascetics, until they reach the River Krauñcā, where they settle and, during autumn, encounter Rāvaṇa's sister, here named Candraṇakhā.[6]

Discussion

Ayodhyā: Ever close

In the Jain accounts, Rāma's visits to various *āśrama*s and sages in the forest have been replaced with visits to cities—and twice, the construction of cities for them (Rāmapuri and Rāmagiri). In these cities, they experience various adventures. In two cases, they restore peace between warring rulers (Vajrakarṇa and Siṃhodara; Vālikhilya and Rudrabhūti). The initiative and agency in these chapters come more from the warrior-like Lakṣmaṇa than from Rāma, but it is Rāma to whom these rulers, as well as Lakṣmaṇa,

5 The building of Rāmagiri is absent from the *PCS*.

6 I discuss the story of Jaṭāyin and his previous birth as Daṇḍaka in De Clercq (2010) and have dealt with the Jain versions of Śūrpaṇakhā, including the integration of the Śambūka story here, in De Clercq (2015).

ultimately bow. In most cases, the city visits end in—and sometimes even revolve around—the marriage of Lakṣmaṇa (and sometimes Rāma) to the cities' princess(es) (for example, Vanamālā and Jitapadmā). Marriages are tried and tested measures of forging political alliances and it appears that in these episodes, too, the visited kings seek to seal their new friendship with an alliance with Lakṣmaṇa and Rāma and, through them, Bharata. In some cases (in the *PCS*, in fact, in almost every visit), the poets explicitly state that Rāma subjected the kings to a *sandhi* ('alliance') with Bharata and Ayodhyā. The underlying presence of Bharata and Ayodhyā in this part of the narrative is the most explicit in the episode of Ativīrya, who initially wants to force Bharata to accept his overlordship, but after the rather comical intervention staged by Rāma of a troupe of crossdressing performers as a kind of 'trojan horse', is forced to accept Bharata's suzerainty. Here, too, an alliance is forged by the marriage of Lakṣmaṇa and Bharata to Ativīrya's daughters. A consequence of this presence of Bharata and Ayodhyā in the background is that, at least in this part of the story, there is barely a sense of separation or distance from Ayodhyā or Bharata, who are somehow always near. The Jain Rāma does not periodically succumb to episodes of sadness, melancholy and sometimes distrust, the way Vālmīki's Rāma does, but is resolute and determined in his mission to protect his father's *satya* ('truthfulness'), strengthening Ayodhyā's long-held supreme political position along the way. According to the Jain universal history, as told in the very first chapters of the three Jain *Rāmāyaṇa*s, Ayodhyā was originally built by Kubera for the first Tīrthaṃkara Ṛṣabha, the founding father of the Ikṣvāku dynasty (PCV, 3–4; *PCR*, 3–4; *PCS*, 2–4). Along this line, this part of Rāma's journey is faintly reminiscent of the *digvijaya* ('world conquest') held by the first Cakravartin, Bharata, the son of Ṛṣabha, which established Ayodhyā as the primary political centre and capital of Bhāratavarṣa.

Ardhacakravartins

Though as a *digvijaya* Rāma's journey from Ayodhyā to the Daṇḍaka Forest lacks some vital features—not in the least the presence of the sacred *cakra* Sudarśana—it could nevertheless have been part of a strategy by the Jain poets to bring their Rāma stories more in line with other narratives of *śalākāpuruṣa*s. One characteristic of every Baladeva, Vāsudeva and Prativāsudeva is that they are considered Ardhacakravartins ('half-universal emperors')—great political leaders who each conquer three of the six regions of Bhāratavarṣa. Rāvaṇa's rise to Ardhacakravartin, including his conquest of half of Bhāratavarṣa, is elaborately described before the beginning of the Rāma narrative proper (*PCV*, 7–14; *PCR*, 7–14; *PCS*, 9–18). When in the ultimate duel Rāvaṇa tries to kill Lakṣmaṇa with his *cakra* Sudarśana, the *cakra* is caught by Lakṣmaṇa, who throws it back, killing Rāvaṇa and subsequently heralding the rise of the new Ardhacakravartin (*PCV*, 72–73; *PCR*, 75–76; *PCS*, 75). When the threesome later returns to Ayodhyā, and after Bharata's renunciation, the city leaders approach Rāma to be consecrated and he suggests that they also consecrate Lakṣmaṇa. Both brothers are then crowned king (*PCV*, 85; *PCR*, 88). A war with the Vidyādhara King Ratnaratha over his rejection of Lakṣmaṇa as a proper bridegroom for his daughter leads to the *digvijaya* of Lakṣmaṇa, again with Rāma present in the background (*PCV*, 90–91; *PCR*, 93–94). The *PCS* (79) deviates from this account: here, Rāma alone is consecrated as king. Yet, the very last line of the chapter (14.9) reads that, as Rāma is consecrated and the royal turban is tied to his head, Lakṣmaṇa rules (lit., 'enjoys') the Earth, endowed with the *cakra*, also indicating some form of joint governance. Moreover, Svayambhū omits the episode of Lakṣmaṇa's rejection as bridegroom, as well as the *digvijaya*. This omission can be explained as one to merely suit the Apabhramsha poetic style, reducing episodes in favour of the poetic elaboration of others, but it could also be an indication of the fact that, for this later poet, it was hard to conceive of a Rāma story in which Rāma shared the kingship with Lakṣmaṇa.

Forest versus city

Coming back to the relative absence of the forest in Rāma's exile, this does not mean that forests were of less importance to the Jains. Jain poets imagined the forest in many ways, as did authors and artists of other South Asian traditions, from paradisiacal to a dangerous wilderness inhabited by fierce, man-eating beasts (Thapar 2015; Parkhill 1980; Falk 1973). In the vein of the latter, the Jain *Rāmāyaṇa*s contain ample descriptions of the forest as a place of danger—for instance, in the famous story of Añjanā, who is cast out by her parents and her in-laws and gives birth to her son Hanumān in the forest (*PCV*, 17; *PCR*, 17; *PCS*, 19), or in the perception of Sītā as she is banished from the kingdom (*PCV*, 94; *PCR*, 97; *PCS*, 81). For Jains, the deep forest is the place of ascetics. The image of Jain ascetics—for instance, Ṛṣabha's giant son, Bāhubali, standing upright in *kāyotsarga* meditation, his limbs covered by creepers and insects—is well known. Also illustrative of this is the account of Lakṣmaṇa's wife Viśalyā, who in a previous life, as Anaṅgaśarā, was abducted and fell from a celestial chariot into the dense forest. With no prospect of being rescued, she does the only thing imaginable in a Jain context as suitable: commits to practising austerities. After thousands of years of asceticism, she dies in *sallekhanā* (*PCS*, 68; *PCR*, 64; *PCV*, 63).[7] Contrary to the Brahmanical ascetics mentioned in the Vālmīki *Rāmāyaṇa*, Jain ascetics did not live in *āśrama*s or monasteries, but were itinerant, except during the monsoon, and often solitary. Nevertheless, echoing Vālmīki's description of the Daṇḍaka Forest, Rāma, too, has two encounters with ascetics—the first with Kulabhūṣana and Deśavibhūṣaṇa on a mountain near Vaṃśasthala, just north of the Daṇḍaka Forest, and the second with Gupti and Sugupti in the Daṇḍaka Forest. Paralleling the Vālmīki *Rāmāyaṇa*, Rāma and Lakṣmaṇa come to the aid of the first pair of ascetics, by driving away the calamities caused by a vengeful god. The second pair, who pass by while Sītā is preparing food, receive a meal from her. Both occasions are accompanied by supernatural occurrences: the first is a visit from the gods after the ascetics become omniscient and the second is a rain of gemstones. Other than this, the episodes with the ascetics form the occasion for the narration of previous birth stories (of the sages themselves, as well as of the vulture Jaṭāyin), illustrating Jain karma theory and some elementary doctrinal teachings. These two encounters summarise the ideal pragmatic relationship between the Jain ascetic and lay communities: the lay community's main task is to facilitate ascetics in their spiritual endeavours by providing subsistence, especially food (*āhāra-dāna*), in exchange for teaching. The first encounter underscores the duty of political leaders to provide security to ascetics. Though the ascetics' omniscience is not directly the result of Rāma and Lakṣmaṇa's intervention, they are rewarded by a god for their benevolence. In this way, these two episodes clearly illustrate the role of Rāma and Sītā as the ideal Jain layman and laywoman, respectively, and serve as instruction for the Jain lay audiences of these texts. That the city or at least the cultivated world, as opposed to the wild forest, is regarded as the only suitable habitat for the lay community also helps in understanding the relative absence of the forest on Rāma's journey. Though Rāma, Sītā and Lakṣmaṇa settle in the Daṇḍaka Forest near the River Krauñcā for the monsoon, their stay is short-lived. After they encounter Candraṇakhā and Rāvaṇa abducts Sītā, Rāma and Lakṣmaṇa are taken by Virādhita—a clear echo of the *gandharva*-turned-demon Virādha in the Vālmīki *Rāmāyaṇa*—to his ancestral city, subterranean Pātālaṅkārapura, the entrance to which is half a *yojana* below in the Daṇḍaka Forest (variants Pātālapura, Alaṃkārapura, Tamalaṅkāra, Pātālalaṅkā, etcetera: *PCV*, 45; *PCR*, 45; *PCS*, 40). It is while residing there that they receive a request for help from Sugrīva of Kiṣkindhā and eventually join forces with the *vānara* people to attack Rāvaṇa in Laṅkā.

7 In *PCS*, she is devoured by a snake.

In the Vālmīki *Rāmāyaṇa*, the journey of Rāma, Sītā and Lakṣmaṇa to and through the forest has a transformative function, changing them from pampered young princes into hardened grownups, fit not just to battle the *rākṣasa*s, but also, for Rama, to eventually excel as a ruler in Ayodhyā, and for Sīta, to survive a second exile. The Jain poets, on the other hand, in their retellings, emphasise the identity of Rāma and Lakṣmaṇa as Baladeva and Vāsudeva, both 'half-universal emperors', and, more importantly, of Rāma and Sītā as ideal Jain laypeople. As laypeople, their habitat is the cultivated world—cities, in particular.

References

Primary texts

Bhatt, G.H. (ed.). (1960–75). *The Vālmīki-Rāmāyaṇa*. [7 vols.] Baroda, India: Oriental Institute.

Bhayani, H.C. (ed.). (1953–60). *Paumacariu of Kavirāja Svayambhūdeva*. [3 vols.] Singhi Jain Series, nr. 34–36. Bombay, India: Singhi Jain Shastra Shikshapith–Bharatiya Vidya Bhavan.

Jacobi, H. and Punyavijayaji, M.S. (eds). (1962–68). *Ācārya Vimalasūri's Paumacariyaṃ with Hindi Translation*. [2 vols.] Prakrit Text Society Series Nos 6 & 12. Varanasi, India: Prakrit Text Society.

Jain, P. (ed.). (1958–59). *Padmapurāṇa of Raviṣeṇācārya with Hindi Translation*. [3 vols.] Jñānapītha Mūrtidevī Jaina Granthamālā, Samskrita Grantha Nos 20, 24 & 26. Kāshī, India: Bhāratīya Jñānapītha.

Secondary texts

Chandra, K.R. (1970). *A Critical Study of Paumacariyaṃ*. Muzaffarpur, India: Research Institute of Prakrit, Jainology and Ahimsa Vaishali.

Clines, G. (2018). The lotus' new bloom: Literary innovation in early modern north India. Unpublished PhD dissertation, Harvard University, Cambridge, MA.

De Clercq, E. (2010). Jaina Jatayus or the story of king Dandaka. In N. Balbir (ed.), *Svasti: Essays in honour of Prof. Hampa Nagarajaiah for his 75th birthday*, pp. 168–75. Karnataka, India: K.S. Muddappa Smaraka Trust.

De Clercq, E. (2015). Śūrpaṇakhā in the Jain Rāmāyaṇas. In M. Brockington and J. Brockington (eds), *Rejection and Response in the Rama Tradition: The Portrayal of Secondary Women*, pp. 18–30. London: Routledge.

De Clercq, E. and Vekemans, T. (forthcoming). Rejecting and appropriating epic lore. In P. Flügel (ed.), *Jaina Narratives*. London: Routledge.

Dundas, P. (2002 [1992]). *The Jains*. London: Routledge. doi.org/10.4324/9780203398272.

Falk, N. (1973). Wilderness and kingship in ancient South Asia. *History of Religions* 13(1): 1–15. doi.org/10.1086/462691.

Kulkarni, V.M. (1990). *The Story of Rāma in Jain Literature*. Ahmedabad, India: Saraswati Pustak Bhandar.

Law, Bimala Churn. (1954). *Historical Geography of Ancient India*. Paris: Société Asiatique de Paris.

Mirashi, V.V. (1968). Rāmagiri in Jaina literature. In A.N. Upadhye, D. Malvania, B.J. Sandesara, U.P. Shah, H.C. Bhayani, R.C. Shah, Sri 'Jayabhikkhu', R.D. Desai and K.D. Korai (eds), *Śrī Mahāvīra Jaina Vidyālaya suvarnamahotsava grantha* [*Shri Mahavira Vidyalaya Golden Jubilee Volume*], pp. 124–29. Bombay, India: Shri Mahavira Jaina Vidyalaya.

Parkhill, Thomas. (1980). The forest threshold: Princes, sages and demons in the Hindu epics. Doctoral dissertation, McMaster University, Hamilton, ON.

Plau, Adrian. (2018). The deeds of Sītā: A critical edition and literary contextual analysis of the Sītācarit by Rāmcand Bālak. Unpublished PhD dissertation, SOAS, University of London.

Pollock, S. (1986). *The Rāmāyaṇa of Vālmīki: An Epic of Ancient India. Volume II: Ayodhyākāṇḍa*. Princeton, NJ: Princeton University Press.

Pollock, S. (1991). *The Rāmāyaṇa of Vālmīki: An Epic of Ancient India. Volume III: Araṇyakāṇḍa*. Princeton, NJ: Princeton University Press.

Thapar, R. (2015). Perceiving the forest: Early India. *Journal of Asian Civilisations* 38(1): 53–73.

12

Gembedded narratives: Jewelled peacetime tales of Rāma's exile and Rāvaṇa's domicile as alternative afterlife anticipations in the *Vālmīki Rāmāyaṇa*

Shubha Pathak

Abstract

While sworn enemies Rāma (Kosala's rightful ruler) and Rāvaṇa (Laṅkā's unrighteous usurper) clash in climactic epic fashion, their most striking existential contention occurs away from the *Vālmīki Rāmāyaṇa*'s battlefield. Each sovereign experiences rest expressed in relation to precious stones to anticipate his ultimate fate. Hence, Rāma leaves his jewelled ancestral capital, Ayodhyā, to live in forest exile on Mount Citrakūṭa, whose rich mineral deposits he likens to gems and whose serenity fosters the equanimity necessary to attain *mokṣa*. Indeed, Rāma eternally is released from reincarnation when he and his younger brothers merge in a heavenly realm with the divine preserver whom they have incarnated partially, Viṣṇu. Divine destroyer Śiva's devotee Rāvaṇa, however, keeps reincarnating—first, earning heavenly and hellish terms on dying by Rāma's hand in battle. Moreover, evanescent Rāvaṇa's rebirth bondage is betokened by his repose within his stolen jewelled residence, as witnessed by sylvan Hanumān, who, with his fellow simians, will burn the whole island stronghold. Scrutinising the *Rāmāyaṇa*'s figurative and literal gembedded features thus reveals its immediate inter-sectarian polemics emblematic of the non-Weberian *nivṛtti* (otherworldliness)/*pravṛtti* (thisworldliness) dynamics seen previously to animate the contemporaneous *Vyāsa Mahābhārata*.

Introduction

Most *Vālmīki Rāmāyaṇa* readers remember, as that poem's most pivotal episode, the epic's outsized battle between Rāma (half of divine preserver Viṣṇu reborn in human form to defend the universe, including his hereditary kingdom, Kosala, from encroaching unrighteousness) and Rāvaṇa (embodiment of that *adharma* as *rākṣasa* [demon] monarch of island stronghold Laṅkā and harasser of the world's human rulers and Rāma's wife, Sītā).[1] Far more consequential, however, for the soteriological courses that the poem plots for those opposed characters are their experiences of resting, away from the battlefield, that are couched in terms concerning gems. Rāma relinquishes the physical jewels encrusted in the walls of his ancestral capital, Ayodhyā, once he is exiled to forested Mount Citrakūṭa, where he figuratively finds gems in mineral caches and where he philosophically concentrates on cultivating the equanimity that he will need when he and his younger brothers merge with their originary deity to attain *mokṣa*. But such liberation from reincarnation is not available to divine destroyer Śiva's devotee Rāvaṇa. Relegated to rebirth after earning a term in heaven for dying while warring with Rāma and a term in hell for tormenting Sītā and others, Rāvaṇa persists in being imprisoned by his physical existence, having been observed already, by forest ape Hanumān, while resting in the jewelled palace that he had seized and that would blaze with the remainder of his island when torched by Hanumān and his fellow primates. In Rāma's metaphorical and Rāvaṇa's literal experiences with jewels in their respective settings, the *Rāmāyaṇa*'s primarily Vaiṣṇava authors vent their tensions with Śaivas by relying on the inter-sectarian dichotomy between non-Weberian *nivṛtti* (otherworldliness) and *pravṛtti* (thisworldliness) seen simultaneously in the primarily Vaiṣṇava *Vyāsa Mahābhārata*.

1 All translations are my own unless otherwise indicated.

Vaiṣṇava *nivṛtti* and Śaiva *pravṛtti* in the primary Sanskrit epics' inter-sectarian mediations of non-Weberian otherworldliness and thisworldliness: Micromosaic and macromosaic interpretative methods

The exaltation of Rāma over and above Rāvaṇa through the former's liberation and the latter's transmigration in the *Rāmāyaṇa* realises implicitly a distinction drawn explicitly in the *Mahābhārata*. Indeed, as both poems were assembled by mainly Vaiṣṇava *brāhmaṇa* (priestly) collectivities mostly between the Maurya (c. 320 – c. 185 BCE) and Gupta (320 – c. 500 CE) empires (Goldman and Goldman 2017: 63; Fitzgerald 2006: 259), the epics' authors approached dissimilarly their common dichotomous topics. The Sanskrit terms for them, *nivṛtti* and *pravṛtti*, are defined primarily in the *Mahābhārata*'s didactic books (12–13), being discussed as such neither in that epic's battle books (6–9) nor in the *Rāmāyaṇa*'s seven *kāṇḍa*s (sections) (Bailey 2005: 581).

In summary, the pair of terms parasol disparate areas of mortal endeavour. The second term, *pravṛtti*, referring to 'active life in the social world', entails a 'system' of 'ritual ... obligation[s]' that are incumbent upon people belonging to the various '*varṇa*[s]' ('classes') and *āśrama*s (life stages) 'organiz[i]n[g]' 'the ancient Indian ... cosmos as well as ... society'—a system that 'centr[es]' on *yajña* (the 'Vedic' fire 'sacrifice'), the main mode of 'reciproc[al]' exchange employed by 'humans' making offerings and 'gods' accepting them and bestowing rewards in return within the saṃsāric cycle (Bailey 2005: 593–604). The first term, *nivṛtti*, designating the 'renunciation of life in the social world', involves the 'attainment of liberation' from that cycle and thus 'is synonymous with absence of rebirth', '*mokṣa*[,] ... [a] condition of being beyond time'—such 'permanen[t]' release being realised through the experiential acquisition of *jñāna* (esoteric 'knowledge') by meditating on Vedic texts (Bailey 2005: 593–603).

As shorthands for these two conceptual nexuses, I, a historian of religions, employ two English terms, 'otherworldliness' and 'thisworldliness', that emerge from Weberian sociologist Reinhard Bendix's (1977) study of Hinduism's portrayal by polymath Max Weber (1864–1920). As considered by the latter thinker, in the view of the former, 'the average Hindu' retained 'interest in this world', even as Hinduism itself evinced 'otherworldliness' (Bendix 1977: 195). The word 'world' here refers to *saṃsāra* (the round of birth, death and rebirth), Hindus' emphases on which differed historically by births into brahmin and non-brahmin statuses. For non-brahmins, who persisted simply in completing 'the ritual duties of everyday life' and thereby possessed 'souls ... thought to endure [individually] throughout the recurrence of births and deaths', that 'immutable world order consisting of the eternal cycle of rebirths' was inescapable. But brahmins could 'aim ... to get away from the world of the senses and passions and to create a state of quiescence that would bring release from th[at cyclical] bustle of life and a union with the Divine' (Bendix 1977: 176–78, 193).

Weber concomitantly dichotomised Hindu divinity, distinguishing 'a personal God' (as exemplified by 'a personal God-Father [*Praj*(*ā*)*pati*] ... thought to have created the world in all its diversity') and 'an impersonal Divine Being' (instantiated as 'Brahman, ... a magical world potency transcending all finite things on earth and in heaven'), while linking the former (as a recipient of ritual offerings) to 'this world' of *saṃsāra* but the latter (as the desired destination in meditative strivings) to the 'other world' of *mokṣa* (Bendix 1977: 177). Yet, Weber's twofold theology is inadequate to the sectarianism expressed in the primary Sanskrit epics, which collapses that divinity distinction.

Happily, however, the intraconnected nature of the epics' simultaneously thisworldly 'personal' and otherworldly 'impersonal' chief deity is reflected better by the corrective that Indologist Greg Bailey (2005: 582, 585) sets forth while inquiring into the 'high[ly] ... Vaiṣṇava' *Nārāyaṇīyaparvan*'s chapter-long disquisition on *pravṛtti* and *nivṛtti* in *Mahābhārata* 12.327. While cataloguing the terms' appearances herein, Bailey (2005: 593–604) identifies, in relation to the remainder of the *Nārāyaṇīyaparvan*, corresponding 'role[s]' that 'Viṣṇu' plays—first, 'as the god who sustains and reaps the rewards of sacrificial activity, ... a symbol of an active commitment to the socio/economic world', and therefore makes possible other gods' ritual participation and, by implication, their other functions (such as Prajāpati's creation); and, second, as 'renunciation''s origin 'synonym[ous]' with *kṣetrajña* (the soul, *ātman*, as it fully knows its field of operation) because of being Brahman.

In the *Rāmāyaṇa*, too, Viṣṇu acts in both capacities, letting half of himself be reborn as human Rāma to quell the threat, to his kingdom and cosmos, of demon Rāvaṇa, and absorbing the Ayodhyan and his brothers when they enact their reincarnation liberation (which is available to them and, as will be discussed below, their fellow exceptional non-brahmins because of their directly divine origins). Nevertheless, apprehending the extents of the idea duo's inter-sectarian dimensions in the primary Sanskrit epics necessitates a different method. Whereas Bailey assembled many fragments of lexical evidence largely from a single *Mahābhārata* chapter into a detailed image of a related programmatic Vaiṣṇava metaphysical episode, I will piece together the distinct outlines of alternative Vaiṣṇava and Śaiva afterlife trajectories symbolised by an array of gemstone references in antagonists' opposed moments of repose in three *Rāmāyaṇa* chapters (2.88–89 and 5.8) and illuminated by relevant events across all seven of that epic's sections. While Bailey's micromosaic method provides a keen god's-eye view of divine existence encapsulated in its most key terms, my macromosaic method affords a glimpse of the entire vista within which human eschatologies diverge when the ideas behind those words are put into contrasting practices. The tendentious picture that ensues monumentalises enduring difference.

Before showcasing the contrasting flashes of Rāma's and Rāvaṇa's afterlives shimmering in these enemies' ornamented moments of living rest, I have a couple of caveats. First, when presenting those portents encoded in metaphorical and literal gems, I implement the sequences of tenses that grammatically ensue then. For clarity's sake, I place in present tenses the central episodes of soteriological concern, to emphasise these incidents' immediacy and importance. Consequently, I discuss preceding and succeeding narrative events in past and future tenses. In so doing, however, I am not making truth claims about those epic occurrences' actual historical or eventual predictive values. Any theologising in my study's subsequent two sections should be ascribed to the predominantly Vaiṣṇava *Rāmāyaṇa* poets themselves, not to me. Second, my focused metaphysical lapidary inquiry is not aspiring to survey every epic gem attestation. Such an overscrupulously inclusive study, in the service of dutiful exhaustiveness if not analytical precision, would weigh unduly many a turned stone that should have remained backgrounded, besides obscuring the salient concepts at hand. Rather, I exercise hermeneutical discretion to highlight those jewel portrayals of most ultimate significance to understanding the subtle inter-sectarian polemics that so permeate certain settings of the epic text as to go undetected and undiscerned. I turn now to the first such setting set, rendered cynosural by its gem mentions indexing Rāma's transition from courtly opulence flush with actual faceted jewels (as signalled by solid single underlining) to sylvan banishment strewn merely with suggestions of unhewn gemstones (as conveyed through dashed underlining).

From regal citadel to exilic hill-forest: Rāma's peaceful progression from physical polished to figurative rough gems

The *mokṣa*-focused portion of my macromosaic depicting the epic's alternative afterlives for mortals departs from Rāma's royal home, happenings at which composed the backstory of the epic hero's central gembedded experience. Rāma, son of divine king Indra's human ally Daśaratha, initially lived a life of luxury, for Daśaratha's capital, Ayodhyā—recalling Indra's city, Amarāvatī—was ornamented with gemmed residences (*Rām* 2.9.9, 1.5.15). Rāma receives his greatest reward, though, while preparing to make whole the divine half of Viṣṇu that he incarnates (1.17.6). Even in seeming penury after being exiled to Daṇḍaka's wilds—a transition requiring Rāma to adopt an ascetic lifestyle and thus give up all earth wealth—he establishes his ashram on pleasant Mount Citrakūṭa, which plentifully provides the roots and fruit that constitute his entire diet there (2.10.28; 2.31.30; 2.50.11–14, 20; 2.48.34; 2.88.26; 2.48.15).

Still more salient than the mountain's status as a source of physical sustenance is Citrakūṭa's condition as a font of spiritual attainment. Sage Bharadvāja identifies the holy hill as housing talented mendicants, implicitly linking with religious insight the delightful sights on all Citrakūṭa's sides and explicitly linking with right thinking the sight of Citrakūṭa's summits (*Rām* 2.48.25, 27). Rāma clarifies for Sītā how such spiritual perspicacity arises. Initially, he explains, seeing the wondrous mountain loosens previous attachments. Hence, in its presence, he no longer feels the stings of having been driven out of Kosala and having been separated from his beloved people there (2.88.1–3). Rāma's sorrows dissipate in faces of Citrakūṭa's craigs, made variegated by their multifarious minerals (2.88.5–6, 20). Although this prince signals the potential expensiveness of some of the mineral veins by likening them in luminescence to the choicest of gems (2.88.5d), the colourful mineral-laden mountain's greatest worth remains as a symbol of life's totality. Home to all manner of animals, plants, blooms, fruits and freshwater (2.88.4ab, 16bc, 7–10, 21, 16ac, 25d, 13), Citrakūṭa, whose entities compose an entire universe writ small, supplies a foretaste of freedom from rebirth's round. Thus, events around this transcendence-tending mountainous terrain form the main story of Rāma's gembedded interactions in my macromosaic section tracing his epic's liberation representation.

Mokṣa's first hypothetical connoisseur here is Sītā—seen already as Rāma's ideal devotee. Since she and Rāma consummated their matrimony, she has had him forever in her heart, displaying double the love for him that he has had for her and ornamenting him as the prosperity goddess Śrī embellishes Viṣṇu (*Rām* 1.76.11, 14–16, 18). The divine couple is evoked on Citrakūṭa as Rāma interacts with Sītā, assuming that accompanying him on that mountain of numerous, various discernible perceptual wonders elicits her bliss. Rāma specifies such happiness's source by observing that woods dwelling amounts to rulers' nectar and conduces to their post-mortem success. Thus, he suggests his own afterlife outcome to be actualised by his own celestial ascent in the extremely attentive Śrī's company (2.88.18–19, 7.99.6ab). Her presence on their way heavenward will be fitting, for she, identified with Viṣṇu's wife Lakṣmī (aka Padmā), already will have been born on Earth as Sītā (6.105.25a), who by then will have merged with her originary deity, as Rāma will on attaining Heaven (7.100.6, 10), as the ideal couple models *mokṣa* (Pathak 2014: 49, 144n.8).

Rāma and Sītā, in anticipation of their reincarnation liberation, undergo *mokṣa* metaphorically while dallying by nearby Mandākinī River. The couple's activities here and at the *Rāmāyaṇa*'s end consequently correspond. More precisely, circumstances surrounding the Mandākinī riverside sights that Rāma shows to Sītā signify events to transpire around when he is released from embodied existence, and there are seven sets of such significations pointing toward the end of my *Rāmāyaṇa* macromosaic's *mokṣa*-centred part—this finale furnishing the forestory of Rāma's gembedded acts.

First, the summary statement of Rāma's reportage to Sītā refers to this prince as the Raghu lineage's magnifier (*Rām* 2.89.19), a station that Rāma symbolically will relinquish while preparing for his final earthly journey. In his possessions' disposition, he, the current sovereign, will transfer enough materials to his twin sons, Kuśa and Lava, so that they will have in their respective kingdoms (Kosala and Uttarakosala) many gems, significant riches and contented, successful populaces (7.97.17–19).

Second, Rāma himself recommends that he and Sītā focus on Citrakūṭa in favour of Ayodhyā and on the Mandākinī rather than the Sarayū, directing her to consider the mountain and its river as the city and its river (*Rām* 2.89.12, 15). Rāma will make a similar mental adjustment at his life's end as he forsakes his Ayodhyan palace and all intermediate means of refreshment for the Sarayū's sacred waters at least 20 kilometres away (7.99.5, 7.100.1).

Third, Rāma's ultimate immersion will be patterned on his earlier Mandākinī submersions. He enters the river to bathe with thrice-daily ritual regularity and adheres to an ascetic fruit-and-root dining regimen. Likewise quelling Rāma's desires to reside in Ayodhyā and to preside over its surrounding kingdom is his accompaniment by Sītā and his younger brother and other ideal devotee, 'prosperity-increasing' (*lakṣmivardhanaḥ*) and 'prosperity-endowed' (*lakṣmisaṃpanno*) Lakṣmaṇa, who, since his boyhood, has been attached deeply to and diligently has served his eldest brother, Rāma (*Rām* 1.17.15d, 1.17.17a, 2.89.17, 1.17.15c–17). Indeed, the devotee duo—obedient Lakṣmaṇa and compliant Sītā—delights Rāma, who by this time has urged Sītā to dive into the river with him in the manner (or, better, womanner) of a female familiar and to go below its lotuses (2.89.16, 13–14). Key qualities of these subservient though regal family members will resurge in the scene of his terminal journey to the Sarayū. Rāma's retinue then will include not only Padmā, Sītā's divine source whose name connects etymologically with the word *padma* (lotus), but also Modesty and Resolve (7.99.6)—attributes that Sītā and Lakṣmaṇa, respectively, will exhibit when proceeding to their own deaths, whose methods Rāma's suicide will combine.

For her part, Sītā will have fulfilled Rāma's request that she display her fidelity to him amid the world before his palace door, entreating—with her eyes lowered, her face turned down and her cupped hands joined, opened and extended in supplication—the earth goddess to inter her for single-mindedly focusing all her romantic attention on Rāma. The goddess, having birthed Sītā from a furrow, will have acknowledged Sītā's faithfulness to Rāma by embracing her and by sharing her unexcelled comprehensively gemmed celestial throne for their descent into Rasātala (the fourth of seven subterranean regions). Sītā's bewildering earth entry will have been seen by all creatures and will have been cheered by all the scene's people and sages (*Rām* 7.88.4; 7.84.5; 7.88.9–10; 1.65.15, 14; 7.88.11–13; 7.App. I.13.1; 7.88.20; 7.App. I.13.1–2). Still, for maintaining her modesty in face of her separation from Rāma by Rāvaṇa, Sītā (whose final resting place will not have been the earth deity's jewelled seat) will reunite with Rāma in her heavenly form, as Śrī (Pathak 2014: 144n.8).

Like Sītā, Lakṣmaṇa will have attained *mokṣa* soon before Rāma will do so. Reputedly resolute Lakṣmaṇa's execution will have been necessitated by the embodiment of Kāla (Time/Death) as an ascetic gravely conditioning his urgent conference with Rāma, about Rāma's ultimate fate, on the pain of death for anyone else accessing this discreet meeting. Certainly, the extenuating circumstance of choleric sage Durvāsas's threat to curse the entire sovereignty and most of its dynasty's present and next generations in the absence of an immediate audience with Rāma will have warranted his commuting of Lakṣmaṇa's capital sentence for interrupting Rāma and Kāla's colloquy to placate the imprecation-prone sage. Nevertheless, the condemned yet condoned prince will have evinced resolve not just in accepting his permanent banishment instead but additionally in exacting himself the penalty originally stipulated for his offence (*Rām* 7.93.1–2, 15; 7.94.13; 7.95.1–2, 6–9; 7.96.1, 3, 12–15). On 'quickly exit[ing]' (*tvaritaḥ prāyāt*) Rāma's palace and heading to the Sarayū, Lakṣmaṇa will have performed, on its banks, *prāya* (yogic self-starvation), prompting Indra to carry him, in his human body, to heaven for his Viṣṇu merger (7.96.14c, 15–18).

Like Lakṣmaṇa, Rāma will proceed to the Sarayū and thereupon will unite with Viṣṇu. Yet, Rāma's *mokṣa* will begin once he ascends to heaven himself and is entreated by divine creator Brahmā to reassume Viṣṇu's form. More specifically, Rāma will walk toward the river, will transport himself to Brahmā's celestial realm and—in his human body—will combine (together with his other younger brothers, Bharata and Śatrughna) with the fieriness tantamount to Viṣṇu, whom Brahmā will equate with Brahman, the universal reality (*Rām* 7.100.5–7, 10, 17). Thus, Rāma will resemble Sītā in requiring the presence of a natural element (water in his case, earth in hers) and the company of at least one relative (for him, Bharata and Śatrughna; for her, her birth mother, the earth goddess) to revert from reborn (Rāma, Sītā) to born (Viṣṇu, Lakṣmī) divinity.

The fourth feature of Rāma's Mandākinī tour for Sītā that prefigures his *saṃsāra* liberation is the enactment of quotidian rituals by ascetics. Some of these seers, as scheduled, bathe daily in the river waters, while others say solar prayers (*Rām* 2.89.6–7). The latter practitioners' performances metonymically represent the Vedic texts that will trail Rāma on his heavenward trek, which themselves will be embodied by the *brāhmaṇas* (priests) reciting them, and will include the Gāyatrī mantra—the sun invocation uttered by boys of ancient Indian society's top three classes (*kṣatriyas* [warriors] and *vaiśyas* [commoners], in addition to *brāhmaṇas*) on initiation into Vedic studenthood and repeated regularly thereafter (7.99.8abd, 9cd). Moreover, the Mandākinī's ritual bathers symbolically reveal the synecdoche encoded in the 'sacred-watered Sarayū' (*sarayūṃ puṇyasalilāṃ*) epithet supplied on Rāma's arrival at the opening of the *Rāmāyaṇa*'s closing chapter (7.100.1c), for what will have rendered the latter river inviolate by then will have been its continual religious use by similar sages. Additionally, the bathing seers and the praying seers whom Rāma sees at the Mandākinī respectively betoken the great mundane sages accompanying him as he makes his way to the Sarayū and the great celestial sages attending his heavenly ascension there (7.99.9, 7.100.2–3).

Rāma's ensuing transcendence of reincarnation is forerun by a fifth image cluster involving the Mandākinī River, where the wind rustles flowers from the shoreside trees, and their blossoms blown into big aerial bursts and down onto the water's centre, where they float to and fro, make Citrakūṭa (the Peak Appearing Extraordinary) look as if it is dancing (*Rām* 2.89.8acd, 10, 8b). Similarly, a wind-dispersed bloom profusion will rain down at the Sarayū River and, as Rāma goes close to the water shortly before his *mokṣa* moment, the air will resonate with trumpet centums and will throng with *gandharvas* (the handsome, heavenly song-makers) and the lovely *apsarās* accompanying them (7.100.4–5).

The sixth link between his future release from the saṃsāric cycle and his current survey of Mandākinī marvels connects the fluvial and celestial biomes. Microcosmically pure-watered, shiny-shored Mandākinī and its immediate environs encompass myriad birds and other animals, fruitful and flowering trees and 'achieved' demidivine creatures called Siddhas (*Rām* 2.89.9abd, 3–5, 9cd). Macrocosmically the utterly pure holiest heaven, Brahmaloka (where Rāma will free himself to reunite with Viṣṇu), will feature all manner of supernatural beings, such as divinities beginning with Sādhyas[2] and including exceptional avians; the neighbouring Sāntānika (Pertaining to Extending) and Santāna (Extending) realms will receive all the mobile and sessile creatures that bodily will have touched the Sarayū with Rāma; and—fittingly, given that Viṣṇu, as Brahman, comprises all entities—the creatures that were reborn on Earth with Rāma (such as apes and demons) and that, too, had immortal sources will coalesce with them after shedding their earthly bodies in the Sarayū and thereby will accomplish *mokṣa* shortly after Rāma (7.100.11–14, 16–17, 23, 18–19, 24).

The emotional valences of the abovementioned transcendence instances are portended by a seventh nexus of associations, in which Mandākinī exuberances are preparatory for confirmatory Sarayū *jouissances*. At the Mandākinī, Rāma maintains that every person witnessing the waters,

2 Their name, To Be Achieved, likely ties etymologically to that of the Siddhas, since the verbal root *sidh* '[a]ppears to be a weakened form of' the verbal root *sādh* (Whitney 1997 [1885]: 187).

the thirsty animals—among which apes as well as regal lions and elephants number—that purposefully arrive on the scene and the thoroughly flowering trees that decorate it obtain relaxation and contentment.[3] At the Sarayū, on whose shores flowers will shower (*Rām* 7.100.1–5), all Ayodhyans (among them, various palace associates) and all apes,[4] having thrilled at the opportunity to devote themselves to pursuing Rāma at his peregrination's end (7.99.10–18), where waters will be within sight, will ascend to heavens. Like Rāma, Bharata and Śatrughna will go to Brahmaloka, will be released from *saṃsāra* there by recombining with Viṣṇu and will go on to experience bliss by thus becoming one with Brahman, which will overarch the other deities' happy reactions to Viṣṇu's reunification; the remaining Ayodhyans will soar to the adjoining Sāntānikas in celestial chariots, having delighted at immersing themselves in the Sarayū and having left their human bodies there first; and the correspondingly contented, submerged and decorporated apes will arrive at heavenly destinations to revert to the divinities from whom they descended, as described earlier (7.100.1, 10, 13, 16, 21, 20, 18, 24).

Present at the different points of the Sarayū sojourns and their associated endpoints will be demons, some of whom will shadow Rāma on his way waterward and ultimately will merge with the divine beings from whom they issued and thus will be liberated from rebirth, while others of whom already will number among the holiest heaven's divine denizens, all of whom will revere Viṣṇu, who—as Brahman—will overspread them all (*Rām* 7.99.18; 7.100.24, 12–13, 11, 7). The possibility of *mokṣa* on ascension to heaven is foreclosed, however, to Rāma's antagonist, Rāvaṇa, who instead must transmigrate forever because he follows the wrong god. Along the way, Rāvaṇa moves from earthly wealth (as evidenced by explicitly perceptible gems, references to which are doubly underlined) to unearthly deserts (as manifested by implicitly intangible jewels, whose construals are dottedly underlined).

3 *Rām* 2.89.18, with the necessary substitution of *paśyan* ('witnessing') for *ramyāṃ* ('delightful') in 2.89.18a made in all 15 *Rāmāyaṇa* 2 manuscripts reflecting the epic's less conservative northern recension.

4 I read at *Rām* 7.99.15, with the Telugu-script manuscript T_3, *snātāḥ pramuditāḥ sarve hṛṣṭāḥ puṣṭāś ca vānarāḥ | dṛptāḥ kilikilāśabdaiḥ sarve rāmam anuvratāḥ* || ('All the apes—having bathed and rejoiced, having delighted and thrived, and having gone wild in their cries of jollity—demonstrated their devotion to Rāma.') instead of *snātaṃ pramuditaṃ sarvaṃ hṛṣṭapuṣṭam anuttamam | dṛptaṃ kilikilāśabdaiḥ sarvaṃ rāmam anuvratam* || ('Every entity—having bathed and rejoiced, having delighted and thrived unexcelled, and having gone wild in its cries of jollity—demonstrated its devotion to Rāma.'), as in the main text of the critical edition's seventh volume.

From simian incursion to soldierly termination: Rāvaṇa's bellicose passage from literal terrestrial to spiritual celestial and infernal jewels

While Śaiva Rāvaṇa is not connected as directly to his deity, Śiva, as is Vaiṣṇava Rāma, semi-incarnating Viṣṇu, to his divinity, that demon's devotion defined him. His identifying story—part of the backstory of the epic villain's central gembedded encounter in my macromosaic's *saṃsāra*-centred section—unfolded as the demon, named Daśagrīva at birth, was stopped when attempting to take his palatial aerial chariot, Puṣpaka, toward Mount Kailāsa. More specifically, the demon monarch was warned away unhesitatingly from the mountain, during Śiva and his wife Pārvatī's lovemaking, by Śiva's powerful ape-faced attendant, Nandin, whose simian appearance elicited Daśagrīva's condescension and amusement. Incensed, Nandin cursed Daśagrīva, who foolhardily had emitted laughter in the manner of a resounding raincloud, and his fellow demons to be killed by apes similarly strong as valorous Nandin (*Rām* 7.9.25; 7.16.3, 7–8, 12–15).

Undeterred, Daśagrīva moved to uproot the mountain, leading Śiva to push down on it mischievously with his big toe and to pin the demon's arms underneath the immense stone. The aggrieved Daśagrīva, on the advice of his astounded councillors, appeased Śiva by praising him with a variety of calming hymns while prostrating himself before him and howling for a millennium. Gratified by the Laṅkan sovereign, Śiva freed him, dubbing this demon 'Rāvaṇa' (Roaring) both because he had shouted out in anger and pain once pinned and because the fear that he had instilled in other beings had caused them, too, to cry out (*Rām* 7.16.17–18, 20–24; 7.317* 3–10[5]; 7.16.25–28). Rāvaṇa, having been granted by Śiva as well a guarantee against being killed by supernaturals, confidently proceeded to harass highly heroic human kings wherever he roamed all over the world, slaying those who stood up to him and sparing those who prudently surrendered before he could mount full-scale attacks on them (7.321* 1–10[6], 7.16.31, 7.322*[7]).

5 This passage is found in 17 of the 20 *Rāmāyaṇa* 7 manuscripts representing the epic's more conservative southern recension.

6 This passage appears in 13 of the 20 *Rāmāyaṇa* 7 manuscripts representing the epic's southern recension.

7 This passage occurs in 17 of the 21 *Rāmāyaṇa* 7 manuscripts representing the epic's northern recension.

Yet, Rāvaṇa's tendency to extend his dominion was longstanding, his want for universal sovereignty having as its kernel his prior, local landgrab. It was rooted in his childhood, when his half-brother, wealth lord Kubera, visited via Puṣpaka, of which he was the original owner. His ostensible resplendence encouraged the then Daśagrīva's mother, the demoness Kaikasī, to urge her young son to work to be like his illustrious semi-sibling. In response to Kaikasī's prodding, Daśagrīva enviously vowed to equal or excel Kubera expeditiously (*Rām* 7.9.31–36).

By then, the could-be role-model already had had a storied career. Born Vaiśravaṇa (son of brahmin sage Viśravas, son of brahmin sage Pulastya, son of Brahmā), this paternal great-grandson of the most well-known Hindu creative deity had engaged in asceticism for millennia, winning from Brahmā supremacy over wealth, the concomitant position as the fourth World Protector, sun-bright celestial vehicle Puṣpaka and status equivalent to that of the 30 primary divinities collectively (*Rām* 7.3.7, 1; 7.2.4; 7.3.10, 15, 17–18). Next, Kubera had moved to gold-and-lapis-gated Laṅkā, had repopulated it with demons to replace those of old who had vacated it when threatened by Viṣṇu and had ruled happily over the newer set of citizens far more content than their panicked antecedents (7.3.24–25, 27–29).

Daśagrīva, bidding to parallel or surpass Kubera, similarly was emboldened by a boon from their paternal great-grandfather, Brahmā. To have the latter god confer impermeability by supernatural beings to him, Daśagrīva (Ten-Necked) performed austerities for 10,000 years, sacrificing one of his 10 heads after each thousand-year span except the last. Also restored to wholeness by the generous god, Daśagrīva stood then in good stead for his conqueror future (*Rām* 7.10.15, 17, 19–20b, 10–12; 7.9.25; 7.10.20c–22).

He first turned his hungry eyes toward his half-brother's abode. The demons displaced from there—led by Daśagrīva's maternal grandfather, Sumālin, whose bright gold earrings had made him look like a dark raincloud and whose glimpse of Kubera's Puṣpaka flying by had incited him to urge his daughter, Kaikasī, to unite with Viśravas and to bear their highly frightful, 10-headed demon son (*Rām* 7.9.1–3, 8, 15, 17–18, 21–22, 25)—implored newly booned Daśagrīva to take over Laṅkā and to reopen it to its erstwhile residents (7.11.1, 3, 7–9). At their behest, Daśagrīva sent a messenger to ask Kubera to cede the city to him without conflict; and Kubera, on their father's recommendation, abandoned Laṅkā and took his demon subjects to Mount

Kailāsa to create a city on another Mandākinī River, enabling Daśagrīva to lord over Laṅkā and to restore it to its prior inhabitants, who likewise looked like dark rainclouds (7.11.20–23, 30, 34–35, 37, 41, 39–40).

Subsequently, Daśagrīva constantly vexed divine beings and wrathfully hacked wonderful celestial parks, provoking Kubera to intervene via envoy to reprove Daśagrīva for his destructive ways and to disclose both his own 800-year worship of Śiva (who, satisfied, now was his ally) and all the gods' deliberation over a countermeasure to kill Daśagrīva (*Rām* 7.13.8–9, 11–12, 16–19b, 21, 25–26, 29, 31–32). Utterly irate, Daśagrīva interpreted Kubera's intervention not as evidence of brotherly love, but as an affront entailing the flaunting of Śiva's friendliness to the wealth deity (7.13.33, 35). Therefore Daśagrīva angrily killed Kubera's messenger; warred, with his forces, against Kubera and his on Kailāsa; and, by committing such aggression, troubled his demonic ministers (7.13.38; 7.14.1–3, 7).

Once Daśagrīva perforated Kubera's capital's gate (a portal composed of gold and dappled with lapis and silver), one of Kubera's warders wrested the gemmed gate from its place, flung that barrier at the invader and hit him with it. Impervious to this assault thanks to Brahmā's boon, Daśagrīva, with the same gate, smashed his opponent, who, effectively having been cremated by that demon, disappeared (*Rām* 7.14.21–24). This sight set Kubera's frightened forces to flee and to enter rivers and caverns, leaving their commander to engage Daśagrīva in head-to-head mace combat after averring that the wayward demon would be compelled to hell (7.14.25; 7.15.23, 13–14, 21). Nonetheless, Daśagrīva employed his demonic illusory capability without compunction, along with his heavy weapon, to clock and fell Kubera, who would be revivified by the divinities overseeing his stores. Meanwhile, Daśagrīva appropriated thought-controlled Puṣpaka—with its auric pillars, lapidary entries, pearl-woven caparison and wishedly fructifying trees—as his success's spoil (7.15.26–31). Assuming ownership of Kubera's vehicle reinforced Daśagrīva's link to Laṅkā, Kubera's former capital, which—like Puṣpaka—had structures of gold, was gated with gems, was encircled in white and contained trees fruiting as desired (3.46.10–11, 12cd).

The episode more keenly betokening Rāvaṇa's afterlife destinations is preceded by certain pivotal conditions. The event catalysing his soteriological causal chain, his abduction of Sītā via a knocked-down Puṣpaka knockoff,[8] was countered collectively in Kiṣkindhā, domain of ape king Sugrīva, semidivine son of sun god Sūrya and thus distant cousin (many times removed) of Solar Dynast Rāma (*Rām* 1.16.19; 1.1.8; 1.5.3, 6). To aid this ally in regaining Sītā from Rāvaṇa, the primate ruler deputed his principal minister, Hanumān, to conscript a large army of simian armies (4.35.4, 7; 4.36.1; 5.45.16; 4.36.9, 16, 33–34; 4.37.24, 27, 29cd, 33). Sugrīva then tetra-directionally sent out his head generals, with their troops, to find Sītā (4.44.7–8). The group led by his nephew Aṅgada and including Hanumān travelled south and learned of Sītā's Laṅkan location (4.40.1, 5, 2b; 4.57.22). Hanumān, son of wind god Vāyu and shapeshifting ape princess Añjanā, grew huge to make the at least 1,300-kilometre leap from the northern to the southern shore of the southern ocean to reach Laṅkā, but regained his regular size before landing (4.65.8–10b, 17–18; 4.1356* 3, 8[9]; 5.1.10, 40, 126; 4.57.23; 4.63.4; 5.2.3, 5; 5.1.185, 187–88). After sunset Hanumān miniaturised himself to dog size to find Sītā in Rāvaṇa's residence; amazedly gazed at the city's golden gates—with their lapis-lined recesses and with their gems, crystals, and pearls—mosaicked with jewels, pinnacled with smelted gold and blanched brilliantly with silver; and beheld Laṅkā's assemblage of gold-and-lapis-netted dwellings suggesting lightning-covered, bird-flecked monsoon clouds (5.2.45, 5.126*[10], 5.2.46ef, 5.3.8–9, 5.6.1).

In Hanumān's eyes, moreover, attention-grabbing golden Puṣpaka, looming like a lofty cloud, was tantamount to Rāvaṇa's might and anticipated both this monarch's loneness on his throne and the figures that this ruler and his wives would strike while reclining in their beds (*Rām* 5.6.5, 7), as detailed below—both of the king's modes of posing centring scenes of him (at rest and work) that Hanumān would undertake to observe. The vehicle's simultaneous likenesses to a terranean heaven—encompassing not only an intricate earth topped with ranging mountains topped with extending trees

8 While Rāvaṇa's return ride was destroyed by the royal vulture Jaṭāyu in his unsuccessful effort to rescue Sītā, whom Rāvaṇa flew himself to Laṅkā, the demon's ill-fated battle vehicle—despite being drawn by goblin-visaged donkeys and driven expressly by a charioteer—was described as being controlled telepathically, jewelled, aerial and palatial, like Puṣpaka (*Rām* 3.47.18–19; 3.49.10–15; 3.50.12; 3.52.11; 3.33.4–7; 3.40.6–7; 3.30.14; 3.46.6; 3.53.29–30; 5.6.5–8, 11; 6.109.9–10; 7.3.18; 7.15.29–31).

9 The latter lines occur in all 14 *Rāmāyaṇa* 4 manuscripts corresponding to the epic's southern recension and, respectively, in six and three of the 18 *Rāmāyaṇa* 4 manuscripts corresponding to the epic's northern recension.

10 This passage appears in all 13 *Rāmāyaṇa* 5 manuscripts reflecting the epic's southern recension.

topped with opened flowers, but also a fourfold menagerie comprising 1) birds crafted from lapis and from silver and coral, as well as lovely-beaked birds whose playfully crooked wings of floral coral and aureal decor seemed to be witnessed by love god Kāma; 2) snakes variegated with different precious substances; 3) fine-bodied horses of various kinds; and 4) blue-lotus-leaf-bearing elephants bedecked with lotus filaments and associated with lotus-bearing, lotus-pond-located Lakṣmī (*Rām* 5.6.9, 12ab, 13, 12cd, 14)—in radiance and bejewelledness and Rāvaṇa in electrically lustrous cloudiness suggested that he would attain celestial experience by dint of his forcefulness (5.6.6ab, 8, 11, 5cd, 7ab).

Yet, Kāma's and Lakṣmī's respective indirect and direct presences in Puṣpaka's jewelwork each intimated the chariot's contemporaneous appropriateness and inappropriateness in Rāvaṇa's possession. Kāma's (Desire's) evocation by Puṣpaka's courting ornate birds implied that the deity presided over its owner Rāvaṇa's happy love life with his many desirable wives desirous of his affections (*Rām* 5.7.66–67). But Kāma apparently would influence Rāvaṇa to be besotted with Sītā after attempting to employ his exalted chariot's simulacrum to abduct her, even though she would remain unwilling to give in to his advances (5.18.6, 5.19.4, 5.20.41). As a consequence, the demon king would seem to be extremely distant from Lakṣmī, whom Sītā incarnated, despite the divinity's immanence in the Ayodhyan princess, much as his mother, when a maiden, had looked like the goddess but had lacked her emblematic lotus (7.9.2). Nevertheless, Lakṣmī was evidenced otherwise in Rāvaṇa's Laṅkā, in whose moats floated red and blue lotuses (5.2.14). And Rāvaṇa's use of Puṣpaka—with its jewelled tribute to that prosperity goddess—perhaps had contributed to the ornateness and capaciousness of his cherished personal assembling hall, whose studded stairflights, gilded latticework, crystal-inset floors, ivory-inset coins, pearl, coral, silver and gold decorations, and countless gemmed pillars were beheld next by Hanumān (5.7.18–20).

Hanumān's aforementioned encounters with Rāvaṇa's city's ornamented entities were portentous for its inhabitants. The following day, after having destroyed the Aśoka Grove, having ripped a gilded pillar from Rāvaṇa's residence and having employed that support's centum of sides to execute a centum of immense palace-sanctuary sentries, exceedingly powerful Hanumān would allow himself to be captured by other Laṅkan demon opponents in order to obtain an audience with their king; would see his heavily jewelled palace; would present himself as Sugrīva's messenger; and would see the enthroned, lustrous Rāvaṇa in all his adorned glory (*Rām* 5.12.1; 5.16.1; 5.41.1, 11, 14–15; 5.46.45, 55, 59; 5.47.14, 9, 2–3, 7–8). Sitting on finely cushioned, clear crystal embellished with jewelled joints, the vigorously energetic demon king would be compared repeatedly to a raincloud and likened to thickened eyeblack; would be crowned with valuable, glittering gold layered with enmeshed pearls; would be decked with preciously gemmed golden ornaments attached with diamond clasps and appearing to be the stuff of dreams; would be dressed in very expensive silk and swathed in ground red sandalwood; would be endowed with sturdy arms bearing close-fitting armlets and shining bracelets, anointed with the best ground sandalwood, and approximating five-headed snakes (presumably because of Rāvaṇa's thick fingers); and would be glistening with his dectet of frightening-looking, bright-fanged, handsome, red-eyed, heavy-lipped, overgrown heads like Mount Mandara's summits when overrun by myriad predators (5.47.9, 14, 7bcd, 7a, 2–4b, 8, 5–6). For his part, prudent Hanumān, once his malefactor captors blazed up his oil-infused tail and paraded him around the city to their self-made shouting din accompanied by conch-shells and kettledrums, would defer to his maternal and paternal heritages—first, expanding to mountain size and then shrinking instantaneously to minusculeness again to free himself from his bonds; and, second, burning and razing the great, golden-netted, pearl-and-gem-constructed, sanctuary-containing Laṅkan dwellings to the ground with the aid of the wind (5.51.8, 16, 36; 5.52.6–11), which would be as fierce here (as a flame fanner) with Rāvaṇa's subjects as it had been and would be gentle (as a flower showerer) with Rāma's followers on Citrakūṭa and near Ayodhyā.

Still worse for Laṅkā would be its last conflagration, engineered and executed by simians. Their sovereign, Sugrīva, would command the strongest, fastest apes to inflame Laṅkā toward the end of the war waged by Rāma and Rāvaṇa (*Rām* 6.62.1, 3); and those torchbearers would do so after sunset (6.62.4, 6), establishing a temporal resemblance to Hanumān's nocturnal scouting of the city, if inverting the bejewelled opulence that he witnessed. The bright mountains formed by the demons' jewelled and coral-embellished homes virtually (or, worse, viciously) scraping against the sun (with their glittering, elevated apartments, aureate lunar and demilunar decorations and porthole windows trimmed with gems of many types)—after kindling, resounding with clinking ornaments and being upended—would disintegrate into cinders (6.62.14cd, 13cd, 12dc, 13a, 14b, 17).

The symbolism of the Laṅkan structures' incineration would be illuminated by a pertinent simile pair. Toward the disintegration narrative's fore, the kindling residences would be compared, from afar, to Himālayan craigs fluorescing with herbed forests. At that splintering account's rear, the city's blazing main gate, sundered and scattered by Rāma's arrows, would be paralleled to Himālayan centrepiece Mount Kailāsa's crest (*Rām* 6.62.6ad, 18, 30). On one significative level, the Himālayan references would strengthen Laṅkā's prior connection to Kailāsa resident Kubera, whom Rāvaṇa, reasserting his demon ancestors' claim to the city, ousted nonviolently, but the honouring of whose right to the Trikūṭa Mountain capital probably would have permitted his more peaceable rule to continue (7.6.14ab, 7.3.27–29). On another meaning-bearing level, the Himālayan mentions would possess Vaiṣṇava valences, suggesting the evanescence of the supremacy of Kailāsan Lord Śiva and his demon followers when Viṣṇu's human manifestation and his simian allies exercise their might. The aggressive, fiery displays that the apes would make while fighting by Rāma's side in peaked Laṅkā would be far war cries from those primates' ultimately tranquil, happy pursuit of the Ayodhyan ruler toward riverine access to heaven and saṃsāric release away from his city.

Rāvaṇa's afterlife outcomes are encoded most tellingly as Hanumān observes the bedecked Laṅkan monarch in his bejewelled bed, which founds the main story of his gembedded (in)activity featured in my macromosaic's *saṃsāra*-concentrated representation. Crystal-constructed and gem-ornamented, the pre-eminent bed resembles both the kind of celestial couch that a heaven-bound person can expect and the ornamented crystal throne that Hanumān will witness waking Rāvaṇa occupying (*Rām* 5.8.1, 5.47.9). Sleeping, red-eyed Rāvaṇa likewise looks like a raincloud (5.47.14, 5b, 7d; 5.8.9bcd, 5cabd, 6cd); is crowned with shining gold and gleaming pearls (5.47.2, 5.8.23abc);[11] is decorated expensively (5.47.3c, 5.8.8b); has been bedaubed with ground red sandalwood (5.47.4b, 5.8.6ab); has substantial arms encircled with gold bracelets and other ornaments, plastered with the best ground sandalwood, and similar to pentacephalous serpents (5.47.8; 5.8.13, 16ab, 17, 16d); and can be compared to Mount Mandara (5.47.5–6, 5.8.7). Yet, fittingly, that mountain's nature in this repose-related context differs. Here, the Mandara full of woodland flora corresponding to the sleeping Rāvaṇa also is at rest, in contrast to the active Mandara teeming with predatory fauna to be seen in

11 Indeed, the phrase *kāñcanena virājatā* ('with shining gold') occupies the same metrical position at 5.47.2b as at 5.8.23b.

comparison to the alert Rāvaṇa. In addition, that inert Mandara is invoked as a comparative standard for the Rāvaṇa compassed by celestial adornments. This metonymic mention of heaven, in concert with certain other of Rāvaṇa's atmospheric attributes in his slumber's description, accents a correspondence set between that demon ruler and his somewhat similarly Śaiva maternal great-grandfather, Sukeśa (7.5.5).

Son of demon couple Vidyutkeśa and Sālakaṭaṃkaṭā, Sukeśa, at his Mandaran birth, was as bright as lightning. But the infant, shining like the autumn sun, cried like a shouting raincloud once his mother forgot him shortly after birthing him and forsook him to have sex with his father. Fortunately for forgotten, forsaken son Sukeśa, however, Śiva, astride his bull vehicle and accompanied by Pārvatī while crossing the sky, spied the crying demon-child and accelerated his ageing until he was as old as his mother. Furthermore, Śiva granted to Sukeśa both immortality and a sky-flying city. Taking pride in these awards, the undying, airborne demon traversed the universe. Before his thoroughgoing journey, Pārvatī ensured that no other demon spawn would suffer his plight, by transforming demonesses into beings who simultaneously would conceive and bear children who instantaneously would age to become their mothers' contemporaries (*Rām* 7.4.22–29, 31, 30).

One such suddenly ageing demon-child was Daśagrīva, born with fiery bright hair nominally recalling his maternal great-great-grandfather, Vidyutkeśa (Lightning-Haired) (*Rām* 7.9.22). Even though time elapsed between Daśagrīva's birth and Kubera's fateful visit with their family via Puṣpaka, Daśagrīva's impetuosity, in aspiring to best his elder half-brother, may reflect this younger sibling's relative immaturity psychologically, if not physically. After exploiting his near-immortality from Brahmā to wrest sky-scaling Laṅkā from Kubera and arrogating Kubera's aerial palace on Mount Kailāsa, Daśagrīva was detained there by Śiva's attendant Nandin—who normally assumed a bull's form and, in spite of his ape face, accordingly was addressed as Cow Lord (*gopate*) (7.16.18d)—to prevent any interference with Śiva and Pārvatī's coitus. Nonetheless, the abovediscussed demon essayed to dislodge the mountain, inclining reclining Śiva to weigh down Daśagrīva's arms and to cause him to cry out in pain, which caused others to cry out in fright. As rewards for the soon-to-be Rāvaṇa's thousand-year obeisance, the god bolstered Brahmā's boon to the demon and thereby enabled him to extend his campaign for world dominion to human kings earth-wide.

Further signalling the similarities between Sukeśa's and pre-Rāvaṇa's early lives are similes emphasising the shared luminary imagery in the limnings of past, prone infant Sukeśa and present, recumbent adult Rāvaṇa. He has the appearance of a raincloud threaded by lightning bolts because of his gold-woven clothes and sparkling earrings, and thereby is reminiscent of raincloud-resembling and lightning-like baby Sukeśa (*Rām* 5.8.6cd, 5abd; 7.4.26d, 24b). And this cloudlike child's ruddy autumn-sun luminescence and his status as a maternal grandson of Saṃdhyā, the goddess personifying twilight, are recapitulated in Rāvaṇa's ground-red-sandalwood coating making him akin to a cloud rouged in the twilight sky (7.4.26bd, 22–24; 5.8.6).

Rāvaṇa's figurative cloudiness connects him in repose both to his enthroned awake self and to the most memorable vehicle through which he has been exercising his will. Hence, in his gemmed bed, he seems similar to a lightning-charged raincloud; on his gemmed throne, he simultaneously will be resplendent unlimitedly and raincloudy; and, in his gemmed chariot, he was housed in a car like a large cloud having an attractive gold lustre and peerless prettiness—a palatial conveyance whose loveliest of women rendered it as luminous as a raincloud lit by lightning strikes (*Rām* 5.8.5abd, 6cd; 5.47.14; 5.6.5, 7).

Also, Puṣpaka's pretties were analogous to Rāvaṇa's striking wives, who likewise shine. More precisely, their pulchritudinous, lunar visages luminesce, and their earrings and bracelets glitter with diamond-and-lapis-inset gold (*Rām* 5.8.29abd, 32, 31). While these sleeping women are draped over their ardent husband's lap and arms and around his feet at night, one of his consorts—appealing, gilded-complexioned Mandodarī—rests alone on an impressive bed separated from the others (5.8.30bd, 28, 48, 46). Her position as chief queen is apparent both in her 'brilliant' (*śubhe*) bed (which matches Rāvaṇa's, which 'brille[s]' [*śuśubhe*], in its attractiveness) and in her pearl-incorporating ornaments (which parallel Rāvaṇa's pearled crown) (5.8.46b, 12ab, 47ab, 23abc; 5.47.2). Additionally, of all Rāvaṇa's queens, only she possesses such exceptional loveliness that she, gleaming with it, seems to bejewel his magnificent palace (5.8.47cd).

Mandodarī's distinction from her co-wives is warranted well, since she, particularly, is key to comprehending her husband's ultimate fates, whose elliptical account forms the forestory of his gembedded positioning—the closing tableau of my macromosaic's saṃsāric tract. Those destinies will follow on Rāvaṇa's death at Rāma's hands. Once the future Kosalan sovereign will have shot the current Laṅkan monarch through the heart with an arrow, the threatening, refulgent Rāvaṇa will perish and will fall earthward from his chariot (not thought-steered, airborne Puṣpaka, but a vehicle driven simply by a charioteer and made for land battling) (*Rām* 6.116.82ab; 6.97.14, 17, 20–21; 6.93.27). Rāvaṇa's bereaved, fearful demon soldiers will retreat to Laṅkā, and their ape adversaries joyfully will announce Rāma's triumph and Rāvaṇa's expiry (6.97.24–25).

Even in death, Rāvaṇa will appear as in life. As his demoness widows happen on his body, it will look, as at birth and on his throne, like piled eyeblack (*Rām* 7.9.22b, 5.47.7a, 6.98.6d). The pained women, before closing their laments over Rāvaṇa, will mimic certain of the positions that they occupied while sleeping around him, clutching his body's various parts, such as his feet (6.98.11, 7–8). Still, Rāvaṇa's distressed senior queen will command individual attention during her mourning as during his bevy's nights with him (6.99.1–2).

She will exert the additional privilege of opining about Rāvaṇa's subsequent destinations. She will open her analysis by ascribing his death to his overreaching Sītā-seizing (*Rām* 6.99.14–17). Sītā's abduction was emblematic of Rāvaṇa's problematic pattern of wanting and obtaining what he should not necessarily have had. All too aware of this tendency, his own half-brother, Kubera, relegated him to the hell-bound (7.15.21). But the airborne chariot that Rāvaṇa wrenched from Kubera, that reflected its new owner's potency and that resembled the terrestrial celestial signified that Rāvaṇa had sufficient might to make right in his afterlife (7.15.29, 5.6.5c–6b). Mandodarī will suggest as much as she cites Rāvaṇa's celebrated prowess (6.99.23ab). Weighing this much-touted martial skill (which Rāvaṇa will have evinced until his own end in battle) against his sheer disregard for the decorum normally ordering his society (which—including his lead wife—will have judged him harshly for harming Sītā, whom he should have esteemed), Mandodarī will conclude that the deceased demon will have proceeded suitably in light of his laudability as well as in dark of his culpability (6.99.24ab). That Rāvaṇa's spiritual journey will have at least two termini will be implied by his corpse's very exterior. His soulless body will continue to seem as celestial as in his jewelled snoozing and ruling, with his golden clothes and radiant bracelets highlight(n)ing his raincloudiness (5.8.5a, 6cd, 5d, 13a;

5.47.14cd, 8c; 6.99.25ab).[12] With Rāvaṇa's skin reddened with blood instead of ground sandalwood, however, his mortal shell will be perceived as infernal, even as he appears as if asleep (5.8.6ab, 5.47.4b, 6.99.25de). What likely will be eternal for Rāvaṇa's soul, then, will be its traversing of different realms, never to settle in one permanently and never to merge with a single divinity.

Conclusion

The disparate lots of epic protagonist Rāma and epic antagonist Rāvaṇa are mapped as these characters dilatorily depart from the paths to their ultimate struggle. Nonetheless, the pair remain counterposed in (pre)views of their diverging afterlives. Rāma's gembedded narrative, consisting in mountainous mineral glints hinting at their richly diverse environs, readily disconnects from the actual jewels of its courtly backstory to attend instead to a liberatory, riverine forestory ahead. Contrastingly, Rāvaṇa's gembedded narrative, composed of myriad precious stones weighing down their pleasure-keen wearers, only sketches its forestory's transmigratory realms, in favour of staying firmly tethered to the sizeable, contested jewelled materials of a considerable backstory pre-enacting inexorable recurrent rebirth's turmoil. Rāma's and Rāvaṇa's differently oriented ornamented main stories, the creations of poets primarily seeking to promote devotion to Viṣṇu above all other immortals, do not adequately accommodate the corresponding loyalty to Śiva as an admirable theological option. Rather, those epic authors leave the latter task to later mythographers, the outlines of whose efforts—I hope—will appear in the theoretical interpretative mosaics offered by my scholarly sectarianism-investigator successors.

References

Primary text

Bhatt, G.H., and Shah, U.P. (eds). (1960–75). *The Vālmīki-Rāmāyaṇa*. [7 vols.] Baroda, India: Oriental Institute.

12 In fact, nearly the same compounds, *jīmūtasaṃkāśaṃ* and *-jīmūtasaṃkāśaḥ* ('like a cloud'), occur in analogous metrical positions in 5.8.5a and 6.99.25a.

Secondary texts

Bailey, Greg. (2005). Contrasting ideologies in the Nārāyaṇīyaparvan (chapter 327 and the definitions of *pravṛtti* and *nivṛtti*). In Ramkaran Sharma (ed.), *Encyclopaedia of Indian Wisdom: Prof. Satya Vrat Shastri Felicitation Volume. Volume 1*, pp. 581–606. Delhi: Bharatiya Vidya Prakashan.

Bendix, Reinhard. (1977). Society and religion in India. In *Max Weber: An Intellectual Portrait*, pp. 142–99. Berkeley, CA: University of California Press.

Fitzgerald, James L. (2006). Negotiating the shape of 'scripture': New perspectives on the development and growth of the *Mahābhārata* between the empires. In Patrick Olivelle (ed.), *Between the Empires: Society in India 300 BCE to 400 CE*, pp. 257–86. New York, NY: Oxford University Press. doi.org/10.1093/acprof:oso/9780195305326.003.0011.

Goldman, Robert P., and Goldman, Sally J. Sutherland. (2017). Introduction to *Uttarakāṇḍa*. In Robert P. Goldman and Sally J. Sutherland Goldman (trans. and eds.), *The Rāmāyaṇa of Vālmīki: An Epic of Ancient India. Volume 7*. Princeton, NJ: Princeton University Press.

Pathak, Shubha. (2014). *Divine Yet Human Epics: Reflections of Poetic Rulers from Ancient Greece and India*. Washington, DC: Center for Hellenic Studies, Trustees for Harvard University.

Whitney, William Dwight. (1997 [1885]). *The Roots, Verb-Forms and Primary Derivatives of the Sanskrit Language (A Supplement to His Sanskrit Grammar)*. Delhi: Motilal Banarsidass.

13

Train stations, enterprising priests and the deadly blows of *kuśa* grass: Reading the purāṇas with a magic-realist lens

Laurie L. Patton

Introduction: The train station and the sacred well

I first read a purāṇa in Banaras (Varanasi) in 1984. I had begun to read the purāṇic texts referring to the pilgrimage sites all around India with one of the major thinkers in Varanasi, the former head priest, or *mahant*, of the Viśvanāth Mandir, a temple to Śiva that stood in the centre of the city. While the *mahant* was retired by then, I understood it was an extraordinary privilege and was always nervous as I walked up the stairway to his residence. I had landed in Banaras after months of pilgrimage treks to sacred river sources, where I spoke with those on the journey with me about their motivations, hopes and dreams for climbing those mountains under harsh conditions.

I had become fascinated by the ways in which so many of the pilgrims referred to the purāṇas as points of reference. Whenever I asked anyone in Badrinath, Kedarnath or Gangotri—all sacred river sources in the Himalaya—they spoke of these authoritative texts, if not by name, then by genre. So, with the enthusiasm and naivety usually only possible in a 23-year-old, I was determined to read as many of those purāṇas as I possibly could. In fact, after landing in Banaras, I had become fascinated with the small wells and ponds that were everywhere in the city. You could find them at almost every turn. They all seemed to have their own legends and played a major role in the lives of the surrounding neighbourhoods (see Singh 1994, among others). In response to my request, my teacher decided that we should read the *Skanda Purāṇa*, in which many of these wells were described. We went over every small well and pond as they were named in that text.[1]

One afternoon, the *mahant* was going over the geographical location of a particular well and said, 'You know, it's near the train station.' I asked him—perhaps with too much of a cheeky sense of humour—whether the train station existed when the *Skanda Purāṇa* was composed. To my surprise, instead of laughing at my irreverent joke, he took the question very seriously. He paused for a long time and said: 'The train station is between the Cantonment and Chetganj.' After a few more seconds of reflection, he said: 'The train station exists for us now, in the Kali Yuga, as a point of reference for this *kupa* ['well'].'

I have never forgotten this encounter. The extraordinary way in which the *mahant* phrased his response has stayed with me. He did not say, 'No, of course not. Trains weren't invented when the *Skanda Purāṇa* was composed.' He could easily have said that, given he was well versed in all forms of historiography—whether Western or Indian. He understood the joke I was trying to make, as he nodded and smiled slightly before he began to think about the question in a serious way. But he took the time to answer it as a serious question, nonetheless. As I have reflected on it over the years, the *mahant* was putting two kinds of time together: the kind of time that is an idealised map of the world (including the Kali Yuga) and the kind of time that is a map of the world as we experience it in contemporary daily life. The train station was both a real referent, between the Cantonment and Chetganj, and one that participated in the sacred geography and time of purāṇic narrative.

The *mahant*'s reply suggested to me a way of reading the purāṇas—a slightly provocative way—which partly addresses some of the dilemma that many people face when reading these texts. Whether rightly or wrongly deserved, the purāṇas have a reputation for being more fantastical, more

1 Sadly, I never wrote up that research, although the conversations and conundrums from that year inform much of what I have written since.

encyclopaedic, more confusing and certainly less wieldy than their epic or literary counterparts in the Sanskrit tradition. In the extreme version of this view, they are more nonsensical for many contemporary readers, regardless of their cultural background. An example from a website chatroom might suffice. Quora is an online chat space (in multiple languages) where one can ask any question and respondents can vote the question, as well as the answers, up or down. The answer with the most votes is posted first, as the best response to the question. A reader of the purāṇas on Quora (2019) asked the following question: 'Is believing the Puranas a mistake? Are the Puranas true?' The answer with the most votes was given by 'Mukunda', who signed off 'with an agnostic mind and a Hindu heart':

> It is not any mistake. But, you have to understand that they are just stories. They didn't happen in real [*sic*], nor are they based on historical events. They are works of fiction. Some were written to explain some subtler concepts, and others due to various other causes. And as in any case, the cause may be a noble one or a selfish one. So, I would say don't take them literally. However, unlike Puranas, the early hindu [*sic*] works like Vedas, Upanishads and others involve a deep and logical thought. So, one should try to learn them as well.
>
> On the other side, Puranas are also useful. They introduce us to the rudimentary hindu [*sic*] thought. For an analogy, kids in school learn that there is no gravity in space. But, later we get to know that objects in space are actually in a state of free fall. Similarly, Puranas may be false sometimes as they are just a crude form of hindu [*sic*] thought meant for children. If you have no time/interest to know more about spiritual aspects of life, then, Puranas do definitely serve your purpose. If not learn some ancient hindu [*sic*] literature at a gurkul [SKT: *gurukul*, traditional school of Hindu learning]. And understand its depth by using your intelligence.
>
> Lastly, I would say, whichever is not logical is not true. But, that logic should be an open and unbiased one. Hence, we should use our openminded logic to test [the] credibility of the source.[2]

There are many concerns a scholar might have with this response—not least the issue of making a hierarchy of texts, comparing the purāṇas to a childlike approach that is crude and thus by implication more primitive, and putting logic at the pinnacle of all the ways we might read a text. To be fair, at the end

2 Available from: www.quora.com/Is-believing-the-Puranas-a-mistake-Are-the-Puranas-true.

of his response, Mukunda does come up with an argument that one can read the purāṇas with another kind of sensibility, and I would certainly give him credit for that attempt.

What is interesting to me is not this respondent's approach to the purāṇas, with which I disagree, but rather his attempt to create a theory of reading about the purāṇas themselves. Wherever we are on the globe, the number of different books and articles about how to read a novel, or how to read an essay, is vast. However, there are very few conversations about how to read a purāṇa. This essay is one attempt to approach the purāṇic texts simply as a reader. I would suggest that, following the train station story, we think about reading the purāṇas in the twenty-first century with a lens refracted by the ideas of magic realism. Or to put it another, reversed and perhaps better way, Indian narratives such as those found in the purāṇas have inspired one of the great magic-realist writers of our time, Salman Rushdie, and that is no accident. They do indeed have something in common.

Magic realism

I use the term 'magic realism' not to impose a contemporary anachronism on the medieval texts of the purāṇas, but rather to ask what they might have in common and to awaken our approach to the purāṇas (the term 'magical realism' is also used). According to one straightforward *Encyclopaedia Britannica* definition, magic realism is a 'chiefly Latin-American narrative strategy that is characterized by the matter-of-fact inclusion of fantastic or mythical elements into seemingly realistic fiction'.[3] The term was first used to describe painting, not writing. In his book *After Expressionism, Magical Realism: Problems of Recent European Paintings*, published in 1925, Franz Roh focused on the contemporary artists of Munich, who chose to paint dreamscapes and fantastic depictions of imaginary worlds. Over time, magic realism also came to describe fiction and was used more in literary circles than artistic ones. Gabriel García Márquez, Alejo Carpentier, Angela Carter, John Fowles, Jorge Luis Borges, Günter Grass, Emma Tennant and Italo Calvino have all been described as magic realists in their combination of everyday and fantastical realities.

3 'Magic realism', *Encyclopaedia Britannica*, available from: www.britannica.com/art/magic-realism.

And, of course, Salman Rushdie. Rushdie is our major point of reference for thinking about this new way of reading the purāṇas, inspired as he is by traditional Indian narratives. As A.G. Ananth (2017: 79) has put it: 'The concept of Magical Realism and other related supernatural elements may feel alienated [*sic*] to the citizens of the various countries, but not for the Indians.' As Rushdie himself and many others have stated, magic realism is often used to describe postcolonial realities, in that it attempts to be a literary vehicle to fuse together two worlds that are often impossible to fuse: the world of the colonised and the world of the colonisers. The only way to represent accurately the fragmented world of the colonised is through this technique, which itself fragments reality.

In a 2020 interview, Rushdie compellingly describes how magic realism works and why he chooses it as a form of narration. Rushdie believes most people think of the 'magic' in the term, but the term 'realism' has just as much weight. The approach is unlike fantasy, which divorces itself completely from the contemporary world, and unlike science fiction, which creates alternative worlds based on scientific ideas. Rather, magic realism bases itself on the reality that we know, but it is frequently interrupted by other layers of reality—such as the supernatural, the celestial, the semidivine or the divine. Magic realism also folds time—that is, it layers everyday times with other times and spaces in the past or the future, or even understandings of the past that are experienced as so 'other' as to be magical. For postcolonial writers and readers, magic realism marks the dual realities of the coloniser and the colonised by fusing mundane historical realities with counterintuitive events. It blends so-called natural historical progressions with supernatural moments and beings, even supernatural talents given to actors in history.

We can see this in so many different examples of Rushdie's work. The main character in *Midnight's Children*, Saleem, has a superhuman capacity to smell and the powers of telepathy. He reads his grandfather Aziz's mind to tell the story of Indian independence. This is the double consciousness of those who lived in the colonial era, which continues in new ways in the postcolonial era, when traditional worlds and ideas interrupt the more Westernised ones and Westernised ideals do the same in return. For example, while the Amritsar massacre is occurring, Aziz is praying, and yet in a folding of time and space, as an 'omen' as it were, he sneezes blood that turns into rubies and cries tears that turn into diamonds. A historical, and sometimes even a 'transactional', everyday event is juxtaposed with a magical, surreal or miraculous one. The scene is also a reference to several traditional Indian motifs where body parts turn into or emerge from the body as jewels.

These are intensified images of India's independence, many of which could not be woven together except through this technique, because they do not 'belong' together in the categories of the historical world. Rushdie is trying to create and represent a world in a way that makes sense of its fragments and yet still represents an experience, both of a person and of a nation.

Yet, Rushdie's inspiration for taking this approach is not only postcolonial in its origin. Rushdie (2021: 160) states that his experience of and love for traditional Indian storytelling are what inspired him to create many of his works. We need only turn to *Haroun and the Great Sea of Stories* (Rushdie 1990) to note this influence. The book is modelled in part on the *Kathāsaritsāgara* ('*The Great Ocean of Stories*'), a collection of tales that have a great deal in common with those in the purāṇas. Tales such as those found in the purāṇas have this same juxtaposition of magical and mundane and their juxtaposition is not just 'encyclopaedic'. Rather, it has the effect of startling the reader into accepting and moving between many worlds.

It is important to be clear here. Am I arguing that the postcolonial motivations for Rushdie's writing and the motivations for composing the purāṇas are the same? Absolutely not. Each purāṇa was trying to establish a primacy of a place, a deity, a temple, and in that way was motivated by understandings of the world very different from postcolonial ones. Rather, I am suggesting that there is a similarity of approach, which helps us read the purāṇas in the twenty-first century. In other words, we can get back to the purāṇas by looking at the tenets of magic realism and its insistence on putting certain forms of reality in juxtaposition to each other.

The coherence problem: The purāṇas as readable texts

Ludo Rocher (1986) and many other experts in the purāṇas have noted an encyclopaedic element to the genre. I have written about this tendency and other early Indian texts, particularly Vedic commentary on texts that used the list or *anukramaṇī* as an organising principle. I have argued in earlier work (Patton 1996) that the reason for this encyclopaedic approach was a totalising one, motivated by a wish to represent the world in its totality and its universalising energy.

That totalising motivation of early Indian authors is true in many ways. The logic of the Vedic text was the list; the various Vedic hymns and the order in which they occurred in the *Saṃhitā*, or collection of hymns, were also the order and logic of the commentarial text. In the case of the purāṇas, however, there is very little of this Vedic organising principle, yet the encyclopaedic multiplicity of topics remains. Moreover, they are accretive texts. Dimmitt and van Buitenen state the classical Indological view well:

> As they exist today, the purāṇas are a stratified literature. Each titled work consists of material that has grown by numerous accretions in successive historical eras. Thus no Purāṇa has a single date of composition ... It is as if they were libraries to which new volumes have been continuously added, not necessarily at the end of the shelf, but randomly. (Dimmitt and van Buitenen 1978: 5)

These characteristics have led many scholarly as well as everyday readers, such as our Quora participant Mukunda, to think of them as fantastical, even whimsical, at best, and illogical at worst. The purāṇas have not survived very well their characterisation as 'being about anything and everything' (Winternitz 1981: 541; Rocher 1986: 134); such a description is not a compliment.

While he does not come to a roaring defence of the coherence of the purāṇas, Rocher does note their complexity rather than their incoherence—a necessary first step in the late twentieth century for these works to be taken seriously as readable documents. He also rightly sees the purāṇas as a living tradition, always changing and being added to. He writes against the idea that, once we find the *ur*-text, and then the right 'layers', we have solved the 'riddle' of any given purāṇa. Because each purāṇa is relevant to its own age and can remain relevant to subsequent ages, a purāṇa cannot be dispensed with once it has been mined for historical and cultural information (Rocher 1986: 8–10).

Rocher also argues that this is in part because of the role of the *sūta* (or 'bard') who created the living part of the living tradition and whose arrival at the edge of a sacrifice usually gives us the occasion for narration (Rocher 1986: 53–55). We can see this as early as the *Vāyu Purāṇa*, a text I will discuss below, in which Lomaharṣaṇa is praised for his conversational excellence and knowledge. The curiosity with which the sages question him shows that the sages, too, want to hear from him and engage in conversation.

In addition, there is a world-creating energy to the purāṇas that is just as interesting to examine. The purāṇas attempt to create a representation of a world that includes plurality. We can read purāṇic texts by thinking about them the way Rushdie did about postcolonial literature, as fragmented and yet with their own associational—even conversational—logic and intentional juxtapositions, the folding of time and space.

Some alternative principles of reading

Several modes of reading follow from this. First, rather than assume that the various topics introduced in a purāṇa do not interact with each other, what if we assumed that the parts did interact and connect in a kind of dialogical momentum between the *sūta* and his interlocutors? What if we looked at this accretive style as its own approach—not as an obstacle to dating, but as an invitation to exploration and the folding of layers? Might it be better to think about the interactions—the associational connections—between various elements in a purāṇa rather than the idea of an encyclopaedia that has failed or only partially succeeded to 'cohere'? Purāṇas have the patterns of conversations and these patterns are not the building blocks of a planned encyclopaedia, but rather a portrayal of a visit between friends where one subject naturally flows to the next. (In fact, Rushdie's *Haroun and the Great Sea of Stories* is a political spoof about speech and conversation.)

Second, what if the sacred geographies described in the purāṇas were intentionally juxtaposing the world of the gods and celestial beings with the world of daily realities? What if the purāṇic authors understood and featured this plural construction of the world that combined the real and the fantastical at the same time? The assumption I am making here is that any reference to a particular geography is a reference to, or an indication of, daily realities in some fashion (remember the train station in Banaras). No matter how sacralised or idealised it is, a geographical reference is still a reference to a real city and creates a mental image as well as an idealised image of that same city (remember Rushdie's admonition that the 'realism' needs just as much emphasis as the 'magic'). Perhaps that is partly why sacred geography is so interesting: it takes the supernatural, the divine and the mundane together in a single piece most of the time. Magic realism does the same. In this way, while writing a postmodern novel of a nation is of course profoundly different from establishing a regional medieval text in praise of a sacred place, Rushdie's *Midnight's Children* (1981) is in many ways like a large and postmodern *māhātmya* ('praise of place') for the State of India and all its ups and downs.

Third, and relatedly, there is also no reason irony and humour cannot be intrinsic to purāṇas, even though we may not be in a cultural position to understand or even appreciate it. The essence of humour is intentional incongruous juxtaposition—and while many of us have read purāṇas as solemn tales with heavy world views, what if that was not always the case? What if, as Paul Veyne (1988: 84) also argues about the Greeks, the purāṇas were to be read with the same combination of credulity and suspicion with which we read journalism today? What if, in our attempt to read the purāṇas only as weighty, 'sacred' texts, we have missed some of the wit that is present?

With these principles of reading, what would it look like to try to read a purāṇa differently? In the following sections, I will attempt to do just that. I have chosen the *Agni Purāṇa*, one of the most 'complex' and 'accretive' texts, to emphasise the conversational, associational logic as well as the unexpectedly descriptive power of sacred geography. I also use one of the oldest purāṇas, the *Vāyu Purāṇa*, to show that this way of reading can illuminate even our most ancient purāṇic tradition.

Agni Purāṇa I: The coherence question revalued as conversation

The *Agni Purāṇa* is, in some ways, the archetype of the complex purāṇa. Its chapters number 382 or 383, depending on which version one quotes. Correspondingly, it has either 12,000 or 15,000 verses. Scholars have long been fascinated by discovering and outlining its layers. Their conjecture is that, since the Persian writer al-Biruni mentions it in his eleventh-century *Kitāb al-Hind*, it must have existed before that. Many argue that its earliest version was likely to have been from about the seventh century and its latest layer was as late as the seventeenth (Rocher 1986: 134–35).

As Gangadharan (1985: vii), a translator of the *Agni Purāṇa*, puts it, this purāṇa, like most of the others, is encyclopaedic in character, containing 'topics of diverse nature'. Nevertheless, he argues that there is unity under diversity. Sections are organised by topics that cohere in themselves, such as architecture in relationship to temple edifices; house building and town planning; creation and the cosmographical accounts of the universe; the sacred places of pilgrimage on the Ganges and the Narmadā; the obligations of a king; atonement for various offences; prayers to Śiva; the king's coronation and duties; the discourse of Rāma to his brother at the battle of Laṅkā; policy and statesmanship; the physiognomy of men and women; royal fans, bows and swords; gems; and the science of archery. Gangadharan names a very 'purāṇa-like' list indeed. A reader encountering the text for the first time could be excused for thinking it is a grab-bag of subjects. However, Gangadharan ends by stating that the wide range of subjects is 'most interesting and informative' and, most importantly for our purposes, that 'the treatment of each topic comprising one or more chapters is lucid and unitary in expression and thought' (1985: viii). I would go further in arguing that the transitions from one topic to another make sense from a conversational point of view and, like magic realism, follow a movement of dialogical narrative.

While it would be possible to make this argument with any of the chapters, the somewhat random example of several chapters of the *Agni Purāṇa* to which Gangadharan refers (Chapters 101–200) is a good place to start our reading process. It begins, as do so many epics and other purāṇas, with a conversation after a bard has visited a sacrifice in the forest hosted by the revered *ṛṣi* Śaunaka. The *sūta* is asked by those attending the sacrifice what are the most important things in the universe. The *sūta* begins with Viṣṇu—certainly not an unpredictable answer. In a first move in this conversational or associational logic, he begins with the avatars of Viṣṇu, then turns to the more extensive avatars of Rāma in the *Rāmāyaṇa*, Kṛṣṇa and the Buddha, and Kalki as the final avatars. The next move—to that of creation—also makes a certain associational sense. The bard notes that in every age (*kalpa*) and era (*manvantara*) Viṣṇu appears. Therefore, it would make sense that the next topic would be that of creation itself. In other words, Viṣṇu appears as needed in different ages and at different times depending on the created world of that moment.

During the narration of the topic of creation, the *sūta* describes the world and the activities of humans in it—in particular, the first king, Pṛthu. His kingdom is the first human activity. A natural next conversational step would be to ask the questions: What does one do in these kingdoms? What is appropriate human activity in relationship to creation? A natural answer to the latter query would be: praying and building temples and sacred images. In this section, the *sūta* says, 'What is the point of gaining money and wealth if one is not going to pray and build temples?' Indeed, there is a mirror logic between this section and the previous one: because Brahmā creates the world, the person attains Brahmaloka in the performance of these activities.

Then, in an elaboration of the topic of prayer, the *sūta* describes the gods to whom one prays, as well as the other gods, just as he described the avatars in the previous chapter. There are more than just prayers, temples and images as forms of holy activity, however. There is also sacred travel, or pilgrimage, as an appropriate human activity in creation. The next chapter is appropriately on pilgrimage places or *tīrtha*s. Not only are they listed, but also one of the most sacred, Gayā, is described and the reason for its sacredness is given in a story.

In another straightforward transition, the *sūta* moves from the sacred geography of *tīrtha*s to the sacred geography of the entire world and Jambūdvīpa and Mount Meru, the 'Rose-Apple Island' and mountain at the centre of the cosmos. In other words, he moves from the smaller (pilgrimage) to the larger (cosmos) sacred geography. In the last part of his sacred geography, the *sūta* describes the skies and the realm of the stars, ending with that which is above Jupiter, the constellation of the Great Bear and the world of Dhruva, the Pole Star.

From this ending in the constellations, it makes sense for the bard to move to the realm of astrology, which is in fact the next chapter. Appropriately, in the section on astrology, the *sūta* discusses how astrology governs human behaviour: when one should be married, the day on which one should have a naming ceremony and so on. These astrological times are also related to the *manvantara*s (or human eras) on a larger scale. As we saw in the smaller and larger forms of sacred geography, in this section, the smaller periods of astrological time are expanded to the larger ones. And, as the *sūta* moves to the next chapter, he reminds the listener that all the Manus who ruled over the *manvantara*s practised *dharma* ('sacred duty'). Their sacred duties are then described. Relatedly, the next chapter focuses on *dharma*'s opposite: the various human sins and how they are atoned for. Again, following a kind of conversational logic, one way to atone for sin and sustain *dharma* is through the performance of vows, and that is the topic of the subsequent chapters.

One could go on showing these transitions for the entirety of the purāṇa. While the specific reasons for moving from one topic to another may not be explicitly given, one can see the conversational sense of the sections of the *Agni Purāṇa* and the implicit transitions the *sūta* makes. Let me describe the transitions in terms of dialogical questions:

- Q: What is the most important thing in creation?
- A: Viṣṇu.
- Q: What are the avatars of Viṣṇu?
- A: Here they are and here are some of their stories. They appear in every age and era.
- Q: How are the ages and eras created?
- A: Here are their stories, including those of the first gods and the first human kingdoms.
- Q: What did people do in those first human kingdoms?
- A: They worshipped gods and built temples, and here is how to make both temples and images of those gods to create sacred places.
- Q: Where were the sacred places on Earth?
- A: Here are the sacred pilgrimages of the Earth.
- Q: What about the sacred places in the larger universe, mentioned above?
- A: Here are the most sacred places in the larger universe, including the Earth and the realm of the stars.
- Q: How do we relate to and interact with the realm of the stars?
- A: Through astrology, and here are some of the rules of astrology, including the ways in which we observe smaller units of time such as the days of the week under those rules.
- Q: What about the larger units of time, such as the eras spoken of earlier?
- A: Each of those areas has a particular *Manu* or human who is the incarnation of the era.
- Q: What did the *Manu*s do in each of their eras?
- A: Each of the *Manu*s practised *dharma* or their sacred duty and here is a description of the different kinds of sacred duties.
- Q: What happens if you do not follow your sacred duty?
- A: You must atone for that straying from *dharma*. You can also keep *dharma* by the following of vows, or *vrata*s, which I describe here.

Put conversationally, or even in terms of associational logic, as I have above, none of this looks random. In fact, it looks quite straightforward as a natural conversation that would be driven by many of the kinds of questions that people would want to ask as each topic is introduced.

Agni Purāṇa II: Praise of place as ironic juxtaposition

Second, let me turn to the idea of sacred geography and the ways in which these descriptions also embody certain tendencies similar to magic realism. As mentioned above, I want to argue that any reference to a particular state or city, even in its sacred or auspicious form, also implies a *particular* place with *particular* challenges. Sacred geography is therefore a combination of the event-like quality of the transactional world and the transcendental quality of the purāṇic divine world.

A story about Gayā, also from the *Agni Purāṇa*, is a wonderful example. *Agni Purāṇa* 114.1–41 tells the following story, which I summarise for the purpose of concision and argument:

> The demon Gayā practised penance and the gods were tormented by the heat (*tapas*) of his penance. They approached the god Viṣṇu, who was lying in the Milky Ocean and asked for protection. Viṣṇu went to the demon Gayā and asked him to request a boon. The demon requested of Viṣṇu that he would become the holiest of all places (*pavitro 'ham bhaveyam sarvatīrthataḥ*), and Viṣṇu granted the wish. Meanwhile, the gods saw that the Earth had become deserted since the demon Gayā had taken it over. Viṣṇu then said to the god Brahmā, 'In order to solve this you should go to the demon Gayā along with all the other gods and ask for his own body in order to be sacrificed' (*yāgārthaṃ daityadehaṃ tvaṃ prārthaya tridaśaiḥ saha*). Brahmā did exactly as Viṣṇu asked, and said to Gayā, 'I am your guest and I would like your pure body in order to offer it in a sacrifice' (*atithiḥ prārthayāmi tvāndehaṃ yāgāya pāvanam*). The demon Gayā answered his request and fell down. Brahmā sacrificed him on his skull. Viṣṇu asked Brahmā to offer the final oblation as the skull was moving. But even in this final act, the demon Gayā was still moving. Viṣṇu then called Dharma and said, 'All of you gods, you all need to support this divine stone. In my club-wielding form along with all the gods, I will be present on the slab of stone.'[4] Dharma then came, responded to Viṣṇu, and supported the slab of stone.
>
> Meanwhile another event occurred. During the same time, Dharma's daughter Dharmavratā was a devoted person who did a lot of penance. She was married to the sage Marīci, son of Brahmā. They

4 *devamayīṃ śilām dhārayadhvaṃ surāḥ sarve yasyāmupari santu te gadādharo madīyātha mūrtiḥ sthāsyatisāmaraiḥ*.

lived together happily until one day Marīci came home very tired and asked Dharmavratā to massage his feet. She did so and he fell asleep. At that very moment, Brahmā came to visit. Dharmavratā was torn between whether she should worship and honour Brahmā (her father-in-law) or whether she should continue to massage her husband's feet. Marīci woke up and was upset that his wife was honouring Brahmā. He cursed her to become a stone (*śilā bhaviṣyasi*). Dharmavratā protested and said, 'After I stopped massaging your feet, I turned to your father (lord). You have cursed me and I am faultless. As a result, you will be cursed by Śiva.'[5] She then performed a long-term penance. As a result, Viṣṇu appeared in front of her and asked her to request a boon. She said, 'Please, let my curse come to an end.' The gods responded that the curse given by Marīci would not end. Instead, they told her, 'You will become a sacred stone bearing the marks of the footprints of Lord Viṣṇu. Dharmavratā, you will be a stone of the gods, the dwelling place of all the gods, with the forms of all the gods, and you will have the spiritual merit for making the demon motionless.'[6] And Dharmavratā accepted this, saying, 'If you are happy with me, then may all the gods stay in me forever' (*yadi tuṣṭāstha me sarva mayī tiṣṭhantu sarvadā*). The divine stone slab of the demon was supported by even more gods as a result.

But the demon still moved on the stone slab and it required one more round of killing, of the demon Gaḍā, and from his bones, a mace was made to kill other demons. Then, after these deaths, the stone was finally steady. Gayā was angry at this and said that the gods had tormented him unnecessarily. But because of all the effort of all the deities to create the steady stone, Gayā was even more sacred than any other place. All the gods and goddesses remain there, and all the sacred places of other parts of India were also there. The sacred place of Gayā extended 5 *krośas* (10 kilometres) and Brahmā gave fees to the priests after performing the sacrifice.

The brahmins at Gayā were cursed by Lord Brahmā when they, on account of their greed, received gifts of money and other benefits of the sacrifice. Brahmā said to them, 'You will be deprived of learning, you will be greedy, the rivers will be bereft of milk and other things, and the mountains will become mere rocks' (*vidyāvivarjitā yūyaṃ tṛṣṇāyuktā bhavisyatha dugdhādivarjitā nadyaḥśailāḥ pāṣāṇarūpinaḥ*). The brahmins said to Lord Brahmā, 'Through this

5 *pādābhyaṅgaṃ parityajya tadgurūpūjitomayā adoṣāhaṃ yatastvaṃ hi śāpaṃ prāpasyasi śaṅkarāt.*

6 *datto marīcinā śāpo bhaviśyati nacānyathā | śilā pavitrā devāṅghrilakṣitā tvaṃ bhaviṣyasi devavratā devaśilā sarvadevādirūpiṇā sarvadevamayī puṇyā niścalāyāsurasya hi ||.*

> curse, all has been lost! Please be kind to us for the sake of our life.' And Brahmā replied to the brahmins, 'You will be dependent on the pilgrims to the sacred place as long as the Moon and Sun exist' (*tīrthāpajīvikā yūyaṃ sacandrākaṃ bhaviṣyatha*). He goes on to say how the pilgrims who come to honour the brahmins at Gayā, through all the right offerings, will elevate their ancestors from Hell into Heaven.

This is a fascinating story that describes the divine origins of a place and its wonders in a multilayered way. Gayā has golden hills, flowing with rivers of milk and honey, reservoirs of curd, clarified butter, plenty of food, the divine tree, the wish-giving cow and a bow made of gold and silver. The city is an idealised place that would be consistent with expected descriptions of sacred geography.

However, the origin story is also fraught with many other more transactional tensions that tend to go with a more political history. First, the result of the sacredness of the stone is because of an ongoing contest with the demons that takes many attempts for the gods to resolve. The stone never becomes steady and the deities never seem to be able to steady it (there is a comical element to the gods all gathered, trying to steady the stone on which they are sacrificing). It takes both the willingness of the demon Gayā to sacrifice himself, the willingness of Dharmavratā to accept her own curse and allow the gods to occupy her as a stone and the final killing of the demon Gaḍā to steady the stone. Like the building of any city, the construction of Gayā proceeds in fits and starts, with anger and misunderstanding, and requires several attempts to get it right.

In addition, in a transactional statement, Gayā is dependent on pilgrims' fees for the brahmins to survive. The purāṇa has no problem stating that the city had fallen from its original state when the area did not suffer such oppressive conditions. So, the sacredness of the city of Gayā is based on multiple tries by the demons and gods, multiple modes of domestic unrest and finally a fall from its original graciousness into a lesser geography and a more desperate priesthood that is dependent on pilgrimage economies and the generosity of the pilgrims who go there. This is a *māhātmya*, yes (and is so indicated in the Sanskrit text as *gayāmāhātmya*), but it is not the effulgent praise of a land with rivers of milk and honey. Gayā is born of struggle and an open description of some decay. Think, too, of the juxtaposition of the economic need of the brahmin priests with their exalted status. It is the same kind of juxtaposition that we see in *Midnight's Children*—of supernatural beings, miraculous events and difficult moments of desperation.

Vāyu Purāṇa: Reading for incongruity

The final magic-realist form of reading involves the possibility of irony and humour. I choose the *Vāyu Purāṇa* due to its age and status as one of the oldest purāṇas. Like the *Agni Purāṇa*, al-Biruni also mentions it in his *Kitab al-Hind*. Scholars note that it is also mentioned much earlier by the seventh-century thinker Bāṇabhaṭṭa, as a text that he heard in his childhood village. They suggest that, given its mention in 3.191 of the *Mahābhārata* and 1.7 of the *Harivaṃśa*, it could have taken shape in the first half of the first millennium CE, from 300–500 (Rocher 1986: 245).

The *Vāyu Purāṇa* is a compelling text with which to think through the principle of reading for irony (or even humour) that we may not otherwise be predisposed to recognise. Like the *Agni Purāṇa*, the *sūta* plays a very important role. In the *Vāyu Purāṇa*, he is named Lomaharṣaṇa, the person who makes one's hair stand on end because of his exciting narration. Lomaharṣaṇa is known for being in command of all the different arenas of the purāṇas, and he knows the epics, the theories of *dharma*, *kāma* ('desire'), *mokṣa* ('liberation') and *artha* ('worldly gain'). The sages had gathered for a long-term sacrifice in the holy land of Kurukṣetra in the precincts of the Naimiṣa Forest. Their ruler was the great-grandson of Janamejaya, himself the great-grandson of Arjuna.

After Lomaharṣaṇa describes the deities and various accounts of creation and the nature of Brahman, the monistic principle animating the universe, the sages remain deeply curious (*paraṃ kautūhalam*) about the story of the earlier sages at the 12-year sacrifice, where Vāyu the wind god recounted the purāṇa to them.[7] Lomaharṣaṇa replies with a story (*Vāyu Purāṇa*, 2.4–41) that I will summarise here:

> In the Naimiṣa Forest, the sages created the universe out of desire and performed a sacrifice for 1,000 years. In that cosmogonic sacrifice, the householder supporting the sacrifice was not a human, but *tapas*, or sacrificial heat itself, personified. The priest who directed the action was no-one less than the god Brahmā, and the goddess Ilā had the status of the consort of the sponsor of the sacrifice. The god of death, Mṛtyu, performed the killing of the sacrificial animal. Naimiṣa was the holy forest where many other sacred events occurred after the universe was created, and Lomaharṣaṇa recounts several of them.

7 *pratyabruvan punah sūtam ṛṣayas te tapodhanāḥ | kutra sattram yeṣām adbhutakarmaṇām | kiyantaṃ caiva tat kālaṃ | kathaṃ samavartata ācacakṣa purāṇaṃ ca | kathaṃ prabhañjanaḥ tebhyaḥ.*

It was in this forest, during the reign of the brave king Purūravas, that the sages decided to perform a sacrifice for 12 years. Even though the king reigned over 18 continents, he was never content, because he was always longing for precious stones (*tutoṣa naiva ratnānāṃ lobhād*). The king was accompanied by Urvaśī, the *apsaras* who loved him.[8] The king himself wanted to perform the sacrifice. During his reign when the sacrifice was being performed, it so happened that the brilliant, shining embryo[9] that the goddess Gaṅgā received in her womb from Agni, the fire god, was put in place on the mountain, and it was transformed into gold. The great divine craftsman Viśvakarman himself made the gold into the sacrificial hall of the sages—literally, the enclosure for the sacrifice. When King Purūravas saw this hall when he was out on a hunting expedition, he lost his senses and was overwhelmed with desire. He tried to take it for himself.

The sages became frustrated at this turn of events. Out of extreme devotion for the success of the sacrifice, at the end of the night, they killed King Purūravas with the *kuśa* grass (which is used in sacrificial procedures) that had become as hard as diamond (*kuśavajra*). Pounded by the diamond-like *kuśa* grass, the king left his mortal body (*vyajahāt tanum*). The sages then made the king's son, who was born of the nymph Urvaśī, the ruler of the Earth. This King Āyu was virtuous, devoted to *dharma* and behaved well with the sages. After honouring the new king, the sages resumed their sacrifice to increase their merit.

In their resumption of the sacrifice, the sages became as wonderful as those who conducted the first sacrifice and thereby created the universe. Many illustrious divine beings attended this new sacrifice, singing hymns and honouring the deities. They were eloquent; they argued philosophy of the mantras and debated with other schools of philosophy. The demons did not perpetuate any misdeeds, nor were there any other aggressors who tried to destroy or plunder the sacrifice. There was no need for correction or expiation due to mistakes in the sacrificial procedure. All the injunctions of the sacrifice were carried out. They paid 10,000 coins as a fee to all the priests.

8 Their story of love in separation is told in the *Mahābhārata* and other purāṇas, as well as the famous Kālidāsa play, *Vikramorvaśīya*. The death of Purūravas because of his quarrel with the *ṛṣis* is also told in the *Mahābhārata* (Sambhavaparvan, 75), but not as elaborately as with this compelling imagery. His death is a result of the brahmins' curse in response to his hunger for power.

9 *garbhe suṣuve gaṅgā pāvakād dīptatejasaṃ, tad ulbaṃ parvate nyastaṃ hiraṇyaṃ pratypadyata.*

Lomaharṣaṇa ends his tale by answering the sages' question about Vāyu:

> After concluding the sacrifice perfectly, they asked the great-souled Lord Vāyu what I have been requested to do by you—to describe the various dynasties of kings.[10] Vāyu then did so. Lomaharṣaṇa then describes Vāyu's many sacred qualities as a bard himself—all-seeing, having perfect control over his senses, sustaining all the worlds of human and non-human species, making beings sustain through his fire, and flowing through the seven regions according to the sacred order, among many others. Lord Vāyu was also expert in the rules of language (*śabdaśāstraviṣaradaḥ*) and knowledgeable in the purāṇa tradition and therefore, with honeyed speech, being grounded in the refuge of the purāṇas, Vāyu pleased the sages.

Even at first glance, this is a story with many layers. First, it depicts three different sacrifices: the one at which Lomaharṣaṇa arrives, the one that creates the universe and the one that Purūravas both hosts and then interrupts by his own greed. In its very structure, the tale involves exuberant layers of time that the best of magic realists would love.

It is also an intriguing story that builds on incongruities—one definition of humour. The first incongruity is that there is something so wonderful about the sacrifice that it has become almost permanent—a kind of gold. This is due to the divine actions of Gaṅgā and Agni, as well as the spiritual merit of the sages, but it is incongruous because the king sees it as part of his collection of jewels. The *Vāyu Purāṇa* presents a story about the opposition between spiritual merit, which results in the gold, and spiritual desire, which results in the stealing of the gold.

A second incongruity is that, even though early Sanskrit literature is rife with the tensions between priests and kings, sages are not known for the murder of kings or gang activities in general. Thus, that they would become so angry as to gang up on the king in response to their sacrificial arena being stolen is not usual behaviour, even from a sage who has been upset. (This would also be a notable moment from the earlier, more basic tale in the *Mahābhārata*.)

Finally, and perhaps most compellingly, is the image of the *kuśa* grass as the murder weapon. While it is strong, *kuśa* grass is usually quite malleable. Its flexibility is what makes it such a good sacrificial substance. It is used to sweep the purified areas, to weave pure mats to sit on and so on. That

10 *samāptayajñās te sarve vāyum eva mahādhipam prapracchur amitātmānam bhavadbhir yad ahaṃ dvijāḥ.*

it would have become as hard as diamonds is a wonderful incongruity. The *kuśa* grass literally becomes like a *vajra*—the diamond weapon of Indra and later Buddhist deities. The fact that *kuśa* grass in its diamond form is the method of killing the king is fascinating. Like the gold that Purūravas himself desires, the grass becomes jewel-like, and it is only in this gemlike state that it is used to kill him. Whether people laughed at this story when it was told is impossible to tell. Yet, within its solemn exterior narration of the 12-year sacrifice, the ironies and incongruities abound.[11]

Final thoughts

We have travelled to witness the energetic conversational patterns of the *sūta* in the *Agni Purāṇa*, the sacred yet powerfully flawed geography and economy of Gayā in that same text and the incongruous gang of sacrificing sages punishing a king with magical blades of *kuśa* grass in the *Vāyu Purāṇa*. In each example, we have found modes of literary composition that resemble the magic realism of a far different century, with far different authorial motivations. As Salman Rushdie put it in 2020, magic realism is 'a new-ish name for a very old thing' (Big Think 2020).

With this purāṇic journey, we return, then, to the train station in the *Skanda Purāṇa*. The year I discussed that small geographical question with the *mahant* in Banaras was during the time that Rushdie's novel was becoming famous and beloved for its careening, joyful, literary clashes of times, minds and civilisations. We often accept an Indological approach to the purāṇas and try to find spaces of coherence or forms of logic to the multilayered narratives, while we do not ask the same of postcolonial literature, embracing it instead as pastiche, creative juxtaposition and fragmentary. The ancient world still needs to 'cohere' in a particular sense for us to understand it. My own thought would be: why wouldn't the self-conscious pastiche, the joy of juxtaposition and plurality be as much a part of compiling a purāṇa as they are of a postmodern novel of magic realism? Perhaps what coheres is not the full narrative logic, but rather the intellectual traveller's or wanderer's logic?

11 I have written in a similar way (Patton 2005: 182) on the context of the use of mantra in Vedic sacrifice: that laughter must have been part of the performances and, given that the purāṇas originated in the 'moments between' the performance of the sacrifices, they, too, must have frequently involved laughter. Certainly, this was the case during all the 'breaks' I witnessed during late twentieth- and early twenty-first-century revivals of Vedic sacrifice.

Seen through this lens, we might read the purāṇas like the associations of the *flâneuse* who creates her world with what she finds, from the worlds of the gods and humans alike.

References

Primary texts

Shastri, Ramaprata Tripathi (ed.). (1987). *Vāyu Purāṇam (Sanskrit Text with Hindi Commentary)*. Prayag, India: Hindi Sahitya Sammelan.

Vedavyas, Shrimanmaharshi (ed.). (1957). *Agni Purana*. Gurumandal Series XVII. Calcutta, India.

Secondary texts

Ananth, A.G. (2017). Traits of magic realism in Salman Rushdie's *Midnight's Children*. *IJCT Journal* 4(3): 79–83.

Big Think. (2020). Salman Rushdie: True stories don't tell the whole truth. [Video interview.] *Big Think*. Available from: bigthink.com/videos/salman-rushdie-on-magical-realism/.

Dimmitt, Corneila and van Buitenen, Edward. (1978). *Classical Hindu Mythology: A Reader in the Sanskrit Purāṇas*. Philadelphia, PA: Temple University Press.

Eaglestone, Robert and McQuillan, Martin. (2013). *Salmon Rushdie: Contemporary Critical Perspectives*. London: Bloomsbury Publishing.

Gangadharan, N. (trans.). (1985). *The Agni Purāṇa. Part I and II*. Delhi: Motilal Banarsidass.

Patton, Laurie. (1996). *Myth as Argument: The Bṛhaddevatā as Canonical Commentary*. Berlin: DeGruyter Mouton. doi.org/10.1515/9783110812756.

Patton, Laurie. (2005). *Bringing the Gods to Mind: Mantra and Ritual in Early Indian Sacrifice*. Berkeley, CA: University of California Press. doi.org/10.1525/9780520930889.

Rocher, Ludo. (1986). *The Purāṇas*. History of Indian Literature Series. Wiesbaden, Germany: Otto Harrasowitz Verlag.

Roh, Franz. (1925). *Nach expressionismus, magischer Realismus: Probleme derneuesten eruopaishcher Maleri* [*After Expressionism, Magical Realism: Problems of Recent European Paintings*]. Munich: Klinkhardt & Bierman.

Rushdie, Salman. (1981). *Midnight's Children*. New York, NY: Alfred Knopf.

Rushdie, Salman. (1990). *Haroun and the Great Sea of Stories*. London: Granta Books.

Rushdie, Salman. (2021). Autobiography and the novel. In *Languages of Truth: Essays 2003–2020*, pp. 148–66. New York, NY: Penguin Random House.

Sharma, Khum Prasad. (2021). Magic realism as rewriting postcolonial identity: A study of Rushdie's *Midnight's Children*. *Scholars: Journal of Arts & Humanities* 3(1): 74–82. doi.org/10.3126/sjah.v3i1.35376.

Singh, Rana P.B. (1994). Water symbolism and sacred landscape in Hinduism: A study of Benares (Vārāṇasī). *Erdkunde* 48(3): 210–27. doi.org/10.3112/erdkunde.1994.03.05.

Slemon, Stephen. (1988). Magic realism as post-colonial discourse. *Canadian Literature* 116: 9–24.

Tagare. G.V. (trans.). (1987). *The Vāyu Purāṇa*. Delhi: Motilal Banarsidass.

Veyne, Paul. (1988). *Did the Greeks Believe in Their Myths? An Essay on the Constitutive Imagination*. Translated by Paula Wissing. Chicago, IL: University of Chicago Press.

Winternitz, Maurice. (1981 [1922]). *History of Indian Literature. Volume 1.* New Delhi: Motilal Banarsidass.

14

Textures of purāṇic transmission: A contemporary vernacular exposition of a Sanskrit purāṇa

Sucharita Adluri

Abstract

It is well known that, contrary to the transmission of the Vedas, the purāṇas continually incorporated ever more information as they circulated as oral texts for centuries. This flexible nature has led to their denotation along with epics as 'fluid texts' or textual and/or cultural 'process[es]'.[1] Integral to popular consumption of purāṇic lore were the exegetes—expounders who were trained in reciting and interpreting the purāṇas and who incorporated material both oral and written in their delivery in temples or other performance spaces. Bailey notes that 'fully understanding the purāṇa as a cultural phenomenon in the development and transmission of Hindu civilisation requires an understanding of how these texts were transmitted to an audience and received' (2010: 141). While it is difficult to reconstruct such historical recitational contexts, it is possible to gain some understanding

1 Coburn (1984) makes a distinction between scripture as immutable and story as dynamic. Classifying the purāṇas, others—such as Doniger (1991: 31–41); Bailey (2003: 139–68; 2010); Matchett (2003: 129–32); Narayana Rao (2004); and Bonazzoli (1983: 269–73)—underscore the importance of medieval purāṇic transmission through their performative traditions.

through the contemporary oral performance repertoire of purāṇas. Moreover, apart from the *Bhāgavata Purāṇa* (*BhP*), there is a dearth of scholarship on this aspect of purāṇas in the study of contemporary Hinduism.[2]

Introduction

This chapter examines a Telugu exposition of the *Viṣṇu Purāṇa* (*VP*) by Samaveda Shanmukha Sharma. As it is not feasible to evaluate his entire discussion of the purāṇa within the confines of this chapter, only his explanation of the story of Dhruva (*Dhruvacaritra*) found in *VP* Book 1, Chapters 11 and 12, is analysed. Using this narrative as a case study, I examine the relationship between the written purāṇa and its oral manifestation. Though Sharma maintains the focus of the story as the young prince Dhruva's devotion to Viṣṇu, his delivery of the myth incorporates significant interpolations and elaborations, beyond the written text. This expansion takes place in four ways: through his use of other textual sources in his reading of the *VP* such as the Vedas, *Bhagavadgītā* (*Bhg*) and the *Bhāgavata Purāṇa*; by means of an Advaita Vedānta philosophical orientation in the characterisation of the deity Viṣṇu; by vernacularising the Sanskrit narrative for a Telugu-speaking audience; and by contemporising an ancient myth on devotion for a modern audience.

The *Viṣṇu Purāṇa* (ca fourth century CE)—classified as one of the 18 great purāṇas (*mahāpurāṇa*) in Sanskrit—is relatively short, comprising six books and 126 chapters (Rocher 1986: 245–49). Presented as a dialogue between the sage Parāśara and his disciple Maitreya, it underscores Viṣṇu's role in the creation, sustenance and dissolution of the universe. Many studies exist that examine the contents of the *Viṣṇu Purāṇa* so only a brief summary of its contents is given here.[3] Of the six books, the first deals with creation, the second with mythic geography, the third details the various accounts of the ages and epochs of existence, the fourth describes the royal lineages, the fifth extols the legend of Kṛṣṇa and the sixth deals with the dissolution of the world. The story of the devotee of Viṣṇu, Dhruva, is found in the first book and forms part of the description of the descendants of the primordial human, Manu, as Dhruva is his grandson.

2 Taylor (2016) is an exception as he explores the contemporary oral performance tradition of the *Bhāgavata Purāṇa*.

3 Such as Rocher (1986); and Schreiner (2013).

Historically, both the written and the oral traditions of purāṇas were important as this genre of scripture existed as manuscripts in Sanskrit as well as their various performative manifestations in the vernacular (Bailey 2010: 144–45; Bonazzoli 1983: 263). According to Narayana Rao, the written text as manuscripts and later paper versions were never the 'complete text' and it is only in its oral extemporisation that the purāṇa 'acquired its fullness' (2004: 114). Thus, through its manifestation as both written text and oral performances, a purāṇa is to be 'understood as a significant process of cultural formation and transmission' (Bailey 2010: 145; Pollock 1984: 5). The aim of the present study is to evaluate such purāṇic transmission in contemporary Hinduism through a study of a Telugu oral exposition of the *Viṣṇu Purāṇa* by Samaveda Shanmukha Sharma.

The earliest mention of a reciter or exegete of purāṇas is the *sūta* ('court-bard'), a scholarly, learned person and a member of one of the mixed castes (Rocher 1986: 53–55; Narayana Rao 2004: 103). Later, purāṇas were recited at temples and other locations by a class of performers called *paurāṇika*s. A 'typical *paurāṇika*, a *paṇḍita* ... well versed in the Purāṇa tradition ... chooses a section of a purāṇa for discourse, reads out a portion of the text in Sanskrit or the regional language, and comments on it' (Narayana Rao 2004: 114). These *paurāṇika*s were *vyākhyātṛ* ('expounders') who explained the Sanskrit purāṇa in a local language (Bonazzoli 1983: 274). In the Telugu region, such a performative style rooted in a text came to be known as *purāṇa pravacana*, which derives its 'authenticity' from its reliance on an 'original text'—in this case, the *Viṣṇu Purāṇa* (Ananth Rao 2011: 133–35).[4]

Samaveda Shanmukha Sharma (b. 1967) is a respected scholar, orator and lyricist. He is a modern-day expounder of not only purāṇas, but also other śāstras.[5] His philosophical outlook is listed as Advaita Vedānta on some of the flyers advertising his discourses.[6] His exposition on the *Viṣṇu Purāṇa* is available as audio recordings on YouTube. There is no video, but a poster-like image of a standing, four-armed Viṣṇu functions as a continuous backdrop throughout the series. Recorded in India, it was posted in its entirety of

4 Narayana Rao mentions another tradition not based on texts.

5 The spiritual training of Samaveda Shanmukha Sharma began early in life. He considers his father, Ramamurthy Sharma, a Sanskrit pandit, as his first guru. www.saamavedam.org.

6 He considers Vivekananda and Sankara as inspirations and codifiers of the various paths of Sanātana Dharma (see: www.saamavedam.org). He established Rushipeetham, an organisation and a monthly magazine in Telugu of the same name that works towards promoting the spiritual heritage of India. He also publishes a pamphlet in English, usually a few pages in length, titled *Aarshavani*, which also publicises his teachings: *Aarshavani* 1(3), April 2015; 1(12), January 2016. Available from: www.saamavedam.org; rushipeetham.org.

11 episodes on YouTube twice, once in 2014 and again in 2017. Sharma's exposition includes a variety of background noises such as temple bells, traffic sounds and everyday din, though his voice is clear and the listener is able to register voice modulations. At times, audience responses to his explanations on specific verses, such as laughter, can also be discerned. His recitation and discussion of the *Viṣṇu Purāṇa* comprise 11 episodes, each about an hour long.[7] The story of Dhruva begins midway through Episode 2 and continues into Episode 3. Before examining his exposition of the myth of Dhruva, we begin with a brief synopsis of this narrative as found in the written purāṇa.

The story of Dhruva (*VP*, 1.11–12)

The narrative of Dhruva is found in *VP* Book 1, Chapters 11–12.[8] King Uttānapāda, the offspring of Manu Svayambhū, had two sons: the eldest, Dhruva, by his queen Sunīti and Uttama by his younger wife, Suruci, whom he favoured excessively. One day, observing his younger brother seated next to his father on the throne, the young prince Dhruva attempts to do the same, but is reproached by his stepmother, Suruci. Her reasoning is that Uttama, born of her, is solely qualified to aspire to the throne and, as Sunīti's offspring, Dhruva is unfit to entertain such ambitions. Humiliated by his stepmother, Dhruva retires to his mother's quarters for comfort (*VP*, 1.11.1–10).[9] Sunīti seeks to console the young boy. She contends that, in a way, Suruci is correct in her assessment of their misfortune, which is a direct result of *pāpa* ('demerit') accrued in their past lives. Whereas Uttama and Suruci enjoy the favour of the king due to their *puṇya* ('merit'), Sunīti and Dhruva are not as fortunate. As a corrective, she urges Dhruva to engage in meritorious action to increase his merit. Inconsolable, the young prince vows to seek a station higher even than that of his father and through his own efforts (1.11.11–28). He leaves the palace and wanders into the forest to achieve his goal. There, he encounters the primordial *sapta ṛṣi-s* ('seven sages'), who instruct him on the nature of Viṣṇu and the way to propitiate this supreme deity through the *japa* ('recitation') of a certain mantra (1.11.29–56). Dhruva sets off for Mathurā on the banks of the Yamunā to begin his austerities to Viṣṇu. This concludes Chapter 11.

7 The first *pravacana* ('exposition') series for the *Viṣṇu Purāṇa* was posted online in December 2014, but I am unsure of the exact date of their delivery.

8 Another version of this mythic narrative to which Sharma refers is found in the *Bhāgavata Purāṇa*, Book 4, Chapters 8–9.

9 The numbering of *Viṣṇu Purāṇa* verses follows the Critical Edition of Pathak (1999).

In Chapter 12, Dhruva's intense meditation agitates the three worlds. Concerned, Indra and the gods attempt to disrupt the young boy's *tapas* ('asceticism') by various illusory means. Unsuccessful, they repair to seek the aid of the creator god, Brahmā, who advises them to take refuge in Hari (*VP*, 1.12.1–30). Viṣṇu promises the gods that he will appease Dhruva by granting him his wish (1.12.31–41). As the supreme deity appears before him, the young boy is overwhelmed and is rendered speechless. Hari, then, enables him to extol his glory by touching his cheek with the tip of his conch (1.12.41–51). Dhruva's praise of Viṣṇu in the following passages is traditionally known as the 'Praise of Dhruva' (*Dhruvastuti*; 1.12.52–75). Finally, pleased with the prince's devotion, Viṣṇu bestows on him and his mother the highest station in the celestial heavens (1.12.76–100). The story concludes with the benefits of listening to and reciting (*phalaśruti*) the story of this young devotee of Hari (1.12.101–2). The outline of the Dhruva narrative as found in the written *Viṣṇu Purāṇa* is the following, along with Sharma's exposition on them.

Table 14.1 Dhruva Narrative (Pathak 1999)

Plot outline	*VP* passages	Sharma's exposition
Setting the scene	1.11.1–28	Episode 2 (2: 29.30–39.30)
The advice of the sages to Dhruva	1.11.29–56	Episode 2 (2: 39.31–57.00)
Dhruva's spiritual practices	1.12.1–52	Episode 3 (3: 0.40–16.53)
Dhruva's hymn to Viṣṇu (*Dhruvastuti*)	1.12.53–75	Episode 3 (3: 16.54–28.13)
Viṣṇu converses with Dhruva	1.12.75–102	Episode 3 (3: 28.14–37.51)

Keeping in mind that this is probably not the first time the audience has heard the story of Dhruva, what takes on importance is Sharma's delivery of the myth. The elaborations, explorations and digressions that constitute Sharma's unique comment on this well-known myth are the significant elements. The questions we need to ask are: What type of elaborations constitute his exposition? Where and when does he introduce digressions and extrapolations and what is their purpose? How do all these factors render Sharma's exposition of the Dhruva narrative similar to but distinct from what is found in the written *Viṣṇu Purāṇa*? As mentioned earlier, there are four ways in which Sharma elaborates and extrapolates on the written purāṇa and these improvisations are examined in the four sections that follow (one–four). However, first, Sharma's perspective on the significance of the purāṇas generally and the *Viṣṇu Purāṇa* in particular is helpful in contextualising his exegetical techniques.

Sharma on the significance of the *Viṣṇu Purāṇa*

Sharma spends considerable time in his introduction on the function and significance of the purāṇas, specifically the *Viṣṇu Purāṇa* (Sharma 2014: Pt 1, 0.12 mins ff.). The three topics of interest for him are the importance of the *Viṣṇu Purāṇa*, the content of the *Viṣṇu Purāṇa* and its relevance, and its relation to another purāṇa, the *Bhāgavata Purāṇa* (ca tenth century CE). First, on the importance and significance of the *Viṣṇu Purāṇa*, he says:

> The *Viṣṇu Purāṇa* is one of the 18 great purāṇas [*mahāpurāṇa*] given by Bhagavān Vyāsa. The characteristic feature of this purāṇa is that it is narrated by Parāśara and hence it is understood as composed by Parāśara [*parāśarakṛta*], meaning that he is the real agent [*kartṛ*]. This text Vyāsa has transmitted to us as part of the purāṇa genre. Like all other purāṇas, the *Viṣṇu Purāṇa*, too, extrapolates on the truths found in the sections [*aṃśa*] of the Vedas. The *Viṣṇu Purāṇa* conveys the essence/root of the Vedas [*vedamūla*] in various ways [*vividha*]. (Sharma 2014: Pt 1, 0.17–50 mins)

> As it has been stated [in the *Mahābhārata*], 'the epics and purāṇas ought to amplify the Veda'. (0.50–58 mins)

These are the traditional views on the origin and transmission of Vedas, the purāṇas and the relationship between these two scriptural traditions, along with the function of the sages Parasara and Vyasa (Rocher 1986: 15).

Second, according to Sharma, the content of the *Viṣṇu Purāṇa* extols the *tattva* ('reality') that is Viṣṇu in an extraordinary way (2014: Pt 1, 0.59 mins):

> The *Viṣṇu Purāṇa*, as the title itself indicates, extols the reality [*tattva*] that is Viṣṇu in a wonderful [*adbhūta*] manner ... (1.12 mins)

> [L]earning about Viṣṇu is itself the gaining of knowledge of Brahman [*brahmavidya*] and that is why this is a text that deals with the knowledge of Brahman [*brahmavidya grantha*]. It conveys information on the supreme Brahman [*parabrahman*] ... [T]he main intent [*uddeśa*] of the purāṇas is not to narrate various stories, simply

> describe various worlds and delineate royal lineages, etcetera. Even though it seems as though that is the case, their main function is to bring about knowledge about the supreme Brahman. This is their main goal. Thus, we cannot say that the content of the purāṇas is one thing and the knowledge regarding Brahman is another. What we need to learn from the purāṇas is also knowledge of Brahman. This is what these verses are all about. (4.03–32 mins)

Sharma refocuses the main function of the purāṇas, including the *Viṣṇu Purāṇa*, as dispensing knowledge of Brahman—a Vedānta enterprise.[10] Purāṇas are not simply mythological texts that deal with cosmological issues, but are philosophical and theological treatises that teach us about the ultimate reality, Brahman.

A third and last point that Sharma introduces in his discussion of purāṇas and their significance is the *Viṣṇu Purāṇa*'s connection to the *Bhāgavata Purāṇa*. Among devotional Vaiṣṇava texts, especially the purāṇas, the latter has more currency than the former and there is much narrative overlap between the two. The *Viṣṇu Purāṇa* is hardly ever mentioned without reference to the *Bhāgavata Purāṇa* and vice versa. For instance, the Dhruva story, is found in both purāṇas. On their relationship, Sharma (2014: Pt 1) says:

> In a sense, this purāṇa [*Viṣṇu Purāṇa*] is the basis for the *Bhāgavata Purāṇa* transmitted to us by Vyāsa. Truly, the *Viṣṇu Purāṇa* is composed to be within the same class of writings as the *Bhāgavata Purāṇa* also. That is why it is possible to think when listening to the *Viṣṇu Purāṇa* that one is listening to the *Bhāgavata Purāṇa*. Given this, you [the audience] may say, 'Must we now, again, listen to the *Bhāgavata Purāṇa* that we've already listened to?' The answer is that the *Viṣṇukathā* is the same everywhere. Listening to it is good fortune [*bhāgya*]. That is why Annamayya has said: (1.12–29 mins)
>
> 'Listen to the Viṣṇukathā, which is our fortune.
> A support like the backbone is this Viṣṇukathā.
> From ancient times, akin to the rituals such as
> the *saṃdhyā* of the Veda, is this Viṣṇukathā.
> Recited by Nārada as he wanders the three worlds,

10 The written commentaries on the *Viṣṇu Purāṇa* articulate its contents from the perspective of either the Vaiṣṇava Advaita Vedānta or Viśiṣṭādvaita Vedānta (Adluri 2019).

such is this Viṣṇukathā.'[11]

Sharma indicates that both the *Viṣṇu Purāṇa* and the *Bhāgavata Purāṇa* are part of an eternal narrative of Viṣṇu that has been sung by Nārada and others in many places and in many ways. Just as Vedic rituals such as the *saṃdhyā* have been performed over two and a half millennia, so has the recitation of the *Viṣṇukathā*; it is a ritual that is both long-lasting and spiritually purificatory (Sharma 2014: Pt 1, 30–55 mins).[12] He finds support for this in a hymn by the South Indian poet-saint Annamayya (ca fifteenth century CE). The significance of this vernacular source is discussed in section three. For now, we must note that Sharma urges the audience to understand the distinction between the *Viṣṇu Purāṇa* and the *Bhāgavata Purāṇa* and particularly the differences in the narrative of Dhruva within this larger context of the numerous articulations that make up the *Viṣṇukathā*. Though there are distinctions between them, they are all connected and united in extolling Viṣṇu. This is Sharma's rationale for drawing on extratextual sources to explain the myth of Dhruva. Texts such as the Vedas, the *Bhagavadgītā* and the *Bhāgavata Purāṇa* are all part of the *Viṣṇukathā* and the relationships between them and the *Viṣṇu Purāṇa* are elucidated by Sharma in his exposition (Pt 1).

Intertextual connections

Sharma infuses his explanation of the purāṇa with content from the Vedas, the *Bhagavadgītā* and the *Bhāgavata Purāṇa*. His intent is to elaborate on the meaning of the *Viṣṇu Purāṇa* passages by making connections to extratextual, scriptural material. The *Bhāgavata Purāṇa* is additionally important not only as a complementary Vaiṣṇava purāṇa to the *Viṣṇu Purāṇa*, but also because the narrative of Dhruva is mentioned in both. Sharma incorporates the Dhruva narrative from the *Bhāgavata Purāṇa* in his explanation of the myth as found in the *Viṣṇu Purāṇa* to discuss variations and contradictions between each telling of the myth.[13] For the audience, such contradictions are not problematic, as long as the exponent contextualises

11 Tel.: *vinaro bhāgyamu viṣṇukathā venubalamidivo viṣṇukathā (pallavi) ādinuṇḍi sandhyādividhulalo vedambaynadi viṣṇukathā nādincīnide nāradādulace vīdhivīdhulane viṣṇukathā* (*caranam* 1) (Sharma 2014: Pt 2, 1.30–55 mins).

12 For the performance of this ritual in ancient India and its attendant myths, see Srinivasan (1973).

13 Ramanujan (2004a) suggests 'tellings' rather than 'variations' and 'versions' because the last two terms suggest that an original exists and all others are simply deviations from this.

and offers a reason for such differences (Narayana Rao 2004: 104). Overall, Sharma reasons that all these variations make up the one *Viṣṇukathā* and he weaves together sources to create a tapestry of Vaiṣṇava *bhakti* that is eternal. It may appear varied, but it is a continuous, unending interwoven tradition. In the following sections, we examine how extratextual sources such as the Vedas, the *Bhagavadgītā* and the *Bhāgavata Purāṇa* are incorporated into Sharma's reading of the *Viṣṇu Purāṇa*, thereby contextualising this one story within the larger landscape of Vaiṣṇava devotion and theology.

Veda

According to Sharma, all Vedic mantras extol the supreme deity, Viṣṇu, and these are conveyed in *śloka* ('verse form') in the purāṇas. Two examples illustrate this in his exposition—the first of which is the verse used for recitation and meditation that is given to Dhruva by the seven sages (*VP*, 1.11.42–54) (Sharma 2014: Pt 2, 43.49–54.31 mins).[14] The second instance is Dhruva's hymn of praise to Viṣṇu, the *Dhruvastuti* (*VP*, 1.12.53–75).[15] Only the first example is considered here. When Dhruva encounters the seven sages on quitting the palace, they advise him that Viṣṇu is the one who can grant him the highest station that he seeks. Asked specifically how to propitiate Viṣṇu, the sages impart to Dhruva a verse for recitation while meditating:

> *hiraṇyagarbhapuruṣapradhānavyaktarūpiṇe* |
> *oṃ namo vāsudevāya śuddhajñānasvabhāvine* ||
>
> [Oṃ, obeisance to Vāsudeva, who is the essence of pure knowledge,
> Whose form is manifest as matter, spirit and Hiraṇyagarbha.]
> (*VP*, 1.11.54)

According to Sharma, this verse has the form of a mantra—that is, it is a mantra in the form of a *śloka*. Moreover, Hiraṇyagarbha—identified in the passage as a form of the ultimate reality, Viṣṇu—is also acknowledged as the very same deity extolled by the Gāyatrī mantra from *Ṛg Veda* 3.62.10: 'May we obtain that excellent effulgence of the god Savitṛ, on whom, may our minds reflect' (*tat savitur vareṇyaṃ bhargo devasya dhīmahi* | *dhiyo yo naḥ*

14 Sharma then identifies this passage as the *dvādaśākṣara* mantra: *oṃ naṃo bhagavate vāsudevāya*. In the *Bhāgavata Purāṇa*, instead of the seven sages, Nārada bestows this exact mantra to Dhruva (*BhP*, 4.8.54).

15 The *Dhruvastuti* is a reformatted as *Puruṣa Sūkta* (Sharma 2014: Pt 3, 16.50–28.01 mins).

pracodayāt ||). This important mantra composed in the Gāyatrī metre and dedicated to the Vedic deity Savitṛ, the sun god, is repeated daily to extol that deity, the source of life and illumination.[16] For Sharma, Hiraṇyagarbha in the *Viṣṇu Purāṇa* passage is a reference to the god Savitṛ of the *Ṛg Veda*, who is ultimately Viṣṇu:

> Hiraṇyagarbha in the *Viṣṇu Purāṇa* passage means that the reality to be known through the Gāyatrī mantra is what is being stated here. Hiraṇyagarbha means 'may we obtain the excellent effulgence of Savitṛ/Sun'—that one who resides in the radiant solar orb that is Hiraṇyagarbha, meaning that it is Nārāyaṇa who resides inside. *Hiraṇya* [golden] means effulgence [*tejas*]—that is, one who is the cause or root [*mūla*] of effulgence [*tejas*]. Here, effulgence [*tejas*] means consciousness [*caitanya*]. The one who is the root of consciousness is Hiraṇyagarbha, meaning Nārāyaṇa ... [W]hat is his essence [*svabhāva*]? It is knowledge that is pure, without any defects and as such he is omniscient [*sarvajñatva*]. Here, pure knowledge [*śuddhajñāna*] means light [*prakāśa* or *bharga*] and thus connects again with Hiraṇyagarbha in the previous line. (Sharma 2014: Pt 2, 53.04–54.31 mins)

The two terms from the *Viṣṇu Purāṇa* passage that Sharma unpacks are 'Hiraṇyagarbha' and 'one whose essence is pure knowledge [*śuddhajñānasvabhāva*]', which refer to Viṣṇu. According to Sharma, *hiraṇya* ('golden') of Hiranyagarbha is a reference to the golden solar orb that is the Vedic god Savitṛ. However, both Hiraṇygarbha and Savitṛ are ultimately Nārāyaṇa. The effulgence of the solar deity, which is the source of life and illumination, is identified as *tejas*, which in turn can mean 'consciousness'. Moreover, Viṣṇu's essence is pure knowledge (*śuddhajñāna*), which Sharma interprets as 'illumination'/'light' and thus sees a connection to the golden (*hiraṇya*) effulgence of Hiraṇyagarbha. Thus, the Vedic deity Savitṛ, Hiraṇyagarbha and Viṣṇu are one and the same and have been hymned in these respective scriptures that form one *Viṣṇukathā*. While in ancient times it was the life-giving power of Viṣṇu that was praised, this effulgence is nothing more than consciousness that is the essence of Viṣṇu, which animates/illuminates us from within.

16 See Gonda (1963) for further discussion of this mantra.

Bhagavadgītā

Sharma also draws from the *Bhagavadgīta* to explain passages of the *Viṣṇu Purāṇa* that address the nature of devotion and the various types of devotees of Viṣṇu (Sharma 2014: Pt 3, 0.41–3.35 mins).[17] In the *Viṣṇu Purāṇa*, unsuccessful initially in his quest for the highest station, Dhruva intensifies his ascetic practice to please Viṣṇu:

> *ātmany aśeṣadeveśaṃ sthitaṃ viṣṇum amanyata* ||
> *ananyacetasas tasya dhyāyato bhagavān hariḥ* |
> *sarvabhūtagato vipra sarvabhāvagato 'bhavat* ||
> *manasy avasthite tasya viṣṇau maitreya yoginaḥ* |
>
> [He contemplated Viṣṇu, the chief god of all, established in himself, O sage, contemplating thus, with undivided thought, the Lord Hari who is in all beings and in all natures. Such a Viṣṇu being present in his (Dhruva's) mind, Maitreya, the earth, supporter of existence could not sustain the weight of the yogin.] (*VP*, 1.12.6cd–8ab)

Sharma elaborates on the nature of Dhruva's devotion to Viṣṇu (2014: Pt 3, 0.57–2.00 mins):

> In whatever way you worship Viṣṇu, the results will be comparable to that practice. Usually, we understand the name Dhruva as a symbol for great perseverance [Tel., *mahāpaṭṭudala saṃketa*]. For Dhruva, the quest for the highest station has led him on the path of Bhagavān. He is set to attain Bhagavān and not anything worldly [*bhautika*]. Some people are led to God because they wish to reach the highest station; others, as a refuge from suffering. When does God come into the mind of the elephant Gajendra? When he is caught in the jaws of a crocodile [a reference to a *Bhāgavata Purāṇa* narrative]. For some, when they are suffering a lot, they think of God. For others, if they want something, they think of God. (Pt 2, 1.47 mins)

The nature of devotion of this young boy has parallels in the *Bhagavadgītā*, in which Kṛṣṇa clarifies the different types of devotees who turn to him: 'Benevolent men of four kinds worship me, O Arjuna: the afflicted [*ārta*], the one desirous of knowledge [*jijñāsu*], the one who desires wealth [*arthārthin*] and the man of wisdom [*jñānin*], O best among the Bharatas' (*caturvidhā bhajante mām janāḥ sukṛtino' rjuna* | *ārto jijñāsur arthārthīm jñānī ca bharatarṣabha* ||; *Bhg*, 7.16).

17 For more on the *Bhagavadgīta*, see Malinar (2007).

According to Sharma, Dhruva, as one who desires the highest station, is one who desires wealth (*arthārthin*)—one of the four types of devotees as categorised by Kṛṣṇa in the *Bhagavadgītā* (2014: Pt 3, 2.00 mins). Though the sages inform Dhruva that meditation and ascetic practice utilising the mantra can lead to liberation, the young prince is initially only intent on acquiring the highest station. This changes later when, having beheld the divine form of Viṣṇu, he realises that he does not have any desires that remain to be fulfilled (*VP*, 1.12.75).

To explain the term for fixed concentration (*ananyacetas*) from *VP* 1.12.7, which refers to the way in which Dhruva meditates, Sharma (2014: Pt 3, 3.11–35 mins) again cites the *Bhagavadgītā*, in which Kṛṣṇa says: 'Those men who worship me, directing their minds to me without other thoughts [*ananya cintayanta*], for them, who are eternally steadfast, I bring to them prosperity' (*ananyaś cintayanto mām ye janāḥ paryupāsate | teṣām nityābhiyuktānām yogakṣemam vahāmy aham ||*; *Bhg*, 9.22).

The term contemplating with 'fixed concentration' (*ananayacetas*) in *VP* 1.12.7 is compared with 'without other thoughts' (*ananya cintayanta*) from the *Bhagavadgītā*. The nature of Dhruva's devotion is focused and uninterrupted; it is a supreme kind of devotion that Kṛṣṇa indicates is most pleasing to him and leads to favourable results for the devotee. Turning to the *Bhagavadgītā*, where Hari himself comments on the nature of devotion and devotee, Sharma classifies Dhruva accordingly. The young boy not only follows the advice of the sages, but also his spiritual practice and mental orientation are in line with what the Lord himself has stated is superior in his dialogue with the hero Arjuna.

Bhāgavata Purāṇa

While the references to the Vedas and the *Bhagavadgītā* mainly extrapolate the content of the *Viṣṇu Purāṇa* passages, Sharma's reference to the *Bhāgavata Purāṇa* is motivated by the fact that it, too, includes a version of the Dhruva narrative. Sharma engages with the differences in the Dhruva storyline between the *Viṣṇu Purāṇa* and the *Bhāgavata Purāṇa* to discuss and offer plausible explanations for their existence. Sometimes he refers to the Sanskrit *Bhāgavata Purāṇa* (ca tenth century) and at others he refers to the Telugu *Bhagavatamu* by Bammera Potana (ca fourteenth century). The latter instances and their significance are addressed in the section on the vernacularising of the *VP* (Pt 3). The provenance of the Sanskrit *Bhāgavata*

Purāṇa dated to about the tenth century CE is South India.[18] Devoted to Kṛṣṇa mythology, it is influenced by the emotional poetry of the Tamil Āḻvār poet-saints. It is also deliberately composed utilising Vedic Sanskrit to heighten its authority and legitimacy (van Buitenen 1988). The Dhruva narrative is found in Book 4, Chapters 8–9. This telling is different from that of the *Viṣṇu Purāṇa* and the audience is aware of this.

In the introduction to his exposition of the Dhruva story, Sharma mentions its *Bhāgavata Purāṇa* counterpart:

> Now, the story that we have heard and known from the *Bhāgavata Purāṇa* is also being stated here [in the *Viṣṇu Purāṇa*]. As soon as we mention the names Priyavrata and Uttānapāda [sons of Manu], people know that it is the story of Dhruva. But there are some differences between the two. We are most familiar with the one stated in the *Bhāgavata Purāṇa*. But we shouldn't err in thinking this is the correct one or the one stated in the *Viṣṇu Purāṇa* is the right one. The story is stated one way in the *Bhāgavata Purāṇa* and in another way in the *Viṣṇu Purāṇa*, but in both cases, it is the narrative of Dhruva only. We have told and retold this myth based on the *Bhāgavata Purāṇa*, but now, by listening to the one that is found in the *Viṣṇu Purāṇa*, we will once again become purified. (Sharma 2014: Pt 2, 29.30–30.43 mins)

The narrative of Dhruva found in the *Bhāgavata Purāṇa* that Sharma relates may be more familiar to the audience, but both are 'the narrative of Dhruva only'. Regardless of the differences, each time this story is heard from either of the purāṇas, it becomes a spiritually purificatory event.

In addition to this mention in his introduction, there is another instance where Sharma invokes the *Bhāgavata Purāṇa* to underscore the relationship between the two purāṇas (2014: Pt 2, 34.13 mins ff.). He does not recite the passages from the *Bhāgavata Purāṇa*, but simply refers to the differences. Hurt by his stepmother, Dhruva repairs to his mother's quarters for consolation. When Dhruva confides to his mother about his father's and stepmother's treatment, she concurs with Suruci and says that, indeed, Dhruva is unlucky to have been born of her and that, lacking merit, they are both treated unjustly by the king. But she offers an antidote to her son's pain:

18 For more on this purāṇa, see Rocher (1986: 138–51). Theodor (2020); and Gupta et al. (2013) could also be of interest.

'If your grief is excessive due to the words of Suruci, then, make an effort to increase merit which yields all kinds of benefits. Be amiable, be virtuous, be a friend, be devoted to beneficence towards all creatures'[19] (*VP*, 1.11.22–23ab).

To all this, Dhruva responds:

amba yat tvam idaṃ prāha praśamāya vaco mama |
naitad durvacasā bhinne hṛdaye mama tiṣṭhati ||
so 'haṃ tathā yatiṣyāmi yathā sarvottamottamam |
sthānaṃ prāpsyāmy aśeṣāṇāṃ jagatām abhipūjitam ||

[Mother, the advice which you addressed to me, to calm me, it does not find a place in my heart broken by harsh speech. I will strive for and obtain that which is the highest of all stations, revered by the whole world.] (*VP*, 1.11.24–25)

There are two differences in the *Bhāgavata Purāṇa* account from that in the *Viṣṇu Purāṇa*. In the *Bhāgavata Purāṇa*, Dhruva's mother does not encourage him to engage in meritorious actions and, second, Dhruva's response to his mother is different. She does not advise her son to engage in meritorious actions, but instead to take refuge in Viṣṇu:

tam eva vatsāśraya bhṛtyavatsalaṃ mumukṣubhir mṛgyapadābjapaddhatim |
ananyabhāve nijadharmabhāvite manasy avasthāpya bhajasva pūruṣam ||

[Son, take refuge in him alone, who cherishes his devotees and the path to whose lotus-feet is striven for by those who seek liberation. Having established him in your mind that is purified by one's dharma, without any other thought, worship the Supreme Person.] (*BhP*, 4.8.22)

This is quite different from the *Viṣṇu Purāṇa*, in which the discussion with his mother is couched in the context of merit and demerit only, though ultimately, the sages do advise Dhruva to take refuge in Viṣṇu.

The second difference between the *Viṣṇu Purāṇa* and the *Bhāgavata Purāṇa* is the young prince's response to his mother. In the *Viṣṇu Purāṇa*, though Dhruva is not satisfied with his mother's advice, he leaves the palace intent on

19 *yadi ced duḥkham atyarthaṃ surucyā vacanāt tava | tat puṇyopacaye yatnaṃ kuru sarvaphalaprade || suśīlo bhava dharmātmā maitraḥ prāṇihite rataḥ |*

attaining the highest station by his own hard work (*VP*, 1.11.24–25). In the *Bhāgavata Purāṇa* on the other hand, Dhruva shows supreme restraint and, 'having controlled his self by his self', he sets out to take refuge in Viṣṇu as his mother suggests: 'Having heard the words of his mother and conversed in this way, on the acquisition of the goal, having restrained his self by his self, he resolutely left his father's kingdom' (*evaṃ sañjalpitaṃ mātur ākarṇyārthāgamaṃ vacaḥ* | *sanniyamyātmanātmānaṃ niścakrāma pituḥ purāt* ||; *BhP*, 4.8.24).

In the *Bhāgavata Purāṇa*, Dhruva does not admit that his heart is broken by his stepmother's harsh words and that he does not find his mother's words consoling in the least. Sharma comments on these differences:

> Now, there are slight differences between the *Bhāgavata Purāṇa* and the *Viṣṇu Purāṇa*. To explore these differences themselves, we have begun this exposition. Even though the story is known already, we still like to listen to it because it is the *Viṣṇukathā*. There are some teachings inherent in exploring these differences. There is no need to break our heads over why such differences exist in the first place. Let's try to be open to what great teachings this purāṇa [*Viṣṇu Purāṇa*] has to teach us. Moreover, for the *Bhāgavata Purāṇa*, the *Viṣṇu Purāṇa* is the source [*mūla*]. The *Bhāgavata Purāṇa* was written later by Vyāsa, for he did not write all purāṇic material, he only arranged what was already existent. We cannot forget that this *Viṣṇu Purāṇa* is recited by Vyāsa's father, Parāśara [implying its precedence to the *Bhāgavata Purāṇa*]. That is why what is found here is stated in a brief [*yathātatha*] manner. This very purāṇa, in order to be enjoyed through *rasa* and shaped with an understanding of devotion, Vyāsa has handed to us in the form of the *Bhāgavata Purāṇa*.[20] In order to convey at every step the experience of Viṣṇu *rasa*, a particular style [*śailini*] is resorted to by Vyāsa. Therefore, this is the difference between the two purāṇas. We should not think of these versions as mutually contradictory [*parasaparaviruddha*] but rather as mutually differenced [*parasparavaividya*]. Each has its own uniqueness [*pratyekata*]. (Sharma 2014: Pt 2, 34.13–35.40 mins)

Sharma provides reasons to legitimise the *Viṣṇu Purāṇa*—first, that it is prior to the *Bhāgavata Purāṇa* and therefore influences it. Second, as an earlier account of Viṣṇu, the content of the *Viṣṇu Purāṇa* is given in a concise (*yathātatha*) way. Third, the *Bhāgavata Purāṇa* amends the content of the

20 Tel.: *rasaramyamugā maḷḷī bhaktiprabodakamugā malachi bhāgavatam dvārā añdiñcāḍu* (Sharma 2014: Pt 2, 34.13–35.40 mins).

Viṣṇu Purāṇa with a novel understanding of devotion to experience the essence of Viṣṇu in a more aesthetic manner. Ultimately, since the style of the two purāṇas is different, the articulation of certain narratives such as that of Dhruva is also distinct, but part of the larger *Viṣṇukathā*. Each has its use and importance and neither is the 'right' one compared with the other. Both must be considered in experiencing devotion to Viṣṇu. In addition to such intertextual connections utilised in his exposition of the *Viṣṇu Purāṇa*, Sharma turns to a well-known Advaita commentary on the *Viṣṇu Purāṇa*.

Reading the *Viṣṇu Purāṇa* through the lens of Advaita Vedānta

Though written Sanskrit commentaries on most purāṇas are rare, the *Viṣṇu Purāṇa* and *Bhāgavata Purāṇa* are exceptions. Sharma, in his exposition, turns to an Advaita Vedānta commentary on the *Viṣṇu Purāṇa* by Śrīdhara (fourteenth century CE) titled the *Ātmaprakāśa*, to read the *Viṣṇu Purāṇa* as an Advaita Vedānta treatise. Two examples are illustrative of the influence of this extratextual source.[21] First, in describing Dhruva's spiritual practice, the *Viṣṇu Purāṇa* states:

> *ātmany aśeṣadeveśaṃ sthitaṃ viṣṇum amanyata* ||
> *ananyacetasas tasya dhyāyato bhagavān hariḥ* |
> *sarvabhūtagato vipra sarvabhāvagato 'bhavat* ||
> *manasy avasthite tasya viṣṇau maitreya yoginaḥ* |
> *na śaśāka dharā bhāram udvoḍhuṃ bhūtadhāriṇī* ||
>
> [He contemplated Viṣṇu, the chief god of all, established in himself, O sage, contemplating thus, with undivided thought, the Lord Hari who is in all beings became one who is of all natures, such a Viṣṇu being present in his (Dhruva's) mind, Maitreya, the earth, supporter of existence could not sustain the weight of the yogin.] (*VP*, 1.12.6cd–8)

The conception of Visnu by Dhruva 'as present in all beings' and, through his meditation, becoming 'present in all natures' is interpreted by Sharma using the concept of the inner ruler/self (*antaryāmin*):

21 A third instance is the comparison of the hymn of Dhruva to the *Puruṣa Sūkta* (Sharma 2014: Pt 3, 16.50 mins ff.).

> The Viṣṇu who is present in all beings [*sarvabhūtagata*] became Viṣṇu who is completely present in the heart of Dhruva. Where is Viṣṇu really? Dhruva does not understand Viṣṇu as he exists in Vaikuṅṭha, but rather as Viṣṇu who pervades all beings. *This* Viṣṇu, Dhruva places within his heart. The Viṣṇu who is the inner self of all [*sarvāntaryāmin*], Dhruva placed within his heart. (Sharma 2014: Pt 3, 2.25–3.11 mins)

The term *antaryāmin* ('inner self') is not found in the Viṣṇu Purāṇa itself and the Advaita Vedānta refers to the *paramātman* ('supreme self'). Dhruva does not worship Viṣṇu envisioning the deity with four arms, holding a conch, discus and so on, residing in his heaven, Vaikuṅṭha. Rather, it is the Viṣṇu who pervades all existence as its inner self/ruler whom Dhruva places within himself. Sharma's use and interpretation of the term inner self are akin to Śrīdhara's Advaita commentary. For instance, on 1.12.74ab, where the *Viṣṇu Purāṇa* describes Viṣṇu:[22] 'The self of all [*sarvātman*], the lord of all beings [*sarvabhūteṣa*], the origin of all existence' (*sarvātman sarvabhūteśa sarvasattvasamudbhava* |). Śrīdhara's interpretation of this verse is as follows: 'It is said that he [Viṣṇu] ought to be praised in this way as of the self of all meaning as existing in the self of all, as the inner-self [*antaryāmin*] of all.'[23]

Here, the fact that Viṣṇu pervades all beings—is all beings—does not mean he is identical with these beings; he is to be understood as their inner self. The concept of inner self is found in the Upaniṣads, where its exact meaning is difficult to discern and each Vedānta school gives it a nuanced interpretation (*Bṛhadāraṇyaka Upaniṣad*, 3.7.3). In Advaita, the *antaryāmin* is the highest self or the internal ruler, Nārāyaṇa, with the 'sole adjunct of wisdom' and is 'one of the closest approaches we have to that which is beyond the purchase of senses and mind', the supreme self (*paramātman*) (Śaṃkara's *Brahmasūtrabhāṣya*, 1.2.18–20; Śaṃkara's *Bṛhadāraṇyakopaniṣadbhāṣya*, 3.7.3; Hirst 2005: 135–36). In so far as we can represent the supreme Brahman in conventional language, the inner self comes closest.[24] Sharma, through this interpretation, wishes to clarify that Dhruva envisions Viṣṇu in this specific Advaita way and not theistically.

22 The Critical Edition parses this passage differently to the commentator. For Śrīdhara (Shastri 2000), *VP* 1.12.73cd and 1.12.74ab constitute passage 74, whereas for the Critical Edition, this passage is 1.12.74cd and 1.12.75ab.

23 *etadeva vivṛṇvan āha sarvātmana sarveṣām ātmabhūta antaryāmin* (Upreti 2018: 104).

24 Though Śaṃkara identifies *antaryāmin* as Nārāyaṇa, he says that this identification is metaphorical (*upalaksanartha*), because in the final analysis, there is the realisation of one's self only; there is no theistic duality that remains (Śaṃkara's *Bṛhadāraṇyakopaniṣadbhāṣya*, 3.7.3).

The second instance of Sharma's dependence on Śrīdhara's Advaita commentary on the *Viṣṇu Purāṇa* occurs in his exposition of 1.12.51 (Sharma 2014: Pt 3, 15.40 mins ff.). Here, Viṣṇu appears before Dhruva, the latter is rendered speechless even though his heart overflows with devotion and he is unable to hymn the praises of the deity. Viṣṇu touches him with the tip of his conch: 'Govinda, the Lord of the world, touched the son of Uttānapāda who was bowing with reverence, with the tip of his conch, O excellent Brahman' (*śaṅkhaprāntena govindas taṃ pasparśa kṛtāñjalim | uttānapādatanayaṃ dvijavarya jagatpatiḥ* ||; *VP*, 1.12.51).

Sharma notes that as Dhruva gazed on Nārāyaṇa, unable to praise him, with eyes full of tears, Viṣṇu touches his cheek with the tip of his conch. The conch symbolises the power of the Veda (*vedaśakti*) and the tip of the conch stands for the end of Veda—that is, the Vedānta or the Upaniṣads.[25] The *paratattva* ('ultimate reality') that is extolled in the Upaniṣads enters Dhruva through this contact (Sharma 2014: Pt 3, 15.40–16.17 mins). Having been touched thus, Dhruva begins his adoration of the supreme being known as the Dhruva Stuti. Sharma's explanation draws from Śrīdhara's commentary on this verse (*VP*, 1.12.51): 'The conch is comprised of all Vedas. With the tip means with the part that is Vedānta. Touched means, causing to obtain the reality of the supreme lord.'[26]

In both cases, Sharma's interpretation of the *Viṣṇu Purāṇa* passages can be traced back to the Advaita commentary on the *Viṣṇu Purāṇa* by Śrīdhara. He chooses to read the narrative of Dhruva through the lens of Advaita ontology to understand how Viṣṇu is imagined from this theological point of view.[27]

Vernacularising the *Viṣṇu Purāṇa* for a Telugu audience

In addition to infusing his explanation with extrascriptural Sanskrit sources, Sharma vernacularises this exposition in two ways. First, his exposition is a translation of the Sanskrit content into Telugu. Second, to unpack the Sanskrit verses, he also relies on extratextual Telugu sources familiar to

25 In *VP* 1.22.68, however, the conch symbolises the *bhūta* ('elements') that make up existence.

26 *sarvavedamayasya saṅkasya prāntena vedāntabhāgena parameśvaratattvapratipādakena pasparśa* (Upreti 2018: 100).

27 For more on the distinction on understanding Viṣṇu from Advaita and Viśiṣṭādvaita perspectives, see Adluri (2019).

the audience. Each of these techniques is examined in more detail. To begin, how does Sharma utilise the Sanskrit verses from the written text in his Telugu explanation?[28] That is, how does his Telugu comment relate to the Sanskrit of the written purāṇa? Of the 158 verses that make up the narrative in *Viṣṇu Purāṇa* 1.11 and 1.12, he recites 70 in their entirety or in part. He skips certain verses altogether or summarises the passages briefly in a line or two, in Telugu.[29] For instance, in the first section of story, which sets the scene of Dhruva's discontent and distress (*VP*, 1.11.1–28), three techniques of vernacularising are evident in Sharma's approach to the written *Viṣṇu Purāṇa*. First, he recites a verse in Sanskrit (partially or in its entirety) and then explains its meaning in Telugu. As an example, in *VP* 1.11.1, the sage Parāśara, narrating the purāṇa to Maitreya, says: 'I have told you of Manu Svayambhū's two sons, Priyavrata and Uttānapāda both of whom possessed great strength and were knowers of dharma' (*priyavratottānapādau manoḥ svāyambhuvasya tu | dvau putrau sumahāvīryau dharmajñau kathitau tava* ||). Sharma, after reciting this entire Sanskrit verse, explains it in Telugu: 'Priyavrata and Uttānapāda are two sons of Manu Svayumbhū who are knowers of *dharma* [*dharmajña*] and great heroes [*mahāvīra*]' (Sharma 2014: Pt 2, 30.43–58 mins).

In the vernacular explanation, he utilises the vocabulary from the Sanskrit verse that characterises Manu's sons and stays close to the verse in extrapolating its meaning.

Second, he skips certain verses altogether, choosing to summarise their meaning in Telugu instead (Sharma 2014: Pt 2, 32.20–59 mins). In the following, Suruci berates Dhruva:

> *kriyate kiṃ vṛthā vatsa mahān eṣa manorathaḥ* |
> *anyastrīgarbhajātena asaṃbhūya mamodare* |
> *uttamottamam aprāpyam aviveko 'bhivāñchasi* ||
> *satyaṃ sutas tvam apy asya kintu na tvaṃ mayā dhṛtaḥ* ||
> *etad rājāsanaṃ sarvabhūbhṛtsaṃśrayaketanam* |

28 Taylor (2012) analyses the role of the written text of the *Bhāgavata Purāṇa* in a vernacular oral performance, comparing their discursive value and their performative function in signalling new narrative units. Flueckiger (1991) also looks at how a written text is used and ideas of what constitutes the boundary of a text at informal and temple *maṇḍalī-s*.

29 Sharma skips or summarises *VP* 1.11.2, 3ab, 5–6, 7cd–15, 17–23, 24cd–26, 30, 31cd–39, 45cd, 49cd–50, 52ab, 55ab and 56cd. In Chapter 12, he skips *VP* 1.12.1–6, 10–13ab, 14, 15cd, 16cd, 17cd, 18cd, 19cd, 20cd, 21cd, 24–28, 29ab, 30cd–31, 32cd, 44, 47–50, 51cd–52ab, 53, 55–56, 58ab, 59cd–68, 69cd, 70cd–71, 73–74, 75cd, 77–81, 87–89, 91cd and 94–100.

yogyaṃ mamaiva putrasya kim ātmā kliśyate tvayā ||
uccair manorathas te 'yaṃ matputrasyeva kiṃ vṛthā |
sunītyām ātmano janma kiṃ tvayā nāvagamyate ||

> [Why child, by being born of another woman's womb, do you uselessly seek this eminent desire; not being born of my womb, lacking discrimination, you aspire to what is suitable for the excellent Uttama only. It is true that you are his (the king's) offspring, however, you have not been born by me. This throne, a symbol of the sovereign of all is suited to my son alone, why torment yourself? Why uselessly do you seek this highest desire? Why is it not recognised by you, who yourself are born of Sunīti?] (*VP*, 1.11.7–10)

Sharma, however, recites only *VP* 1.11.7ab of the above; the rest he summarises in Telugu without highlighting any Sanskrit vocabulary found therein. He explains in Telugu:

> Once when Uttānapāda was on his throne, Suruci's son, Uttama, was seated on his lap. Seeing this, Dhruva also attempts to do the same. While Uttānapāda exhibits his dislike [mentioned in *VP*, 1.11.3], at the same time, Sunīki arrives and says, son you are not worthy of that seat. She says, why are you unnecessarily entertaining this thought. This is not possible for you. Because, apart from one born to me, no-one else can aspire to that royal seat. Only if one has the merit to be born of me, only they can aspire to this high station. (Sharma 2014: Pt 2, 32.20–59 mins)

His vernacular explanation captures the intent of the Sanskrit passages but does not utilise specific Sanskrit vocabulary from them.

Third, he does not recite the Sanskrit verse, choosing to simply explain it in Telugu. But in so doing, he relies on the Sanskrit vocabulary from the purāṇa (Sharma 2014: Pt 2, 35.42–36.08 mins). As an illustration, when Dhruva's mother tries to appease her son after his encounter with his stepmother, she advises him to increase his own merit by performing meritorious actions: 'Acquire a good disposition [*suśīla bhāva*], become virtuous [*dharmātma*], be friendly [*maitra*], be well-disposed to others [*prāṇihita*]' (*suśīlo bhava dharmātmā maitraḥ prāṇihite rataḥ | nimnaṃ yathāpaḥ pravaṇāḥ pātram āyānti saṃpadaḥ||*; *VP*, 1.11.23). Without reciting the Sanskrit passage, Sharma says:

> Sunīti says to her son, Dhruva, your stepmother, Suruci, is right. Those kind of things [affection of the king] happen only to those who have merit [*puṇya*]. Because Uttama has merit, he is sitting in his father's lap. You, my son, do not have merit as you have been born to me … [W]hat kind of merit does Sunīti want Dhruva to acquire? She urges her son to become a man of good disposition [Tel., *śīlavān*], to be virtuous [Tel., *dharmātma*], to be friendly [Tel., *maitra*] and to be one who wishes for the wellbeing of others [Tel., *prāṇulahita*]. (Sharma 2014: Pt 2, 36.08 mins ff.)

Sharma utilises Sanskrit vocabulary from the passage to convey the meaning of the verse in Telugu but does not recite it. Sharma's exposition unpacks the Sanskrit of the written purāṇa for those in the audience who may not understand it. He does, however, use the written text as a roadmap in that he follows it closely, even though he skips certain passages.

In addition to explaining the Sanskrit purāṇa in Telugu, Sharma localises it with use of local and regional sources. In his study of oral and performative traditions of epics, Ramanujan (2004b: 496–506) notes that when classical myths are told by folk performers, they localise pan-Indian narratives to include local and regional motifs. Localising or regionalising can include insertion of local geographic names, culinary details, local flora and fauna, local rituals and local histories (Richman 2015: 35; Sax 2001; Shah 2015: 46–53; Das 2015: 56–59; Ghulam-Sarwar 2015: 87). Sharma vernacularises his exposition of the Sanskrit purāṇa through the use of two important Telugu-language sources: the Telugu *Bhāgavata Purāṇa* called *Bhāgavatamu* by Bammera Potana (ca fourteenth century CE) and selections from the *pada* ('hymns') of the poet-saint Annamayya (ca fifteenth century CE).[30]

Telugu literature in the fourteenth to seventeenth centuries was dominated by two parallel traditions: that of the court poets and that of the temple poets. The former catered to an elite audience and were sustained by royal patronage. For the temple poets, God was the sole patron and was thought to speak through them (Narayana Rao and Shulman 2002: 56–57). Both Potana's and Annamayya's works were meant for oral recitation or, in the case of the latter, were set to music and used for singing and dancing in entertaining the deity (Narayana Rao and Shulman 2012: 165; 2002: 233). Potana's *Bhāgavatamu* is a 'work of passionate devotion … meant to evoke or actually to conjure up fully and realistically … the latent and hidden

30 For more on Annamayya's translated hymns, see Narayana Rao and Shulman (2005); and Jackson (1999).

presence of the god' (Narayana Rao and Shulman 2002: 57). Devotion here is 'distinct from Sanskrit and Tamil Āḻvārs and Nāyaṉmārs' in that it 'is at once emotional and open to the senses, but not rooted in separation' (Shulman 1993: 153–55). Annamayya's hymns are 'meant as direct communication to the god he worships' and the simple and accessible language illustrates an intimate familiarity with the supreme deity who yet transcends all human thought, underscoring a distinctively Telugu mode of devotional context (Narayana Rao and Shulman 2002: 58–60; Annamayya 2005: 520–25 [Kindle edition]). Both these extratextual sources underscore a unique devotional milieu and Sharma's use of them to explain the Sanskrit *Viṣṇu Purāṇa* taps into a characteristically Telugu devotional idiom.

In his introduction to the exposition of the *Viṣṇu Purāṇa* itself, Sharma turns to both Potana and Annamayya. We saw earlier that Sharma cites a hymn by Annamayya to characterise all Vaiṣṇava purāṇas as *Viṣṇukathā* (see the section on the significance of the *Viṣṇu Purāṇa*).[31] In this hymn, identifying Viṣṇu, Kṛṣṇa and Venkaṭeśvara, the local/regional form of Viṣṇu as one and the same deity, the poet indicates that this deity has been continuously adored and praised over aeons in the form of *Viṣṇukathā*. After citing this hymn of Annamayya's, Sharma asks, what does listening to the *Viṣṇukathā* accomplish? In answer, he cites Potana: '[L]istening to *Viṣṇukathā* is the same as ritually bathing in the River Ganges' (Sharma 2014: Pt 1, 1.55 mins).[32] The use of both these stalwarts of Telugu devotion is an opportunity for Sharma to ensconce the Sanskrit *Viṣṇu Purāṇa* within a unique understanding of Telugu *bhakti*. Though these instances of localising are found in the introduction to the *Viṣṇu Purāṇa* exposition, Sharma depends on them in his exposition of the Dhruva narrative as well—for instance, in his comment on *VP* 1.12.42, when Viṣṇu appears before Dhruva: 'Son of Uttānapāda, may you be prosperous. Delighted with your *tapas*, I, giver of boons, have arrived, choose a boon O steadfast one of vows [*suvrata*]' (*auttānapāde bhadraṃ te tapasā paritoṣitaḥ* | *varado 'ham anuprāpto varaṃ varaya suvrata* ||).

To gloss the term 'steadfast one of vows' (*suvrata*), Sharma recites a verse from Potana's *Bhāgavatamu*—the story of the liberation of Gajendra ('Gajendramokṣa'). The elephant Gajendra, bathing in the waters of a spring,

31 Tel.: *vinaro bhāgyamu viṣṇukathā venubalamidivo viṣṇukathā (pallavi) ādinuṇḍi sandhyādividhulalo vedambaynadi viṣṇukathā nādincīnide nāradādulace vīdhivīdhulane viṣṇukathā (caranam 1)* (Sharma 2014: Pt 2, 1.30–55 mins).

32 Tel.: *viṣṇupadi jalamunangi vimulalajeyan viṣṇukathā saṃpraṣṭam.*

is mauled by a crocodile. Having exhausted all means to escape its powerful jaws, Gajendra turns to Viṣṇu for refuge. One of the verses the elephant hymns and which Sharma quotes is the following:

> *muktasaṅgulaina munulu didṛkṣulu sarvabhūtahitulu sādhucittulu*
> *asadṛṣavratādhulai kolturu evvani divyapadamu vāṃdu dikku nāku*
>
> [The sages who are free from desires, who are desirous of seeing him, who are well-wishers of all beings, who are of sound mind and incomparable in their vows, he whose divine feet they worship, that one, is my refuge.] (Tel.: *BhP*, 8.77)

He reads the term 'steadfast one of vows' (*suvrata*) considering the seers whom Gajendra extols as devotees of Viṣṇu and who are incomparable in their vows (*asadṛṣavrata*). By so doing, he connects the plight and devotional fervour of Gajendra with that of Dhruva (Sharma 2014: Pt 3, 13.45–14.39 mins). Both are steadfast devotees of Viṣṇu. Examining the connection between the Sanskrit and the Telugu purāṇas on the narrative of Gajendra, Shulman notes that the Telugu *Bhāgavatamu* is 'softer, sweeter, and more lyrical' than the Sanskrit original and establishes 'an intimacy and familiarity between Gajendra and Viṣṇu ... [T]he essential message of the text ... is god's proximity, familiarity, immediate availability, his being as it were as close to us as our innermost intimately sensed reality.' This is the hallmark of the Telugu purāṇa (Shulman 1993: 150–53). In Potana's version, hearing Gajendra's pleas, Viṣṇu, who is in the middle of sporting with his consort Śrī, hurries, dragging a dishevelled goddess with him. This detail, which is not found in the Sanskrit *Bhāgavata Purāṇa*, signals Viṣṇu's immediate availability, his reflex to abandon all matters when he hears the cries of his devotees (Shulman 1993: 146–48). Sharma invokes all these emotions as he references this passage from the story of Gajendra, linking Dhruva's plight to that of the great elephant and Viṣṇu's willingness to hastily tend to the concerns of the young prince.

In the Dhruva narrative, in the last passages that summarise the merit generated on hearing this story (*phalaśruti*), Sharma once again references Annamayya. The last two passages of the *Viṣṇu Purāṇa* summarise the merit generated in listening to the story of Dhruva:

> *yaś caitat kīrtayen nityaṃ dhruvasyārohaṇaṃ divi* |
> *sarvapāpavinirmuktaḥ svargaloke mahīyate* ||
> *sthānabhraṃśaṃ na cāpnoti divi vā yadi vā bhuvi* |
> *sarvakalyāṇasaṃyukto dīrghakālaṃ ca jīvati* ||

> [He who shall recite constantly, the ascent of Dhruva into heaven, he, freed of all sin, will be welcomed in heaven. He shall not fall from that station whether in heaven or on earth and lives a long life possessed of every fortune.] (*VP*, 1.12.101–2)

According to Sharma, whoever worships Viṣṇu will never be a *bhraṣṭa* (one who fails). Why? Because the worship of Viṣṇu will lead only to an elevated station, never to failure. He quotes the poet-saint as support: '[N]o matter which purāṇa one searches, devotees of Śrī's husband never suffer' (Sharma 2014: Pt 3, 35.12 mins).[33] Such incorporation of regional materials in the explanation of a pan-Hindu text allows for 'readings between the [purāṇic] lines' and domesticates the Sanskrit myth (Lutgendorf 1991: 213).

Contemporising the *Viṣṇu Purāṇa* for a modern audience

It is highly likely that Sharma's audience has heard the narrative of Dhruva on other occasions and is aware of the plot. Sharma himself mentions this in his introduction. Given this, how he delivers an already known story becomes important. In addition to some of his expository techniques discussed earlier, he contemporises the Sanskrit myth for a modern audience. Following Ramanujan (2004b: 506), Lutgendorf (1991: 221) and Richman (2015: 37) define contemporising as 'making the story seem as if it relates to life at the present moment'. Sharma, in the introduction to his exposition, states that the purāṇic stories are not about characters from aeons ago, but have relevance for contemporary life. Dhruva's devotion is a model on which to fashion our own spiritual life. Two examples illustrate this principle in his exposition. Dhruva's discussion with his mother about his stepmother's insult offers Sharma an opportunity to do just this (2014: Pt 2, 32.59–34.12; 35.42–38.50 mins). Sunīti says to Dhruva: 'What Suruci said is true. You are unfortunate, son. Indeed, you are not endowed with merit, son, as has been stated by the co-wife' (*suruciḥ satyam āhedaṃ svalpabhāgyo 'si putraka | na hi puṇyavatāṃ vatsa sapatnair evam ucyate ||*; *VP*, 1.11.16). Sharma elaborates on and contemporises the content of this passage for his audience:

> We are enjoying a lot of luxuries and happiness, and these happen because of merit. Merit [*puṇya*] and demerit [*pāpa*] drive the comforts [*sukha*] and discomforts [*duḥkha*] of life. Otherwise, without such

33 Tel.: *yē purāṇmula eṇta vedikinā śrīpati dāsulu cedarennaḍu*.

> karma, everyone would be the same. Because of karma, there is a gradation [*tāratamya*] of happiness, suffering, etcetera. That is why to only those who have accrued merit is the experience of happiness, wealth, etcetera available. (Sharma 2014: Pt 2, 32.59 mins ff.)

> If you experience any kind of suffering, recognise that by this a demerit [*pāpa*] has been reduced/exhausted [*kṣaya*]. If you experience happiness, it means you have expended some merit that you had previously accrued. So, if you really want to experience happiness, perform meritorious actions. (Sharma 2014: Pt 2, 36.52 mins ff.)

Sharma quotes a well-known adage to support this stance: 'By performing extreme actions, whether good or bad, one experiences the results in this life itself' (*atyutkaṭaiḥ puṇyapāpaiḥ ihaiva phalam ucyate*) (2014: Pt 2, 36.08 mins). Contemporising further, he says that these days, mothers do not give such advice to their kids:

> They may say, 'Could you not have forcefully pulled the kid off your father's lap?' [This elicits laughter from the audience.] The mother's words are affecting Dhruva in the way that they should be. In life, for every mood [*bhava*], there are two components/aspects [*bhāga*]: positive and negative. The mood fear has two aspects: positive and negative. To experience positive fear means that you refrain from committing *adharma*. This is called healthy fear in English and it is good. Because Dhruva is not thinking of how to destroy his brother—negative aspect—but instead chooses to accomplish what he desires through his own efforts, he channels everything in a positive way. This is what needs to be remembered in life. (Sharma 2014: Pt 2, 37.15 mins ff.)

An ancient story about a disillusioned young prince is updated as the exposition of the *Viṣṇu Purāṇa* serves as enjoyment, entertainment and education.

The second example of contemporising occurs in the section in which Dhruva's intense meditation begins to disrupt and agitate the worlds and the gods, taking Indra's advice, decide to interrupt his asceticism (Sharma 2014: Pt 3, 8.36–10.00 mins). They use different means of *māyā* ('illusion') to sway his focus. One such distraction includes an illusory manifestation of the prince's mother, Sunīti, who attempts to dissuade him from further meditation. In passages 1.12.15–21, she begs her son to quit his austerities. This apparition of Sunīti tries to persuade the prince to cease his *tapas*, claiming that his young age is not commensurate with such rigorous penance and he should not take the remarks of his stepmother to heart but instead return to the palace to play and enjoy his childhood. She cites play, study, *bhoga* ('enjoyment') and then *tapas* as the normal sequence of activities with which one needs to engage in life. She claims that Dhruva's main goal as a young boy must be to please his mother and that is his supreme *dharma*; turning away from this, he is committing *adharma*. She pleads with him to desist. Dhruva, however, is unmoved. Sharma elaborates on this reasoning of the illusory Sunīti:

> In our society we may hear things said such as, 'Why engage in harsh spiritual practices from now itself? At this present time?' That is, first play, then study, enjoy life and then think about spiritual practice; think about *tapas* later in life. But when is the right time? No-one knows! The distinction is between let's do it versus let's see if we can do it [Tel., *cesukundām* versus *cusukundām*; this alliteration elicits laughter from the audience.] (2014: Pt 3, 8.36–59 mins)

> Normally, when you have taken up, say, a vow of fasting [*upavāsa*], you may hear someone say to you, 'Oh, you look wiped out [*nirāsa*].' You immediately give up fasting, stating, 'Okay, this one time, listening to you, I will stop this fasting today itself. But next time even if you say such things, I will not heed your advice' [the audience roars with laughter]. Māyā takes so many forms and hinders our practice [*sadhana*]. (9.30–10.00 mins)

> ... [W]hat we need to learn from Dhruva is how to persevere/to be firm [*sthira*] in one's devotion. Even when Dhruva intensified his meditation at first, Viṣṇu did not appear and yet we do so little to propitiate God and then quickly conclude that he must not exist. (8.35 mins)

Just as the illusory Sunīti's advice to Dhruva was an obstacle to his spiritual practice, so one's acquaintances and their remarks can be obstacles in spiritual practice today. In his explanation of how we usually are tempted to put off spiritual practice, while at the same time eager to get on with secular activities, Sharma uses alliteration to get his point across, eliciting laughter from the audience. Through such humour and playful sarcasm, Sharma entertains and educates the audience.

This exposition is clearly not a silent reception of the text. Furthermore, his voice modulation in the recitation of the verses and their explanation keeps the audience interested and focused on a story that they have heard perhaps many times before. There is evidence of engagement from a second type of audience of the exposition—namely, those who listen to the recordings of the lectures posted on YouTube. The first three episodes register between 18,000 and 51,000 views and include 145–313 'likes' and 9–32 'dislikes'. Posted comments include praise for Sharma's exposition of the *Viṣṇu Purāṇa*, emojis of flowers and *namaskāra* gestures made as offerings to Viṣṇu and Sharma, who is referred to as a 'guru'. Several listeners also posted various Sanskrit mantras such as *Oṃ namo nārāyaṇāya*, which perhaps could have been uttered if they were present for the live discourse.

Concluding remarks

To better comprehend the continuing interaction between a written purāṇa and its oral manifestations, this study examines a modern-day exposition of the *Viṣṇu Purāṇa* by Samaveda Shanmukha Sharma. The narrative of Dhruva (*Dhruvacaritra*) offers a window into this larger 'performative process' of purāṇas as Sanskrit 'books' embedded in specific vernacular cultures (Bailey 2010: 127). Each section evaluates the ways in which the exposition comments on and adds to the written purāṇa. In the first section, using extratextual materials, Sharma makes connections to the Vedas, the *Bhagavadgītā* and the *Bhāgavata Purāṇa* to broaden the context within which the *Viṣṇu Purāṇa* and specifically the story of Dhruva must be understood. As different articulations of the one *Viṣṇukathā*, each of these scriptures intersects with the other on the nature of deity and devotion and aids Sharma in situating the story and the *Viṣṇu Purāṇa* within the larger landscape of Hindu theology. The interpretation of the purāṇa through an Advaita Vedānta perspective by use of Śrīdhara's commentary, in the second section, allows Sharma and the audience to envision the narrative with an added philosophical dimension. Sharma vernacularizes and contemporizes a myth that has been heard several times earlier but is reimagined anew through his exposition.

While the written text remains important in Sharma's explanation, it becomes a stepping-stone for a unique vernacular telling. The Dhruva narrative—a tale of devotion to Viṣṇu—remains just that, but it is transformed by an infusion of extrascriptural material and philosophy such as Advaita Vedānta, packaged for vernacular and contemporary consumption using Telugu literary sources. All these techniques and their implementation in the telling of the narrative of Dhruva are unique to this expositor's encounter with the written *Viṣṇu Purāṇa*. The purāṇic text, then, is a starting point, but becomes a meaningful whole, with consideration of these recitational and performative manifestations.

References

Primary texts

Bhāgavatamu. (1983). *Bammera Potana's Śrīmad Mahābhāgavatamu*. Hyderabad, India: Telugu Sahitya Akademi.

Pathak, M.M. (1999). *Critical Edition of the Visnu Purana*. Vadodara, India: Oriental Institute.

Sadhale, G.S. (1935). *The Bhagavadgītā with Eleven Commentaries*. [2 Vols.] Bombay, India: Gujrati Press.

Shastri, J.L. (2000). *Bhāgavata Purāṇa with Sanskrit Commentary: Bhāvārthabodhinī of Śrīdhara Svāmin*. New Delhi: Motilal Banarsidass.

Secondary texts

Adluri, S. (2019). Who is the Viṣṇu of the Viṣṇu Purāṇa? In R. Balakaran and M. Taylor (eds), *Purāṇic Studies: Proceedings of the 17th World Sanskrit Conference*, pp. 45–76. Vancouver, BC: Department of Asian Studies, University of British Columbia.

Ananth Rao, C.R. (2011). Oral performance of ancient texts. *Journal of the Oriental Society of Australia* 43: 131–45.

Annamayya. (2005). *God on the Hill: Temple Poems from Tirupati*. Translated by V. Narayana Rao and D. Shulman. Oxford, UK: Oxford University Press.

Bailey, G. (2003). The purāṇas: A study in the development of Hinduism. In Arvind Sharma (ed.), *The Study of Hinduism*, pp. 139–69. Columbia: University of South Carolina Press.

Bailey, G. (2010). The purāṇas. In Knut A. Jacobsen, Helene Basu, Angelika Malinar and Vasudha Narayanan (eds), *The Brill Encyclopedia of Hinduism. Volume II*, pp. 127–52. Leiden, Netherlands: Brill Publishers.

Bhattacarya, J.V. (1875). *Bṛhadāraṇyakopaniṣat-Śaṃkarācāryabhāṣya-sahitāanand agirikṛtatīkāyālaṃkṛtāñca*. Calcutta, India: Vinayantra Mudrita.

Bonazzoli, G. (1983). Composition, transmission and recitation of purāṇas. *Purāṇam* 25(2): 254–80.

Coburn, T.B. (1984). 'Scripture' in India: Towards a typology of the word in Hindu life. *Journal of the American Academy of Religion* 52(3): 435–59. doi.org/10.1093/jaarel/52.3.435.

Das, A.K. (2015). Rāma legend in Assam: Tangible and intangible. In Molly Kaushal, Alok Bhalla and Ramakar Pant (eds), *Ramkatha in Narrative, Performance, and Pictorial Traditions*, pp. 55–62. New Delhi: Aryan Books International.

Doniger, W. (1991). Fluid and fixed texts in India. In Joyce Burkhalter Flueckiger and Laurie Sears (eds), *Boundaries of the Text: Epic Performances in South and Southeast Asia*, pp. 31–42. Ann Arbor, MI: University of Michigan Center for South and Southeast Asian Studies.

Doniger, W. (1993). Introduction. In Wendy Doniger (ed.), *Purāṇa Perennis: Reciprocity and Transformation of Hindu and Jaina Texts*, pp. vii–xii. New Delhi: Sri Satguru Publications. doi.org/10.2307/1178575.

Flueckiger, J.B. (1991). Literacy and the changing concept of a text. In Joyce Burkhalter Flueckiger and Laurie Sears (eds), *Boundaries of the Text: Epic Performances in South and Southeast Asia*, pp. 43–60. Ann Arbor, MI: University of Michigan Center for South and Southeast Asian Studies. doi.org/10.3998/mpub.19503.

Ghulam-Sarwar, Y. (2015). Rāmāyaṇa in Southeast Asian traditional theatre performances: Adaptation and localization. In Molly Kaushal, Alok Bhalla and Ramakar Pant (eds), *Ramkatha in Narrative, Performance, and Pictorial Traditions*, pp. 85–96. New Delhi: Aryan Books International.

Gonda, J. (1963). The Indian mantra. *Oriens* 16: 244–97. doi.org/10.1163/18778372-01601016.

Gupta, Ravi M. and Valpey, Kenneth R. (eds). (2013). *The Bhāgavata Purāṇa: Sacred Text and Living Tradition*. New York, NY: Columbia University Press.

Hirst, J.S. (2005). *Śaṃkara's Advaita Vedānta: A Way of Teaching*. Oxford, UK: Routledge. doi.org/10.4324/9780203001929.

Jackson, W. (1999). *Songs of the Three Great South Indian Saints*. New Delhi: Oxford University Press.

Lutgendorf, P. (1991). Words made flesh: The Banares Rāmlīlā as epic commentary. In Joyce B. Flueckiger and Laurie Sears (eds), *Boundaries of the Text: Epic Performance in South and Southeast Asia*, pp. 85–105. Ann Arbor, MI: University of Michigan Center for South and Southeast Asian Studies. doi.org/10.3998/mpub.19503.

Malinar, A. (2007). *The Bhagavadgītā: Doctrines and Contexts*. Cambridge, UK: Cambridge University Press. doi.org/10.1017/CBO9780511488290.

Matchett, F. (2003). The purāṇas. In Gavin Flood (ed.), *The Blackwell Companion to Hinduism*, pp. 129–43. Oxford, UK: Blackwell Publishing. doi.org/10.1002/9780470998694.ch7.

Muller, M.F. (1965). *Ṛgveda Saṃhitā*. Kashi Sanskrit Series 167. Varanasi, India: Chowkhamba Sanskrit Series Office.

Narayana Rao, V. (2004). Purāṇa. In Sushil Mittal and Gene Thursby (eds), *The Hindu World*, pp. 97–115. Oxford, UK: Routledge.

Narayana Rao, V. and Shulman, D. (2002). *Classical Telugu Poetry: An Anthology*. New Delhi: Oxford University Press.

Narayana Rao, V. and Shulman, D. (2005). *God on the Hill: Temple Poems from Tirupati*. Oxford, UK: Oxford University Press.

Narayana Rao, V. and Shulman, D. (2012). *Śrīnātha: The Poet Who Made Gods and Kings*. Oxford, UK: Oxford University Press.

Olivelle, P. (1998). *The Early Upaniṣads: Annotated Text and Translation*. Oxford, UK: Oxford University Press.

Pauwels, H. (2004). 'Only you': The wedding of Rāma and Sītā, past and present. In Mandrakanta Bose (ed.), *The Rāmāyaṇa Revisited*, pp. 165–218. Oxford, UK: Oxford University Press. doi.org/10.1093/0195168321.003.0008.

Pollock, S. (1984). The problem of the Āraṇyakāṇḍa. In Robert P. Goldman (ed.), *The Rāmāyaṇa of Vālmīki: Āraṇyakāṇḍa*. Princeton, NJ: Princeton University Press.

Ramanujan, A.K. (2004a). Three hundred Rāmāyaṇas: Five examples and three thoughts on translation. In Vinay Dharwadker (ed.), *The Collected Essays of A.K. Ramanujan*, pp. 131–60. New Delhi: Oxford University Press.

Ramanujan, A.K. (2004b). Two realms of Kannada folklore. In Vinay Dharwadker (ed.), *The Collected Essays of A.K. Ramanujan*, pp. 485–512. New Delhi: Oxford University Press.

Richman, P. (2015). Rāmkathā alive in performance. In Molly Kaushal, Alok Bhalla and Ramakar Pant (eds), *Ramkatha in Narrative, Performance, and Pictorial Traditions*, pp. 31–45. New Delhi: Aryan Books International.

Rocher, L. (1986). *The Purāṇas. Volume II. Fasc. 3: A History of Indian Literature*. Edited by Jan Gonda. Wiesbaden, Germany: Otto Harrassowitz.

Sastri, D. (1929). *Śrīmadśaṃkarācāryabrahmasūtrabhāṣya*. [2 Vols.] Varanasi, India: Caukambha Sanskrit Series.

Sax, W.S. (2001). The Pāṇḍav Līlā in Uttarkhand. In Molly Kaushal (ed.), *Chanted Narratives: The Living 'Katha-Vachana' Tradition*, pp. 165–74. New Delhi: Indira Gandhi National Center for Arts.

Schreiner, P. (2013). *Viṣṇupurāṇa althergebrachte Kunde über Viṣṇu* [*Viṣṇupurāṇa: Ancient Lore about Viṣṇu*]. Berlin: Verlag der Weltreligionen im Insel Verlag.

Shah, N. (2015). Living Rāmāyaṇas of the Adivasis of Gujarat: A study. In Molly Kaushal, Alok Bhalla and Ramakar Pant (eds), *Ramkatha in Narrative, Performance, and Pictorial Traditions*, pp. 46–54. New Delhi: Aryan Books International.

Sharma, S. (2014). Viṣṇu Purāṇa Pravacana. YouTube. Available from: www.youtube.com/watch?v=0Ve0ZY2gRFo [Part 1/11]; www.youtube.com/watch?v=m4FVu5fZGmA&t=2331s [Part 2/11]; www.youtube.com/watch?v=UQGtIqC9ZK8&t=1457s [Part 3/11].

Shulman, D. (1993). Remaking a purāṇa: The rescue of Gajendra in Potana's Telugu Mahābhāgavatamu. In Wendy Doniger (ed.), *Purāṇa Perennis: Reciprocity and Transformation in Hindu and Jaina Texts*, pp. 121–58. New Delhi: Sri Satguru Publications.

Srinivasan, D. (1973). Saṃdhyā: Myth and ritual. *Indo-Iranian Journal* 15(3): 161–78. doi.org/10.1163/000000073790079125.

Taylor, M. (2012). Empowering the sacred: The function of the Sanskrit text in a contemporary exposition of the Bhāgavatapurāṇa. In Elizabeth Minchin (ed.), *Orality, Literacy and Performance in the Ancient World*, pp. 129–50. Leiden, Netherlands: Brill Publishers.

Taylor, M. (2016). *Seven Days of Nectar: Contemporary Oral Performance of the Bhāgavata Purāṇa*. Oxford, UK: Oxford University Press. doi.org/10.1093/acprof:oso/9780190611910.001.0001.

Theodor, I. (2020). *The Fifth Veda of Hinduism: Poetry, Philosophy and Devotion in the Bhāgavata Purāṇa*. London: I.B. Tauris.

Upreti, T. (2018). *Viṣṇumahāpurāṇam of Mahārṣi Vedavyāsa with Sanskrit Commentary Ātmaprakāśa of Śrīdharācārya*. [2 Vols.] New Delhi: Parimal Publications.

van Buitenen, J.A.B. (1988). On the archaism of the Bhāgavata Purāṇa. In Ludo Rocher (ed.), *Studies in Indian Literature and Philosophy*, pp. 223–43. New Delhi: Motilal Banarsidass.

15

The Śivaśarmopākhyāna of the *Padma Purāṇa* as a bizarre compendium of epic and purāṇic tales of *Pitṛbhakti*

Nicolas Dejenne

Abstract

The *Padma Purāṇa* displays in its second section, in didactic as well as narrative passages, a considerable interest in the question of the devotion and obedience of children to their parents. The initial story in this section (2.1–5), the story of brahmin Śivaśarman and his testing of the obedience of his five sons, deserves an in-depth analysis in this respect. We will show how this story seems to gather and encapsulate motives and features that are important in several epic and purāṇic legends that deal with 'family matters' and that controversially highlight to which lengths, in the Hindu Brahmanical world view, a son's *pitṛbhakti* ('devotion to the father') is supposed to go. The very structure of the story also appears typical of such tales—the 'four plus one' structure in which the fifth son adopts a different attitude to the first four and they are diversely rewarded by their father. Eventually, we will underscore how, despite these analogies, the story of Śivaśarman remains quite original and, in some respects, unique among these *pitṛbhakti* tales.

Introduction

The *Padma Purāṇa* (*PP*) is among the largest purāṇas, with a total of 55,000 verses. Of its two recensions, the Western and the Bengali, the Bengali remains in manuscripts only while the Western one has been edited and published several times.[1] The Veṅkaṭeśvara Press edition has provided the source text for the complete English translation by D.N. Deshpande, in 10 volumes (Volumes 39–48), in the Ancient Indian Tradition and Mythology series.[2] In the Western recension, on which we will exclusively focus in this chapter, the second *khaṇḍa* ('portion') of the *PP*, the 125 *adhyāya*-long Bhūmikhaṇḍa ('Section on the Earth'), displays, in didactic as well as narrative passages, a considerable interest in the question of the devotion and obedience of children to their parents or, more precisely, of sons to their fathers. More than 20 chapters (2.62–84)—mostly concerned with a retelling of Yayāti's story—are even grouped in one section labelled as concerning *mātāpitṛtīrtha* ('mother and father as holy sites').[3] Significantly, the initial subsection in this *khaṇḍa* (2.1–5) consists of the story of a brahmin named Śivaśarman and his testing of the obedience of his five sons against the strong background of the importance of Viṣṇubhakti.

This Śivaśarmopākhyāna (as it is called in the Ānandāśrama Sanskrit Series), which seems to be found only in, and is thus most likely an original production of, the *PP*, deserves in-depth analysis in this respect. The story gathers and encapsulates motives and features that are important in some very famous epic and purāṇic legends—notably, Yayāti's and Jamadagni's, showing dramatically how far, in the Hindu orthodox Brahmanical world view, a son's *pitṛbhakti* ('filial devotion') is supposed to go. The very structure of the story also strongly reminds one of such legends—what we can call the

1 For a general presentation of the *Padma Purāṇa*, its editions and the limited scholarly work about to it, see Rocher (1986: 206–14). If we leave aside the various contributions to the debate about the possible borrowings, and their direction, between the *PP* and Kālidāsa's *Śakuntalā* and *Raghuvaṃśa* (Rocher 1986: 209–10), Chatterjee (1967) seems to be the only full-length monograph devoted to the *PP* (considering the manuscript of the Bengali recension as well as the Western one and displaying the most useful summary of several works traditionally ascribed to the *PP*).

2 For the sake of convenience, the references to verses in the article will be to the Veṅkaṭeśvar Press edition (Kṣemarāja Śrīkṛṣṇadāsa 1895) and their translation by D.N. Deshpande (1988–92), except where indicated. The Ānandāśrama Sanskrit Series edition (Viśvanātha Nārāyaṇa Maṇḍalīka 1893–94), published in Pune, and very close to the former one as far as the Bhūmikhaṇḍa is concerned, has also been consulted.

3 In Viśvanātha Nārāyaṇa Maṇḍalīka (1893–94), according to the *adhyāyas*' colophons, we find the phrases *mātāpitṛtīrtha* (67, 69, 71–73, 76–77), *mātāpitṛtīrthamāhātmya* (62, 66, 84) or *mātāpitṛtīrthakathana* (64–65). Some other *adhyāyas* are restricted to the mention of the father (*pitṛtīrtha*; 70, 78–83).

'four plus one' structure, in which the first four sons usually adopt a different attitude to the fifth and as a consequence are diversely rewarded by their exacting father.

As the story of Śīvaśarman and his sons is not well known and does not seem to have attracted much academic attention, the first part of this chapter will provide detailed summary of its main episodes. This summary will form the basis for the comparisons and analogies that will be drawn in the second part, with emblematic epic and purāṇic narratives that we can soundly suppose to be the implicit references to and perhaps the sources of Śivaśarman's story. In the final portion of the chapter, we will highlight the main idiosyncrasies of this *PP* story as well as some difficulties for its interpretation.

Summary of the Śivaśarmopākhyāna

At the very beginning of the Bhūmikhaṇḍa,[4] narrated in the classical framework of a discussion between the *sūta* Ugraśravas and a group of *ṛṣi*s in the Naimiṣa Forest, the sages ask a question about the fate of Prahlāda, Hiraṇyakaśipu's son, against the background of the cosmic conflict opposing *deva*s and *asura*s. They are somewhat baffled by the fact that, after being killed in the battle by Viṣṇu, Prahlāda immediately entered Viṣṇu's body. Rather than engaging directly with Prahlāda's story, which is otherwise briefly narrated in the *PP* in Uttarakhaṇḍa's *adhyāya* presenting Narasiṃhāvatāra (6.238), the *sūta* decides to narrate the birth and life of Prahlāda in the previous *kalpa* and begins to tell the story of the brahmin Śivaśarman, without specifying at this point which character in this story will be reborn as Prahlāda.

Śivaśarman, a brahmin endowed with eminent qualities and deeply devoted to Viṣṇu, lives near Dvārakā with his wife[5] and their five sons, Yajñaśarman, Vedaśarman, Dharmaśarman, Viṣṇuśarman and Somaśarman, in descending age order. While all are presented as knowing 'no other duty than devotion to their father' (1.15), Śivaśarman decides one day to test the depth of his sons' *bhakti* towards him as well as towards Viṣṇu, leading to a series of five trials. He resorts to *māyā* thanks to his possession of 'all superhuman

4 The rationale behind the title of this *khaṇḍa*—accepted in all editions of the *PP*—remains obscure as it does not deal with descriptions or the geography of the Earth. The *adhyāyas* comprising praises of specific *tīrtha*s, which are so numerous in other *khaṇḍa*s of the *PP*, are even rather few in the Bhūmikhaṇḍa.

5 The name of Śivaśarman's wife is not given in the *upākhyāna*.

faculties' through the favour of Viṣṇu, and he first displays in front of his sons the corpse of their mother, supposedly dead of a sudden onset of disease. The grieving sons are obviously in shock. The five tests are described below.

1. Yajñaśarman (*PP*, 1.20–27). Śivaśarman summons his eldest son, Yajñaśarman, and, rather strangely, orders him to cut his mother's body into pieces and throw the limbs here and there. Yajñaśarman does not vent his feelings about or refuse this cruel command but immediately obeys his father. After completing the task, he returns to his father and expresses his readiness to accomplish any other command of his, however harsh it may be.
2. Vedaśarman (*PP*, 1.28–56). Śivaśarman, who has not expressed any judgement of Yajñaśarman's behaviour and obedience, calls his next son, Vedaśarman, and explains to him that, after the death of his wife, he cannot bear loneliness and needs the company of a woman. He once more secretly uses his *māyā* to create a beautiful young woman and asks Vedaśarman to approach her and bring her back to him (1.28–30). The son immediately goes to the young woman and conveys to her his father's desire, but the woman (who remains unnamed in the passage) is not much interested in going with an old, sick, disgruntled man and would rather enjoy the company of the young and handsome Vedaśarman (1.31–38). Outraged by the woman's straightforwardness, Vedaśarman censures her but tries to strike a deal with her: if she witnesses his *balam* ('power'), attested by his calling the gods, she should agree to live with his father. As announced by Vedaśarman, Indra and the other gods appear in front of them and offer a boon to Vedaśarman, who unhesitatingly requests to remain steadfast in his devotion to his father (1.39–47). The woman remains unimpressed and exacts a more gruelling toll from him: if Vedaśarman wants her to sport with his father, he must behead himself! Vedaśarman readily and happily complies and offers his own head to the woman (1.48–51), who then proceeds towards Śivaśarman's hermitage. She shows him Vedaśarman's bleeding head and invites him to enjoy her. The father is satisfied with Vedaśarman's devotion to him while his brothers stand by impressed by and somewhat envious of his *pitṛbhakti* (1.51–56).
3. Dharmaśarman (*PP*, 1.57–58 and 2.1–17). Śivaśarman asks his third son, Dharmaśarman, to grasp Vedaśarman's head without intimating what he should do with it (1.57–58). Dharmaśarman leaves for the forest with the severed head and invokes the god Dharma, who is satisfied with him and grants a boon to him. By an act of truth, Dharmaśarman

exhorts Dharma to resuscitate his brother Vedaśarman (2.1–6) and then demands, as another boon, the deepening of his devotion to his father (2.7–10). As soon as Vedaśarman is revived, his first inquiry concerns the fate of the young woman and the situation of his father—a testimony to his filial devotion (2.10–12). Both brothers, who are delighted by Dharma's boons, quickly return to the hermitage and Dharmaśarman can proudly proclaim that he has obtained the revival of Vedaśarman (2.13–17). Though he is satisfied with Dharmaśarman's devotion, Śivaśarman remains silent and begins to think of the next test (2.17–18).

4. Viṣṇuśarman (*PP*, 2.18–27 and 3.1–38). Śivaśarman is confronted with a problem in his relationship with the young woman with whom he was provided thanks to Vedaśarman's effort: his old age and weakness make him unattractive to her. He thus prompts Viṣṇuśarman, his fourth son, to visit Indra's heaven to obtain and bring back *amṛta* so that he can please and enjoy his mate (18–23). Thanks to his own *tapas*, the obliging Viṣṇuśarman immediately reaches Indra's kingdom (2.24–27 and 3.1) but the god does not intend to hand out the precious nectar. He enjoins the famed *apsaras* Menakā to try to seduce Viṣṇuśarman to divert him from his aim (3.2–6). The young brahmin is very aware of Menakā's mission and virtuously rebuffs her, explaining he is committed to celibacy (3.7–16). After Indra tries to deter him with various obstacles (3.17–21), Viṣṇuśarman threatens to deprive Indra of his divine kingship (3.22–26). Indra is humbled and lectured by Viṣṇuśarman about the superiority and unlimited power of brahmins (especially the ones devoted to their father; 3.30). The god then grants a boon to Viṣṇuśarman: he requires a pitcher of *amṛta* and, like his brothers, he wants to remain unswerving in his devotion to his father (3.27–38). Viṣṇuśarman's success in his mission greatly pleases Śivaśarman, who declares his satisfaction with his four sons, who have amply proved that they are *pitṛbhaktiyutāḥ* (3.40). Offered a boon by their father, the sons—including Somaśarman, it seems—instantly and unanimously demand the coming back to life and good health of their mother and they also ask to be reborn life after life as children of the same parents (3.43–47). Śivaśarman, who has never avowed his use of *māyā*, 'revives' his wife, who delivers to her sons a discourse on the duties of wives and children (3.47–58). The four elder sons, granted another boon by their delighted father, ask to be directly sent to Goloka, Viṣṇu's heaven. Viṣṇu himself comes mounted on Garuḍa—endowed with conch, discus and mace—to drive them to Goloka. He also asks Śivaśarman and his wife to accompany their sons

(3.59–64) but the brahmin decides to spend some more time on Earth in the company of his revived wife and his youngest son, Somaśarman. The four elder sons 'enter Viṣṇu's place due to their devotion to their father' (*gatās te vaiṣṇavaṃ dhāma pitṛbhaktyā dvijottamāḥ*; 3.69) and become absorbed in the god (3.64–71).

5. Somaśarman[6] (*PP*, 4 and 5.1–6). The trial of Somaśarman can be said to be a multifarious one and thus can be divided into three 'subtests'. First, Śivaśarman asks Somaśarman to guard the hermitage and the *amṛta* pot while he goes with his wife on a pilgrimage and practices penance with her (4.1–5). Second, after 10 years, the parents return, horribly afflicted by a disfiguring leprosy (*kuṣṭharoga*)—once more a production of Śivaśarman's *māyā* without the knowledge of his son. Somaśarman is deeply disturbed to see his meritorious parents, devoted to penance, in such a pitiful condition, but he readily accepts the command of his father to nurse them (4.6–19). For years, Somaśarman unfailingly and selflessly attends to his parents' needs, takes care of them, washing their wounds and ulcers, carrying them to various *tīrtha*s and helping them to bathe in rivers (4.19–29). Despite such kind behaviour, Śivaśarman often insults and sometimes even beats Somaśarman, who, against all odds, never strays from his filial duty (4.29–34). Reflections are made *in petto* by Śivaśarman on the compared merits of his sons after the tests he has imposed, and he seems to opine that Somaśarman's constancy in taking care of his sick parents is the most admirable. He nevertheless decides to submit Somaśarman to a final test (4.35–46).

In this final test, Śivaśarman asks Somaśarman to give him the precious *amṛta* that had been brought back by Viṣṇuśarman from Indra's heaven, as it will cure him of leprosy (*PP*, 4.47–50). However, once more owing to Śivaśarman's *māyā*, the pot appears empty when Somaśarman reaches for it. After a painful moment of doubt and anxiety, Somaśarman resorts to an act of truth, vindicating the sincerity of his behaviour and of his service to his parents, and the pitcher is then refilled with *amṛta* (4.51–56), which magically cures Śivaśarman and his wife (4.57–60). Somaśarman has achieved all the tests and is deemed by Śivaśarman as the most devoted of his sons due to his unswerving loyalty and patience.

---

6 This Somaśarman must not be confused with another Brahmanical character of the same name, whose story is also told at length in the Bhūmikhaṇḍa of the *PP* (*adh.* 11–20). The focus of this story is how the sonless Somaśarman, born in Kauśika's family, manages, through his devotion to Viṣṇu and with the help of his *pativratā* wife Sumanā, to obtain the birth of a very meritorious son named Suvrata.

The time has now come for Śivaśarman and his wife to end their earthly life and reach Viṣṇu's abode (*PP*, 5.1–6). Left alone on Earth, Somaśarman resettles in Śāligrāma, where he practices intense *tapas* and attains complete detachment from the objects of the senses. However, at the hour of his death, the words uttered by Dānavas and Daityas penetrate his ear, producing fear in him. Due to that very final thought, Somaśarman is reborn as Prahlāda, the son of the Daitya King Hiraṇyakaśipu (5.7–18). Prahlāda, when he contemplates Viṣṇu in his universal form (*viśvarūpa*) during the fight between gods and Daityas, recollects his former birth as Somaśarman, which concludes the narration by the *sūta* of the story of Śivaśarman and his sons (5.19–22).

If we sum up the trials of Śivaśarman's sons, several of which are facilitated or produced by Śivaśarman's *māyā*, we can underscore that: 1) the eldest son, Yajñaśarman, is ordered to cut into pieces and scatter the limbs of his dead mother; 2) the second son, Vedaśarman, is requested to bring to his father a young woman as a new life-partner, but when the woman expresses her own interest in Vedaśarman, the young brahmin remains adamant and accepts her command to behead himself for the sake of her union with Śivaśarman; 3) the third son, Dharmaśarman, who is entrusted by his father with the severed head of Vedaśarman, obtains from the god Dharma the resuscitation of his elder brother; 4) Viṣṇuśarman is assigned the task of reaching Indra's heaven to bring back the precious *amṛta* that will enable his father to fully enjoy the company of his young female mate; and 5) Somaśarman displays unswerving selflessness and helpfulness in taking care for years of his parents afflicted by leprosy, and he is able to obtain the reappearance of the *amṛta* that had momentarily vanished from the pitcher.

Themes and motives of the Śivaśarmopākhyāna emblematic of tales of *pitṛbhakti*

Based on this summary of the Śivaśarmopākhyāna, we can proceed to highlight elements of the story that are strongly reminiscent of far more famous epic and purāṇic tales of filial devotion. Among such tales, King Yayāti's exchange of his old age for his son Pūru's youth to enjoy at length a pleasurable life, and brahmin Jamadagni's order to his son Paraśurāma to slay his mother, Reṇukā, stand out. Their antiquity—both are crucial parts of well-known upākhyānas of the *Mahābhārata* (1.78–80 and 3.115–116, respectively)—and their pan-Indian fame encourage us to identify echoes and analogies between them and the Śivaśarmopākhyāna, although in a somewhat bizarre guise for parts of the narrative. This reflection on tales of *pitṛbhakti* is inspired by Goldman's (1978) article on 'Fathers, sons and gurus' in the Sanskrit epics, even if we will not focus here on the most psychoanalytical aspects of this article on the specific Indian form of Oedipal conflicts. We are more interested in identifying and locating common significant themes, features and narrative organisation.

As mentioned at the start of this chapter, the Śivaśarmopākhyāna stands at the beginning of the *Bhūmikhaṇḍa*, which is replete with stories and discourses on the theme of devotion towards one's parents, especially one's father, and the conception of parents as *tīrtha*s in their own right. The topic is obviously not absent from other parts of the voluminous *PP*, but it is paramount, bordering on the obsessive, in large sections of the Bhūmikhaṇḍa only. If we admit that *khaṇḍa*s 5, 6 and 7 of the *PP* (depending on the editions and manuscripts) are largely autonomous (Rocher 1986: 207–8), taking for analysis the Śivaśarmopākhyāna in a textual whole limited to the long 125-*adhyāya* Bhūmikhaṇḍa (BhKh) will not seem unreasonable. In addition to the story of Śivaśarman and his sons, a much developed and peculiar version of the Yayāticarita occupies the *adhyāya*s 64–83 of the BhKh; strong didactic considerations on the topic of reverence and devotion to parents conspicuously mark off and surround the Yayāti narrative as the preceding *adhyāya*s, 62 and 63, are devoted, respectively, to 'parents as sacred places of pilgrimage' and 'merit resulting from service to parents' and the concluding *adhyāya*, 84, espouses once more the 'glorification of devotion to parents'.[7]

Similarly, in the Śivaśarmopākhyāna, the phrase *pitṛbhakti* recurs throughout, either in the description of characters or in their prayers. Every time Śivaśarman's sons are granted a boon—a well-known ubiquitous feature of epic and purāṇic literature—either by a god or by their own father, they ask for a deepening and solidification of their reverence for their father. It is the case for Vedaśarman bidding Indra and the other gods (*yadi devāḥ prasannāḥ me … | imāṃ tu vipulāṃ bhaktiṃ pādayoḥ pitur eva me* ||; *PP*, 1.46), Dharmaśarman to the god Dharma (*dehi me tv acalāṃ bhaktiṃ pituḥ pādārhaṇe punaḥ* |; 2.9), Viṣṇuśarman to Indra (*amṛtaṃ dehi devendra pitṛbhaktiṃ tathā'calām* ||; 3.33) and the sons to their father, Śivaśarman

7 I use here the titles of the *adhyāya* in Deshpande's (1988–92) translation.

(3.44–45).[8] In the semantically close field of the acts of truth, in which a character solemnly proclaims his good faith to obtain fair treatment or the reparation of a wrong, Śivaśarman's sons always invoke their devotion to their elders. Such is the pattern in the scenes just referred to as well as in Somaśarman's mental stance to make the *amṛta* reappear in the pitcher to cure his parents of leprosy (4.54–55).[9] In all these cases, it must be noted that the invocation of filial devotion, or the request for even deeper *pitṛbhakti*, is always accompanied by more immediate, urgent and practical demands: the resurrection of Vedaśarman by the god Dharma, the resurrection of the seemingly dead mother by the *māyāvid* Śivaśarman or the reappearance of *amṛta* in the pitcher through Somaśarman's declaration.

Boons and their ominous counterparts, curses, pervade the tales of *pitṛbhakti* according to a rather simple grid. The most obedient and self-denying *pitṛbhakta* will be rewarded while the rebellious or even only reluctant sons will be severely or definitively chastised. A typical pattern in the tales of *pitṛbhakti*, which has been amply illustrated and analysed in Goldman (1978) and which has contributed to the definition of the Indian 'negative Oedipal son', is a demand by the father that implies the denial of his own desire and material, as well as the psychological wellbeing of his son. Bhīṣma's decision to give up not only his legitimate right to kingship but also having his progeny comply with his father Śāntanu's wish to marry Satyavatī is one of the most famous stories of this kind. Yayāti's myth is another case in point, in which Yayāti prompts his sons to exchange their youth for his old age so that he can enjoy all sensual pleasures for longer. The perfect *pitṛbhakta* son is thus ready and sometimes willing to give up, for a period (*Pūru*) or forever (*Bhīṣma*), his own access to *kāma* for the sake of an egoistic, demanding and lustful father.

The Śivaśarmopākhyāna provides us with two occurrences of the same mindset and of implicit rivalry between father and sons in the trials undergone by Vedaśarman and Viṣṇuśarman. Vedaśarman is sent by his father to bring him

8 *bhavān pitā iyaṃ mātā janmajanmāntare pitaḥ/vayaṃ sutā bhavameti sarve puṇyakṛtas tathā* || (43). The demand is here a little different but expresses movingly the permanent attachment of the sons to their parents: 'O father, may you be [our] father, and this one [our] mother, even in existence after existence, and may we be your meritorious sons.'

9 *yadi me satyam astīti guruśuśrūṣaṇaṃ yadi* | *tapas taptaṃ mayā pūrvaṃ nirvyalīkena cetasā* || (54) *damaśaucādibhiḥ satyaṃ dharmaṃ eva prapālitam* | *tadā ghaṭo'mṛtayuto bhavatv eṣa na saṃśayaḥ* || (55). Guruśuśrūṣaṇam can here be understood as 'obedience to elders'—more so for being the guru of his sons than for being their father. It is only here that it is one of the virtues underscored by Somaśarman, beside 'truthfulness, practise of *tapas* with a sincere mind, observance of the proper code of conduct by means of restraint, purity, etcetera'.

back a very beautiful young woman to replace his deceased wife.[10] Acting as the loyal and devoted messenger of his father, Vedaśarman makes abundantly clear to the woman what his mission is and how he wants to stick to it, even when the woman boldly expresses her desire for him and a lack of interest in the old father. The woman's assertiveness puts Vedaśarman in competition with his father for her. When she dares him to behead himself to fulfill Śivaśarman's wish of enjoying her, Vedaśarman, by happily complying and offering his head, refuses to rival or defy his father.[11] The trial of the fourth brother, Viṣṇuśarman, can be seen as the extension of Śivaśarman's desire to enjoy the young woman. Confronted with the risk of being cheated on or forsaken because of his old age, he needs the rejuvenating *amṛta*.[12] On his way to Indra's heaven, Viṣṇuśarman meets Menakā, the *apsaras* famous for her radiance and her ability to interrupt sages in their *tapas*, who has been sent by Indra to seduce Viṣṇuśarman. Like his older brother, the young brahmin underscores that he is going to Heaven for his father (*PP*, 3.9) and, when Menakā becomes more insistent, he proclaims his determination to stick to celibacy, as the proud son of Śivaśarman (3.13–15). Once more, we witness the case of a son who is so focused on the mission assigned by his lustful father that he does not ponder for a minute the possibility of having an affair with a resplendent *apsaras* or other woman.

Among the most conspicuous and dramatic cases of a *pitṛbhakti* put to extreme lengths we can count the very few episodes in which the total obedience to the father involves offending or even killing the mother. In such a situation, the tried son must make a terrible choice about which of his parents deserves greater reverence and *pitṛbhakti* is opposed to, and deemed superior to, *mātṛbhakti* ('devotion to one's mother'). The story of the beheading of Reṇukā by Paraśurāma at the command of Jamadagni stands out in the *Mahābhārata* (in the Vanaparvan account; it is absent from the *Mbh* 12.49 narrative) and in the purāṇas, which have retained the matricidal act in their retelling of Paraśurāmāvatāra. This is, quite noticeably, not the

10 As in Yayāti's case, the fact the self-denial expected of and exacted from the sons is aimed at enabling the father to enjoy the company of a woman other than his legitimate wife (and their mother) makes even more difficult the effort on the sons' side.

11 The religious, ritual and devotional overtones of voluntary head-offering could be fruitfully explored, but they fall outside the scope of this chapter.

12 The desire of an old man to obtain rejuvenation of some kind to cohabit with a younger woman is widely illustrated in epics and purāṇas—also outside the field of tales of *pitṛbhakti* (cf. the story of Cyavana, who is given back his youth by the Aśvins to please his young wife, Sukanyā).

case for the *PP* in a textual portion situated far from the BhKh, the *adhyāya* 241 of the Uttarakhaṇḍa, where the episode of Reṇukā's death is missing from Paraśurāma's narrative.

We find in the Śivaśarmopākhyāna a strange and faint echo of an offence towards the mother, here displaced and transposed towards her dead body. Śivaśarman does not order his sons to kill their mother but cruelly displays by *māyā* her corpse and then urges his eldest, Yajñaśarman, to cut her limbs into pieces 'with a very sharp and whetted weapon' (*anenāpi sutīkṣṇena śastreṇa niśitena*; *PP*, 1.25) and scatter them nearby. Absolutely no rationale is advanced by Śivaśarman to justify such an unusual and disrespectful way to dispose of the body of a parent, and neither Yajñaśarman nor any of his brothers asks for an explanation.[13] The silent and immediate compliance of Yajñaśarman contributes—like Paraśurāma's in the Vanaparvan account—to making this short scene more striking. In the afterthought reflections that Śivaśarman entertains in *adhyāya*s 4.35–46 on the respective acts of obedience of his sons, he underscores that by striking and scattering his mother's body, Yajñaśarman did not show compassion to her (*tena kṛtā na mātari kṛpā*; 4.37), which points in the direction of a trial involving a 'matricidal' side. The theme of the contest between *pitṛbhakti* and *mātṛbhakti* through a matricidal order by the father also figures in the Yayāticarita of the BhKh in an episode unique to this version.[14]

In *adhyāya* 80, observing the dissension between his wives, Devayānī and Śarmiṣṭhā, on the one side, and his concubine, the divine nymph Aśrubindumatī, on the other, Yayāti is willing to solve the problem by ordering Yadu to kill both his mothers (the biological one, Devayānī, and his stepmother, Śarmiṣṭhā). This rather expeditive and rough solution is forcefully rejected by Yadu, who reminds Yayāti of the total prohibition by the sages (*vedapaṇḍitaiḥ*; 80.9) of killing one's mother, even if she had committed 'one thousand sins' (*doṣāṇāṃ sahasreṇa*; 80.10). Because of his refusal, Yadu is once more angrily cursed by Yayāti—this time, to 'enjoy a portion of [his] mother' (*mātur aṃśaṃ bhajasva*; 80.13). The dramatic and

13 In the Śivaśarmopākhyāna, it is difficult to ascertain whether the nature of the trial of each son is known to the others, as the text specifies that Śivaśarman summons the sons individually and in succession. We cannot ascertain whether he has a private discussion with each son or whether he speaks to each in front of the others.

14 In his study of the myth of Yayāti in epic and purāṇic literature, strongly inspired by Madeleine Biardeau's reading, Michel Defourny (1978) has rightly underscored the originality of the retelling of Yayāti story in the *PP*.

uxoricidal outburst of Yayāti does not have further consequences as he does not reiterate his requests with his other sons and returns to his life of pleasure with Aśrubindumatī.

Correlative to the topic of loss of life or at least of senses, the theme of revival and resurrection is a regular one in the tales of *pitṛbhakti*. When the mother has died, either of disease (Śivaśarmopākhyāna) or from killing (Paraśurāma), the episode cannot but involve her resuscitation, which is very much longed for by her sons. Reṇukā's resurrection on Paraśurāma's request after Jamadagni has calmed down fulfills the crucial role of proving that his act of matricide was exclusively the sign of his total devotion to his father and not of enmity for her. The situation is less tragic in the Śivaśarmopākhyāna, but in this case, too, the call for their mother's resurrection to full health by the brothers bears witness to their attachment to her. It also undoes (as with Reṇukā's beheading) the gruesome cutting into pieces of her corpse by Yajñaśarman. Such a resurrection is not limited to the mother in the Śivaśarmopākhyāna, in which Dharmaśarman obtains the revival of his elder brother Vedaśarman and obviously the binding back together of his body and his head. We could call it an instance of *bhrātṛbhakti*, which is a kind of derivative of *pitṛbhakti* when it concerns the devotion of a younger brother towards an older one (Goldman 1978: 328 ff.). An analogous act of *bhrātṛbhakti* also occurs when Paraśurāma requests from Jamadagni the restoration to their full physical and mental capacities of his brothers previously cursed by him to lose their consciences and their thinking abilities.

The analogies and echoes between the Śivaśarmopākhyāna and the more classical tales of *pitṛbhakti* are not limited to themes and episodes. As far as the structure of the Śivaśarmopākhyāna is concerned, the successive trials of the five sons of Śivaśarman, from the eldest to the youngest, are also reminiscent of Yayāti's and Jamadagni's 'four plus one' narrative structure. In fact, when Yayāti wants to be given the youth of one of his sons, he also summons them in order of their seniority. The first four (Yadu, Turvasu, Druhyu and Anudruhyu) refuse what they see as an unfair demand, while the youngest one, Pūru, complies with his father's wishes and will be rewarded by kingship and (after a very long gap) the return of his youth once Yayāti finally decides to renounce earthly satisfactions. When Jamadagni wants his sons to punish the supposedly unfaithful Reṇukā by slaying their own mother, he resorts to the same process: interrogation of the sons from the oldest to the youngest, the first four of whom (Rumaṇvan, Suṣeṇa, Vasu and Viśvāvasu, in *Mbh*, 3.116.10) remain aghast and are cursed to become mindless, after which Paraśurāma obeys the command without protesting. The 'four plus one' structure could be the most visible in Jamadagni and Reṇukā's story because the four elder sons seem to be deprived of individuality and even of identity in their first mention in *Mbh* 3.116.4 (*tasyāḥ kumārāś catvāro jajñire rāmapañcamaḥ* | *sarveṣāṃ ajaghanyas tu rāma āsīj jaghanyajaḥ* |), where the purpose is clearly to exalt the youngest, Rāma, as the last born (*jaghanyaja*) but not the least (*ajaghanya*) son. In Yayāti's story, the curses thrown at the four elder sons, if they clearly demean them compared with Pūru, are individualised and do not deter Yadu from becoming the founder of a prestigious lineage from which Kṛṣṇa will be born. In the Śivaśarmopākhyāna, we can also clearly identify in the construction of the narrative a 'four plus one' structure. Right from the enumeration of Śivaśarman's sons, Somaśarman stands somewhat apart from his elder brothers mentioned in the same verse: 'He had five sons who were well-versed in [all] branches of knowledge. [They were] Yajñaśarman, Vedaśarman, Dharmaśarman, the glorious Viṣṇuśarman, who knew their own duties. The fifth one was Somaśarman, who was greatly devoted to his father' (*PP*, 1.13b–15).[15] Beside this distinction at a very small scale, a clearer one appears at the level of the *adhyāya* organisation of the whole *upākhyāna*. The trials of the four elder brothers are narrated in the first three *adhyāya*s, at the end of which they have proved their filial devotion, obtained the resuscitation of their mother and leave for Goloka under the guidance of Viṣṇu himself. Śivaśarman does not want to join this journey to Goloka because he prefers to stay longer on Earth with his wife and with Somaśarman, who is thus tested separately from his brothers. However, the analogies in the general structure between Śivaśarman's, Yayāti's and Jamadagni's stories, in which the youngest son stands apart from the four elder ones, must be qualified and nuanced in the case of the Śivaśarmopākhyāna whose peculiarities and sometimes apparent oddities must be considered on their own.

15 *tasyāpi pañca putrās tu babhūvuḥ śāstrakovidāḥ* | *yajñaśarmā vedaśarmā dharmaśarmā tathaiva ca* | (14) *viṣṇuśarmā mahābhāga nunaṃ tatkarmakovidāḥ* | *pañcamaḥ Somaśarmeti pitṛbhakti parāyaṇaḥ* | (15).

Idiosyncrasies and discrepancies in the Śivaśarmopākhyāna

Reflecting on the twists given to the 'four plus one' structure in the Śivaśarmopākhyāna can provide a good entry point to what makes this *PP* story peculiar, idiosyncratic and, in some respects, bizarre or fuzzy. The qualification of the 'four plus one' scheme, compared with the canonical Yayāti and Jamadagni narratives, consists mainly of two observations. First, in the Śivaśarmopākhyāna, each son must undergo a personal trial and the first four do not constitute a group of disobedient elders compared with the outshining youngest. As a corollary, the brothers are not involved in or tricked into direct rivalry by a single paternal request like the bid for youth or the slaying of Reṇukā, even if it may roll out as such if a son refuses to satisfy his father's order or wish. But, second, in a clear divergence from the narrative model, in the Śivaśarmopākhyāna, no son fails his own trial, none of the first four sons is cursed by his father and the collective success built by the individual achievements of the four elder brothers results in the resurrection of the mother granted by Śivaśarman (quite differently here from the request formulated by the lone Paraśurāma in favour of the revival of Reṇukā in *Mbh* 3.116).

In addition, the differentiation induced by the various tests of the five sons in the Śivaśarmopākhyāna allows for a far more nuanced appreciation and assessment of the devotion of the sons than in the 'either/or' scheme of the classical accounts of Yayāti or Jamadagni, which create a significant gap between the disobedient sons and the obedient one. Here, the fact that all the sons have passed the test and satisfied their father does not preclude Śivaśarman from establishing a hierarchy between them in a passage worth quoting. He first thought: 'Viṣṇuśarman brought nectar for me. That righteous one [Somaśarman] has religious merit and is always devoted to me [his father].' After the passage of hundreds of days of Somaśarman unfailingly caring for his parents, Śivaśarman ranks Yajñaśarman, Vedaśarman and Somaśarman. As seen above, he notices Yajñaśarman's apparent lack of compassion for his mother when he dismembered her corpse to obey him and adds:

> *amṛtaṃ matkṛte cāpi hy ānītaṃ Viṣṇuśarmaṇā* |
> *puṇyayuktaḥ sa dharmātmā pitṛbhaktiparaḥ sadā* || (35)
> *madvākyaṃ pālitaṃ tena kṛtā na mātari kṛpā* |
> *etat svalpataraṃ duḥkhaṃ nirjīve ghātam icchatā* || (38)
> *sāhasaṃ tu kṛtaṃ tena putreṇa Vedaśarmaṇā* |

asyādhikam ahaṃ manye yato'yaṃ calate na ca || (39)
nimeṣamātram evāpi sāhasaṃ kārayet punaḥ |
asyādhikas tu saṃpannaḥ prabhāvas tapasaḥ paraḥ || (40)
duḥsahaṃ vacanaṃ mahyaṃ dāruṇaṃ sahate sadā || (45)
kutsane tāḍane caiva sadā miṣṭapravācakaḥ |

[This grief of one who desires to give strikes on an inanimate body is smaller, but that son Vedaśarman did a bold act (beheaded himself), but I think that this one (Somaśarman) is superior since he does not swerve (from duty) even for a moment ... Even in everyday attendance he appears excelling (the others) ... (Even though I) reproached and beat him, he always talks pleasing words.] (*PP*, 4.35–45)

Śivaśarman, who in his comparison seems to have left aside or forgotten the third son, Dharmaśarman, assesses Somaśarman as his most devoted son due to his infallible patience and constant attention to his father,[16] which surpass the sometimes more dramatic but also more isolated acts of devotion of his brothers.

A very striking feature of the Śivaśarmopākhyāna, even in the most casual reading, is the prominent role played in it by the *māyā* of Śivaśarman. Most of the trials undergone by his sons have their origin in his power of illusion, which is conspicuous in the display of the dead mother (which bewilders all the sons and leads Yajñaśarman to dismember her body), the creation of the young woman whom Vedaśarman must bring to his father and, in the trial of Somaśarman, the appearance of Śivaśarman and his wife disfigured and sullied by leprosy and the final disappearance of the *amṛta* in the pitcher. This recurrence and even the pervasiveness of *māyā* offer a strong contrast with the classical epic tales of *pitṛbhakti* of Yayāti, Jamadagni or Bhīṣma in which the events seem to have far more weight. Even if the *kāma*, so strong in Yayāti's and Śāntanu's stories, always involves some illusion and *moha* ('confusion'), the feelings of those kings, and hence their actions and requests, are not produced almost *ex nihilo* as in the Śivaśarmopākhyāna, in which Śivaśarman behaves as both an actor and the playwright of a drama or even like a *bhakti* god playing with his devotees and testing them at will

16 The qualities that are most valued by Śivaśarman here are the same as those highlighted and praised in another kind of epic and purāṇic narrative, the tales of hospitality in which an abusive and irascible guest (most often a *ṛṣi* or a god in disguise) tests the patience of his host and rewards him. The host cannot be blamed in any way.

for reasons they cannot understand. It must nevertheless be noted that the term *līlā* ('god's play')—so important in *bhakti* texts, especially in Vaiṣṇava contexts—does not appear in the Śivaśarmopākhyāna.

The repeated use—bordering on the overuse—of *māyā* in the story creates in the reader the awkward impression that the trials undergone by Śivaśarman's sons are devoid of any real import, even if much is obviously at stake for the sons, who are unaware of the illusions produced by their father. The fact that the father, in contrast with the usual behaviour of the *bhakti* god, does not tell the truth to his sons after they have managed the test, leaves one with a feeling of unfulfillment because the brothers leaving for Viṣṇu's abode are not informed that their trials were not the vital ones they imagined.[17]

A final element of 'awkwardness', or at least a feature difficult to understand, in the Śivaśarmopākhyāna is the following: Somaśarman, the model of *pitṛbhakti* put forward by the *upākhyāna*, is reborn as Prahlāda, an archetype of *Viṣṇubhakti*, but also one of the least obedient sons in Hindu mythology due to his refusal to give up his devotion to Viṣṇu despite the command of his father, the Daitya King Hiraṇyakaśipu. Ironically enough, the link established between Somaśarman and Prahlāda could almost extend here to a tentative inversion (or subversion?) of the classical framework in which the youngest son is unquestionably the best. Somaśarman, whom his father has declared his most devoted son (in keeping with the 'four plus one' structure), is reborn as a Daitya because of an incident at the time of his death, while his elder brothers have been immersed in Viṣṇu. The virtuous Daitya devoted to Viṣṇu will know the same fortunate fate only after his opposition to his Daitya father and a mortal fight with Viṣṇu.

The relationship and intertwining between *pitṛbhakti* and *Viṣṇubhakti* appear complex and not homogeneous in the beginning of the BhKh. Both *bhakti*s are either intimately linked in Śivaśarman's story proper (*pitṛbhakti* is rewarded by direct access to Goloka and fusion into Viṣṇu's body for the four elder sons) or seem to be in conflict in Prahlāda's story, in which *Viṣṇubhakti* is clearly assessed as superior to *pitṛbhakti* if the devotion to the father implies

17 The idea that the use of *māyā* by a 'testing' character in a story diminishes the gravity of an action entailed by such a manufactured test pervades some modern retellings of Paraśurāma's story, where the episode of the beheading of Reṇukā is presented as a result of an illusion created by Jamadagni. Consequently, Reṇukā was never 'really' dead and Paraśurāma's action thus cannot be technically labelled as matricide (Dejenne 2009).

giving up devotion to Viṣṇu. Prāhlada would then be a counterexample to an overwhelming conception of *pitṛbhakti* as dwarfing all other dharmic duties and obligations.

The Śivaśarmopākhyāna can be characterised as a kind of meta-myth (to use Goldman's 1977 labelling of Paraśurāma's myth as a Bhārgava meta-myth) or at least a narrative construction whose building blocks, themes, features and junctures are recognisable, even in a strange guise, as borrowed from various more well-known epic and purāṇic tales of *pitṛbhakti*. These include the self-denial of the sons, up to accepting death, to enable the father to enjoy for longer youth and sensual pleasures; the curse of the rebellious or reluctant sons and rewarding of the most obedient one; the offence towards the mother followed by her restoration to her initial condition; and the narrative structure itself ('four plus one').

However, in the context of the Śivaśarmopākhyāna, the recurring use of *māyā* by Śivaśarman to test his sons' devotion runs the risk of depriving most of its episodes of real weight, particularly compared with their epic inspirations. Could this be one reason such a spectacular compendium of mythemes from diverse *pitṛbhakti* stories has not gained more fame?

This chapter has drawn attention, through and beyond the Śivaśarmopākhyāna, to the Bhūmikhaṇḍa and more largely to the *Padma Purāṇa* itself. As well as the story of Śivaśarman and his sons, this purāṇa offers many other original legends, as well as idiosyncratic retellings of some of the most famous Hindu myths (like Yayāti's or the *avatāras*' stories) and texts (like an elaborate rewriting of Rāma Dāśarathi's *aśvamedha* in the Pātālakhaṇḍa). It deserves to be studied in more depth. Nevertheless, for this voluminous purāṇa, the main *khaṇḍa*s of which clearly spring from diverse cultural and religious contexts—although dominantly Vaiṣṇava—the *PP* retains very old Brāhma passages while others display a Śaiva bias. Studies at the level of *khaṇḍa*s, or even smaller and more homogeneous portions of *khaṇḍa*s, could prove to be the most fruitful way to shed light on their dominant themes and organisation.

References

Primary texts

Deshpande, N.A. (trans. and ed.). (1988–92). *Padma Purāṇa*. Ancient Indian Tradition and Mythology, Volumes 39–48. Delhi: Motilal Banarsidass. [The translation of the Bhūmikhaṇḍa occupies the whole of Vol. 41 (Part III), *adhyāyas* 1–90, and Vol. 42 (Part IV), *adhyāyas* 90–125, pp. 1241–349.]

Kṣemarāja Śrīkṛṣṇadāsa (ed.). (1895). *Padma Purāṇa*. Bombay, India: Veṅkaṭeśvara Press.

Viśvanātha Nārāyaṇa Maṇḍalīka (ed.). (1893–94). *Padma Purāṇa*. [4 vols.] Poona, India: Anandasrama Sanskrit Series [Vol. 1: Ādikhaṇḍa and Bhūmikhaṇḍa, 1893].

Secondary texts

Chatterjee, Asoke. (1967). *Padma-Purāṇa: A Study*. Calcutta Sanskrit College Research Series No. LVIII. Calcutta, India: Calcutta Sanskrit College.

Defourny, Michel. (1978). *Le mythe de Yayāti dans la littérature épique et purāṇique. Étude de mythologie hindoue* [*The Yayāti Myth in Epic and Purāṇic Literature: Study of Hindu Mythology*]. Paris: Les Belles-Lettres. doi.org/10.4000/books.pulg.111.

Dejenne, Nicolas. (2009). Paraśurāma torchbearer of a regenerated Bhārat in a contemporary retelling of his narratives. In P. Koskikallio (ed.), *Parallels and Comparisons: Proceedings of the Fourth DICSEP (September 2005)*, pp. 447–68. Zagreb: Croatian Academy of Sciences and Arts.

Goldman, Robert P. (1977). *Gods, Priests and Warriors. The Bhṛgus of the Mahābhārata*. New York, NY: Columbia University Press.

Goldman, Robert P. (1978). Fathers, sons and gurus: Oedipal conflict in the Sanskrit epics. *Journal of Indian Philosophy* 6: 325–92. doi.org/10.1007/BF00218428.

Rocher, Ludo. (1986). *The Purāṇas*. A History of Indian Literature, Vol. II, Fasc. 3. Wiesbaden, Germany: Otto Harrassowitz.

16

Same, same but different: The Tamil *Kāñcippurāṇam* and its Sanskrit source

Jonas Buchholz[1]

Abstract

This chapter investigates the relationship of two mythological texts (*sthalamāhātmya*/*talapurāṇam*) on the city of Kanchipuram in Sanskrit and Tamil. The Tamil *Kāñcippurāṇam*, composed in the eighteenth century by the influential author Civañāṉa Muṉivar, is demonstrably based on the Sanskrit *Kāñcīmāhātmya* and follows its source rather closely on a narrative level. However, the two texts differ considerably in terms of their literary agendas. Unlike the rather utilitarian *Kāñcīmāhātmya*, the *Kāñcippurāṇam* is a sophisticated literary work, composed in a complex poetic style, which is typical of Tamil *talapurāṇam*s. It will therefore be argued that the differences between the Tamil and the Sanskrit texts are more interesting than their parallels. Using the examples of the *Kāñcippurāṇam* and the *Kāñcīmāhātmya*, this chapter addresses the relationship of Tamil *talapurāṇam*s to Sanskrit *sthalamāhātmya*s in the larger context of the literary cultures of which these texts formed part.

1 Research for this chapter was funded by the Deutsche Forschungsgemeinschaft (DFG, German Research Foundation), project number 428328143, and the Academies Programme of the Union of the German Academies of Sciences and Humanities.

Introduction

There is perhaps no other area in which the Tamil and Sanskrit literatures have been in closer contact than the genre of texts that tell the legendary stories of holy places, known as *sthalamāhātmya* in Sanskrit and *talapurāṇam* (from Skt., *sthalapurāṇa*) in Tamil. A great number of such texts exists about numerous places across Tamil Nadu in both Sanskrit and Tamil.[2] In Tamil, *talapurāṇams* were an extremely productive genre between the sixteenth and nineteenth centuries, and many of these Tamil texts were based on Sanskrit sources. Yet, the *sthalamāhātmyas* and *talapurāṇams* of Tamil Nadu are a largely neglected field of study. Moreover, the Sanskrit and Tamil texts have mostly been studied in isolation.[3] With the exception of a recent PhD thesis (Ramesh 2020) and a handful of short individual studies (Harman 1987; Younger 1995: Ch. 5; Wilden 2015; Fisher 2017: Ch. 4), little attempt has been made to systematically investigate the relationship between Tamil *talapurāṇams* and Sanskrit *sthalamāhātmyas*.

This chapter aims to contribute to a better understanding of that relationship through an investigation of the *Kāñcippurāṇam* (*KP*), a Tamil *talapurāṇam* on the South Indian temple town of Kanchipuram, and its Sanskrit source, the *Kāñcīmāhātmya* (*KM*).[4] The *KP* was composed during the second half of the eighteenth century by Civañāṉa Muṉivar (d. 1785) based on the *KM*.[5] The latter is an anonymous and undated Sanskrit *sthalamāhātmya* that describes Kanchipuram's sacred space from a Śaiva perspective, dealing with the mythical origin stories of more than 100 Śiva temples in Kanchipuram and its surroundings, culminating with the great

2 For an overview of the Tamil *talapurāṇam* genre, see Kiruṣṇacāmi (1974); Shulman (1980); Mātavaṉ (1995); and Nachimuthu (2022). Sanskrit *sthalamāhātmyas* are representative of a wider genre known as *māhātmya* ('glorification'). Literature on *māhātmyas* in general is scarce and mostly confined to short overviews in literary histories (for example, Gonda 1977: 277–83; Rocher 1986: 70–72). Probably the best overview is found in an unpublished MA thesis (Wiig 1981).

3 It is telling that, for example, Hermann Kulke's substantial study of the *Cidambaramāhātmya* (1970) does not mention the Tamil parallel text, Umāpati Civācāriyar's *Kōyiṟpurāṇam*, with a single word. On the *Cidambaramāhātmya* and the *Kōyiṟpurāṇam*, see also Younger (1995: Ch. 5); and Ganesan (2022: 90–93).

4 For an overview of the *sthalamāhātmyas* and *talapurāṇams* of Kanchipuram and a more detailed description of the *KP* and the *KM*, see Buchholz (2022).

5 In fact, the *KP* contains two books (*kāṇṭam*), the first composed by Civañāṉa Muṉivar and the second by his pupil Kacciyappa Muṉivar. However, as I have shown elsewhere (Buchholz 2022: 27–29), the second book is a self-contained composition that is based on a different, so far unpublished, Sanskrit source. In this chapter, I am not concerned with the second book of the *KP*. Wherever I speak of the *KP*, I refer only to the first book by Civañāṉa Muṉivar.

Ekāmranātha (or Ekāmbaranātha) temple, the city's main Śaiva sanctuary.[6] While the *KM* has received little scholarly attention,[7] a French summary of the *KP* by Dessigane et al. (1964) and a copious study in Tamil by Cāmi Aiyā (1989) exist. However, the nature of the relationship between the *KP* and its Sanskrit source, the *KM*, has so far not been investigated in detail—a lacuna that the present chapter aims to fill.

The *KM* as the source of the *KP*

That the *KP* is based on the *KM* is noted by Dessigane et al. (1964: vi–vii), who point out that the narrative structure of the *KP* closely corresponds with that of the *KM*. They also state that the *KP* follows the *KM* '*très fidèlement jusque dans le detail* [very faithfully down to the detail]', while at the same time describing the *KP* as '*beaucoup plus élaboré du point de vue littéraire* [much more elaborate from the literary point of view]'. As I will show in this chapter, Dessigane et al.'s assessment is essentially correct. However, it is precisely the tension between the Tamil text's faithful adherence to its Sanskrit source and its much more ambitious poetic agenda that makes the case of the *KM* and the *KP* interesting, calling for a more detailed investigation.

The *KP* itself also acknowledges its Sanskrit source, albeit in a somewhat oblique way. Its prefatory section (*pāyiram*) contains a verse (*KP*, 1.22) in which Civañāṉa Muṉivar states that he composed his work because local dignitaries from Kanchipuram had asked him to 'tell the *purāṇam* of peerless Kacci [Kanchipuram] in luxuriant Tamil' (*poruv il kacciyam purāṇam vaṇ ṭamiḻiṉiṟ pukal*).[8] Such verses describing the circumstances of the text's composition are a standard element of Tamil *talapurāṇams*, and they often refer to a Sanskrit source that the author has rendered into Tamil. Here, no source is named, but the fact that Civañāṉa Muṉivar says he composed his work in Tamil implies that the text was originally in another language—namely, Sanskrit. Elsewhere, Civañāṉa Muṉivar explicitly states that he has translated (*moḻipeyarttu*) the stories that were told by Sūta (the mythical narrator of

6 There is another *sthalamāhātmya* of Kanchipuram, of Vaiṣṇava orientation, which also bears the title *Kāñcīmāhātmya*. Apart from the title, this text has nothing in common with the Śaiva *KM* and therefore is of no concern to us. Wherever I speak of the *KM* in this chapter, I mean the Śaiva *KM*.

7 The only major exception is Kerstin Schier's (2018) study of the marriage festival at the Ekāmranātha temple, which draws on the *KM* in its discussion of the temple's central myth.

8 Note that the numbering of the chapters of the *KP* differs depending on whether the *pāyiram* is included in the chapter count. I follow Dessigane et al. (1964) in counting the *pāyiram* as chapter number one.

the purāṇas) for the benefit of those well versed in Tamil.[9] Although some scholars have dismissed the claim of a Sanskrit source as a mere convention (for example, Harman 1987), there is ample evidence of Tamil *talapurāṇam*s that were based on Sanskrit sources. The *KP* is a case in point as it is based on an identifiable Sanskrit text—namely, the *KM*. As such, the *KM* and the *KP* provide an excellent starting point for an investigation of the relationship between Sanskrit *sthalamāhātmya*s and Tamil *talapurāṇam*s.

How can we be sure that the *KP* is based on the *KM*? The close parallels between the two texts make it abundantly clear that they are related, but could the *KM* not be based on the *KP*, rather than the other way around? This possibility can be safely ruled out. First, the *KP* is a relatively late text, composed during the second half of the eighteenth century, and an even later date for the *KM* seems unlikely. More importantly, a direct comparison of the two texts makes the direction of borrowing rather clear. As we will see, the *KP* takes the narrative of the *KM* as its starting point but expands it by adding ornamentation and descriptive passages. It seems natural to assume that such additions were made when the *KM* was rendered into Tamil, whereas the opposite process is much more difficult to imagine. This will become clear from the following discussion of the *KM* and the *KP*.[10]

Parallels between the *KM* and the *KP*

Reading the *KM* and the *KP* in parallel

To understand the exact nature of the relationship between the *KM* and the *KP*, a close parallel reading of a selected passage seems in order. Let us therefore consider the beginning of the origin myth of the Tirumēṟṟaḷīśvara temple (or Paścimālaya),[11] which relates how Viṣṇu performed austerities to obtain Śiva's form. In the *KM* (15.49–55), the passage in question reads as follows:

> *atra pūrvaṃ mahāviṣṇuḥ paścimālayasaṃjñake* |
> *tapaś cacāra sārupyasamprāptyai śūlino hariḥ* ||

9 *KP*, 3.126: *cūtaṉ aṉṟ' uraittav āṟē mut tamiḻ aṟiñar tēṟa moḻipeyartt' uraippēṉ uyntēṉ*.

10 This is not to say that there cannot be Sanskrit *sthalamāhātmya*s that are based on Tamil *talapurāṇams* (for a possible case in point, see Wilden 2015), although this direction of borrowing seems to have been much rarer. What is needed is an unprejudiced investigation of the texts that neither uncritically accepts the Tamil texts' claims to a Sanskrit source nor dismisses them without looking into the Sanskrit parallel texts.

11 The Tirumēṟṟaḷīśvara temple is a Śiva temple in Kanchipuram's Piḷḷaiyārpāḷaiyam neighbourhood. This site is mentioned in the *Tēvāram* (seventh/eight century) under the name Tirumēṟṟaḷi. The name Paścimālaya, which appears in the *KM*, seems to be a Sanskrit calque of the Tamil name Tirumēṟṟaḷi, which can be interpreted as 'western temple' (< *mēl* + *taḷi*).

śānto dānto jitakrodho bhasmoddhūḷitavigrahaḥ |
rudrākṣamālābharaṇo rudrādhyayanatatparaḥ ||
hṛtpuṇḍarīkanilayaṃ viśvākṣaṃ viśvatomukham |
viśvataḥpāṇipādaṃ taṃ viśvarūpam umāpatim ||
dhyāyamāno divārātraṃ tatāpa paramaṃ tapaḥ |
tapasā tasya saṃtuṣṭaḥ prāhāvirbhūya śūladhṛt ||
vatsa viṣṇo prasanno 'smi varaṃ varaya suvrata |
tvam atīva priyo 'smākaṃ pārvatyāś ca viśeṣataḥ ||
iti devavacaś śrutvā murāriḥ prītamānasaḥ |
praṇamya girijādhīśaṃ pṛṣṭavān varam uttamam ||
bhagavan deva sarvajña viśveśvara maheśvara |
sārūpyaṃ mahyam īśāna prasīda tava śaṅkara ||

[There, in the place named Paścimālaya, Hari, the great Viṣṇu, once performed austerities in order to achieve identity of form with the trident-bearer (Śiva). Pacified, restrained, his anger subdued, his body besmeared with ashes, wearing a garland of *rudrākṣa* beads, engaged in reciting the Rudra(-mantra), he performed extreme austerities, meditating day and night on the one who lived in the lotus of his heart, the one who had eyes everywhere, the one whose face is turned everywhere, the one whose hands and feet are everywhere, that one who has all forms, the husband of Umā (Śiva). Pleased by his austerities, the trident-bearer (Śiva) manifested himself (and said:) 'Viṣṇu, my dear, I am pleased. You who are strict in observing your vows! Choose a boon. You are very dear to us, and particularly to Pārvatī.' When the enemy of Mura (Viṣṇu) heard these divine words, his mind was gratified. He bowed down before the lord of the daughter of the mountain (Śiva) and asked for an excellent boon: 'Lord! God! Omniscient one! Lord of the universe! Great lord! Master! Grace me with identity of form with you, Śaṅkara!']

Compare this with the parallel passage in the *KP* (28.5–8):

navilum at talatt' eyti muṉ ṉāk' aṇaip puttēḷ
kavir itaḻc ciṟu nuṇuk' iṭaik kavuri taṉ kaḷapak
kuvi mulait taṭac cuvaṭu tōy kuricil cārūpam
puvimicaip peṟa viḻaintu meyt tavam purintaṉaṉāl.
aim pulaṉkaḷaiy aṭakki niṉṟ' aṟu pakai tuṟantu
nampu nīṟṟ' aṇiy akka mālikaiyuṭa ṉayantu
kampiyāt' uruttiraṅ kaṇitt' itaya naṟ kamalatt'
empirāṉ aruḷ vaṭiviṉaiy iṭaiy aṟāt' irutti;

āṟṟ' arun tavam iyaṟṟuḷiy aḻal viḻit taṟukaṭ
kūṟṟai veṉṟ' aruḷ paramporuḷ karuṇai kūrnt' aṭal āṉ
ēṟṟiṉ mīt' eḻunt' aruḷiy emm aṭiyariṟ ciṟantōy
nōṟṟu nontaṉai vēṭṭaṉa nuvaṟiy eṉṟ' aruḷa;
unti pūttavaṉ aḷapp' arum uvakaiyuṭ ṭiḷaittuc
canta mā malar aṭimicai vīḻntu tāḻnt' eḻuntāṉ
entai nī tara muḻuvatum peṟṟ' uḷēṉ in nāḷ
antil eṉ ṟaṉakk' aḷitt' aruḷ aiya niṉṉ uruvam.

[In this famous site (Tirumēṟṟaḷi), the god who rests on a snake (Viṣṇu) once arrived and performed austerities with the wish to obtain identity of form with the lord (Śiva) who bears the large impression of the perfumed round breasts of Gaurī, who has lips like flowers of the coral tree and a small, minute waist. Keeping his five senses under control, having renounced the six enemies (emotions), adorned with desirable ashes, having a garland of *rudrākṣa* beads, reciting the Rudra(-mantra) without fail, having constantly placed our lord's gracious form in the good lotus of his heart, he performed austerities that were difficult to endure. Then the highest being that graciously overcame the cruel-fiery eyed god of death (Śiva), graciously mounted his victorious bull and said: 'You who have excelled among my servants! You have practised great austerities. Say what you wish for!' He who had a flower in his navel (Viṣṇu) rejoiced with immeasurable joy, fell to his beautiful large lotus feet, rose again, and said: 'My father! I have obtained everything by you. Lord! Bestow me today identity of form with you.']

The narrative outlined by the *KM* and the *KP* is identical: Viṣṇu performs austerities because he wants to obtain identity of form with Śiva; pleased by Viṣṇu's austerities, Śiva grants him a boon; Viṣṇu then asks for identity of form with Śiva. Apart from the basic outline of the narrative, we also find numerous phrasal parallels between the two texts. For example, both texts describe Viṣṇu as performing austerities in the way of a Śaiva ascetic, using almost the same terms in the same sequence. Compare the following phrases:

- *śānto dāntaḥ* ('pacified and restrained') (*KM*) *aim pulaṉkaḷaiy aṭakki niṉṟu* ('keeping his five senses under control') (*KP*)
- *jitakrodhaḥ* ('having subdued his anger') (*KM*) *aṟu pakai tuṟantu* ('having renounced the six enemies [that is, emotions]) (*KP*)
- *bhasmoddhūḷitavigrahaḥ* ('having a body that is besmeared with ashes') (*KM*) *nampu nīṟṟ' aṇi* ('adorned with desirable ashes') (*KP*)

- *rudrākṣamālābharaṇaḥ* ('adorned with a garland of *rudrākṣa* beads') (*KM*) *akka mālikaiyuṭa ṉayantu* ('having a garland of *rudrākṣa* beads') (*KP*)
- *rudrādhyayanatatparaḥ* ('devoted to reciting the *Rudra*[*-mantra*]) (*KM*) *kampiyāt' uruttiraṅ kaṇittu* ('reciting the *Rudra*[*-mantra*] without fail) (*KP*)

The parallels between the two texts thus go beyond the narrative level and extend to the phrase level. Civañāṉa Muṉivar did not just retell the narrative that is also found in the *KM*; he also must have had the Sanskrit text in front of him and rendered it into Tamil phrase by phrase.

At the same time, the *KP* is not a literal translation of the *KM*. First, the diction of the *KP* is much more florid than that of the *KM*; I will return to this point later. Second, while the Tamil text for the most part closely follows its Sanskrit source, it occasionally adds or omits individual phrases or simply says things in a different manner. Consider, for example, Śiva's words to Viṣṇu: in the *KM*, he tells him, 'You are very dear to us, and particularly to Pārvatī' (*tvam atīva priyo 'smākaṃ pārvatyāś ca viśeṣataḥ*), whereas in the *KP*, he says, 'You have excelled among my servants' (*emm aṭiyariṟ ciṟantōy*). Such differences of course do not really change the message, but they show that while Civañāṉa Muṉivar was closely guided by the Sanskrit text, he did not try to render it into Tamil word by word. Describing the *KP* as a 'translation' of the *KM* (cf. Zvelebil 1975: 248) could therefore fall short. While I do not want to enter this issue here, the Sanskrit *sthalamāhātmya*s and Tamil *talapurāṇam*s certainly provide ample opportunity to reflect on the concept of translation (cf. Ramesh 2020: Ch. 3).

The *KP* as an interpretational aid and textual witness for the *KM*

The close relationship between the *KM* and the *KP* means that the *KP* can help solve problems of interpretation or even textual problems with the *KM* when the texts are read side by side. Consider, for example, the following passage from the *KM* (3.79c–81b), which describes the rivers flowing in Kanchipuram and its vicinity:

> *kampayā kampayā puṇyajalayā niśayāvṛtā* ||
> *vegavatyā viśeṣeṇa puṇyakoṭīśamānyayā* |
> *kṣīranadyā mahatyā ca skandanadyā ca saṃyutā* ||
> *mālābhir abhita svacchasumābhir iva māninī* |

This passage poses several problems. The word *kampayā* can be easily discerned as the instrumental of *kampā* (the name of a river), but its reduplication is difficult to explain. Moreover, it is not entirely clear which of the words in the instrumental are names of rivers and which are attributes describing the rivers. Is *puṇyajalā* (lit., 'having holy water') a river or does the word *puṇyajalayā* simply qualify the following *niśayā*? And how is *niśayā* to be understood? The usual meaning of *niśā* ('night') seems hardly fitting. For all these problems, the parallel passage in the *KP* (7.23a–b) is illuminating:

> *pampai kampai puṇṇiyanīr mañcaṇati vēkavati pāli cēyāṟ'*
> *eṉpaṉav ēḻ ulakum iṭum ēḻ mālaiy eṉav oḻukum*
>
> [Pampai, Kampai, Puṇṇiyanīr, Mañcaṇati, Vēkavati, Pāli and Cēyāṟu
> flow like seven garlands that are put on the seven worlds]

First, the problematic phrase *kampayā kampayā* in the *KM* is echoed by the phrase *pampai kampai* in the *KP*. This suggests that the name of the first river should be *pampā* in Sanskrit (Tamilised as *pampai*) and that *kampayā kampayā* is a corruption of *pampayā kampayā*. Second, the *KP* clarifies that the rivers are seven in number: this becomes clear from the comparison, where the rivers are likened to seven garlands (*ēḻ mālai*). To arrive at the number seven, *puṇyajalā* (or *puṇṇiyanīr* in the *KP*) must be taken as a part of the enumeration of rivers. Furthermore, the obscure *niśayā* is glossed by *mañcaṇati* (< *mañcaḷ* + *nati*), which suggests that the word *niśā* is here used in the rare meaning of 'turmeric' (*mañcaḷ* in Tamil) and stands for a river named 'Turmeric River'. All this helps us to arrive at the following translation for the *KM* passage cited above:

> [Kanchipuram] is enclosed by the Pampā [read *pampayā*], Kampā, Puṇyajalā, and Niśā rivers,
> and by the Vegavatī, which is particularly dear to Puṇyakoṭīśa,
> and it is joined by the great Kṣīranadī and the Skandanadī
> like a haughty woman [is adorned] with bright flower garlands all over.[12]

12 Of these rivers, the identification of Pampā/Pampai and Puṇyajalā/Puṇṇiyanīr is unclear. Kampā/Kampai is the name of a mythical river (or possibly a river that existed formerly but has since disappeared) that features prominently in the myth of the Ekāmranātha temple; today it is the name of one of the Ekāmranātha temple's tanks. Niśā/Mañcaṇīr stands for the now canalised rivulet presently known as Mañcaḷ Nīr Kālvāy, which flows through central Kanchipuram. Vegavatī/Vēkavati is the name of a river in the southern part of Kanchipuram (Puṇyakoṭīśa being Śiva's name in the main Śiva temple of this area). Kṣīranadī/Pāli is the Palar (Pālāṟu) River to the south of Kanchipuram and Skandanadī is the Cheyyar (Cēyāṟu) River, a tributary of the Palar that runs further south.

This example shows that the *KP* can serve both as an interpretational aid and as a textual witness for the *KM*. In many cases, the Tamil paraphrase helps us to understand the meaning of the Sanskrit text that might otherwise be unclear. Of course, the interpretation found in the *KP* does not always have to be compelling: in the case of the passage discussed above, for example, it is possible that Civañāṉa Muṉivar simply misinterpreted *puṇyajalā* to be the name of a river (especially since a river of that name cannot be presently found).[13] When he composed the *KP*, Civañāṉa Muṉivar could have been faced with the same problems regarding the interpretation of the *KM* as we are, and we are free to challenge his choices. However, it seems wise to assume that Civañāṉa Muṉivar and his interlocutors in eighteenth-century Kanchipuram were in a better position to understand the *KM* than we are today and his interpretation often gives us a better understanding of the Sanskrit text.

Not only does the *KP* show us how Civañāṉa Muṉivar understood the *KM*, in some cases, it is even possible to reconstruct what form of the text he must have had before him. In our example, the fact that the *KP* has *pampai* suggests that the version of the *KM* to which Civañāṉa Muṉivar had access contained the reading *pampayā* instead of the first, *kampayā*.[14] Therefore, although all manuscripts of the *KM* that I have been able to examine support the reading *kampayā kampayā*, we must consider *pampayā kampayā* as a variant reading that is attested by the Tamil parallel. Even though the identification of the Pampā River is unclear, this reading seems preferable since the reduplication of *kampayā* cannot be satisfactorily explained.[15] Other such examples can be found from a parallel reading of the *KM* and the *KP*. If a critical edition of the *KM* were to be produced, it therefore must consider the testimonia provided by the *KP*. Although the value of Tamil parallel texts for the textual criticism of the Sanskrit purāṇas was noted by V. Raghavan as early as 1959, this approach has only rarely been used with Sanskrit and Tamil texts—quite in contrast, for example, to Buddhist texts in Sanskrit, Tibetan and Chinese.

13 Given that the enumeration of rivers moves from north to south, the Puṇyajalā River should flow between the Ekāmranātha temple (where the semi-mythical Kampā River is located) and the Mañcaḷ Nīr Kālvāy, but no river is presently found in this area. However, Kanchipuram's urban landscape has changed considerably over the centuries and it cannot be ruled out that there once was a watercourse here.

14 Another possible explanation is that Civañāṉa Muṉivar had access to a manuscript that contained the reading *kampayā kampayā* but opted for the conjectural emendation *pampayā kampayā* because he could not make sense of the reading in the manuscript.

15 As it stands at the beginning of the enumeration, the Pampā River should be found to the north of Kanchipuram, but I am not aware of a river of that name in this area. However, *pampā* is a plausible name since a river of that name is mentioned in the *Rāmāyaṇa* and several rivers in India bear that name (see Eck 2012: 419–21).

Recensions of the *KM*

In some cases, it is possible to discern that the *KP* is based on a recension of the *KM* that is different from the printed version. Purāṇic texts in Sanskrit such as the *KM* were subject to a process that Hans Bakker (1989) has described as 'composition in transmission' and therefore often exist in several widely divergent versions. The textual history of the *KM* remains to be investigated in detail, but my preliminary findings, based on an investigation of three manuscripts held by the Institut français de Pondichéry, suggest that at least two different recensions of the *KM* exist. One of the three manuscripts, RE 30565, transmits a recension that is rather like the text of the printed editions (henceforth, 'Recension A'), whereas the two other manuscripts, RE 30550 and RE 39684, represent a different recension (henceforth, 'Recension B'). Significantly, the *KP* seems to be based on a version of the *KM* that is closer to Recension B than to the printed text. Consider, for example, the passage *KM* 13.12c–13b, which is part of the section on Kanchipuram's Kāyārohaṇeśvara temple, which reads as follows in the printed edition:

> *atrārṇavasamudbhūtāṃ lakṣmīm ārādhya vai purā* ||
> *bilvapatrair mahādevam arcayet prītaye sukham* |
>
> [Here, one should first (*purā*?) worship sea-born Lakṣmī and (then) happily honour Mahādeva (Śiva) with *bilva* leaves for (his) satisfaction.]

This version of the text contains an injunction to worship the goddess Lakṣmī before worshipping Śiva in the Kāyārohaṇeśvara temple. As such, it seems to reflect the unusual fact that the Kāyārohaṇeśvara temple houses a shrine for Mahālakṣmī. On the other hand, in Recension B, the passage in question refers to a mythical event that explains Lakṣmī's connection with the Kāyārohaṇeśvara temple:

> *atrārṇavasamudbhūtā lakṣmīr ārādhya vai purā* ||
> *bilvapatrair mahādevam priyā viṣṇor abhūt sukham* |
>
> [Here, seaborn Lakṣmī once worshipped Mahādeva (Śiva) with *bilva* leaves and (thus) happily became Viṣṇu's beloved.]

The parallel passage in the *KP* (19.7c–d) closely matches the text of Recension B, suggesting that the manuscript of the *KM* that Civañāṉa Muṉivar had at his disposal contained the latter version of the text:

> *cītaḷa kamalap pokuṭṭ' aṇaik kiḻatti ceñ caṭaip pirāṉai villattāṟ*
> *kōt' aṟa vaḻipaṭṭ' accutaṉ ṟaṉakkuk koḻunaṉāp peṟṟaṉaḷ aṅkaṇ*

> [The lady who is seated on the pericarp of the cool lotus flower (Lakṣmī) faultlessly worshipped the lord who has reddish matted hair (Śiva) with *bilva* leaves there and (thus) got Acyuta (Viṣṇu) as her husband.]

In several cases, the printed text of the *KM* contains passages that are not reflected by the *KP*. Significantly, this sometimes concerns entire sections about particular temples. For example, the twelfth chapter of the *KM* describes, among other things, three temples named Aṣṭabhujeśvara, Nārasiṃheśvara and Jaigiṣivyeśvara, supposedly located in the Tumpaivaṉam neighbourhood of Kanchipuram. However, the *KP* does not mention these temples.[16] To some extent, this corresponds to differences between the recensions of the *KM*: the sections on the Aṣṭabhujeśvara and Jaigiṣivyeśvara temples (*KM*, 12.1–7 and 12.23–48) are also missing from Recension B. However, the section on the Nārasiṃheśvara temple (*KM*, 12.19–22) *is* found in both recensions of the *KM*. Similarly, at the end of the seventh chapter of the *KM* (7.79–95), we find a section describing three sites to the south of Kanchipuram, named Kuraṅgaṇīgoṣṭha (identifiable with the Valīśvara temple in the village of Kuraṅkaṇilmuṭṭam), Tāḷīvaneśa (identifiable with the Tāḷapurīśvara temple in the village of Tiruppaṉaṅkāṭu) and Jīvatpākeśvara (so far not identified). This section, too, is included in both recensions of the *KM*, but is nevertheless missing from the *KP*. The situation therefore seems to be more complicated. Possibly the copy of the *KM* that Civañāṉa Muṉivar had at his disposal when he composed the *KP* represented a third recension that was even further removed from the printed text than that of Recension B.[17] Be that as it may, these findings show that a detailed comparison of the *KM* and the *KP* must consider the complex and so far unstudied textual history of the *KM*.[18]

16 Notably, the three temples cannot be presently located. This raises the question of whether the temples were omitted from the text because they had already ceased to exist or whether they were forgotten precisely because they are not mentioned in the *KP*.

17 An alternative explanation would be that the passages in question were found in Civañāṉa Muṉivar's source, but he decided to omit them. However, given how closely Civañāṉa Muṉivar otherwise follows the *KM*, it seems unlikely that he left out passages unless he had a reason to do so. This is conceivable in the case of sections describing temples that had ceased to exist in Civañāṉa Muṉivar's time or that were otherwise obscure, but not in the case of the Kuraṅkaṇilmuṭṭam and Tiruppaṉaṅkāṭu temples, which belong to the holy places of Tamil Śaivism (*pāṭal peṟṟa stalam*) and therefore must have been known to Civañāṉa Muṉivar (see below).

18 Schier (2018: 85) notes two deviations between the *KM* and the *KP* in the Ekāmranātha temple's myth and speculates that the *KP* could have been composed based on a different version of the *KM*. As far as I can see, the relevant passages (*KM*, 45.11–16b and 45.90–92) are found in both available recensions of the *KM*, but in this case, too, it is possible that Civañāṉa Muṉivar had access to an unknown third recension.

Differences between the *KM* and the *KP*

We have seen that, except for some deviations that are caused by the inherent variation of the source text, the *KP* closely follows the narrative of the *KM*. At the same time, however, there are marked differences between the two texts. These are essentially of two kinds: differences in the poetic style and the addition of passages in the *KP* that are not found in the *KM*. As I will argue, these differences are even more interesting than the similarities because they tell us something about the intended uses of the two texts and the different milieus in which they were produced. However, before we discuss the implications, we must have a closer look at the ways in which the *KM* and the *KP* differ from each other.

The style of the *KP* and the *KM*

The poetic style of the *KP* is far more complex than that of the *KM*. This can be seen in the fact that the *KP* employs more complicated and varied metres than the *KM*. The *KM*, like other Sanskrit *māhātmyas*, is composed almost entirely in the simple *anuṣṭubh* or *śloka* metre. Moreover, the number of verses that employ an irregular pattern (*vipulā*) is relatively high. Other more ornate metres (for example, *vasantatilakā*) are used only for the last verse of each chapter and rarely for eulogies or philosophical passages that are inserted into the narrative. By contrast, the *KP* employs several different variations of the *āciriyaviruttam*, *kaliviruttam* and *kalitturai* metres. These metres are not only much longer than the *anuṣṭubh* metre of the Sanskrit text, but also employ a more rigid metrical scheme and require obligatory line-initial rhyme (*etukai*). Other sound figures such as alliteration (*mōṉai*) are also extensively used in the *KP*.

Moreover, as we have already seen, the *KP* employs a much more florid diction than the *KM*. For example, while the *KM* refers to the gods and other mythological characters that feature in its narratives with varying short names, the *KP* employs much more verbose expressions, which often refer to the gods' mythical deeds. For example, in the parallel passage that was quoted before, the *KM* refers to Śiva with stock epithets such as *śūlin* ('the trident-bearer') or *umāpati* ('the husband of Umā'), whereas the *KP* calls him 'the highest being that graciously overcame the cruel fiery-eyed god of death' (*aḻal viḻit taṟukaṭ kūṟṟai veṉṟ' aruḷ paramporuḷ*) or even 'the lord who bears the large impression of the perfumed round breasts of Gaurī, who has lips like flowers of the coral tree and a small, minute waist' (*kavir itaḻc ciṟu nuṇuk' iṭaik kavuri taṉ kaḷapak kuvi mulait taṭac cuvaṭu tōy kuricil*).[19] Similar expressions can be found in many places in the *KP*.

In the same way, the places mentioned in the *KP* regularly receive long, ornate attributes that have no parallel in the *KM*. Thus, a temple can be said to be 'surrounded by tanks with flowers that, when the bees stir them up with their legs, burst open their buds and blossom, spitting out nectar from all the mouths that are their long petals' (*ñimiṟu kāl uḻakka mukaiy uṭaint' alarntu neṭṭ' itaḻ vāytoṟum naṟavam umiḻ malart taṭañ cūḻ*; *KP*, 12.1). Similarly, a temple tank can be described as a place 'with clear waters and roaring floods, on whose sides the waves break while heaps of brilliant pearls noisily set forth by pot-like conches emit intense white moonlight, dispelling the spreading darkness' (*kuṭa vaḷaiy alaṟiy īṉṟa kurūu maṇit taraḷak kuppai paṭalai veṇ ṇilavu kāṉṟu paṭar iruḷ irippa ñāṅkar uṭai tiraiy otukkun teṇ ṇīr oli puṉal*; *KP*, 48.2). Such expressions are not only indicative of the extremely ornate poetic style of the *KP*, but also build on ancient Tamil literary conventions. For example, the hyperbolic trope of the pearls that are washed ashore and dispel the darkness of the night through their luminance is found in early Tamil texts such as the *Tiṇaimālai Nūṟṟaimpatu*, a poetic work of the late-classical *Kīḻkkaṇakku* corpus possibly composed in the seventh or eighth century (cf. *Tiṇaimālai Nūṟṟaimpatu* 48 and 49).

The examples that we have seen make it clear that the poetic style of the *KP* differs starkly from that of the *KM*. At the same time, it would be wrong to qualify the *KM* as devoid of poetic ambition. Although Sanskrit *māhātmya*s have often been described as crude, artless or even dull, such an evaluation could amount to an overgeneralisation. Thus, Travis LaMar Smith (2007: 156–60) has pointed out that the *Kāśīkhaṇḍa*—perhaps the best-known of all Sanskrit *sthalamāhātmya*s—is a text of considerably literary appeal. The *KM*, too, has at least some degree of poetic quality. We can note that the text quite often uses sound figures such as alliterations (for example, *pradakṣiṇaṃ prakurutaṃ pratyahaṃ prītamānasau*; *KM*, 16.73) or assonances (for example, *akhaṇḍajagadaṇḍānāṃ piṇḍīkaraṇapaṇḍitaḥ*; *KM*, 4.78). It also quite frequently employs wordplays of the *yamaka* type where two words that are similar in sound but different in meaning are used next to

19 The first expression refers to the well-known purāṇic myth of Śiva's destruction of Yama. The second refers to the Ekāmranātha temple's central myth, which tells how Pārvatī (Gaurī) firmly embraced a *liṅga* made of sand to protect it against a flood that Śiva had sent to test her devotion, leaving the marks of her breasts on the *liṅga* (see Schier 2018: 73 ff.).

each other—for example, *kṣamasvāgaḥ kṣamākānta* ('forgive [*kṣamasva*] my sin, husband of the Earth [*kṣamā*]') (*KM*, 31.63). The occasional descriptive passages such as the depiction of Kanchipuram in *KM* 3.68–104 or eulogies of Śiva that are inserted in the narrative are also relatively ornate. Yet, it is a long way from the *KM* to the hyper-sophisticated style of the *KP*. Thus, while Civañāṉa Muṉivar used a Sanskrit source and followed it very closely on a narrative level, he rendered it into a much more ambitious poetic text in Tamil. *What* is said in the *KP* may be the same as in the *KM*, but *how* it is said is very different.

Additions to the *KP*

Apart from using a more ornate style in his retelling of the narratives that are also found in the *KM*, Civañāṉa Muṉivar made several additions, including both entire new chapters and additional descriptive passages that are inserted into existing narratives. Thus, the first four chapters of the *KP* have no equivalent in the *KM*. They comprise a prefatory section (*pāyiram*), two lengthy chapters that describe the region around Kanchipuram and the city itself (titled Tirunāṭṭuppaṭalam, 'Chapter on the Sacred Country', and Tirunakarappaṭalam, 'Chapter on the Sacred City', respectively) and an introduction (*patikam*) that summarises the contents of the text. All these chapters are conventional elements of Tamil *talapurāṇams* and *kāppiyams* (long narrative poems). Among these chapters, the Tirunāṭṭuppaṭalam and the Tirunakarappaṭalam are particularly noteworthy for the way in which they frame the *KP* using Tamil literary conventions.

The Tirunāṭṭuppaṭalam and the Tirunakarappaṭalam

The Tirunāṭṭuppaṭalam and the Tirunakarappaṭalam contain an elaborate description of the Toṇṭai country (the region around Kanchipuram) and of the city of Kanchipuram, comprising 145 and 126 verses, respectively. The two chapters draw heavily on Tamil literary conventions and are rife with intertextual references to other Tamil literary texts. Thus, the Tirunāṭṭuppaṭalam begins with a description of the rainclouds, whose downpour on the Nandi Hills causes the origin of the Palar River (*KP*, 2.2–17). The same trope is found in numerous other Tamil *talapurāṇams* and *kāppiyams*; ultimately, it goes back to the *Kamparāmāyaṇam*, the Tamil version of the *Rāmāyaṇa*, which was composed by Kampaṉ probably in the twelfth century (cf. *Kamparāmāyaṇam*, 1.1.2–11). The passage in the *KP* is clearly modelled after the *Kamparāmāyaṇam*: both texts describe how the white clouds set out and return as dark rainclouds after they have absorbed water from the sea, how the clouds cling to a mountain range (the Nandi Hills in the *KP*; the Himalaya in the *Kamparāmāyaṇam*) and how the rain poured by the clouds flows forth as a river (the Palar and the Sarayū, respectively).[20] It is interesting to note that Civañāṉa Muṉivar modelled his work after the *Kamparāmāyaṇam*. While the *Kamparāmāyaṇam* was highly esteemed for its literary value and was as such also read in Śaiva circles (Cutler 2003: 279), Kampaṉ's Tamil adaptation of the *Rāmāyaṇa* was a Vaiṣṇava text that the staunch Śaivite Civañāṉa Muṉivar appears to have opposed on religious grounds. Indeed, he even composed—allegedly after a debate with the Vaiṣṇava scholars of Kanchipuram—a polemic in which he pointed out no less than 22 poetic flaws in the first verse of the *Kamparāmāyaṇam*.[21] Seen against this background, the fact that the *KP* borrows from the *Kamparāmāyaṇam* can be seen as an attempt by Civañāṉa Muṉivar to outdo Kampaṉ's work.

After describing the origin of the Palar, the Tirunāṭṭuppaṭalam of the *KP* follows the river on its course through the Toṇṭai country. In its description of the Toṇṭai country, the *KP*, like many other Tamil *talapurāṇams* and *kāppiyams*, draws on the ancient convention of the five *tiṇai*s or poetic landscapes. This concept is found in the *Caṅkam* texts, the oldest stratum of Tamil literature (possibly composed between the first and sixth centuries CE) and becomes regularised in subsequent works such as those of the late-classical *Kīḻkkaṇakku* corpus. The *tiṇai* concept is also discussed at length in the Tamil poetological treatises, which served as a guide for later poets such as Civañāṉa Muṉivar. According to the *tiṇai* system, poetic compositions deal with five landscapes (the hills, the wasteland, the woodlands, the agricultural tract and the seashore), each associated with particular elements and particular poetic themes.[22] The Tirunāṭṭuppaṭalam of the *KP* includes a section on each of the five landscapes (2.38–127) as well as a section in which elements of different landscapes appear in various combinations—a feature that is also sanctioned by Tamil poetics under the name *tiṇaimayakkam* or 'mixture of *tiṇai*s' (*KP*, 2.128–42). These landscape descriptions do not aim at a realistic

20 The description of the origin of the Sarayū River in the *Kamparāmāyaṇam* also served as a model for many other Tamil texts—for example, the *Cīṟāppurāṇam*, a seventeenth-century hagiography of the Islamic prophet Mohammed by the author Umaṟup Pulavar (see Narayanan 2000: 82–85).

21 On this polemic (titled *Kamparāmāyaṇa mutaṟ ceyyuḷ caṅkōttara virutti*), see Āravintaṉ (1968: 426–29).

22 For an introduction to the *tiṇai* system as it is found in classical Tamil literature, see Ramanujan (1967: 105–8); and Zvelebil (1973: 85–110).

portrayal of the Toṇṭai country but are entirely made up of conventional *tiṇai* elements. Thus, the section on the mountain landscape begins with a description of the millet fields, which the hillmen have ploughed after cutting down sandalwood trees and where the women who have been sent to the fields to chase away the parrots have amorous adventures with the men who have come to the forest to hunt (*KP*, 2.39–41). Anyone familiar with classical Tamil literature will recognise these conventional tropes, which are attested in the *Caṅkam* and *Kīḻkkaṇakku* works. As such, the *KP* forms part of a continuous Tamil literary tradition that reaches back to the beginning of the first millennium.[23] At the same time, there is a marked contrast between the heavy and hyperbolic style of the *KP* and the naturalistic and unmediated imagery of the *Caṅkam* works, highlighting the fact that, in spite of all continuities, Tamil literature underwent a major transformation during this period.

The descriptions of the Toṇṭai country and the city of Kanchipuram also provide Civañāṉa Muṉivar with an opportunity to employ many sophisticated poetic devices; this part of the *KP* is filled with numerous elaborate similes and hyperbolic images. On several occasions, we also find verses employing the stylistic device of *śleṣa* (Tam., *cilēṭai*) or paronomasia, which skilfully uses homonyms to convey two different meanings at the same time.[24] Consider, for example, the following verse (*KP*, 2.19), which can be read simultaneously as a description of the Palar River flowing through the landscape and of a king going to battle with his retinue:

> *aracukaḷ cūḻntu cellav aruṅ kaṇi malar vāy viḷḷac*
> *cari kuḻar kuṟa miṉṉārkaḷ paṟpala tāṉai veḷḷam*
> *virav' iṭap pariya kāl āṇ mētaku mākkaḷ attiy*
> *iru puṭai taḻuvip pōtav ikal koṭu vaiyam ūrntu.*

> [While it is surrounded by *aracu* trees (while he is surrounded by [other] kings),
>
> while precious *vēṅkai* trees blossom (while expert astrologers open their mouths),

23 See also Ebeling (2010: 90–101) for the use of classical poetic conventions in nineteenth-century Tamil literature.

24 For a comprehensive study of *śleṣa* in Sanskrit and other Indian literature, see Bronner (2010). For *śleṣa* in nineteenth-century Tamil literature, see Ebeling (2010: 43–45).

> while the clothes of *kuṟava* women with flowing hair join the flood (while *kuṟava* women with flowing hair mingle with the army),
>
> while *āṉ* trees with sturdy trunks, excellent mango trees, and fig trees flank it on both sides (while sturdy foot-soldiers, excellent horses, and elephants flank him on both sides),
>
> it (the river) flows on earth with strength (he [the king] mounts his chariot with hostility).]

By beginning his work with a description of the country and the city with which the text deals, Civañāṉa Muṉivar follows a well-established Tamil poetic convention and thus frames the *KP* as a distinctly Tamil poetic composition. At the same time, the extensive descriptive passages give him ample opportunity to showcase his poetic skills and to explore his creative imagination in a way that is not possible in the other chapters of the *KP*, where the outline of the narrative is predetermined by the Sanskrit source text.

Other additions in the *KP*

Just as the *KP* begins with an ornate description of the Toṇṭai country and the city of Kanchipuram, several individual chapters of the text begin with a passage that describes the setting of the subsequent narrative. Unlike the narrative portions of these chapters, the descriptive passages are not based on the *KM*, but have been added by Civañāṉa Muṉivar. Thus, the Purāṇavaralāṟṟuppaṭalam, which deals with the purāṇic frame story, begins with an elaborate description of the Naimiṣa Forest, the place where the sages have assembled to hear the narration of the purāṇa (*KP*, 5.1–7). The Canaṟkumārappaṭalam, which tells the story of the sage Sanatkumāra, begins with a description of Mount Meru, Sanatkumāra's dwelling place (*KP*, 6.1–11). Similarly, the Talavicēṭappaṭalam, in which Śiva explains the greatness of Kanchipuram to Pārvatī, begins with a description of Śiva's throne hall (*KP*, 7.1–10). As in the case of the Tirunāṭṭuppaṭalam and the Tirunakarappaṭalam, these descriptive passages allow Civañāṉa Muṉivar to display his poetic ability by employing numerous striking images and elaborate comparisons. Consider, for example, the description of Śiva's throne hall in *KP* 7.1–10, which is too long to quote in full, but which can be summarised as follows:

> The gods, who had assembled to worship Śiva in his golden hall, were bedazzled by the splendour of the many jewels there and feared that they had become mortal every time they had to blink [1]. Śiva's

> lion throne looked as though Narasiṃha was resting at Śiva's feet, wishing to eradicate the impurities of his soul [2]. Śiva's white parasol looked as though the full moon was consoling the crescent moon on Śiva's head, which was troubled by the waves of the Gaṅgā [3]. The yak-tail fans that were waved for Śiva looked as though Śiva's fame were moving to and fro, unable to find space because he had already accumulated so much of it [4]. Skanda and Gaṇeśa were standing on Śiva's sides, displaying their tusk and lance that destroyed demons like Gajamukha and Sūrapadma, as if to remind the gods not to become arrogant after they had received boons from Śiva [5]. Śiva's hideous *gaṇa*s were standing next to him while Brahmā and the other gods were standing at a distance, showing that true greatness comes through Śiva's grace, not from outer appearances [6]. Seeing Śiva's beauty, Viṣṇu contemplated becoming Mohinī again, but gave up his plan when he realised how beautiful Pārvatī was [7]. Urvaśī and the other Apsaras resorted to *abhinaya* gestures to conceal that they were unable to dance because they were infatuated by Śiva's dance [8]. Thus, Śiva presided over the assembly on Mount Kailāsa while Nandī was holding back the multitudes of gods who placed their crowned heads on Śiva's feet until they hurt [9]. There, Pārvatī praised Śiva's feet and started speaking [10].

The most elaborate addition is found at the beginning of the Curakarīcappaṭalam (*KP*, 25.1–25), where we find a description of Mount Mandara, the place where the following myth of the Jvaraharīśvara temple is set. This section uses classical *tiṇai* imagery related to the mountain landscape and at the same time employs an array of increasingly more complex poetic figures. Thus, we find verses composed in the *citrakāvya* (Tam., *cittirakkavi*) mode, in which the syllables are arranged according to particular patterns—for example, as complex palindromes or in the form of two intertwined snakes. Other verses employ a limited set of sounds. Consider the following verse (*KP*, 25.11), which manages to depict a vivid scene of the mountain landscape, ripe with conventional *tiṇai* elements, while only employing the consonant *t*:

> *tattai tittittat' ōt' itai tātu tēt*
> *tott' utittut titittat' attittu tūt*
> *tuttitt' ētatta tīt' utai tīt tatt' att'*
> *otta tātu tataittut tutittatē.*

> [The millet field (*itai*), where the parrots (*tattai*) call with sweet voices (*tittittat' ōtu*), (the field) that is guarded (*titittatu*) while flower-clusters with pollen and nectar (*tātu tēt tottu*) appear (*utittu*),

is worthy of praise (*tutittatē*) because it abounds (*tataittu*) in (ivory) that comes from elephants (*attittu*), pure (gems) that come from cobras' hoods (*tūt tuttittu*), and (gold) ore (*tātu*) that resembles (*otta*) the red colour (*attu*) that is emitted by fire (*tīt tattu*), which destroys (*utai*) the evil of suffering (*ētatta tītu*).]

Such examples of extremely constrained writing are also known from many other works of South Asian literature. They are also found in other Tamil *talapurāṇam*s—for example, Ti. Mīṉāṭcicuntaram Piḷḷai's *Amparppurāṇam* (see Ebeling 2010: 46 ff.). What is significant, however, is that in Sanskrit literature, such verbal feasts are a hallmark of high poetry (*kāvya*), whereas they are never found in *māhātmya*s or other purāṇic texts. Evidently, we are dealing with two rather different literary registers.

Comparison of the *KP* and the *KM*

The above examples should have made it clear that the *KP* follows a poetic agenda that is radically different from that of the *KM*. While the two texts closely correspond on a narrative level, the style of the *KM* is relatively pedestrian, whereas the *KP* is an extremely sophisticated poetic composition that can be easily characterised as high literature. Such a difference is typical of the relationship between Tamil *talapurāṇam*s and Sanskrit *sthalamāhātmya*s. As George L. Hart (1976: 343) has pointed out, Tamil *talapurāṇam*s are much more akin to Sanskrit *kāvya* than to purāṇic literature. These insights invite questions about the respective literary cultures in which Tamil *talapurāṇam*s and Sanskrit *sthalamāhātmya*s originated. In this regard, it seems useful to investigate the respective milieus in which the *KM* and the *KP* were produced.

The milieus of the *KM* and the *KP*

Of the two texts that are the subject of this chapter, the *KM* is far more elusive because of its anonymity. As we do not know when and by whom it was composed, it is difficult to say anything about the milieu from which the text arose. However, as with other Sanskrit *māhātmya*s, it does not seem far-fetched to assume that the text was produced by members of the Brahman caste. In the case of the *KP*, we are in a much better position to assess the text's milieu as we have ample information about its author and the institution with which he was affiliated. At the same time, contrasting the *KP* with the *KM* can help us understand how the world views of the two texts' respective authors differed. Let us therefore consider what we know about Civañāṉa Muṉivar and his milieu, and how his background influenced his rendering of the *KM*.

Civañāṉa Muṉivar's biography

Civañāṉa Muṉivar, the author of the *KP*, was perhaps the most influential Tamil intellectual of the eighteenth century, and we are therefore relatively well informed about his biography.[25] Born to a Śaiva family of the Vēḷāḷar caste—a prominent landowning community—in Vikkiramaciṅkapuram, near Tirunelveli in southern Tamil Nadu, Civañāṉa Muṉivar joined at a young age the Tiruvāvaṭuturai Ātīṉam, a Śaiva monastery (*maṭha*) in the Kaveri Delta region of central Tamil Nadu. In Tiruvāvaṭuturai, he was trained in Tamil, Sanskrit and Śaiva Siddhānta philosophy and soon became an eminent scholar. Civañāṉa Muṉivar spent the rest of his life in Tiruvāvaṭuturai and other places where the Ātīṉam maintained branch monasteries, including Kanchipuram, where he composed the *KP*. He died in Tiruvāvaṭuturai in 1785 CE.

Civañāṉa Muṉivar is best known as a Śaiva Siddhānta scholar: his *Civañāṉa Māpāṭiyam* is considered the most important commentary on Meykaṇṭatēvar's *Civañāṉapōtam*, which is the seminal text of the Tamil Śaiva Siddhānta school. He also authored several other Śaiva Siddhānta commentaries and translations of Sanskrit philosophical treatises, as well as grammatical commentaries and scholarly polemics. He also excelled as a poet: in addition to the *KP*, his only *talapurāṇam*, he composed about a dozen shorter works of devotional poetry. As such, Civañāṉa Muṉivar embodies the traditional idea of a Tamil *pulavar* ('scholar-poet') who is versed both in theoretical treatises and in poetical composition.

Civañāṉa Muṉivar's milieu

The Tiruvāvaṭuturai Ātīṉam, to which Civañāṉa Muṉivar belonged, was (and still is) an influential Śaiva institution, run by an ascetic brotherhood of initiated members who belong to certain elite non-Brahman castes (most importantly, the Vēḷāḷar).[26] Since its formation in the sixteenth century, the

25 On Civañāṉa Muṉivar's biography and works, see Cuppiramaṇiya Piḷḷai (1955); and Cāmi Aiyā (1989: 11–39).

26 For a study of the *Tiruvāvaṭuturai Ātīṉam* and other non-Brahman Śaiva *maṭhas* in Tamil Nadu, see Koppedrayer (1990). For the present role of the *Tiruvāvaṭuturai Ātīṉam*, see Klöber (2019).

Tiruvāvaṭuturai Ātīṉam has been a seat of religious authority and a place of learning, which has fostered the philosophical school of Śaiva Siddhānta as well as Tamil literature and scholarship. The Tiruvāvaṭuturai Ātīṉam promotes a form of Śaivism that is characterised by its adherence to the philosophical school of Śaiva Siddhānta and a specifically Tamil form of devotionalism that is based on the veneration of the Tamil Śaiva saints (the 63 *nāyaṉmār*) and the acceptance of a Tamil Śaiva canon (the *Tirumuṟai*). As I will show, all these elements can be found in Civañāṉa Muṉivar's *KP*.

Śaiva Siddhānta philosophy

As we have seen, Civañāṉa Muṉivar was himself an influential Śaiva Siddhānta scholar. His *KP* also contains references to Śaiva Siddhānta doctrines, often in the form of similes in the text's descriptive passages. For example, *KP* 2.12, a verse of the Tirunāṭṭuppaṭalam that describes the aftermath of the rains, refers to the central Śaiva Siddhānta concept of the three impurities of the soul (*malam*; Skt., *mala*), which can be removed by attaining knowledge of Śiva (*civañāṉam*; Skt., *śivajñāna*), when it says that the birds and other animals continue to suffer even after the rains have stopped because raindrops remain on the trees just like a karmic imprint (*vātaṉai*; Skt., *vāsanā*) remains even after a person has overcome the impurities of the soul through the means of knowledge. It may seem surprising to find such philosophical references in a poetic text, but the fact that Civañāṉa Muṉivar found a way to include Śaiva Siddhānta concepts in the *KP* shows their importance to his intellectual world.

Devotion to the Tamil Śaiva saints

Civañāṉa Muṉivar's devotion to the Tamil Śaiva saints becomes clear from the fact that the *KP*, like most Śaiva *talapurāṇams* in Tamil, includes invocation verses to Tiruñāṉacampantar, Tirunāvukkaracar, Cuntarar and Māṇikkavācakar (the four most important poet-saints), the 63 *nāyaṉmār* as a group and Cēkkiḻār, who composed the canonised hagiography of the Śaiva saints (the *Periyapurāṇam*), as part of its *pāyiram* section (*KP*, 1.12–17). Elsewhere, Civañāṉa Muṉivar also alludes to the stories of Śaiva saints that are outlined in the *Periyapurāṇam*. For example, *KP* 2.139, part of the *tiṇaimayakkam* section of the Tirunāṭṭuppaṭalam, contains an elaborate comparison, in which three types of flowers from different landscapes are correlated with the story of the saint Ceruttuṇai, who cut off the nose of a queen because she had smelt a flower that was meant as an offering to Śiva.[27] Such references make it clear that Civañāṉa Muṉivar was familiar with the stories of the *nāyaṉmār*, most likely through the *Periyapurāṇam*, whose author, Cēkkiḻār, he praised in the introductory section of his work.

Notably, two temples in Kanchipuram relate to the life stories of specific Śaiva saints: the saint Tirukkuṟipputtoṇṭar is said to have attained liberation in the Muktīśvara temple and the saint Cākkiyar in the Vīraṭṭāneśvara temple. The story of Tirukkuṟipputtoṇṭar, a washerman whom Śiva liberated after he had tested his devotion, is told in the *Periyapurāṇam* (1078–1205). In the *KM*, on the other hand, the story associated with the Muktīśvara temple (here also called Garuḍeśvara) is an entirely different one, dealing with Garuḍa, who worshipped Śiva.[28] However, the *KM* also briefly refers to the story of Tirukkuṟipputtoṇṭar when it states that 'a certain washerman' (*kāruḥ kaścit*) attained liberation in this place (*KM*, 12.71).[29] Whoever composed this passage of the *KM* clearly was aware of the Tirukkuṟipputtoṇṭar story, but apparently did not deem it very important and, as the distanced tone suggests, did not have an emotional relation to it. Similarly, the section of the *KM* that deals with the Vīraṭṭāṉeśvara temple (here called Vīrāṭṭahāseśvara) does not contain any reference to Cākkiyar, the Śaiva saint who is said to have been liberated there. In contrast, Civañāṉa Muṉivar must have been aware of the stories of the two Tamil saints. This can be seen from the fact that he explicitly names the washerman who was liberated in the Muktīśvara temple as Tirukkuṟipputtoṇṭar (*KP*, 17.17) and briefly refers to the Vīraṭṭāṉeśvara temple as the place where Cākkiyar attained liberation (54.1). However, since he closely follows the narrative of the *KM*, he does not elaborate on these stories further.

27 The story of Ceruttuṇai is told in *Periyapurāṇam*, 4120–26. In the *KP* verse, *kumiḻ* flowers from the forest tract are compared to the queen's nose, *kaitai* flowers from the seashore with the sword that Ceruttuṇai used to cut off the queen's nose and *tōṉṟi* flowers from the mountains with the hand holding the sword. The flower of the *kumiḻ* tree (*Gmelina asiatica*) is a conventional element of the forest landscape and often serves as the object of comparison for a woman's nose. The *kaitai* or screw pine (*Pandanus odorifer*) is found in coastal tracts and has flowers with long silvery bracts. The *tōṉṟi* flower or glory lily (*Gloriosa superba*) is associated with the mountains; its long petals are often compared to fingers.

28 In the *KM*, the names Garuḍeśvara and Muktīśvara seem to be used interchangeably. Today, the temple is known as Muktīśvara and is mainly associated with the story of Tirukkuṟipputtoṇṭar's liberation, whereas Garuḍeśvara is the name of a side shrine in this temple.

29 Incidentally, the word *kāru* shows the limitations of the standard Sanskrit dictionaries when dealing with regional materials. In Monier Monier-Williams's *Sanskrit–English Dictionary* (2009), *kāru* is defined as 'maker, doer, artisan, mechanic', but here it clearly must be understood as 'washerman'. That the word *kāru* was used in this meaning in the Tamil-speaking area is shown by the *Tamil Lexicon* (1924–36), which lists the Sanskrit loanword *kāru* and gives its meaning as 'washerman'.

The Tamil Śaiva canon

Another case where the different priorities of the authors of the *KM* and the *KP* become evident are the sites that are associated with the *Tēvāram*. The *Tēvāram*, a collection of hymns to Śiva composed by the three poet-saints Tiruñāṉacampantar, Tirunāvukkaracar and Cuntarar during the seventh and eighth centuries, is the most important part of the Tamil Śaiva canon. Most of its hymns are dedicated to Śiva in a particular place, and the 274 (or 276) sites that are mentioned in the *Tēvāram*, termed *pāṭal peṟṟa stalams* ('places that have received a song'), are considered particularly important in the Tamil Śaiva tradition.[30] Eight such sites in Kanchipuram and its surrounds feature among the temples mentioned in the *KM* and the *KP*.[31] Importantly, the status of these temples as *pāṭal peṟṟa stalams* did not seem to be a relevant category for the author(s) of the *KM*. The only exception is the Tirumēṟṟaḷīśvara temple (called Paścimālaya in the *KM*), where the temple's myth (*KM*, 15.49–64) refers to the site's association with the *Tēvāram*: it states that Viṣṇu obtained Śiva's form in that place after Śiva's devotee Sambandha (Tiruñāṉacampantar) had praised him with Tamil hymns (*drāviḍastutibhiḥ*). However, it is ironical that Tiruñāṉacampantar was the only *Tēvāram* author who did *not* compose hymns on the Tirumēṟṟaḷīśvara temple.[32] It seems that the person who composed this passage of the *KM* was aware of the site's association with the *Tēvāram* but did not have any firsthand knowledge of the hymns. In the case of the other *pāṭal peṟṟa stalams*, the *KM* makes no mention of their *Tēvāram* connection. In contrast, Civañāṉa Muṉivar must have been very much familiar with the *Tēvāram* and he clearly was aware of the identity of the *pāṭal peṟṟa stalams* in Kanchipuram. This can be seen from the fact that the *KP* refers to these sites under the Tamil names that are used in the *Tēvāram*, whereas it uses the Tamilised forms of the Sanskrit names from the *KM* for all other temples. Otherwise Civañāṉa Muṉivar does not address the *pāṭal peṟṟa stalam* status of these temples any more than does the *KM*. In other words, even though sites that were associated with Śaiva saints or with the hymns of the *Tēvāram* had special significance for Civañāṉa Muṉivar, his strict adherence to the narrative of the *KM* prevented him from giving them more space in the *KP*.

30 For a comprehensive list of the *pāṭal peṟṟa stalams*, see Chevillard and Sarma (2007).

31 They are Tiruvēkampam (the Ekāmranātha temple), Tirumēṟṟaḷi, Tiruvōṇakāntaṉtaḷi, Aṉēkataṅkāvatam, Tiruneṟikkāraikkāṭu, Tirumākaṟal, Tiruvōttūr and Tirumāṟpēṟu. Two more *pāṭal peṟṟa stalams*, Kuraṅkaṇilmuṭṭam and Tiruppaṉaṅkāṭṭūr, are mentioned only in the *KM* and not in the *KP* (see above).

32 The Tirumēṟṟaḷīśvara temple has received one Tēvāram hymn each, by Tirunāvukkaracar (4:43) and Cuntarar (7:21).

Comparison of the *KM* and the *KP*

What we can witness here is a tension between Civañāṉa Muṉivar's adherence to the narrative of the *KM* and the differences between his belief system and that of the author(s) of the *KM*. It seems that the *KM* originated in a (presumably Brahmanical) milieu, in which certain concepts that were central for the non-Brahman tradition to which Civañāṉa Muṉivar belonged, such as the veneration of the Tamil Śaiva saints and the acceptance of the Tamil Śaiva canon, did not play a great role. In this respect, one has to be very careful to not overstate a Brahman/non-Brahman dichotomy, particularly in light of the strong polarisation this issue has undergone in Tamil Nadu since the twentieth century.[33] While modern proponents of Tamil cultural nationalism (including some Śaiva practitioners) have postulated a fundamental opposition between Brahmans and non-Brahmans, associated with Sanskrit and Tamil culture, respectively, such antagonism did not exist in the eighteenth century when Civañāṉa Muṉivar composed his *KP*. Non-Brahman institutions such as the Tiruvāvaṭuturai Ātīṉam at that time accepted Brahmanical values such as the system of the social classes (*varṇa*) and stages of life (*āśrama*) or the high status of the Sanskrit language; at the same time, however, they tried to reinterpret some aspects of this world view to their own benefit. The category of *varṇa* was particularly delicate for the Vēḷāḷar members of the non-Brahman *maṭhas*, as despite their high social status as members of a landowning community, they were classified as *śūdra*s—that is, members of the lowest *varṇa*, who were not entitled to renunciation (*sannyāsa*) according to orthodox Brahmanical norms.[34] A century before Civañāṉa Muṉivar's time, Tiruvampala Tēcikar, the head of the Dharmapuram Ātīṉam, another Vēḷāḷar-led Śaiva *maṭha*, composed a Sanskrit text titled *Varṇāśramacandrika*, in which he argued for the right of *śūdra*s to receive all levels of Śaiva initiation (see Koppedrayer 1991). In his text, Tiruvampala Tēcikar did not question the Vēḷāḷar's status as *śūdra*s but contended that 'pure' (*sat-*) *śūdra*s were eligible for initiation just like the members of the higher *varṇa*s. As such, he found a way to justify his

33 In fact, even the category of 'non-Brahman' is, strictly speaking, an anachronism when speaking about Civañāṉa Muṉivar's times. While caste identity certainly was meaningful in eighteenth-century Tamil Nadu, a collective identity of castes other than the Brahmans as 'non-Brahmans' emerged only during the twentieth century.

34 In South Indian society, the two middle *varṇa*s, viz. *kṣatriya*s and *vaiśya*s, are almost entirely absent.

institution's existence without openly subverting Brahmanical orthodoxy. Some examples of this tension between Brahmanical norms and non-Brahman self-reassurance can also be seen in the *KP*.

The *KM* clearly affirms the *varṇāśrama* system and the notion of Brahman superiority. This can be seen most clearly from its Chapter 47, a kind of dharmaśāstric appendix that describes the rules of conduct appropriate for the inhabitants of Kanchipuram relative to their caste (*varṇa*) and stage of life (*āśrama*), but also from other references in the text. In line with its faithfulness to its source, the *KP* generally adopts these passages as they stand. In some cases, however, Civañāṉa Muṉivar has made small changes that alter the text's outlook in a subtle but significant way. For example, *KM* 33.82 states that outcastes can become Brahmans in the course of seven rebirths by visiting a particular temple in Kanchipuram, whereas Brahmans will be liberated at once.[35] This statement is closely mirrored by *KP* 58.25, except that Civañāṉa Muṉivar extends the promise of instant liberation to 'Brahmans and others' (*tiru maṟaiyōr mutal āṉōr*), which the modern commentary understands as referring to the members of the four *varṇa*s. It thus emerges that Civañāṉa Muṉivar was fundamentally willing to accept the orthodox Brahmanical undertone of the *KM*, but also made strategic changes at selected points that reflected on the status of his fellow Vēḷāḷars.

The way in which Civañāṉa Muṉivar renders the Sanskrit *KM* into Tamil can be seen as the outcome of a similar process. Purāṇic texts are framed as the speech of mythical sages and deities, and the fact that they are composed in Sanskrit—the proverbial 'language of the gods'—justifies their divine origins. The authors of Tamil *talapurāṇams* seem to affirm the high status of the Sanskrit language as they frame their works as Tamil renderings of Sanskrit purāṇas. As such, Tamil *talapurāṇams* derive their religious authority from their dependence on Sanskrit sources. At the same time, however, Tamil literati like Civañāṉa Muṉivar preferred Tamil as their language of expression and cultivated it as a highly sophisticated literary language. By turning their Sanskrit sources into refined poetic works, the authors of Tamil *talapurāṇams* showed that Tamil could easily compete with, if not surpass, Sanskrit as a medium of poetic expression. As such, they could assert the status of the Tamil language while at the same time nominally accepting the axiom of Sanskrit's linguistic supremacy.

35 *caṇḍālo 'pi bhavet saptajanmāḍhyo brāhmaṇottamaḥ | brāhmaṇā vā vimuktāghā mucyante nātra saṃśayaḥ ||*.

Conclusion

To sum up, we have seen that the *KP* is based on the *KM* and closely follows its Sanskrit source on a narrative level. At the same time, however, it radically differs from the *KM* in terms of its poetic agenda. Civañāṉa Muṉivar, like many authors of Tamil *talapurāṇam*s, relied on a Sanskrit source, but rendered it into a much more sophisticated poetic text. As such, the case of the Tamil *talapurāṇam*s and the Sanskrit *sthalamāhātmya*s refutes the still prevalent cliché of Sanskrit as the transregional 'elite' language and the regional Indian languages as ordinary 'vernaculars', for the Tamil *talapurāṇam*s are, in fact, far more elite than the Sanskrit texts on which they are based.

The case of the *KM* and the *KP* shows what can be gained by studying Sanskrit *sthalamāhātmya*s and Tamil *talapurāṇam*s in conjunction. The close relation of the two texts' narratives means they can be read in parallel, allowing us to use the *KP* as an interpretational aid and even a textual witness for the *KM*—an approach so far rarely applied to Tamil and Sanskrit texts. At the same time, the differences between the *KM* and the *KP* inform us about the different priorities of the two texts' authors, allowing us to draw conclusions about the different milieus in which the texts were produced. How representative the case of the *KM* and the *KP* is remains to be seen. Other authors of Tamil *talapurāṇam*s may have employed different strategies when rendering Sanskrit texts into Tamil (and of course not all Tamil *talapurāṇam*s are necessarily based on Sanskrit sources). What is needed is more in-depth research that allows us to understand the relationship between Sanskrit *sthalamāhātmya*s and Tamil *talapurāṇam*s in a broader perspective.

References

Primary texts

Buchholz, Jonas. (2017). Tiṇaimālai Nūṟṟaimpatu: Tiṇaimālai Nūṟṟaimpatu: Critical edition and annotated translation. PhD thesis, University of Hamburg. Available from: ediss.sub.uni-hamburg.de/handle/ediss/6333.

Cuppiramaṇiya Mutaliyār, C.K. (ed.). (1937–53). *Periyapurāṇam: Tiruttoṇṭar purāṇam eṉṉum Periyapurāṇam*. [7 vols.] Kōyamuttūr, India: Kōvait Tamiḻccaṅkam.

Gopal Iyer, T.V. (ed.). (1984–91). *Tēvāram. Hymnes śivaïtes du pays tamoul* [*Tēvāram: Saiva Hymns from the Tamil Country*]. [3 vols.] Pondicherry, India: Insitut Français d'Indologie.

Kōpālakiruṣṇamācāryar, Vai. Mu. (ed.). (1962–67). *Kamparāmāyaṇam: Śri Kamparāmāyaṇam*. [7 vols.] Chennai, India: Vai. Mu. Kōpālakiruṣṇamācāriyar Kampeṉi.

Piḷḷai, Ālālacuntaram (ed.). (1900). *Tirukailacaparamparait Tiruvāvaṭuturai Ātīṉattu Tirāviṭamahāpāṣyakarttarākiya Civañāṉa Yōkikaḷ aruḷicceyta Kāñcippurāṇam. Cupparāya Ceṭṭiyār and Kā*. Madras, India: Paṇṭitamittira yantiracālai, Vikāri varuṣam.

Vēṅkaṭrāmayya, Īdara (ed.). (1967). [Kāncīmāhātmya (KM):] *Śriskāndapurāṇāntargataṃ Śrīkāñcīmāhātmyam (Śrīrudrakoṭimahimādarśaḥ)*. [In Telugu script.] Vijayawada, India: Vēṅkaṭrāma aṇḍ kō.

Secondary texts

Āravintaṉ, Mu. Vai. (1968). *Uraiyāciriyarkaḷ*. Citamparam, India: Maṇivācakar Nūlakam.

Bakker, Hans. (1989). Some methodological considerations with respect to the critical edition of puranic literature. In Einar von Schuler (ed.), XXIII Deutscher Orientalistentag vom 16. bis 20. September 1985 in Würzburg. Ausgewählte Vorträge [XXIII German Orientalist Day from September 16th to 20th, 1985 in Würzburg: Selected Lectures], pp. 329–41. Stuttgart, Germany: Franz Steiner Verlag Wiesbaden.

Bronner, Yigal. (2010). *Extreme Poetry: The South Asian Movement of Simultaneous Narration*. New York, NY: Columbia University Press. doi.org/10.7312/bron15160.

Buchholz, Jonas. (2022). Sthalamāhātmyas and talapurāṇams of Kanchipuram: A network of texts. In Malini Ambach, Jonas Buchholz and Ute Hüsken (eds), *Temples, Texts, and Networks: South Indian Perspectives*, pp. 11–40. Heidelberg, Germany: Heidelberg Asian Studies Publishing. doi.org/10.11588/hasp.906.c13934.

Cāmi Aiyā, Cu. (1989). Civañāṉa Muṉivariṉ Kāñcippurāṇam: ōr āyvu. Aṇṇāmalainakar, India: Aṇṇāmalaip Palkalaikkaḻakam.

Chevillard, Jean-Luc and Sarma, S.A.S. (eds). (2007). *Digital Tēvāram/Kaṉiṉit Tēvāram. With the Complete English Gloss of the Late V.M. Subramanya Ayyar (IFP) and Furnished with a Full Concordance of the Tamil Text*. Pondicherry, India: École française d'Extrême-Orient/Institut français de Pondichéry. Available from: www.ifpindia.org/digitaldb/site/digital_tevaram/.

Cuppiramaṇiya Piḷḷai, Kā. (1955 [1932]). *Civañāṉa Cuvāmikaḷ Varalāṟu*. Reprint. Tirunelveli, India: Tirunelvēlit Teṉṉintiya Caivacittānta Nūṟpatippuk Kaḻakam.

Cutler, Norman. (2003). Three moments in the genealogy of Tamil literary culture. In Sheldon Pollock (ed.), *Literary Cultures in History: Reconstructions from South Asia*, pp. 271–322. Berkeley, CA: University of California Press.

Dessigane, R., Pattabiramin, P.Z. and Filliozat, Jean. (1964). Les légendes çivaïtes de Kāñcipuram. Analyse de textes et iconographie [The Saiva Legends of Kāñcipuram: Analysis of Texts and Iconography]. Pondicherry, India: Institut français de Pondichéry. doi.org/10.4000/books.ifp.2409.

Ebeling, Sascha. (2010). *Colonizing the Realm of Words: The Transformation of Tamil Literature in Nineteenth-Century South India*. Albany: SUNY Press.

Eck, Diana. (2012). *India: A Sacred Geography*. New York, NY: Harmony Books.

Fisher, Elaine M. (2017). *Hindu Pluralism: Religion and the Public Sphere in Early Modern South India*. Oakland, CA: University of California Press. doi.org/10.1525/luminos.24.

Ganesan, T. (2022). Innovations & reformulations in translation: Some sthalapurāṇas in Tamil. In Malini Ambach, Jonas Buchholz and Ute Hüsken (eds), *Temples, Texts, and Networks: South Indian Perspectives*, pp. 77–94. Heidelberg, Germany: Heidelberg Asian Studies Publishing. doi.org/10.11588/hasp.906.c13936.

Gonda, Jan. (1977). *Medieval Religious Literature in Sanskrit*. Wiesbaden, Germany: Harrassowitz.

Harman, William. (1987). The authority of Sanskrit in Tamil Hinduism: A case study in tracing a text to its sources. *The Mankind Quarterly* 27(3): 295–315. doi.org/10.46469/mq.1987.27.3.4.

Hart, George L. (1976). *The Relation between Tamil and Classical Sanskrit Literature*. Wiesbaden, Germany: Harrassowitz.

Kiruṣṇacāmi, Ve. (1974). *Tamiḻil talapurāṇa ilakkiyam*. Muttucāmipuram, India: A. Vēluk Kōṉār.

Klöber, Rafael. (2019). Sivaismus im Wandel. Der tamilische Saiva Siddhanta seit dem 19. *Jahrhundert* [*Saivism in Transition: The Tamil Saiva Siddhanta Since the 19th Century*]. Halle, Germany: Frankesche Stiftungen zu Halle.

Koppedrayer, Kathleen Iva. (1990). The sacred presence of the guru: The Velala lineages of Tiruvavatuturai, Dharmapuram, and Tiruppanantal. PhD thesis, McMaster University, Hamilton, ON. Available from: hdl.handle.net/11375/8299.

Koppedrayer, Kathleen Iva. (1991). The Varṇāśramacandrika and the Śūdra's right to preceptorhood: The social background of a philosophical debate in late medieval South India. *Journal of Indian Philosophy* 19: 297–314. doi.org/10.1007/BF00180493.

Kulke, Hermann. (1970). *Cidambaramāhātmya. Eine Untersuchung der religionsgeschichtlichen und historischen Hintergründe für die Entstehung der Tradition einer südindischen Tempelstadt [Cidabaramāhātmya: An Investigation of the Religious History and Historical Background for the Emergence of the Tradition of a South Indian Temple City*]. Wiesbaden, Germany: Otto Harrassowitz.

Mātavaṉ, Vē. Irā. (1995). *Tamiḻil talapuraṇaṅkaḷ*. [2 vols.] Thanjavur, India: Pāvai.

Monier-Williams, Monier. (2009). *An English–Sanskrit Dictionary*. New Delhi: Asian Educational Services.

Nachimuthu, K. (2022). A survey of the sthalapurāṇa literature in Tamil. In Malini Ambach, Jonas Buchholz and Ute Hüsken (eds), *Temples, Texts, and Networks: South Indian Perspectives*, pp. 41–76. Heidelberg, Germany: Heidelberg Asian Studies Publishing. doi.org/10.11588/hasp.906.c13935.

Narayanan, Vasudha. (2000). Religious vocabulary and regional identity: A study of the Tamil Cirappuranam. In David Gilmartin and Bruce B. Lawrence (eds), *Beyond Turk and Hindu: Rethinking Religious Identities in Islamicate South Asia*, pp. 74–97. Gainesville, FL: University Press of Florida.

Raghavan, V. (1959). An unique two-khaṇḍa version of the Matsya Purāṇa. *Purāṇa* 1(1): 42–57.

Ramanujan, A.K. (1967). *The Interior Landscape: Love Poems from a Classical Tamil Anthology*. Bloomington, IN: Indiana University Press.

Ramesh, Jay. (2020). Abodes of Śiva: Monuments and memory in medieval and early modern South Indian purāṇas. PhD thesis, Columbia University, New York, NY. doi.org/10.7916/d8-h0zf-pg97.

Rocher, Ludo. (1986). *The Purāṇas*. Wiesbaden, Germany: Harrassowitz.

Schier, Kerstin. (2018). *The Goddess's Embrace: Multifaceted Relations at the Ekāmranātha Temple Festival in Kanchipuram*. Wiesbaden, Germany: Harrassowitz. doi.org/10.2307/j.ctvcm4fcn.

Shulman, David. (1980). *Tamil Temple Myths: Sacrifice and Divine Marriage in the South Indian Śaiva Tradition*. Princeton, NJ: Princeton University Press. doi.org/10.1515/9781400856923.

Smith, Travis LaMar. (2007). The sacred center and its peripheries: Śaivism and the Vārāṇasī Sthala-Purāṇas. PhD thesis, Columbia University, New York, NY.

Tamil Lexicon. (1924–36). [6 vols.] Madras, India: University of Madras.

Wiig, Linda. (1981). Māhātmyas: A preliminary descriptive survey (including a list of māhātmyas from Aufrecht's Catalogus Catalogorum). MA thesis, University of Pennsylvania, Philadelphia. Available from: repository.upenn.edu/southasia_theses/1.

Wilden, Eva. (2015). Translation and transcultural adaptation in a multicultural lingual environment: Tamil and Sanskrit versions of the Tiruviḷaiyāṭaṟpurāṇam. In Émilie Aussant (ed.), *La traduction dans l'histoire des idées linguistiques. Représentations et practiques [Translation in the History of Linguistic Ideas: Representations and Practices]*, pp. 93–110. Paris: Paul Geuthner.

Younger, Paul. (1995). *The Home of Dancing Śivaṉ: The Traditions of the Hindu Temple in Citamparam*. New York, NY: Oxford University Press.

Zvelebil, Kamil V. (1973). *The Smile of Murugan: On Tamil Literature of South India*. Leiden, Netherlands: Brill.

Zvelebil, Kamil V. (1975). *Tamil Literature*. Leiden, Netherlands: E.J. Brill. doi.org/10.1163/9789004492981.

17

The 'purāṇification' of the death of Kṛṣṇa

Christopher R. Austin

Abstract

Popular Hindu mythology tends to understand the death of Kṛṣṇa as initiating the turnover from the Dvāpara to the Kali Yuga. Additionally, this Kali Yuga discourse of dharmic devolution often attracts the related theme of *pralaya* or cosmic dissolution. It is often assumed that these yugic and cosmic implications of Kṛṣṇa's death are established in the *Mahābhārata*. This chapter seeks to historicise the material by tracing a pattern of amplification from the *Mahābhārata* to the *Harivaṃśa* and finally to the *Viṣṇu Purāṇa*, wherein we find the most explicit setting of Kṛṣṇa's death against both Kali Yuga and *pralaya* discourse. As such, this chapter demonstrates that the *Harivaṃśa* mediates between the *itihāsa* and purāṇa genres and that the *Mahābhārata*, while partaking to an extent of the language and mythos of the purāṇas, is not so thoroughly purāṇified as is often assumed.

> *Après moi, le déluge*
> —attr. Louis XV

Introduction[1]

Popular conceptions of the *Mahābhārata* (*Mbh*) and the life of Kṛṣṇa understand the great war and death of Kṛṣṇa to take place during, or even prompt, the turnover from the Dvāpara to the Kali Yuga. That the war took place at this moment is stated very early in the epic:

> *antare caiva saṃprāpte kalidvāparayor abhūt |*
> *samantapañcake yuddhaṃ kurupāṇḍavasenayoḥ ||*
>
> In the interval of the Kali and Dvāpara there was
> at Samantapañcaka a battle between the armies of the Kurus and the Pāṇḍavas. (*Mbh*, 1.2.9)[2]

These and a handful of other passages in the epic (taken up below) appear to link the events of the war to the yugic turn. Elsewhere in purāṇic and Hindu tradition, various sources link the yugic turn into the Kali Age with the appearance of Kṛṣṇa at this moment of human history, occasionally suggesting he is born in the Dvāpara (for example, *dvāparaṃ yugam āsādya … avatīrṇaḥ sa … vasudevakule*; *Brahma Purāṇa* [Schreiner and Söhnen 1987], 176.52–53). Thus, it is commonly understood that there is a link between the onset of the Kali Age and the bloody war and/or life of Kṛṣṇa on Earth, and we see this carried forward by popular works such as Iravati Karve's *Yuganta* (2017). It is, moreover, common to read the destructive imagery of the *Mahābhārata* as a transposition, or human-scale equivalent, of a cosmic *pralaya* ('universal destruction'), at least in poetic or imagistic terms. Such readings owe much to Madeleine Biardeau, whose reading of the epic privileged the mythology of cosmic temporal cycles within a larger universe of *bhakti* (see especially Biardeau 1976, 1978b). Thus, while yugic–dharmic social devolution and universal cosmic dissolution operate on two completely different levels in Hindu mythology, it is often assumed that both constitute key reference points for understanding the great war and life of Kṛṣṇa.

In what follows, I will be concerned not so much with the larger and by now well-worked theme of time in the *Mahābhārata*, but particularly with the yugic and cosmic temporal framings of Kṛṣṇa's death.[3] That is, I hope to

1 I am grateful to John Brockington and André Couture for their helpful comments on earlier drafts of this chapter.

2 All *Mahābhārata* references are to the Critical Edition (Sukthankar 1933–66).

3 On the topic of yugic–social and cosmic time cycles in the *Mahābhārata*, see Koskikallio (1994); Vassilkov (1999); González-Reimann (2002, 2009, 2010); Yano (2003); Thomas (2007); Kloetzli (2013); Hudson (2013: 146–77); and Hiltebeitel (2011a: 243–336).

track a pattern of amplification that results in the (ca fifth century CE) *Viṣṇu Purāṇa* (*VP*), wherein we find an explicit framing of Kṛṣṇa's death against both Kali Yuga discourse and cosmic *pralaya* processes. As I will demonstrate, this framing builds on the *Harivaṃśa* (*HV*), which in turn supplements the *Mahābhārata* in which the yugic and pralayic imagery around the death of Kṛṣṇa are absent or at best decidedly understated. In this way, it will become clear that the *Harivaṃśa* is a kind of mediating work between the *Mahābhārata*'s world and that of the purāṇas. My final purpose is not to attempt a wholescale debunking, but simply to underline the fact of the yugic and pralayic thematic amplification across these three sources (*Mbh*, *HV* and *VP*). If we can sketch a kind of genealogy of the death of Kṛṣṇa, it will be possible to identify more clearly where the constructs of *yuga* and *pralaya* are truly operative in early Kṛṣṇa mythology, and where they are not.

Purāṇic temporal constructs in the *Mahābhārata*: Popular and critical views

The work I propose here carries forward from that of Luis González-Reimann, who challenged more thoroughly than any other scholar the notion that yugic cycles are fundamental to the *Mahābhārata*'s mythology. Hence, before looking at the death of Kṛṣṇa in *Mbh* 16, I would like to take up some of González-Reimann's observations, as well as those of Yaroslav Vassilkov.

The value of Vassilkov's (1999) work for my purposes is its articulation of the theme of destructive time—the *kālavāda* or doctrine of time in the *Mahābhārata*—as wholly independent of the notion of devolving *yuga*s and the Kali Age. Vassilkov assembles and examines the *Mahābhārata*'s many passages treating the theme of time as the ultimate power. In so doing, he demonstrates that 'the *kālavāda* and the teaching of the omnipotent Fate (*daiva*) related to it are constitutive for the epic, being the quintessence of the epic *Weltanschauung*' (Vassilkov 1999: 26). But this coherent set of ideas—fatalism, the inevitability of decay and death and the advocacy of resigned stoicism in the face of all-powerful time—appears to reach back as far as the *Atharvaveda* (Vassilkov 1999: 18) and is genetically independent of the *yuga* doctrine. In other words, *kāla* fatalism is a dominant theme in the *Mahābhārata* and appears over and over in both narrative and didactic passages across the entire text without any reference to the Kali Yuga or to the better-known theme of four devolving *yuga*s. Certainly, the *yuga* doctrine is conceptually continuous with the *kālavāda*, but Vassilkov's evidence can leave little doubt as to the antiquity and genetic independence of the *Mahābhārata*'s *kālavāda* from *yuga* mythology.

González-Reimann likewise observes that this theme of time, destiny and the ineluctable forces of nature, decay and death, all circulating around the construct of *kāla*, indeed pervades the *Mahābhārata*, but this is a separate matter from that of the Kali Yuga as such (González-Reimann 2002: 20–50).[4] Similarly, the notion of *kali* itself—conflict, misfortune, war and the causes thereof, as well as the associated notion of the losing throw of dice—pervades the text, largely without reference to *yuga*s or cyclic time frames (González-Reimann 2002: 139). In short, between Vassilkov and González-Reimann, we are given good reason to be wary of simply inserting 'Kali Yuga' into any and every occurrence of the terms *kāla* and *kali*, which clearly have their own rich registers of meaning and are pervasive throughout the epic without any reference to yugic cycles.

González-Reimann demonstrates that the principal or most common mode in which the construct of *yuga* appears in the *Mahābhārata* is not in any explicit placing of the epic events in or between the Dvāpara and the Kali, but as a poetic and generic simile for describing terrible destruction—'*yugānte ... iva*' ('as at the end of a *yuga*') being an especially common formula (2002: 51–85). And for this to make any sense, the *yuga* image must refer to the termination of what in popular Hindu cosmology would be called not a *yuga* but a *kalpa*, since there is no *pralaya* or universal destruction marking the end of a mere human-scale single *yuga* (González-Reimann 2002: 71). Thus, the most frequently encountered usage of the notion of *yuga* in the *Mahābhārata* is poetic, imagistic and refers to cosmic destruction and not to the four devolving social–dharmic eras, much less do they assert anything at all about the yugic–temporal placement of the *Mahābhārata*'s events.[5]

4 See González-Reimann (2010) for a précis of the salient points of the 2002 monograph.

5 On the related point of the relationship between kings and *yuga*s in the *Mahābhārata*, Lynn Thomas (2007) critiques González-Reimann, but in so doing confirms what for my purposes is the most important aspect of his overall hypothesis—namely, that the *Mahābhārata*'s construction of *yuga*s is too complex for any pat homogenisation. She argues that several passages of the *Mahābhārata* in fact understand the yugic alternations to be the product not of automatic temporal cycles but of the virtues of kings—in other words, 'the king makes the age' (for example, *Mbh*, 12.70.6; Thomas 2007: 190–91). Thomas develops a well-defended argument for understanding these passages as asserting a real cause–effect relationship between a king's rule and the dharmic–yugic state of the cosmos (Thomas 2007: 192–93), but this makes it clearer that the *Mahābhārata*'s concept of *yuga*s is too complex and heterogeneous to support any notion of a single monolithic *yuga* mythology for it, which in my view is the most significant argument made by González-Reimann.

The *Mahābhārata* does, however, at times explicitly place its events in the Kali Yuga or at the turn of the Kali from the Dvāpara—this much is clear from the quote at the start of this chapter (*Mbh*, 1.2.9). Similarly, it does state occasionally that Kṛṣṇa appears on Earth at this time. What does González-Reimann make of such statements? He recognises nine in total (González-Reimann 2002: 86–102), including this first already mentioned (*Mbh*, 1.2.9). The others are found at *Mbh* 3.148.37 (Hanumān explains to Bhīma that the Kali Age will begin soon), 3.186–189 (a substantial treatment of the *yuga*s delivered by Mārkaṇḍeya in which Yudhiṣṭhira at least suggests he is presently living in the Kali Yuga), 6.11.5–7 (Saṃjaya states that the Kali is the current era), 6.62.39 (Kṛṣṇa appears at the start of the Kali Yuga), 9.59.21 (Kṛṣṇa tells Saṃkarṣaṇa that the Kali Yuga has arrived), 12.326.82 (Kṛṣṇa will appear towards the end of the *saṃdhi* of the Dvāpara and Kali), 12.337.42–44 (Vyāsa will be born in the Kali Age when the great war occurs) and 13.143.9 (Kṛṣṇa is said to be *adharma* in the Kali Yuga). In assessing these passages that appear to compromise his hypothesis, González-Reimann largely deploys the notion of their lateness to minimise their integrity as a part of the fabric of the basic text, and states:

> Whatever the exact circumstances of each one of our quotes, the fact remains that they are too few and too conflicting to be an organic part of the story. If placing the action historically according to the yuga system were crucial to the Epic, one would expect more consistency, especially when the references are so scarce. This lack of agreement suggests that the yuga theory is only loosely connected to the Epic, and that this connection was probably late and came from various sources. (González-Reimann 2002: 103)

All nine passages are part of the critically edited text and as such they must be taken as part of our evidence; I would not seek to reject them or otherwise dismiss them from consideration. But even insisting on the organic integrity of these verses alongside everything else, the basic point González-Reimann wishes to make stands: a mere nine passages, most of them in *upākhyāna* and didactic portions, is surprisingly meagre. Why do we not see this yugic specification everywhere in the Pāṇḍava narrative? While pursuing a different agenda, Emily Hudson makes much the same point. Referring particularly to the two most substantial of González-Reimann's nine passages (the Hanuman lesson at *Mbh* 3.148 and Mārkaṇḍeya's at 3.186–89), she states:

> Given the tendency of both modern scholarship and received tradition to explain various narrative events, particularly the tragic conflict and the war, in terms of the influence of the Kali *yuga*, it is

> surprising that there are only two extensive discussions of the *yugas* in the *Mahābhārata*. Neither is located 'in the thick of things,' that is, in the midst of the heat of the action of the central narrative ... [and] neither ... explicitly link[s] the war or any other key narrative event explicitly to the approaching Kali *yuga*. (Hudson 2013: 151)

I am convinced by these arguments that, if we are speaking about the Critical Edition of the Sanskrit *Mahābhārata*, there are few compelling grounds to assert that yugic–temporal concerns were fundamental to the epic's initial creation and design. What we can say is that, in the text as we have it now, the idea of the war and Kṛṣṇa's life as Dvāpara–Kali events is emerging, but the nine passages are not wholly consistent and they point to a mythology in formation, not a *fait accompli*. González-Reimann was right to draw our attention to the complexity of the source itself, which does not withstand scrutiny if we are going to insist that, start to finish, the poet-composers of the *Mahābhārata* always understood that the war, together with the life and death of Kṛṣṇa, took place at the transition between the Dvāpara and the Kali, and that such yugic–mythic constructs are deep in the DNA of the poem. The seeds of the idea—or shall we say, perhaps, a small sapling—appear to be here, although to phrase things this way always runs the risk of a teleological fallacy. It happens that they did grow into a clear purāṇic theology in the *Viṣṇu Purāṇa*'s account of the death of Kṛṣṇa, but we must always ask what our reading of the *Mahābhārata* would be if no such purāṇas existed. Were it possible for someone to read the entire Critical Edition of the *Mahābhārata*, bringing to that raw reading no prior knowledge of Hindu mythology, would they decide that the turn of the Kali Age is essential to the epic's design and identity? I have difficulty imagining such a thing. What I wish to make clear—and I am indebted to González-Reimann's work on this point—is that the mytheme of the Mahābhārata war as a Kali Age event is at best a seed or a sapling and not a tree in the *Mahābhārata*.

All this has to do with the human-scale *yuga* cycle, which, again, is thematically connected to larger cycles of time that could be labelled 'kalpic'—that is, the exponentially larger periods of the *sarga* ('creation') and *pralaya* ('dissolution') of the entire cosmos that become standard topics in most purāṇas. The idea that the *Mahābhārata* is fundamentally shaped and informed by the mythology of such larger cycles is traceable to Madeleine Biardeau (1968, 1971, 1976, 1978b), although her views on this are more complex than is often recognised and some of what I wish to argue about the 'purāṇification' of the death of Kṛṣṇa is in fact continuous with certain of her claims rather than critical of them. Where English readers are familiar with her notions of *pralaya* and apocalyptic imagery in the *Mahābhārata*, they have largely depended on the mediation of Alf Hiltebeitel, whose engagement with Biardeau is creative and adaptive and does not simply re-present her ideas in a neutral way. Biardeau argued that purāṇic *pralaya* imagery, as part of a larger *bhakti avatāra* soteriology, was fundamental to the epic, even while recognising its complex and at times contradictory nature. Hiltebeitel (particularly 1976: 299–360; see also 1980; 1984) engaged with this work in various ways, initially putting Biardeau's ideas into productive conversation with the work of Dumézil, from whom Biardeau differed vastly in methodology and approach.[6] It is fair to say that, Hiltebeitel's adaptive mediation notwithstanding, Biardeau is a key thinker for those who wish to argue for the centrality of kalpic–pralayic imagery in the *Mahābhārata*. The premise here is that the *Mahābhārata* is essentially, and not accidentally or secondarily, a purāṇic myth of cosmic destruction, of avatāric intervention and renewal.

But as Hiltebeitel has observed (1976: 310–11)—indeed, as even Biardeau has conceded occasionally—it is very difficult to sustain any reading that insists the epic's authors were transposing one fundamental mythic structure or that there is a single key to unlocking the meaning of the vast story.[7] Thus, to

6 It is important to note as well that Hiltebeitel's early engagement with her thought, as represented in Hiltebeitel (1976), was based on an understanding of Biardeau's work in progress. See Biardeau (1978a) for her initial response to Hiltebeitel and Hiltebeitel (2011b) for a more recent review of the dialogue between the two.

7 Biardeau recognised the points of tension in the *Mahābhārata* between human-scale yugic cycles and cosmic-scale dynamics such as *pralaya*, generally emphasising the integrity of the latter over the former for understanding the epic's more basic concerns, but often expressing such things in an exploratory or hypothetical mode: '*Et s'il est vrai que l'événement central du récit est la fin d'un yuga (ou comme la fin d'un yuga), il est assez piquant de constater que nous risquerions de manquer le sens de toute l'histoire si nous ne connaissions déjà le cadre de référence qui lui est essentiel: l'alternance des créations et des résorptions purâniques. S'il est un point de vue selon lequel il est vrai de dire que l'épopée est antérieure aux purâna, ce n'est certainement pas celui du contenu doctrinal* [And if it is true that the central event of the narrative is the end of a yuga (or like the end of a yuga), it is quite surprising to note that we might miss the meaning of the whole story if we did not already know the frame of reference, which is essential to it: the alternation of creations and purāṇic resorptions. If there is a point of view according to which it is true to say that the epic pre-dates the purāṇas, it is certainly not that of the doctrinal content]' (Biardeau 1976: 135). The quote—a hedged and somewhat noncommittal statement making gestures towards the epic's complexity but driving nonetheless at a deep conviction of an 'essential frame of reference', which is decidedly purāṇic—is representative of the difficulties one can encounter in understanding Biardeau's position. Thus, it could be that González-Reimann misread Biardeau on certain key points, as she charged in Biardeau (2003–04). The chief issue of contention here was the degree to which Biardeau actually asserted the coherence of the *yuga* construct in the *Mahābhārata* and its centrality to its overall mythos. While a review from Biardeau of González-Reimann's book might have presented a good opportunity for clearing the air about what precisely Biardeau did and did not believe, her response took the shape not of a review properly speaking, but of a personal and broad-brushed reaction.

over-privilege the imagery of *pralaya* as a truly essential structuring principle of the entire *Mahābhārata* can lead to contradictions and distortions, and we would do well to heed the same kinds of caveats that were raised around yugic mythology in the epic: just because something is in the *Mahābhārata* does not mean it is absolutely essential to the text's basic identity and design. Tieken expresses the matter succinctly in observing that 'the *pralaya* myth is indeed present in the *Mahābhārata* but rather as a by-product of the epic story than as the source of it' (2004: 7).[8]

Yet, there did occur in the *Harivaṃśa* and *Viṣṇu Purāṇa* a gradual 'purāṇification' process, whereby the principal events of the *Mahābhārata*, and particularly the account of Kṛṣṇa's death, came to be framed ever more explicitly within the constructs of both the Kali Yuga and pralayic destruction. In what follows, I review the key materials involved here—the *Mahābhārata*, *Harivaṃśa* and *Viṣṇu Purāṇa*—and hope to demonstrate how these sources deepen and amplify the apocalyptic language and significance surrounding Kṛṣṇa's death, whereby the discourse on the social ills of the Kali Yuga come to be tied to the much larger theme of cosmic destruction. By highlighting this amplification pattern, I hope at least to offer a historicising nuance to the ongoing conversation about purāṇic constructs in the epics.

The death of Kṛṣṇa and the Vṛṣṇis in *Mahābhārata* 16

At first glance, one might well believe that the death of Kṛṣṇa in the *Mahābhārata* marks the beginning of the Kali Yuga. The account of the Critical Edition *Mbh* 16 is grim, laden with doom and gloom, and marks the death of the Vṛṣṇi clan with bad omens. This is initially a matter of unusual meteorological phenomena, freak weather and so on (*Mbh*, 16.1–6). The destruction heralded by these signs will be the result of two curses: the first was levied 36 years earlier against Kṛṣṇa by Gāndhārī (*Mbh*, 11.25.38–42) and the second is cast on the Vṛṣṇis early in Book 16 when three sages are insulted by prankster Vṛṣṇi boys who have dressed up Kṛṣṇa's son Sāmba as a pregnant woman and asked the sages 'what she will give birth to' (*kim iyaṃ janayiṣyati*; *Mbh*, 16.2.6).[9] The sages reply that Sāmba will give birth to an

8 On this point, see also Johnson (1998: xxxiii–xxxv).

9 The prank itself is an odd one, which I will not endeavour to decode here. For one intriguing attempt at such a decoding, see von Simson (2007).

iron club that will destroy the Vṛṣṇis and Andhakas, including Halāyudha (Saṃkarṣaṇa) and Kṛṣṇa. Time itself then begins stalking about Dvārakā in fearful human form (*kālo ... karālo vikaṭo muṇḍaḥ puruṣaḥ kṛṣṇapiṅgalaḥ*; *Mbh*, 16.3.1–2) and more bad omens appear—again, of the inauspicious type encountered elsewhere in the epic. Brahmins are mistreated (*Mbh*, 16.3.8). Kṛṣṇa, when realising 36 years have passed since Gāndhārī's curse, ties the inauspicious omens of the present moment to those occurring many years before during the great war (*Mbh*, 16.3.16–20):

> Hṛṣīkeśaḥ, seeing thusly how his time was up [*saṃprāptaṃ kālaparyayam*] and having noted it was a new-moon on the 13th of the fortnight [*trayodaśyām amāvāsyāṃ*], said:
>
> 'The fourteenth [day of the month] has been made into the fifteenth by Rāhu, as during the Bhārata war, and occurring again today for our destruction.'
>
> Reflecting on the time [*vimṛśann eva kālaṃ*] and remembering, Janārdana Slayer of Keśi thought: 'The 36 years have elapsed.
>
> 'That curse has now arrived, which was cast by distraught Gāndhārī, her family slain and herself utterly ruined by grief over her sons.
>
> 'This has now come to pass—what Yudhiṣṭhira said in the past amidst the armies in formation, having seen terrible omens.'

The Vṛṣṇi women have nightmares of a frightful female figure, *kālī strī* (*Mbh*, 16.4.1), whom we might be tempted to assume is the goddess Kālī. Tieken (2004: 17) makes this mistake, but she is better understood simply as 'a black woman with white teeth' (Smith 2009: 759). Much less can she be thought of as an embodiment of the Kali Yuga as the term *yuga* is used nowhere in *Mbh* 16. Standards and other implements of Kṛṣṇa and Saṃkarṣaṇa begin to disappear of their own accord. Eventually, the clan takes a seaside holiday at Prabhāsa and destroys itself in a drunken brawl with the clubs after which the *parvan* takes its name. Kṛṣṇa sends for Arjuna and arranges for the protection of the women of Dvārakā, and subsequently finds his brother Rāma trading in his mortal coil for a serpentine one, returning to the ocean in multiheaded snake form. Fully aware that the soles of his feet are especially vulnerable,[10]

10 Kṛṣṇa 'remembered what was said by Durvāsas when [he was] smeared over by the remains of his rice pudding' (*durvāsasā pāyasocchiṣṭalipte yac cāpy uktaṁ tac ca sasmāra kṛṣṇaḥ*; 16.5.17cd). See *Mbh* 13.144 for this incident, which bears an intriguing resemblance to that of the child Achilles.

Kṛṣṇa enters a yogic state, is shot in the sole of his foot by the hunter Jarā (lit., 'Old Age') and ascends to Heaven, where he is greeted by all the gods (*Mbh*, 16.5.22–25).

The remainder of the *parvan* focuses on the ageing Arjuna and his pathos-laden interactions with the survivors. The key issues I wish to highlight here are the eventual flooding of Kṛṣṇa's now-abandoned city of Dvārakā, which returns to the ocean from which it was claimed (*Mbh*, 16.8.40), and the persisting stress on fate and destiny as Arjuna and other bereaved characters bemoan the loss of Kṛṣṇa and the Vṛṣṇis. The *parvan* closes with a conversation between Arjuna and Vyāsa, in which the latter explains that Arjuna should not grieve over what has come to pass; Kṛṣṇa knew all and could have changed things if he had wanted to. In particular, Vyāsa says that Kṛṣṇa's task in relieving the Earth is now complete (*Mbh*, 16.9.29) and that the time for the Pāṇḍavas to depart has arrived (*gamanaṃ prāptakālaṃ*; 16.9.31). He continues:

> O Bhārata, strength, wisdom, majesty and knowledge come about in their proper times and perish in the end [*bhavanti bhavakāleṣu vipadyante viparyaye*].
>
> Dhanaṃjaya, this is the whole root of time. Time alone restores the seed of the world again spontaneously [*jagadbījaṃ ... kāla eva samādatte punar eva yadṛcchayā*].
>
> A man becomes strong and then weak, a lord and then directed by others.
>
> Your departed weapons have done what they were meant to do, now returned whence they came. They will return to your hand when the time comes about once again [*punar eṣyanti te hastaṃ yadā kālo bhaviṣyati*].
>
> O Bhārata, for you noble [Pāṇḍavas] as well the time has come to set out upon the highest path. This is what is best and ideal for you, I believe, O Bull of the Bharatas. (*Mbh*, 16.9.32–36)

The Mausalaparvan raises any number of theological, moral, ritual and mythological questions, some of which have been treated in scholarship (see, for example, von Simson 2007; Granoff 2008, 2010; Sharma 2020). My present concern, however, is with the episode's degree of engagement with explicit yugic and pralayic imagery and terminology. A casual reading certainly gives a first impression of a kaliyugic disaster but, confirming what we have already learned from González-Reimann above, what we find on inspection is that, for all its darkness and mood of resignation in the face of ineluctable forces, the Mausalaparvan nowhere mentions the Kali Yuga or sets the inauspicious death of Kṛṣṇa within a larger pattern of ages.

The term *kāla* is the catchword throughout (occurring some 30-odd times) for fate, the inevitability of the curses' fructification, decay and so on, without ever being deployed in a yugic–temporal sense. To be sure, the omens and ill-boding perversities read something like a Kali Yuga text, particularly insofar as brahmins are abused (*Mbh*, 16.3.8). Also noteworthy is the fact that Kṛṣṇa himself links the coming destruction to that of the great war, noting the same omens that Yudhiṣṭhira had observed years ago. As such, Kṛṣṇa recognises the link between his own death and the violence of the great war, which popular tradition indeed binds together as markers of the transition to the Kali Age. But what we see here is a very liberal use of *kāla* forms, none of which designates a yugic framing. It is very odd that the poets consciously understood this event to mark the beginning of the Kali Yuga and did not once state this clearly amid the 30 or so occasions when they used related forms of *kāla*. Clearly, the dominant construct here is Vassilkov's *kālavāda* and not the popular four-age *yuga* cycle. Vyāsa's concluding lesson to Arjuna does hint at renewal of some kind (*Mbh*, 16.9.33), but in fact suggests that this could even occur within Arjuna's lifetime, which of course it does not (*punar* [*astrāṇi*] *eṣyanti te hastaṃ yadā kālo bhaviṣyati*; 16.9.35). Moreover, the pattern of decay and loss he repeatedly emphasises concerns a single human lifespan, not a large cosmic process or dharmic attenuation. Arjuna will carry his despondent *kālavāda* resignation into the Mahāprasthānikaparvan, chanting '*kāla*, *kāla*!' (*Mbh*, 17.1.4) to prompt his brothers to renounce the world, and the remainder of the epic told in Books 17 and 18 unfolds with no mention of any yugic turnover.[11]

As for pralayic imagery, there is certainly a fit of destructive violence here, as well as the flood imagery of Dvārakā returning to the ocean. Biardeau identifies the massacre of Kṛṣṇa and the Yādavas with the apocalyptic violence of the Sauptikaparvan, conscripting it into her stock of examples of the transposed myth, and she reads the flooding of Dvārakā as a pralayic inundation (1978b: 194n.3). However, the text makes no clear gesture towards such imagery, not even using the common '*yugānt*[*e*] *iva*' simile when describing the violence of the Vṛṣṇis' civil war. I would not exclude

11 'It is very significant that neither [*Mbh* Book 16 or 17] (nor the very last Svargārohaṇa Parvan) makes any mention whatsoever of the Kali Yuga or, for that matter, of any other yuga or the yugas in general. In the final three books of the *Mahābhārata* the yugas are never mentioned, let alone invoked as the cause of events' (González-Reimann 2002: 52).

the possibility that the poets had seen a parallel between the inundation of Dvārakā (*Mbh*, 16.8.40) and other significant mythological expressions of waters as chaos, of which there are indeed examples elsewhere in the *Mahābhārata*. But this does not amount to evidence that the death of Kṛṣṇa 'is' or consciously transposes the kalpic–purāṇic imagery of universal flood.

The dominant themes and concerns lying clearly on the surface of the basic text as we have it are the unchangeable nature of fate and predestination, the power of curses and the corrosive effects of time on a single individual throughout his or her life, as well as the enlightened equanimity of Kṛṣṇa, who understands all this and makes no attempt to change the course of things. And behind it all is the soon-to-be concluded theological frame of the *aṃśāvataraṇa* or *ad hoc* descent of the portions of the gods, according to which the entire stock of epic characters, not only Kṛṣṇa, are portions of deities descended to complete the great task of relieving the Earth of her burden (*Mbh*, 1.61).[12] What the poets are concerned with in relating the death of Kṛṣṇa and the Pāṇḍavas in Books 16–18 is first and foremost the return of the semi-human characters to their divine origins, following their ascent back to Heaven, where they are reunited with the divinities from whom they have descended (Austin 2009). One could argue that a Kaliyugic darkness is suggested here in Book 16, but it is never named as such and, moreover, we see no clear invocation of cosmic-scale destruction.

The *Harivaṃśa*'s Kṛṣṇa portrait as an itihāsa–purāṇa mediation

My next source, the *Harivaṃśa*, does not relate the death of Kṛṣṇa at all but, for reasons that will become clear, it is extremely important if we wish to understand how and why later *paurāṇika*s came to set the affair of the clubs directly and explicitly against apocalyptic yugic and cosmic devolutions. The *Harivaṃśa* carries forward the *Mahābhārata*'s *aṃśāvataraṇa* mythology, but advances towards what we might call a more classically purāṇic sensibility in at least two ways. First, it deepens the Vaiṣṇava theological framework

12 The theme of the overburdened Earth is possibly an Indo-European inheritance (Dumézil 1968), while the general structure of descent, intervention and return provides the basis for the later (but not much later) Vaiṣṇava doctrine of the *avatāra* (Hacker 1960). The *Mahābhārata* descent mythology captures an intriguing moment—perhaps in the second or third century CE—on the edge of the fully articulated purāṇic universe, in many respects pointing directly towards it and in others still fundamentally shaped by much older Vedic and Indo-European paradigms (*pace* Biardeau).

behind and around the descent of the multiple gods by developing an elaborate mythic narrative of and rationale for Viṣṇu's descent as Kṛṣṇa (*HV*, 30–45).[13] The *Harivaṃśa* poets appear to have felt that Viṣṇu's centrality in this affair needed clarification, and the result is a more explicitly and vigorously Vaiṣṇava casting for the epic story. Second, the *Harivaṃśa* precedes its rendering of Kṛṣṇa's life with materials that become typical of the purāṇic genre: an opening account of universal creation (*HV*, 1–3), Manvantara enumerations (7) and genealogical lists of both the solar (8–10) and the lunar (20–29) lines, with the latter culminating in the person of Kṛṣṇa. While one hesitates to speak of 'transition' texts, the *Harivaṃśa* does provide a crucial linking or mediating point between the complex and heterogeneous mythology of the epic and the more homogenised purāṇic portraits of a universe articulated around a single, all-controlling deity.

The *Harivaṃśa*'s yugic setting of the events of the war is, like the *Mahābhārata*'s, still somewhat conflicted. One *Harivaṃśa* passage states that Viṣṇu sleeps through the Kṛta and Tretā, but awakens at the end of the Dvāpara (*dvāparaparyante*; *HV*, 40.36). In a second, Brahmā states that the great destruction of the war will occur at the end of the Dvāpara (*dvāparasya yugasyānte*; *HV*, 43.56) and, when Aśvatthāman slaughters the sleeping Pāṇḍava camp, this will mark the end of the Dvāpara or third *yuga* (*samāptam idam ... tṛtīyaṃ dvāparaṃ yugam*; 43.58). Later, however, a young and unmarried Kṛṣṇa states to the sleepy sage Mucukunda that it is already the Kali Age (*HV* 85.59). This conversation occurs before the founding of Dvārakā and therefore many years before the war and the night-raid marked out by Brahmā as the end of the Dvāpara. Clearly, the notion here is of a general orientation around the third and fourth ages, but we do not yet have a consistent temporal setting.

More significantly, the *Harivaṃśa* does not relate the inauspicious death of Kṛṣṇa, nor does it repeat in detail any episode of the *Mahābhārata*, functioning as it does to provide only what is not related in the epic: substantial genealogies, the mythological background of the descent of Viṣṇu and the gods and the episodes, untold in the *Mahābhārata*, of Kṛṣṇa's birth, youth and adult life. We have here in the *Harivaṃśa* plenty of fighting, but none of it is agonised over or prompts any wringing of hands in the manner of the dharmically sensitive Yudhiṣṭhira and Arjuna. Bad guys are killed, Kṛṣṇa wins and everyone is happy. There is throughout the *Harivaṃśa* none of the moral darkness that besets the larger epic, very little of the *kālavāda*

13 All *Harivaṃśa* references are to the Critical Edition (Vaidya 1969–71) unless indicated otherwise.

sensibility of fatalism and, without any rendering of the *mausala* affair, the *Harivaṃśa*'s life story of Kṛṣṇa ends on a happy note, seeing him returned to Dvārakā after rescuing his grandson Aniruddha and defeating Bāṇāsura (*HV*, 113). I do not mean to suggest that the authors of this biography knew nothing of any yugic setting for Kṛṣṇa's life, but clearly the task they set themselves—to supplement the *Mahābhārata*'s tantalisingly patchy portrait of Kṛṣṇa—did not inspire them to explore or deepen the inauspicious aspects of his character, much less to do so in relation to the yugic turnover.[14]

The *Harivaṃśa*, however, does not end with the conclusion of Kṛṣṇa's life story. In *Harivaṃśa* 20–29, the lunar line had been related down to the generation of Kṛṣṇa and now that his life story has been related (46–113), attention turns to the future descendants of Janamejaya (114). This is followed by an account of Janamejaya's attempt at a horse sacrifice, on which occasion Vyāsa arrives to warn him that this proposed rite will be attacked by Indra, and in fact the entire institution of the horse sacrifice will fall into disuse and will never again be offered by *kṣatriya*s so long as the Earth remains. Janamejaya asks whether there will be a restoration of the ritual (*yajñasya punarāvṛtti*[*ḥ*]; 115.38). Vyāsa explains that it will be revived in the Kali Yuga by a Kāśyapa brahmin army general (115.40), which is not a good thing of course, as it is only proper for *kṣatriya*s to undertake such ceremonies, not brahmins. This somewhat perverse restoration will, rather, be a sign of the times, when *dharma* will become unstable (*pravicaliṣyati*; 115.44). Consequently, the discussion turns to the Kali Yuga itself—described by Vyāsa in some detail in *HV* 116 and 117, with its usual qualities, all in the future tense.[15] Naturally, no mention is made here of the Mahābhārata war or of Kṛṣṇa. Occasionally, Vyāsa gestures towards the eventual turn back into the Kṛta, which will occur seamlessly when virtue is restored from the nadir of perversion; no cosmic-scale process of fire or flood is involved or referred to (for example, 117.42–44). Once this prediction is concluded, we hear the details in the last book of the poem (118) of how Janamejaya's horse sacrifice debacle leads to the cessation of the ritual's observance among *kṣatriya*s and several *phalaśruti* verses then conclude the *Harivaṃśa*.

14 Even amid the voluminous appendix material to the *Harivaṃśa*, we do not see any concern on the part of later poets to append a Kṛṣṇa death sequence. Many supplementary episodes are added after the period represented by the CE text (roughly from the fourth century CE onwards), but it is noteworthy that in all this activity, there appeared to be a consensus about the *mausala* affair: it does not belong in the *Harivaṃśa*.

15 Indeed, the traditional designation for this section of the text in manuscript colophons and in the Vulgate edition (Kinjawadekar 1936) is Bhaviṣyaparvan or 'Book of the Future'. The *Mahābhārata*'s own *anukramaṇī* list of its contents gives this title as well ('Bhaviṣyatparvan'; *Mbh*, 1.2.69).

Where Vaiśaṃpāyana and Vyāsa sit vis-à-vis the anticipated turn of the age is not clear, and Janamejaya says as much, remarking that he does not know whether the time of *yugānta* is near or far off (*HV*, 116.1). Certainly, Vyāsa sets the entire Kali Yuga discourse consistently in the future tense and the notion of a restoration of the Vedic rite after its disappearance (*yajñasya punarāvṛtti*[*ḥ*]; 115.38; *aśvamedhaṃ kaliyuge punaḥ pratyāhariṣyati*; 115.40) indicates a considerable gap between the end of Janamejaya's life and the Kali Yuga revival by the upstart brahmin general. There is an investment in the topic here, but it does not sit well with Kṛṣṇa's earlier statement that it is already the Kali Yuga (*HV* 85.59), which, moreover, we have seen is problematic when set against verses in *HV* 40 and 43.

Apart from the matter of timing, it is significant that the substantial treatment of the Kali Yuga in the *Harivaṃśa* is tied directly and only to the proper and improper performance of the horse sacrifice, and not the Bhārata war or the death of Kṛṣṇa. The reason we find an account of the Kali Age soon after the end of the Kṛṣṇa biography is not because the work ends with the inauspicious death of Kṛṣṇa. No such death is related and, again, the *Harivaṃśa*'s biography is marked by a vigorous and uncomplicated heroism perturbed by neither the *kālavāda* fatalism nor the dharmic quandaries and violations of its parent text. Vyāsa's *HV* 115–17 discourse on these future woes turns on an anticipated *varṇasaṃkara* violation of social–ritual distinctions that will occur many years after Janamejaya—himself already three generations removed from the time of the war and Kṛṣṇa's life. Additionally, it is worth observing that none of this carries any hint of a yugic–pralayic coordination or symbolic or literal association between the social ills of the fourth age and the cosmic processes of *pralaya*, even though explanations of *sarga* or cosmic creation opened the *Harivaṃśa*.

The *mausala* battle in the *Viṣṇu Purāṇa*: A death of cosmic significance

With the *Viṣṇu Purāṇa*, we turn a significant corner into a fully and classically purāṇic universe in which the epic's *aṃśāvatarana* theology is replaced with, or develops into, a robustly articulated Viṣṇu-centric cosmos. As a perhaps fifth-century CE text, the *Viṣṇu Purāṇa* follows closely on the heels of the *Harivaṃśa* and takes it as its model, repackaging the life of Kṛṣṇa into a comprehensive portrait of a universe that is the very body of Viṣṇu. Such visions of Viṣṇu–Nārāyaṇa can of course be found in the *Mahābhārata* (for example, 3.186–87), but the *Viṣṇu Purāṇa* is unprecedented in the monolithic focus it places on Viṣṇu, the totality of its vision and the subordinating incorporation of other philosophical systems into its theology. What is significant for my purposes is the *Viṣṇu Purāṇa*'s marshalling of received mythemes, structures and materials from the *Mahābhārata* and *Harivaṃśa*, which are reconfigured in such a way as to render the demise of Kṛṣṇa explicitly as a death of cosmic significance, tied directly to both the human–social miseries of the Kali Yuga and the *pralaya* that is its cosmic analogue.

A full account of this purāṇa is not possible here, although thankfully we now have available a new English translation, including an excellent introduction to which readers can turn for an up-to-date overview of the text's themes, dating and theology (Taylor 2021: 1–41). In the briefest possible terms, the *Viṣṇu Purāṇa*'s Kṛṣṇa biography (Book 5)[16] follows a full account of the creation and constitution of the universe and the human world (Books 1–3), the solar dynasty (4.1–5) and the lunar dynasty into which Kṛṣṇa and the Pāṇḍavas are born (4.6–24). In broad terms, this is derived from the *Harivaṃśa*, but with the addition of much new material. Especially important is the Somavaṃśa account, which is expanded and creatively adapted, with the poets choosing to project well beyond the Pāṇḍava–Vāsudeva period into future generations of the lunar line. This future-tense account (*VP*, 4.24) becomes increasingly disheartening as we learn that *śūdra*s will rule the Earth, and the list of degraded rulers flows into a more generic description of the Kali Age. This in fact has already begun and will conclude at the time of the intervention of Viṣṇu's manifestation as Kalkin, who will restore the Kṛta Yuga (4.24.20). The narrator Parāśara then provides the precise astronomical markers of when this age began: at the time of the birth of Janamejaya's father, Parīkṣit, and more precisely when Kṛṣṇa died and went to Heaven (4.24.27–28; 32ab):

> When that aspect of Lord Viṣṇu born in the family of Vasudeva returned to heaven, brahmin, the Kali age descended on the world.
>
> But as long as his two feet trod this earth, the Kali age had no effect upon it.
>
> … The day that Kṛṣṇa went to heaven was the very day that Kali started. (translation by Taylor 2021: 333)

16 All *Viṣṇu Purāṇa* references are to the Critical Edition (Pathak 1997–99).

A few sage words of advice about royal ambition then conclude the chapter and, with it, Book 4, and the Kṛṣṇa biography (Book 5) begins immediately thereafter.

What we see here is a creative reshaping of the lunar line, carried over from *HV* 20–29 but incorporating now the future or post-Kṛṣṇa generations immediately, rather than waiting until after the Kṛṣṇa story (as in *HV*, 114), and certainly treating them in greater detail. With this *Viṣṇu Purāṇa* projection of lunar kings to come we have again the associated question of the Kali devolution across these generations—the whole downturn explicitly identified as having begun with the death of Kṛṣṇa. We saw this connection between future generations and the Kali Yuga in *HV* 114–17, but in that text this was not tied to Kṛṣṇa's rather cheerfully rendered life as such, and certainly not his death. Hence, the *Viṣṇu Purāṇa*'s life story of Kṛṣṇa is marked at the outset by a yugic flag-setting, which provides the basic reference point and initiating spark for the entire biography. It might even be fair to say that the most significant thing about Kṛṣṇa's life, for the *Viṣṇu Purāṇa* poets, is its *yuga*-inducing termination. Additionally, it is important to note that it is Kṛṣṇa's departure from the world that is the trigger, the sense being that his presence on Earth prevents the dharmic devolution out of the Dvāpara. So, we see here a simple and elegant solution to the problem of how a *dharma*-restoring *avatāra* of Viṣṇu could cause the Kali Yuga: he does not cause it, but rather holds it at bay until his death.

The *Viṣṇu Purāṇa*'s Kṛṣṇa biography follows the *Harivaṃśa* very closely, tending to shorten the episodes while occasionally introducing the odd novelty (for example, *VP*, 5.34). As such, the *Viṣṇu Purāṇa*, while wholly independent of the *Mahābhārata*, carries over the *Harivaṃśa*'s strict policy on 'double-dipping', recounting no episodes from the great epic, save of course for the death of Kṛṣṇa, which the poets clearly felt needed to be reintroduced (*VP*, 5.37–38). This is quite faithful to *Mbh* 16, and all the fundamental units of the original are here: omens, the sense of doom and predestination, the curse of the three sages, the mysterious 'birth' of the club from Sāmba, the ill-fated pilgrimage to Prabhāsa, the drinking and fighting, the return of Saṃkarṣaṇa to a snake form at his death, the arrow of Jarā in Kṛṣṇa's foot as well as the grieving Arjuna's misadventures thereafter and Vyāsa's sermon on time. There are some explicative additions to the *Mahābhārata*'s content here, but what is most significant is the mere fact of the Mausalaparvan's reincorporation into the Kṛṣṇa biography, even where the *Viṣṇu Purāṇa* otherwise follows the *Harivaṃśa* so closely in eschewing *Mahābhārata* content. While we can imagine that this reincorporation of the Vṛṣṇis' death is simply prompted by a desire for totality, it is important to recognise that a whole *Mahābhārata–Harivaṃśa* composite is not what the *Viṣṇu Purāṇa* poets were after. No other *Mahābhārata* episode is introduced and the contrast with the later *Bhāgavata Purāṇa* (*BhP*), which does more liberally fold other *Mahābhārata* scenes into its Book 10 biography of Kṛṣṇa (most notably, key events of *Mbh* 2 and 3 at *BhP* 10.69–74), is instructive.

Most important of all is *VP* Book 6, which reclaims the yugic flag set out at *VP* 4.24.27–32. Now that Kṛṣṇa's death has been related in *VP* 5.37–38, we turn immediately in 6.1–5 to the Kali Yuga and its woes, and this progresses directly into the cosmic register of *pralaya*. As soon as he hears the story of Kṛṣṇa's death, Maitreya asks about cosmic or universal destruction (*śrotum icchām*[*i*] ... *upasaṃhṛtim mahāpralayasaṃjñāṃ* ... *kalpānte*; *VP*, 6.1.2). Parāśara begins this explanation with a Kali Yuga discourse (6.1.9–6.2), which then turns to the three types of *pratisaṃcara* ('reabsorption') and the usual pralayic sequence of fire, desiccation, downpour, inundation and finally the sleeping Viṣṇu resting on the *ekārṇava* ('cosmic ocean'). This is designated as the *avāntara pralaya*, and two more types of *pralaya* (the *naimittika* and *prākṛta*) follow (6.4–5). We see here a seamless sequence of Kṛṣṇa's yugically initiating death, the Kali Age discourse and the immediate graduation as it were of the human-scale unravelling into the register of kalpic destruction. The *Mahābhārata–Harivaṃśa aṃśāvataraṇa* theology has yielded to a fully purāṇic one in which Kṛṣṇa's death is framed so as to activate a yugic–kalpic symmetry as well as the closure of an entire account of the nature of the universe.

Conclusion

How 'purāṇically' should we read the *Mahābhārata*? How would we understand the meaning of *Mbh* 16—or indeed any episode of the epic—if there were no *Harivaṃśa* or purāṇas to set alongside it? Does the difficulty we have in dating these texts require us to collapse them all into a corporate mass of common mythology? Just how much ideological, theological and temporal distance is loaded into the dash separating itihāsa–purāṇa? These are difficult questions that I do not claim to have answered in any detail here. In fact, I do not claim even to have presented a novel hypothesis, but simply to have illustrated a process of development across three sources. But this in itself implies a measured response to some of these difficult questions.

The three sources, in sum, give us the following picture: first, *Mbh* 16 loads the death of Kṛṣṇa with abundant darkness, foreboding and a sense of the inevitable decaying effects of time, as we see so often elsewhere in the epic. This is suggestive but exemplifies first and foremost the *kālavāda* diagnosed by Vassilkov; there is no mention of a yugic turnover here, nor of any connection to cosmic processes. The *aṃśāvataraṇa* theology is, rather, the reference point for understanding Kṛṣṇa's death and heavenly ascent. However, we do have elsewhere in the larger epic a few scattered if not entirely consistent statements that the events of the war have transpired in either the late Dvāpara or the Kali Age. Second, the *Harivaṃśa* carries forward the *aṃśāvataraṇa* complex, only now significantly Vaiṣṇavising it and preceding it with an *ādisarga* account of creation and royal lineages down to the time of Kṛṣṇa. His life is marked by a much brighter and sunnier heroism than in the *Mahābhārata* and his death is not related. The text nonetheless perpetuates—again, with some disagreements on the precise timing—the Dvāpara or Kali temporal placement of the events overall. The last episode of Kṛṣṇa's life—a tale of felicitous triumph—is followed by a Kali Yuga discourse, but this is truly a projection of future events connected only with social and ritual violations and not the *Mahābhārata* war or Kṛṣṇa's life. No *pralaya* account matches or answers the *HV*'s opening *sarga* cosmogony. Third, following but expanding the template of the *Harivaṃśa*, the *Viṣṇu Purāṇa* creates a monolithically Vaiṣṇava universe that opens with extensive *sarga* processes and follows through the same royal lineages down to Kṛṣṇa—whose death is cited as the moment of the onset of the Kali Yuga—and beyond to the unfortunate generations living in that (really, this) degenerate age. This leads directly to the narrative of his life that follows very closely the structure and contents of the *Harivaṃśa*, with the crucial exception being the reintroduction of his death, based directly on *Mbh* 16. This leads seamlessly into a resumption of the Kali Yuga discourse, which is tied directly to an account of cosmic dissolution and pralayic destruction. In no uncertain terms now, the death of Kṛṣṇa is loaded with both human–social and cosmic significance.

How I might be tempted to answer some of the difficult methodological questions posed above is suggested by the fact that I have found it a worthwhile exercise to trace this development across the three texts. Although they are closely placed in the second to fifth-century CE period, I do see here a movement that should at least provide nuance and historicise somewhat the popular mythic reading of the epic, which tends to privilege purāṇic constructs. The 'purāṇification' process involves a shift away from the *Mahābhārata*'s *kālavāda* and *aṃśāvataraṇa* constructs, which nonetheless deserve to be examined and understood on their own terms. The *Mahābhārata* is not a story about the end of the world, and how the yugic mythology of the epic connects to the death of Kṛṣṇa is not at all clear until the *Viṣṇu Purāṇa*. It can of course be argued that everything we see in the *Viṣṇu Purāṇa* is already 'implicit' in the *Mahābhārata* and *Harivaṃśa*, or that these earlier texts are in some sense 'anticipating' purāṇic exposition.[17] But does this mean there are only quantitative differences between these sources? It could also be worthwhile to consider a reversal of this reading strategy and imagine what sense we would make of these texts if we were compelled to read them in complete isolation from one another, as this could help us to see that the *Mahābhārata*, *Harivaṃśa* and *Viṣṇu Purāṇa* are in fact three unique creations even while they stand in creative relationship with one another.

References

Primary texts

Kinjawadekar, Pandit Ramachandrashāstri (ed.). (1936). *Harivanshaparvan with Bhārata Bhāwadeepa by Neelakantha*. Poona, India: Shankar Narhar Joshi (Citrashala Press).

Pathak, M.M. (ed.). (1997–99). *The Critical Edition of the Viṣṇupurāṇam*. [2 vols.] Vadodara, India: Oriental Institute.

Schreiner, Peter and Söhnen, Renate (eds). (1987). *Sanskrit Indices and Text of the Brahmapurāṇa. Volume 1*. Purāṇa Research Publications. Wiesbaden, Germany: Otto Harrassowitz.

Shastree (Bambhania), K.K. (ed.). (1997). *The Bhāgavata [Śrīmad Bhāgavata Mahāpurāṇam]*. Critical Edition. Vol. IV [Skandha X]. Ahmadabad, India: B.J. Institute of Learning and Research.

Sukthankar, Vishnu Sitaram (ed.). (1933–66). *The Mahābhārata*. [19 vols.] Poona, India: Bhandarkar Oriental Research Institute.

17 Thus, for example, Biardeau (2003–04: 514), speaking of *yugas* and *kalpas* in the *Mbh*: '*Tout se passe comme s'il savait qu'il aura des successeurs pour compléter son elaboration* [Everything happens as if it knew that it would have successors to complete its elaboration].'

Vaidya, Parashuram Lakshman (ed.). (1969–71). *The Harivaṃśa: Being the Khila, or Supplement to the Mahābhārata*. [Critical Edition.] [2 vols.] Poona, India: Bhandarkar Oriental Research Institute.

Secondary texts

Austin, Christopher R. (2009). Janamejaya's last question. *Journal of Indian Philosophy* 37(6): 597–625. doi.org/10.1007/s10781-009-9075-y.

Biardeau, Madeleine. (1968). Études de mythologie hindoue [Studies in Hindu mythology]. *Bulletin de l'École française d'Extrême-Orient* [*Bulletin of the French School of the Far East*] 54: 19–45. doi.org/10.3406/befeo.1968.3775.

Biardeau, Madeleine. (1971). Études de mythologie hindoue [Studies in Hindu mythology] (III). *Bulletin de l'École française d'Extrême-Orient* [*Bulletin of the French School of the Far East*] 58: 17–89. doi.org/10.3406/befeo.1971.5074.

Biardeau, Madeleine. (1976). Études de mythologie hindoue [Studies in Hindu mythology] (IV). *Bulletin de l'École française d'Extrême-Orient* [*Bulletin of the French School of the Far East*] 63: 111–263. doi.org/10.3406/befeo.1976.3888.

Biardeau, Madeleine. (1978a). Compte rendu [Review]: *The Ritual of Battle* by Alf Hiltebeitel. *L'Homme* 18(1–2): 208–14.

Biardeau, Madeleine. (1978b). Études de mythologie hindoue [Studies in Hindu mythology] (V). *Bulletin de l'École française d'Extrême-Orient* [*Bulletin of the French School of the Far East*] 65(1): 87–238. doi.org/10.3406/befeo.1978.3906.

Biardeau, Madeleine. (2003–04). Review: Luis González-Reimann, *The Mahābhārata and the Yugas, India's Great Epic Poem and the Hindu System of World Ages*. *Bulletin de l'École française d'Extrême-Orient* [*Bulletin of the French School of the Far East*] 90–91: 510–15.

Dumézil, Georges. (1968). *Myth et épopée: l'idéologie des trois fonctions dans les épopées des peuples indo-européens* [*Myth and Epic: The Ideology of the Three Functions in the Epics of the Indo-European Peoples*]. *Volume 1*. 5th edn. Paris: Éditions Gallimard.

González-Reimann, Luis. (2002). *The Mahābhārata and the Yugas: India's Great Epic Poem and the Hindu System of World Ages*. New York, NY: Peter Lang.

González-Reimann, Luis. (2009). Cosmic cycles, cosmology and cosmography. In Knut A. Jacobsen (ed.), *Brill's Encyclopedia of Hinduism*, pp. 411–28. Leiden, Netherlands: Brill.

González-Reimann, Luis. (2010). Time in the Mahābhārata and the time of the Mahābhārata. In Sheldon Pollock (ed.), *Epic and Argument in Sanskrit Literary History: Essays in Honour of Robert P. Goldman*, pp. 61–73. New Delhi: Manohar.

Granoff, Phyllis. (2008). The Mausalaparvan between story and theology. *Asiatische Studien/Études Asiatiques* 62(2): 545–62.

Granoff, Phyllis. (2010). Karma, curse, or divine illusion: The destruction of the Buddha's clan and the slaughter of the Yādavas. In Sheldon Pollock (ed.), *Epic and Argument in Sanskrit Literary History: Essays in Honour of Robert P. Goldman*, pp. 75–90. New Delhi: Manohar.

Hacker, Paul. (1960). Zur Entwicklung der Avatāralehre [On the development of the avatāra doctrine]. *Archiv für Indische Philosophie* [*Archives of Indian Philosophy*] 4(14): 47–70. [Reprinted in *Paul Hacker: Kleine Schriften: Herausgegeben von Lambert Schmithausen* [*Paul Hacker: Small Writings. Edited by Lambert Schmithausen*, 404–27. Wiesbaden: Steiner, 1978.]

Hiltebeitel, Alf. (1976). *The Ritual of Battle: Krishna in the Mahābhārata*. Ithaca, NY: Cornell University Press.

Hiltebeitel, Alf. (1980). Śiva, the goddess, and the disguises of the Pāṇḍavas and Draupadī. *History of Religions* 20(1–2): 147–74. doi.org/10.1086/462866.

Hiltebeitel, Alf. (1984). The two Kṛṣṇas on one chariot: Upaniṣadic imagery and epic mythology. *History of Religions* 24(1): 1–26. doi.org/10.1086/462971.

Hiltebeitel, Alf. (2011a). *Dharma: Its Early History in Law, Religion, and Narrative*. New York, NY: Oxford University Press.

Hiltebeitel, Alf. (2011b). 'You have to read the whole thing': Some reflections on Madeleine Biardeau's Mahābhārata. In *Du texte au terrain, du terrain au texte: Dialogues disciplinaires autour de l'œuvre de Madeleine Biardeau* [*From Text to Field, from Field to Text: Disciplinary Dialogues around the Work of Madeleine Biardeau*]. 5 May. Paris: Centre for South Asian Studies. Available from: ceias.ehess.fr/docannexe/file/3137/journee_biardeau_intervention_alf_hiltebeitel.pdf.

Hudson, Emily T. (2013). *Disorienting Dharma: Ethics and the Aesthetics of Suffering in the Mahābhārata*. New York, NY: Oxford University Press. doi.org/10.1093/acprof:oso/9780199860760.001.0001.

Johnson, W.J. (trans.). (1998). *The Sauptikaparvan of the Mahābhārata: The Massacre at Night*. New York, NY: Oxford University Press.

Karve, Iravati. (2017 [1969]). *Yuganta: The End of an Epoch*. Translated from the Marathi by Irawati Karve. Hyderabad, India: Orient BlackSwan (Deshmukh Prakashan).

Kloetzli, W.R. (2013). Myriad concerns: Indian macro-time intervals (yugas, sandhyās and kalpas) as systems of number. *Journal of Indian Philosophy* 41: 631–53. doi.org/10.1007/s10781-013-9196-1.

Koskikallio, Petteri. (1994). When time turns: Yugas, ideologies, sacrifices. *Studia Orientalia Electronica* 73: 253–72. Available from: journal.fi/store/article/view/45094.

Sharma, Vishal. (2020). The problem of the indifference to suffering in the Mahābhārata tradition. *International Journal of Hindu Studies* 24: 177–97. doi.org/10.1007/s11407-020-09276-2.

Smith, John D. (trans. and ed.). (2009). *The Mahābhārata*. London: Penguin Classics.

Taylor, McComas (trans.). (2021). *The Viṣṇu Purāṇa: Ancient Annals of the God with Lotus Eyes*. Canberra: ANU Press. doi.org/10.22459/VP.2021.

Thomas, Lynn. (2007). Does the age make the king or the king make the age? Exploring the relationship between the king and the yugas in the Mahābhārata. *Religions of South Asia* 1(2): 183–201. doi.org/10.1558/rosa.v1i2.183.

Tieken, Herman. (2004). The Mahābhārata after the great battle. *Wiener Zeitschrift für die Kunde Südasiens* [*Vienna Journal of South Asian Studies*] 48: 5–46. doi.org/10.1553/wzksXLVIIIs5.

Vassilkov, Yaroslav. (1999). Kālavāda (the doctrine of cyclical time) in the Mahābhārata and the concept of heroic didactics. In Mary Brockington and Peter Schreiner (eds), *Composing A Tradition: Concepts, Techniques and Relationships. Proceedings of the First Dubrovnik International Conference on the Sanskrit Epics and Purāṇas, August 1997*, pp. 17–33. Zagreb: Croatian Academy of Sciences and Arts.

von Simson, Georg. (2007). Kṛṣṇa's son Sāmba: Faked gender and other ambiguities on the background of lunar and solar myth. In Simon Brodbeck and Brian Black (eds), *Gender and Narrative in the Mahābhārata*, pp. 230–57. London: Routledge.

Yano, Michio. (2003). Calendar, astronomy and astrology. In Gavin Flood (ed.), *The Blackwell Companion to Hinduism*, pp. 376–92. Oxford, UK: Blackwell. doi.org/10.1002/9780470998694.ch19.

18

Lambs, lightning, nakedness and fire: Polythetic networks and literary elaborations of the Purūravas–Urvaśī narrative

McComas Taylor

Abstract

The enigmatic Vedic narrative of King Purūravas and his divine lover, Urvaśī, has been reproduced in many Sanskrit literary genres. In the epic tradition of the *Harivaṃśa*, the narrative highlights Purūravas's kingly virtues. In the *Viṣṇu Purāṇa*, tellability is paramount and romantic elements are added. The *Kathāsaritsāgara*, a collection that exists primarily to entertain, adds details that accord with its own predilection for the supernatural and the sensational. The *Padma* and *Matsya* purāṇas add a 'purāṇic' touch by introducing Dharma, Artha and Kāma (Virtue, Profit and Love) in corporeal form. Kālidāsa recasts the narrative for dramatic effect in his *Vikramorvaśīya*, while the *Skanda Purāṇa* reproduces the narrative as 'advertorials' for various sacred sites. This chapter aims to show that a single mythic narrative, recurring in multiple contexts, is not a constant, stable unit. Its constituent mythemes form a polythetic network, which are reordered and reshaped to advance the transcreators' discursive projects.

Introduction

The more enigmatic, obscure and open-ended a narrative, the more diverse are the interpretations it invites. For the past three millennia, commentators, writers and scholars have found their own ways to make sense of the Vedic dialogue between the mortal king Purūravas and his divine lover, Urvaśī. Possibly the world's oldest marital squabble, this exchange is contained in the tenth book of the *Ṛg Veda*, dating from at least 1000 BCE. Like an aria from a lost opera or an episode cut adrift from a miniseries, the context for the dialogue is missing. This ambiguity has provided a fertile field for interpretation. It shows how close reading of narratives can destabilise the idea that myths are constant and unchanging. Mythemes are generative and spark new creations when they appear in new literary ecosystems.

Described as an 'obscure song' (*dunkle Lied*) (Geldner 1889: 243), an 'odd hymn' (Kosambi 1962: 53), a 'curious dialogue' (Macdonell and Keith 1912: 3) and a 'brief masterpiece' (Jamison and Brereton 2014: 1548), the dialogue has fascinated Western scholars since the early days of Indology. For many centuries before Western Indological interest, Sanskrit authors transcreated, embellished and recast the dialogue and its surrounding narrative to tell their own stories and to satisfy their own discursive projects. There is already a substantial literature on the various versions of the Purūravas–Urvaśī narrative, including surveys by Geldner (1889), Penzer (1926), Kosambi (1962) and Gaur (1974). These scholars describe the various transcreations, but in this chapter, I propose to explore the reasons for the variations and to demonstrate how they relate to the context in which the narrative is embedded.

Beginning with the Vedic dialogue itself and its significant elaboration in the *Śatapatha Brāhmaṇa* (*ŚPB*) of about 700 BCE, I will explore these different versions in roughly chronological order, bearing in mind the inherent difficulty of dating these sources. Drawing all this material together, we can discern a polythetic network of tropes—a category that is multiply (*poly*) composed (*thetic*) (Stormer 2016: 302). Members of such categories may share some but not necessarily all of a specific group of characteristics. This is a useful way of tying together and discerning commonalities among many diverse narratives from different eras that share certain tropes and images, including, in this case, lambs, lightning, nakedness and fire.

There are many references to Purūravas and Urvaśī scattered throughout the Sanskrit literary archive. Many focus on Purūravas's curious birth from his mother, Ilā, who was previously a man named Ila or Sudyumna. Purūravas is also often mentioned in lists of paradigmatic kings and progenitors. He is said to have fed the *pitṛ*s in Heaven and to have stolen gold or a sacrificial altar from brahmins who killed him in revenge. There are also many mentions of Urvaśī, who appeared on Earth after the deities Mitra and Varuṇa spied on her and ejaculated into a clump of grass. In the *Mahābhārata*, she was Arjuna's lover, and elsewhere appears in lists of prominent *apsaras*es.[1] There are other occasional brief mentions of the relationship between Purūravas and Urvaśī in the archive, but for the purposes of this investigation, I focus on the more detailed accounts of their relationship. Before doing so, it is necessary to introduce the foundational dialogue in the *Ṛg Veda*.

The source of the narrative: *Ṛg Veda* 10.95

Trying to discern Vedic society through the medium of its literary traces is, at best, like trying to describe a room while peering through a keyhole. The view is partial, limited and tantalising. The Purūravas–Urvaśī dialogue could only have made sense if the audience supplied or invented a backstory that has not survived. Vedic audiences would have recognised the two bickering characters. Purūravas, a mortal king, like Prometheus in the European tradition, was the giver of fire and a legendary progenitor of humankind. His troubled spouse was Urvaśī, a semidivine female being known as an *apsaras*. Immortal, airborne and sexual, *apsaras*es are also in some ill-defined way aquatic, riverine and fluid, as their name *ap-sara* ('going among the waters') suggests.

The interchange between Purūravas and Urvaśī is found in the final book, the tenth *maṇḍala*, of the *Ṛg Veda*. It is one of a small number of famous and well-studied 'dialogue hymns' or *saṃvāda-sūkta* (Jamison and Brereton 2014: 1548–50).

Of the 18 verses of the song, all but the final constitute the dialogue itself. The last verse functions retrospectively as a narrative frame and reveals that the dialogue is being repeated by an anonymous voice. The speaker explains to Purūravas why a group of assembled deities—'these gods here' (*devā̱*

1 Useful guides to locating Purūravas and Urvaśī in Sanskrit literature include Macdonell and Keith (1912); and Ramachandra Dikshitar (1995).

imá)—have just reminded him he will die the death of a mortal being, his offspring will sacrifice to the gods and he will eventually 'rejoice in Heaven' (*svargá u tvám ápi mādayāse*).

In the following paragraphs, I will summarise the above verses and point out some features that become important in later retellings. The song begins with Purūravas pursuing his angry wife. He tries to mollify her and suggests they talk things over: 'Hey, wife! Stand still, you cruel-minded woman! Let us two now exchange words. These thoughts, if unuttered, will not bring us joy even on a distant day' (*hayé jā̱ye mánasā tíṣṭha ghore vácāṃsi miśrā̱ kṛṇavāvahai nú*) (1). Urvaśī refuses to discuss the situation and tells him to go home, saying: 'I am as hard to attain as the wind' (*durāpanā̱ vā̱ta ivāhám asmí*) (2). Purūravas adds that she is as unstoppable as a victorious arrow or a battle charge: no man can control her. She will keep on howling, Purūravas predicts, just like ewes keep on bleating (3). This throwaway simile assumes an important role in later versions.

Reflecting fondly on their relationship, Purūravas observes that Urvaśī had served her father-in-law conscientiously, was happy at home and 'day and night she was pierced by my reed' (*dívā náktam śnathitā̱ vaitaséna*) (4). Urvaśī has no such happy recollections and complains that she was required to have sex three times a day, even though she had no desire for it: 'You were then the king of my body', she says, calling Purūravas—perhaps ironically as Jamison and Brereton (2014: 1548) suggest—a 'hero' (*rājā' me vīra ta̱nvas tad ā́sīḥ*) (5).

At this point, Purūravas's mind wanders and he imagines life without Urvaśī. His thoughts stray towards the attractive and amenable ranks of *apsaras*es (6). Urvaśī tries to distract him from his reverie by reminding him that those same watery, riverine beings were present at the birth of his son. If the *apsaras*es knew that Purūravas had a child, would he be a less attractive partner or is Urvaśī reminding him of his parental responsibilities? Even though Urvaśī flatters Purūravas, reminding him that the gods made him strong (7), he remains captive to his reverie. He continues to fantasise about undressing and caressing the *apsaras*es, recalling how they pranced and nipped like ponies (8–9).

Purūravas now begins to recall more fondly that Urvaśī, who has given him a son, Āyu, was also one of those divine beings (10), and Urvaśī reminds him that, as a husband, he was duty-bound to protect his wife, but on the contrary, he forced himself on her. His efforts to woo her back are a waste of breath, she says (11). The mention of his son seems to soften Purūravas's resolve. He worries that if Urvaśī leaves him, he will also lose the boy. Should not married couples stick together (12)? Urvaśī remains unmoved and abruptly offers to send him the child, referring to Āyu (callously?) in the neuter as 'it' (*tát*). Again, she urges Purūravas to give up and go home (13).

Purūravas now changes tack and resorts to emotional blackmail. If he left for some distant place, he says, he might end up in the lap of disaster or be eaten by wolves (14). This has the desired effect and Urvaśī's heart begins to melt. She implores him not to leave: 'Purūravas, please don't die. Please don't fly away. Don't let those cruel wolves devour you' (*púrūravo mā́ mr̥thā mā́ prápapto mā́ tvā vŕ̥kāso áśivāsa u kṣan*). She adds an odd chaser: 'There is no friendship with women: they have the hearts of jackals' (*ná vái stráiṇāni sakhyā́ni santi sālāvr̥kā́ṇām hŕ̥dayānyetā́*). It is unclear whether she is apologising for the failure of their relationship or warning Purūravas off other females (15). Urvaśī then reminds Purūravas of the four years they spent together and how she was the ultimate cheap date, being satisfied with just a little ghee each day. Like the simile of the ewe in Verse 3 above, this seemingly insignificant mention of ghee also plays an important part in later retellings (16). Now it is Purūravas's turn to soften. He flatters Urvaśī, claiming that the 'good deed' (*suukr̥ta*) of her returning home will be repaid in the long term (17).

The concluding verse, as mentioned above, provides an outer narrative frame. The narrator (himself a deity?) explains to Purūravas why 'these gods here' said he would die like any other mortal. They know that Urvaśī did indeed return to Purūravas and that he had vowed to live in whichever realm she had chosen. As she elected the world of mortals, Purūravas willingly gave up his chance of immortality and acquired the 'bond to death' (*mr̥tyúbaandhuḥ*) mentioned by the gods. The deities had told Purūravas that his progeny would offer sacrifices to the gods with oblations because he 'discovered' the threefold sacred fire, and that he would 'rejoice in Heaven' (18).

Creating a context: *Śatapatha Brāhmaṇa* 11.5.1

Later transcreations of the Purūravas–Urvaśī narrative, while ultimately derived from the Vedic verses, are mediated through a version found in the *Śatapatha Brāhmaṇa*. The Brāhmaṇas are defined as 'running prose commentary' on the four main Vedas and present 'explanations of the meaning and usage of the liturgical texts' (Proferes 2018; Lubin 2019) or, as stated by Witzel: 'The Brāhmaṇa style prose texts thus are the oldest explanations, in fact native commentaries, of the literal meaning of the Mantras, of their ritual applications, and of their often hidden secret import' (2003: 81).

In the case of the Purūravas–Urvaśī dialogue, the *Śatapatha Brāhmaṇa* provides a commentary, explanation and embellishment in 17 verses of prose narrative. There are three aspects to the *Śatapatha Brāhmaṇa*'s treatment. First, it makes explicit what I described above as the assumed knowledge of Vedic audiences—that is, the background information required to make sense of the song. Second, it quotes several lines directly from the song and places these in a broader context. Third, it elaborates on the original by extrapolating from specific words or phrases or by adding entirely new twists to the dialogue. In the following paragraphs, I summarise the dialogue as preserved in the *Śatapatha Brāhmaṇa* and point out these three features.

The dialogue is situated in a section of the *Śatapatha Brāhmaṇa* that deals with the Agnihotra sacrifice generally. The narrative seems to be adapted to explain the origin of the sacred fire used in these rituals, hence the connection with Purūravas. The English translation below is based on Eggeling (1900), but I have updated and de-bowdlerised it with reference to the Sanskrit text from the Göttingen Register of Electronic Texts in Indian Languages and the Venkateshwar Steam Press (1940) edition. Direct quotations from the *Ṛg Veda* are given in italics. The *gandharvas* mentioned in the text are semidivine beings—often seen as the male counterparts of the *apsarases*:

> The *apsaras* Urvaśī loved Purūravas, the son of Iḍā. When she married him, she said, 'Pound me three times a day with your "reed-rod", but do not lie with me against my will. And do not let me see you naked, for this is the way to behave to us women.'
>
> She then lived with him for a long time, and became pregnant to him, so long had they been together. Then the *gandharvas* said to one another, 'This Urvaśī has indeed lived among men for a long time. Devise some means so that she may return to us.' Now, a ewe with twin lambs was tied to her bed, and the *gandharvas* then carried off one of the two.
>
> 'Alas,' she cried, 'as if in a place without a hero or a man, they are taking away my son!' When they carried off the second lamb, she said the same thing again.

Then this [Purūravas] thought to himself, 'How can a place be without a hero or a man if I am here?' And thinking that it would take too long to get dressed, he leapt up after them, completely naked. The *gandharva*s caused a flash of lightning, and she beheld him naked as if by daylight, and immediately vanished. 'I'm back!' he said, but behold! she had disappeared. Wailing with sorrow he wandered all over Kurukṣetra. There was a lotus-lake called Anyataḥplakṣā. He walked along its bank, and there *apsarase*s were swimming about in the form of waterbirds.

She [Urvaśī] recognised him and said, 'This is the man I lived with.' They then said, 'Let us appear to him!' 'So be it!' she replied, and they appeared to him.

He then recognised her and implored her, '*Hey, wife! Stand still, you cruel-minded woman! Let us two now exchange words. These thoughts, if unuttered, will not bring us joy even on a distant day.*' That is what he said to her.

The other replied to him, '*What shall I do with this speech of yours? I have stepped forth, like the foremost of the dawns. Go home again, Purūravas. I am like the wind, difficult to catch.* You did not do what I said. Now it is difficult for you to catch me. Go home again.' That is what she implied to him.

He then said with sadness, '*If I, dear to the gods, should fly away today, never to return, to go to the most distant distance, then I might lie in the lap of Nirṛti, Goddess of Death. Then again the ravening wolves might eat me.* Sudeva might string himself up, or he might flee, and then wolves or dogs might devour him.' That is what he implied.

The other replied to him, '*Don't die, Purūravas. Don't fly away. Don't let the cruel wolves eat you. There are no friendships with women. They have the hearts of jackals.* Don't take this to heart. There is no friendship with women. Go home again.' That is what she implied to him.

'*When in different form I walked among mortals and spent the nights there for four autumns, once a day I ate a drop of ghee. From that alone I am still sated now.*' This is the fifteen-verse dialogue that was handed down by the Bahvṛcas. Her heart began to soften.[2]

---

2 The Vedic dialogue has 18 verses. Various attempts have been made to explain this discrepancy.

She said, 'Come here in the evening one year from now. Then you will lie with me for one night, and a son will be born to you.' He came at night one year later and there stood a golden palace. They then said to him alone, 'Go inside!' and urged her to join him.

She then said, 'Tomorrow morning the *gandharvas* will grant you a boon, and you must make a choice.' He said, 'You must choose for me.' She replied, 'Say, "Let me become one of you."' In the morning the *gandharvas* granted him a boon, and he said, 'Let me become one of you.'

They said, 'Surely there is not among men that sacred form of fire by sacrificing with which one may become one of us.' They put fire into a vessel, and gave it to him saying, 'By sacrificing with this, you will become one of us.' He took it [the fire] and his son, and set off for home. He then placed the fire in the forest, and went to the village with the boy, saying 'I will go back' [but on reaching the forest], behold!, the fire had disappeared. What had been the fire was an *aśvattha* tree, and what had been the vessel was a *śamī* tree. He then returned to the *gandharvas*.

They said, 'For one year cook enough rice for four people. Take three sticks each time from this *aśvattha* tree, anoint them with ghee, and put them on the fire with verses containing the words "stick" and "ghee". The fire which results from these will be that [very fire which is required].'

They said, 'But that is indeed secret knowledge. Instead, make a spindle of *aśvattha* wood, and a hearth board of *sami* wood. The fire which results from these will be that [very fire].'

They said, 'But that also is secret knowledge. Instead, make a spindle of *aśvattha* wood, and a hearth board of *aśvattha* wood. The fire which results from these will be that [very fire].'

He then made a spindle of *aśvattha* wood, and a hearth board of *aśvattha* wood, and the fire which resulted from these was that [very fire]. By offering with that, he became one of the *gandharvas*. One should therefore make a spindle and a hearth board of *aśvattha* wood, and the fire which results from these will be that [very fire]. By offering with that, one becomes one of the *gandharvas*. (*ŚPB*, 11.5.1.1–17)

How does this account in the *Śatapatha Brāhmaṇa* relate to the *Ṛg Veda*? First, as mentioned above, it serves the *Śatapatha Brāhmaṇa*'s purposes in the elaboration of Agni in that the Purūravas–Urvaśī narrative explains how the threefold sacred fire came into the world. This version appears as a 'prequel' to the Vedic dialogue. Here, Urvaśī sets the ground rules for their marriage: they may have sexual intercourse three times a day, but it must be consensual. In the *Ṛg Veda*, Urvaśī looks back on their failed relationship and lists the complaints against Purūravas, which include 'piercing' her with his 'reed' without consent. The *Śatapatha Brāhmaṇa* adds a new twist, or possibly reveals an element that could have been prior knowledge to the audience of the *Ṛg Veda* but was not made explicit: the prohibition on Purūravas appearing naked. In the *Veda*, Urvaśī gives nonconsensual sex as one of her reasons for leaving Purūravas. In the *Śatapatha Brāhmaṇa*, the fact that Purūravas appeared naked and broke their agreement was added as a second reason for her departure.

In the older version, Purūravas observes that Urvaśī will keep up her complaints just as a ewe will keep bleating. This throwaway line has morphed into an integral part of the more developed plot in the *brāhmaṇa* in the form of Urvaśī's pet sheep and the twin lambs at her bedside. Purūravas's eventual discovery of Urvaśī and the *apsaras*es in the form of waterbirds accords with the watery, riverine aspects of their natures. Here again, an image in the *Veda* is echoed or amplified in the *brāhmaṇa*: the postcoital *apsaras*es are compared to waterbirds, possibly 'ducks', preening themselves.[3]

Once the prequel has concluded, the *Śatapatha Brāhmaṇa* begins its own interaction with the main narrative from the *Veda*. In this sense, it is now doing what *brāhmaṇa*s are supposed to do. Having provided a context for the Vedic text, it now explains the meaning by quoting directly from the dialogue and providing a summary with some additional explanation. It created an entire backstory to the Vedic text by sketching Purūravas and Uravśī's marriage, their prenuptial pact, the *gandharva*s' scheme to win her back, the theft of the lambs and the breaking of the pact. This provides an explanation for their estrangement and creates the setting for the Vedic dialogue on the shores of Lake Anyataḥplakṣā.

3 The word is *ā̱tayo̱* from *āti* (f.), given by Monier-Williams (2009) as 'a waterbird', with the cognate *anas, anati-s* ('duck') in Latin. This episode spawned a whole cottage industry of 'swan maiden' studies. See Fass Leavy (1994).

In addition to the ewe and lambs, the *brāhmaṇa* lifted other key words from the Vedic account, weaving them into a more complex literary narrative. The metaphor of lightning, to which Urvaśī is compared in the earlier text, reappears as the dazzling flash created by the *gandharva*s to reveal Purūravas's nakedness. The word 'hero', sarcastically (?) thrown in Purūravas's face in the *Veda*, occurs again when Urvaśī laments the lack of heroes after her lambs have been stolen.

To summarise the *Śatapatha Brāhmaṇa*'s contribution to the development of the Purūravas–Urvaśī narrative, first, it explains and provides a context for the Vedic root text. It does so by supplying a prequel to the dialogue that explains how, where and why the marital squabble took place. In addition to providing explanation and context, it introduces several important tropes, ultimately derived from the Vedic song, but greatly elaborated. It either invented or clarified the reason for Urvaśī's departure: the compact she made with Purūravas and its rupture. The simile of Urvaśī bleating like a ewe was substantiated into her pet sheep and its two lambs. Purūravas's statement that Urvaśī will 'flash forth' was reconceived as the *gandharva*s' bolt of lightning. Finally, the *brāhmaṇa* also greatly expanded on the idea of sacrificial fire, which was merely hinted at in the original. As we will see in the following paragraphs, all these innovations become key tropes in the later development of the narrative.

Epic elaboration: The *Harivaṃśa* and *Vāyu Purāṇa*

The *Harivaṃśa* (*HV*) styles itself as a *khila* or supplement to the *Mahābhārata*, but its content and style closely follow the model of a purāṇa. In the opening verses, the sage Śaunaka says to the son of the *sūta*, the traditional narrator of the *Mahābhārata*: '[In the epic] you described the birth of the Kurus, son of Lomaharṣaṇa, but not of the Vṛṣṇis and Andhakas. It befits you to speak of them' (*HV*, 1.17).[4] These two lineages or *vaṃśa* culminate in Kṛṣṇa (Hari), the account of whose deeds occupies a large part of the text.

4 *tatra janma kurūṇām vai tvayoktaṃ laumharṣṇe | na tu vṛṣṇyandhakānāṃ ca tad bhavan vaktum arhati* || (*HV*, 1.17).

The *Harivaṃśa* is of indeterminate age but is younger than the epics and probably contemporaneous with the earlier purāṇas. Like members of the latter genre, the *Harivaṃśa* also describes the creation and cyclical destruction of the universe, the dimensions of the world, the historical lineages and so on. Some versions, such as the 1967 Gita Press edition, include a substantial account of the Purūravas–Urvaśī narrative. The Critical Edition also has a version of the story, but it is much shorter and omits most, if not all, of the drama (Vaidya 1969: 21.1–10). True to the style of the *Mahābhārata*, the narrative in the *Harivaṃśa* is recounted by Vaiśampāyana, the original narrator of the epic, to King Janamejaya. The *Harivaṃśa* version, which extends to 49 verses, comes towards the beginning of a purāṇic description of the world and its peopling by the descendants of the patriarch Manu.

A similar version of the narrative appears in the same context in the *Vāyu Purāṇa* (*VaP*, 2.29.1–45). This version has the generic purāṇic framing device in which the narrative is related by the *sūta* to an assembly of sages. It is four verses shorter than the *Harivamśa*'s, but the wording in both sources is nearly identical and the differences are trivial. Either one was copied from the other or they share a common origin.

The discursive function of both the *Harivaṃśa* and the *Vāyu Purāṇa* at the point at which the narrative is included is to magnify the importance of Manu's descendants and to describe their kingly virtues as part of the leadup to the advent of Kṛṣṇa. Among the innovative features of the narrative as it appears in these sources are the four opening verses. In this context, the addition of stereotypical verses in praise of Purūravas's regal qualities furthers the discursive objectives of the *Harivaṃśa* and *Vāyu Purāṇa* at this point:

> Vaiśampāyana said: Budha's son Purūravas was learned, energetic and generous, your majesty, and performed sacrifices with lavish fees. He was conversant with *brahman*, powerful and his enemies could not defeat him in battle. That king maintained the sacred fires in his house and undertook many sacrifices. He was truthful, pious, attractive and his sexual urges were controlled. At that time none in the three worlds equalled him in glory. Having cast off her pride, the illustrious Urvaśī chose as her partner that devout, patient, virtuous and truthful man. (*HV*, 1.17.1–4)

The account as it appears in these two sources fast-forwards to Purūravas's relationship with Urvaśī, adding a flowery description of all the mythical locations in which they spent time together. In response to a question about how this relationship between Purūravas and Urvaśī came about, the narrator in both versions picks up the story, in the main, from the *Śatapatha Brāhmaṇa*. The 'pounding with the reed-rod' has been dropped, but three conditions are stated. First, that her sheep never leave her bedside—but 'sheep', no longer 'lambs'. Second, she must never see Purūravas naked, which is also carried over from the earlier source, as is the ban on nonconsensual sex. Finally, she only eats butter. The Veda's seemingly idle reflection on the economical nature of her existence has been elevated to become the third condition of their relationship.

The *gandharvas*' desire to win Urvaśī back and their plot to snatch the sheep have been retained, with the introduction of a *gandharva* named Viśvāvasu to carry out the raid. The flash of lightning, the breaking of the pact, Urvaśī's disappearance, Purūravas's search and her eventual discovery were retained, but the name of the lake—Anyataḥplakṣā in the earlier source—appears as Haimavatī, with a sacred ford called Plakṣatīrtha. The tantalising suggestion that the *apsaras*es were in the form of waterbirds has been dropped, as have all but one of the citations from the *Ṛg Veda*. Even the remaining one is truncated and garbled. These versions give *jāye tiṣṭha manasā ghore vacasi tiṣṭha ha* where the Veda has *hayé jā̃ye mánasā tíṣṭha ghore vácāṃsi miśrā̃ kṛṇavāvahai nú*.

The remaining tropes—the couple's reunion after a year, the *gandharvas*' boon, the fire pan and the *aśvattha* and *śamī* trees—have all been retained. The *gandharvas*' inexplicable demand for rice for four people and their first suggestion for fire-making have been dropped. In the *Śatapatha Brāhmaṇa*, Purūravas creates a single fire to attain the realm of *gandharvas*, but in these later versions, he divides the fire in three, thereby providing an origin myth for the practice of maintaining three sacrificial fires known as *tretāgni*.

Romantic twists: *Viṣṇu Purāṇa*

The *Viṣṇu Purāṇa*, dating from about the middle of the first millennium CE, is one of the more purāṇic purāṇas, as the bulk of its six books conform to the *pañca-lakṣaṇa* or five characteristic topics covered by the genre: the creation of the world, its periodic destruction and re-creation, the origin of gods and men, the cosmic cycles and the royal dynasties. There is significant dilation on this last topic in the fifth book, which is devoted to the deeds of Kṛṣṇa.

As a purported history of the universe, the *Viṣṇu Purāṇa* is prolix and literary. One senses it was created to entertain as well as to uplift. As such, the *Viṣṇu Purāṇa* takes the narrative up a level. As with the previous versions, the Purūravas–Urvaśī narrative in the *Viṣṇu Purāṇa* (4.6.23–50) is placed in a 'chronological' account of the Lunar Dynasty, the descendants of Manu and Soma. This elaborate prose narrative in 27 verses is a romance. We glimpse Urvaśī's backstory with Mitra and Varuṇa, the deities who 'shed their seed' and cursed her to live on Earth. This episode exists in a different context in the *Ṛg Veda* (7.34.11) but is first integrated with the Purūravas–Urvaśī narrative in this purāṇa. Purūravas falls in love with Urvaśī at first sight, and she with him, but their relationship is subject to the three conditions that have by now become canonical: the sheep, the prohibition on nakedness and the provision of ghee.

The *Viṣṇu Purāṇa* continues to add details to the basic plot. The entry of the naked king has been amplified and elaborated: now he is wielding a sword and shouting, 'Thief! Thief! You're dead!' (*duṣṭa duṣṭa hato 'sīti*). While Purūravas is searching for Urvaśī, he is both frenzied and naked. She is swimming with four *apsaras*es. At this point, Purūravas shouts the famous words from the Veda: '*Hey! That's my wife! Wait, you hardhearted woman. Wait! Speak to me!*' To this, the *Viṣṇu Purāṇa* adds 'and so on' (*vacasīty anekaprakāraṃ sūktam avocat*), suggesting that the audience will recognise this speech. In this version, Urvaśī is already pregnant when Purūravas finds her swimming in the lake. She tells him to come back in a year to meet his son and to spend another night together. Purūravas does so, meets his son Āyus (note the slight name change) and they conceive another five sons. As above, Urvaśī suggested that Purūravas ask the *gandharva*s for a boon so that he might become one of them to stay with her forever.

The aspect of the narrative dealing with the sacred fire is also considerably elaborated in the *Viṣṇu Purāṇa*. We have much more of Purūravas's internal monologue as he purposely abandons the pan of fire in the forest, later regrets this decision and returns to retrieve it. There is also interesting detail not found elsewhere about the creation of the fire-sticks: 'Measuring with his thumb as he chanted the Gāyatrī mantra, he made a fire-stick twenty-four inches long, as that is the number of syllables in the verse' (*tatpramāṇaṃ cāṅgulaiḥ kurvan gāyatrīm apaṭhat*; *VP*, 4.6.48). The narrative closes with a quote from an unidentified source: 'That's why they say, "In the beginning there was just a single fire, but during the current Manvantara, Ilā's son divided it in three"' (*eko 'gnir ādāv abhavad ailena tv atra manvantare tredhā pravartita iti*; *VP*, 4.6.50).

Pure entertainment: *Kathāsaritsāgara*

While the *Viṣṇu Purāṇa* both informs and entertains, the *Kathāsaritsāgara* (*KSS*) (the '*Ocean of Streams of Stories*') was created to provide amusement. Dating from the eleventh century CE, this vast rambling compendium of 22,000 verses consists of multiply embedded narratives collated from all corners of the Sanskrit literary archive.[5]

In this source, the King of Vatsa was reflecting on a recent period of separation from his wife Vāsavadattā (*KSS*, 3.3). He related this version of the Purūravas–Urvaśī narrative as a parallel to his own condition of loss and misery. His situation is used as a framing device to accommodate the narrative, but it also fulfills the discursive function of the *Kathāsaritsāgara* as an encyclopaedic accumulation. This is also a common narrative technique in the *Mahābhārata*, in which characters reflect on their own situation by repeating a story of others in similar circumstances. As the summary below will demonstrate, there are numerous elaborations and embellishments, all of which heighten the narrative's 'tellability'.

Purūravas, 'a devotee of Viṣṇu', first spied Urvaśī in Nandana, Indra's pleasure grove, and was attracted to her. Viṣṇu instructed the divine seer Nārada to tell Indra to find a way to unite the couple. The sage did so, and the happy pair descended to Earth together. Purūravas subsequently returned to Heaven to aid Indra in a war against his eternal adversaries, the demons known as Dānavas. After they had been defeated, Purūravas saw the *apsaras* Rambhā dancing at Indra's victory festival. Purūravas insulted the dancing instructor, a *gandharva* by the name of Tumburu, by suggesting that he, Purūravas, could do a better job himself. Tumburu cursed Purūravas to be separated from Urvaśī 'until he worships Kṛṣṇa' (*KSS*, 3.3.23). Many of these events are also found with slight variation in Kālidāsa's *Vikramorvaśīya* (see below).

When Purūravas informed Urvaśī of the curse, it struck her 'like a bolt from the blue' (*akālāśanipāta*; *KSS*, 3.3.24)—a simile that seems to resonate with the lightning of other versions. The *gandharva*s conducted Urvaśī to their own realm, while Purūravas performed austerities for Viṣṇu. Urvaśī waited like a 'female *cakravāka*' (3.3.28)—a waterbird often invoked as a symbol of marital fidelity. This provides another source of resonance with earlier

5 For an overview of the Purūravas–Urvaśī narrative in the *KSS*, see Penzer (1926: Vol. 2, pp. 34–36). For the Sanskrit text, see Prasad (1930: 55–56).

retellings. Viṣṇu was gratified by Purūravas's austerities and caused the *gandharvas* to return Urvaśī to Purūravas. The happy couple was reunited on Earth.

Almost all that survives of the original story are the union between Purūravas and Urvaśī, a curse and a reunion, with hints (possibly coincidental) of lightning and waterbirds. The above synopsis includes many innovative features and florid literary detail. The role of Viṣṇu is worthy of note. As mentioned, Purūravas is described as a 'devotee of Viṣṇu', this same deity brings about their happy union and the curse of separation will not be lifted until Purūravas propitiates Kṛṣṇa (Viṣṇu in another form). It is unclear why the *Kathāsaritsāgara* would introduce this sectarian angle, as it is not a particularly sectarian text and is more concerned with the miracles and sensations. The appearance of the *Kathāsaritsāgara* in the eleventh century CE roughly coincides with an uptick in Vaiṣṇava traditions and *bhakti* yoga—exemplified by the *Bhāgavata Purāṇa*. One possibility is that the interpolation of Viṣṇu into the narrative lends it a canonical air and aligns it with narratives found in other popular Vaiṣṇava sources. Alternatively, it also accords well with the *Kathāsaritsāgara*'s own predilection for the supernatural and the sensational.

Purāṇic touches: *Padma* and *Matsya* purāṇas

The *Padma Purāṇa* (*PP*) and *Matsya Purāṇa* (*MP*) contain almost identical versions of the Purūravas–Urvaśī narrative in *śloka* metre (*PP*, 1.12.51–75; *MP*, 24.9–33). They create an elaborate narrative around the separation of the couple and constitute a truly purāṇic take on the story. In these versions, Purūravas, the perfect king, performed 100 horse sacrifices, propitiated Brahmā, became lord of the whole world and wedded Urvaśī. He served as Brahmā's personal carrier and bearer of his chowrie. The deity even offered the king half his throne as a mark of respect. Purūravas was visited by Dharma, Artha and Kāma, the three goals of life—virtue, profit and love—in corporeal form. Because Purūravas offered slightly superior worship to Dharma, Artha cursed him to die from greed and Kāma cursed him with madness following his separation from Urvaśī. Dharma intervened, saying that because Purūravas had led a good life, his affliction would last only 60 years. All these appear to be innovations.

Many features of these two purāṇic versions are familiar from the *Kathāsaritsāgara*. Purūravas befriended Indra and one day, while riding in the deity's chariot, Purūravas saw the demon Keśin abducting Urvaśī. Purūravas defeated the demon and presented Urvaśī to Indra, who promptly gave her back. In Indra's palace, Bharata, the famous author of the *Nāṭyaśāstra*, cast three *apsaras*es, Menakā, Ūrvaśī and Rambhā, in a play called 'Lakṣmī's Svayaṃvara'—a parallel to the 'victory festival' in the *Kathāsaritsāgara*. During the performance, Urvaśī, who was playing the leading part of Lakṣmī, saw Purūravas in the audience and was so overcome with love that she forgot her lines. Bharata was furious and cursed her to separate from Purūravas and to live on Earth for 55 years in the form of a creeper. We will shortly see a similar version in Kālidāsa's *Vikramorvaśīya*. After the curse had run its course, Urvaśī was reunited with Purūravas and bore him eight sons.

Compared with other versions of the narrative, this account further complicates the story. It expands on the idea of Purūravas's madness—only hinted at in earlier versions—but sets a time limit on it. It also explains why Urvaśī came to Earth in the first place, because of a failed performance, but with much elaboration. While dressing up these two curses, many other tropes are assumed or subsumed: the compact, the split, the lambs, lightning, the waterbirds and fires.

One key feature here is the very purāṇic role played by the various deities. Purūravas befriends both Brahmā and Indra and the three goals of human existence, the *trivarga*, appear in bodily form. The active role of deities and their involvement in the world of mortals are typical features of the purāṇic genre, in which the gods are often 'brought down to Earth'. The appearance of Bharata as director of his own musical, in the place of the *gandharva* Tumburu, is also worthy of note.

Finally, the only significant difference between these two purāṇic texts is that the *Matsya Purāṇa* has slightly more sectarian colour. It includes two references to Viṣṇu-Kṛṣṇa: *samārādhya janārdanam* ('having propitiated Janārdana'; *MP*, 24.11) and *viṣṇoḥ prasādāt* ('by the grace of Viṣṇu'; 24.14). In parallel passages, the *Padma Purāṇa* references Brahmā *samārādhya pitāmaham* (*PP*, 1.12.53) and *brahma-prasādāt* (1.12.56). By referencing Viṣṇu, the *Matsya Purāṇa* may resonate more with a Vaiṣṇava audience. Brahmā is a generic deity of mythology, rather than an object of devotion, and by invoking him, the Padma may have avoided alienating devotees of any tradition.

The narrative in drama: Kālidāsa's *Vikramorvaśīya*

Like the *Kathāsaritsāgara*, the play *Vikramorvaśīya* ('*Urvaśī Won through Valour*') exists for pure entertainment. Its author, Kālidāsa, is usually dated to the fourth or fifth century CE. Whether his adaptation of the narrative predates or postdates the versions above is a moot point, owing to the difficulty of dating any of these sources accurately, except the *Kathāsaritsāgara*. We can, however, draw attention to its position in the polythetic network. As will be seen from the summary below, Kālidāsa's version shares many features with other tellings, but also introduces numerous innovations to add to the dramatic quality of the work. The summary below is drastically simplified and is limited to elements that concern Purūravas and Urvaśī directly. Comprehensive studies of the drama were undertaken by Kale (1915) and Kosambi (1962).

The play opens with the anguished cries of *apsaras*es fleeing from demons. Purūravas heard their calls and they reported that Urvaśī had been captured by Keśin. Purūravas rescued her, but before she returned to Heaven, their love was kindled. Purūravas repaired to a park and Urvaśī appeared overhead. She wrote him a love message on a birch leaf (an interesting early example of female literacy) and let it fall. Purūravas read the message and Urvaśī revealed herself to him. At that moment, a heavenly messenger reported that Indra required Urvaśī to act in a play directed by Bharata, 'Lakṣmī's Svayaṃvara', as above. Playing the part of the leading lady, Urvaśī committed an early Freudian slip and accidently referred to the hero Puruṣottama as 'Purūravas'. Bharata cursed her to go back to Earth, where she was reunited with Purūravas, and together the couple resorted to the Gandhamādana Forest. One day, Urvaśī caught Purūravas eyeing another girl and stormed off to the sacred forest—usually forbidden to females—where she was turned into a creeper.

Purūravas wandered like a madman while searching for his lover. This section, Act 4, is really the heart of the play, as the mad king, like Lear, questions plants, birds and animals for news of his beloved. The play almost seems to have been created to allow this display of poetic virtuosity in 34 verses. Purūravas eventually comes across a magic gemstone that, when worn, brings about union with one's beloved. He puts it on and embraces a creeper, which turns out to be Urvaśī herself. The reunited lovers return to the king's city of Pratiṣṭhāna.

Some time later, the gemstone was carried off by a vulture. The king called for the bird to be shot and the arrow that brought it down bore an inscription: 'This arrow belongs to Ayus, son of Aila and Urvaśī.' Thus, Purūravas discovered he had a son. We learn that Urvaśī had concealed the child on account of a former pact by which Indra had declared that she must return to Heaven as soon as Purūravas beheld his son. But just as they were about to part unhappily, Nārada arrived to report that Indra had changed his mind and allowed Purūravas and Urvaśī to live together on Earth.

Only traces remain from the earliest strata of the narrative: the union, separation and reunion of the couple, plus the birth of a son. With later versions, the *Vikramorvaśīya* shares a clash with demons, the various appearances of Indra, the play in Indra's palace, the curse that resulted in Urvaśī's fall to Earth and her transformation into a creeper and, in particular, the king's madness. Many of the standard tropes—including the compact, lambs/sheep, nakedness, lightning and fires—have disappeared. Kālidāsa has filled his account with innovations to heighten the dramatic interest of the piece—notably, the 34 verses of Purūravas's lament, the gemstone, its theft and the inscribed arrow, not to mention the completely new elements of the queen and Purūravas's confidant, the *vidūṣaka*, whom I have omitted from this summary.

Advertorials in the *Skanda Purāṇa*

The third section or *khaṇḍa* of the *Skanda Purāṇa* (*SkP*) is a guide to pilgrimage sites in and around the presumed site of Rāma's bridge to Lankā (modern Rameswaram in Tamil Nadu). Twenty-four sacred bathing places or *tīrtha*s are described in this region, many on the slopes of Mount Gandhamādana, which is the physical, earthly manifestation of the mythical mountain of the same name. The *khaṇḍa* describes a circuit around the *tīrtha*s and the practices to be undertaken. For each location, the *sūta* (the purāṇic narrator) tells an assembly of sages a story to exemplify the greatness (the *māhātmya*) of the site.

The *Skanda Purāṇa* draws on a wide range of narratives and characters including Yudhiṣṭhira and the Pāṇḍavas from the *Mahābhārata*, Rāma and Lakṣmaṇa from the *Rāmāyaṇa*, Kṛṣṇa and Kaṃsa from the *Viṣṇu Purāṇa*, Śuka from the *Bhāgavata Purāṇa* and Yaugandharāyaṇa and other characters from the *Kathāsaritsāgara*. In each case, these characters undergo a ritual bath at a given *tīrtha*, are cleansed of their misdeeds or misfortunes and attain a higher state, thereby demonstrating the efficacy of the location. Some narratives and rewards won from these pilgrimages lean more towards the Śaiva side, some towards the Vaiṣṇava and others seem non-sectarian. In other words, this pilgrimage circuit is pitched as one that will benefit devotees of any tradition.

The *Skanda Purāna* recasts the Purūravas–Urvaśī narrative to glorify a sacred bathing place called Sādhyāmṛta Tīrtha (*SkP*, 3.1.28). The first half of the narrative is as it appears in the *Viṣṇu Purāṇa*, but after Purūravas reached the realms of *gandharvas* with Urvaśī, there was a second dramatic performance, like the one in *Kathāsaritsāgara* and *Vikramorvaśīya*.

The chapter begins with the *sūta* telling his audience of assembled sages that a person who bathes at the Sādhyāmṛta Tirtha will receive all that he desires. He gives the example of Purūravas, who was freed from the curse of Tumburu and was subsequently reunited with Urvaśī as the result of bathing there. The sages ask how the couple met, why Tumburu cursed them and how they overcame their separation. In response, the *sūta* relates a version of the narrative that, while it shares many passages verbatim with the *Viṣṇu Purāṇa*, as mentioned, includes some interesting twists.

Purūravas, the perfect king, met Urvaśī, who had appeared on Earth because of the curse of Mitra and Varuṇa, as we have seen. He proposed to her, she agreed, with the usual three conditions: the rams, the nakedness and the ghee. They spent 61 years together. The *gandharvas* missed her, stole the sheep, caused a flash of lightning, Urvaśī disappeared, Purūravas wandered like a madman and found her in a lake in Kurukṣetra with four companions. He uttered the words from the *Ṛg Veda* 10.95: '*Hey wife! Stand still, you cruel-minded woman!*' Urvaśī told Purūravas that she was already pregnant and to come back in a year to meet his son and spend one more night with her. He did what he was told, they spent the night together and she bore him five more sons. He asked the *gandharvas* for a boon, they gave him the brazier—all this is familiar from other versions.

The next passage is interesting as it offers an explanation of why Purūravas abandoned the fire—always a puzzling aspect in other versions. In the middle of the forest, he said to himself: 'Alas, I'm such a fool. I still haven't got Urvaśī, so what's the use of this brazier?'[6] But he woke in the middle of the night, had

6 *aho batātimūḍho 'ham iti madhyevanaṃ nṛpaḥ | urvaśī na mayā labdhā vahnisthālyā* kimplalam || (*SkP*, 3.1.28.60).

a change of heart, went back to retrieve the *agniṣṭhālī*, found the two trees, made the three fires with fire-sticks, attained the world of the *gandharva*s and was reunited with Urvaśī.

Until this point, the *Skanda Purāṇa* has followed the 'normative' Purūravas–Urvaśī narrative, but now adds an interesting innovation. Instead of the story finishing here, it incorporates the dancing episode with an additional twist. In this version, Indra was watching the performance in his assembly hall. Purūravas had also come to watch Urvaśī dance. Tumburu, the dance instructor (not Bharata), saw the pair smiling at one another and cursed them to be separated. Purūravas begged Indra to intervene. The deity explained that a ritual bath at Sādhyāmṛta would release Purūravas from Tumburu's curse. Purūravas made the pilgrimage and was immediately reunited with Urvaśī, and together they flew to Indra's realm of Amarāvatī on a sky-going chariot.

The fifth book of the *Skanda Purāṇa*, which describes sacred places in Avantī (modern Madhya Pradesh), has a second version of the Purūravas–Urvaśī narrative (*SkP*, 5.1.9.27–81). This one advertises the efficacy of the Mahākālavana Tīrtha, which is said to confer conjugal bliss and to overcome separation. In this account, Urvaśī was born from contact between Nara's thigh and a mango blossom. Nara gave her to Indra, in whose palace she learned to dance. Purūravas, while visiting Indra, saw Urvaśī and fell in love with her, but when she looked at him, she fell off the stage. Purūravas wandered the world like a madman for 60 years and finally came to Mahākālavana. Urvaśi, who had been pining in Heaven, also came to the *tīrtha*, where they were reunited. The tropes of Indra, the dance performance, the separation and the reunion are all familiar; at the same time, many others—including the contract, lambs, lightning, curse and fire—are missing.

Purūravas as devotee: The *Bhāgavata Purāṇa*

The ninth book of the *Bhāgavata Purāṇa*, dating from the sixth to tenth centuries, also has an account of the Lunar Dynasty, which includes a version of the narrative (*BhP*, 9.14.15–49). This version in 34 *śloka*s is surprisingly straightforward both in terms of diction and in the fact that it is relatively unelaborated. It covers all the main moves of the typical versions described above—the compact, the sheep, the lakeside, the fire-sticks and fires—and it closely resembles a versified version of the prose account in the *Viṣṇu Purāṇa*.

Of more interest to us, however, is a passage in the eleventh book, known as the Aila-gītā ('The Song of the Son of Ilā') (*BhP*, 11.26.3–35). In this section, Kṛṣṇa is delivering a series of discourses to his disciple Uddhava on devotion and renunciation as the means to attain liberation. To illustrate the point, Kṛṣṇa cites Purūravas's long lament. Purūravas finally grasps the futility of his infatuation with Urvaśī and, through the realisation of Viṣṇu-Kṛṣṇa, renounces the world and attains the state of a *jīvan-mukta*—one who is liberated while still living. A thorough investigation of this version of the narrative has been undertaken by Gupta (2018).

Singing this song, Purūravas realised that the Lord was 'the Self within himself', and he attained the state of liberation. This creative elaboration and deployment of the narrative are in direct service of the *Bhāgavata Purāṇa*'s discursive aims. Purūravas's union with Urvaśī in the realm of the *gandharva*s is taken as the paradigm of highest sensual pleasure, only to be found meaningless. The happy couple's union is where the narrative often ends, but the *Bhāgavata Purāṇa* has added this sequel, as even this state of bliss proves unsatisfactory. Through his devotion to Viṣṇu-Kṛṣṇa, Purūravas ultimately realised the futility of physical attraction and romantic love and achieved a state of union with the divine—the ultimate goal of this tradition of Vaiṣṇava practice.

Conclusion

The Vedic dialogue between Purūravas and Urvaśī tantalises us with images of lambs, lightning, butter and lakes, but its vagueness has invited and stimulated creative responses through the millennia. From the earliest days, Sanskrit authors created prequels and sequels to explain the dialogue and fill the gaps in the story. Who were the protagonists? How did they come together? What drove them apart? How were they reunited? In so doing, authors produced a polythetic network, a body of literature in which some but not all of a set of tropes are deployed. Each of the re-creations is embedded in a particular context, and the context and discursive objectives of the authors shaped their transcreations.

The primary function of the genre of texts known as *brāhmaṇas* is to contextualise and elucidate Vedic *sūktas*. Accordingly, the *Śatapatha Brāhmaṇa* took the raw material of the Vedic dialogue and crafted a highly influential backstory for it, with a time, place and scene in which the words of the dialogue could be delivered. The *Harivaṃśa* and *Vāyu Purāṇa*, dedicated to the lineage of Viṣṇu-Kṛṣṇa, valorise the deity by providing an unbroken lineage of descent from Manu, the progenitor of the Lunar Dynasty. This includes each successive monarch, illustrating his greatness. Purūravas is an early member of this lineage and, accordingly, in their retelling of the Purūravas–Urvaśī narrative, these two texts dwell at length on Purūravas's heroic, kingly characteristics. The *Viṣṇu Purāṇa* is also dedicated to the lineage of Viṣṇu-Kṛṣṇa, but in line with the purāṇic genre more generally, it likes to spin a good tale. Hence, the *Viṣṇu Purāṇa* adds elements of drama and romance—for example, in amplifying the speech of Purūravas on hearing that Urvaśī's sheep had been stolen.

While the above sources all have pious intentions to varying degrees, the collection of stories known as the *Kathāsaritsāgara* and Kālidāsa's play *Vikramorvaśīya* exist primarily to entertain. Thus, their versions of the narrative contain many flourishes and innovations to enhance its 'tellability' and dramatic nature. The version shared by the *Padma* and *Matysa* purāṇas has what I call 'purāṇic' innovations in which deities are actively involved in human affairs. In addition to Viṣṇu, Brahmā and Indra, the three goals of life—love, wealth and virtue—appear in the narrative in bodily form as the deities Kāma, Artha and Dharma.

The relevant books of the *Skanda Purāṇa* describe the greatness (*māhātmya*) of various pilgrimage sites. Here, we see the narrative deployed in two different contexts to promote sacred fords or *tīrtha* in Tamil Nadu and the Avantī country, respectively. In contrast to the worldly orientation of the *Skanda Purāṇa*, the *Bhāgavata Purāṇa* is dedicated to the cultivation of intense personal devotion to Viṣṇu-Kṛṣṇa. As part of this project, the *Bhāgavata* adds a sequel to the narrative in which Purūravas laments the futility of his relationship with Urvaśī and achieves liberation. In all these sources, authors have access to a certain set of tropes from their literary inheritance. They accept or reject these images and add their own innovations to progress their discursive projects: to glorify the deity, to amuse their audience or to validate a sacred place. In so doing, each has contributed in their own way to that seemingly limitless quality we might call the Sanskritic literary genius.

References

Primary texts

Goswami, C. (2005). *Śrīmad Bhāgavata Mahāpurāṇa*. Gorakhpur, India: Gita Press.

Kale, M. (1915). *The Vikramorvaśiya of Kālidāsa*. Bombay, India: Oriental Publishing Company.

Mahābhārata-khilabhāga Harivaṃśa. (1967). Gorakhpur, India: Gita Press.

Matsya Purāṇam. (1876). Calcutta, India: Śrījīvānanda Vidyāsāgarabhaṭṭācārya.

The Padmamahāpurāṇam. (1984). Delhi: Nag Publishers.

Pathak, M. (1997–99). *The Critical Edition of the Viṣṇupurāṇam*. Vadodara, India: Oriental Institute.

Prasad, D. (1930). *The Kathâsaritsâgara of Somadevabhatta*. Bombay, India: Nirnaya Sagara Press.

Satapatha Brāhmaṇa. (1970). New Delhi: Ram Swarup Sharma.

The Skandamahāpurāṇam. (1986). Delhi: Nag Publishers.

Śrīmad Vāyu Mahāpurānam. (n.d.). Mumbai, India: Kṣemarāja Śrīkṛṣṇadāsa.

Vaidya, L. (1969). *The Harivaṃśa: Being the Khila or Supplement to the Mahābhārata*. [Critical Edition.] Poona, India: Bhandarkar Oriental Research Institute.

Secondary texts

Brodbeck, S. (2019). *Krishna's Lineage: The Harivamsha of Vyāsa's Mahābhārata*. New York, NY: Oxford University Press.

Eggeling, J. (1900). *The Satapatha Brâhmana According to the Text of the Mâdhyandina School. Part V.* Oxford, UK: Clarendon Press.

Fass Leavy, B. (1994). *In Search of the Swan Maiden: A Narrative on Folklore and Gender*. New York, NY: New York University Press.

Gaur, R. (1974). The legend of Purūravas and Urvaśī: And interpretation. *Journal of the Royal Asiatic Society of Great Britain and Ireland* 106(2): 142–52. doi.org/10.1017/S0035869X00131983.

Geldner, K. (1889). Purûravas und Urvaçî. In R. Pischel and K. Geldner, *Vedische Studien* [*Vedic Studies*], pp. 243–95. Stuttgart, Germany: Verlag von W. Kohlhammer.

Gupta, R. (2018). Restoring sight to blinding love: The Bhāgavata Purāṇa's transformation of the Urvaśī–Purūravas narrative. *Journal of Hindu Studies* 11: 67–79. doi.org/10.1093/jhs/hiy004.

Jamison, S. and Brereton, J. (2014). *The Rigveda: The Earliest Religious Poetry of India.* New York, NY: Oxford University Press.

Kosambi, D. (1962). *Myth and Reality: Studies in the Formation of Indian Culture.* Bombay, India: Popular Prakashan.

Lubin, T. (2019). Brāhmaṇa as commentary. In L. Bausch (ed.), *Self, Sacrifice, and Cosmos: Vedic Thought, Ritual, and Philosophy*, pp. 22–39. Delhi: Primus Books.

Macdonell, A.A. and Keith, A.B. (1912). *Vedic Index of Names and Subjects.* London: John Murray.

Monier-Williams, Monier. (2009). *An English–Sanskrit Dictionary.* New Delhi: Asian Educational Services.

Penzer, N. (1926). *The Ocean of Story: Being C.H. Tawney's Translation of Somadeva's Kathā Sarit Sāgara.* London: Privately printed for subscribers.

Pischel, R. and Geldner, K. (1889). *Vedische Studien* [*Vedic Studies*]. *Volume 1.* Stuttgart, Germany: Verlag von W. Kohlhammer.

Proferes, T. (2018). Vedas and brāhmaṇas. In K. Jakobsen, H. Basu and A. Malinar (eds), *Brill's Encyclopedia of Hinduism Online.* Leiden, Netherlands: Brill. Available from: referenceworks.brillonline.com/browse/brill-s-encyclopedia-of-hinduism.

Ramachandra Dikshitar, V.R. (1995). *The Purana Index.* Madras, India: University of Madras.

Stormer, N. (2016). Rhetoric's diverse materiality: Polythetic ontology and genealogy. *Review of Communication* 16(4): 299–316. doi.org/10.1080/15358593.2016.1207359.

Taylor, M. (trans.). (2021). *The Viṣṇu Purāṇa: Ancient Annals of the God with Lotus Eyes.* Canberra: ANU Press. doi.org/10.22459/VP.2021.

Weber, A. (1850). *Indische Studien: Zeitschrift für die Kunde des Indischen Alterthums* [*Indian Studies: Journal of the Knowledge of Indian Antiquities*]. Berlin: Dümmler.

Witzel, M. (1995). Early Indian history: Linguistic and textual parameters. In G. Erdosy (ed.), *The Indo-Aryans of Ancient South Asia: Language, Material Culture and Ethnicity*, pp. 85–271. Berlin: Walter de Gruyter. doi.org/10.1515/9783110816433.85.

Witzel, M. (2003). Vedas and upaniṣads. In G. Flood (ed.), *The Blackwell Companion to Hinduism*, pp. 68–98. Oxford, UK: Blackwell.

Wright, J. (1957). Purūravas and Urvaśī. *Bulletin of the School of Oriental and African Studies* 30: 526–47. doi.org/10.1017/S0041977X00132033.

www.ingramcontent.com/pod-product-compliance
Lightning Source LLC
Chambersburg PA
CBHW052009290426
44112CB00014B/2176
* 9 7 8 1 7 6 0 4 6 5 8 9 6 *